M. LIB. GUIDE
Part I

M. LIB. GUIDE
Part I

Riyazuddin Khan
Pankaj Kumar Singh

Ess Ess Publications
New Delhi

M. LIB. GUIDE
Part I

ISBN: 978-81-7000-743-2

₹ 450/-

First Published 2015

Published by:
Ess Ess Publications
4831/24, Ansari Road,
Darya Ganj,
New Delhi-110 002.
INDIA
Phones: 23260807, 41563444
Fax: 41563334
E-mail: info@essessreference.com
www.essessreference.com

Cover Design by *Patch Creative Unit*

Printed and bound in India at Salasar Imaging Systems.

CONTENTS

Part - Two

PREFACE

Library and Information science is an interdisciplinary or multidisciplinary area that applies the practices, perspectives and tools of management, information technology, education and other areas to libraries; in collection, organisation, preservation and dissemination of information resources; and also in other domains of information.

In today's world, the subject: Library and Information Science has comparatively higher job prospects. After completion of the post-graduate programme, with UGC norms, one can be absorbed in the job market, quite easily. This is the reason, behind the phenomenal growth of the number of students, taking admission in various departments of Library and Information Science, in different universities of the country.

There are many a book, available in print, along with many more online resources, which a student can access freely. Even then, there is a dearth for comprehensive, reader-friendly books.

In fact, Library and Information Science (LIS) is a confluence of the two fields; Library Science and Information Science. The phrase, 'Library and Information Science' is associated with schools of library and information science (abbreviated as, SLIS), which has generally developed from professional training programmes, in various institutions, during the second half of the 20th century. In the last phase of seventh decade, schools of librarianship began to add the term 'information science' to their nomenclature in 1980s, and by the 1990s, almost all library schools in USA had added 'Information Science' to their names. The trend was more for the adoption of information technology, rather than the concept of a science. A similar development has taken place in other parts of the world, including India.

This book is aimed at filling the vacuum for a good student-oriented book. Particularly, prepared for the aspirants, seeking admission to higher courses in Library and Information science, such as M.Lib. Further, this book should prove to be useful for the hopefuls, appearing for UGC NET, SLET and other courses.

I am indebted to all scholars, authors and compilers, whose valuable contributions, I have benefited from, while preparing this book. I am also thankful to the publishers and website operators, whose works, I have referred to, during the compilation of this book. And last but not the least, the undersigned expresses a wholehearted gratitude to all the associates, who extended their full cooperation, in shaping and finalising this project. This book is destined to be acknowledged, by all concerned circles. Enlightening comments and suggestive remarks are heartily solicited.

—*Editor*

PART – ONE

1

INTRODUCTION

Library and Information Science (LIS) is a profession that is full of people passionate about making a positive change to the world around them, and they tend to be wildly happy about what they do. According to one recent survey, over 85 per cent of information professionals questioned said if they had the choice, they'd do it again.

Information professionals and librarians in particular are in a unique position to bridge the gaps that exist between people, information and technology. In their professional lives, information professionals work to:

- Help scholars locate archival and other resources crucial to their work;
- Design and develop knowledge-organisation systems that allow organisations to more easily find and use resources developed by their members;
- Help doctors more quickly locate health information in critical situations;
- Create reader's advisory resources to encourage young students to develop a lifelong love of reading and learning;
- Identify sources of assistance in family and personal crises.

Library and information science (LIS) (sometimes given as the plural library and information sciences) is a merging of the two fields library science and information science. The phrase "library and information science" is associated with schools of library and information science (abbreviated to "SLIS"), which generally developed from professional training programmes (not academic disciplines) to university institutions during the second half of the 20th century. In the last part of 1960s schools of librarianship began to add the term "information science" to their names. The first school to do this was at the University of Pittsburgh in 1964. More schools followed during the 1970s and 1980s, and by the 1990s almost all library schools in the USA had added information science to their names. The trend was more for the adoption of information technology rather than the concept of a science. Library and information science (LIS). The study and practice of professional methods in the use and exploitation of information, whether from an institutional base or not, for the benefit of users. An umbrella term and used to cover terms such as library science, librarianship, information science, information work, etc. (tabinda naveed).

A similar development has taken place in large parts of the world. In Denmark, for example, the 'Royal School of Librarianship' in 1997 changed its English name to The Royal School of Library and Information Science. Another indication of this name shift is that *Library Science Abstracts* in 1969 changed its name to Library and Information Science Abstracts. In spite of this merge are the two original disciplines (library science and information science) still by some considered to be separate fields while the main tendency today is to use the terms as synonyms, but with different connotations.

In some parts of the world the development has been somewhat different. In France, for example, information science and communication studies form one interdiscipline. In Tromsø, Norway documentation science is preferred as the name of the field.

In the beginning of the 21st century one tendency has been to drop the term "library" and to speak about *information departments* or *I-schools*. There has also been an attempt to revive the concept of documentation and speak of Library, information and documentation studies (or science). Another tendency, for example in Sweden, is to merge the fields of Archival science, Library science and Museology to develop an integrated field: Archival, Library and Museum studies.

Library Science, Information Science and LIS

Tefko Saracevic (1992, p. 13) argued that library science and information science are separate fields:

> "The common ground between library science and information science, which is a strong one, is in the sharing of their social role and in their general concern with the problems of effective utilisation of graphic records. But there are also very significant differences in several critical respects, among them in: (1) selection of problems addressed and in the way they were defined; (2) theoretical questions asked and frameworks established; (3) the nature and degree of experimentation and empirical development and the resulting practical knowledge/competencies derived; (4) tools and approaches used; and (5) the nature and strength of interdisciplinary relations established and the dependence of the progress and evolution of interdisciplinary approaches. All of these differences warrant the conclusion that librarianship and information science are two different fields in a strong interdisciplinary relation, rather than one and the same field, or one being a special case of the other."

Another indication of the different uses of the two terms are the indexing in UMI's Dissertations Abstracts. In *Dissertations Abstracts Online* on November 2011 were 4888 dissertations indexed with the descriptor LIBRARY SCIENCE and 9053 with the descriptor INFORMATION SCIENCE. For the year 2009 the numbers were 104 LIBRARY SCIENCE and 514 INFORMATION SCIENCE. 891 dissertations were indexed with both terms (36 in 2009).

It should be considered that information science grew out of documentation science and therefore has a tradition for considering scientific and scholarly communication, bibliographic databases, subject knowledge and terminology, etc. Library science, on the other hand has mostly concentrated on libraries and their internal processes and best practices. It is also relevant to consider that information science used to be done by scientists, while librarianship has been split between public libraries and scholarly research libraries. Library schools have mainly educated librarians for public libraries and not shown much interest in scientific communication and documentation. When information scientists from 1964 entered library schools, they brought with them competencies in relation to information retrieval in subject databases, including concepts such as recall and precision, boolean search techniques, query formulation and related issues. Subject bibliographic databases and citation indexes provided a major step forward in information dissemination - and also in the curriculum at library schools.

Julian Warner (2010) suggests that the information and computer science tradition in information retrieval may broadly be characterised as query transformation, with the query articulated verbally by the user in advance of searching and then transformed by a system into a set of records. From librarianship and indexing, on the other hand, has been an implicit stress on selection power enabling the user to make relevant selections.

Difficulties in Defining LIS

"The question, "What is library and information science?" does not elicit responses of the same internal conceptual coherence as similar enquiries as to the nature of other fields, e.g., "What is chemistry?", "What is economics?", "What is medicine?" Each of those fields, though broad in scope, has clear ties to basic concerns of their field. [...] Neither LIS theory nor practice is perceived to be monolithic nor unified by a common literature or set of professional skills. Occasionally, LIS scholars (many of whom do not self-identify as members of an interreading LIS community, or prefer names other than LIS), attempt, but are unable, to find core concepts in common. Some believe that computing and internetworking concepts and skills underlie virtually every important aspect of LIS, indeed see LIS as a sub-field of computer science! [Footnote III.1] Others claim that LIS is principally a social science accompanied by practical skills such as ethnography and interviewing. Historically, traditions of public service, bibliography, documentalism, and information science have viewed their mission, their philosophical toolsets, and their domain of research differently. Still others deny the existence of a greater metropolitan LIS, viewing LIS instead as a loosely organised collection of specialised interests often unified by nothing more than their shared (and fought-over) use of the descriptor information. Indeed, claims occasionally arise to the effect that the field even has no theory of its own. " (Konrad, 2007, p. 652-653).

A Multidisciplinary, Interdisciplinary or Monodisciplinary Areas

The Swedish researcher Emin Tengström (1993). described cross-disciplinary research as a process, not a state or structure. He differentiates three levels of ambition regarding cross-disciplinary research:

- The "Pluridisciplinary" or "multidisciplinarity" level;
- The genuine cross-disciplinary level: "interdisciplinarity";
- The discipline-forming level "transdisciplinarity".

What is described here is a view of social fields as dynamic and changing. Library and information science is viewed as a field that started as a multidisciplinary field based on literature, psychology, sociology, management, computer science, etc., which is developing towards an academic discipline in its own right. However, the following quote seems to indicate that LIS is actually developing in the opposite direction:

> Chua and Yang (2008) studied papers published in *Journal of the American Society for Information Science and Technology* in the period 1988-1997 and found, among other things: "Top authors have grown in diversity from those being affiliated predominantly

with library/information-related departments to include those from information systems management, information technology, business, and the humanities. Amid heterogeneous clusters of collaboration among top authors, strongly connected crossdisciplinary coauthor pairs have become more prevalent. Correspondingly, the distribution of top keywords' occurrences that leans heavily on core information science has shifted towards other subdisciplines such as information technology and sociobehavioural science."

As a field with its own body of interrelated concepts, techniques, journals, and professional associations, LIS is clearly a discipline. But by the nature of its subject matter and methods LIS is just as clearly an interdiscipline, drawing on many adjacent fields.

A Fragmented Adhocracy

Richard Whitley (1984, 2000) classified scientific fields according to their intellectual and social organisation and described management studies as a 'fragmented adhocracy', a field with a low level of coordination around a diffuse set of goals and a non-specialised terminology; but with strong connections to the practice in the business sector. Åström (2006) applied this conception to the description of LIS.

Scattering of Literature

Meho and Spurgin (2005) found that in a list of 2,625 items published between 1982 and 2002 by 68 faculty members of 18 schools of library and information science, only 10 databases provided significant coverage of the LIS literature. Results also show that restricting the data sources to one, two, or even three databases leads to inaccurate rankings and erroneous conclusions. Because no database provides comprehensive coverage of the LIS literature, researchers must rely on a wide range of disciplinary and multidisciplinary databases for ranking and other research purposes. Even when the nine most comprehensive databases in LIS was searched and combined, 27.0 per cent (or 710 of 2,635) of the publications remain not found.

"The study confirms earlier research that LIS literature is highly scattered and is not limited to standard LIS databases. What was not known or verified before, however, is that a significant amount of this literature is indexed in the interdisciplinary or multidisciplinary databases of Inside Conferences and INSPEC. Other interdisciplinary databases, such as America: History and Life, were also found to be very useful and complementary to traditional LIS databases, particularly in the areas of archives and library history." (Meho & Spurgin, 2005, p. 1329).

Unique Concerns of Library and Information Science

"Concern for people becoming informed is not unique to LIS, and thus is insufficient to differentiate LIS from other fields. LIS are a part of a larger enterprise." (Konrad, 2007, p. 655).

"The unique concern of LIS is recognised as: Statement of the core concern of LIS: Humans becoming informed (constructing meaning) via intermediation between enquirers and instrumented records. No other field has this as its concern. " (Konrad, 2007, p. 660)

"Note that the promiscuous term *information* does not appear in the above statement circumscribing the field's central concerns: The detrimental effects of the ambiguity this term provokes are discussed above (Part III). Furner [Furner 2004, 427] has shown that discourse in the field is improved where specific terms are utilised in place of the i-word for specific senses of that term." (Konrad, 2007, p. 661).

Michael Buckland wrote: "Educational programmes in library, information and documentation are concerned with what people know, are not limited to technology, and require wide-ranging expertise. They differ fundamentally and importantly from computer science programmes and from the information systems programmes found in business schools."

Historical Background

17th Century

Gabriel Naude (2 February 1600 – 10 July 1653) wrote the first textbook on library science: *Advice on Establishing a Library* (1627). A French librarian and scholar, Naude wrote prolifically, producing works on many subjects including politics, religion, history and the supernatural. He put into practice all the ideas he put forth in *Advice* when given the opportunity to build and maintain the library of Cardinal Jules Mazarin.

19th Century

Martin Schrettinger wrote the second textbook (the first in German) on the subject from 1808 to 1829.

Thomas Jefferson, whose library at Monticello consisted of thousands of books, devised a classification system inspired by the Baconian method, which grouped books more or less by subject rather than alphabetically, as it was previously done.

The Jefferson collection provided the start of what became the Library of Congress.

The first American school of librarianship opened January 1, 1887 as the *School of Library Economy*. The term library economy was used for library science in USA until 1942. The Dewey Decimal Classification (DDC) used the term "Library economy" from 1876 and to 1942; thereafter using the term *Library Science* until 1965.

20th Century

Later, the term was used in the title of S.R. Ranganathan's *The Five Laws of Library Science*, published in 1931, and in the title of Lee Pierce Butler's 1933 book, *An introduction to library science* (University of Chicago Press).

Shiyali Ramamrita Ranganathan conceived five laws of library science and the development of the first major analytico-synthetic classification system, the colon classification. In India, he is considered to be the father of library science, documentation, and information science and is widely known throughout the rest of the world for his fundamental thinking in the field.

In the United States, Lee Pierce Butler's new approach advocated research using quantitative methods and ideas in the social sciences with the aim of using librarianship to address society's information needs. He was one of the first faculty at the University of Chicago Graduate Library School, which changed the structure and focus of education for librarianship in the twentieth century. This research agenda went against the more procedure-based approach of "library economy," which was mostly confined to practical problems in the administration of libraries.

William Stetson Merrill's *A Code for Classifiers*, released in several editions from 1914 to 1939, is an example of a more pragmatic approach, where arguments stemming from in-depth knowledge about each field of study are employed to recommend a system of classification. While Ranganathan's approach was philosophical it was also tied more to the day-to-day business of running a library. A reworking of Raganathan's laws was published in 1995 which removes the constant references to books. Michael Gorman's *Our Enduring Values: Librarianship in the 21st Century*, features his 8 principles necessary by library professionals and incorporate knowledge and information in all their forms, allowing for digital information to be considered. In more recent years, with the growth of digital technology, the field has been greatly influenced by information science concepts. In the English speaking world the term "library science" seems to have been used for the first time in a book in 1916 in the *Panjab Library Primer* written by Asa Don Dickinson and published by the University of the Punjab, Lahore, Pakistan. This university was the first in Asia to begin teaching 'library science'. The *Panjab Library Primer* was the first textbook on library science published in English anywhere in the world. The first textbook in the United States was the *Manual of Library Economy* which was published in 1929. In 1923, C.C. Williamson, who was appointed by the Carnegie Corporation, published an assessment of library science education entitled, "The Williamson Report," which designated that universities should provide library science training. This report had a significant impact on Library Science training and education. Library research and practical work, the area of information science has remained largely distinct both in training and in research interests.

21st Century

The digital age has transformed how information is accessed and retrieved. "The library is now a part of a complex and dynamic educational, recreational, and informational infrastructure." The evolution of the library sciences maintains its mission of access equity and community space, as well as, the new means for information retrieval called Information Literacy Skills. All catalogues, databases, and a growing number of books are all available on the Internet. Information literacy is the ability to "determine the extent of information needed, access the needed information effectively and efficiently, evaluate information and its sources critically, incorporate selected information into one's knowledge base, use information effectively to accomplish a specific purpose, and understand the economic, legal, and social issues surrounding the use of information, and access and use information ethically and legally."

History of Libraries

Library history is a subdiscipline within library science and library and information science focusing on the history of libraries and their role in societies and cultures. Some see the field as a subset of information history. Library history is an academic discipline and should not be confused with its object of study (history of libraries): the discipline is much younger than the libraries it studies. Library history begins in ancient societies through contemporary issues facing libraries today. Topics include recording mediums, cataloguing systems, scholars, scribes, library supporters and librarians.

Various Kinds of Libraries

Branch Libraries: Every village, suburb or hamlet cannot expect the establishment of a full-fledged library for the use of its inhabitants mainly due to economic reasons. These small areas cannot be viable units. But the provision of reading materials to every person, irrespective of the fact that he lives in a city, town, village far flung from the library centres, is essential. In all developed countries, librarians have been making efforts to make available books to persons living in such areas through the establishment of branch or mobile libraries or other Library Network.

Administration of a Branch Library: "A branch public library is usually defined as an agency in its own building or rooms with a substantial and permanent book stock with paid staff members, and open to the public on a regular schedule of hours."

A branch library may either serve as a small public library, offering reference and other special services as does the central library or as an agency for circulating popular books at the neighbourhood level. "A branch library of the first kind should offer a full range of library service and materials. It should have a wide selection of books, vertical file materials, current and back issues of magazines and newspapers, photograph records, flat pictures and maps; and it should be able to borrow promptly any materials in the rest of the system. It should offer all the usual circulation services, including reading guidance, for children, high school students and adults... It should regularly offer book-centred programmes for children and adults, tailored to the interests and needs of its neighbourhood, and there should be active cooperation with the schools, social agencies, clubs and organisations in the community."

Mobile Libraries: "Mobile libraries are collection of books arranged in vehicles and so staffed as to provide a library service capable of being directed to communities which are often, though not exclusively, rural. They are used by some municipal and many county library systems in the UK. In many areas abroad they are making a notable contribution to the development of library services in large parts of Asia, Africa and the Middle East. In county library practice a distinction is drawn between mobile branch libraries and travelling libraries. The mobile branch library is a medium-to-large vehicle with a shelf stock of upwards of 2,000 books used over reasonably good roads to serve villages and hamlets. The travelling library is a smaller vehicle with a limited stock used in the service of scattered communities and providing, in some cases, a house-to-house service in remote and upland areas. "Bringing books to people by book mobile is the most dramatic and colourful and evidently the most efficient and economical type of everyday public library service." However, in hilly tracts, some mode of communication is required.

Construction of Book Mobiles: The chassis used may range from 25 cwt. to 6 tons. Both trailer type and caravan mobile libraries have been used in addition to rigid ones, In many cases a passenger bus chassis is employed and, because of its economy in running, the 3 tons vehicle is a popular choice... In the United Kingdom however, the standard practice is to provide a body into which the reader can enter. The shelves, therefore, face inwards and generally run round three sides of the vehicle, the fourth usually reserved for the issue desk assembly. The shelves are generally tilted backwards, some 1 in. to 1½ in. from front to back. This helps to keep the stock in position while the vehicle is in motion. Natural light is provided by roof lights which may be flush or of the projecting 'lantern' variety... Artificial lighting is normally electrical using either filament type bulbs or fluorescent tubes.

Cost and Operation of Mobile Van: In America, "Book mobiles range in size from a panel truck of a ton or less, costing about $ 2,500 and capable of carrying only several hundred books, to large vehicles built on a bus chassis, costing perhaps $ 20,000 and carrying 4,000 books or more. A popular model but with a book capacity of only 1,600 volumes cost $ 7,500 in 1959." The analysis of costs and operation of a librachine in the Delhi Public Library system throws enough light on the problem in India.

Such a vehicle has a capacity of carrying 3,000 books. The total cost of chassis (₹ 43,300) and body building (₹ 32,000) comes to ₹ 75,000. A librachine consumes ₹ 1,500 worth of diesel every year and for the two years the repair costs are ₹ 1,500 per year. After the first two years, these repair costs go up nearly three times. An expenditure of ₹ 60,000 is incurred on the initial book stock of 10,000 volumes. Every year a sum of ₹ 6,000 is spent in buying books. Another sum of ₹ 1,500 is spent on bookbinding. The salary of the personnel including the Librarian who manages the job, the driver, the cleaner, etc., comes to ₹ 13,900 per year.

Dr. Ranganathan suggests that a librachine can visit 10 places in a week @ 2 places a day for 5 days in a week. It visits each place fortnightly. On 6th day, the vehicle is serviced and the stock is replenished. Seventh day is a rest day for the staff. A librachine carries about 2,000 volumes. It costs ₹ 30,000. For India as a whole, a fleet of more than 12,000 vehicles is required.

The economics of book mobiles suggest:

(1) That they should have a capacity of 3,000 to 4,000 volumes, and that none be undertaken with space for less than 2,500;

(2) That they be planned and operated to serve as many adults as children and to lend as many adult books as children's;

(3) That school stops and the mass movement of children through the bus at the rate of one a minute no longer be acceptable book mobile service;

(4) That the investment in equipment, stock and salaries be better capitalised on by an all afternoon and evening schedule of stops, at fortnightly intervals, at points where adults can and will visit the book mobiles;

(5) That a trained person be present at all book mobile stops, and staff schedules adjusted for this 1-9 P.M. duty;

(6) That every book mobile carry materials to render quick everyday reference service, e.g., Collier's Encyclopaedia, World Book, World Almanac, Reader's Guide, a few handbooks and two vertical file trays of informational pamphlets, and that the substantial type of library service be emphasised and publicised.

With these shifts in emphasis, the worth of our book mobiles to society would be greatly stepped up.

Administration of Book Mobile Service: The book mobile service creates many administrative problems.

These include the following:

1. The maintenance and repair of a book mobile is essential. Repairs should be got done without any delay. It should be regularly serviced either weekly or fortnightly.
2. The life of a book mobile is very short. Adequate finance should be made available for its replacement at convenient intervals.
3. Proper facilities should be provided for housing the vehicle.
4. Proper and adequate staff should be provided. The staff members should have physical stamina, adequate knowledge and love of books and readers. Some other suitable staff members should be kept in reserve to relieve the librarian and the driver of the book mobile.
5. Exact timetable for the book mobile should be chalked out and adhered to minutely. Routes to be followed must be adhered to strictly.
6. Stops for the book mobile should be fixed before hand. These should be indicated boldly on crossings. The information should show the day, time and place of the stoppage of the book mobile. A printed programme should be distributed among the readers of the area of its operation.
7. The book stock should be replenished regularly and should be kept up-to-date.

Different Types of Libraries

Public Library: The study of librarianship for public libraries covers issues such as cataloguing; collection development for a diverse community; information literacy; readers' advisory; community standards; public services-focused librarianship; serving a diverse community of adults, children, and teens; intellectual freedom; censorship; and legal and budgeting issues. The public library as a commons or public sphere based on the work of Jurgen Habermas has become a central metaphor in the 21st century.

School/Media Library

The study of school librarianship covers library services for children in schools through secondary school. In some regions, the local government may have stricter standards for the education and certification of school librarians (who are often considered a special case of teacher), than for other librarians, and the educational programme will include those local criteria. School librarianship may also include issues of intellectual freedom, pedagogy, information literacy, and how to build a cooperative curriculum with the teaching staff.

Academic Library

The study of academic librarianship covers library services for colleges and universities. Issues of special importance to the field may include copyright; technology, digital libraries, and digital repositories; academic freedom; open access to scholarly works; as well as specialised knowledge of subject areas important to the institution and the relevant reference works. Librarians often divide focus individually as liaisons on particular schools within a college or university.

Some academic librarians are considered faculty, and hold similar academic ranks to those of professors, while others are not. In either case, the minimal qualification is a Master of Arts in Library Studies or Masters of Arts in Library and Information Science. Some academic libraries may only require a master's degree in a specific academic field or a related field, such as educational technology.

Special Library

Special librarians include almost any other form of librarianship, including those who serve in medical libraries (and hospitals or medical schools), corporations, news agencies, government organisations, or other special collections. The issues at these libraries will be specific to the industries they inhabit, but may include solo work; corporate financing; specialised collection development; and extensive self-promotion to potential patrons.

Archives

The study of archives includes the training of archivists, librarians specially trained to maintain and build archives of records intended for historical preservation. Special issues include physical preservation of materials and mass deacidification; specialist catalogues; solo work; access; and appraisal. Many archivists are also trained historians specialising in the period covered by the archive.

Preservation

Preservation librarians most often work in academic libraries. Their focus is on the management of preservation activities that seek to maintain access to content within books, manuscripts, archival materials, and other library resources. Examples of activities managed by preservation librarians include binding, conservation, digital and analogue reformatting, digital preservation, and environmental monitoring.

Theory and Practice

Many practising librarians do not contribute to LIS scholarship, but focus on daily operations within their own libraries or library systems. Other practising librarians, particularly in academic libraries, do perform original scholarly LIS research and contribute to the academic end of the field.

On this basis, it has sometimes been proposed that LIS is distinct from librarianship, in a way analogous to the difference between medicine and doctoring. In this view, librarianship, the application of library science, would comprise the practical *services* rendered by librarians in their day-to-day attempts to meet the needs of library patrons.

Whether or not individual professional librarians contribute to scholarly research and publication, many are involved with and contribute to the advancement of the profession and of library science and information science through local, state, regional, national and international library or information organisations.

Other uses of these terms do not make the distinction and treat them as synonyms.

Powell's widely used introductory textbook does not make a formal distinction, but its bibliography uses the word librarianship as the heading for articles about the library profession.

Library science is very closely related to issues of knowledge organisation; however, the latter is a broader term which covers how knowledge is represented and stored (computer science/ linguistics), how it might be automatically processed (artificial intelligence), and how it is organised outside the library in global systems such as the internet. In addition, library science typically refers to a specific community engaged in managing holdings as they are found in university and government libraries, while knowledge organisation in general refers to this and also to other communities (such as publishers) and other systems (such as the Internet). The Library system is thus one socio-technical structure for knowledge organisation.

Common Relations

'Mitra-Mandal' Libraries: As a result, a number of public libraries started appearing in various parts of the country. Notable among them are the 'Mitra Mandal Libraries' opened in Gujarat. About 150 libraries were opened under this banner in different parts of Gujarat. This scheme was engineered by Mr. Motibhai Amin and his associates. Under this scheme, a village has to contribute ₹ 10 or ₹ 15 a year and get in return newspapers, periodicals and books worth double the amount. The loss was met from concessions secured from the editors of the papers, authors of books and from funds privately raised for the purpose. A similar movement under the name of "Gokhale Libraries" were started under the guidance of Mr. I.K. Yagnik by the Kalavani Mandal.

Royal Patronage: The Sayaji Rao Gaikwad of Baroda is regarded as an "Apostle of Indian Library Movement". He introduced the free primary compulsory education in his princely state in the year 1907. In 1908, while touring in America wired to his Prime-Minister to open circulating libraries in villages of the Baroda State for diffusion of knowledge among the masses forthwith sanctioning ₹ 30,000 for this very project.

The Education Department of the State thereupon worked out the scheme of establishing libraries in the State and offered ₹ 24 a year for periodicals, provided the villagers contributed a similar sum and also a set of new books worth ₹ 100 each on payment of ₹ 25 made by the people. He brought with him Mr. W.A. Borden from America for organising the 'library system' of the State. Mr. Borden had established the State Central Library, and a number of branch libraries. He organised library training classes and a journal by name 'Library Miscellany'. He also designed a classification scheme suitable to the local needs and an alphabetical list of author's surnames. Children and Womens' libraries were also organised. In about 20 years almost all the towns and about 1,100 villages in the State had a library of their own.

Mysore State: At the recommendation of the Education Committee of the Economic Conference the State of Mysore had sanctioned grants for a period of three years, to all the then existing public libraries in the State with, the aim of providing 'free book service for all'.

Peoples Movement in Andhra: The public library movement in Andhra is regarded as a "People's Movement" as the Library consciousness in Andhra arose as a mass movement. It was carried to the nook and corner of the State by enthusiastic library. The Andhra Desa Library Association founded in 1914 is the first of its kind in India. Soon after its formation the Association had compiled a Directory of Andhra Libraries and started the publication of its monthly organ Granthalaya Sarvaswamu in 1915. They had also organised library training classes and the All India Public Library Association (in 1919). Of the various activities which the Association had carried out in the early days, the 'library pilgrimages' can be regarded as unique and superb. This consisted of six sections and their activities were in short as follows:

> The advance party first used to enter into a village, paste down the posters, etc. and meet the local libraries, elders and officers of the village and discuss about the library matters in general and about the programme of the pilgrimage. The second party consisted of Exhibition Section, which used to arrange an exhibition in order to arouse public interest in libraries. The third party used to play gramophone records to attract people for the meeting.
>
> The fourth one which is called as 'Bhajan Section' used to go round the village with songs and bhajans and reach the place of meeting by time. The 'Lecturing Section' consisted of eminent personalities who used to deliver lectures for the establishment of libraries, inspect the various local libraries if there were any and give suggestions for their improvement. After the meeting the 'Magic Lantern Section' used to exhibit informative pictures on library propaganda, health, cooperation, etc. 'Ibis is a unique ingenious method of library extension technique devised by the Andhra Desa Library Association.

Other State-level Associations: The Andhra Desa Library Association also took lead in convening the first All India Library Conference in Madras which converged into the formation of the All India Public Library Association. It has also started the first full fledged professional periodical in English in 1925 under the title Indian Library Journal. This Association had also encouraged the formation of the Bengal Library Association, Madras Library Association and the revival of Punjab Library Association.

Bengal Library Association: The Bengal Library Association founded in 1925 took an active part in spreading the library movement in that part of the country. It has organised regular conferences and periodical training classes for library workers. Kumara Munindra Deb Roy Mahasay took keen interest in library matters and gave a lead in the early days of its activities.

Madras Library Association: The Madras Library Association, formed in the year 1928 had done yeoman service in 1940s under the able leadership of its Secretary Dr. S.R. Ranganathan. This Association apart from running the library training classes introduced the first mobile library service at Mannergudi in 1931 and prison and hospital library services in 1931-32.

Punjab Library Association: The Punjab Library Association after its reorganisation in 1929 had done a commendable work. It had hosted in the 7th All India Public Libraries Conference in December, 1929 and published its organ the Modern Librarian successfully for about a decade. It was the only journal in English when it was started in 1930.

Indian Library Association: The Indian Library Association was founded in the year 1933 with its headquarters in Calcutta. In the earlier years it had compiled a directory of libraries and encouraged training of Library personnel in the country. It had organised conferences in alternative years. In 1943, it had started its quarterly organ the Library Bulletin. After the partition of the Country in 1947, the then Secretary, Mr. K.M. Asadullah had resigned and left for Pakistan. The office of the Association was shifted to Delhi. Under the Presidentship of Dr. Ranganathan, the Association had done a lot of work.

The organ of the Association was started under the title Abgila (this included a Hindi section also) in 1949. Conferences were held regularly. Symposia were organised along with the Conferences. The association had started its publication, series and a few publications were brought out in English and Hindi. It also took up the project of the compilation of the Union Catalogue of Scientific Periodicals in S.E. Asia in collaboration with the UNESCO. Using the good offices of ILA Dr. Ranganathan initiated the Delhi Public Library project and the INSDOC. The Association became inactive after 1954. In the recent part Mr. D.R. Kalia had rejuvenated the organisation by creating various Sectional Committees and also provided a house to the Organisation.

Working Group on Libraries: While preparing the Fourth Five Year Plan, the Planning Commission had appointed a Working Group on Libraries in 1964 with Dr. V.K.R.V. Rao as its Chairman. After conducting an intensive survey, this Group had put forth the following objectives before the Planning Commission for preparing a Library Plan:

1. Sharing of the responsibility among the Centre and the States of providing adequate public library service to the citizens;
2. Setting up an All India Library Advisory Council at the Centre; and State Library Advisory Councils in the States;
3. Financing Library Legislation for providing adequate library service; and
4. Promotion of book production.

The working Group envisaged that within a period of ten years all the villages over two thousand population will have their own libraries, with an estimated expenditure of 310 Million Rupees.

National Advisory Board for Libraries: In pursuance of the Recommendations of the Working Group on Libraries, the Union Government had constituted a National Advisory Board for Libraries with the Union Education Minister as its Chairman in 1966 for advising the Union and State Governments on matters relating to the reorganisation and coordinated development of libraries in the country. To promote closer contacts between different libraries, and closer association of Government and the public with the activities of the different libraries in India. The members of the Board included five nominees of the Union Government: two Members of Lok Sabha: one Member of the Rajya Sabha: a nominee each of the UGC: Librarian of the National Library, and one representative each of the ILA, All India Federation of Publishers and Book Sellers' Association, the NCERT, the Indian Adult Education Association, the National Book Trust, and the Children's Book Trust.

Raja Ram Mohan Roy Library Foundation: The Raja Ram Mohan Roy Library Foundation was set up as a part of the bureaucracy celebration of the birth anniversary of Raja Ram Mohan Roy. The main objective of the foundation is to promote and support the public library services in the country particularly in the non-metropolitan areas. The foundation is assisted by the State Library Planning Committees set-up in each State, which consists of a representative of the foundation and of the State Government. The officer-in-charge of the library services in the State is the Convener of the Committee. It is the responsibility of the Committee to recommend proposals for assistance to the libraries of the State by the foundation.

The foundation has taken up the following programmes during the fifth Five Year Plan period:

1. Assistance towards building up of adequate stock of books and reading and visual material in the District Libraries and the Nehru Yuvak Kendras.
2. Assistance towards development of the Rural Book Deposit Centres and Mobile Library Services;
3. Assistance towards processing, binding, preservation of out-of-print and rare books and of manuscripts, and
4. Assistance to rural libraries run by voluntary organisations.

The organisation since its inception in 1972 to the middle of 1977 covered more than 6,000 libraries at various levels all over the country.

National Library, Calcutta: Soon after independence, the Government of India had passed the National Library Act in 1948 with the effect of which the Imperial Library was renamed as the National Library of India. Today this (National) Library is having 1.5 million collection and a staff of over 700 including technical and non-technical. In 1958 the Central Reference Library was established in Calcutta at the National Library which took up the work of the compilation and issue of Indian National Bibliography on the lines of BNB. The first issue of the Bibliography was released on 15th August.

Heaven of Books

Today there are about 6,00,000 primary schools, 80,000 secondary schools and 223 universities in India. All the universities have good library facilities. Their collection range from few thousands to a million. The growth of the university libraries is very rapid on account of the generous grants from the UGC. Statistics with regard to school libraries is unfortunately not available.

However, we can say that very few schools have good library facilities and even in those schools where there are libraries, they have been playing a very insignificant role. Most of these are managed by unqualified people. Almost all the colleges numbering 10,000 are having library facilities though their contributions to the development of education and skills is not much.

Important Libraries

Most of the special libraries are those run by the Government Departments or Quasi-Government organisations and research institutions. There are a few run by learned societies and business houses. All the Union and State Governments are having their own libraries. Government is the main agency supporting research in this country as like in any other State. There are number of special libraries attached to these organisations. There are about 34 research establishments under CSIR which include national and regional laboratories, institutions, organisations, and two information centres. The ICAR has 25 research establishments under its control. Two more are in offing.

The ICMR has several permanent and semi-permanent research institutions that are being organised by the Union Government in different fields like, Food, Family Planning, Housing, Mines, Observations, Oil and Gas Standards, etc. These are equipped with good libraries. The Atomic and Space Research organisations are also having big libraries with best facilities.

2

FUNDAMENTALS OF LIBRARY AND INFORMATION SCIENCE

Meaning, Nature and Characteristics of Library

General Aspects

The term 'library' means different things to different people depending on where they stand on the enlightenment spectrum. To some, it is a bookstore; a building where books are kept for safe custody over-seen by a stern-looking watchman in the name of a librarian, essentially ensuring that the books are not tampered with unduly. To many, the library is a place of reading and studying; where examination-writing candidates make their second homes to read their textbooks and notebooks in preparation. This explains why many libraries have seasonal uses as their patrons have a well-known pattern of visits and usage, which are at the designated examination periods. Only a few others conceive of the library as an organisation of information resources meant for use.

The Issues

The above perceptions underpin the justification for a variety of definitions of the library by different people. The answer to such question as "what is a library" may seem quite simple and straightforward to provide; since many would quickly jump to the conclusion "a room or building where books are kept", "a reading room", "a storehouse of books", etc. Even though these conceptions of a library are not completely wrong in themselves, they however provide the foundations upon which the highly misrepresented and misconceived idea of what a library truly is was laid. Even the Librarian Glossary was not spared of this tendency in defining a library as "a collection of books and other literary materials kept for reading, study and consultation", "a place, building, room or rooms set apart for the keeping and use of a collection of books".

Incidentally, there is an historical antecedent to this line of conception of what a library is. Evidence of this can be readily found in the Oxford English Dictionary, which affirmed that the word "library" has been used in English in the sense of being a place where books were kept for "reading, study, or reference" since 1374. By the 19th Century, the understanding metamorphosed into "a building, room, or set of rooms containing a collection of books for the use of the public or some portion of it, or the members of society; ... a public institution or establishment charged with the care of a collection of books." Then, as time went by, additional concepts of "circulation" and "administration" featured in the definition of a library.

No doubt therefore that the concept 'library' has long been established in our language, and the more reason for the age-long misconceptions about the true nature of the library, which is essentially dynamic (thus, ever-changing); and for which those definitions, though correct to some extent, are no longer sacrosanct in the face of an avalanche of new additions to the world of the library and the librarianship profession today. These new additions have impacted tremendously on the nature of the modern-day library; thereby rendering those either definitions inadequate for capturing the true essence of what a typical library has come to represent. Hence, the need for a re-examination of the concept towards a redefinition that will reflect the emerging trends.

Concept of Library

In so far as control over information forms the basis of managerial authority, the technologies which process it are inherently political. Indeed, business organisations are under pressure to change their decision-making structures as a direct consequence of information technology implementation. These 'subversive' effects on organisational structures are not immediately obvious to management. They arise as the new technology changes the established work practices and consequently creates different relationships on the organisation's information network. Management is then faced with a dual threat:

1. A new pool of knowledge outside its formal control structures. Employees are able to access information without hindrance.
2. Power is shifting from line managers to those who control the information technology, such as the technicians in the DP departments or knowledgeable users.

Management's response has been weak and incremental. The control of information generated by computer technologies increasingly reflected the new power structures that these technologies established. On the one hand, functional control (allocation, budget, etc.) remains with general management. On the other, operational control (how and what is processed) is left to the technicians in the DP departments. The pervasive nature of the technology spreading through all levels of the organisation established those who controlled it as important powerbrokers or gatekeepers. Newcastle Business School research has shown that senior managers are often unwilling to become involved. They served their apprenticeship in computerless or, at best, early mainframe-driven organisations and therefore do not always fully understand or appreciate the new technologies. Despite the obvious need for new control structures the traditional methods are adhered to.

The dichotomy between the established management structures and the changed (and changing) technological structures is therefore maintained and often worsened. Such opposing forces create a complex environment and place considerable constraints on management action. The dichotomy quickly becomes institutionalised. Lack of management action causes other user employees to perceive themselves as powerless in any dealings with the new technologies. This serves to enhance the influence of the technicians and is built into the organisation's structures. Business action then tends to become increasingly inflexible; user managers are reluctant to take risks in an environment they do not understand, and many operational decisions are left to the technicians.

This area of decision-taking is also built into the firm's task structure. Meanwhile the new networked systems demand increasing flexibility in order to work but are instead being faced with increasingly inflexible and decision-shy managements. To appreciate the nature of this threat and how profound its impact can be on the organisation, it is essential to grasp the characteristics of technology, in particular its integrative nature with any social entity whether it be an organisation or something else. Explore this area, but it also then distinguishes between different types of technology, highlighting the perceptual characteristics of information technology. It concludes that to control information technology we must realise that we cannot treat it as just another piece of machinery.

The relationship between technology and an organisation has, indeed, been thoroughly explored. It is obvious that a firm's structure is characterised by the many forces emanating from its operating environment. What is perhaps not so obvious is that technology is one of those forces. This is because it is quite often seen as a locally owned, physical resource. The machine on the shop-floor is just that and not part of a more complex social process. Within the framework of this perspective technology is a tool, totally predictable and controllable by management.

The physical technology alone (e.g., machinery or computers) will not explain how organisations are affected by it. As Weizenbaum suggested, a computer or telecommunication system (or any form of technology) is merely junk without the people to relate to them. It is how those people relate to their technology, how they use it, their perceptions of it, and so on, that are important. These aspects govern not only the technological process but also the characteristics of the organisation structure. In the same way, structure should not be seen merely in a physical sense. The dividing of a firm into departments and functions, although of interest, does not capture the essence of an organisation, which is to be found within the minds of its employees. The relationship between technology and structure is thus not physical but perceptual because it is within people's minds that the links are made. Our understanding of such techno behavioural forces is not great. This is partly because of the hegemonic view of business organisations as hierarchies in organisation theory. It would seem, therefore, that we have not as yet learnt to examine organisations in an appropriate dimension which can highlight the effects of information and its technology.

The traditionalist's view of an organisation is typically presented by Schein as a rational co-ordination of activities. This emphasises the hierarchical and functionally-bound aspects. Butler, on the other hand, discussed the lack of understanding of such models determining that all the interrelationships are not adequately identified. They tend to portray firms as static entities without the turbulence of opposing forces. In particular, technology is seen as a side issue, if at all, and not central to the fundamental mechanisms of an organisation.

A more appropriate model in Butler's mind is Udy's, which puts technology at the centre of an interactive environment of production objectives, social setting, physical exigencies and work organisation. Technology, not the structure, sets the constraints ('trade-offs' as Butler calls them) upon an organisation. Thus, a certain structure can be considered suitable for a given technology. For example, a company using mass production techniques, such as Ford, will best be structured to suit the needs of mass production technology. The relationship does not end there, however, as in Pugh's model, because he suggests that it is technology which drives the organisation.

Where this model fails is in not identifying with sufficient clarity the perceptual aspects of an organisation's technology. It is only within this domain that useful links can be established between technology and structure. The perceptual aspects of structure must also be emphasised for this to be successful since within any physical domain technology can only be seen as a resource and structure as a functional framework. It will then demonstrate that employees' perception of their structure determines the consequent structural characteristics. This chapter also suggests, however, that the relationship is two-way, in that an established structure can itself influence and change the perception of the employees. The impact of information technology is then again introduced. Already it has been established that such technology can change the way that individuals perceive their environments. A link with the present chapter is that since an employee's perception of the environment can be changed through information technology, his/her perception of the firm's structure must also change. The post-implementation structure that emerges may be profoundly different from any previous structure.

This control-theoretic view of information technology's impact is particularly relevant to the devolution of management authority. The impact of the new technology may radically affect the power structure or the political relationships between management and staff (but not the functional relationships) thus creating an imbalance between the perceptual and physical aspects of the organisation. Through the perceptual domain, information technology has also infiltrated the cultural base of organisations and has thus had the potential to alter cultural objectives, which are the consequence of existing value systems. For example, it may be the formal objective of one firm to produce good quality products at the expense of higher profits. This objective has arisen from the organisation's culture, but any form of technology, especially information technology, is not sensitive to cultural requirements.

Managers may try to fit the technology into their companies but it is generally within a framework provided by the physical domain. The objectives suitable for the technology do not always match existing cultural needs. To seek an explanation of the technological impact, therefore, we should no longer look at organisations in terms of departments and divisions. Any boundary established by such a definition may be rendered irrelevant. It is more sensible to consider an organisation as a network of perceptual maps, dependent on an information network which is itself part of a wider network within the region, market, industry, and so on.

The need for such an outlook is underlined by the number of firms accessing information beyond their established functional boundaries. Internally, this involves different departments accessing a common pool from the company database; externally, employees gain entrance to public databases such as Prestel. It is increasingly difficult to understand these organisations as physically controllable entities. The problem, however, extends beyond management. If it is accepted that our models of organisation are also too limiting because of their inability to highlight the dichotomy between the perceptual and the physical, then we must develop new models, which is one of the major proposals of the book. In order to do this we must first establish an appropriate methodology. The analysis which must be pursued is wide- ranging. It extends beyond the convenient boundaries that traditional theory has established. The tidy logic of an organisation reaches only into the physical domain, beyond that is a vast perceptual arena which can be understood only as a network of relationships.

Five Laws of Library Science

The Five laws of library science is a theory proposed by S. R. Ranganathan in 1931, detailing the principles of operating a library system. Many librarians worldwide accept them as the foundations of their philosophy.

These laws are:

1. Books are for use.
2. Every reader his [or her] book.

3. Every book its reader.
4. Save the time of the reader.
5. The library is a growing organism.

First Law

The first law constitutes the basis for the library services. Dr. Ranganathan observed that books were often chained to prevent their removal and that the emphasis was on storage and preservation rather than use. He did not reject the notion that preservation and storage were important, but he asserted that the purpose of such activities was to promote the use of them. Without the use of materials, there is little value in the item. By emphasising use, Dr. Ranganathan refocused the attention of the field to access-related issues, such as the library's location, loan policies, hours and days of operation, as well as such mundanities as library furniture and the quality of staffing.

First law of library science Books are for use This means that Books in Libraries are not meant to be shut away from people.

Second Law: Every Reader his or her Book

This law suggests that every member of the community should be able to obtain materials needed. Dr. Ranganathan felt that all individuals from all social environments were entitled to library service, and that the basis of library use was education, to which all were entitled. These entitlements were not without some important obligations for both libraries/librarians and library patrons. Librarians should have excellent first-hand knowledge of the people to be served. Collections should meet the special interests of the community, and libraries should promote and advertise their services extensively to attract a wide range of readers.

Second law of library science Every reader his (or her) book This means we don't judge what someone wants to read. Everyone has different tastes and differences and we should respect that.

Third Law: Every Book its Reader

This principle is closely related to the second law but it focuses on the item itself, suggesting that each item in a library has an individual or individuals who would find that item useful. Dr. Ranganathan argued that the library could devise many methods to ensure that each item finds it appropriate reader. One method involved the basic rules for access to the collection, most notably the need for open shelving.

Third law of library science Every book its reader This means we should have books in the library even if there is just one person who wants to read it. We shouldn't just have popular books.

Fourth Law: Save the Time of the Reader

This law is a recognition that part of the excellence of library service is its ability to meet the needs of the library user efficiently. To this end, Dr. Ranganathan recommended the use of appropriate business methods to improve library management. He observed that centralising the library collection in one location provided distinct advantages. He also noted that excellent staff would not only include those who possess strong reference skills, but also strong technical skills in cataloguing, cross-referencing, ordering, accessioning, and the circulation of materials.

Fourth law of library science Save the time of the user. This means it should be as easy as possible to find what you want in the library and the library should be accessible to all.

Fifth Law: The Library is a Growing Organism

This law focused more on the need for internal change than on changes in the environment itself. Dr. Ranganathan argued that library organisations must accommodate growth in staff, the physical collection, and patron use. This involved allowing for growth in the physical building, reading areas, shelving, and in space for the catalogue.

Fifth law of library science The library is a growing organism. This means that a library is always changing. The books need to be updated over time, new books should be bought and old books replaced.

Variants

Librarian Michael Gorman (past president of the American Library Association, 2005–2006), and Walt Crawford recommended the following laws in addition to Ranganathan's five in *Future Libraries: Dreams, Madness, and Realities* [American Library Association, 1995], Gorman later repeated them in his small book, *Our Singular Strengths* [American Library Association, 1998].

1. Libraries serve humanity.
2. Respect all forms by which knowledge is communicated.
3. Use technology intelligently to enhance service.
4. Protect free access to knowledge.
5. Honour the past and create the future.

In 2004, librarian Alireza Noruzi recommended applying Ranganathan's laws to the Web in his paper, "Application of Ranganathan's Laws to the Web":

1. Web resources are for use.
2. Every user has his or her web resource.
3. Every web resource its user.
4. Save the time of the user.
5. The Web is a growing organism.

In 2008, librarian Carol Simpson recommended that editing be done to Ranganathan's law due to media richness. The following were:

1. Media are for use.
2. Every patron his information.
3. Every medium its user.
4. Save the time of the patron.
5. The library is a growing organism.

Elements of Dynamic Nature

Before its presentation, however, there are other factors which must be addressed. The point has already been made that an organisation is a fluid and ever-changing entity. The components so far discussed form the framework of the organisation but they are no more than boxes in an analyst's model. Other forces exist which breathe life into these concepts. They can be termed as the dynamics of an organisation. People are the organisation, and as such their perceptions, aspirations, alliances and conflicts form an important dynamic. It suggests that the outcome for any organisation is not through a rational process, although that may seem to be apparent within the physical domain, but rather as a consequence of perceptual interaction between individuals or groups. These can be dysfunctional as well as functional.

For managers the issue is how such diverse forces can be controlled. They can only directly access the physical domain and therefore have to attempt to manipulate this in some way to have any impact upon the perceptual domain. One area, however, which allows a controllable linkage between the two domains is the information network. The quality, quantity and content of information, amongst other factors such as historicity, will determine an individual or group perception. On the other hand, the network itself can be physically manipulated thus affecting the quality, quantity and content of information. Its control is therefore of considerable importance to management.

Its particular emphasis is on the use of computer technology to generate information. Other forms of generated information through manual methods can also be controlled as information management, but because of the computer's ability to generate so much information other important forces come into play which are not present in a manual system.

The ways in which employees regard the characteristics of their information will determine in part the nature of their information network and ultimately the organisation structure itself. Management must be aware of this and develop strategies through training and computer technology implementation which are sensitive to this. Information, however, is only part of the process. On its own it is not particularly a dynamic of the organisation. Individuals may receive information and do nothing with it. A firm, therefore, does not change because of information. Information must be used. Action or behaviour is the consequence of information being used in the physical domain. In the perceptual domain, information being used is manifest through the decision process. There are no actions without decisions, no matter how minor or simple they may be, so that an organisation, which can be analysed in terms of its actions, is driven by its decision processes.

In any context there is no such thing as an individual decision, even if the person involved is on a deserted island. Especially within a complex social process such as an organisation, a decision is based upon a range of perceptual and physical influences. A person's experience coming to bear in a decision, for example, is the consequence of previous interactions with other people and institutions. Therefore one cannot fully control the decision process by controlling those individuals who are seen to own it. Their actions might be constrained but the source of their decisions is to be found in the perceptual domain. This is particularly important when such processes are affected by computer technology. Managers tend to develop mechanisms around the physical aspects of the technology and ignore the wider perceptual impact. It then places these ideas in the context of the other major components of a firm, in particular the information network, by highlighting the close relationship between a decision and information.

We have so far developed the framework of an organisational structure dominated by two domains: the physical and the perceptual. In a similar fashion to matter and anti-matter, their forces to Conflict and contradict one another. Management must maintain the narrow ground between the two, because it is only here that long-term stability is established. At this point the forces of both domains are in equilibrium, which for the purposes of the model has been termed balance. The achievement of such a state is one of the key outcomes to be identified.

The domination of one domain over another could lead to long-term instability, the degree of which depends upon a range of factors unique to specific organisations. For example, if there is no balance and an organisation is dominated by its physical domain, then its short-term survival, at least, will depend upon how effective that domain is in dealing with the firm's particular environment. In the longer term, however, all firms must achieve an equilibrium whether the dominant domain is in tune with the environment or not. This is because the cost of not achieving equilibrium will be manifest in the dysfunctional relationship between the two domains. Forces will come into play that will undermine stability. It shows a complex social entity driven by an abstract relationship between two sets of forces. Much of this arena exists within the minds of the employees, of course, but like other societal phenomena its logic extends beyond them.

The forces can exist independently of particular individuals in that they are perpetuated by culture, technology and training. Individuals may come and go, some people may contribute more than others, but the logic of the organisation as a separate entity remains consistent. It is proposed that an, organisation can pass a significant point, the virtuality point, whereby its survival does not depend upon a particular set of individuals. This is a different world from the one portrayed by established theory. It comprises many of the same elements, such as structure and technology, recognised by conventional wisdom, but it is the perspective, the way in which those elements are arranged, that is different.

The emphasis is upon a force field relationship rather than the aspects of one domain or another. By having this different framework, we can also analyse the effects of change in other ways. In particular, the impact of information technology is shown to have a far wider effect upon organisations than the traditional models may lead us to suppose. Much of it is common sense, gleaned from the working environment and from those in it. Nevertheless, the model is placed before all management as a challenge: to use the ideas this book presents as a basis for analysing the worth of their information technology.

Role of Librarian

A librarian is a person who works professionally in a library, and may hold a degree in librarianship (known either as library science or library and information science). Traditionally, a librarian is associated with collections of books, as demonstrated by the etymology of the word "librarian" (from the Latin *liber*, "book"). The role of a librarian is continually evolving to meet social and technological needs: a modern librarian may deal with information in many formats, including books, magazines, newspapers, audio recordings (both musical and spoken word), video recordings, maps, manuscripts, photographs and other graphic material, bibliographic databases, web searching, and digital resources.

A librarian may provide other information services, including computer provision and training, coordination of public programmes, basic literacy education, assistive equipment for people with disabilities, and help with finding and using community resources. Appreciation for librarians is often included by authors and scholars in the Acknowledgment (creative arts and sciences) sections of books.

Historical Backdrop

The Sumerians: The Sumerians were the first to train clerks to keep records of accounts. "Masters of the books" or "Keepers of the Tablets" were scribes or priests who were trained to handle the vast amount and complexity of these records. It is unknown, however, what their specific duties were.

Assyrian, Greek and Egyptian Eras

Sometime in the 8th century BC Ashurbanipal, King of Assyria, created a library at his palace in Nineveh in Mesopotamia. Ashurbanipal was the first individual in history to introduce librarianship as a profession. We know of at least one "keeper of the books" who was employed to oversee the thousands of tablets on Sumerian and Babylonian materials, including literary texts, history, omens, astronomical calculations, mathematical tables, grammatical and linguistic tables, and dictionaries, and commercial records and laws. All of these tablets were catalogued and arranged in logical order by subject or type, each having an identification tag.

The Great Library of Alexandria, created by Ptolemy I after the death of Alexander in 323 BC, was created to house the entirety of Greek literature. It was notable for its famous librarians: Demetrius, Zenodotus, Eratosthenes, Apollonius, Aristophanes, Aristarchus, and Callimachus. Although librarianship was an accidental aspect of their career, these scholars contributed significantly to the collection and cataloguing of the wide variety of scrolls in the library at Alexandria. Most notably, Callimachus created what is considered to be the first subject catalogue of the library holdings, called the pinakes, which contained 120 scrolls arranged into ten subject classes. Each class was then subdivided listing authors alphabetically by titles. The librarians at Alexandria were considered the "custodians of learning".

Roman Era

Near the end of the Roman Republic and the beginning of the Roman Empire, many Roman aristocrats had private libraries in their home. Many of these aristocrats, such as Cicero, kept his library to himself, only boasting of the enormity of his collection. Others, such as Lucullus, took on the role of librarian by lending out scrolls in their collection. Many Roman Emperors included public libraries into their political propaganda to win favour from citizens. While librarians worked in the various Emperors' libraries, there was no specific office or role that qualified an individual to be a librarian. For example, Pompeius Macer, the first librarian of Augustus' library, was a praetor (an office that combined both military and judicial duties). A later librarian of the same library was Gaius Julius Hyginus, a grammarian.

Middle Ages

Christian monasteries in Europe are credited with keeping libraries alive as an institution after the fall of the Roman Empire. During this time we see the first book (as opposed to scroll), the parchment codex. The role of librarian was often filled by an overseer of the scriptorium where monks would copy out books cover to cover. Anastasias was a very learned librarian who took on the title of *Bibliothecarius,* for his translations of the Greek Authors. We also learn about the introduction of the lectern system, in which books were chained to desks for security. In general during the early Middle Ages books were arranged according to subjects alphabetically, and were inventoried by a basic check list. Later on, however, a librarian, referred to as a *librarius,* began cataloguing by taking inventory and classifying the books.

Most libraries had been associated with churches, but around the 14th century universities began to emerge and they had libraries, and employed librarians. At the same time Princes, nobles and jurists began to establish libraries of their own as status symbols. King Charles V of France began his own library, and he kept his collection as a *bibliophile,* an attribute that is closely connected to librarians of this time.

Renaissance Age

The Renaissance is considered to be a time of aristocratic enthusiasm, during which great private libraries were developed in Europe by figures such as Petrarch and Boccaccio. These libraries were sponsored by popes, Princes, or dukes who sent agents throughout Western Europe to track down manuscripts in deteriorating monastic libraries. As a result, Renaissance libraries were filled with a wealth of texts. While these libraries were mostly restricted they were open to the public, and so librarians were needed to plan and organise libraries to meet public needs. This was also why libraries were often catalogued: the first catalogue appeared in 1595.

17th Century: During the 17th century in France the idea of *Bibliotheca Universalis* emerged from well-established academics and librarians: Conrad Gessner, Gabriel Naude, John Dury, and Gottfried Leibniz. With the approach of *Bibliotheca Universalis,* libraries changed: the content of libraries would become less selective, and they would include literature of entertainment as well as academic value. At this time libraries also became fully open to the public, with access not, as previously, restricted to a small circle of readers. The four librarians responsible for establishing the *Bibliotheca Universalis* are important figures in librarianship. Gabriel Naude published *Avis pour dresser une bibliotheque,* the first printed monograph on librarianship. In this monograph, Naude advocated collecting all kinds of books, old and new, of famous, more obscure, and heretical authors. He also contributed to the idea of organisation and administration of libraries which led to the development of library collections. It was also in part thanks to Naude that some libraries began to lend books outside of the precincts of the library. John Dury is considered to be the first English library theorist. He wrote two letters to Samuel Hartlib concerning the duties of a professional librarian, which were published in 1650 as "The Reformed Librarie-Keeper". He held that librarians should not only care for the books, but should also be well educated and accomplished to raise the standards of librarianship. Furthermore, he advocated that librarians deserve a living wage in order to use their energy to perform their duties to the fullest extent. Gottfried Leibniz upheld that the librarian was the most important factor in the aid of learning. He is credited as including science texts in addition to conventional literature within library collections. Another key figure of this time was Sir Thomas Bodley, who gave up his career as a diplomat and established Oxford's Bodleian library. He is credited as creating the first functional library of modern times. Subsequent librarians following Bodley were called *Protobibliothecarius Bodleianus,* Bodley's Librarian. They would earn £40 a year.

18th Century - France: In 18th century France two librarians, Hubert-Pascal Ameilhon and Joseph Van Praet, selected and identified over 300,000 books and manuscripts that became the property of the people in the *Bibliotheque Nationale.* During the French Revolution, librarians were solely responsible for the bibliographic planning of the nation. Out of this came the implementation of the concept of library service: the democratic extension of library services to the general public, regardless of wealth or education.

19th Century - US and Canada: In the 19th century, librarianship began to emerge as a profession. Male librarians called "bookmen" were found in sophisticated academic institutions around the middle of the 19th century. Like the librarians of Alexandria, they were scholars, not custodians of the library in which they worked. At that time there was no formal training for librarians: just by experience; they were self-taught or learned from the example of other librarians. But experienced librarians quite often recruited trainees. In 1872, Publishers Weekly, an instructional publication focusing on the publishing industry, began to devote small sections to librarians. The US Office of Education published "Public Libraries in the United States of America: Their History, Condition, and Management", a study for practising librarians, which included a manual with articles on management, administration, history, cataloguing, popular reading, and library buildings, written by notable authorities on librarianship. Also in the middle of the 19th century, the businessman Andrew Carnegie funded the construction of nearly 3000 libraries throughout the world. With this substantial increase in libraries, library workers were established as a permanent workforce. While Carnegie provided the institutions where librarianship as a profession blossomed, it was Melvil Dewey who was a primary force in the professionalisation of librarians and library education in the US. Dewey believed that librarians are meant to provide patrons with "better" books to improve people and their way of life. As part of his contribution to librarianship, Dewey, along with Justin Winsor, founded the creation of the American Library Association (ALA). Not only did the ALA provide national visibility and recognition to the field of librarianship, but it substantially strengthened the professional identity among the library practitioners. Dewey also had a hand in creating the first major professional publication for librarians: *The American Library Journal*, which was intended to assist librarians in their daily work. Moreover, Dewey had first-hand experience in opening the first library school, *The School of Library Economy*, which opened January 1, 1887. The programmes offered by the library school took three months, and students had to take an internship of up to 2 years to gain exposure to and familiarity with professional tasks.

The situation in Canada was different at that time. Canada did not have the advancement of library schools that the US did, and in the earlier half of the 19th century there was no formal training or education for potential librarians. The Toronto Public Library held competitive examinations for librarian hopefuls. The first exam was held December 15, 1887 and tested candidates on writing, arithmetic, reading, and English Literature. In 1890 they added a qualification for exam graduation: candidates were required to be at least 5'3" (160 cm) tall. Although successful candidates were referred to American library schools for training, they also had the option of serving as apprentices and learning on the job.

20th Century - US and Canada: After Dewey's library school, four more library schools were opened by 1900: Albany, Pratt Institute, Drexel University, and the Armour Institute. By 1919, there were 15 more programmes in the United States. These programmes varied by length of programme, type of degree or certificate awarded, and requirements for admission. On completion of most programmes, students became Bachelor's of Library Science. At the time, the degree of Master of Library Science was not awarded anywhere but Albany.

In recognition of the rise of Library education programmes, ALA created the ALA Committee on Library Training in which members would review the various educational programmes. This led to ALA's "Standards for Library Education", which established separate standards for the different types of training programmes. He neutral approach that ALA took to the Library Schools, however, influenced the schools to band together and create their own organisation: the Association of American Library Schools. The Williamson Report, created for the Carnegie Corporation, however, was the most important review of library education programmes. In the Williamson report, C.C. Williamson criticises the quality of many established programmes, and designates a university graduate degree, not a college bachelor's degree, as the appropriate education for professional librarians. The Graduate Library School, University of Chicago, 1928–1989. was founded to respond to this need. It was thanks to the Williamson report that librarians were required to receive one year of post-graduate education in librarianship. By the 1950s most library schools in the US awarded a Master's degree.

It was at this point in history that the notion of library science was established as the study for future librarians. In addition to professional librarians, faculty in Library Science programmes included other academics such as sociologists and historians. Because the faculty consisted mostly of scholars, they contributed a considerable amount of research which formed the foundation of the field of library science.

Another notable progression that arose after the "Williamson Report" was the establishment of The Hampton Institute Library School, the first library school to train African-American librarians in the US. After the establishment of the Hampton Institute Library School, more African-Americans were accepted to library schools, including Edward Christopher Williams, a graduate of the New York State Library School, who went on to become the director of the library at Howard University in 1916.

With the expanding economy, the baby boom, and the important federal legislation supporting the development of education institutions and their libraries, library schools reached their heyday in the 1950s to 1960s. These factors lead to an increased need for librarians. By the 1970s, there were more than 70 accredited library schools with master's programmes in US and Canada. By 1999, however, there were only 56 ALA-accredited library school programmes in the US and Canada. As library schools were never high-profile departments, these closures were a result of universities' efforts to reduce costs during the recessions of the 1980s.

While library schools were established in the US as early as the 19th century, library schools in Canada were not established until the 20th century. The starting push to establish library schools in Canada came from George Locke, chief librarian of the Toronto Public Library from 1908–1937. When Locke started his reign as chief librarian at TPL, training for librarians was still limited to on the job training. He believed, however, that librarians should be formally trained in educational programmes like those of the US. He favoured librarians that had a formal educational background in librarianship. In 1909, Locke recruited Winnifred Barnstead, a Canadian graduate of a two-year training course for librarians at Princeton University, to head the cataloguing department. Locke also hired Lillian H. Smith, a Canadian graduate from the training school at the Carnegie Library of Pittsburgh, to head the Children's department. With the help of Barnstead and Smith, Locke began his own training programme through the Toronto Public Library.

A contemporary of Locke was Edwin A. Hardy, secretary of the Ontario Library Association from its inception in 1901 to 1925, then as President from 1925–1926. Hardy was vocal in his opinion of formal educational training for librarians, and desperately desired a library school in Canada for fear of losing Canadian librarians trained in the US to the US. He was active in establishing library institutes, one-day regional workshops, through Ontario departments of Education, the first of which was held in Brantford, Ontario in 1907.

These institutes, however, proved insufficient, and there was a formal request for Departments of Education to begin a summer library school. The first of these summer schools ran in 1911; it was a hybrid programme modelled after American schools and normal schools which educated teachers in Ontario. This programme ran for four weeks in the summer when libraries were able to spare staff for training and eligible candidates were only those already employed in libraries. In 1919, it was extended to be a 3 month programme and became the Ontario Library School.

Library schools in Canada at this time, however, were unique to those in the US because they were under complete control of the Department of Education. For this reason, library schools in Canada fell under the jurisdiction of the Department of Education. While the Department of Education always provided funding for the library school, librarians were not able to push their own ideas or agenda. A course was established in the Ontario College of Education, located on the University of Toronto campus, to provide an academic and professional compliment to the already established technical training of librarians. Barnstead became the first director, but all financial, hiring, and curriculum matters were made by the Dean of the College of Education and the Minister of Education. Graduates of the programme did not receive a degree; they received a librarian's certificate from the Minister of Education and a diploma from the University of

Toronto. It was not until the 1930s that the library school became a separate entity from the Department and Ministry of Education. In 1937, the library school at the University of Toronto received ALA accreditation and Canadian students began to receive a professional degree - The Bachelor of Library Science.

Roles and Responsibilities

Positions and Duties: Specific duties vary depending on the size and type of library. Olivia Crosby described librarians as "Information experts in the information age". Most librarians spend their time working in one of the following areas of a library: Archivists can be specialised librarians who deal with archival materials, such as manuscripts, documents and records, though this varies from country to country, and there are other routes to the archival profession.

Collections development librarians monitor the selection of books and electronic resources. Large libraries often use approval plans, which involve the librarian for a specific subject creating a profile that allows publishers to send relevant books to the library without any additional vetting. Librarians can then see those books when they arrive and decide if they will become part of the collection or not. All collections librarians also have a certain amount of funding to allow them to purchase books and materials that don't arrive via approval.

Electronic resources librarians manage the databases that libraries license from third-party vendors. School librarians work in school libraries and perform duties as teachers, information technology specialists, and advocates for literacy. Instruction librarians teach information literacy skills in face-to-face classes and/or through the creation of online learning objects. They instruct library users on how to find, evaluate and use information effectively. They are most common in academic libraries. Media specialists teach students to find and analyse information, purchase books and other resources for the school library, supervise library assistants, and are responsible for all aspects of running the library/media centre. Both library media teachers (LMTs) and young adult public librarians order books and other materials that will interest their young adult patrons. They also must help YAs find relevant and authoritative Internet resources. Helping this age group to become lifelong learners and readers is a main objective of professionals in this library speciality.

Outreach librarians are charged with providing library and information services for underrepresented groups, such as people with disabilities, low income neighbourhoods, home bound adults and seniors, incarcerated and ex-offenders, and homeless and rural communities. In academic libraries, outreach librarians might focus on high school students, transfer students, first-generation college students, and minorities.

Public service librarians work with the public, frequently at the reference desk of lending libraries. Some specialise in serving adults or children. Children's librarians provide appropriate material for children at all age levels, include pre-readers, conduct specialised programmes and work with the children (and often their parents) to help foster interest and competence in the young reader. (In larger libraries, some specialise in teen services, periodicals, or other special collections.)

Reference or research librarians help people doing research to find the information they need, through a structured conversation called a reference interview. The help may take the form of research on a specific question, providing direction on the use of databases and other electronic information resources; obtaining specialised materials from other sources; or providing access to and care of delicate or expensive materials. These services are sometimes provided by other library staff that have been given a certain amount of special training; some have criticised this trend. Systems librarians develop, troubleshoot and maintain library systems, including the library catalogue and related systems. Technical service librarians work "behind the scenes" ordering library materials and database subscriptions, computers and other equipment, and supervise the cataloguing and physical processing of new materials.

A young adult or YA librarian serves patrons who are between 12 and 18 years old. Young adults are those patrons that look to library services to give them direction and guidance towards recreation, education, and emancipation. A young adult librarian could work in several different institutions; one might be a school library/media teacher, a member of a public library team, or a librarian in a penal institution. Licensing for library/media teacher includes a Bachelor or Master of Arts in Teaching and additional higher-level course work in library science. YA librarians who work in public libraries are expected to have a Master's degree in Library and/or Information Science (MLIS), relevant work experience, or a related credential.

Additional Responsibilities

Experienced librarians may take administrative positions such as library or information centre director. Similar to the management of any other organisation, they are concerned with the long-term planning of the library, and its relationship with its parent organisation (the city or county for a public library, the college/university for an academic library, or the organisation served by a special library). In smaller or specialised libraries, librarians typically perform a wide range of the different duties.

Representative examples of librarian responsibilities:

- Researching topics of interest for their constituencies.
- Referring patrons to other community organisations and government offices.
- Suggesting appropriate books ("readers' advisory") for children of different reading levels, and recommending novels for recreational reading.
- Facilitating and promoting reading clubs.
- Developing programmes for library users of all ages and backgrounds.
- Managing access to electronic information resources.
- Building collections to respond to changing community needs or demands.
- Creating pathfinders.
- Writing grants to gain funding for expanded programme or collections.
- Digitising collections for online access.
- Answering incoming reference questions via telephone, postal mail, *e*-mail, fax, and chat.
- Making and enforcing computer appointments on the public access Internet computers.

Workplaces: Basic categories of workplace settings for librarians are routinely classified around the world as: public, academic, school, and special. Some librarians will start and operate their own business. They often call themselves information brokers, research specialists, knowledge management, competitive intelligence or independent information professionals. Below are the basic differences between the types of libraries.

Public Library: Public libraries are created through legislation within the jurisdiction they serve. Accordingly, they are given certain benefits, such as taxpayer funding, but must adhere to service standards and meet a wide group of client needs. They are usually overseen by a board of directors or library commission from the community. Mission statements, service and collection policies are the fundamental administrative features of public libraries. Occasionally private lending libraries serve the public in the manner of public libraries. In the United States, public librarians and public libraries are represented by the Public Library Association. Public library staffing is structured in response to community needs. Libraries bridge traditional divisions between technical and public services positions by adopting new technologies such as mobile library services and reconfigure organisations depending on the local situation.

Academic Library: An academic library is a library that is an integral part of a college, university, or other institution of post-secondary education, administered to meet the information and research needs of its students, faculty, and staff. In the United States, the professional association for academic libraries and librarians is the Association of College and Research Libraries. Depending upon the institution, the library may serve a particular faculty or the entire institution. Many different types, sizes, and collections are found in academic libraries and some academic librarians are specialists in these collections and archives. A university librarian, or chief librarian, is responsible for the library within the college structure, and may also be called the Dean of Libraries. Some post-secondary institutions treat librarians as faculty, and they may be called professor or other academic ranks, which may or may not increase their salary and benefits. Some universities make similar demands of academic librarians for research and professional service as are required of faculty. Academic librarians administer various levels of service and privilege to faculty, students, alumni and the public.

School Library: A school library exclusively serve the needs of a public or private school. The primary purpose is to support the students, teachers, and curriculum of the school or school district. In addition to library administration, certificated teacher-librarians instruct individual students, groups and classes, and faculty in effective research methods, often referred to as information literacy skills. Audiovisual equipment service and/or textbook circulation may also be included in a school librarian's responsibilities. Often, teacher-librarians are qualified teachers who take academic courses for school library certification and/or earn a Master's degree in Library Science.

Special Library: Special libraries include news, law, medical, government, non-governmental organisation, prison, corporate, museum or any other type of library owned and operated by an organisation. They can be highly specialised, serving a discrete user group with a restricted collection area. In an increasingly global and virtual workplace, many special librarians may not even work in a library at all but instead manage and facilitate the use of electronic collections. Funding for special libraries varies widely. Librarians in some types of special libraries may be required to have additional training, such as a law degree for a librarian in an academic law library or appropriate subject degrees for subject specialities such as chemistry, engineering, etc. Many belong to the Special Libraries Association. There are also more specific associations such as the American Association of Law Libraries, Art Libraries Society of North America, the Medical Library Association, or the Visual Resources Association.

Education:

The US and Canada: In the United States and Canada, a librarian might have a one or two-year (more common) master's degree in library and information science, library science or information science (called an MI, MLS, MALIS, MSLS, MIS, MSIS, MS-LIS, MISt, MLIS, or MILS) from an accredited university. These degrees are accredited by the American Library Association and can have specialisations within fields such as archival studies, records management, information architecture, public librarianship, medical librarianship, law librarianship, special librarianship, academic librarianship, or school (K-12) librarianship. School librarians often are required to have a teaching credential; however, for the most part, a library science degree is not required. Many, if not most, academic librarians also have a second, subject-based master's degree. This is especially true of four-year colleges. The first doctoral degree in library science was offered by the Graduate Library School (GLS) at the University of Chicago beginning in 1928 until the GLS closure in 1989.

Australia: In Australia, a professional librarian must meet the requirements set out by the Australian Library and Information Association (ALIA). There are three ways in which these requirements can be met: the individual must obtain an ALIA-recognised bachelor degree in library and information studies, complete a first degree in any discipline followed by an ALIA-recognised post-graduate diploma or masters course, or gain an ALIA-recognised library technician qualifications (undertaken at a Technical and Further Education (TAFE) college/institute followed by an ALIA-recognised bachelor degree in library and information studies. ALIA is responsible for accreditation of library specific qualifications for both librarians and library technicians. Professional Australian teacher-librarians require slightly different qualifications. In addition to having a degree that meets ALIA's accreditation process, teacher librarians must also hold recognised teaching qualifications.

Advanced Degrees: It is also possible to earn a doctorate in library and information science. The first doctoral degree in library science was offered by the Graduate Library School, University of Chicago, 1928–1989. Graduates with Ph.Ds usually become teaching faculty in schools of library and information science, or sometimes occupy the directorship or deanship of university libraries. Those undertaking research at the doctoral level can pursue a very wide range of interests including information technology, government information policy, social research into information use among particular segments of society, information in organisations and corporate settings, and the history of books and printing.

Beta Phi Mu, the international honour society for library and information science and information technology, honours faculty for distinguished service to education for librarianship with the annual Beta Phi Mu Award. It is common in academic and other research libraries to require the librarians to obtain Master's degrees in some academic subject, sometimes but not necessarily related to their professional responsibilities; in major research libraries, some of the librarians will hold Ph.D. degrees in subject fields. Other advanced degrees often taken in conjunction with a degree in librarianship are law, management, health administration or public administration.

Library-related Positions: Library associates, library technicians, and library assistants often have college diplomas but usually do not hold library-related degrees. Occasionally they also hold undergraduate or graduate degrees in other disciplines. These workers, sometimes referred to as paraprofessionals, perform duties such as database management, library cataloguing, ready reference, and serials and monograph processing.

Professional Organisations and Activities: The two largest library associations in the United States are the American Library Association (ALA) and the Special Libraries Association. YALSA The Young Adult Library Services Association serves Young Adult librarians, and is part of the American Library Association. Many US states have their own library association as well. Librarians may also join such organisations as the Association of College and Research Libraries and the Public Library Association and the Art Libraries Society. The Canadian Library Association serves Canada and there are provincial associations as well, such as the Ontario Library Association. In the United Kingdom, the professional body for Librarians is the Chartered Institute of Library and Information Professionals (formerly known as the Library Association). The International Federation of Library Associations and Institutions (IFLA) represents the interests of libraries and librarians internationally.

Recent issues of concern for US libraries include implementation of the Patriot Act and the Children's Internet Protection Act. Many librarians around the world share American librarians' concern over ethical issues surrounding censorship and privacy. Some librarians join activist organisations like the UK-based Information for Social Change and the North American-based Progressive Librarians Guild. The Progressive Librarians Guild covers the actions of union library workers in its journal and blog, *Union Library Workers*.

Within the American Library Association (ALA), some also join the Social Responsibilities Round Table (SSRT). SRRT came into being amid the social ferment of the 1960s and is often critical of the American Library Association for not living up to its professed ideals. Another important activist organisation is the Social Responsibilities Special Interest Section of the American Association of Law Libraries (AALL). These activist organisations are viewed as controversial by some librarians, while others view them as a natural extension and outgrowth of their own deeply-held library ethics. Librarians in the United States who as political actors in our times provide examples of a commitment to equality, the right to know or social justice include Peter Chase, George Christian, Janet Nocek, and Barbara Bailey. In the Doe v. Gonzales case, these librarians challenged the constitutionality of the non-disclosure provisions of the National Security Letters issued by the government under the USA Patriot Act in terrorist or other investigations. The four received the Roger Baldwin Medal of Liberty from the American Civil Liberties Union in June 2007.

Technology: The increasing role of technology in libraries has a significant impact on the changing roles of librarians. New technologies are dramatically increasing the accessibility of information, and librarians are adapting to the evolving needs of users that emerge from the adoption of these new technologies. One of the most significant examples of how technology has changed the role of librarians in the last 50 years has been the move from traditional card catalogues to online public access catalogues (OPACs). Librarians had to develop software and the MARC standards for cataloguing records electronically. They had to purchase and run the computers necessary to use the software. They had to teach the public how to use the new technologies and move to more virtual working environments.

The same could be said of other technology developments, from electronic databases (including the Internet), to logistical functions such as bar codes (or in the near future RFID). Many librarians provide virtual reference services (via web-based chat, instant messaging, text messaging, and *e*-mail), work in digitising initiatives for works in the public domain, teach information literacy and technology classes to their users, and work on the development of information architectures for improving access and search functionality. These examples illustrate some of the ways in which librarians are using technology to fulfil and expand upon their historical roles.

Librarians must continually adapt to new formats for information, such as electronic journals and *e*-books, which present both challenges and opportunities in providing access and promoting them to library patrons. Increasing technological advance has presented the possibility of automating some aspects of traditional libraries. In 2004 a group of researchers in Spain developed the UJI Online Robot. This robot is able to navigate the library, look for the specified book, and upon its discovery, carefully take it from the shelf and deliver it to the user. Because of the robot's extremely limited function, its introduction into libraries poses little risk of the employment of librarians, whose duties are not defined by menial tasks such as the retrieval of books.

Popular Culture

Gender and Librarianship: Librarianship manifests a dual career structure for men and women in the United States. While the ratio of female to male librarians remains roughly 4:1, top positions such as Librarian of Congress have been held by men since the establishment of the Library of

Congress. Women, however, have made continuous progress towards equality. Women have been largely left out of standard histories of US librarianship, but Hildenbrand's scholarly assessment of the work done by women expanded the historical record. The Committee on the Status of Women in Librarianship (COSWL) of the American Library Association represents the diversity of women's interest within ALA and ensures that the Association considers the rights of the majority (women) in the library field; to promote and initiate the collection, analysis, dissemination, and coordination of information on the status of women in librarianship. The bibliographic history of women in US librarianship and women librarians developing services for women has been well-documented in the series of publications initially issued by the Social Responsibilities Round Table Task Force on Women and later continued by COSWL.

Library Assessment

Library assessment is a process undertaken by libraries to learn about the needs of users (and non-users) and to evaluate how well they support these needs, in order to improve library facilities, services and resources. In many libraries successful library assessment is dependent on the existence of a 'culture of assessment' in the library whose goal is to involve the entire library staff in the assessment process and to improve customer service.

Although most academic libraries have collected data on the size and use of their collections for decades, it is only since the late–1990s that many have embarked on a systematic process of assessment by surveying their users as well as their collections. Today, many academic libraries have created the position of Library Assessment Manager in order to coordinate and oversee their assessment activities. In addition, many libraries publish on their websites the improvements that were implemented following their surveys as a way of demonstrating accountability to survey participants. Several libraries have undertaken renovation or expansion projects as a result of their assessment activities as well as enhance resource discovery tools, improve website usability and stop redundant services.

Tools

In order to determine what is important to library users and how satisfied they are with services, resources and physical space, library assessment utilises a variety of research methods such as: website usability testing, observation, 'In-Library Use' surveys, focus groups, interviews, way finding, balanced scorecard, furniture usability, photo and mapping surveys, organisational climate, statistics and satisfaction surveys. The most widely used library satisfaction survey is LibQUAL+, a service quality evaluation survey developed by the Association of Research Libraries (ARL) based on ServQUAL. Other satisfaction surveys are: the SCONUL Satisfaction Survey, Insync Surveys (formerly Rodski), and Counting Opinions LibSat survey.

In USA, UK, Australia and Israel

Although library assessment has become almost ubiquitous in USA, Australia, UK and some European countries such as Italy and Denmark since 2000, it is still relatively uncommon elsewhere. Below are a selection of library assessment sites that show the multitude of activities undertaken by assessment teams: University of Washington, USA; University of Virginia, USA; University of York, UK, Council of Australian University Libraries (CAUL).

One notable exception is Israel whose University of Haifa Younes and Soraya Nazarian Library began a systematic process of library assessment in 2007, and has been conducting a Hebrew version of the University of Washington's 'In-Library Use' survey since 2008, and LibQUAL+ Lite (also in Hebrew) since 2009 in three-yearly cycles.

Conferences

The library assessment community holds two biennial conferences: the *Library Assessment Conference (LAC)* in USA and the *Northumbria Performance Measurement Conference* which is generally held in Europe. Also relevant are the annual *Qualitative and Quantitative Methods in Libraries Conference* (QQML) and the annual *Evidence Based Library and Information Practice Conference* (EBLIP).

Courses

Although courses on library assessment are not commonplace on the curricula of library schools, in the past few years several schools have opened courses, such as: the University of North Carolina at Chapel Hill School of Information and Library Science and the joint Digital Library Programme of Oslo and Akershus University College of Applied Sciences, Norway, Tallinn University, Estonia, and the University of Parma, Italy.

3

Concept and Perception

Traditionally there are three main branches in the profession-archivists, librarians and documentalists, within which certain specialisations such as bibliographer or indexer have become occupations in their own right. Today, however, people are more willing to accept that the information occupations all belong to a single profession. Before going into the details of the present information profession, let us look into some of the basic issues of our profession.

Concept of Librarianship

There is a long standing dispute, whether librarianship is a profession or vocation. In order to resolve this, let us see what characterises a profession and as to what is vocation.

Profession: A Profession warrants:

(a) A specialised knowledge of the field-scientific, historical or scholarly;

(b) Intensive preparation for acquiring needed skills and methods to put the knowledge to work;

(c) A set of principles, a social code or ethics;

(d) An organisation that will bind all the numbers together for:

- (i) Concerted opinion.
- (ii) To achieve high standards in performance;
- (iii) To act as a force to achieve common good and work for collective thinking; and

(e) Working with the prime purpose of rendering a public service.

Vocation: A vocation involves:

(a) An activity of some kind-routine, physical or scholarly;

(b) A craft, trade or profession;

(c) Need certain or no skills; and

(d) Mainly an activity involving service against fee or free.

Custodian of Library

From the above discussion we can safely conclude that librarianship is a profession rather than a vocation. Because:

(a) It needs a specialised knowledge-imparted in various library schools;

(b) It needs intensive training and continued practice to gain mastery over the skills needed for successful librarianship;

(c) A set of principles professional ethics have been drawn;

(d) A large number of organisations at various levels and of different groups are in existence; and

(e) It is service oriented.

Not Very Old: Librarianship may be regarded as the one, as old as the book. But librarianship as a profession is just a little over hundred years old. Earlier it was only an occupation. The organisation of librarianship as a profession started with the establishment of the American Library Association in 1876. The imparting of specialised knowledge started with the establishment of the first library school in 1887 by Dr. Melvil Dewey. Most of the national library associations drew a set of professional ethics. During the last hundred years, it has grown rapidly and established itself as a notable profession.

The choicest few working in special libraries, who enjoy a status on par with the executives or scientists have been trying to keep themselves away from the common core of the profession. Mr. J. Farradane in Britain started advocating since 1953 that "information work is distinct from librarianship and should in no way be confused with it." He took initiative to form the 'Institute of Information Scientists Ltd.' as distinct from The Library Association in 1958. The Library Association Record of 1953 and 1954 carried a spate of letters for and mostly against the arguments of Mr. Farradane. Some described that "Farradane was thumping a rather lonely tub."

Unified View: Many librarians in UK and USA, and Dr. Ranganathan and others in India were of the opinion that the difference between librarianship and information work was one of degree not kind. Information activity is rather an extension of library activity.

The Experts: Messrs Guinchat and Menou says that the current term for the unified profession of librarians, documentalists and information personnel, for want of a better, is 'Information Specialist'.

The general type of work of all information specialists is similar. They are:

(i) Process documents and information and must therefore master the technical skills involved;

(ii) Serve users and hence needs a gift for and interest in human relations; and

(iii) Need to work effectively on orderly and methodical turn of mind, a sense of organisation and imagination.

People Friendly:

Service: An information specialist works nearly always for other people and this can occasionally be frustrating. He should continue to be useful.

Communication Skills: Personal relations of the information specialist with the users and producers of information have more decisive influence on the effectiveness of the service. Information specialist must be capable of understanding other people, mixing socially and inspiring confidence-in short of communicating.

Judgement: There are many factors that influence information and communication. These factors change so rapidly that there is never a ready-made solution or a simple rule-of-thumb for every situation. An information scientist should take decisions on taking into account of all the criteria and visualising all the implications of his judgement.

Curiosity: The information specialist should have curiosity to know people, organisations, things, facts, ideas and techniques so that he can make use of the right means and method for providing service.

Adaptability: The needs of the users change from time to time. So too are the knowledge and techniques employed for dissemination of information. The information specialist should have an adaptive and flexible mind.

Perseverance and Modesty: Information work is always demanding: yet its immediate results are often far from impressive; besides, it is frequently the user who reaps the benefit and the praise.

Main Features

Sound Theory: Librarianship for long was based on rules-of-thumb and practices were involved or improved on trial and error basis. Practical librarianship was by way of apprenticeship or by observation and adaptation of practices in vogue in popular and big libraries. Some of the librarians started publishing manuals and guides on several library practices for the benefit of their fellow professionals. Establishment of library associations gave opportunities for professionals to meet and discuss matters of mutual interest. Some of the leaders in the profession started bringing out basic works of guidance. The establishment of library schools gave sound and well rounded theory. Research in librarianship was initiated. Laws, rules and regulations were framed so as to assist in the day-to-day management of libraries. Work of documentation brought-in scientists from diverse professions into the library and documentation profession. This helped the profession to understand the users better and to evolve new systems and services to meet their demands. Information science enhanced the boundaries of the profession and disciplines. The demands of the users started changing fast. With the result there has been a great thrust on library, documentation and information professionals to understand users needs better, understand the technology, adapt and refine them from time to time to provide pin pointed information in an expeditious manner.

Due Status

Library and information science (LIS) has attained due status in the universe of subjects at par with tradition disciplines. Education in library and information science is offered at various levels from school to university. At school and college level LIS is offered as an optional subject along with traditional disciplines. Special courses are also offered after school leaving certificate, post-degree programmes; as well as post-graduate courses in LIS. Research in LIS has also picked up and several areas in the discipline are being investigated with great emphasis and vigour. Apart from the regular courses, in-service refresher courses, orientation courses into the new areas of the discipline, etc. are also being organised on regular basis. New technology brought in specialists in computer, communication, repro and micrography and several other fields into information activity. Some of the subject Specialists are also involved in processing data; information analysis, condensation, repacking, etc.; providing liaison, referral and other services.

The Set-up

Today almost all countries, regions and states have professional organisations-not one, but many. Sometimes, unhealthy competition and rivalries are also observed among the various associations. Objectives of professional associations are also different. There is a need for unified approach among various organisations. The dichotomy between library and information workers should be removed. These organisations should strive to achieve high standards in service; service to the society/nation by way of providing right information to the right user, at right time; and bring the professionals together for close association and collective thinking.

Jobs Assigned

Tasks in the professional work are defined by level of complexity, the general and technical knowledge required and their related responsibilities.

There are fairly elementary routines of manipulative tasks usually performed by subordinate personnel or assistants. Technical tasks calling for professional qualifications and in certain cases for a general one too-cataloguing, indexing, bibliographic searches, etc.

Supervision, control and organisation of the various functions of the documentary chain. These tasks require a sound professional and general training together with some experience. Technical tasks requiring high level training and social experience in the fields or disciplines concerned, e.g., Evaluation of information; Liaison with users, etc.

Overall design and management of the unit; teaching and research; training, internship, etc.

In all information units there is a natural tendency for these divisions to overlap, with the result the profession contains a large number of generalists.

The Gradation

Broadly speaking there are four grades of professionals:

(1) Para-professional (assistants);

(2) Professional Juniors (Minimum qualification of graduation in LIS);

(3) Professional Seniors-grade II (Generally post-graduates in LIS with minimum 5 years of professional experience);

(4) Professional Seniors-grade I (Managers).

The Beginning

There are quite a few who enter the profession at the lower level and gradually climb up to the higher levels.

At professional junior level, the entry may be direct. They need proper orientation into the system, services and professional ethics.

At the professional senior level, the entry is by selection among experienced professionals. Their entry and their success will depend upon the maturity which they may demonstrate in their work and behaviour.

Quite sometimes, people in other professions particularly those with computer science, reprography, publishing and book trade, audiovisual media, etc. background enter the LIS profession. They undergo initial training at the appropriate level in an educational institution specialising in LIS or receive in-service training in conjunction with *ad hoc* courses. Some of them may enter the profession at the fag-end of their career into library and information field. Sometimes their experience, their competence as specialists can be an asset to the organisation. But often they may not be able to cope up with the work and the demand of the profession.

The Specialists

In this profession specialist skills reflect the type of information unit; the functions of the documentary chain which it covers; and its subject fields. These criteria can, of course be combined.

The major specialisations are archival administration; library administration; information management; documentation services, etc. Particularly in the fields of information and documentation (I&D) persons with the special knowledge in the concerned discipline are preferred.

Another area of specialisation is teaching and research in LIS. Lately with the development of large information systems and networks; and the creation of complex agencies to formulate information policy, a new specialist field has emerged-the planner or manager of information. Some of the retired professionals have started offering consultancy service and liaison service. The new occupation requires an excellent specialist background, advanced training in information science and powers of synthesis.

Levels of Responsibility

The status of the profession is the reflection of rules which define levels of responsibility, qualifications, career prospects, duties and rewards of each position and the level of training and amount of experience required.

A few countries have established rules at the national level for a particular branch of activity or for particular organisation. In the majority of countries, unfortunately, they are either not defined at all or only partly defined at the three levels. A recognised professional status is very important since it clarifies the relative standing of the profession and makes it possible to attract and keep staff with requisite qualities. Without such a formal framework, there is the risk, especially for new occupations, that each individual will be dealt with a haphazard fashion with a natural tendency to diminish his socio-professional standing. The danger of this is increased by the fact that the profession is too small to form a sufficiently powerful pressure group.

Developmental Programmes

Policy is a statement of general principle of intent that helps translate programme objectives into accomplishments. An objective is a desirable future condition. To achieve an objective, we have to draw a course of action. The course of action we may describe as a plan. The plan has to be implemented. The process of implementation needs a programme. A programme warrants several procedures.

The Weaknesses

For the most part, information agencies have not developed or used policies. They are guided by rules of thumb or were following trial and error method. Scientific management brought in the concept of policies, planning, implementation, evaluation, etc.

Basic Policy Questions: Policies can be formulated at different levels, say, at local, regional, state, national and international. At the local level, different institutions may have different policies. Thus, the policies of different institutions may differ. However, there will be some basic policy questions in general which even evolved separately may come out to be common.

Policy Statement: Policy statements provide the basis for orderly, smooth and thoughtful change. They further assist and enable longer range management planning. There can be policies to cover every decision or to meet every contingency.

The following basic premises are likely to be useful:

1. Programmes and activities must operate within one framework and be directed towards a common set of objectives.
2. The establishment of performance goals and the determination of priorities is contingent upon a clear understanding of general policies.
3. Consistency and efficiency of operations are ultimately dependent upon the existence of a sound body of policies.
4. Clear policy statement reinforce and protect the information service in matters where its position is questioned or challenged.

Value of Policies: Policies are of value in a number of ways. To name a few:

(i) They standardise activities;
(ii) Facilitate decision-making;
(iii) Minimise confusion;
(iv) Coordinate the activities of various units; and
(v) Conserve time in training personnel.

Policy Questions: Information organisations must address themselves to the following basic policy questions:

1. What is the major role of the information service?
2. What are the components of the information system? And how are they related?
3. What information services are provided? And how?
4. What are the different categories of users served?
5. Which levels of services are to be provided?
6. What role is to be played by the Information Unit in relation to the services available from outside agencies?
7. What are the roles, responsibilities and relationship of the users vis-a-vis the information services administration and staff.
8. What are the lines of authority and process of decision-making?

Issues for a Policy Statement: As mentioned earlier, policy statements are to be formulated at the institutional level, regional, state, national and international level. Whatever may be the level at which the policy has to be formulated, it should comprehend a set of basic issues. Some of these are illustrated below:

1. Identification of the objectives and thrust areas of the institution.
2. Requirement of the users.
3. Existing infrastructure and new infrastructure to be developed.
4. Manpower, material and monetary requirements.
5. Increased control of locally generated information.
6. Access to databases and databanks.
7. Information dissemination methods.
8. Information analysis and consolidation.

9. User studies and identification of user needs.
10. Improving access to new technologies.
11. Guidance for utilisation of the new technologies.
12. New services with new technologies.
13. Sharing of resources and services.
14. Increasing training of manpower.
15. Initiation into new technological developments.
16. Organising continuing education programmes.
17. Training in user training.
18. Training of trainers.
19. Guidelines for policy formulation.
20. Study and evaluation of systems and services.
21. Reviewing of the policy and its effectiveness.
22. Preparation of policy manual.
23. Cooperation and coordination with organisations at different levels and in different fields.

Process of Policy Formulation: The following framework for policy formation may be adopted:

Initiation of Policy Development: Involves preparation of a plan of action.

Review of Existing Policies: Covers identification of existing formal and informal policies.

Analysis of Existing Policies: A staff group may take up this task and identify the areas of the existing policy which may need to be rewritten or modified; as well as, new areas to be comprehended in the revision. Such decisions should primarily be based on the judgement of the effectiveness of each item of the present policy statement.

Recommendation of the New and Revised Policies: Areas in the policy that need to be rewritten or modified are to be drafted. Policy has to be formulated.

Process of Formulating Policies: A priority list of written policies that need to be drafted and outline of areas that need policy statements should be formulated.

Preparing a Policy Manual: This will form an ideal tool for management. Such a manual should comprehend objectives, planning, implementation, evaluation and revision of the policy; areas like institutional framework and linkages, services, systems and networks: personnel and management.

Dissemination of the Policy: Once the manual has been published the same need to be circulated widely for review and expert opinion.

Finalisation of the Policy: Valuable suggestions extended by reviewers and peers should be incorporated and the policy statement should be implemented.

Periodic Review of the Policy: The policy implemented has to be closely monitored for its performance. A policy review and revision programme has to be worked out. It is increasingly being realised that information is vital for national development as like energy and manpower. Most of the nations started evolving national policies for information generation, organisation and dissemination. In spite of restrictions trans-border data flow has become imperative and common.

Important Necessities

By and large nations have realised that the progress, if a nation depends upon the information it generates, disseminates to the users, and puts it to work. Lack of information is going to adversely affect the development. Secondly, the cost of information is directly related to its use or application. Generation of new information needs lot of inputs by way of research, gathering, processing and storage. Information dissemination is governed by the factor of recovery of investments in research, gathering, processing and storage costs. The cost of information make it imperative to share the information in a planned manner and coordination of information activities within a nation.

In almost all countries national governments are the major investors and disseminators of information. As such, each country should evolve a national policy of its own taking into consideration the developments at national and international level.

The Guidelines

Guidelines for the National Information Policy: A national information policy should comprehend the following:

1. Identification of the information needs of different socio-professional groups.
2. Establish priorities in regard to these needs.
3. Visualise a 'National Information System' with various subsystems, sectorial systems, etc.
4. Services to be offered and methods to provide the services.
5. Keep a watch on the capacity of the national information infrastructure (manpower, material, money, etc.)
6. Decide the measures needed to enable the national information system to perform its role and ensure compatibility among the various information systems in the country.
7. Decide as to how the national information system should be further developed.
8. Development and improvement of primary publications and ensure generally of the availability of information and data.
9. Strengthening the collections and improve the accessibility.
10. Policy regarding access to foreign collections of documents and databases.
11. Development of translation services; databases; networks; preservation, dissemination and conservation of documents.
12. Bibliographical control of documents generated in the country.
13. Coordination between various information units and subsystems.
14. Establishment of standards for information processing and communication of information.
15. Manpower planning.
16. Financing of information systems and pricing of the services.
17. Enacting appropriate legislation for regulation of information activities.
18. Promotion of user education and services.
19. Encouragement of education and research in library and information science.
20. Cooperation with other national and international organisations and institutions.

National Policy Initiative: The Department of Culture, Government of India setup a Committee on National Policy on Library and Information Systems (Conpolis) on 7th October 1985 under the

Chairmanship of Prof. D.P. Chattopadhyaya, Chairman RRRLF. During the period between December 1985 and February 1986, the Committee toured different parts of the country and discussed with cross-sections of people. Suggestions were also received from several individuals and institutions. An interim report was submitted in March and the final Report on 30th May 1986.

Salient Features of the Report

1. The most important task before the Government is to establish, maintain and strengthen the free public libraries in the country and enable them to work as a system.
2. The main thrust in this area should go to the rural public library. A village or a village cluster with an adequate population should have a community library which will also serve as an information centre. Resources of different agencies engaged in the work of public health, adult education, local self-government and such others may be pooled to build up this composite centre.
3. An important link should be established between the community library of the village and the village primary school. If the school does not have a library of its own, the community library should provide the children with an adequate book-corner.
4. The community library should also importantly cater for adult education and make-adequate audiovisual aids available to attract the illiterate villages.
5. The district library should serve as an apex library for each district with public libraries at city, town and village levels constituting important components in the district library system. In addition to the usual services to be rèndered by it, it should also provide for learning facilities and recreation for the handicapped, wherever possible, district libraries and comparable city public libraries should provide literature in Braille. The district library and branch libraries serve within its area wherever it is necessary and feasible. Special services should be rendered to hospitals, prisons and the infirm in their homes.
6. Libraries for special groups should be built in areas of tribal concentration or of minority communities to develop their distinctive cultures. Government will provide all encouragement for such communities to develop their own libraries through voluntary effort.
7. Each public library should have a section for children and, in addition, separate libraries for children with attractive books and audiovisual supporting material should be established wherever possible.
8. The district library will take the leadership in establishing linkages between all other public libraries of the district and work towards resource sharing within the area.
9. The key role of public libraries as chief sustaining agencies of distance education should be recognised and they should be adequately equipped with the relevant resources for this purpose.
10. All the libraries within a state should form part of a network extending from the community library of the village through intermediary levels to the district and to the State Central Library. This state network should eventually be connected with the national level network.
11. The role of the State Central Library is crucial in networking and the establishment of uniform library procedures within the State. The State Central Library or Directorate of Public Libraries has to perform as the co-ordinating agency for public libraries in the state.
12. To bring about the development of the public libraries in a state it is vital that each enacts its own library legislation. The Central Government should revise the Model Public Library

Bill, which it has already prepared, in the light of experience gained in recent years and urge upon the states the importance of enacting such legislation. Finances for library development should be funded by each state either from its general revenues or from local taxation.

13. The Central Government should assist the state in the development of public libraries in a larger way than it has done so far. The Raja Rammohan Roy Library Foundation as the national agency for co-ordinating and assisting the development of public libraries be suitably strengthened enabling it to discharge its responsibilities effectively.

Powerful Persons

The Department of Culture, GOI appointed an Empowered Committee in November 1986 again under the Chairmanship of Prof. D.P. Chattopadhyaya to lay down the programme of action for the implementation of the recommendations made in policy statement. The Empowered Committee submitted its Report in April 1988.

Active People

On examination of the Empowered Committee's decisions, the Department of Culture felt that certain decision would be difficult to implement in the form envisaged by the Empowered Committee. It was accordingly decided to constitute a Working Group to go through carefully each decision of the Empowered Committee and indicate how best to implement them. This Working Group was chaired by Ms. Komal Anand (Jt. Secretary to the Govt. of India, Department of Culture).

The President ILA was a Member of the Group. The Working Group discussed the whole matter in four sittings between July-September 1992 and submitted its suggestions in December 1992. These have since been accepted by the Government for implementation. Salient features of the Empowered Committee Report as accepted by the Working Group are given below:

1. Declaring Director, National Library as the Head of the Central Reference Library.
2. Initiating action for creation of National Commission on Library Documentation and Informatics within the Government set-up.
3. Establish, maintain and strengthen public libraries in the country and enable them to work as a system.
4. Making rural library service available in each village under the "Minimum Needs Programme" by 2001 AD by Central and State Government agencies.
5. Every rural public library should have a children's section.
6. Community Centre Libraries should have AV material and equipment. Such libraries should have an important role in Adult Education Programme.
7. District Libraries should provide more facilities for the handicapped and underprivileged classes.
8. Public libraries should act as chief sustaining agencies for distance education and should be adequately equipped.
9. State Central Library should play an important role in networking, establishment of uniform library procedures and standards within the state.
10. RRRLF may establish 100 model rural libraries in collaboration with state agencies.
11. The Central Government may revise Model Public Library Bill in the light of the experience gained in the recent years.

12. The Central Government in collaboration with State Governments may establish at least one multilingual library in each state.
13. Every school and college must have a library and a qualified librarian.
14. Association of Indian Universities may take up a project evolving academic library norms on priority basis.
15. To begin with, a few selected University Library Science Departments may be provided with adequate resources as part of manpower development programme.
16. The National Library, INSDOC, DST and ICSSR may take suitable steps to create national databases.
17. There should be a National Library System (NLS) consisting of the National Library, National Depository Libraries in Delhi, Mumbai and Chennai; National subject libraries and other libraries of national importance.
18. There is a strong need of having a national R&D Centre for Library and Information Science. National Commission on Libraries once established may consider this proposal.
19. A national 'Grid' of public libraries be developed linking village community centre library with national grid.
20. The Department of Culture may take suitable steps in preparing the Draft Bill on National Commission on Libraries (NCL) giving the detailed provision under powers and function of the NCL; Bodies of NCL; Finances of NCL, etc.
21. Department of Culture has been requested to constitute a "Library Unit" which will be entrusted with the implementation of Empowered Committee's decisions.

Most of the recommendations of the Empowered Committee are of general nature. It seems no action has been initiated either in creating the envisaged "Library Unit" or in the establishment of NCL. The Department of Culture was vested with the responsibility of preparing the Draft Bill on NCL. The Department of Culture should appoint a 'Committee of Experts" to draft the Bill. The proposed NCL should have more of ex-officio members rather than *ad hoc* nominations. Professional associations and senior professionals should have place in the NCL. In fact, the Department of Culture should appoint yet another committee to draft a National Library Plan giving long-term and short-term programmes, spelling out details of a "National Library System' networking: norms for cooperation and coordination of services; etc.

Moral Aspects

A set of moral principles and a code of conduct is a necessary guide to professional behaviour. Many of the countries have evolved written codes or ethics. Special codes were also drawn for some of the special branches of the profession. It is desirable to have a written professional code. These codes cover from general principles of dedication, devotion, determination and commitment to the profession; General social ethics of understanding the users; Social obligations of the library; Social behaviour, equality before service, etc.; Moral responsibilities of the professionals; Professional goals and objectives and means of achieving them. The code of ethics should be prefaced with the nobility of the profession and responsibilities of the professionals. These ethics time and again remind the professional his role, responsibilities and social commitment. The professional should keep the code of ethics before him so that they remind him the expectations of the profession. If possible an oath be administered to the new entrants in the profession to live up to the code of ethics of the profession.

4

Evolution of Libraries, through the Ages

Ancient Period

The discovery of innumerable seals from Mohenjodaro, Harappa, Lothal and other places confirm the fact that writing was well known in the so-called pre-historic India and Indians had the conception of reduplication on the basis of a printing technique.

Universities: By 700 BC universities or centres of learning were started in Panchala, Kuru, Videha, Matsya, Usinara, Taxila, Naimisharanya, Kasi and other places.

Scribes: Vinaya Pitika and Nikayas mention a list of games of which one is called 'Akharika' (= lettering). It was guessing of letters in the air or in a play fellows back. The great grammarian Panini used the term 'Lipikara' for scribes in the eighth chapter of his work.

Libraries: Acharya Nagarjuna, the founder of Mahayana Buddhism is known to have maintained a library on the top-floor of the university building. Taxila was one of the most important seats of learning in Ancient India. It was in existence from 700 BC. The teaching was mostly in Vedic literature, philosophy and eighteen shilpas. It was said that there was a rich library. The great grammarian Panini and great economist Kautilya were students of this university. Another important library of great significance was that of the Nalanda University established in the fourth century AD. The area of the library was called as "Dharma Ganja" (= Mast of religion). The library was said to be in three grandest buildings named as 'Ratna-Sagar', Ratna Dadhi' and 'Ratna Ranjaka'. Of these, the last one is said to be of nine storied building. The other important academic libraries of ancient India were Odantapuri, Vikramasila, Somapuri, Jagadala, etc.

Medieval Age

Muslim Contribution: Muslim rulers were patrons of education, literature and libraries. Babur brought with him to India all the specimen he could collect from the library of his ancestors. He authored many works on jurisprudence and prosody. He encouraged calligraphy and himself invented a new type of writing called Baburi Hand. Humayun was also a lover of books and it is said that he converted a pleasure house in purana-qila in Delhi into a library. Akbar maintained an "Imperial Library" and Mulla Pir Muhammad was his Librarian. The books in his library were classified and catalogued according to a scheme developed by them. He encouraged translations and illustration of manuscripts. Jahangir is said to have maintained a personal library which moved with him wherever he went. Aurangazeb also encouraged, libraries and Islamic learning.

Printing Press in India: Christian missionaries were responsible for the introduction of printing press in India. The first press arrived in Goa on September 6, 1556 from Portugal. It was accidental. The press which was landed in India was bound for Abyssinia. By the time the press reached Goa, the relations between the Abyssinian ruler and the Portuguese missionaries were strained and the press was retained in Goa.

David Library: The East India Company established the fort St. David Library at Cuddalore in 1707. In the year 1709, The Society for Promotion Christian Knowledge sent out a circulating library to Calcutta, the first of its kind in India.

The Asiatic Society, Calcutta was established in 1784. It started Asiatic Researches, a scientific journal in 1787 which continued till 1939.

Early Libraries: The concept of 'public libraries is an exotic one. It was the British who introduced this concept by starting a few public libraries in the chief metropolitan cities of this country in the late 18th Century. Prior to these, there were libraries, rich in many ways but were purely private, owned by the native rulers, their officials and a few feudal lords. The access was-to a chosen few.

Modern Times

When the British established their rule and started settling in big colonies in this country, felt the need of libraries. The residents of Kolkata made an appeal to the Society for the Promotion of Christian Knowledge to dispatch a 'circulating library" to meet their reading demands. The Society had conceded to their request and sent on in the year 1709. The concept of libraries for all had dawned on this soil. Subsequently a number of such libraries were established in this country. Notable among them are fort St. George Library (1714), East India Company's Library, Bombay (1715); John Andrews Circulating Library at Fort Williams, Calcutta (1770), The Calcutta Circulating Library started by Messrs Cock, Marxwell & Co. (1787); and The Calcutta Literary Society's Library (1818).

Academic Libraries: The East India Company had faced administrative difficulties on account of language barrier. As a solution they started establishing schools to train local people in English who can serve as the middle men between the Government and the public. The first school to be started thus was the one at fort St. George in 1715. This was followed by the Fort William School in Calcutta founded in 1729. Thereafter a number of schools, colleges and universities were started in the course of time by the rulers as well as by the public. The first college to be started in this country is the fort William College in 1800. The first three modern universities were started in 1857 in Calcutta, Bombay and Madras successively.

Research Libraries: The Asiatic Society was established in Calcutta in the year 1784. Mr. Warren Hastings was its first Patron and Sir William Jones, Judge of the Calcutta's Supreme Court was its first President, which post he retained till his death. This society has started building-up a good research library since its inception. The Asiatic Society, Bombay founded in 1804 also developed a good library. The first technical library to be founded in this country is the Victoria Technical Library in Nagpur in 1806. The Madras Literary Society had founded its library in 1812.

Registration of Libraries: The Government of Bombay Province started a scheme for registering libraries in 1808 with the intention of supplying copies of books to be published from the "fund for the Encouragement of Literature" This has been the first attempt to register the libraries and assist them with literature by the Government.

Public Libraries: The subscription Library started at the Fort Williams in 1770 was later on converted into a public library in the early 19th century. A few public libraries started appearing sporadically here and there during the same period in this country. Notable among them are: The Asha Granthalaya, Waltair (1800); United Services Library, Poona (1818); Raghunandan Library, Puri (1821); Bombay General Library (1830). These were followed by those started in Cochin, Ernakulam, Serampore, Trichur and Nasik.

Calcutta Public Library: Mr. J.H. Stocquel, the editor of the local daily Englishman drafted a scheme for the establishment of a public library in Calcutta and convened a general meeting at Town Hall on 31 October. Indians and Europeans all supported the scheme. As a result a public library was established and was first house in the lower apartment of Dr. E.P. Strang's house at Esplanade, Calcutta. The Government of India put the final seal to the Imperial Library Act in 1902 under which it became the owners of the Calcutta Public Library and its building. The new library was renamed as the 'Imperial Library'.

Gradual Development

The library consciousness has started developing from the beginning of this century. There are various reasons for this. Important among them are:

> The division of Bengal in the early part of this century brought in the people a smouldering political consciousness, which culminated into a struggle for freedom. The leaders of the nation, spearheading the movement realised that the literacy of the masses is an essential prerequisite to arouse public consciousness in this direction and the libraries will play a vital role in educating the masses and creating political consciousness among the people.

Evolution of Academic Libraries in 21st Century

As The ALA Glossary of Library and Information Science states, a library is "a collection of materials organised to provide physical, bibliographic, and intellectual access to a target group, with a staff that is trained to provide services and programmes related to the information needs of the target group." A library is not worthy of the name if it is not organised and administered according to sound principles of library and information science. Without such organising principles, collections of information resources of any substantial size cannot be used effectively or efficiently.

Without such organising principles, you don't have an effective library-you have the Internet. Information retrieval becomes an arduous process of hit and miss, of trial and error, with no assurance that the search-engine-of-the-day has really turned up all relevant sites. But organising and administering information resources is becoming increasingly challenging due to the explosion in recent years of new publications, both in paper and electronic formats. In reality, no academic library is capable any longer of meeting all the needs of its users, if that was ever possible. Even the great research libraries log thousands of interlibrary loan and document delivery requests every year. In short, truly effective academic libraries are more reliant than ever on highly skilled and well trained professionals who are sensitive to the needs of library constituents. The primary mission of the library faculty and staff as we enter the 21st Century should be to support educational goals and priorities through whatever media, means, and services are most appropriate, and to accomplish this mission the library faculty and staff must be an integral part of institutional planning and decision-making. I believe that those of us who try to carry out this academic library mission will find that while the surface veneer of our work will continue to change in dramatic and often stressful ways, we will also continue to be guided most wisely by the values and principles that have been the library's bedrock for decades. Consider S.R. Ranganathan's five laws of library science, which he published in 1931:

1. Books Are For Use.
2. Every Reader His/Her Book.
3. Every Book Its Reader.
4. Save The Time Of The Reader.
5. The Library Is A Growing Organism.

Maurice Line underscored the validity of these laws by turning them on their heads to describe what he believed to be the reality of too many libraries:

1. Books Are For Collecting.
2. Some Readers Their Books.
3. Some Books Their Readers.
4. Waste The Time of the Reader.
5. The Library Is A Growing Mausoleum.

The laws of Ranganathan and Line assert in their own ways that the academic library should be measured by the extent to which it selects resources on the basis of user needs, organises the resources so they may be identified and accessed efficiently, promotes and exposes resources to potential users, engages its users in an ongoing dialogue regarding evolving user needs, and responds to social and technological trends affecting higher education. Not only does that describe the ideal academic library of today, but I believe adherence to Ranganathan's laws will continue to provide the best guide to achieving the ideal library in the 21st Century. The balance of this paper will expand on that assertion.

Consider the first law, Books Are For Use. This means there should be no unnecessary barriers or constraints on the use of information resources. The ideal academic library seeks the best balance between preservation concerns and the need for patrons to use materials efficiently and effectively. Rare or irreplaceable materials require greater emphasis on preservation than on user convenience, but so far as our general collections are concerned the ideal academic library tailors its loan and related service policies to maximise the opportunities for students and faculty to use materials. A new but very important aspect of eliminating barriers and constraints on access is the negotiation of favourable license terms for electronic databases.

Many of the standard contracts which vendors present us contain restrictions that go beyond a copyright owner's statutory rights and infringe upon fair use. In response, we should insist upon license terms that protect fair use without affecting the vendor's right to a fair profit or its competitiveness in the marketplace. I am encouraged that a number of experts have published sample license terms that are intended to accomplish just that task. I hope that as academic libraries in the early 21st Century assert their rights and reject such dangerous requirements as indemnification of vendors against lawsuits, we will find standardised language in license agreements that is more realistic and less one-sided. Another constraint on access involves the authentication of eligible users of electronic resources. As we rely more and more on electronic databases, both for users on campus and for remote students enrolled in distance learning programmes, we must perfect authentication techniques such as web access management programmes.

The academic library will continue to be a vanguard in the protection of free access to knowledge. First, consider that the people in the future will only know about us that which we preserve. Allowing the records of the past to disappear is a form of censorship. We must beware of being too selective about what we collect and preserve. The universe of academic libraries must preserve all records of all societies and communities and make those records available to all. This will be a major challenge in the future since we can expect the trend towards managing and controlling information as a commodity will continue. Libraries must be responsible for ensuring information is archived and doesn't simply disappear because a commercial vendor goes out of business. And libraries must strive to make information as accessible as possible, so that in the Information Economy about which we hear so much, there is not an unnecessary chasm between haves and have-nots.

A related issue of information preservation is that of data permanence. The May 1999 issue of *American Libraries* records some facts that should give pause to anyone who thinks the paperless society will be within reach in the first decade of the 21st Century:

- Magnetic media such as floppy disks have a data life span of five years or less. According to data-preservation scientist J.W.C. Van Bogart, even in extreme circumstances high quality paper lasts 10 times longer than the best magnetic media used for commercial and scientific data storage.
- Optical media, such as CD-ROM and DVD-ROM, are proving to be far less durable than originally expected. The longest warranty in the industry for CD-ROM products only guarantees for 25 years, in spite of the claims that CD disks are good for more than a century. DVD's can be expected to have a shorter life span since increased data density has been proven to be associated with shorter life spans. In contrast, the life span of acid paper, which libraries have tried to avoid collecting for decades, is 50 to 100 years.
- As of the end of 1999, Kodak still stated on its website, "Digital storage media impose a strict discipline that human-readable records do not: their rapid evolution creates a continual progression of technology that cannot safely be ignored for too long." In other words, according to Van Bogart, libraries seeking to use digital media for long-term data and information storage could be faced every 10-20 years with either
  (a) copying such data to the latest formats, or
  (b) purchasing the latest programme for uploading data on obsolete formats to the latest medium.

Even given the obvious advantages of electronic media for remote access and searching for specific information, will we be able to justify this new kind of "planned obsolescence" to our funding authorities? The academic library in the first five years of the 21st Century will need to make tough decisions about what resources will need to be archived for the long term, and in what format. I suggest to you that paper will continue to be one of our most important long term data storage formats.

Let us now reflect on the second law, Every Reader His/Her Book. Here Ranganathan is telling us we are obliged to help find the resources that meet a user's need, and that may include going beyond the resources that are easily at hand. As I said earlier, no academic library is able to collect comprehensively. We must engage our constituents in the development of our collection development policy and ensure that when class assignments are made there will be adequate information resources to support them. We should try to stay abreast of the research needs of the faculty and support those needs as much as possible through materials purchases and subscriptions, and also through fast, accurate, and (to the user at least) free document delivery systems. The ideal academic library, particularly one that is a member of a state-supported university system, will help build an infrastructure of policies and procedures that facilitate resource sharing among the system's libraries.

The library should take full advantage of the dialogues that are possible with library advisory committees, through focus groups and surveys, suggestion boxes and *e*-mail addresses, informal communication of all kinds, and by the library faculty and staff being fully engaged in the academic community. The dominant ethic of librarianship is service to the individual, community, and society as a whole. This is especially true for publicly supported academic institutions. This requires attention to quality and living up to-and even surpassing-the expectations of library users. I would add that it also requires a commitment to human diversity and multiculturalism, which should be reflected in collection development policies and respected in our patron services.

The third law is Every Book Its Reader. In the ideal academic library, the librarians seek to match information materials with their potential users. New acquisitions which could be helpful to someone's ongoing research should be brought to that individual's attention. We should be as concerned with the exposure and promotion of our resources as we are with their accessibility. Over the course of the next five years, and indeed into the foreseeable future, this goal will not only be more difficult but also more urgent due to the remarkable proliferation of paper and electronic publications. As Richard Dougherty wrote: "There is a striking contradiction between our professional imperative of providing free and easy access to infonnation and the rising tide of information that is rapidly engulfing us... we need to face the reality that more and more people haven't the time, the expertise, or the psychological make-up to find the information that best serves their needs."

Through such means as electronic and printed bibliographies, current awareness services, and liaison programmes with academic departments, librarians should be the matchmakers that bring materials to the people who could use them.

Law number 4 is Save The Time Of The Reader. Information services must satisfy needs as efficiently as possible. Clearly this relates back to my earlier comment about the difference between a library and an unorganised collection of materials.

An important way in which an academic library will save the time of the reader is by bringing greater bibliographic order to the Internet and World Wide Web. As marvellous as these are, they leave much to be desired as efficient and orderly means of archiving and retrieving information. I enjoyed Will Manley's humorous take on the Internet, to wit: "If we were to go about acquiring the Internet like any other resource we would probably try to read a review of it. What would the objective reviewer say? 'The Internet is a vast informational network with millions of entries on a myriad of diverse subjects. It is loosely and unreliably indexed and is awkward to use because of the increasingly slow response time. While some of the entries are well researched by reliable authors, many others are poorly written by people with no literary or academic credentials who have a pronounced proclivity to punctuate their points with the repeated use of the words cool and suck.'" In summary, says Manley, "the Internet is the global village's vanity press. It has no editorial board and no editorial principles."

Given the vastness of the Internet and its resources, we cannot rely on existing Internet search engines to help us find all of the best information available to meet our needs. A 1999 study sponsored by the NEC Research Institute of 11 search engines revealed that none of the 11 indexed more than 16 per cent of the World Wide Web. I think over the course of the next several years we will need to re-double our efforts to save the time of our users by identifying those reliable Internet sites that are likely to be of the greatest utility and facilitating access to those sites.

This can be done through subject bibliographies that are printed as well as mounted on the library's web page with links to the sites. It can be done through creative proposals like Dan Hazen's selective scanning. In this scheme, digitising front matter like tables of contents could result in quicker and cheaper cataloguing, and in the enhancement of the information that cataloguers can provide users trying to make informed choices of which materials to examine in depth. It can also be done by helping users learn advanced searching skills and evaluate critically the results of their searches. And it certainly should be done through working as partners with commercial vendors and campus computer centres to design, test, and implement improved search capabilities, user interfaces, and ergonomic hardware.

In the future we must certainly continue to use technology intelligently to enhance our services. We must reject the false dichotomy of having to pick between two sides; in reality, we do not have to choose between being a Luddite or a technocrat. I agree with Michael Gorman's view, "electronic methods are best for...giving access to data and small, discrete packets of textual, numeric, and visual information (such as those found in many reference works). Each of the other media has areas in which it is the best. In particular, print on paper is and will be the pre-eminent medium for the communication of cumulative knowledge by means of sustained reading."

Finally, law number 5 states that The Library Is A Growing Organism. While all of Ranganathan's laws, as I interpret them, imply the need to be prepared for change, this fifth law reinforces that need explicitly. We will need to continue to adapt to new social conditions, technological developments, and changing needs of the clientele. The number of challenges we face can seem daunting at times, but change is the norm in the library world and we must not delude ourselves into hoping that we are ever going to reach a steady-state plateau.

A clear implication of this law is that the ideal academic library will make a major ongoing investment in the continuing development of faculty and staff knowledge and skills. We must take advantage of workshops and seminars offered on and off campus-some of which are now offered electronically. We must attend professional conferences, engage in informal networking with peers, and learn from the literatures of our own and other appropriate disciplines.

The academic library of the future will use all kinds of carriers of knowledge and information, with each new means of communication enhancing and supplementing the strengths of all previous means. To quote Michael Gorman again, "There is no reason to cling to print on paper, images on film, or grooves on discs in cases when it can be demonstrated clearly that technology offers a cost-beneficial alternative. What is the point, however, in replacing print on paper, etc., when new technology is less effective, more costly, or has other disadvantages? The best approach to the future of libraries lies in this utilitarianism."

The academic library in a publicly supported university will find itself increasingly called upon to serve the citizens of the region and to engage in cooperative ventures with other post-secondary institutions in the state. For example, GALILEO is the paradigmatic example of the benefits of libraries working cooperatively and with the state to establish an electronic network that brings enormous information resources to all citizens of the state, at a fraction of the full cost that the individual libraries would have paid for those resources. In the future, I think such collaborative efforts will become ever more important means of maximising access to information and controlling costs. Within such initiatives, an individual academic library must be prepared to demonstrate leadership, contribute whatever strengths of personnel and collections it may have, and continue to keep its primary users' unique set of priorities in mind as it works with other libraries for the good of the entire state.

Another intriguing challenge to academic libraries is the growing tendency of superstores like Barnes and Noble or Borders to usurp the academic library as the favoured location for students to study. Renee Feinberg, a reference librarian at Brooklyn College, has reported on her interviews with college students she encounters at B&N superstores, and not surprisingly to those of us who have enjoyed patronising these stores, the students indicate a preference for B&N over their campus libraries because of the more comfortable and congenial settings, good coffee, the buzz of conversation, and in some cases even the more convenient hours of operation. Perhaps most disturbing, however, is the recurring statement that B&N has better and more accessible monograph holdings, especially of recently published materials.

This is worth bearing in mind when we hear the stories of how our X Generation students are plugged into technology to the point of ignoring printed resources. The truth may fall somewhere in between these two extremes. As Feinberg states: "Students want their books. If libraries choose to weaken their book collections in favour of increased electronic information, they will lose patrons who would support them as they argue for protection of collections." What libraries can learn from these bookstores, as Leonard Kniffel wrote, is to return to the niceties we appear to have abandoned: tasteful signs, cozy spots, comfort, elegance, and the human touch. We in academic libraries should concede nothing to Barnes and Noble in terms of comfort, convenience, and service, and we certainly should not bow to B&N's holdings of scholarly books.

Conclusion

As academic libraries evolve to meet new challenges, they must retain the best of the past and a sense of the history of libraries and of scholarly communication. With a sense of history, and a knowledge of enduring values and the continuity of our mission, there must also be the acceptance of the challenge of innovation. If the library ever ceases to be a growing organism, then it really will become Maurice Line's growing mausoleum.

Evolution of Library Science, as a Subject

Pre-independence Days

The first ever library school was started by Melvil Dewey in USA in 1887. WA Bordon, a disciple of Dewey initiated training in librarianship in India in 1911 at Baroda to create a cadre of men to man the newly established libraries in the State library system. In 1913, another training class for working librarians of town libraries, was started. These classes continued even after the departure of Bordon. However, the existence of in-service training was initiated by John Macfarlane, the first librarian of the Imperial Library (now National Library) at Calcutta from 1901 to 1906 as mentioned in some reports. In subsequent years, the training programme was opened to the staff of other libraries and even to non-librarians but dealing in books and other documents.

Punjab University: A more systematic training programme was initiated by another American librarian by name Asa Don Dickenson at Punjab University, Lahore (now in Pakistan). This happens to be the first university course in India. Mr. Dickenson also prepared a manual for the use of students namely, The Punjab Library Primer.

Andhra Desa: Library movement in Andhra is described as the 'peoples movement' because, it was the common man who took lead in the establishment of the libraries and the reading rooms. With the coming-up of innumerable libraries, there arose the need for people with some background knowledge and technique of library management. The Andhra Desa Library Association (founded in 1914) started conducting 'training classes' for the library workers in the state in 1920 at Vijayawada. The classes covered a module on running adult education classes in addition to library techniques.

Mysore State: In the same year, i.e., in 1920, a course for the training of librarians was conducted at Bangalore under the 'programme of library development' initiated by the then Dewan of Mysore, M. Visweswarayya.

Madras Library Association (MALA): A regular certificate course in Library Science was organised by MALA from 1929. A 'Summer School' for college librarians and Lecturers-in-charge of college libraries in Madras was held in 1928 and repeated in 1930. University of Madras took-up the training course of MALA in 1931 and started offering the course on a regular basis.

Andhra University: Andhra University started a certificate course in 1935. But, the course was abandoned shortly, thereafter. In 1970 the university started B Lib Sc Course.

Imperial Library, Calcutta: The Imperial Library, Calcutta started a training class under the supervision of its Librarian Mr. K.M. Asadullah in 1935. It was a full time regular Diploma Course in Librarianship at the Imperial Library (now National Library), Calcutta. It continued till 1946.

Bengal Library Association: The Bengal Library Association under the leadership of Kumara Munindra Deb Rat Mahasay arranged a 'Library Training Camp' at Banasberia in 1935.

University of Madras: With the experience in conducting the certificate course, the University Librarian, S.R. Ranganathan proposed to the University of Madras to introduce a post-graduate degree course in 1936. This was not accepted then on the ground that "the subject is not a discipline of sufficient calibre for which the university can give a degree" However, undaunted Ranganathan could succeed in convincing the authorities in the next year, i.e., in 1937 and the university introduced a one year post-graduate diploma course in place of the certificate course of three months duration.

Banaras Hindu University and Bombay University: The second university to start a post-graduate diploma course was the Banaras Hindu University in 1942. University of Bombay initiated a similar diploma course in 1943.

Delhi University: Sir Maurice Gwyer, the then Vice-chancellor of University of Delhi invited Dr. S.S. Ranganathan to organise a Department of Library Science. The Department was started in 1947 to conduct Post-Graduate Diploma in Library Science. Dr. S.R. Ranganathan worked as Hon. Professor at the University during 1947–1955.

First Degree Course: The University of Delhi instituted the first post-diploma degree course in 1948. In 1949 the structure was changed. The programme of Master of Library Science was introduced as a two year course with the first year leading to Post-Graduate Diploma in Library Science (later changed into Bachelor of Library Science).

GOI's In-service Training Course: The Government of India Libraries Association approached the Union Government to start an in-service training course for the staff working in various government organisations to meet the shortage of qualified librarians. Accordingly, a training course was started in 1953. This course was recognised as equivalent to the university diploma course.

Institute of Library Science

An Institute of Library Science was established at the University of Delhi with a grant from the Union Ministry of Education. Its main objectives were to train public librarians and to prepare teaching aids and materials. This Institute was inaugurated in 1959. Unfortunately this Institute was closed down in 1964 and the staff was got merged with the University Department of Library Science.

Diploma to Degree: The full-time one year Diploma Course was converted to degree course (B Lib. Sc.) in 1960 by Madras University. By mid-1960s many other universities had fallen in line with University of Madras and the recommendation of Review Committee Report of UGC.

First B.Lib. Sc. Course: In 1957 Aligarh Muslim University started B Lib Sc. Course for the first time in the country. It had been conducting certificate course since 1951.

Polytechnic Diploma Courses: The Government Polytechnics for women at Ambala, Bangalore, Chandigarh, Delhi, Jallandar and Rourkela started post-matric Diploma courses of two year duration in late 1960s.

DRTC Course: Dr. Ranganathan started Documentation Research and Training Centre (DRTC) at Bangalore in 1962 under the auspices of Indian Statistical Institute (ISI) Calcutta. Its training course was of 14 months duration (Recently it has been made a two year programme).

INSDOC Course: INSDOC conducted a short-term course for Asian documentalists in 1963. Later in 1964, it started a one year post-graduate course in 'Documentation and Reprography' leading to "Associateship in Documentation and Reprography." Now it is called "Course, in Information Science."

University Courses

Bachelor of Library and Information Science: Most of the university departments today are offering Bachelor of Library and Information Science (BLI Sc) course, though in some universities still they are calling it as Bachelor of Library Science (B Lib Sc) course (e.g. Punjab University, SNDT Women's University, Bombay University, Delhi University, etc.). This course is of one academic year in duration. In addition, there are a few universities which are offering BLISc as a Correspondence Course. Two open universities are also offering this course. Some colleges are also conducting BLISc programme. Presently there are 78 universities in India offering BLISc programme at 86 institutions.

Master of Library and Information Science (Earlier M.Lib. Sc.): There were only three schools offering M Lib Sc course till the end of 1960s. These were University of Delhi (1948); Banaras Hindu University (1965); and University of Bombay (1967). However a large number of schools initiated MLISc Course in 1970s. Four universities namely Aligarh, Karnataka, Mysore and Vikram started M Lib Sc in 1971. Today there are about 40 universities offering this programme through 44 institutions.

M.Phil Programme: With the recommendation of the Sen Committee (UGC), M.Phil programmes were initiated in various disciplines in different universities. University of Delhi was the first to introduce M.Phil programme in library and information science in 1980. Today 5 more universities are offering this programme.

Ph.D. Programme: University of Delhi instituted doctoral programme leading to Ph.D. in 1951. Dr. D.B. Krishnarao was the first awardee of Ph.D. in library science from University of Delhi in

1958. Then it could be only after 19 years in India that Dr. Pandey, S.K. Sharma became the second person to receive Ph.D. in library science from Punjab University in 1977, however, 1970s marked the beginning of research programmes in library science in several universities. Today there are 30 universities in India offering Ph.D. programme.

Role of Commissions

UGC Review Committee Report: There was no written document laying down certain norms and prescribed standards or projecting a policy, etc., till 1958. A policy on library science education was partially covered by the UGC Libraries Committee headed by Dr. Ranganathan in 1957. A Review Committee on Library Science was appointed by the UGC in 1961 again under the chairmanship of Dr. Ranganathan. This Committee in its report laid down for the first time in the country a detailed pattern for library and information science education. The report of this committee was published by the UGC under the title Library Science in Indian Universities (1965).

Salient Features of the Report: The Report in its introduction mentioned the importance of proper training for librarians; and the growing need for qualified and competent librarians in the country with the developing network of libraries, democratisation, research institutions and nevertheless the planners and policy-makers. It also gave a brief historical account of library science education in India. It identified the following problems with library science education in 1960s:

(a) No assessment of the value of training programmes was made till then. There is no uniformity with regard to admission qualifications, scope of practical training, quality of teachers, etc.

(b) The quality of entrants to the schools was poor.

(c) Teaching in most of the schools was conducted by part-time staff drawn from the university library.

(d) Certificate course was being conducted in certain universities along with high level courses.

(e) Need for more intensified research.

The Committee laid-down the following three-fold functions for a department of library science:

(i) To train professional librarians;

(ii) To prepare the holders of B.Lib.Sc. degree for the additional course leading to the degree of M.Lib.Sc.; and

(iii) To engage in research and to train the professionally qualified staff to do research.

A questionnaire was issued by the committee (the same was given as appendix 1) and the replies received were analysed and presented under the title "Existing Facilities of Teaching and Research." Following are some of the important findings:

1. Five universities were conducting Certificate course; eleven were offering Diploma course; only University of Delhi was offering Master's degree and Ph.D. programme.
2. The number of papers to be offered at Certificate level ranged from 3-7; whereas, at B.Lib Sc./ Diploma level they ranged from 7–9, and at M.Lib.Sc. there were in all 8 papers including one optional and one literature survey.
3. The duration varied from 3–4 months in case of certificate course; one full academic year in case of Diploma/B.Lib Sc. and M.Lib.Sc.

4. The total number of hours assigned to course work in majority of the schools were found to be inadequate.

Scheme of Papers: The scheme of papers suggested by the Committee for each course was given. Though research was at its lowest off in 1960s, the Committee detailed and discussed the various areas of research in the field.

University Courses: The Committee laid down the minimum qualification for admission to various courses and recommended that the universities should be concerned only with the Ph.D., M.Lib.Sc. and B.Lib.Sc. courses.

Equivalence of Diploma and Bachelor's Degree: The Post-Graduate Diploma courses in the universities should be redesignated as the post-graduate B.Lib.Sc. course and should enjoy the same status for all purposes.

Non-professional Subjects: Non-professional subjects like general knowledge, language, cultural history, etc. should be dropped as in those days only graduates were being admitted and such courses increase the load beyond the proper limit.

Staff Requirement

Staff-student Ratio (full time)

At B.Lib.Sc.	1:10
At M.Lib.Sc.	1:5

Minimum Staff (full-time):

For B.Lib.Sc.	One reader and two lecturers.
For M.Lib.Sc.	One professor, two readers and four lecturers.

Cooperation between the Department and the University Library: There should be a close cooperation between the library and the department of library science in a university. It would be useful for the teachers to work in the library for short periods and similarly, it would be useful for the librarians to maintain an academic interest in the subject by delivering a few lectures in the department.

The Functions: The Review Committee tried to enumerate the functions of a library science department and objectives of various courses. It has not recommended any major change in the scheme of papers. Interestingly it devoted a full chapter on sectors for research, even though the research work was almost nil in library science departments. Suggestions for discontinuation of Certificate course by university departments; equivalence of diploma and degree; dropping of non-professional subjects, staff-student ratio, grant to books, training of teachers and desired cooperation between the school and the university library are some of the important recommendations.

UGC Panel on Library and Information Science (1979): The Department of University of Delhi organised two national seminars with the financial support of UGC in 1973 and 1977 on the themes mentioned below:

(i) All India Workshop on Methods of Teaching and Evaluation in Library Science. May 15–30, 1973: and

(ii) All India Seminar on Library and Information Science Education in India. October 3–8, 1977.

The recommendations of these programmes along with the proposed syllabi for various courses were discussed by the Panel on Library and Information Science of UGC at its meeting held from 17–18 December 1979. The Panel made a number of recommendations.

The Guidelines: Two Year Integrated Programme: While accepting the usefulness of Bachelor's and Master's courses of one year duration the panel recognised the need for a two year integrated programme leading to M.L.I.Sc. and recommended that the universities having adequate facilities may start such a course on an experimental basis.

Independent Status to the Department: A university department of library and information science should be the constituent department of the university having the same status, privileges as other departments in the university and should have adequate full time teaching staff and also a full-time Head.

Change in the Nomenclature of the Department: Taking into consideration the introduction of the new areas of study of information science, it would be appropriated if the nomenclature of the department is suitably changed to reflect such changes in its curriculum.

Promotion of Research: Research programmes leading to the award of M.Phil and Ph.D. degree should be undertaken by departments having adequate facilities. Research projects also be undertaken by the university departments in order to raise the quality of teaching and to relate the educational programmes to the needs of the society.

New Components

Towards the late 1970s, the demand of information science component was increasingly felt. Many library schools giving room for the 'new technology' and even started changing the nomenclature of the departments to 'department of library and information science'. The new component of the curriculum made the syllabi heavy. The panel recommended for a two year integrated programme leading to Master of Library and Information Science. The panel stressed on the independent status of the department. The syllabus do not carry any drastic change, except introduction of new subject areas like information storage and retrieval, computer application, operation research and systems analysis, etc. It was right in recommending to UGC to support a survey to study utilisation of the product from the schools, standards and guidelines for schools to raise the quality of their educational programmes, and financial assistance for continuing education programmes. The suggestion for cooperative programmes among library schools is a welcome one. The Panel made an elaborate and detailed recommendation with regard to space requirement and budget.

New Policy

An All India Seminar on 'National Policy for Library and Information Science Education' was organised by the Department of Library and Information Science, Nagpur University, Nagpur from 23–26 September 1983 in collaboration with Indian Association of Teachers of Library and Information Science (IATLIS) under the sponsorship of UGC. This seminar discussed in detail the need for a national policy; levels of training and agencies that should handle, bibliographic organisation and control in LIS: policy for research and training: and monitoring evaluation and standardisation.

RRRLF and ILA: The Raja Rammohun Roy Library Foundation and Indian Library Association brought out separate drafts on national library and information policy in 1985. Both these drafts touched upon library and information science education.

Conpolis of Ministry of Human Resource Development: Government of India set-up a Committee on National Policy on Library and Information System (CONPOLIS) in October, 1985 under the chairmanship of Prof. D.P. Chattopadhyaya with Dr. B.P. Barua as the Member-Secretary. After a series of seminars, symposia and meetings, the Committee submitted to Government its report entitled "National Policy on Library and Information System-A Presentation" on 30 May 1986. Thereafter, the Government of India set-up an Empowered Committee again under the chairmanship of Professor D.P. Chattopadhyaya to assess the policy document and draw-up an action plan. The Empowered Committee submitted its report in March, 1988.

Recommendations on LIS

- In view of the rapidly expanding library and information services and the fast changing character of library and information science, the development of manpower in a planned manner becomes essential. The Indian librarian and information scientist in particular will face the difficult task of carrying the literacy drive on the one hand and dealing with the technological revolution on the other.
- The literary and information science courses run by the universities and comparable institutions at the post-graduate level should continue to maintain the high standards that have been reached and improve their quality, in particular by the incorporation of advancing information technology.
- Para-professional training courses may be undertaken by other appropriate agencies, but care must be taken to ensure uniformity and quality of such training all over the country.
- In view of the challenging and dynamic situation in the profession, the Indian library and information professional must be given every facility to refresh his/her expertise, so as to keep abreast of advancing knowledge by a planned development of continuing education programmes in the field.
- Considering the fact that library and information science courses tend to proliferate, introducing on occasions a dilution of standards, there should be an accreditation agency to ensure the standard and the quality of the training imparted.
- The national need of furthering higher education and research in library and information science may be undertaken by a National Centre to be established for the purpose.
- Library and Information Science professionals should be given the status and pay scales as well as academic facilities commensurate with their responsibilities with due regard to the fact that every library is an academic/research centre and has to function as such.
- The Government of India should recognise the need for the creation of an All India Library Service and implement the plan when feasible. The creation of such a service will strengthen the national network of library and information systems.

Norms and Standards

ILA: The Central Sectional Committee on Library and Information Science (E&T) of Indian Library Association organised a workshop on "Norms, Guidelines and Standards of Library and Information Science Education" on 31 July 1991 in Nagpur. The CSC prepared a working document covering a brief history of education for library and information science in India, present educational frame work, admission criteria, enrolment, medium of instruction course contents, structure of papers, research, working hours, teaching methods, teaching aids, teaching staff, library, workshop, physical facilities, accreditation, standards for evaluation of library schools, etc. These were further discussed at the All India Library Conference held at Pune in 1989.

IATIS Seminar on Standards in LIS Education: The IX National Seminar on IATLIS held at Visakhapatnam in August 1991, discussed in detail the problems and procedure for accreditation.

CDC of the UGC: On the recommendation of the Panel on Library and Information Science, UGC constituted a Curriculum Development Committee on L.I.Sc. in Sept., 1990. The committee was to:

(i) Review the existing curricula of L.I.Sc. in the university system,

(ii) Take the responsibility of modifying or changing the existing curriculum by incorporating the changes in the field of L.I.Sc. and to meet the manpower needs of libraries and information centres in the modern age,

(iii) Develop model curricula for course programmes at various levels,

(iv) Prepare the report of the Curriculum Development Committee on the following terms of references,

(v) Achieve the objectives that the "Libraries should be transformed into information centres and steps to link the library with various departments through modern communication technology, library service be strengthened to extend its access with a view to making it whole-day institution working with modern facilities including computer search and documentation services."

ILA Guidelines: The guidelines prepared by the ILA Central Sectional Committee on Library and Information Science and discussed at the All India Library Conference at Pune in 1989 set-out certain guidelines for LIS Schools.

The Requirements

1. Starting of new courses, and the number of seats in each of the existing course is to be decided by conducting a study of the manpower needs of the region and its employment potential.

   Not the demand from students, but the demand for qualified personnel should decide the intake of library schools.

2. As subject background is going to play an important role in special libraries and in handling specific needs of subject specialists, students with varied backgrounds be admitted in the courses. A proportion of 2:1:1 be followed for candidates with science, social and arts (including commerce) background. Special consideration be given to candidates from the fields of medicine, engineering, agriculture, technology, etc.

The Objects: Each LIS school should spell out the basic objectives of each course being offered by them. Such a set of objectives should indicate:

(i) Aims;

(ii) Level of professionals to be developed;

(iii) Jobs for which they will be suitable;

(iv) Skills to be developed;

(v) Means of achievement; etc.

Note: Objectives stated under norms are illustrative.

Admission Criteria

Certificate Course: SSC should be the minimum qualification for admission to CLSc course.

Degree Course

1. Bachelor's degree or its equivalent qualification. However, preference be given to postgraduates. The following order of preference be followed:
   - (i) Master's degree holders with first division;
   - (ii) Degree holders with first division;
   - (iii) Master's degree holders with second division;
   - (iv) Degree holders with second division.
2. The following reservation criteria be followed

(i)	Backward classes	40%
(ii)	Working/deputed	10%
(iii)	Defence personnel/wards	10%
(iv)	Science graduates	20%
(v)	Social sciences	10%
(vi)	Arts/Commerce	10%

3. Selection be based on the academic achievement, admission test and interview.

   The following scale be applied for these criteria:

(i)	Academic achievement	50%
(ii)	Admission test	40%
(iii)	Interview	10%

4. Weightage be given to CLISc holders among equals.

Postgraduate Course: Basing on the demand from working librarians, a maximum of 50 per cent seats be reserved for them.

Selection of working librarians be based on:

(i) Experience;

(ii) Qualification; and

(iii) Interview.

Freshers be selected on the basis of:

(i) Qualification;

(ii) Admission test; and

(iii) Interview.

About 5 per cent of the seats be spared for candidates seeking admission from outside the university area, both at BLISc and MLISc level.

Enrolment: The staff-student ratio suggested by the UGC Review Committee (1: 10 at the BLISc level and 1:5 at the MLI Sc level) be followed scrupulously. Taking note of the present day employment market, the following enrolment is suggested for various courses:

BLISc	20-30
MLISc	5-10
M.Phil	5

Medium of Instruction

CLSC	English or regional language
+2, +3, BLISc level	Preferably English
MLISc, M. Phil	English only

Curriculum: It is not desirable to prescribe uniform syllabi for various LIS courses run in our country. However, a set of core and optional papers can be listed here. The individual school will have the freedom to choose.

CLSC: At CLSc level there be five theory and one or two practical papers:

(i) Library Administration and Organisation;

(ii) Classification (Theory);

(iii) Cataloguing (Theory);

(iv) Bibliography and Book Selection;

(v) Reference Sources and Services;

(vi) Practical test in Classification and Cataloguing.

BLISC

There is almost uniformity in the content of BLISc courses run by various universities.

Foundation Course: Library and Society

Core Courses:

1. Library Organisation and Management;
2. Library Classification;
3. Library Cataloguing;
4. Documentation;
5. Reference Sources and Service.

Auxiliary Courses:

1. Bibliography;
2. Book Selection.

Applied Courses:

1. Classification Practice;
2. Cataloguing Practice;
3. Bibliography/Bibliographical essay;
4. Library records;
5. Evaluation of reference sources;
6. Fact finding;
7. Book Selection.

Optionals/Electives:

1. Information Science;
2. Subject indexing/ Indexing theory;
3. Computer applications.

Work Experience:

1. Educational tour;
2. Internship.

MLISc

Foundation Courses:

1. Universe of Knowledge;
2. Research Methodology;
3. Statistical Methods;
4. Systems Analysis;
5. Comparative Librarianship;
6. Management Techniques;
7. Operations Research;
8. Linguistics;
9. Behavioural Science;
10. Communication Theory.

Core Courses:

1. Classification, Advanced/Depth;
2. Cataloguing, Advanced;
3. Information Science and Technology;
4. Information systems and programmes.

Applied Courses:

1. Classification, Advanced/Depth (Practical);
2. Cataloguing, Advanced (Practical).

Optionals Electives:

1. Information and literature sources in:
   (i) Humanities,
   (ii) Social Science,
   (iii) Science,
   (iv) Medical Science,
   (v) Engineering and Technology,
   (vi) Agricultural Science, etc.
2. Computer Applications;
3. Library and Information Science Education;
4. Library systems:
   (i) Public,
   (ii) Academic,
   (iii) Research and technical,
   (iv) Agricultural,

(v) Medical,
(vi) Engineering and technology,
(vii) Medical, etc.

5. Bibliographical control.

Work Experience:

1. Seminar;
2. Project.

M.PHIL

Foundation Course: Research methods.

Core Courses: Library Planning and Management.

Optionals:

1. University and college library system;
2. Research and technical library system;
3. Public library system;
4. Information processing and organisation;
5. Information transfer and dissemination;
6. Comparative librarianship;
7. Education for library and information science.

Work Experience: Dissertation.

Projections:

1. Internship programme of 1–3 months be introduced at BLISc level.
2. Educational tours and visits to local libraries be carried out on regular basis.

Approaches for Teaching

1. Last 15 minutes of the lecture hour be spared for discussion.
2. Weekly seminars be organised.
3. Initiate group discussions and cooperative projects.
4. Tutorials be organised on regular basis.
5. New techniques like role-playing, management games, etc. be used.
6. Computer simulations be developed to provide 'hands-on' experience to students.

Tools for Teaching

The departments of library science should possess and use the following teaching aids to make teaching-learning process more effective:

(i) Overhead projector;
(ii) Slide projector (with synchroniser);
(iii) Video equipment;
(iv) Personal Computer, etc.

Necessary software be prepared locally.

Role of Teachers

1. No new department or course be started without proper infrastructural facilities and availability of qualified full-time staff.
2. The recommendation of the UGC Panel on Library and Information science (1982) be followed with regard to staff requirement.
3. General UGC recommendations issued be time with regard to qualifications shall have, followed.

Main Points of Concern

Finances: Non-recurring Expenditure. Provision should be made for the following non-recurring expenditure while planning for a new department or for further strengthening the existing department:

(i) Department's Library;

(ii) Workshop/ Laboratory.

Recurring: In addition to the provision such as salaries, contingencies, office/library equipment, etc. the budget of a department of library and information science should include provisions for expenditure for the following purposes:

(i) Establishment and maintenance of:

(a) Department's Library ₹ 25,000/

(b) Workshop/ Laboratory ₹ 6,000/

(ii) *Ad hoc* grants for acquiring the editions of manuals, reference tools, etc., like, classification schedules, catalogue codes, subject heading list, etc., should be calculated on the basis of actual need by the department (UGC Panel, 1982).

Building Accommodation: It will be ideal to have a separate, building for the department of library and information science. If not, the minimum accommodation prescribed by the UGC Panel in 1982 should be provided.

Research: Apart from the research for the award of Ph.D., pragmatic, applied, empirical and a priori research should be done by teachers, students of library and information science, as well as, practising librarians. Such studies should have a direct bearing on day-to-day library organisation and management, application of new technology, introducing new services, building-up vital statistical data on library and information services, and the profession in general.

Examination Programme

UGC, Curriculum Development Committee (India) (1992): The UGC's Curriculum Development Committee on Library and Information Science in its Report gave separate schemes of papers and Bachelor of Library and Information Science and Master of Library and Information Science.

(a) Bachelor of Library and Information Science:

(i) Library and Information Society,

(ii) Library and Information Management,

(iii) Library Classification-Theory and Practice,

(iv) Library Cataloguing and Subject Indexing-Theory and Practice,

(v) Information Sources and Services,

(vi) Computer Application.

(b) Master of Library and Information Science:

(i) Information and Communication: Evolution and Development,
(ii) Library and Information Management: Sources and Services,
(iii) Computer Technology, Library Automation and Information Systems,
(iv) Information Processing and Retrieval,
(v) Research Methodology and Informatics.

Electives: In addition, the following electives were suggested at the Bachelor of Library and Information Science Level:

(i) School and children libraries;
(ii) University and college libraries;
(iii) Public library system;
(iv) Government department libraries;
(v) Research and development libraries;
(vi) Archives Librarianship;
(vii) Engineering and Technology Information System;
(viii) Medical librarianship;
(ix) Agricultural Library and Information System;
(x) Law libraries;
(xi) Music libraries;
(xii) Industrial Library and Information System;
(xiii) Manuscriptology;
(xiv) Library buildings, fittings and furniture;
(xv) Local studies librarianship;
(xvi) Non-book materials;

The following electives were suggested at Master of Library and Information Science Level:

(i) Comparative and International Librarianship;
(ii) Higher Education and Academic Library System;
(iii) Communication, Mass Media and Public Library;
(iv) Bibliographic control;
(v) User Education and User Studies;
(vi) Education for Library and Information Science.

In the above curricula, one can observe a gradual shifting from documentation work to total information oriented syllabus from the one suggested by Prof. Foskett to the 'criteria' suggested by the Institution of Information Scientists (UK). However, in the syllabus suggested by UGC's CDC (India) still a large part is devoted to librarianship, which is justified considering local needs and local situation. It is essential to think loudly whether there is a need for specialised courses for information science parallel to librarianship. If the present practice is to be continued, how to incorporate the new technology and trends in information science in the Library and Information Science courses?

UGC Model Curriculum (2001): UGC constituted a Curriculum Development Committee as per the recommendations of the Subject Panel in 1998. Dr. C.R. Karisiddappa was the 'nodal person' (Convenor). This committee recommended an integrated 2 year (=4 Semester) programme leading to Master of Library and Information Science.

The scheme of papers is as following:

Module Nomenclature of the Paper:

1. Foundations of Library and Information Science;
2. Knowledge Organisation, Information Processing and Retrieval (T);
3. Knowledge Organisation, Information Processing and Retrieval (P);
4. Information Technology: Basics;
5. Management of Library and Information Centres;
6. Information Sources and Services (T);
7. Information Sources and Services (P);
8. Library and Users;
9. Fundamentals of Information Science;
10. Information Analysis, Repackaging, Consolidation;
11. Information Retrieval;
12. Research Methods and Statistical Techniques;
13. Information Technology Applications (T);
14. Information Technology Applications (P);
15. Elective;
16. Dissertation/Project Work.

5

LIBRARY CULTURE

Library, an Institution

The Library which is to be spoken of in these pages, is all unlike the halls which a Spencer or a Huth fills with treasure beyond price. The age of great libraries has gone by, and where a collector of the old school survives, he is usually a man of enormous wealth, who might, if he pleased, be distinguished in Parliament, in society, on the turf itself, or in any of the pursuits where unlimited supplies of money are strictly necessary. The old amateurs, whom La Bruyere was wont to sneer at, were not satisfied unless they possessed many thousands of books. For a collector like Cardinal Mazarin, Naude bought up the whole stock of many a bookseller, and left great towns as bare of printed paper as if a tornado had passed, and blown the leaves away. In our modern times, as the industrious Bibliophile Jacob, says, the fashion of book-collecting has changed; "from the vast hall that it was, the library of the amateur has shrunk to a closet, to a mere book-case. Nothing but a neat article of furniture is needed now, where a great gallery or a long suite of rooms was once required.

The book has become, as it were, a jewel, and is kept in a kind of jewel-case." It is not quantity of pages, nor lofty piles of ordinary binding, nor theological folios and classic quartos, that the modern amateur desires. He is content with but a few books of distinction and elegance, masterpieces of printing and binding, or relics of famous old collectors, of statesmen, philosophers, beautiful dead ladies; or, again, he buys illustrated books, or first editions of the modern classics. No one, not the Duc d'Aumale, or M. James Rothschild himself, with his 100 books worth 40,000 pounds, can possess very many copies of books which are inevitably rare.

Thus the adviser who would offer suggestions to the amateur, need scarcely write, like Naude and the old authorities, about the size and due position of the library. He need hardly warn the builder to make the salle face the east, "because the eastern winds, being warm and dry of their nature, greatly temper the air, fortify the senses, make subtle the humours, purify the spirits, preserve a healthy disposition of the whole body, and, to say all in one word, are most wholesome and salubrious." The east wind, like the fashion of book- collecting, has altered in character a good deal since the days when Naude was librarian to Cardinal Mazarin. One might as well repeat the learned Isidorus his counsels about the panels of green marble (that refreshes the eye), and Boethius his censures on library walls of ivory and glass, as fall back on the ancient ideas of librarians dead and gone.

The amateur, then, is the person we have in our eye, and especially the bibliophile who has but lately been bitten with this pleasant mania of collecting. We would teach him how to arrange and keep his books orderly and in good case, and would tell him what to buy and what to avoid. By the LIBRARY we do not understand a study where no one goes, and where the master of the house keeps his boots, an assortment of walking-sticks, the "Waverley Novels," "Pearson on the Creed," "Hume's Essays," and a collection of sermons. In, alas! too many English homes, the Library is no more than this, and each generation passes without adding a book, except now and then a Bradshaw or a railway novel, to the collection on the shelves.

The success, perhaps, of circulating libraries, or, it may be, the Aryan tendencies of our race, "which does not read, and lives in the open air," have made books the rarest of possessions in many houses. There are relics of the age before circulating libraries, there are fragments of the lettered store of some scholarly great-grandfather, and these, with a few odd numbers of magazines, a few primers and manuals, some sermons and novels, make up the ordinary library of an English household. But the amateur, whom we have in our thoughts, can never be satisfied with these commonplace supplies. He has a taste for books more or less rare, and for books neatly bound; in short, for books, in the fabrication of which ART has not been absent. He loves to have his study, like Montaigne's, remote from the interruption of servants, wife, and children; a kind of shrine, where he may be at home with himself, with the illustrious dead, and with the genius of literature.

The room may look east, west, or south, provided that it be dry, warm, light, and airy. Among the many enemies of books the first great foe is DAMP, and we must describe the necessary precautions to be taken against this peril. We will suppose that the amateur keeps his ordinary working books, modern tomes, and all that serve him as literary tools, on open shelves. These may reach the roof, if he has books to fill them, and it is only necessary to see that the back of the bookcases are slightly removed from contact with the walls.

The more precious and beautifully bound treasures will naturally be stored in a case with closely-fitting glass-doors. The shelves should be lined with velvet or chamois leather, that the delicate edges of the books may not suffer from contact with the wood. A leather lining, fitted to the back of the case, will also help to keep out humidity. Most writers recommend that the bookcases should be made of wood close in the grain, such as well-seasoned oak; or, for smaller tabernacles of literature, of mahogany, satin-wood lined with cedar, ebony, and so forth. These close-grained woods are less easily penetrated by insects, and it is fancied that bookworms dislike the aromatic scents of cedar, sandal wood, and Russia leather.

There was once a bibliophile who said that a man could only love one book at a time, and the darling of the moment he used to carry about in a charming leather case. Others, men of few books, preserve them in long boxes with glass fronts, which may be removed from place to place as readily as the household gods of Laban. But the amateur who not only worships but reads books, needs larger receptacles; and in the open oak cases for modern authors, and for books with common modern papers and bindings, in the closed armoire for books of rarity and price, he will find, we think, the most useful mode of arranging his treasures. His shelves will decline in height from the lowest, where huge folios stand at case, to the top ranges, while Elzevirs repose on a level with the eye. It is well that each upper shelf should have a leather fringe to keep the dust away.

As to the shape of the bookcases, and the furniture, and ornaments of the library, every amateur will please himself. Perhaps the satin-wood or mahogany tabernacles of rare books are best made after the model of what furniture-dealers indifferently call the "Queen Anne" or the "Chippendale" style. There is a pleasant quaintness in the carved architectural ornaments of the top, and the inlaid flowers of marquetry go well with the pretty florid editions of the last century, the books that were illustrated by Stothard and Gravelot. Ebony suits theological tomes very well, especially when they are bound in white vellum. As to furniture, people who can afford it will imitate the arrangements of Lucullus, in Mr. Hill Burton's charming volume "The Book-hunter" (Blackwood, Edinburgh, 1862).—"Everything is of perfect finish,—the mahogany-railed gallery, the tiny ladders, the broad winged lecterns, with leathern cushions on the edges to keep the wood from grazing the rich bindings, the books themselves, each shelf uniform with its facings, or rather backings, like well-dressed lines at a review."

The late Sir William Stirling-Maxwell, a famous bibliophile, invented a very nice library chair. It is most comfortable to sit on; and, as the top of the back is broad and flat, it can be used as a ladder of two high steps, when one wants to reach a book on a lofty shelf. A kind of square revolving bookcase, an American invention, manufactured by Messrs. Trubner, is useful to the working man of letters. Made in oak, stained green, it is not unsightly. As to ornaments, every man to his taste. You may have a "pallid bust of Pallas" above your classical collection, or fill the niches in a shrine of old French light literature, pastoral and comedy, with delicate shepherdesses in Chelsea china. On such matters a modest writer, like Mr. Jingle when Mr. Pickwick ordered dinner, "will not presume to dictate."

Next to damp, dust and dirt are the chief enemies of books. At short intervals, books and shelves ought to be dusted by the amateur himself. Even Dr. Johnson, who was careless of his person, and of volumes lent to him, was careful about the cleanliness of his own books. Boswell found him one day with big gloves on his hands beating the dust out of his library, as was his custom. There is nothing so hideous as a dirty thumb-mark on a white page. These marks are commonly made, not because the reader has unwashed hands, but because the dust which settles on the top edge of books falls in, and is smudged when they are opened. Gilt-top edges should be smoothed with a handkerchief, and a small brush should be kept for brushing the tops of books with rough edges, before they are opened.

But it were well that all books had the top edge gilt. There is no better preservative against dust. Dust not only dirties books, it seems to supply what Mr. Spencer would call a fitting environment for bookworms. The works of bookworms speak for themselves, and are manifest to all. How many a rare and valuable volume is spoiled by neat round holes drilled through cover and leaves! But as to the nature of your worm, authorities differ greatly. The ancients knew this plague, of which Lucian speaks. Mr. Blades mentions a white bookworm, slain by the librarian of the Bodleian. In Byzantium the black sort prevailed. Evenus, the grammarian, wrote an epigram against the black bookworm ("Anthol. Pal.," ix. 251):

Pest of the Muses, devourer of pages, in crannies that lurkest, Fruits of the Muses to taint, labour of learning to spoil; Wherefore, oh black-fleshed worm! wert thou born for the evil thou workest? Wherefore thine own foul form shap'st thou with envious toil? The learned Mentzelius says he hath heard the bookworm crow like a cock unto his mate, and "I knew not," says he, "whether some local fowl was clamouring or whether there was but a beating in mine ears. Even at that moment, all uncertain as I was, I perceived, in the paper whereon I was writing, a little insect that ceased not to carol like very chanticleer, until, taking a magnifying glass, I assiduously observed him. He is about the bigness of a mite, and carries a grey crest, and the head low, bowed over the bosom; as to his crowing noise, it comes of his clashing his wings against each other with an incessant din." Thus far Mentzelius, and more to the same purpose, as may be read in the "Memoirs of famous Foreign Academies" (Dijon, 1755-59, 13 vol. in quarto).

But, in our times, the learned Mr. Blades having a desire to exhibit bookworms in the body to the Caxtonians at the Caxton celebration, could find few men that had so much as seen a bookworm, much less heard him utter his native wood-notes wild. Yet, in his "Enemies of Books," he describes some rare encounters with the worm. Dirty books, damp books, dusty books, and books that the owner never opens, are most exposed to the enemy; and "the worm, the proud worm, is the conqueror still," as a didactic poet sings, in an ode on man's mortality. As we have quoted Mentzelius, it may not be amiss to give D'Alembert's theory of bookworms: "I believe," he says, "that a little beetle lays her eggs in books in August, thence is hatched a mite, like the cheese-mite, which devours books merely because it is compelled to gnaw its way out into the air." Bookworms like the paste which binders employ, but D'Alembert adds that they cannot endure absinthe. Mr. Blades finds too that they disdain to devour our adulterate modern paper.

"Say, shall I sing of rats," asked Grainger, when reading to Johnson his epic, the "Sugar-cane." "No," said the Doctor; and though rats are the foe of the bibliophile, at least as much as of the sugar- planter, we do not propose to sing of them. M. Fertiault has done so already in "Les Sonnets d'un Bibliophile," where the reader must be pleased with the beautiful etchings of rats devouring an illuminated MS., and battening on morocco bindings stamped with the bees of De Thou. It is unnecessary and it would be undignified, to give hints on rat-catching, but the amateur must not forget that these animals have a passion for bindings.

The book-collector must avoid gas, which deposits a filthy coat of oil that catches dust. Mr. Blades found that three jets of gas in a small room soon reduced the leather on his book-shelves to a powder of the consistency of snuff, and made the backs of books come away in his hand. Shaded lamps give the best and most suitable light for the library. As to the risks which books run at the hands of the owner himself, we surely need not repeat the advice of Richard de Bury. Living in an age when tubs (if not unknown as M. Michelet declares) were far from being common, the old collector inveighed against the dirty hands of readers, and against their habit of marking their place in a book with filthy straws, or setting down a beer pot in the middle of the volume to keep the pages open.

But the amateur, however refined himself, must beware of men who love not fly leaves neither regard margins, but write notes over the latter, and light their pipes with the former. After seeing the wreck of a book which these persons have been busy with, one appreciates the fine Greek hyperbole. The Greeks did not speak of "thumbing" but of "walking up and down" on a volume.

To such fellows it matters not that they make a book dirty and greasy, cutting the pages with their fingers, and holding the boards over the fire till they crack. All these slatternly practices, though they destroy a book as surely as the flames of Caesar's soldiers at Alexandria, seem fine manly acts to the grobians who use them. What says Jules Janin, who has written "Contre l'indifference des Philistins," "il faut a l'homme sage et studieux un tome honourable et digne de sa louange."

The amateur, and all decent men, will beware of lending books to such rude workers; and this consideration brings us to these great foes of books, the borrowers and robbers. The lending of books, and of other property, has been defended by some great authorities; thus Panurge himself says, "it would prove much more easy in nature to have fish entertained in the air, and bullocks fed in the bottom of the ocean, than to support or tolerate a rascally rabble of people that will not lend." Pirckheimer, too, for whom Albert Durer designed a bookplate, was a lender, and took for his device Sibi et Amicis; and Jo. Grolierii et amicorum, was the motto of the renowned Grolier, whom mistaken writers vainly but frequently report to have been a bookbinder. But as Mr. Leicester Warren says, in his "Study of Book-plates" (Pearson, 1880), "Christian Charles de Savigny leaves all the rest behind, exclaiming non mihi sed aliis."

But the majority of amateurs have chosen wiser, though more churlish devices, as "the ungodly borroweth and payeth not again," or "go to them that sell, and buy for yourselves." David Garrick engraved on his bookplate, beside a bust of Shakspeare, these words of Menage, "La premiere chose qu'on doit faire, quand on a emprunte' un livre, c'est de le lire, afin de pouvoir le rendre plutot." But the borrower is so minded that the last thing he thinks of is to read a borrowed book, and the penultimate subject of his reflections is its restoration. Menage (Menagiana, Paris, 1729, vol. i. p. 265), mentions, as if it were a notable misdeed, this of Angelo Politian's, "he borrowed a 'Lucretius' from Pomponius Laetus, and kept it for four years." Four years! in the sight of the borrower it is but a moment. Menage reports that a friend kept his "Pausanias" for three years, whereas four months was long enough.

"At quarto saltem mense redire decet."

There is no satisfaction in lending a book; for it is rarely that borrowers, while they deface your volumes, gather honey for new stores, as De Quincey did, and Coleridge, and even Dr. Johnson, who "greased and dogs-eared such volumes as were confided to his tender mercies, with the same indifference wherewith he singed his own wigs." But there is a race of mortals more annoying to a conscientious man than borrowers. These are the spontaneous lenders, who insist that you shall borrow their tomes. For my own part, when I am oppressed with the charity of such, I lock their books up in a drawer, and behold them not again till the day of their return. There is no security against borrowers, unless a man like Guibert de Pixerecourt steadfastly refuses to lend. The device of Pixerecourt was un livre est un ami qui ne change jamais. But he knew that our books change when they have been borrowed, like our friends when they have been married; when "a lady borrows them," as the fairy Queen says in the ballad of "Tamlane."

"But had I kenn'd, Tamlane," she says, "A lady wad borrowed thee, I wad ta'en out thy twa gray een, Put in twa een o' tree!

"Had I but kenn'd, Tamlane," she says, "Before ye came frae hame, I wad ta'en out your heart o' flesh, Put in a heart o' stane!"

Above the lintel of his library door, Pixerecourt had this couplet carved -

"Tel est le triste sort de tout livre prete, Souvent il est perdu, toujours il est gate."

M. Paul Lacroix says he would not have lent a book to his own daughter. Once Lacroix asked for the loan of a work of little value. Pixerecourt frowned, and led his friend beneath the doorway, pointing to the motto. "Yes," said M. Lacroix, "but I thought that verse applied to every one but me." So Pixerecourt made him a present of the volume.

We cannot all imitate this "immense" but unamiable amateur. Therefore, bibliophiles have consoled themselves with the inventions of book-plates, quaint representations, perhaps heraldic, perhaps fanciful, of their claims to the possession of their own dear volumes. Mr. Leicester Warren and M. Poulet Malassis have written the history of these slender works of art, and each bibliophile may have his own engraved, and may formulate his own anathemas on people who borrow and restore not again. The process is futile, but may comfort the heart, like the curses against thieves which the Greeks were wont to scratch on leaden tablets, and deposit in the temple of Demeter. Each amateur can exercise his own taste in the design of a bookplate; and for such as love and collect rare editions of "Homer," I venture to suggest this motto, which may move the heart of the borrower to send back an Aldine copy of the epic -

Mr. William Blades, in his pleasant volume, "The Enemies of Books" (Trubner), makes no account of the book-thief or biblioklept. "If they injure the owners," says Mr. Blades, with real tolerance, "they do no harm to the books themselves, by merely transferring them from one set of book-shelves to another." This sentence has naturally caused us to reflect on the ethical character of the biblioklept. He is not always a bad man. In old times, when language had its delicacies, and moralists were not devoid of sensibility, the French did not say "un voleur de livres," but "un chipeur de livres;" as the papers call lady shoplifters "kleptomaniacs." There are distinctions. M. Jules Janin mentions a great Parisian bookseller who had an amiable weakness. He was a bibliokleptomaniac. His first motion when he saw a book within reach was to put it in his pocket.

Every one knew his habit, and when a volume was lost at a sale the auctioneer duly announced it, and knocked it down to the enthusiast, who regularly paid the price. When he went to a private view of books about to be sold, the officials at the door would ask him, as he was going out, if he did not happen to have an Elzevir Horace or an Aldine Ovid in his pocket. Then he would search those receptacles and exclaim, "Yes, yes, here it is; so much obliged to you; I am so absent." M. Janin mentions an English noble, a "Sir Fitzgerald," who had the same tastes, but who unluckily fell into the hands of the police. Yet M. Janin has a tenderness for the book-stealer, who, after all, is a lover of books. The moral position of the malefactor is so delicate and difficult that we shall attempt to treat of it in the severe, though rococo, manner of Aristotle's "Ethics." Here follows an extract from the lost Aristotelian treatise "Concerning Books":-

"Among the contemplative virtues we reckon the love of books. Now this virtue, like courage or liberality, has its mean, its excess, and its defect. The defect is indifference, and the man who is defective as to the love of books has no name in common parlance. Therefore, we may call him the Robustious Philistine. This man will cut the leaves of his own or his friend's volumes with the butter- knife at breakfast. Also he is just the person wilfully to mistake the double sense of the term 'fly-leaves,' and to stick the 'fly- leaves' of his volumes full of fly-hooks. He also loves dogs'-ears, and marks his place with his pipe when he shuts a book in a hurry; or he will set the leg of his chair on a page to keep it open. He praises those who tear off margins for pipe-lights, and he makes cigarettes with the tissue-paper that covers engravings. When his books are bound, he sees that the margin is cut to the quick. He tells you too, that 'HE buys books to read them.' But he does not say why he thinks it needful to spoil them. Also he will drag off bindings—or should we perhaps call this crime, or brutality, rather than mere vice? for vice is essentially human, but to tear off bindings is bestial. Thus they still speak of a certain monster who lived during the French Revolution, and who, having purchased volumes attired in morocco, and stamped with the devices of the oligarchs, would rip off the leather or vellum, and throw them into the fire or out of the window, saying that 'now he could read with unwashed hands at his ease.' Such a person, then, is the man indifferent to books, and he sins by way of defect, being deficient in the contemplative virtue of book-loving. As to the man who is exactly in the right mean, we call him the book-lover. His happiness consists not in reading, which is an active virtue, but in the contemplation of bindings, and illustrations, and title-pages. Thus his felicity partakes of the nature of the bliss we attribute to the gods, for that also is contemplative, and we call the book- lover 'happy,' and even 'blessed,' but within the limits of mortal happiness. But, just as in the matter of absence of fear there is a mean which we call courage, and a defect which we call cowardice, and an excess which is known as foolhardiness; so it is in the case of the love of books.

As to the mean, we have seen that it is the virtue of the true book-lover, while the defect constitutes the sin of the Robustious Philistine. But the extreme is found in covetousness, and the covetous man who is in the extreme state of book-loving, is the biblioklept, or book-stealer. Now his vice shows itself, not in contemplation (for of contemplation there can be no excess), but in action. For books are procured, as we say, by purchase, or by barter, and these are voluntary exchanges, both the seller and the buyer being willing to deal. But books are, again, procured in another way, by involuntary contract—that is, when the owner of the book is unwilling to part with it, but he whose own the book is not is determined to take it.

The book-stealer is such a man as this, and he possesses himself of books with which the owner does not intend to part, by virtue of a series of involuntary contracts. Again, the question may be raised, whether is the Robustious Philistine who despises books, or the biblioklept who adores them out of measure and excessively, the worse citizen? Now, if we are to look to the consequences of actions only (as the followers of Bentham advise), clearly the Robustious Philistine is the worse citizen, for he mangles, and dirties, and destroys books which it is the interest of the State to preserve. But the biblioklept treasures and adorns the books he has acquired; and when he dies, or goes to prison, the State receives the benefit at his sale. Thus Libri, who was the greatest of biblioklepts, rescued many of the books he stole from dirt and misuse, and had them bound royally in purple and gold. Also, it may be argued that books naturally belong to him who can appreciate them; and if good books are in a dull or indifferent man's keeping, this is the sort of slavery which we call "unnatural" in our POLITICS, and which is not to be endured. Shall we say, then, that the Robustious Philistine is the worse citizen, while the Biblioklept is the worse man? But this is perhaps matter for a separate disquisition."

This fragment of the lost Aristotelian treatise "Concerning Books," shows what a difficulty the Stagirite had in determining the precise nature of the moral offence of the biblioklept. Indeed, both as a collector and as an intuitive moralist, Aristotle must have found it rather difficult to condemn the book-thief. He, doubtless, went on to draw distinctions between the man who steals books to sell them again for mere pecuniary profit (which he would call "chrematistic," or "unnatural," book-stealing), and the man who steals them because he feels that he is their proper and natural possessor. The same distinction is taken by Jules Janin, who was a more constant student of Horace than of Aristotle. In his imaginary dialogue of bibliophiles, Janin introduces a character who announces the death of M. Libri.

The tolerant person who brings the sad news proposes "to cast a few flowers on the melancholy tomb. He was a bibliophile, after all. What do you say to it? Many a good fellow has stolen books, and died in grace at the last." "Yes," replies the president of the club, "but the good fellows did not sell the books they stole. .. Cest une grande honte, une grande misere." This Libri was an Inspector-General of French Libraries under Louis Philippe. When he was tried, in 1848, it was calculated that the sum of his known thefts amounted to 20,000 pounds. Many of his robberies escaped notice at the time. It is not long since Lord Ashburnham, according to a French journal, "Le Livre," found in his collection some fragments of a Pentateuch. These relics had been in the possession of the Lyons Library, whence Libri stole them in 1847. The late Lord Ashburnham bought them, without the faintest idea of Libri's dishonesty; and when, after eleven years, the present peer discovered the proper owners of his treasure, he immediately restored the Pentateuch to the Lyons Library.

Many eminent characters have been biblioklepts. When Innocent X. was still Monsignor Pamphilio, he stole a book—so says Tallemant des Reaux—from Du Monstier, the painter. The amusing thing is that Du Monstier himself was a book-thief. He used to tell how he had lifted a book, of which he had long been in search, from a stall on the Pont-Neuf; "but," says Tallemant (whom Janin does not seem to have consulted), "there are many people who don't think it thieving to steal a book unless you sell it afterwards." But Du Monstier took a less liberal view where his own books were concerned. The Cardinal Barberini came to Paris as legate, and brought in his suite Monsignor Pamphilio, who afterwards became Innocent X. The Cardinal paid a visit to Du Monstier in his studio, where Monsignor Pamphilio spied, on a table, "L'Histoire du Concile de Trent"—the good edition, the London one. "What a pity," thought the young ecclesiastic, "that such a man should be, by some accident, the possessor of so valuable a book." With these sentiments Monsignor Pamphilio slipped the work under his soutane. But little Du Monstier observed him, and said furiously to the Cardinal, that a holy man should not bring thieves and robbers in his company. With these words, and with others of a violent and libellous character, he recovered the "History of the Council of Trent," and kicked out the future Pope. Amelot de la Houssaie traces to this incident the hatred borne by Innocent X. to the Crown and the people of France. Another Pope, while only a cardinal, stole a book from Menage—so M. Janin reports—but we have not been able to discover Menage's own account of the larceny.

The anecdotist is not so truthful that cardinals need flush a deeper scarlet, like the roses in Bion's "Lament for Adonis," on account of a scandal resting on the authority of Menage. Among Royal persons, Catherine de Medici, according to Brantome, was a biblioklept. "The Marshal Strozzi had a very fine library, and after his death the Queen-Mother seized it, promising some day to pay the value to his son, who never got a farthing of the money." The Ptolemies, too, were thieves on a large scale. A department of the Alexandrian Library was called "The Books from the Ships," and was filled with rare volumes stolen from passengers in vessels that touched at the port. True, the owners were given copies of their ancient MSS., but the exchange, as Aristotle says, was an "involuntary" one, and not distinct from robbery.

The great pattern of biblioklepts, a man who carried his passion to the most regrettable excesses, was a Spanish priest, Don Vincente, of the convent of Pobla, in Aragon. When the Spanish revolution despoiled the convent libraries, Don Vincente established himself at Barcelona, under the pillars of Los Encantes, where are the stalls of the merchants of bric-a-brac and the seats of them that sell books. In a gloomy den the Don stored up treasures which he hated to sell. Once he was present at an auction where he was out-bid in the competition for a rare, perhaps a unique, volume. Three nights after that, the people of Barcelona were awakened by cries of "Fire!" The house and shop of the man who had bought "Ordinacions per los gloriosos reys de Arago" were blazing. When the fire was extinguished, the body of the owner of the house was found, with a pipe in his blackened hand, and some money beside him. Every one said, "He must have set the house on fire with a spark from his pipe." Time went on, and week by week the police found the bodies of slain men, now in the street, now in a ditch, now in the river. There were young men and old, all had been harmless and inoffensive in their lives, and—all had been bibliophiles. A dagger in an invisible hand had reached their hearts but the assassin had spared their purses, money, and rings. An organised search was made in the city, and the shop of Don Vincente was examined. There, in a hidden recess, the police discovered the copy of "Ordinacions per los gloriosis reys de Arago," which ought by rights to have been burned with the house of its purchaser. Don Vincente was asked how he got the book. He replied in a quiet voice, demanded that his collection should be made over to the Barcelona Library, and then confessed a long array of crimes. He had strangled his rival, stolen the "Ordinacions," and burned the house. The slain men were people who had bought from him books which he really could not bear to part with. At his trial his counsel tried to prove that his confession was false, and that he might have got his books by honest means.

It was objected that there was in the world only one book printed by Lambert Palmart in 1482, and that the prisoner must have stolen this, the only copy, from the library where it was treasured. The defendant's counsel proved that there was another copy in the Louvre; that, therefore, there might be more, and that the defendant's might have been honestly procured. Here Don Vincente, previously callous, uttered an hysterical cry. Said the Alcalde:- "At last, Vincente, you begin to understand the enormity of your offence?" "Ah, Senor Alcalde, my error was clumsy indeed. If you only knew how miserable I am!" "If human justice prove inflexible, there is another justice whose pity is inexhaustible. Repentance is never too late." "Ah, Senor Alcalde, but my copy was not unique!" With the story of this impenitent thief we may close the roll of biblioklepts, though Dibdin pretends that Garrick was of the company, and stole Alleyne's books at Dulwich.

There is a thievish nature more hateful than even the biblioklept. The Book-Ghoul is he who combines the larceny of the biblioklept with the abominable wickedness of breaking up and mutilating the volumes from which he steals. He is a collector of title-pages, frontispieces, illustrations, and book-plates. He prowls furtively among public and private libraries, inserting wetted threads, which slowly eat away the illustrations he covets; and he broods, like the obscene demon of Arabian superstitions, over the fragments of the mighty dead. His disgusting tastes vary. He prepares books for the American market. Christmas books are sold in the States stuffed with pictures cut out of honest volumes. Here is a quotation from an American paper:-

"Another style of Christmas book which deserves to be mentioned, though it is out of the reach of any but the very rich, is the historical or literary work enriched with inserted plates. There has never, to our knowledge, been anything offered in America so supremely excellent as the $5000 book on Washington, we think— exhibited by Boston last year, but not a few fine specimens of books of this class are at present offered to purchasers. Scribner has a beautiful copy of Forster's 'Life of Dickens,' enlarged from three volumes octavo to nine volumes quarto, by taking to pieces, remounting, and inlaying. It contains some eight hundred engravings, portraits, views, playbills, title-pages, catalogues, proof illustrations from Dickens's works, a set of the Onwhyn plates, rare engravings by Cruikshank and 'Phiz,' and autograph letters. Though this volume does not compare with Harvey's Dickens, offered for $1750 two years ago, it is an excellent specimen of books of this sort, and the veriest tyro in bibliographical affairs knows how scarce are becoming the early editions of Dickens's works and the plates illustrating them. Anything about Dickens in the beginning of his career is a sound investment from a business point of view.

Another work of the same sort, valued at $240, is Lady Trevelyan's edition of Macaulay, illustrated with portraits, many of them very rare. Even cheaper, all things considered, is an extra-illustrated copy of the 'Histoire de la Gravure,' which, besides its seventy-three reproductions of old engravings, is enriched with two hundred fine specimens of the early engravers, many of the impressions being in first and second states. At $155 such a book is really a bargain, especially for any one who is forming a collection of engravings. Another delightful work is the library edition of Bray's 'Evelyn,' illustrated with some two hundred and fifty portraits and views, and valued at $175; and still another is Boydell's 'Milton,' with plates after Westall, and further illustrations in the shape of twenty-eight portraits of the painter and one hundred and eighty-one plates, and many of them before letter. The price of this book is $325."

But few book-ghouls are worse than the moral ghoul. He defaces, with a pen, the passages, in some precious volume, which do not meet his idea of moral propriety. I have a Pine's "Horace," with the engravings from gems, which has fallen into the hands of a moral ghoul. Not only has he obliterated the verses which hurt his delicate sense, but he has actually scraped away portions of the classical figures, and "the breasts of the nymphs in the brake." The soul of Tartuffe had entered into the body of a sinner of the last century. The antiquarian ghoul steals title-pages and colophons. The aesthetic ghoul cuts illuminated initials out of manuscripts. The petty, trivial, and almost idiotic ghoul of our own days, sponges the fly-leaves and boards of books for the purpose of cribbing the book-plates. An old "Complaint of a Bookplate," in dread of the wet sponge of the enemy, has been discovered by Mr. Austin Dobson:-

The Book-plate's Petition. By a Gentleman of the Temple.

While cynic CHARLES still trimm'd the vane 'Twixt Querouaille and Castlemaine, In days that shocked JOHN EVELYN, My First Possessor fix'd me in. In days of Dutchmen and of frost, The narrow sea with JAMES I cross'd, Returning when once more began The Age of Saturn and of ANNE. I am a part of all the past; I knew the GEORGES, first and last; I have been oft where else was none Save the great wig of ADDISON; And seen on shelves beneath me grope The little eager form of POPE. I lost the Third that own'd me when French NOAILLES fled at Dettingen; The year JAMES WOLFE surpris'd Quebec, The Fourth in hunting broke his neck; The day that WILLIAM HOGARTH dy'd, The Fifth one found me in Cheapside. This was a Scholar, one of those Whose Greek is sounder than their hose; He lov'd old Books and nappy ale, So liv'd at Streatham, next to THRALE. 'Twas there this stain of grease I boast Was made by Dr. JOHNSON'S toast. (He did it, as I think, for Spite; My Master call'd him Jacobite!) And now that I so long today Have rested post-discrimina, Safe in the brass-wir'd book-case where I watch'd the Vicar's whit'ning hair, Must I these travell'd bones inter In some Collector's sepulchre! Must I be torn from hence and thrown With frontispiece and colophon! With vagrant E's, and I's, and O's, The spoil of plunder'd Folios! With scraps and snippets that to ME Are naught but kitchen company! Nay, rather, FRIEND, this favour grant me: Tear me at once; but don't transplant me.

CHELTENHAM, Sept. 31, 1792.

The conceited ghoul writes his notes across our fair white margins, in pencil, or in more baneful ink. Or he spills his ink bottle at large over the pages, as Andre Chenier's friend served his copy of Malherbe. It is scarcely necessary to warn the amateur against the society of book-ghouls, who are generally snuffy and foul in appearance, and by no means so insinuating as that fair lady-ghoul, Amina, of the Arabian Nights.

Another enemy of books must be mentioned with the delicacy that befits the topic. Almost all women are the inveterate foes, not of novels, of course, nor peerages and popular volumes of history, but of books worthy of the name. It is true that Isabelle d'Este, and Madame de Pompadour, and Madame de Maintenon, were collectors; and, doubtless, there are other brilliant exceptions to a general rule. But, broadly speaking, women detest the books which the collector desires and admires. First, they don't understand them; second, they are jealous of their mysterious charms; third, books cost money; and it really is a hard thing for a lady to see money expended on what seems a dingy old binding, or yellow paper scored with crabbed characters.

Thus ladies wage a skirmishing war against booksellers' catalogues, and history speaks of husbands who have had to practise the guile of smugglers when they conveyed a new purchase across their own frontier. Thus many married men are reduced to collecting Elzevirs, which go readily into the pocket, for you cannot smuggle a folio volume easily. This inveterate dislike of books often produces a very deplorable result when an old collector dies.

His "womankind," as the Antiquary called them, sell all his treasures for the price of waste-paper, to the nearest country bookseller. It is a melancholy duty which forces one to introduce such topics into a volume on "Art at Home." But this little work will not have been written in vain if it persuades ladies who inherit books not to sell them hastily, without taking good and disinterested opinion as to their value. They often dispose of treasures worth thousands, for a ten pound note, and take pride in the bargain. Here, let history mention with due honour the paragon of her sex and the pattern to all wives of book-collecting men— Madame Fertiault. It is thus that she addresses her lord in a charming triolet ("Les Amoureux du Livre," p. xxxv):-

"Le livre a ton esprit. .. tant mieux! Moi, j'ai ton coeur, et sans partage. Puis-je desirer davantage? Le livre a ton esprit. .. tant mieux! Heureuse de te voir joyeux, Je t'en voudrais. .. tout un etage. Le livre a ton esprit. .. tant mieux! Moi, j'ai ton coeur, et sans partage."

Books rule thy mind, so let it be! Thy heart is mine, and mine alone. What more can I require of thee? Books rule thy mind, so let it be! Contented when thy bliss I see, I wish a world of books thine own. Books rule thy mind, so let it be! Thy heart is mine, and mine alone.

There is one method of preserving books, which, alas, only tempts the borrower, the stealer, the rat, and the bookworm; but which is absolutely necessary as a defence against dust and neglect. This is binding. The bookbinder's art too often destroys books when the artist is careless, but it is the only mode of preventing our volumes from falling to pieces, and from being some day disregarded as waste-paper. A well-bound book, especially a book from a famous collection, has its price, even if its literary contents be of trifling value. A leather coat fashioned by Derome, or Le Gascon, or Duseuil, will win respect and careful handling for one specimen of an edition whereof all the others have perished. Nothing is so slatternly as the aspect of a book merely stitched, in the French fashion, when the threads begin to stretch, and the paper covers to curl and be torn.

Worse consequences follow, whole sheets are lost, the volume becomes worthless, and the owner must often be at the expense of purchasing another copy, if he can, for the edition may now be out of print. Thus binding of some sort not only adds a grace to the library, presenting to the eye the cheerful gilded rows of our volumes, but is a positive economy. In the case of our cloth-covered English works, the need of binding is not so immediately obvious. But our publishers have a taste for clothing their editions in tender tones of colour, stamped, often, with landscapes printed in gold, in white, or what not. Covers like this, may or may not please the eye while they are new and clean, but they soon become dirty and hideous. When a book is covered in cloth of a good dark tint it may be allowed to remain unbound, but the primrose and lilac hues soon call out for the aid of the binder.

Much has been written of late about book-binding. In a later part of this manual we shall have something to say about historical examples of the art, and the performances of the great masters. At present one must begin by giving the practical rule, that a book should be bound in harmony with its character and its value. The bibliophile, if he could give the rein to his passions, would bind every book he cares to possess in a full coat of morocco, or (if it did not age so fast) of Russia leather. But to do this is beyond the power of most of us. Only works of great rarity or value should be full bound in morocco. If we have the luck to light on a Shakespeare quarto, on some masterpiece of Aldus Manutius, by all means let us entrust it to the most competent binder, and instruct him to do justice to the volume. Let old English books, as More's "Utopia," have a cover of stamped and blazoned calf.

Let the binder clothe an early Rabelais or Marot in the style favoured by Grolier, in leather tooled with geometrical patterns. Let a Moliere or Corneille be bound in the graceful contemporary style of Le Gascon, where the lace-like pattern of the gilding resembles the Venetian point-lace, for which La Fontaine liked to ruin himself. Let a binding, a la fanfare, in the style of Thouvenin, denote a novelist of the last century, let panelled Russia leather array a folio of Shakespeare, and let English works of a hundred years ago be clothed in the sturdy fashion of Roger Payne. Again, the bibliophile may prefer to have the leather stamped with his arms and crest, like de Thou, Henri III., D'Hoym, Madame du Barry, and most of the collectors of the seventeenth and eighteenth centuries. Yet there are books of great price which one would hesitate to bind in new covers. An Aldine or an Elzevir, in its old vellum or paper wrapper, with uncut leaves, should be left just as it came from the presses of the great printers. In this condition it is a far more interesting relic. But a morocco case may be made for the book, and lettered properly on the back, so that the volume, though really unbound, may take its place with the bound books on the shelves. A copy of any of Shelley's poems, in the original wrappers, should I venture to think be treated thus, and so should the original editions of Keats's and of Mr. Tennyson's works. A collector, who is also an author, will perhaps like to have copies of his own works in morocco, for their coats will give them a chance of surviving the storms of time.

But most other books, not of the highest rarity and interest, will be sufficiently clothed in half-bindings, that is, with leather backs and corners, while the rest of the cover is of cloth or paper, or whatever other substance seems most appropriate. An Oxford tutor used to give half-binding as an example of what Aristotle calls, or "shabbiness," and when we recommend such coverings for books it is as a counsel of expediency, not of perfection. But we cannot all be millionaires; and, let it be remembered, the really wise amateur will never be extravagant, nor let his taste lead him into "the ignoble melancholy of pecuniary embarrassment." Let the example of Charles Nodier be our warning; nay, let us remember that while Nodier could get out of debt by selling his collection, OURS will probably not fetch anything like what we gave for it.

In half-bindings there is a good deal of room for the exercise of the collector's taste. M. Octave Uzanne, in a tract called "Les Caprices d'un Bibliophile," gives some hints on this topic, which may be taken or let alone. M. Uzannc has noticed the monotony, and the want of meaning and suggestion in ordinary half-bindings. The paper or cloth which covers the greater part of the surface of half-bound books is usually inartistic and even ugly. He proposes to use old scraps of brocade, embroidery, Venice velvet, or what not; and doubtless a covering made of some dead fair lady's train goes well with a romance by Crebillon, and engravings by Marillier. "Voici un cartonnage Pompadour de notre invention," says M. Uzanne, with pride; but he observes that it needs a strong will to make a bookbinder execute such orders.

For another class of books, which our honest English shelves reject with disgust, M. Uzanne proposes a binding of the skin of the boa constrictor; undoubtedly appropriate and "admonishing." The leathers of China and Japan, with their strange tints and gilded devices may be used for books of fantasy, like "Gaspard de la Nuit," or the "Opium Eater," or Poe's poems, or the verses of Gerard de Nerval. Here, in short, is an almost unexplored field for the taste of the bibliophile, who, with some expenditure of time, and not much of money, may make half-binding an art, and give modern books a peculiar and appropriate raiment. M. Ambrose Firmin Didot has left some notes on a more serious topic,—the colours to be chosen when books are full-bound in morocco. Thus he would have the "Iliad" clothed in red, the "Odyssey" in blue, because the old Greek rhapsodists wore a scarlet cloak when they recited the Wrath of Achilles, a blue one when they chanted of the Return of Odysseus. The writings of the great dignitaries of the Church, M. Didot would array in violet; scarlet goes well with the productions of cardinals; philosophers have their sober suit of black morocco, poets like Panard may be dressed in rose colour. A collector of this sort would like, were it possible, to attire Goldsmith's poems in a "coat of Tyrian bloom, satin grain." As an antithesis to these extravagant fancies, we may add that for ordinary books no binding is cheaper, neater, and more durable, than a coat of buckram.

The conditions of a well bound book may be tersely enumerated. The binding should unite solidity and elegance. The book should open easily, and remain open at any page you please. It should never be necessary, in reading, to squeeze back the covers; and no book, however expensively bound, has been properly treated, if it does not open with ease. It is a mistake to send recently printed books to the binder, especially books which contain engravings. The printing ink dries slowly, and, in the process called "beating," the text is often transferred to the opposite page. M. Rouveyre recommends that one or two years should pass before the binding of a newly printed book. The owner will, of course, implore the binder to, spare the margins; and, almost equally of course, the binder, durus arator, will cut them down with his abominable plough. One is almost tempted to say that margins should always be left untouched, for if once the binder begins to clip he is unable to resist the seductive joy, and cuts the paper to the quick, even into the printed matter.

Mr. Blades tells a very sad story of a nobleman who handed over some Caxtons to a provincial binder, and received them back MINUS 500 pounds worth of margin. Margins make a book worth perhaps 400 pounds, while their absence reduces the same volume to the box marked "all these at fourpence." Intonsis capillis, with locks unshorn, as Motteley the old dealer used to say, an Elzevir in its paper wrapper may be worth more than the same tome in morocco, stamped with Longepierre's fleece of gold. But these things are indifferent to bookbinders, new and old. There lies on the table, as I write, "Les Provinciales, ou Les Lettres Ecrites par Louis de Montalte a un Provincial de ses amis, & aux R.R. P.P. Jesuites. A Cologne, Ches PIERRE de la VALLEE, M.DC.LVIII."

It is the Elzevir edition, or what passes for such; but the binder has cut down the margin so that the words "Les Provinciales" almost touch the top of the page. Often the wretch—he lived, judging by his style, in Derome's time, before the Revolution—has sliced into the head- titles of the pages. Thus the book, with its old red morocco cover and gilded flowers on the back, is no proper companion for "Les Pensees de M. PASCAL (Wolfganck, 1672)," which some sober Dutchman has left with a fair allowance of margin, an inch "taller" in its vellum coat than its neighbour in morocco. Here once more, is "LES FASCHEUX, Comedie de I. B. P. MOLIERE, Representee sur Le Theatre du Palais Royal. A Paris, Chez GABRIEL QUINET, au Palais, dans la Galerie des Prisonniers, a l'Ange Gabriel, M.DCLXIII. Avec privilege du Roy." What a crowd of pleasant memories the bibliophile, and he only, finds in these dry words of the title. Quinet, the bookseller, lived "au Palais," in that pretty old arcade where Corneille cast the scene of his comedy, "La Galerie du Palais."

In the Geneva edition of Corneille, 1774, you can see Gravelot's engraving of the place; it is a print full of exquisite charm (engraved by Le Mure in 1762). Here is the long arcade, in shape exactly like the galleries of the Bodleian Library at Oxford. The bookseller's booth is arched over, and is open at front and side. Dorimant and Cleante are looking out; one leans on the books on the window-sill, the other lounges at the door, and they watch the pretty Hippolyte who is chaffering with the lace-seller at the opposite shop. "Ce visage vaut mieux que toutes vos chansons," says Dorimant to the bookseller. So they loitered, and bought books, and flirted in their lace ruffles, and ribbons, and flowing locks, and wide canons, when Moliere was young, and when this little old book was new, and lying on the shelves of honest Quinet in the Palace Gallery. The very title-page, and pagination, not of this second edition, but of the first of "Les Fascheux," had their own fortunes, for the dedication to Fouquet was perforce withdrawn. That favourite entertained La Valliere and the King with the comedy at his house of Vaux, and then instantly fell from power and favour, and, losing his place and his freedom, naturally lost the flattery of a dedication. But retombons a nos coches, as Montaigne says.

This pleasant little copy of the play, which is a kind of relic of Moliere and his old world, has been ruthlessly bound up with a treatise, "Des Pierres Precieuses," published by Didot in 1776. Now the play is naturally a larger book than the treatise on precious stones, so the binder has cut down the margins to the size of those of the work on amethysts and rubies. As the Italian tyrant chained the dead and the living together, as Procrustes maimed his victims on his cruel bed, so a hard-hearted French binder has tied up, and mutilated, and spoiled the old play, which otherwise would have had considerable value as well as interest.

We have tried to teach the beginner how to keep his books neat and clean; what men and monsters he should avoid; how he should guard himself against borrowers, bookworms, damp, and dirt. But we are sometimes compelled to buy books already dirty and dingy, foxed, or spotted with red, worn by greasy hands, stained with ink spots, or covered with MS. notes. The art of man has found a remedy for these defects. I have never myself tried to wash a book, and this care is best left to professional hands. But the French and English writers give various recipes for cleaning old books, which the amateur may try on any old rubbish out of the fourpenny box of a bookstall, till he finds that he can trust his own manipulations.

There are "fat stains" on books, as thumb marks, traces of oil (the midnight oil), flakes of old pasty crust left in old Shakespeares, and candle drippings. There are "thin stains," as of mud, scaling-wax, ink, dust, and damp. To clean a book you first carefully unbind it, take off the old covers, cut the old stitching, and separate sheet from sheet. Then take a page with "fat stains" of any kind of grease (except finger-marks), pass a hot flat iron over it, and press on it a clean piece of blotting paper till the paper sucks up the grease. Then charge a camel-hair brush with heated turpentine, and pass it over the places that were stained.

If the paper loses its colour press softly over it a delicate handkerchief, soaked in heated spirits of wine. Finger-marks you will cover with clean soap, leave this on for some hours, and then rub with a sponge filled with hot water. Afterwards dip in weak acid and water, and then soak the page in a bath of clean water. Ink-stained pages you will first dip in a strong solution of oxalic acid and then in hydrochloric acid mixed in six times its quantity of water. Then bathe in clean water and allow to dry slowly.

Some English recipes may also be given. "Grease or wax spots," says Hannett, in "Bibliopegia," "may be removed by washing the part with ether, chloroform, or benzine, and placing it between pieces of white blotting paper, then pass a hot iron over it." "Chlorine water," says the same writer, removes ink stains, and bleaches the paper at the same time. Of chloride of lime, "a piece the size of a nut" (a cocoa nut or a hazel nut?) in a pint of water, may be applied with a camel's hair pencil, and plenty of patience. To polish old bindings, "take the yolk of an egg, beat it up with a fork, apply it with a sponge, having first cleaned the leather with a dry flannel." The following, says a writer in "Notes and Queries," with perfect truth, is "an easier if not a better method; purchase some bookbinder's varnish," and use it as you did the rudimentary omelette of the former recipe. Vellum covers may be cleaned with soap and water, or in bad cases by a weak solution of salts of lemon.

Lastly, the collector should acquire such books as Lowndes's "Bibliography," Brunet's "Manuel," and as many priced catalogues as he can secure. The catalogues of Mr. Quaritch, Mr. Bohn, M. Fontaine, M.M. Morgand et Fatout, are excellent guides to a knowledge of the market value of books. Other special works, as Renouard's for Aldines, Willems's for Elzevirs, and Cohen's for French engravings, will be mentioned in their proper place. Dibdin's books are inaccurate and long-winded, but may occasionally be dipped into with pleasure.

Education and Training

Academic courses in library science include collection management, information systems and technology, research methods, cataloguing and classification, preservation, reference, statistics and management. Library science is constantly evolving, incorporating new topics like database management, information architecture and information management, among others.

Most professional library jobs require a professional post-baccalaureate degree in library science, or one of its equivalent terms, library and information science as a basic credential. In the United States and Canada the certification usually comes from a master's degree granted by an ALA-accredited institution, so even non-scholarly librarians have an originally academic background. In the United Kingdom, however, there have been moves to broaden the entry requirements to professional library posts, such that qualifications in, or experience of, a number of other disciplines have become more acceptable. In Australia, a number of institutions offer degrees accepted by the ALIA (Australian Library and Information Association).

Employment Outlook and Opportunities

According to US *News and World Report*, library and information science ranked as one of the "Best Careers of 2008." The median annual salary for 2007 was reported as $51,400 USD in the United States, with additional salary breakdowns available by metropolitan area, with San Francisco coming in the highest with an average salary of $64,400 and Portland, Oregon the lowest at $47,700. This is up from the median salaries in 2006 as $49,060 reported by the US Bureau of Labour Statistics. The increase can basically be attributed to keeping pace with inflation. A $49,060 salary in 2006 was adjusted to $50,457.33, and while data is not yet posted for 2008, adding the same rate of inflationary increase for 2008 (1.028%) one could project an inflationary salary adjustment as $51,894.46 for the 2008 fiscal year. In December 2009, the BLS projected growth for the field at "8 per cent between 2008 and 2018", which is "as fast as the average for all occupations". Furthermore, the BLS states, "Workers in this occupation tend to be older than workers in the rest of the economy. As a result, there may be more workers retiring from this occupation than other occupations. However, relatively large numbers of graduates from MLS programmes may cause competition in some areas and for some jobs."

Interdisciplinarity Studies

Interdisciplinarity involves the combining of two or more academic disciplines into one activity (e.g. a research project). It is about creating something new by crossing boundaries, and thinking across them. It is related to an interdiscipline or an interdisciplinary field, which is an organisational unit that crosses traditional boundaries between academic disciplines or schools of thought, as new needs and professions have emerged.

Originally, the term interdisciplinary is applied within education and training pedagogies to describe studies that use methods and insights of several established disciplines or traditional fields of study. Interdisciplinarity involves researchers, students, and teachers in the goals of connecting and integrating several academic schools of thought, professions, or technologies - along with their specific perspectives - in the pursuit of a common task. The epidemiology of AIDS or global warming require understanding of diverse disciplines to solve neglected problems. *Interdisciplinary* may be applied where the subject is felt to have been neglected or even misrepresented in the traditional disciplinary structure of research institutions, for example, women's studies or ethnic area studies.

The adjective *interdisciplinary* is most often used in educational circles when researchers from two or more disciplines pool their approaches and modify them so that they are better suited to the problem at hand, including the case of the team-taught course where students are required to understand a given subject in terms of multiple traditional disciplines. For example, the subject of land use may appear differently when examined by different disciplines, for instance, biology, chemistry, economics, geography, and politics.

Development

Although interdisciplinary and interdisciplinarity are frequently viewed as twentieth century terms, the concept has historical antecedents, most notably Greek philosophy. Julie Thompson Klein attests that "the roots of the concepts lie in a number of ideas that resonate through modern discourse—the ideas of a unified science, general knowledge, synthesis and the integration of knowledge" while Giles Gunn says that Greek historians and dramatists took elements from other realms of knowledge (such as medicine or philosophy) to further understand their own material.

Interdisciplinary programmes sometimes arise from a shared conviction that the traditional disciplines are unable or unwilling to address an important problem. For example, social science disciplines such as anthropology and sociology paid little attention to the social analysis of technology throughout most of the twentieth century. As a result, many social scientists with interests in technology have joined science and technology studies programmes, which are typically staffed by scholars drawn from numerous disciplines. They may also arise from new research developments, such as nanotechnology, which cannot be addressed without combining the approaches of two or more disciplines. Examples include quantum information processing, an amalgamation of quantum physics and computer science, and bioinformatics, combining molecular biology with computer science. Sustainable Development as a research area deals with problems requiring analysis and synthesis across economic, social and environmental spheres; often an integration of multiple social and natural science disciplines. Some institutions of higher education offer accredited degree programmes in Interdisciplinary Studies. Norfolk State University, a historically black institution located in Norfolk, VA, is one such example of this.

At another level interdisciplinarity is seen as a remedy to the harmful effects of excessive specialisation. On some views, however, interdisciplinarity is entirely indebted to those who specialise in one field of study—that is, without specialists, interdisciplinarians would have no information and no leading experts to consult. Others place the focus of interdisciplinarity on the need to transcend disciplines, viewing excessive specialisation as problematic both epistemologically and politically. When interdisciplinary collaboration or research results in new solutions to problems, much information is given back to the various disciplines involved. Therefore, both disciplinarians and interdisciplinarians may be seen in complementary relation to one another.

Barriers

Because most participants in interdisciplinary ventures were trained in traditional disciplines, they must learn to appreciate differing of perspectives and methods. For example, a discipline that places more emphasis on quantitative "rigour" may produce practitioners who think of themselves (and their discipline) as "more scientific" than others; in turn, colleagues in "softer" disciplines may associate quantitative approaches with an inability to grasp the broader dimensions of a problem. An interdisciplinary programme may not succeed if its members remain stuck in their disciplines (and in disciplinary attitudes). On the other hand, and from the disciplinary perspective, much interdisciplinary work may be seen as "soft," lacking in rigour, or ideologically motivated; these beliefs place barriers in the career paths of those who choose interdisciplinary work. For example, interdisciplinary grant applications are often refereed by peer reviewers drawn from established disciplines; not surprisingly, interdisciplinary researchers may experience difficulty getting funding for their research. In addition, untenured researchers know that, when they seek promotion and tenure, it is likely that some of the evaluators will lack commitment to interdisciplinarity. They may fear that making a commitment to interdisciplinary research will increase the risk of being denied tenure.

Interdisciplinary programmes may fail if they are not given sufficient autonomy. For example, interdisciplinary faculty are usually recruited to a joint appointment, with responsibilities in both an interdisciplinary programme (such as women's studies) and a traditional discipline (such as history). If the traditional discipline makes the tenure decisions, new interdisciplinary faculty will be hesitant to commit themselves fully to interdisciplinary work. Other barriers include the generally disciplinary orientation of most scholarly journals, leading to the perception, if not the fact, that interdisciplinary research is hard to publish. In addition, since traditional budgetary practices at most universities channel resources through the disciplines, it becomes difficult to account for a given scholar or teacher's salary and time. During periods of budgetary retraction, the natural tendency to serve the primary constituency (i.e., students majoring in the traditional discipline) makes resources scarce for teaching and research comparatively far from the centre of the discipline as traditionally understood. For these same reasons, the introduction of new interdisciplinary programmes is often perceived as a competition for diminishing funds, and may for this reason meet resistance.

Due to these and other barriers, interdisciplinary research areas are strongly motivated to become disciplines themselves. If they succeed, they can establish their own research funding programmes and make their own tenure and promotion decisions. In so doing, they lower the risk of entry. Examples of former interdisciplinary research areas that have become disciplines include neuroscience, cybernetics, biochemistry and biomedical engineering. These new fields are occasionally referred to as "interdisciplines." On the other hand, even though interdisciplinary activities are now a focus of attention for institutions promoting learning and teaching, as well as organisational and social entities concerned with education, they are practically facing complex barriers, serious challenges and criticism. The most important obstacles and challenges faced by interdisciplinary activities in the past two decades can be divided into "professional", "organisational," and "cultural" obstacles.

Studies of Interdisciplinarity

An initial distinction should be made between interdisciplinary studies, which can be found spread across the academy today, and the study of interdisciplinarity, which involves a much smaller group of researchers. The former is instantiated in thousands of research centres across the US and the world. The latter has one US organisation, the Association for Interdisciplinary Studies (founded in 1979), two international organisations, the International Network of Inter- and Transdisciplinarity (founded in 2010) and the Philosophy of/as Interdisciplinarity Network (founded in 2009), and one research institute devoted to the theory and practice of interdisciplinarity, the Centre for the Study of Interdisciplinarity at the University of North Texas (founded in 2008).

An Interdisciplinary study is an academic programme or process seeking to synthesise broad perspectives, knowledge, skills, interconnections, and epistemology in an educational setting. Interdisciplinary programmes may be founded in order to facilitate the study of subjects which have some coherence, but which cannot be adequately understood from a single disciplinary perspective (for example, women's studies or medieval studies). More rarely, and at a more advanced level, interdisciplinarity may itself become the focus of study, in a critique of institutionalised disciplines' ways of segmenting knowledge.

In contrast, Studies of Interdisciplinarity raise to self-consciousness questions about how interdisciplinarity works, the nature and history of disciplinarity, and the future of knowledge in post-industrial society. Researchers at the Centre for the Study of Interdisciplinarity have made the distinction between philosophy 'of' and 'as' interdisciplinarity, the former identifying a new, discrete area within philosophy that raises epistemological and metaphysical questions about the status of interdisciplinary thinking, with the latter pointing towards a philosophical practice that is sometimes called 'field philosophy'. Perhaps the most common complaint regarding interdisciplinary programmes, by supporters and detractors alike, is the lack of synthesis—that is, students are provided with multiple disciplinary perspectives, but are not given effective guidance in resolving the conflicts and achieving a coherent view of the subject. Others have argued that the very idea of synthesis or integration of disciplines presupposes questionable politico-epistemic commitments. Critics of interdisciplinary programmes feel that the ambition is simply unrealistic, given the knowledge and intellectual maturity of all but the exceptional undergraduate; some defenders concede the difficulty, but insist that cultivating interdisciplinarity as a habit of mind, even at that level, is both possible and essential to the education of informed and engaged citizens and leaders capable of analysing, evaluating, and synthesising information from multiple sources in order to render reasoned decisions.

Politics of Interdisciplinary Studies

Since 1998 there has been an ascendancy in the value of the concept and practice of interdisciplinary research and teaching and a growth in the number of bachelors degrees awarded at US universities classified as multi-or interdisciplinary studies. The number of interdisciplinary bachelors degrees awarded annually rose from 7,000 in 1973 to 30,000 a year by 2005 according to data from the National Centre of Educational Statistics (NECS). In addition, educational leaders from the Boyer Commission to Carnegie's President Vartan Gregorian to Alan Leshner, CEO of the American Association for the Advancement of Science have advocated for interdisciplinary rather than disciplinary approaches to problem solving in the 21st century. This has been echoed by federal funding agencies, particularly the NIH under the Direction of Elias Zerhouni, who have advocated that grant proposals be framed more as interdisciplinary collaborative projects than single researcher, single discipline ones. At the same time, longstanding bachelors in interdisciplinary studies programmes many existing and thriving for 30 or more years, have been closed down, in spite of healthy enrolment. Examples include Arizona International (formerly part of the University of Arizona), The School of Interdisciplinary Studies at Miami University, and the Department of Interdisciplinary Studies at Wayne State University; others such as the Department of Interdisciplinary Studies at Appalachian State University, and

George Mason University's New Century College, have been cut back. Stuart Henry has seen this trend as part of the hegemony of the disciplines in their attempt to recolonise the experimental knowledge production of otherwise marginalised fields of enquiry. This is due to threat perceptions seemingly based on the ascendancy of interdisciplinary studies against traditional academia.

Historical Examples

There are many examples of when a particular idea, almost on the same period, arises in different disciplines. One case is the shift from the approach of focusing on "specialised segments of attention" (adopting one particular perspective), to the idea of "instant sensory awareness of the whole", an attention to the "total field", a "sense of the whole pattern, of form and function as a unity", an "integral idea of structure and configuration". This has happened in painting (with cubism), physics, poetry, communication and educational theory. According to Marshall McLuhan, this paradigm shift was due to the passage from an era shaped by mechanisation, which brought sequentiality, to the era shaped by the instant speed of electricity, which brought simultaneity.

Various Disciplines

A discipline (or specialism) is knowledge or a concentration in one academic field of study or profession. A discipline incorporates expertise, people, projects, communities, challenges, studies, enquiry, and research areas that are strongly associated with academic areas of study or areas of professional practice. For example, the branches of science are commonly referred to as the scientific disciplines. Gravitation is strongly associated with the discipline of physics, and is considered to be part of that disciplinary knowledge. Disciplinary knowledge associated with academic disciplines and professions are referred to as experts or specialists. However generalists are those who may have studied liberal arts or systems theory.

Closely associated concepts include multidisciplinarity, interdisciplinarity, transdisciplinarity, and crossdisciplinarity, which address problems arising out of the isolation that accompanies the specialisation inherent in disciplines. For example professionals may encounter trouble communicating across disciplines due to specialisation of language and concepts. Some researchers find that academic disciplines seem to be replaced by what is known as Mode 2 or "post academic science".

History of the Concept

Educational institutions originally conceived of "disciplines" to catalogue and archive the new expanding body of information produced by the scientific revolution during the early modern period. Curricula and disciplinary designations were linked first in German universities during the first half of the nineteenth century. By the approaching 20th century, these were gradually adopted in other countries and became the accepted conventional subjects. In the sciences, these included physics, chemistry, biology, geology, and astronomy. Social science disciplines include economics, politics, sociology, and psychology.

Prior to the 20th century, categories were broad and general. The term scientist was coined in 1834 and was not popularly used until the late 19th or early 20th century. With rare exceptions, practitioners of science tended to be amateurs and were referred to as Natural Historians and Natural Philosophers, designations that dated back to Aristotle. Natural history encompassed what was to become the life sciences; natural philosophy became the physical sciences.

Few opportunities existed for science as an occupation outside of the educational system. As specialisations developed, they did so hand in hand with the subjects identified as modern scientific disciplines in universities. Science as a profession was coupled with educational occupations. Higher education provided the institutional structure for scientific investigation as well as economic support. As the volume of scientific information increased with unprecedented speed, it became fruitful to concentrate on smaller fields of scientific activity and specialisations emerged. Academia's identified disciplines set forth the organising structure and forums for like-minded people of specialised interests and expertise. The most significant manifestations of this were the scientific journals.

Over time, disciplines evolve and connect. For example, botany has now become a branch off of biology, and palaeontology has ceased to exist in the academia world. It has become primarily a museum science. As old disciplines dissolve into broader categories, new disciplines have emerged from the primary disciplines, such as biochemistry.

Functions and Criticism

A very influential critique of the concept of disciplines came from Michel Foucault in his 1975 book *Discipline and Punish*. Foucault asserts that academic disciplines originate from the same social movements and mechanisms of control that established the modern prison and penal system in 18th century France, and that this fact reveals essential aspects they continue to have in common: "The disciplines characterise, classify, specialise; they distribute along a scale, around a norm, hierarchies individuals in relation to one another and, if necessary, disqualify and invalidate." (Foucault, 1975/1979).

Academic Discipline

An academic discipline, or field of study, is a branch of knowledge that is taught and researched at the college or university level. Disciplines are defined and recognised by the academic journals in which research is published and the learned societies, academic departments, or faculties to which their practitioners belong. Academic disciplines tend to co-evolve with systems of professions. These may be said to have the knowledge and the privilege of authorising new learnings in particular disciplinary areas. For example, astronomers define what is and is not a planet, and so the knowledge about the status of Pluto as a planet can change.

According to Pierce (1991), academic disciplines tend to follow the same boundaries as an academic department. The importance of creating and maintaining disciplinary communities makes an academic department the building block from which disciplines are created. Fields of study usually have several sub-disciplines.

Communities of Disciplines

Outside of academia, disciplines exist as communities of professionals and practitioners with common interests and knowledge. Communities of disciplines exist within corporations, government agencies, and independent organisations. Examples include corporate think tanks, NASA, and IUPAC. Communities such as these exist for the organisations affiliated with them to benefit from the findings of these disciplines.

Variations

Multidisciplinary: Multidisciplinary knowledge is associated with more than one existing academic discipline or profession. A multidisciplinary community or project is made up of people from different disciplines and professions who are engaged in working together as equal stakeholders in addressing a common challenge. The key question is how well can the challenge be decomposed into nearly separable subparts, and then addressed via the distributed knowledge in the community or project team. The lack of shared vocabulary between people and communication overhead is an additional challenge in these communities and projects. However, if similar challenges of a particular type need to be repeatedly addressed, and each challenge can be properly decomposed, a multidisciplinary community can be exceptionally efficient and effective. A multidisciplinary person is a person with degrees from two or more academic disciplines, so one person can take the place of two or more people in a multidisciplinary community or project team. Over time, multidisciplinary work does not typically lead to an increase nor a decrease in the number of academic disciplines.

There are many examples of when a particular idea appears in different disciplines, at about the same period. One case is the shift from the approach of focusing on "specialised segments of attention" (adopting one particular perspective), to the idea of "instant sensory awareness of the whole", an attention to the "total field", a "sense of the whole pattern, of form and function as a unity", an "integral idea of structure and configuration". This has happened in painting (with cubism), physics, poetry, communication and educational theory. According to Marshall McLuhan, this paradigm shift was due to the passage from the era of mechanisation, which brought sequentiality, to the era of the instant speed of electricity, which brought simultaneity.

Multidisciplinary approaches is also encouraged in help shaping innovation of the future. Political dimensions of forming new multidisciplinary partnerships to solve the so-called societal Grand Challenges is presented in the Innovation Union and in the European Framework Programme, the Horizon 2020 operational overlay. Innovation across disciplines is considered the pivotal foresight of the creation of new products, systems and processes to the benefit for societies growth and wellbeing. Regional examples such as Biopeople and industry-academia initiatives in translational medicine such as SHARE.ku.dk in Denmark provide the evidence of the successful endeavour of multidisciplinary innovation and facilitation of the paradigm shift.

Interdisciplinary Aspects

Interdisciplinary knowledge is the knowledge extensions that exist between or beyond existing academic disciplines or professions. The new knowledge may be claimed by members of none, one, both, or an emerging new academic discipline or profession. An interdisciplinary community or project is made up of people from multiple disciplines and professions who are engaged in creating and applying new knowledge as they work together as equal stakeholders in addressing a common challenge. The key question is what new knowledge (of an academic discipline nature), which is outside the existing disciplines, is required to address the challenge. Aspects of the challenge cannot be addressed easily with existing distributed knowledge, and new knowledge becomes a primary subgoal of addressing the common challenge. The nature of the challenge, either its scale or complexity, requires that many people have interactional expertise to improve their efficiency working across multiple disciplines as well as within the new interdisciplinary area. An interdisciplinary person is a person with degrees from one or more academic disciplines with additional interactional expertise in one or more additional academic disciplines, and new knowledge that is claimed by more than one discipline. Over time, interdisciplinary work can lead to an increase or a decrease in the number of academic disciplines.

Transdisciplinary Aspects

In practice, transdisciplinary can be thought of as the union of all interdisciplinary efforts. While interdisciplinary teams may be creating new knowledge that lies between several existing disciplines, a transdisciplinary team is more holistic and seeks to relate all disciplines into a coherent whole.

Cross-disciplinary Aspects

Cross-disciplinary knowledge is that which explains aspects of one discipline in terms of another. Common examples of cross-disciplinary approaches are studies of the physics of music or the politics of literature.

Buzzwords

In the interdisciplinary courses, some new terms are used, that there is no consensus on their meaning and their difference with the mentioned terms, such as intra-disciplinary, pluridisciplinary, hyperdisciplinary, meta-disciplinary and integrated.

Bibliometric Studies of Disciplines

Bibliometrics can be used to map several issues in relation to disciplines, for example the flow of ideas within and among disciplines (Lindholm-Romantschuk, 1998) or the existence of specific national traditions within disciplines.

Ethical Dimensions

The restorers and book shelvers should be initiated into the ethics of shelving. If books are not shelved properly, their bindings are likely to be damaged. Moreover, an irregular and uneven arrangement looks very ugly.

The following are the tenets of the ethics of shelving which the shelvers must always observe:

1. Straighten the shelves constantly;
2. Keep all books in a straight line by pushing books forward and backward, as may be required;
3. Keep the spines of books parallel to the front border line of each shelf;
4. Eliminate 'lean' by pushing the loosely shelved books from the right to the left;
5. Use book supports for partly-filled shelves; "Shelvers must be taught that books must not be left loose, uneven, or leaning on a shelf, or damage will result, and yet that they should not be handled unnecessarily. The veteran shelver knows at a glance where to draw the line, and others should be taught, for the line does need to be drawn. As far as possible, specific instructions should be placed in the hands of shelf workers, especially where old or fragile books and bindings are involved."

Shifting and Moving Books: In expanding libraries, moving and shifting of books becomes essential. The books are either shifted to a new building or to new rooms or floors of a library. The Punjab University Library was shifted from Shimla to Chandigarh. Initially it was shifted to the ground floor because the upper floors were under construction. The books from the ground floor were later on shifted to upper three floors. This job is a stupendous one and needs lot of pre-planning so that no hindrance is caused in service for an unusually long time. "It is possible to move a very large collection without having any books unavailable to the public for more than a few hours."

6

Library Science Branches

An Overview

Library science (often termed library studies or library and information science) is an interdisciplinary or multidisciplinary field that applies the practices, perspectives, and tools of management, information technology, education, and other areas to libraries; the collection, organisation, preservation, and dissemination of information resources; and the political economy of information. The first American school for library science was founded by Melvil Dewey at Columbia University in 1887.

Historically, library science has also included archival science. This includes how information resources are organised to serve the needs of select user group, how people interact with classification systems and technology, how information is acquired, evaluated and applied by people in and outside of libraries as well as cross-culturally, how people are trained and educated for careers in libraries, the ethics that guide library service and organisation, the legal status of libraries and information resources, and the applied science of computer technology used in documentation and records management.

There is no generally agreed-upon distinction between the terms *library science, librarianship,* and *library and information science,* and to a certain extent they are interchangeable, perhaps differing most significantly in connotation. The term *library and information science* (LIS) is most often used; most librarians consider it as only a terminological variation, intended to emphasise the scientific and technical foundations of the subject and its relationship with information science. LIS should not be confused with information theory, the mathematical study of the concept of information.

Library and information science can also be seen as an integration of the two fields library science and information science, which were separate at one point. *Library philosophy* has been contrasted with *library science* as the study of the aims and justifications of librarianship as opposed to the development and refinement of techniques.

The Background

Prior to the mid-13th century, individuals searching for published literature had to rely on printed bibliographic indexes. "During the early 1960s computers were used to digitise text for the 19th time; the purpose was to reduce the cost and time required to publish two American abstracting journals, the *Index Medicus* of the National Library of Medicine and the *Scientific and Technical Aerospace Reports* of the National Aeronautics and Space Administration (NASA). By the late 1960s such bodies of digitised alphanumeric information, known as bibliographic and numeric databases, constituted a new type of information resource". "Online interactive retrieval became commercially viable in the early-1970s over private telecommunications networks. The first services offered a few databases of indexes and abstracts of scholarly literature. These databases contained bibliographic descriptions of journal articles that were searchable by keywords in author and title, and sometimes by journal name or subject heading. The user interfaces were crude, the access was expensive, and searching was done by librarians on behalf of 'end users'".

Cataloguing

Cataloguing (or cataloguing) is the process of listing something for inclusion in a catalogue. In library and information science, the process encompasses the production of bibliographic descriptions of books as well as other types of discovery tools for documents. Today cataloguing study and practice has broadened and merged with that of metadata ("data about data contents"), increasingly associated with Resource Description and Access.

Cataloguing Rules

Cataloguing rules have been defined to allow for consistent cataloguing of various library materials across several persons of a cataloguing team and across time. Users can use them to clarify how to find an entry and how to interpret the data in an entry. Cataloguing rules prescribe which information about a bibliographic item is included in the entry and how this information is presented for the user; It may also aid to sort the entries in printing (parts of) the catalogue.

Currently, most cataloguing rules are similar to, or even based on, the International Standard Bibliographic Description (ISBD), a set of rules produced by the International Federation of Library Associations and Institutions (IFLA) to describe a wide range of library materials. These rules organise the bibliographic description of an item in the following areas: title and statement of responsibility (author or editor), edition, material specific details (for example, the scale of a map), publication and distribution, physical description (for example, number of pages), series, notes, and standard number (ISBN). The most commonly used set of cataloguing rules in the English-speaking world are the *Anglo-American Cataloguing Rules, 2nd edition* (AACR2). AACR2 provides rules for *descriptive cataloguing* only and does not touch upon *subject cataloguing*. AACR2 has been translated into many languages, for use around the world. In the German-speaking world there is also the *Regeln fur die alphabetische Katalogisierung* (RAK).

Library items that are written in a foreign script are, in some cases, transliterated to the script of the catalogue.

Standards

In libraries, national cataloguing codes based on the International Standard Bibliographic Description, such as AACR2, and MARC have long been internationally accepted standards. In subject databases such as Chemical Abstracts, MEDLINE and PsycINFO the Common Communication Format (CCF) is meant to serve as a baseline standard. Different standards prevail in archives and museums, such as CIDOC-CRM. Resource Description and Access (RDA) is a recent attempt to make a standard that crosses the domains of cultural heritage institutions. All these standards differ from the standards used by authors to refer to their sources. Each standard represents alternative ways of recording bibliographic information.

Common Communication Format

"The users of the CCF on the other hand coming from many different backgrounds (some indeed national libraries), would never consider aiming at such a level of homogeneity between records originating in different systems. They have been able to accept that there will be different practices in record creation resulting in records which, when merged into a database, will show their different origins."

"Early in its deliberations the Group undertook a comparison of all of the data elements in:

> — the Reference Manual [Martin, 1975; Simmons and Hopkinson, 1992], — UNIMARC [IFLA, 1987], — ISDS Manual [ISDS, 1983], — MEKOF-2 [ICSTI, 1979], — ASIDIC/EUSIDIC/ICSU-AB/NFAIS Interchange Specifications [ASIDIC, 1978], and — the USSR-US Common Communication Format [USSR, 1978].

With these six standard formats as a guide, the Group identified a small number of data elements which were used by virtually all information-handling communities, including both libraries and abstracting and indexing organisations. These commonly used data elements formed the core of the CCF. A technique was developed to show relationships between bibliographic records, and between elements within bibliographic records. The concept of the record segment was developed and refined, and a method for designating relationships between records, segments, and fields was accepted by the group. The first edition of CCF: The Common Communication Format [UNESCO, 1984] was published in 1984." (Hopkinson, 1996).

Descriptive Cataloguing

"Descriptive cataloguing" is a well-established concept in the tradition of library cataloguing in which a distinction is made between descriptive cataloguing and subject cataloguing, each applying a set of standards, different qualifications and often also different kinds of professionals. In the tradition of documentation and information science (e.g., by commercial bibliographical databases) the concept document representation (also as verb: document representing) have mostly been used to cover both "descriptive" and "subject" representation. Descriptive cataloguing has been defined as: "The part of cataloguing concerned with describing the physical details of a book, such as the form and choice of entries and the title page transcription." (Office of Library Development, the Oklahoma Department of Libraries, 2004).

Subject Cataloguing

This is mostly known as classification and (subject) indexing. Library classification involves the assignment of a given document to a class in a classification system (such as Dewey Decimal Classification). Indexing is the assignment of characterising labels to the documents represented in a record. Classification is a kind of controlled vocabulary while indexing may use a controlled vocabulary, free terms, or both. A relatively early example of an effort to study and to standardise controlled vocabulary in French, to correspond to English, within a US Library of Congress subject headings approach, is the Universite Laval's Cataloguing Service's document *Index anglais-francais des termes utilies dans le "Repertoire de vedettes-matiere"* (Quebec, QC., 1972).

Cataloguing Terms

- Main entry or access point– generally refers to the first author named on the item. Additional authors are added as "added entries." In cases where no clear author is named, the title of the work is considered the main entry.

Archival Science

Archival science, or archival studies, is the study and theory of building and curating archives, which are collections of recordings and data storage devices.

To build and curate an archive, one must acquire and evaluate recorded materials, and be able to access them later. To this end, archival science seeks to improve methods for appraising, storing, preserving, and cataloguing recorded materials.

An archival record preserves data that is not intended to change. In order to be of value to society, archives must be trustworthy. Therefore, an archivist has a responsibility to authenticate archival materials, such as historical documents, and to ensure their reliability, integrity, and usability. Archival records must be what they claim to be; accurately represent the activity they were created for; present a coherent picture through an array of content; and be in usable condition in an accessible location. An archive curator is called an *archivist;* the curation of an archive is called *archive administration.*

Background

History: Archival science emerged from diplomatics, the critical analysis of documents.

In 1540, Jacob von Rammingen (1510–1582) wrote the manuscript of the earliest known archival manual. He was an expert on *registries* (*Registraturen*), the German word for what later became known as *archives.*

Rammingen elaborated a registry for the Augsburg city council. However, since he could not attend the council meeting, he described the structure and management of the archives in writing. Although this is not the first work about archival science (Rammingen himself refers to earlier literature about record-keeping), earlier manuals were usually not published. Archival science had no formal beginning. Jacob von Rammingen's manual was printed in Heidelberg in 1571.

Traditionally, archival science has involved the study of methods for preserving items in climate-controlled storage facilities. It is also the study of cataloguing and accession, of retrieval and safe handling. The advent of digital documents along with the development of electronic databases has caused the field to re-evaluate its means and ends. While generally associated with museums and libraries, the field also can pertain to individuals who maintain private collections or business archives. Archival Science is taught in colleges and universities, usually under the umbrella of Information Science or paired with a History programme.

Standards

There is no universal set of laws or standards that governs the form or mission of archival institutions. The forms, functions, and mandates of archival programmes and institutions tend to differ based on geographical location and language, the nature of the society in which they exist and the objectives of those in control of the archives. Instead, the current standards that have been provided and are most widely followed, such as the ICA standard, ISO standard, and DIRKS standard, act as working guidelines for archives to follow and adapt in ways that would best suit their respective needs. When cataloguing archives, archivists are expected to follow a set of standards. Rules of Archival Description, also known as RAD, provides archivists with a set of rules which aim to provide a consistent and common foundation for the description of archival material within a fond, based on traditional archival principles. These standards are in place to provide archivists with the tools for finding and making accessible archival material to the public.

Metadata provides archivists with the contextual data surrounding a record or aggregate of records. Standards such as Machine-Readable Cataloguing (MARC format), Encoded Archival Description (EAD), and Dublin core are standards for archival metadata which provide archivists with appropriate descriptions in regards to collections.

Provenance in Archival Science

Provenance in archival science refers to the "origin or source of something; information regarding the origins, custody, and ownership of an item or collection." As a fundamental principle of archives, provenance refers to the individual, family, or organisation that created or received the items in a collection. In practice, provenance dictates that records of different origins should be kept separate to preserve their context. As a methodology, provenance becomes a means of describing records at the series level.

Principle of Provenance: Describing records at the series level to ensure that records of different origins are kept separate, provided an alternative to item-level manuscript cataloguing. The practice of provenance has two major concepts: "*respect des fonds*", and "original order". "*Respect des fonds*" rose from the conviction that records entering an archive should be described at the series level, where archivists respect the person or office that generated and used the records. Records from former or existing units are given a separate archival grouping, or "fonds", wherein their records are placed. "Original order", refers to keeping records "as nearly as possible in the same order of classification as obtained in the offices of origin," gives additional credibility to preserved records and to their originating "fonds". Records must be kept in the same order they were placed in the course of the official activity of the agency concerned; records are not to be artificially reorganised. Records kept in their original order are more likely to reveal the nature of the organisations which created them, and more importantly, of the order of activities out of which they emerged.

Not infrequently, practical considerations of storage mean that it is impossible to maintain the original order of records physically. In such cases, however, the original order should still be respected intellectually in the structure and arrangement of finding aids.

Practices before the Emergence of Provenance: Following the French Revolution, a newfound appreciation for historical records emerged in French society. Speaking to the past, records began to "acquire the dignity of national monuments" and their care was entrusted to scholars who were trained in libraries. With an emphasis on historical research, it seemed obvious at the time that records should be arranged and catalogued in a manner that would "facilitate every kind of scholarly use." To support research, artificial systematic collections, often arranged by topic, were established and records were catalogued into these schemes. With archival documents approached from a librarianship perspective, records were organised according to classification schemes and their original context of creation were frequently lost or obscured. This form of archival arrangement has come to be known as the "historical manuscripts tradition".

Emergence of Provenance: The principle of "*respect des fonds*" and of "original order" was adopted in Belgium and France about 1840 and spread throughout Europe during the following decades. Following the rise of state-run archives in France and Prussia, the rising volume of modern records entering the archive made the adherence to the manuscript tradition impossible; there were not enough resources to organise and classify each record. Provenance received its most pointed expression in the "Manual for the Arrangement and Description of Archives", a Dutch text published in 1898 and written by three Dutch archivists, Samuel Muller, Johan Feith, and Robert Fruin. This text provided the first description of the principle of provenance and argued that "original order" is an essential trait of archival arrangement and description.

Complementing the work of the Dutch archivists and supporting the concept of provenance were the historians of the era. Though subject-based classification aided research, historians began to concern themselves with objectivity in their source material. For its advocates, provenance provided an objective alternative to the generally subjective classification schemes borrowed from librarianship. Historians increasingly felt that records should be maintained in their original order to better reflect the activity out of which they emerged.

Debates

Although original order is a generally accepted principle, there has been some debate surrounding this theory in regards to personal archives. It has been argued that original order is not always ideal for personal archives as they are far more complex than organisational archives. However, others prefer to remain loyal to the principle of original order and maintain that personal records are created and maintained for much the same reason as organisational archives and should therefore follow the same principles.

Preservation in Archival Science

Preservation, as defined by the Society of American Archivists (SAA), is the discipline of protecting materials from physical deterioration or loss of information, ideally in a non-invasive way. The goal of preservation is to maintain as much originality as possible while maintaining all the information which the material has to offer. Both scientific principles and professional practices are applied to this technique to obtain maximum effectiveness. In an archival sense, preservation refers to the care of all the aggregates within a collection. Conservation can be included in this practice and often these two definitions overlap.

Beginnings of Preservation

Preservation emerged with the establishment of the first central archives. In 1789, during the French Revolution, the Archives Nationales was established and later, in 1794, transformed into a central archives. This was the first independent national archives and their goal was to preserve and store documents and records as they were. This trend gained popularity and soon other countries began establishing national archives for the same reasons, to maintain and preserve their records as they were created and received.

Cultural and scientific change also helped to bring about the idea and practice of preservation. In the late eighteenth century, many museums, national libraries, and national archives were established in Europe; therefore ensuring the preservation of their cultural heritage.

Archival Preservation

Preservation, like provenance, is concerned with the proper representation of archival materials. Archivists are primarily concerned with maintaining the record, along with the context in which it was produced, and making this information accessible to the user.

Tout ensemble is a definition relating to preservation. This definition encompasses the idea of context and the importance of maintaining context. When a record is removed from its fellow records, it loses its meaning. In order to preserve a record it must be preserved in its original entirety or else it may lose its significance. This definition relates to the principle of provenance and *respect des fonds* as it similarly emphasises the idea of the original record.

Metadata is key for the preservation of context within archival science. Metadata, as defined by the SAA, is "data about data." This data can help archivists locate a specific record, or a variety of records within a certain category. By assigning appropriate metadata to records or record aggregates, the archivist successfully preserves the entirety of the record and the context in which it was created. This allows for better accessibility and improves the authenticity of the record.

Physical maintenance is another key feature of preservation. There are many strategies in place to preserve archives properly; such as rehousing items in acid-free containers, storing items in climate controlled areas, and copying deteriorating items. These preservation techniques are to be carried out with respect to provenance.

Digital Preservation

Digital preservation involves the implementation of policies, strategies, and actions in order to ensure that digitised documents remain accurate and accessible over time. Due to emerging technologies, archives began to expand and require new forms of preservation. Archival collections spread to include new media such as microfilm, audiofiles, visualfiles, moving images, and digital documents. Many of these new types of media suffer from a shorter life expectancy than paper. With the quick advancement of our technological society, old media is becoming obsolete. Therefore, migration from old formats to new formats is necessary for the preservation of these digital medias so they can remain accurate and accessible.

Metadata is an important part of digital preservation as it preserves the context, usage, and migration of a digital record. Similarly to traditional preservation, metadata is required to preserve the context, authenticity, and accessibility of a record.

Professional Associations

Professional archivist associations seek to foster study and professional development:

- Archives and Records Association (UK and Ireland);
- Archives and Records Association, Ireland;
- Association of Moving Image Archivists;
- Association of Records Managers and Administrators;
- Association of Canadian Archivists;
- International Association of Sound and Audiovisual Archives;
- International Council on Archives;
- Society of American Archivists;
- Society of North Carolina Archivists.

In 2002, the Society of American Archivists published guidelines for a graduate programme in archival studies, but as of 2007 these guidelines have not been adopted by many universities. Practitioners of archival science might come from such academic backgrounds as library science, history, or museology.

Archival Appraisal

In the archival sense, appraisal is a process usually conducted by a member of the record-holding institution (often a professional archivist) in which a body of records are examined to determine their value. Some considerations when conducting appraisal include how to meet the record-granting body's organisational needs, how to uphold requirements of organisational accountability (be they legal, institutional, or determined by archival ethics), and how to meet the expectations of the record-using community.

Appraisal is considered a core archival function (alongside acquisition, arrangement and description, preservation, reference, and public programming) although the task of records appraisal is somewhat slippery and can occur within the process of acquiring records, during arrangement and description, and for the sake of preservation; further, public programming projects often prompt the reappraisal process. The official definition from the Society of American Archivists is as follows:

> "In an archival context, appraisal is the process of determining whether records and other materials have permanent (archival) value. Appraisal may be done at the collection, creator, series, file, or item level. Appraisal can take place prior to donation and prior to physical transfer, at or after accessioning. The basis of appraisal decisions may include a number of factors, including the records' provenance and content, their authenticity and reliability, their order and completeness, their condition and costs to preserve them, and their intrinsic value. Appraisal often takes place within a larger institutional collecting policy and mission statement."

History of Appraisal Theory

Muller, Feith and Fruin – Dutch Manual, 1898: Mostly concerned with the records of government bodies, the Dutch Manual assumed, generally, that the archives would keep each record it acquired. Before the era of mass duplication, this text was primarily concerned with the arrangement and description of records.

Sir Hilary Jenkinson, 1922: Sir Hilary Jenkinson was the Deputy Keeper of the Public Record Office during the early twentieth century. His best-known work, entitled *Manual of Archive Administration,* argues that archives are "documents which formed part of an official transaction and were preserved for official reference." For Jenkinson, the records creator is responsible for determining which records should be transferred to the archives for preservation. Since in his view records are "impartial" the task of selection is merely a matter of choosing documents that best describe "what happened".

T.R. Schellenberg, 1956: T.R. Schellenberg authored *Modern Archives* in 1956, and represents a departure from Jenkinson's approach, necessitated by the advent of mass duplication and an overwhelming influx of documents into archives. In his work, he divides records' values into primary values (the original value for the creator for their administrative, fiscal, and operating uses) and secondary values (their lasting value after they are no longer in current use, for those other than the original creator). He defines evidential value as deriving from the "evidence records contain of the organisation and functioning of the Government body that produced them," and informational value as related to the "information records contain on persons, corporate bodies, things, problems, conditions, and the like, with which the Government body dealt." After defining the terms, Schellenberg details the manner in which an archivist could perform appraisal based on these criteria, placing a stress in every case on the importance of research and analysis on the part of the archivist.

According to Schellenberg, informational value is based on three criteria:

- *Uniqueness*: The information in the record cannot be found anywhere else and must also be unique in form (i.e., not duplicated elsewhere).
- *Form*: An archivist must, according to Schellenberg, consider the form of the information (the degree to which the information is concentrated) as well as the form of the records itself (whether or not they can easily be read by others, e.g., punch cards and tape recordings would involve the use of expensive machinery to decipher).
- *Importance*: When appraising records, one must judge records first based on the needs of the government itself, then on the needs of historians/social scientists, as well as local historians and genealogists; he encourages archivists to be wary of records with sentimental value.

Some Current Approaches to Appraisal

Macro-appraisal: According to Terry Cook, North American appraisal theory is unplanned, taxonomic, random and fragmented, and has rarely embodied the concepts of institutional and societal dynamics which would lead archivists to a working model that would allow them to appraise the broad spectrum of human experience. His model is a top-down approach, which focuses on key processes through which a particular function is expressed by intersecting with structures and individuals. This requires a planned, logical approach—archivists embarking upon appraisals are equipped with an understanding of the record creator, its mandate and functions, its structure and decision-making processes, the way it creates records, and changes to these processes over time. The benefits of this process are theoretical (identifying the important functions in society which should be documented) and practical (the ability to focus appraisal activities on records of the highest potential archival value).

Documentation Strategy

Connected with the writings of Helen Samuels, documentation strategy aims to reach beyond institutional frameworks when appraising collections. In the past, she says, archivists have been passive, concentrating on researchers' needs rather than understanding a document in context. This has led to a circular problem, as researchers state their needs based on the context that they deduce from the archives, and as the archives create an artificial context based on researchers' stated needs. "Archivists are challenged to select a lasting record," Samuels says, "but they lack techniques to support this decision-making" (1992). Samuels argues that while archivists once needed to know and understand the complex bureaucratic structures of organisations, they must now understand the structures between organisations and ignore institutional boundaries.

However, this is increasingly impossible; archivists need to examine documentation in a comprehensive manner. A documentation strategy is, then, "a plan formulated to assure the documentation of an ongoing issue, activity or geographic area" (ibid). Its development includes records creators, archivists, and users, and it is carried out through a system-wide understanding of the intended life-cycle of the record.

Bibliographic Database

A bibliographic database is a database of bibliographic records, an organised digital collection of references to published literature, including journal and newspaper articles, conference proceedings, reports, government and legal publications, patents, books, etc. In contrast to library catalogue entries, a large proportion of the bibliographic records in bibliographic databases describe articles, conference papers, etc., rather than complete monographs, and they generally contain very rich subject descriptions in the form of keywords, subject classification terms, or abstracts.

A bibliographic database may be general in scope or cover a specific academic discipline. A significant number of bibliographic databases are still proprietary, available by licensing agreement from vendors, or directly from the indexing and abstracting services that create them.

Many bibliographic databases evolve into digital libraries, providing the full-text of the indexed contents. Others converge with non-bibliographic scholarly databases to create more complete disciplinary search engine systems, such as Chemical Abstracts or Entrez.

Library Instructions

Library instruction, also called bibliographic instruction (BI), user education and library orientation, consists of "instructional programmes designed to teach library users how to locate the information they need quickly and effectively. It usually covers the library's system of organising materials, the structure of the literature of the field, research methodologies appropriate to the academic discipline, and specific resources and finding tools (library catalogue, indexes and abstracting services, bibliographic databases, etc.)". It prepares individuals to make immediate and lifelong use of information effectively by teaching the concepts and logic of information access and evaluation, and by fostering information independence and critical thinking.

The Background

Library instruction "began in the nineteenth century, with instruction in library use offered by a number of libraries in the United States between 1876 and 1910, and then ramped up in the early twentieth century". In a 1912 American Library Association survey, 57 per cent of respondents offered required or elective library instruction courses.

"Academic library instruction was for the most part dormant in the library profession from the late–1930s until the early 1960s. Some librarians were still participating in classroom instruction but the literature shows little activity on the topic.... Academic library instruction mushroomed during the 1960s and early–1970s. This resulted in the founding of the Library Orientation Exchange (LOEX), a non-profit, self-supporting educational clearing house, in the early–1970s. The first conference was held at Eastern Michigan in 1973 and has been held annually around the United States ever since. The LOEX borrowing collection consists of print materials such as one page handouts, bibliographies, and subject guides; instructional videos and audio tapes; and CD-ROMS. By 1999, LOEX had over 650 members in the United States, Canada, the Caribbean, Europe, Australia, Israel, Lebanon, and South Africa."

"During the 1970s and 1980s, prior to widespread public use of computers, [library instruction] went far beyond teaching the mechanics of identifying and locating materials in the physical library. It also included critical thinking, active (participatory) learning, and the teaching of concepts, such as controlled vocabularies. It focused on the physical library, as for the most part, that was all that users could try out during instruction. However, the goal was always teaching so that users would transfer what they learned to new situations, reference tools, and environments new to them—that is, they would learn how to learn." Library instruction pioneer Miriam Sue Dudley's library instruction materials, originally produced in 1970 for a Chicano student group at UCLA, are an example of such materials now available online.

Library instruction is evolving to adapt to the changing concepts of information use and understanding. Model programmes, in order to be meaningful and effective, should respond to the changing information environment. New methods of library instruction, such as the Cephalonian method, reflect changes in instructional technology and education theory. Information and communication technology literacy (ICT) is an example of a modern approach to library instruction. ICT extends information literacy to the use of computer technology in a variety of forms to manipulate, deliver, and receive information and ideas. A model library instruction programme utilises complementary tools and resources to deliver memorable, interactive instruction. These resources are necessary to engage the attention of contemporary patrons immersed in a media environment.

Relationship to Information Literacy

An information literate person is "able to recognise when information is needed and have the ability to locate, evaluate, and use effectively the needed information". Currently there are debates about whether instruction on how to use library systems is necessary, or if efforts are better spent making systems easier to use so that they require no instruction.

Formats

Library instruction "occurs in various forms such as formal class settings, small group sessions, one-on-one encounters, written guides and brochures, audiovisual presentations, and computer-assisted instruction (CAI)". "Course-related instruction has long been viewed as one of the most effective user education methods. A complication of course-related instruction, however, is the requirement for faculty cooperation and the faculty member's authority to decide when instruction is given and who receives it. In short, librarians have limited control over course-related instruction. These forms of instruction are also very staff-intensive, and this is exacerbated by the high ratio of students to librarians that exists in most institutions". Some university libraries offer specialised instructional sessions. At these sessions the librarian works one-on-one with a user to assist him or her with specific research goals. These sessions are sometimes referred to as a "term paper clinic" or a "research consultation."

Another option for library instruction consists of *one-shot* instruction sessions. This slang term refers to "formal instruction given in a single session, as opposed to instruction extended over two or more sessions". These class meetings are often held just before a term paper is assigned, and the goal of the librarian is to orient the class to the best library sources for use in a term paper.

References

Reference is a relation between objects in which one object designates, or acts as a means by which to connect to or link to, another object. The first object in this relation is said to *refer to* the second object. The second object – the one to which the first object refers – is called the referent of the first object. The term *reference* is used in many spheres of human knowledge, adopting shades of meaning particular to the contexts in which it is used.

References can take on many forms, including: a thought, a sensory perception that is audible (onomatopoeia), visual (text), olfactory, or tactile, emotional state, relationship with other, spacetime coordinate, symbolic or alphanumeric, a physical object or an energy projection; but, other concrete and abstract contexts exist as methods of defining references within the scope of the various fields that require an origin, point of departure, or an original form. This includes methods that intentionally hide the reference from some observers, as in cryptography.

The following sections give specific usages of *reference* in different subjects.

Etymology

The word reference is derived from Middle English *referren*, from Middle French *referer*, from Latin *referre*, "to carry back", formed from the prefix *re*-and *ferre*, "to bear". A large number of words derive from this root, including referee, referent, referendum, all retaining the basic meaning of the original Latin as "a point, place or source of origin" in terms of which something of comparable nature can be defined. A referee is the provider of this source of origin, and a referent is the possessor of the source of origin, whether it is knowledge, matter or energy.

Library and Information Science

In a library, "reference" may refer to a dictionary, an encyclopaedia or other reference work, that contains many brief articles that cover a broad scope of knowledge in one book, or a set of books. However, the word *reference* is also used to mean a book that cannot be taken from the room, or from the building. Many of the books in the *reference department* of a library are reference works, but some are books that are simply too large or valuable to loan out. Conversely, selected reference works may be shelved with other circulating books, and may be loaned out.

References to many types of printed matter may come in an electronic or machine-readable form. For books, there exists the ISBN and for journal articles, the Digital object identifier (DOI) is gaining relevance. Information on the Internet may be referred to by a Uniform Resource Identifier (URI). Librarians also conduct reference interviews at the library reference desks, to help people find the information they seek. Help may also be available outside the library though virtual reference and digital reference services.

Computer Science

In computer science, references are data types that refer to an object elsewhere in memory and are used to construct a wide variety of data structures, such as linked lists. Generally, a reference is a value that enables a programme to directly access the particular data item. Most programming languages support some form of reference.

The C++ programming language has a specific type of reference also referred to as a "reference".

The notion of reference is also important in relational database theory.

Bibliographies

Bibliographies are special reference works that are used to identify as many published works on a given subject as possible, and serve as compilations for other authors or researchers.

Encyclopaedias and Books of Facts

Some published sources are produced as reference works that allow quick access to essential information about given subjects, sometimes compiled as topical collections, and sometimes as general collections of entries.

Psychology

In terms of mental processing, a self-reference is used in psychology to establish identification with a mental state during self-analysis. This seeks to allow the individual to develop own frames of reference in a greater state of immediate awareness. However, it can laso lead to circular reasoning, preventing evolution of thought.

Economics and Business

In the labour market, potential employers often ask job applicants for references or recommendations, so that their suitability can be verified independently. The references can be a written letter, but are often just a contact telephone number. Employers can ask for professional references, which are from former employers, or for character references, which are from people of distinction such as doctors or teachers. The source of the reference must be well known to the applicant and able to vouch for their abilities during employment.

In business administration, terms of reference describe the purpose and structure of a project, committee, meeting, negotiation, or any similar collection of people who have agreed to work together to accomplish a shared goal. The terms of reference of a project are often referred to as the project charter. In business marketing and public procurement and tenders references are often used within the field of engineering, consultancy, industry and construction contracts. References are used to examine a company's ability to deliver the required level of service. Very often bigger companies will have hundreds or even thousands of references and will often try to categorise and manage them with reference management software.

Education

In academics and scholarship, an author-title-date information in bibliographies and footnotes, specifying complete works of other people. Copying of material by another author without proper citation or without required permissions is plagiarism. Keeping a diary allows an individual to use references for personal organisation, whether or not anyone else understands the systems of reference used. However, scholars have studied methods of reference because of their key role in communication and co-operation between *different* people, and also because of misunderstandings that can arise. Modern academic study of reference has been developing since the 19th Century.

In scholarship, a reference may be a citation of a text that has been used in the creation of a piece of work such as an essay, report, or oration. Its primary purpose is to allow people who read such work to examine the author's sources, either for validity or to learn more about the subject. Such items are often listed at the end of an article or book in a section marked "Bibliography" or "References". A bibliographical section often contains works not cited by the author, but used as background reading or listed as potentially useful to the reader. A reference section contains all of the works and only those works cited by the author(s) in the main text.

Law

In law, references are documents or people providing *witness to character*. This connotation is also used in employment. In patent law, a reference is a document that can be used to show the state of knowledge at a given time and that therefore may make a claimed invention obvious or anticipated. Examples of references are patents of any country, magazine articles, Ph.D. theses that are indexed and thus accessible to those interested in finding information about the subject matter, and to some extent Internet material that is similarly accessible. In Canadian law, a reference question is a procedure through which the government can submit legal questions to the Supreme Court of Canada and provincial governments to the provincial courts of appeal.

Semantics

In semantics, reference is generally construed as the relationships between nouns or pronouns and objects that are named by them. Hence, the word "John" refers to John. The word "it" refers to some previously specified object. The object referred to is called the "referent" of the word. Sometimes the word-object relation is called "denotation"; the word denotes the object. The converse relation, the relation from object to word, is called "exemplification"; the object exemplifies what the word denotes. In syntactic analysis, if a word refers to a previous word, the previous word is called the "antecedent".

Meaning

Gottlob Frege argued that reference cannot be treated as identical with meaning: "Hesperus" (an ancient Greek name for the evening star) and "Phosphorus" (an ancient Greek name for the morning star) both refer to Venus, but the astronomical fact that '"Hesperus" is "Phosphorus"' can still be informative, even if the "meanings" of "Hesperus" and "Phosphorus" are already known.

This problem led Frege to distinguish between the sense and reference of a word. Some cases seem to be too complicated to be classified within this framework; the acceptance of the notion of secondary reference may be necessary to fill the gap.

Absent Referent

Words can often be meaningful without having a concrete here-and-now referent. Fictional and mythological names such as "Bo-Peep" and "Hercules" illustrate this possibility. Sign links with absent referents also allow for discussing abstract ideas ("love," "peace") as well as people and events of the past and future.

For those who argue that one cannot directly experience the divine (e.g. God), the sign "God" can serve as an example of a reference with an absent referent. Additionally, certain sects of Judaism and other religions consider it sinful to write, discard, or deface the name of the divine. To avoid this problem, the signifier G-d is sometimes used, though this could be seen as a sign that refers to another sign with an absent referent.

Linguistic Sign

The very concept of the linguistic sign is the combination of content and expression, the former of which may refer entities in the world or refer more abstract concepts, e.g., thought. Certain parts of speech exist only to express reference, namely anaphora such as pronouns. The subset of reflexives expresses co-reference of two participants in a sentence. These could be the agent (actor) and patient (acted on), as in "The man washed himself", the theme and recipient, as in "I showed Mary to herself", or various other possible combinations.

Mathematics

In mathematics, the absent referent can be seen with the symbol for zero, "0" or the empty set, "{ }".

A reference point in Geometry is a location used to describe another point, by giving the relative position. Similarly there is the concept of frame of reference (both in physics and figuratively) and benchmark (in surveying and figuratively).

Engineering

In engineering a reference design is often used during the pre-production phase of design development to test design features against original specifications.

Arts

In Art, a reference is an item from which a work is based. This may include:

- An existing artwork;
- A reproduction (i.e., photo);
- Directly observed object (i.e., person); or
- The artist's memory.

Another example of reference is samples of various musical works being incorporated into a new one.

Literature and Rhetoric

In academic literature, a reference is a previously published written work within academic publishing that has been used as a source for theory or claims referred to that are used in the text. References contain complete bibliographic information so the interested reader can find them in a library. References can be added either at the end of the publication or as footnotes.

In publishing, a reference is *citation* of a work, in a footnote, from which an idea was taken.

Readers' Advisory

Readers' advisory (sometimes spelled readers advisory or reader's advisory) is a service which involves suggesting fiction and non-fiction titles to a reader through direct or indirect means. This service is a fundamental library service; however, readers' advisory also occurs in commercial contexts such as bookstores. Currently, almost all North American public libraries offer some form of readers' advisory.

The Background

North America: "Setting a date for the start of what we now call readers advisory service, particularly readers advisory in the public library, is at best a frustrating, almost arbitrary exercise. Efforts at historical precision can founder on such basic issues as the absence of common definitions. For example, answcrs to such questions as 'What exactly is a public library?" or "What really is readers advisory?" have long been disputed." (Bill Crowley, from his 2005 journal article "Rediscovering the History of Readers Advisory Service").

Opposing Viewpoints

The historical period divisions and merits of different types of readers' advisory services is a hotly debated topic among librarians.

Bill Crowley, in his 2005 article, "Rediscovering the History of Readers Advisory Service," breaks down the historical period divisions of the service into four eras:

- 1876 to 1920 - "Inventing" Readers' Advisory;
- 1920 to 1940 - "Privileging Non-fiction" in Readers' Advisory;
- 1940 to 1984 - Readers' Advisory "'Lost' in Adult Services";
- 1984 to 2005 (current at time of article) - "Reviving Readers' Advisory".

Juris Dilevko and Candice Magowan question the merits of the current readers' advisory emphasis on popular fiction materials in their book "Readers' Advisory Service in North American Public Libraries, 1870–2005." They subdivide the history as:

- 1870 to 1916 - "The Formative Years";
- 1917 to 1962 - "The Commitment to Systematic Adult Education";
- 1963 to 2005 - "The Devolution into Entertainment".

Dilevko and Mogowan write about "readers' advisory systematically committing itself to meaningful adult education through serious and purposeful reading" up until the 1960s, when emphasis on "popular culture resulted in the 'Give 'Em What They Want' approach" and the "The Devolution into Entertainment."

1897–1920: In 1897, the ALA President stated that "the personal influence of librarians who assisted and advised readers was the most potent force in moulding community reading."

1920–1980: Organised readers' advisory programmes have been documented dating back to the 1920s. Between 1922–1926 readers' advisory programmes were experimentally introduced into seven urban libraries (Cleveland and Detroit, in 1922, Indianapolis, Milwaukee, and Chicago, in 1923 and 1924, and Cincinnati and Portland, OR). The Adult Education Movement emerged in the 1920s in public libraries and was frequently discussed in American Library Association professional publications.

The 1924 report *The American Public Library and the Diffusion of Knowledge* by William Learned to the Carnegie Corporation sought to establish adult education as the focus of the public library, with personalised readers' advisory service to adult readers by "reference experts" who would make up a "community intelligence service."

The 1926 American Library Association "book-length" commission report *Libraries and Adult Education* placed high importance on readers' advisory services in Adult Education. Judson T. Jennings provided a summary of the work, observing that the "library's contribution to adult education resolved itself into three major activities":

1. An information service regarding local opportunities for adult students.
2. Service to other agencies engaged in adult education.
3. Service to individual readers and students.

This new professional interest during the 1920s spurred the creation of specialised full-time readers' advisory positions in major public libraries. By 1936, an estiminated, 50 public libraries had established readers' advisory services. Until the early 1960s, readers' advisory focused on non-fiction materials and continuing adult education.

1980s–2000s: Some librarians consider the early–1980s to be the beginning of a revival in readers' advisory and praise the inclusion of fiction (including genre fiction: fantasy, mystery, romance, etc.) and write that historically readers' advisory was biased in favour of non-fiction.

Others disapprove of the new approaches and changes in service. Dilevko and Magowan write "Post–1980 readers' advisory thus became an opportunity to converse with patrons about 'light, quick, escapist' books — popular and ephemeral fiction and non-fiction for entertainment, pleasure, and recreation — because such conversations were not 'too burdensome'."

In 1982, the term "genreflecting" was first coined by Betty Rosenberg, who authored: Genreflecting: A Guide to Reading Interests in Genre Fiction (Libraries Unlimited, 1982). Another major influence on the spread and revival of readers' advisory was the Adult Reading Round Table (ARRT), founded by a group of Chicago public librarians in 1984. The group organised workshops, seminars, and genre-study groups.

Current Interest

Interest in readers' advisory continues to grow. Libraries Unlimited Genreflecting Advisory Series has grown to 27 titles as of July 2008 (from 15 titles in 2005). Beyond traditional genres (fantasy, mystery, romance), some of the diverse, unique, and niche offerings now include: Gay, Lesbian, Bisexual, and Transgendered Literature A Genre Guide, Graphic Novels: A Genre Guide to Comic Books, Manga, and More, and Christian Fiction A Guide to the Genre.

> "...contemporary readers advisory service is best understood as an organised programme promoting both fiction and non-fiction discretionary reading for the dual purposes of satisfying reader needs and advancing a culture's goal of a literate population." (Bill Crowley, from his 2005 journal article "Rediscovering the History of Readers Advisory Service").

Various Types

Direct Readers' Advisory: Direct readers' advisory is based on a non-judgemental assessment of the personal preferences of the reader through a series of questions, called a readers advisory conversation. The assessment focuses on reader likes and dislikes with regard to a number of factors, including, subject, reading level, genre, writing style, the level of characterisation, plot elements, storyline, pace, tone, frame, and setting. The hoped-for outcome of this interview is the identification of three or more appropriate suggestions (sometimes referred to as "readalikes"—especially when the interview was initiated by patron interest in new authors/titles similar to one enjoyed in the past). In identifying suitable suggestions, a readers' advisor combines personal knowledge of material with a variety of specialised print and online resources to come up with appropriate suggestions. The goal of direct readers advisory is to *suggest* titles based on a readers' individual interests and tastes. Librarians who simply recommend their favourite books with little or no regard for the patron's own interests are not performing readers' advisory.

For example, if a patron requests "a good book," the readers' advisor might ask the reader to describe a book they have enjoyed. The focus of the conversation is not on recitation of plot, but on the aforementioned appeal elements (i.e. pace, subject, tone, writing style, etc.). In our example, the patron tells the readers' advisor of a humorous mystery novel with a sharp-tongued female protagonist. Our readers' advisor also learns that the patron prefers fast-paced dialogue to excessive descriptive passages. Once the appeal elements have been identified (i.e. a humorous mystery featuring snappy dialogue and a female protagonist), the readers' advisor will suggest appropriate titles in the collection by drawing on personal knowledge and/or by consulting appropriate print and online resources. Even though the patron requested a mystery, a skilled readers advisor will often offer a suggestion or two that point the reader to new a new vista outside of a mentioned genre or milieu.

Readers' advisory can also be performed across multiple media. For example, a patron who likes the movie *Matilda* might be unaware that it is based on a book by Roald Dahl. Other patrons who enjoy audio books may be introduced to other titles read by the same person.

Questions for Advisory Interview

In the 2005 edition of *Readers' Advisory Services in the Public Library*, Joyce Saricks lists some questions for advisors to consider, such as:

- Are characters and plot quickly revealed or slowly unveiled? (Identifying Pacing);
- Is there more dialogue or more description? (Identifying Pacing);

- Is there a focus on a single character or on several whose lives are intertwined (Identify Characterisation);
- Is the focus of the story more interior and psychological or exterior and action oriented? (Identifying Story Line).

Indirect Readers' Advisory

Indirect readers' advisory involves the creation of displays, bookmarks, and annotated book lists that a reader/patron can pick up and peruse on their own without actively engaging a readers' advisor. Indirect readers' advisory aids, particularly annotated book lists, focus on appeal elements rather than providing extensive plot summaries. Recently, some public libraries (like the Williamsburg Regional Library in Virginia) have begun experimenting with form-based readers' advisory, which allows for a richer indirect readers advisory experience.

Maintaining a Staff Recommendations display is another way to improve a library's readers' advisory service. Since many readers are browsers, staff recommendations make it easier to select a book. In their 2001 article "Reader's Advisory: Matching Mood and Material," Ross and Chelton recommend placing books in four areas of the library in order to make the most of merchandising. These four areas are the entrance, the ends of stacks, high traffic areas, and the circulation desk. Placing the display in these areas ensure that patrons will see and, hopefully, utilise the books on display. Ross and Chelton also note that books, not posters and announcements, should be here because merchandised titles will circulate very quickly.

Readers' Advisory Resources

There are numerous books, online subscription databases, and websites dedicated to readers' advisory.

Print Resources: Popular print resources include the *What Do I Read Next?* series of reference books (published by Thomson Gale), the *Genreflecting* series (published by Libraries Unlimited), and the *Readers' Advisory Guides* (published by the American Library Association).

Seattle Librarian Nancy Pearl achieved broad fame and recognition for her readers guides, *Book Lust* and *More Book Lust,* which recommend "reading for every mood, moment, and reason." Both have been popular with the general public and can be found at most book stores and libraries. Also of note are Pearl's guides to contemporary fiction: *Now Read This: A Guide to Mainstream Fiction, 1978–1998* and *Now Read This II: A Guide to Mainstream Fiction, 1990–2001.*

Internet Resources:

- Fiction_L is the Morton Grove Public Library's electronic mailing list for readers' advisory discussions, developed by Roberta S. Johnson and the Reader's Services staff of the library. The List encompasses fiction, as well as "all aspects of reader's advisory for children, young adults and adults, including non-fiction materials." Many booklists discussed on the listerv are indexed on the library website, in the following categories: Genre, Character, Setting, Subject, Author, Audience, "Best of," and Miscellaneous. The list is a powerful resource for a worldwide community of librarians and other readers, because of its accessibility and searchable archives. Given some basic information, almost every enquiry receives a response, often within minutes.
- Booklist Online "delivers highly searchable and creatively linked reviews, columns, and features—all designed to help users find exactly the right book."

- Novelist is a database of reading recommendations, available through libraries around the world. It is a comprehensive source of information about books, and genres that includes read-alikes, expert recommendations, recommended reads lists, professional reviews, feature articles, author bios, complete series information, and lots more. Novelist Plus includes both fiction and non-fiction titles. There is also a companion service, Novelist Select, that adds these recommendations to a library's catalogue.
- BookBrowse.com offers a customised subscription service for libraries. Its readers' advisory database includes read-alikes, browsing by 100+ themes, in-depth reviews, previews, back-stories, book club advice, author bios, interviews and pronunciation guide and ezines.
- ALA Recommended Reading compiles different reading lists for all ages, especially children and teens. Most lists are available on the ALA website.
- LibraryThing is a social networking website for cataloguing and sharing personal and institutional library collections. The site contains a "Suggester" feature which provides book recommendations based on user catalogues with similar books. The broader your catalogue, the more specific suggestions you will receive.
- NextReads is an *e*-mail newsletter service that delivers more than 25 themed book recommendation newsletters to readers. Libraries can customise the newsletters to include only items in the library's catalogue, and also add information about related events and programmes happening in the library.
- Wowbrary is a weekly *e*-mail newsletter showing the new books, movies, and CDs selected by a library in the previous week. Because these items are all in the library's catalogue, newsletter recipients can be among the first to place holds, even if the items have not arrived yet.
- What's Next is a free resource from the Kent District Library System in Michigan that helps users in finding quality series fiction. "A series is two or more books linked by character(s), settings, or other common traits."
- Fantastic Fiction maintains bibliographies for over 30,000 authors and is an easy way to track series by authors and authors who write under different pseudonyms.
- BookSpot.com is a free resource "that simplifies the search for the best book-related content on the Web" and directs users to where they can find audiobooks, free first chapters, and specific lists such as award winners and the top 150 bestsellers of the week.
- Some libraries have developed online indirect readers' advisory websites based on specific titles, series, or authors. For example, the Allen County Public Library's *Lemony Snicket Read-Alikes and Supplements* page answers the question of 'what to read next' with annotated book lists based around different genre and stylistic aspects of the series (mystery books, books about "Orphans or kids living without much help from adults," humorous books). They also refer readers to non-fiction works on related topics from the *Lemony Snicket* series. For example, the book *Using Ropes and Knots* is recommended because.

  "In The Bad Beginning (A Series of Unfortunate Events, Book the First) Violet Baudelaire found herself in the unfortunate circumstance of trying to rescue her baby sister Sunny from a perilous perch. Violet was able to invent a grappling hook and attach it to a rope with the proper knot. It will be unfortunate if you do not read this book and you find yourself trying to rescue your baby sister."

Blogs: Reading and/or maintaining a readers' advisory blog for a library can be beneficial for both patrons and librarians. Patrons gain access to book reviews and recommendations and librarians stay current on new releases and improve their readers' advisory skills.

- The Early Word is a blog run by Nora Rawlinson and Fred Ciporen that includes loads of reading lists as well as links to news on upcoming releases and reviews.
- Readers' Advisor Online blog from Libraries Unlimited offers essential news, tips, fun stuff, and a community for exploring RA issues.
- Readers' Advisory for All blog.

Wikis:

- Read Me;
- Book Lust Community;
- ALA Reader's Advisory Committee;
- Readers' Advisory Services;
- Readers' Advisory - Professionaltips - ALA;
- LISWiki - Readers' advisory (Library and Information Science Wiki).

Chat:

- The Florida Ask a Librarian Service provides live, real-time chat with librarians throughout the state, offering reference services which include readers' advisory.

7

STRUCTURAL SET-UP OF LIBRARY

This chapter briefly indicates the fundamental problems of data communications, and gives an overview of the broad approaches which have been taken towards them. A computer network is intended to connect together a wide range of information technology equipment, which varies in the design and operation of the equipment itself, in the information types it handles, and in the internal processing which it undertakes. In order to be able to communicate successfully, these various systems must have a common 'language' for the exchange of information, while retaining their local independence.

As well as an agreed form for communication the network units must also agree on the *process* of communicating—the rules which govern the procedures for the exchange of information and the co-ordination of action between participants. In daily communication we use a language to express our ideas and intentions, and the voice as a means of transmitting this information to other people. To ensure that the communication is successful, we must converse in an agreed language which the hearer is able to understand, and we must be able to respond to messages asking for clarification, repetition, and so on. In any conversation, there are well-understood rules which govern the process of communication—taking turns, allowing others a chance to speak, indicating that one has finished speaking, waiting until another has finished before speaking oneself, and so on. These signals are often given implicitly, through signs such as gestures or tone of voice.

The data communication process has to be much more structured and organised in style, spelled out in every detail, since these tacit factors are missing from a machine-based process. The rules for communication must be well defined and standardised; there is little room for 'working out' what a participant in the exchange really meant to say. This process underlies the development of sophisticated and 'user-friendly' applications which depend on network communication, even though this may not be immediately apparent.

A goal of information networking is to allow users to work in this medium as naturally as possible, finding the least obtrusive fit with the natural work environment. A dialogue which is mediated by computer communication places certain structural constraints on the process due to these underlying factors; the task of design is to find ways of incorporating the equivalent of the contextual factors which inform human communication while working within these constraints. A basic model of the communication process identifies the entities involved, and their respective roles. There are *three main elements:*

- A sender, which originates the message, and is responsible for representing the content of the message in an agreed format;
- A channel, which carries the message from sender to recipient through some physical medium;
- A recipient, which receives the message, and is responsible for interpreting the format in order to extract the information content.

The communication is not simply one way, and the roles will at times be reversed: the recipient may wish to send a reply to the original message.

In network communications explicit signals and format rules are vital to the success of the communications process. For a computing machine to manage this role effectively, rules governing these issues must be highly detailed and agreed in advance, and encapsulated in software programmes. Data and communications software must be able to deal with management of the exchange process, not only by sending and receiving messages for transmission but also by encoding and decoding between the internal format used by the computer and the format used for external communication. It is also necessary to monitor the quality of the exchange and to co-ordinate activity between participants at each end of the process for longer data exchanges. This is problematic because the channel which links the participants will have characteristics of its own which may affect the communication process.

The sender and recipient exchange the encoded message as a physical signal transmitted in some way through a common channel. The environment of this channel can potentially interfere with and distort the signals in the process, resulting in the loss of some information content and delivery of a corrupted message. This kind of interference is known as noise—the general effect of corruption and garbling of the signal which occurs after it has been transmitted, and before it is received. For example, noise may result in the appearance of unreadable characters on a computer screen in the midst of a normal text message, as the receiving system attempts to interpret corrupted signalling codes.

Although the use of more reliable technology for the transmission medium has reduced the problem of noise in recent years, the rules which govern the process of communication must still be capable of detecting and recovering from the effects of noise by returning a message to its original form. This requires the communications software to have some means of matching the two versions of the message—that sent and that received—and entails the addition of control information to the actual data content by one means or another. Thus the exchange will consist of more than the simple data content of the message.

Techniques for dealing with the effects of noise are concerned to preserve the quality of the message by ensuring that the integrity of the signs used to represent the information content have not been compromised. The communication process must also therefore be concerned with co-ordinating the system of codes which is used to express the semantic qualities of the data exchange—what might be loosely called the 'meaning' of the message; with the physical representation of the chosen coding system as transmittable signals; and with any control information which binds different elements of the message together. There are various different coding systems for the task of mapping information generated by user applications into the binary codes used by the computer. For text, the ASCII (American Standard Character Set for Information Interchange) is widely used both within a computer and for data interchange purposes; however, completely different character sets are used in some circumstances, for instance the EBCDIC character set which dominates the IBM mainframe world.

There are several different representation formats for graphics, which may be either bit patterns or geometric coordinates, and for other forms such as video signals and multimedia information. For meaningful information to be exchanged there must be agreement between the end systems on the method by which the message is represented for transmission, even though this may not affect the actual exchange of data symbols through the channel. Since there is little standardisation in the internal processes of computer equipment itself, the actual physical signals which the end systems generate must also be standardised for inter-operability, and may need translation between different physical forms in order to make use of different communication channels.

Library Building

It is an important role, for although a librarian does not draw plans or instruct builders, it is to his conception of the new library what it is to hold and what it is do that an architect creates the final building.

Various Functions

In the first place the librarian has to define the purpose which the library is being created to fulfil, and he has to identify the many and various functions which it has to perform, to show the relative importance of each and the relationship between them. Not least, he has to forecast the future, so that a library can be planned to serve not only today's needs, but the needs of the next twenty, thirty or forty years. This is a serious and complicated task for which the librarian must equip himself. In the first place it is essential that he should attack it in a systematic manner.

Because a library building is created for a specific need, so the whole of the planning and design will differ with the essential difference between libraries. A great multinational library, created to hold millions of books and other materials for a long time, a college library designed to serve the ever-changing needs of students in a technological age, a branch public library to bring books and other materials to a community which has a wide range of reading levels and abilities—the needs of these three libraries are so very different. Yet in fact they have in common their basic, and identifiable, features; if treated systematically, the same planning methods are applicable to each.

One of the most important of the librarian's task, and the earliest, is to make sure that the architect knows exactly what it is that the library is being created to do. This may seem so obvious that it is not always taken seriously; the complexity of the task which lies before the architect and the enormous range of problems which he has to solve, mean that he must have a very clear picture of the proposed library's purpose. . Only with this film in mind can he create, not only an efficient machine in terms of stone, brick, glass and mechanical equipment, but also a building which by its design works aesthetically towards the end which he clearly appreciates.

Clear Account

The librarian should, then, write as clear an account as it is possible for him to do of the purpose of the library; if the library is to form part of an institution such as a college, school or university, then it is also important to define, not only the part which the library is to play in that institution's life, but also the purpose, aims and range of activities of the institution itself.

It is equally important that the librarian defines for the architect the community the library is to serve, its size and its potential requirements. Standards, national and international, official and unofficial, exist to recommend the number of books, the number of seats, the overall space and so on, to be provided not only for the community as a whole, but (especially in the case of educational establishments) for the proportion of that community which may be expected to make use of the facilities at anyone time; the librarian must know of these standards and see that the architect knows of them. Every library has to house materials and to make them available under varying conditions to certain types of readers. By identifying the readers and by listing systematically the numbers, times and conditions under which they can be expected to use the various facilities, the librarian will give to the architect the information which he needs to be able to create the machine to do the job which has already been identified.

We talk about library buildings, but there are several important kinds of libraries which seldom, if ever, have separate buildings to themselves. The libraries and resource-centres which acquire, hold and exploit materials to fulfil the purpose of schools, small colleges, hospitals, welfare institutions, private firms and so on, seldom have separate buildings. In many cases, public branch libraries are built as integral parts of community and art centres. In every one of these cases it is essential that the part of the building which is allocated to the library should be given as-much care in its planning as if it were a separate building. Similarly, when we talk about a new building, we may equally be referring to the conversion of an old library, or the adaptation of an entirely different building. In times of shortage of money, or, equally important, lack of empty sites for libraries conversions may be more common than new construction. The principles of planning remain the same; it is for the architect to devise an acceptable solution to the structural problems.

Basic Principles

The basic principles of library building design are:

Functional: A library building should have functional design rather than a monumental one. Thus functional requirements should get preference.

In beginning, the university library building constructions were massive library structures, which gave an impression of monumentality. The factors which are important in a good library such as functionality and expandibility were not given much importance. However, in recent days, building constructions have taken into consideration these factors to a certain extent.

Open Access: A library building designed for 'open access system' is also considered useful for a 'close access system'. Provision of 'open access system' has certain implications. There should be one entrance and one exit to keep a proper control on incoming and outgoing users. The height of the book rack should be such that a person of normal height should be able to pick up books from topmost shelf.

Future Growth: A library building should be planned for at least next 10 years, keeping in view the rate of stock development, number of readers, future use of microforms, etc.. The, building should be extendable to allow for future growth with minimum of disruption.

Flexible: In case a change in library functions takes place, then it should be possible to adjust the layout without carrying major structural operations. This means interchangeability of all major stack areas, service areas, reading areas and staff areas. There should be no interior load bearing walls but building should be able to bear stack load anywhere. Uniform standards of lighting ventilation and flooring are necessary to meet the criteria of inter changeability.

Provision of Areas: There should be provision for documents, users, staff, service areas, library tools like public catalogue, microfilm-reader, xerox machine, etc.

Accessible: Building should be accessible from outside and from the entrance to different parts of the building by means of a simple and easy to understand plan requiring only a few directions or guides.

Modular: The basic dimensions of library building furniture and fittings should be in multiples or submultiples of 10-cm module. This would be the case for tables, chairs, book racks, book trolleys, doors, windows, etc. The dimensions of different items should register with one another. A column spacing of between 22½ to 23 feet from centre to centre has been suggested. A building based on modular system is the one supported by columns placed at regular interval.

Economic: Design should be economical to carry out and result in a building which can be maintained with minimum of staff and finance.

In a systematic approach to the planning of the library we have to answer in detail the following questions:

1. What has the library to accommodate? How much material, of what sort, and in what physical conditions?
2. How many users must it cater for? How many at peak times, how many at less busy times? How many will sit, or sit and write, how many will choose books and leave? What hours will the library be open, and how many of each category of user can be expected to use it, at what hours of the day and at what times of the year?
3. What physical conditions, (heat, light, humidity, etc.) must be provided?
4. How much security is needed, and how much interference with ease of access is acceptable in order to get it?
5. How much money is available to build the library, and to what extent is absolute economy to be the prime criterion in its proposed operations?

Let us take the five questions and sketch out answers, bearing in mind the enormous difference of emphasis on every point according to the considered needs and priorities of the particular library.

The Protocol

Essentially, a protocol is one attempt to address the basic problems of data communications which are relevant to networking within a particular arena. Since there is no universally applicable solution to these problems which will be effective in all situations, a range of protocols have arisen which have proved effective in specialised areas within the current feasible limits of technology. Since the development of communication protocols has been carried out within the context of perceived practical problems, there is a tendency for the available offerings to be predicated on the use of particular types and make of equipment.

Computer manufacturers have devised their own proprietary protocol suites intended to interconnect only their own Computer makes; and more generally applicable protocols have emerged for broader categories of computer, such as for local networks of microcomputers. Although a protocol is a logical specification rather than a particular implementation in software, the protocol is likely to make assumptions about available levels of functionality and processing capabilities. As both computing technology and information applications have led to more complicated and sophisticated systems, so the communications process between systems has also developed a parallel level of complexity. The complexity of modern networking has led to the use of a layered approach to protocol specification. A *layered protocol* aims to analyse the overall communications process into well-defined and semi-autonomous functional modules, each of which provides a specialised service in the overall scheme and works in conjunction with the other modules. Network communications can then be split into constituent activities, and these may be implemented on different parts of the system in different ways, not necessarily all together on the same piece of equipment. Any particular layer may potentially contain alternative specifications for reaching the same goals, each of which is more appropriate for a particular environment or system arrangement. As long as the module provides the appropriate service to its co-operating modules in the process, the way in which it achieves this, need not concern the other elements involved. This kind of arrangement provides a greater flexibility in interconnecting different types of system which conform to the same layered framework. There is not, unfortunately, any universal or even dominant agreement on one scheme for dividing logical functions up into different layers.

The growing need for the capability of interconnecting computer systems and networks whatever their local characteristics has led to several initiatives aiming to develop a degree of standardisation between the major alternatives, and to encourage the conformity of new products to these standards. These initiatives aim to develop a framework within which the most widely accepted and established 'industry standard' protocols can fit as alternative options. At the present time *networking protocols fall into two main groups:*

- Those emanating from or supported by national and international standards making bodies, which are more 'open' in nature with published specifications;
- Those emerging as proprietary standards from major computer manufacturers, which are 'closed' by virtue of their confidential specification and non-participative development.

A set of protocols will deal with aspects which are more closely related to the physical aspects of data and network communications and those which are more related to the information transfer aspects of user activity. At the lower layers, the data communications aspects can be seen as falling into three main areas: the physical connection, basic data management, and routing through the network. The *physical level* is concerned with producing, receiving and monitoring the physical signals which are actually transmitted between systems, and with the standardisation of methods for representing data in this form.

A well-known example of this is the RS-232C standard, which defines the electrical interface on equipment as a multi-pin connection and assigns a particular function to each pin. The *data link level* is concerned with error control and recovery, and with flow control. In order to achieve this, most protocols encapsulate the user data in frames by dividing the stream of data into units of a pre-defined size and adding control information for use by the receiving system.

Since the network connection will be conveying data frames from other network users, the frames also contain header information ensuring delivery to the correct destination. Special frames may also be used to send only control information, for example to establish and terminate links with a remote computer. The frames produced by this layer are passed down to the physical layer for transmission. Error control is important at this level, since noise on the channel may result in the loss or corruption of frames; one purpose of splitting the whole message up into data frames is to retain control of the transmission as it develops, and take any remedial action necessary. Error control takes a number of simpler or more sophisticated forms, some of which require feedback from the receiver, for example:

- Echo checking reflects characters received back to the sender for display on the user's screen, so that any corruption can be noticed and re-transmitted;
- Acknowledgment schemes require the receiver to send an acknowledgment token back to the sender for each frame, before the next is transmitted;
- Check digits can be added to the data frame by the sender, based on a computation carried out on the user data itself, and which the receiver can also use to check comparability.

Flow control is concerned to ensure that the data is not sent faster than it can be received; this function can make use of some of these devices, for instance acknowledgment schemes, or add features of its own to the exchange process. The network level is concerned with the management and control of routing through the network. The extent to which this is relevant will depend on the type of network in use and the mode in which it is operating. There are two broad *modes within which a network can operate*, providing two types of service:

- *Connectionless mode,* in which the data is dispatched by the sender with the appropriate destination address, but no direct connection is made between them;
- *Connection-oriented mode,* in which the two end systems behave as though directly connected by a physical medium and work in co-operation with each other.

A network may offer both these types of service as alternatives, but cannot normally support mixing between the two types. The network layer will typically organise the user data into packets, splitting up a long message into several units in this way, and adding source and destination information to each packet to control its path through the network. The user data is then made transparent to the network itself, which is only concerned with the 'external' address information. Different packets which constitute parts of the same message are then treated as independent units, and may travel through the network at different speeds and by different routes.

The receiving system takes delivery of the packets and reconstitutes the message in its original format using the control information added by the sender. An X.25 network is an example of this arrangement. The network layer passes the packets down to the data link layer for the addition of error and flow control information, once it has completed its own responsibilities. In this way, user data is passed between layers between both sender and receiver, with only one actual physical network connection among them. In wider area networks, these three layers are also contained within the intermediate stages internal to the network, as well as in the end systems. The specific protocols which implement these broad functions within an individual context will depend on the particular elements of the system which is in use, and the equipment available to it. A range of protocols are implemented either as software in communications packages, or as hardware built into data communications equipment. Some have achieved a greater popularity and therefore a *de facto* standardisation over time.

In order for the communication process to be successful, both systems which intend to exchange data must be capable of running the same protocol, and therefore require communications packages or hardware which are compatible with each other; larger systems may offer a range of communication alternatives which can sense the method used by a caller and select the appropriate option. The *types of device* which have a role to play in the entire networking process can be placed into two categories: 1. Data terminating equipment (DTE) describes the devices which originate, or provide the final destination for, a transmitted message; either that operated by an end-user, or a computer system working autonomously. Typical examples of DTE devices would be a desktop microcomputer, a mainframe computer system, a visual display unit terminal, a printer, or a facsimile machine. 2. Data communicating equipment (DCE) describes the devices which are used to support onwards communication of a message received from some DTE device type—acting as 'steps in the chain' rather than as end-controllers of the process. This may be a device attached to the end-user's system, or some intermediate step within the network itself.

The data communicating equipment acts as a common interface for unlike data terminating equipment, they even out the differences through the common use of a standard protocol. In this way, dissimilar types of information technology equipment can be used for information networking without requiring an end user to be aware of the physical characteristics of the receiving system; the more widely used and open the standard protocol which is used, the wider range of equipment which can interface in this way. The kind of equipment which falls into this category fulfils specialised roles in the communications process: some of these are integral to the internal functioning of the network element itself while others are associated with user end systems. Some of the more commonly found types are described here, as indicative of the range.

The multiplexor is a device for concentrating a number of terminal devices onto a higher bandwidth line, to make the most effective use of this capacity and to remove the need for installing many duplicate lines (one for each device) in parallel with each other. This arrangement would typically be used to connect several terminals situated near each other to a central computer which is located at some distance.

The multiplexor is responsible for apportioning the line on an equitable basis between all the terminals connected. There are two main *methods of multiplexing:*

- Time-division multiplexing, in which each terminal is allotted the full capacity of the channel for a fixed period of time, in a rotating sequence;
- Frequency division multiplexing, in which the full channel capacity is divided between users by allowing simultaneous transmissions on different frequencies.

The most appropriate form to use depends on the applications which are using the system; commonly asynchronous enquiry-type applications, where activity is in unpredictable short bursts, use a time-division form of multiplexing. A multiplexor must be installed at the receiving end, to separate out the different terminal signals for processing. A modem is another communicating device which allows one kind of DTE equipment, typically a personal computer, to establish a temporary connection with another remote computer system by using the normal telephone line. Since the telephone system was originally designed solely for voice traffic, which is analogue in nature, some conversion process must be used to translate digital computer data into a form suitable for analogue transmission. Digital signals are in a binary form, having two states—on and off—which can be represented as changes in voltage signals on a cable. Since the normal telephone line is designed for transmission of sound waves, these binary signals must be transformed into an audible tone by the modem. This process is known as modulation; a modem (modulator—demodulator) must be placed at both ends of the telephone link, acting as the interface between the end systems and the line, encoding and decoding the digital data signals. A series of standard recommendations have been produced by the CCITT (Comite Consultatif Internationale de Telegraphie et Telephonic), a Geneva-based international organisation concerned with issues in telecommunications development, for the use of modems.

The cost of modem technology falls steadily, faster transmission speeds are achieved at a higher expense due not only to the price of equipment but also to the additional communications processing which is necessary at higher speeds. Higher transmission speeds are achieved by a panoply of special techniques which require more sophisticated error checking capabilities to counter the increased influence of noise. While the CCITT recommendations are standard within Europe, the existence of a separate set of standards in North America, developed by the Bell Communications Corporation complicates the international situation. The most common of these are the Bell 203 (1200 bps) and Bell 212 (2400 bps) standards; although working at the same speeds they do not have an exact correspondence to V-series standards and are not compatible. A final example of data communicating equipment is the use of an independent computer processor to handle the communications loading of a large computer system. This would typically be used where a mainframe computer is accessed by a large number of remote callers; for example, a system which makes an online bibliographic database available to users on a global basis through the use of modems over a telecommunications network.

A smaller computer—such as a minicomputer—is dedicated to the task of dealing with the network communications, so that the mainframe does not become overloaded by this task, and is free to concentrate on database activity. The front end processor handles the external contact, passing queries back to the database machine and forwarding results to the remote caller. The remote caller is, of course, not aware of the separation of functions.

Communication of Synchronous Nature

The additional control information which is appended to the user data content carries information used in processing the message, and must also conform to some agreed system. A simple text message, for example, may contain an, overhead of information which is used to indicate boundaries between characters or chunks of text; this will appear as binary digits apparently identical to the data content unless there is some common method of 'reading' the stream of symbols.

A multimedia message which contains both sound and video elements requires control information to synchronise timing of the audio output with the screen display, which must be interpreted correctly. There is a need to synchronise the flow of information between the two end systems, so that signals which will conflict with each other are not generated simultaneously, and so that the receiver is ready and capable of processing the incoming signals at the rate which they are sent—controlling the 'turn taking'.

Communication can take place in one of two alternative patterns, and in each of these synchronisation is achieved in different ways. Asynchronous communication might be characterised as 'on demand' use of the communications channel. All network users have equal access to the channel, and use it to send messages at random intervals, characterised by short bursts of activity with quiet periods of varying length in between. The receiver waits passively once the connection is made, and is activated by the receipt of some message. A typical example of this type of activity would result from a user seated at a terminal screen, alternating interaction with a remote computer with periods of planning and thinking.

Synchronous communication depends on a fixed cycle, in which each user, and both sender and receiver, have access to the channel at defined time intervals for a fixed period. A typical use for this approach would be for large data file transfers in situations where the transfer is being managed completely by the computer systems as a background process, with no human intervention, or for the synchronisation of composite sound and video signals in video-conferencing systems. This synchronicity characteristic delineates the time/response dimension of the process, defining the appropriate activities in the end systems to control the process; there is also a characteristic of the communication channel which will affect the process.

Communication of Channel and Network

Communication through a transmission channel can occur in one of three different modes determining the allowed direction of, and activity in, the transmission. Each of these requires a different level of sophistication in control of the communication process:

- In simplex mode, the communication is in one direction only;
- In half-duplex mode, the communication can be bi-directional, but at alternate times only;
- In full-duplex mode, the communication is bi-directional, and both end systems may transmit simultaneously.

The term *channel* is normally used to denote the more abstract concept of a logical channel rather than the actual physical media. One physical link may potentially offer several logical communication channels, which can be thought of as separate entities. Since a network is a medium which is shared by many users, management of the communication process is a more complex affair than is suggested by the simplified one-to-one model. As well as agreeing on the terms by which the exchange will be conducted, the communication programme must be able to supervise and regulate the dynamic elements of the process, making necessary adjustments as the exchange develops and operating conditions fluctuate. The communications programme must be able to:

- Establish and maintain a connection across the communications channel between the sender and recipient, agree the terms on which the exchange is to be conducted, and terminate the connection-once the transaction is completed;
- Regulate the flow of information, between the two participants to prevent overloading of data by the recipient, if it is unable to process it quickly enough, causing a possible loss of information;
- Control the quality of information received by checking for the presence of errors and taking corrective action as necessary, perhaps by requesting a re-transmission of corrupted information.

The term bandwidth is an indication of the information capacity of an individual element in the process: the higher the bandwidth of the channel, for example, the higher is its information carrying capacity. The overall communication process (including the end systems) can only utilise the information-carrying capacity of the element with the least available bandwidth in any particular situation; either the transmitter, the receiver, or the channel will have a more limited bandwidth and will define the overall information exchange rate. In many situations, the bandwidth of the communication channel will be the limiting factor.

The capacity of a channel is normally expressed as the number of distinct symbols per second which can be passed along it. This maximum *data transfer rate* is usually given as a figure measured in bits per second, since the number of bits which make up a useful 'unit' of information will differ according to the information type—between characters of text and scanned images in bit-map form, for instance. In this way, a channel which is described as having a particular data transfer rate can be matched to different information transfer processes through a common comparable measure. In some circumstances, particularly in modem communications, the term *baud rate* is popularly used as an equivalent to this measure of bits per second; although this is not a strictly accurate use of the term, it can normally be taken to mean the same thing. Transmission channels can also be characterised by the method of signalling which is used. In *baseband* signalling the capacity of the channel is monopolised by a single message for the duration of the transmission, typically by varying the voltage along an electrical cable in a predetermined pattern. Broadband signalling enables a physical medium to be shared by more than one transmission by varying the frequency of the signals to ensure separation of one from the other—as a radio can distinguish different frequency transmissions. Broadband offers a higher bandwidth, and is therefore more associated with information networking applications which require higher capacities, such as multimedia. A goal of advanced network technology is to support a flexible, use of bandwidth among multiple users according to fluctuating demand, changing the allocation dynamically according to the transmission needs of the moment.

A communication channel is a logical concept that can be implemented on a variety of physical media, each of which has its own particular characteristics, such as bandwidth. The choice of which to adopt depends on the purposes of the network and the kind of applications it must support, the predicted traffic and data rates together with required response times, and a cost/benefit calculation on the relative importance between these factors. *The most widely used physical transmission media* are mentioned here:

1. The *twisted pair* is the simplest form of transmission cable, two simple electrical cables carrying small voltage signals. This is a very cheap method of connecting individual computer devices to a network, and is easy to install, but is not suitable for carrying traffic from many devices due to the limited bandwidth which it possesses, nor for applications which require more than a 1 Megabit per second (Mbps) data rate.
2. *Co-axial cable* uses a more substantial copper cable to offer a higher bandwidth suitable for multiple access from a limited number of nodes on a local network; and for the transmission of information forms which require a higher throughput of data, such as video signals, at data rates of up to 10 Mbps. This higher capacity is bought, at the expense of a higher material cost and a more complex installation process.
3. *Optical fibre cable* provides a means of transcending the physical limits of electrical cable, by conveying signals on a fluctuating light beam enclosed within a very fine glass fibre. Since light waves have a much higher potential bandwidth than electrical waves, data rates up to and beyond 100 Mbps are possible, as well as providing a lower susceptibility to noisy or sensitive environments.

   A single glass fibre, smaller in dimension than a human hair, is provided for each signal, and an installed optical cable may consist of several hundred fibres bundled together, providing *a* high throughput for existing services and spare capacity for future growth. While optical fibre provides a means of building very high bandwidth networks which can support sophisticated multimedia services, it is expensive and more difficult to install, requiring special interface equipment between cable and computer.
4. Microwave transmission offers a non-terrestrial alternative to a physical point-to-point link. Data is conveyed on radio waves through free space, and is normally used in conjunction with geostationary satellites. The data is transmitted from a ground station, called an uplink, to an orbiting satellite which is in direct line-of-sight, and the signal is bounced back to a receiving station (the downlink) at some different geographical ground location. These re-transmissions can be broadcast over a wide area for receiving by many destinations simultaneously, or be highly focused onto a single site.

   Satellite relay is commonly used to leap across long distances, such as in establishing connections between the United Kingdom and North America or the Far East, or where the laying of a physical cable would be costly or impossible across difficult geographic terrain. Microwave transmission may also be used on a ground-to ground basis, between stations situated on high ground within line of sight of each other.
5. Network communications have also been achieved by the use of infrared and broadcast radio signals; there is a growing interest in the use of such 'wireless' communications. Some use is also made of radio data broadcasting at a national level.

8

LIBRARY MAINTENANCE

The importance of the Maintenance Section of a library needs no emphasis. If proper care is not taken to organise and administer it on sound lines, the library property would become unserviceable in no time. In the Maintenance Section, the books are properly shelved when received from the Processing Section or when returned after being used. In other words, the books are properly stored and displayed. It is continually watched that books are correctly shelved on the book racks. This is very important especially if open access system is practised.

> "The objectives of the shelf work like the overall objectives of the library are to give adequate and efficient service to the library user. More specifically the shelf worker is primarily concerned with delivering a book when it is wanted, returning it to its assigned place when it is no longer needed, and seeing that it is properly cared for until it is wanted again."

> "A shelf supervisor is responsible for, or shares decisions concerning the arrangement of the collection so as to bring the most used book near service points without too much disregard of the classification scheme; the special shelving of oversized books; housing and arrangement of non-book materials: the exploitation of architectural and aesthetic possibilities of building areas in which readers are in direct contact with books; order and cleanliness within his areas and the training and supervision of his staff. He also has such other duties as planning and executing of major shifts or moving of the book collection and inventory with its follow-up."

Besides, the Maintenance Section is responsible for conserving the reading material. This function is one of the important functions which a librarian is expected to perform. "Conservation..........is only library function which should be continuously at work twenty-four hours a day. It is the only function which should be concerned with every piece of material in the library from the moment the selector becomes aware of its existence to the day it is discarded. The reason this sounds so exaggerated is that it is a forgotten platitude. It applies to any library collection, whether it be of Egyptian papyrus, of the third grade classroom in a low village, or a University's incunabula."

The Planning

It is advisable to prepare all the requisite plans before hand in order to avoid any confusion. This is essential because books being in thousands, if mixed, will cause much confusion. In larger libraries, the Chief of the Circulation Section may be made Incharge of all planning in this regard and a committee of senior officials be constituted to assist him, while in small libraries the Head Librarian will have to plan it by himself. Sometimes, a contractor is engaged for this purpose and the senior staff members provide him necessary guidance and help.

"The basic information needed for planning to shift a collection should include:

1. The number of sections or shelves of books in each subject classification;
2. The number of sections or shelves available on each tier;
3. Decisions regarding the new locations of the several classes of books; and
4. Decisions regarding distribution of free space among the various classes."

While shifting books from one place to another, it should be ensured, that enough free space is left out and special provision is made for shelving oversize books and periodicals. Certain sections need more space for expansion. Enough space should be left out so that the new additions made during a period of about every five years may be absorbed easily.

It is advisable to "prepare duplicate drawing of floor plans for each stack level. A large scale was used (¼ inch to ten feet) so there would be ample space for indicating the inclusive classification numbers for each section. A general plan for dividing the book collection among the several floors was then made, based on account of the number of sections occupied by each classification. It was formed desirable to put these figures, as well as the capacities of each stack level, on a separate sheet since this helped in explaining the shifting. Finally, using the duplicate plans, the new location for each class of book was written in the spaces representing each section. It was decided to leave some space vacant on each shelf in order to prolong the time before another shift would be necessary. The amount of space left on each shelf was determined by dividing the amount of free space by the total space available. Assuming that a particular stack level contains 150 sections and that 120 sections of books are to be shelved on this level, there would be 30 sections of free shelf space. These 30 sections, divided by the total space, 150 sections, allow for 20 per cent free space, which may be distributed as desired."

Similarly plan was prepared for moving the Toledo Public Library from its old building to a new building. "This move was complicated by the need for increasing the number of subject service areas from four to eleven and inter-shelving a number of branch library collections. Horizontally perforated, coloured, gummed labels were made to use in identifying related subject areas: yellow signified art, music and the humanities; green, history, travel, biography, etc. Each service head was made responsible for measuring his collections in the old building.

In addition, estimates of the amount of space required for expansion of each collection were made and added to the measurements of the collections. This total was then measured on the shelves in the new building and since the shelves were numbered with chalk, a notation was made of the inclusive numbers of shelves to be occupied. The day before the actual moving started, the proper coloured labels were affixed by the narrow portion above the perforation to the individual wooden shelves beneath the volumes in the old building.

Each of these labels bore in pencil the number of the shelf in the new building. Thus when the movers packed a shelf of books in the container, retaining the proper sequence of books on the shelf, they had only to tear the label off, moisten the back of it, and affix it to the end of the box. By its colour it showed to which service area the container should be sent, and upon which shelf the books should be placed when unpacked." Similarly, arrangements were made when the Punjab University Library, as already referred to, was shifted from its Shimla abode to a new building at Chandigarh. Different subject areas were divided amongst various Assistants and books were arranged in containers and clear indications were given on the outer cover of the containers. The inclusive call numbers along with subject names were written. The boxes were also consecutively numbered and corresponding lists were prepared. The shifting was accomplished very smoothly.

Equipment and Methods of Shifting: If books are to be shifted from one floor to another, ordinary boxes or containers may be used. If book elevators are available in the library, these should be made use of for carrying the books, otherwise some other trolleys and book trucks may be used, but if books are to be shifted from fairly long distances, it is advisable to carry the books in specially prepared standard containers:

> "In the Teledo Public Library, where shelf of books was considered as the unit in moving, special containers of corrugated card board were used because of possible danger to books and to the floors of the new building. These boxes were made in two sizes, the one for standard size books being 36 inches long, 10½ inches wide, and 9 inches deep, and the one for large books, 36 inches long, 15 inches wide, and 12 inches deep. All had regular flap covers so that the books could be protected from the weather."

Various sizes of containers have been used by many libraries, e.g., The Pennsylvania State College Library used wooden boxes measuring 38 inches by 14 inches by 12 inches. "During the general shifting and moving at Brown University in 1938–40, boxes 3 feet in length requiring two men for handling were discarded and replaced by boxes made for half inch pine with inside measurements of 1 foot by 1 foot by 8 inches.

Since one worker could carry two of these; the new boxes increased by one-half foot the number of books each person was able to carry. When filled, a box of this size balanced itself so that it could be carried by its edge without spilling the books. A human chain was used to forward the boxes of books from packer to shelver." Similar method was used by the Punjab University Library in 1960–61 when it moved its book stock from the ground floor to the stack areas on the other three floors. It is evident that proper planning and provision of suitable equipment are essential if the shifting and moving of books are to be carried out smoothly.

Procedures Followed in Maintenance Section

Multiple Sequences: The processed books are received from the Processing Section for shelving. In almost all libraries, books are shelved in more than one sequence. These sequences pertain to:

1. Reference books and Reports, marked as 'R' and 'RR' respectively.
2. Rare Books, marked as 'Rare'.
3. Paintings and illustrations, marked as 'P' or 'R'.
4. Manuscripts, marked as 'MSS'.
5. Films, Filmstrips, Microcards, Microfilms and Photographs marked as 'Closed Collections'.
6. Undersized or oversized books, marked by underlying or overlining their call numbers.

Reasons: The reasons for having multiple sequences are:

(i) Nature of thought-content i.e., whether these books are to be read through or are to be consulted off and on.

(ii) Nature of material on which the information is printed or written, i.e., whether it is on paper, film or card, etc.

(iii) Size of the books and other reading materials, i.e., undersized oversized books.

(iv) Age and availability of the books, i.e., whether the books to be shelved are very old and/ or rare books.

(v) Manuscripts or printed, i.e., whether the books are originally handwritten or printed ones.

Duties of the Shelving Staff: The junior staff members deputed to shelve the books should be asked to perform the following duties:

1. Dusting and cleaning of the shelves for which they are responsible.
2. To bring the newly processed books from the Processing Section.
   2.1 To arrange these books in a classified manner.
   2.2 To shelve these books in a proper manner.
3. To fetch the returned books from the Return Counter.
4. To regularly read the shelves and rectify the shelving.
5. To take out the torn and otherwise mutilated books for sending the same to the Binding Section for mending purposes.
6. Renewal of tags.
7. To reshuffle the existing books and merging of new books by making room for them. The existing books are to be shifted from one shelf to the other.
8. To arrange 'Topical Sequences' containing books on various important subjects or which pertain to various special festivals and occasions.
9. To make arrangement for stock-taking.
10. In case of closed access, those books are to be sent to the Issue Counter for which requisition slips have been handed over by the readers at the Issue Counter.

The books received from either the Processing Section or the Reference and Reading tables, Issue and Return Counters and Binding Section, etc., must be shelved at the earliest moments so that the needy readers find the books on the shelves.

Tools for Proper Functioning of the Section: The Maintenance Section should be provided with the following articles for ensuring proper functioning:

1. *Book Ends or Book Supports:* These should be provided in large numbers. At least two book supports are required for one plank so that the books are made to stand erect.
2. *Book-lifts and Trolleys:* If the book stacks are spread over many floors, it is desirable that book lifts or dumb elevators, as these are called, should be provided. Similarly, to carry books from one end to the other end of each floor, there should be a book trolley so that the time and energy of the staff are not wasted unnecessarily in performing those jobs which can be done quickly through machine operations.

3. *Shelving Tables:* One small table for sorting out books for shelving should be provided in each bay of stacks. Even when books are in the process of shelving, these can be used by the readers.
4. *Guide Boards:* In order to bring to the notice of the readers the books on all subjects, the following guides should be provided:

Tier Guides: In case of more than one tier of stacks, Tier Guide Board should be provided on each tier. One combined Tier Guide Board should be affixed at the entrance on the ground floor so that a reader gets the overall view of the arrangement of books on the shelves.

Gangway Guide Boards: All gangways should be provided with Gangway Guides so that the readers know easily as to which books on particular subjects are arranged on right, left, front and back of the gangways. The boards should contain the names of subjects along with the inclusive main class numbers.

Bay Guides: Every bay of shelves should be provided with a Bay Guides which should be of hard card board and it should contain the concerned class number and its equivalent terms in common parlance. These should be inclusive of the subjects on both the ends. Such Bay Guides should be put up at the beginning of each bay in the stack room.

Shelf Guide: Every shelf should be provided with a Shelf Guide which should contain the class numbers 'denoting the subject on which the books are found in particular shelf.

Plank Guide: Selection of books would be further facilitated if Plank Guides are also provided.

General Instructions Guides: The Maintenance Section should provide the following guides; i.e., one in each bay:

(a) 'No smoking please'.

(b) 'Silence please'.

(c) 'Readers are advised not to shelve the books by themselves'.

(d) 'No spitting, please'.

(e) 'Readers are advised to sit for study in the reading room only'.

> "The stack room is a place for browsing and selecting books only. The place for study is in the adjoining reading room. Readers are frequently to be reminded of this in as polite a manner as possible. They do not easily realise the obstruction they cause to others settling down to read in the stack room".

Open Access versus Closed Access: It is the duty of the Maintenance Section to make arrangements for supervising the readers who handle books, especially in open access libraries because there always remains a danger of mutilation and damage of books by unscrupulous readers. To avoid it, the Maintenance Section should arrange for sufficient staff members for keeping close watch for all the time if the open access is to be made a success and if the fruits of the open access system are to be reaped. In open access system, implications of the Five Laws of Library Science enunciated by Dr. S.R. Ranganathan are fulfilled as books are put to best use. All the readers have got the liberty to consult the books, and in this manner, they can select their appropriate reading materials.

"The popularity of open stacks seems to be founded on the following sentiment as stated by a Librarian: "Our policy, in general, is to eliminate as many barriers between the books and readers as possible." Their valuable time is also saved as they have not to wait for the books to be brought by the pages because the readers can go direct to the stack room for bringing the requisite books. It does not take much time if the books are arranged in a helpful order.

Their time which is liable is to wasted in closed access, can be saved if open access system is followed. In closed access, a reader by consulting the catalogue, gives a requisition slip and he gets the book issued for home reading. But on perusing the book, he may find that it does not serve his purpose. He returns the book on the next day and selects another book by consulting the catalogue. It is possible that the second book may also not be useful to him. In this way, lot of his time is wasted and he feels disappointed because he does not have any opportunity to have close communion with the books.

Moreover, the page or the restorer who has to bring the requisite books from the shelves has to cater to the needs of so many readers at one and the same time. He naturally is liable to consume a lot of time, thereby forcing the reader to wait for a longer time. In an open access system, the Third Law of Library Science is also satisfied because every book has got the chance of being used by its readers. "According to it, readers frequently "discover" books if allowed to walk amidst them in the stack room". The Fourth Law stresses that the subjective loss of time is more painful than its objective loss. According to it, open access allows readers to adventure among books. In this adventure, they do not feel the flight of time. This makes them love going to the library again and again. The pressure of the Fifth Law grows out of considerations of economy. In open access, there is no need to have special staff, book-lifters, as they are called in North India—to take out and bring the books needed by readers. For, the readers take them out themselves.

Even the staff for replacing books can be reduced considerably. For, in the open access system, all books returned by readers are kept temporarily in special book-racks near the entrance (These) are the books much in demand for the time being. All readers, therefore, go to these book-racks first. Nearly three-fourths of the returned books go into circulation in this way. Thus, the staff time for replacing is reduced by more than half."

Tenets of Open Access: An open access system is definitely better than the closed one. But its basic tenets must be observed if its fruits are to be reaped. The essence of an open access system consists of:

1. Putting the books in open book-racks free from doors and locks;
2. Admitting the reader inside the stack room;
3. Freedom for readers to walk amidst the books in the open shelves;
4. Browsing by readers without let or hindrance;
5. Guidance to readers by the reference librarian, both in anticipation and on demand; and
6. Right of readers to take away any book to the reading room for study or to circulation counter to get it issued for study at home.

Besides, an open access system implies proper classification and cataloguing of books. It demands efficient and correct arrangement and rearrangement of books.

Safeguards for an Open Access Library: Open access is not a licence for handling the books roughly. It is a freedom with some essential corresponding obligations on the part of the library staff members and readers.

Safeguards by Library Staff

Design of the Library Building: Open access, no doubt, carries with it a certain risk of loss. The loss likely to occur in an open access library should be minimised by the very design of the building. All entrance and exits to and from the library are to be only through controlled wicket-gates. All the other doors and windows are to be made book-proof. They should be fitted with mesh-shutters."

Separation of Rare Books and Manuscripts: Another safeguard should be taken to minimise the loss of valuable books. "Rare and costly books, pamphlets and undersize books, books with too many plates and other weakly built books, are not to be given open access. They are to be kept in closed shelves and issued only against formal application."

Replacement of Books: Generally in an open access system, if not properly run, books are likely to be misplaced knowingly or unknowingly by the users. The reason of such a situation is the freedom to the readers to replace the books by themselves. The readers cannot be expected to know the technicalities and niceties of shelf-arrangement.

Moreover, they are generally in a hurry to go. So they cannot be expected to replace the books at correct places. Its remedy lies in prohibiting readers to replace books themselves. They should, on the other hand, be instructed not to shelve the books but to place them on the shelving tables kept in each bay of stacks.

Shelf-rectification: In an open access system, it is certain that a large number of books will be taken out of their respective places. These may also be replaced at wrong places deliberately or otherwise. In order to avoid it, the used books must be replaced at regular short intervals. Moreover, shelf-rectification should be carried out in a planned manner. These will minimise misplacement of books.

Different Services

Vigilance Service: In an open access library, there are chances of stealing, mutilating or hiding of books, because readers are given full freedom to handle books in the stacks and reading rooms. These evils can be overcome if proper vigilance is kept over them. Enough maintenance staff should be posted for the purpose at vantage points in stacks and reading rooms. This can be achieved easily if the library building design itself provides proper vigilance facilities with minimum staff.

Reference Service: "The provision of ample reference service is the best human safeguard. The kind reference service will wean away many, who are not confirmed criminals, from stealing, mutilating or hiding books. Apart from this, the constant movement of the reference staff in the stack room provides incidently some vigilance service."

Change in Subject Sequences: To get the full benefit of the open access system for the Third Law, the sequence of the subjects in the stack room should be changed at convenient intervals. Change in the arrangement of books will evoke new curiosity even as the shaking of a Kaleidoscope. The Third Law will bless the librarian for this.

Conclusion: Due to the superiority of the open access system over the closed one it has led most of the library administrators of today to introduce it in spite of the danger of loss or mutilation of books. One should not lose heart if his first experiment does not provide complete success. It must be practised perseveringly and steadfastly with full faith in the efficacy of the open access system.

Staff Management

Relation with other Sections: The maintenance work is related to many sections of a library. Processing Section feeds the Maintenance Section with new books and creates problems of shelving when books on a particular subject are received in large numbers and it is not possible to accommodate them without disturbing the existing order. The Circulation Section draws books from the stacks and sends back the returned books to the stacks. In libraries practising closed access, the maintenance staff has also to do the paging job i.e., the job of carrying requisitioned books from one place to another place. The disturbance of the existing order demands proper shelving and reshelving. The maintenance staff remains mainly busy in shelving and reshelving the books returned on the Return Counter of the Circulation Section. Maintenance Section is also related to the Reference Section. The books taken by the readers for consultation within the library premises are in so large numbers that the maintenance staff remains always busy in shelving them.

Workplace Management

"Shelf work in small and medium-sized libraries is normally assigned to the Circulation Department. It is done by the personnel who serve at the Circulation desk or by one or more shelf workers who are a part of the Circulation staff. The two principal reasons for this are:

(1) Good administrative practice requires that this part-time work be done by someone doing related work, or that no separate administrative unit be set up for such a small staff, as the case applies;

(2) Since those who shelve the books are in most cases the same assistants who page the books and since paging is an integral part of circulation, the assistants doing shelf work logically belong to the circulation department.

But in large libraries, more shelf workers are required. In order to have smooth working, it would be advisable to have a separate department under the charge of either an independent Assistant Librarian or Circulation Department Incharge or the Incharge of the Readers Services:

> "The universality of shelf-work makes it a natural and relatively simple area of work in which a certain amount of consistency can be attained, even if the responsibility cannot be vested centrally. The more rapidly a collection is growing the more desirable it becomes to consider possible advantages of centralising shelving responsibility, for growth creates and intensifies problems of shelf-work."

Besides an Incharge of shelf-work, enough number, of junior staff members should be appointed who should be trained in the art of shelving. Even if they are unskilled workers, they can be initiated into shelving practices, but they must be literate. It must be brought to their notice that they will have to do the dusting work also. In case of small libraries, two or three persons should be appointed for this work, depending upon the number of books in stock and number of books issued and returned. In bigger libraries and especially having multistoreyed stacks, at least one shelf worker must be provided for one wing of the stack. He should be made responsible for the proper upkeep and arrangement of books of his section. In addition to it, one or two semi-professionals should be appointed who should continually read the shelves. They should rectify the arrangement also.

In bigger libraries, more persons may be provided to do this job because this is a very important job in the sense that if a book is misplaced either knowingly or unknowingly, it is lost for ever for a reader and until and unless it is placed at its proper place, the readers will be unable to get this book, thereby affecting library service. Their work should be checked occasionally by Section Incharge, so that certain mistakes are rectified which are likely to be committed by junior members of the library staff.

Stacking Methods and Materials: In ancient and medieval times, libraries were mere store houses of books. The books were considered treasure troves and these were not allowed to be read by the common people. Rather these were considered as 'forbidden fruit' for the man in the street as imparting of education and learning in ancient times was the monopoly of the rich (Brahmins in India). The books were collected for preservation sake and were naturally kept in closed almirahs and safes and were heavily guarded. In the 16th century there were 'chained libraries' in which books were actually kept in brass frames which were fastened by iron chains with the almirahs.

These could not be removed away in any manner. The stacking of books was influenced by the conditions prevalent in those times. Printing press was still not there and due to the difficulty of duplicating them, the books were not issued out. So, the furniture required for keeping the books was of such a kind that the books could be stored safely. Later on, safes and alcoves gave way to shelves so that the books could be stored in better hygienic conditions and could be issued out to the readers, though to the privileged few. Again, in the shelves, some arrangement was provided so that the time of the readers could be saved, A lot of time was wasted earlier when the books were stored in boxes and safes in which no desirable arrangement was possible and books were mixed with each other. 'Once the shelf has evolved from the book-rests of the medieval library nearly four centuries were to pass before any further significant step was taken in storage methods.'

With the invention of the printing press and the advent of Renaissance and democracy, the production of books began to increase. Libraries which were once considered 'forts of rebellions' were opened in large numbers. These libraries acquired books in large numbers. "With the growth of library stocks the height of shelving came to be increased, access to the upper levels being afforded by galleries, and during the nineteenth century cast-iron construction was introduced, to be superseded in its turn by steel and concrete. Much space continued to be unprofitable taken up by the gangways and aisles required to give access to shelving, and it was eventually realised that the proportion of shelving in relation to the total volume of a book store could be increased by using movable presses in addition to fixed ones.'

With the change in the purpose of a library from 'preservation' to 'use,' the sizes, shapes and kinds of stacking equipment also underwent a revolution. Proper rooms meant for stacking books were built so that books could not be eaten away by white-ants and other bookworms. Similarly, stacking furniture was designed in such a manner that books could be used without any difficulty and without any wastage of space.

Principles of Stacking: "In order to ensure an efficient and economical scheme it is necessary, when planning a new building, that there be collaboration between the architect, the librarian and the equipment manufacturers. Briefly:

(a) A library must be designed to accommodate books and folios of every description.

(b) Planned to give ready access to every volume and easy communication with cataloguing, reading and delivery rooms.

(c) A ventilating system ensuring adequate fresh air, free of dust, with temperature and humidity control.

(d) A lighting system whereby the titles of books are easily read.

(e) Adequate provision for expansion.

The first principle implies that the planks of shelves should be adjustable so that books and folios of every description could be shelved without any wastage. Alternatively, shelves with planks at various distances should be provided in a library.

The second principle implies that the shelves should be such that the shelved books were within the reach of persons of normal height. This means that the height of the shelves should not be more than 7 feet, because a person of normal height could have access of even those volumes which might be shelved on the upper most, planks of shelves.

The third principle is mainly concerned with the structure of a building. But it has implications on the shape and construction of book shelves also. This means that the book shelves should have enough vacant space so that fresh air and light might reach each volume. So far as keeping the books free from dust and controlling temperature and humidity are concerned, the stack room should be air-conditioned. Vacuum cleaners and exhaust fans should be provided for keeping books in a normal condition. The shelves with glass panes can also save the books from dirt, dust, variation of temperature and humidity but this system violates the very spirit of modern librarianship because it entails unnecessary expenditure and hindrance to the readers.

The fourth principle implies that the lighting arrangement should be such in the stack room that every title could be easily read. This can be possible only if sky ventilation, glass walls and other natural and artificial lighting arrangements are made. Slanting light should be thrown on the spines of all books arranged in the shelves. It also implies that the book shelves should be rack type i.e., without doors.

The fifth principle lays down that adequate provision should be made for expansion. The implication of this principle in relation to book shelves is that the book shelves should be of standard size and should be in consonance with the size of the module used for constructing the library building, especially the stack room. In this way, any number of new racks can be added to accommodate newly acquired books.

The following may be added to the above-mentioned principles:

1. Wastage of space should be avoided to as much extent as possible.
2. Maximum number of books should be shelved in minimum amount of space.
3. The shelves should be as much attractive, functional and durable as possible.

The first out of these principles implies that the shelves should be of uniform size and shape so that any number of racks could be fixed without taking undue space. In other words, it means that the length, breadth and depth of the shelves should be in accordance with the sizes of the books to be shelved. The shelves should also be double-faced so that space could be saved which would otherwise be wasted if each shelf was fixed separately. The partition between two sides of the racks may be of mesh wire because it will take lesser space.

The second principle implies that the shelves should be such which could either be folded after use or could be arranged in a vertical manner. These also enable the libraries to make use of other methods such a Rolling Stacks, Bracket Stacks, Compact Shelving equipments. The last principle lays down that the material and make-up of the shelves should be such that these could give a fine and attractive finish and also could be durable. This can be ensured only if these are made either of seasoned wood or of steel with enamelled colours.

For normal shelving in general libraries, the standard racks or shelves made of either seasoned teak or Sheesham wood can prove useful and functional. The steel rack are manufactured in India, by M/s. Godrej Co. Bombay, M/s. J.K.S. Company, Hubli, M/s. Siddeshwar and Co. Pvt. Ltd., Hubli Decor Steel Pvt. Ltd. New Delhi and Chandigarh and M/s. Vinar Limited, Delhi. The last mentioned company claims nine distinct advantages of its steel equipment. These are:

1. Built to last— especially phosphate against rust and corrosion, strengthened with a hand baked enamel finish.

2. Built in sturdy side rests and back stoppers for better care of books.
3. Range indicators and index pockets are provided on each 'Vinarak' for easier cataloguing.
4. Label holder for each shelf is provided for efficient classification.
5. There are no dirt-trapping ridges or corners.
6. Adjustability of shelves is possible at every 19 mm (3/4).
7. There is an ease of arranging continuous bays.
8. There is an ease of assembling and dismantling.
9. Special grey finish is provided to match the most modern decor.

M/s. Curzon & Co. Madras has been manufacturing wooden Unit Book Racks.

Dr. S.R. Ranganathan's specifications of a standard Teakwood Book Rack which he designed for the Madras University Library in 1926 can also be used in manufacturing wooden book racks.

The Indian Standards Institution, Delhi has laid down a standard for wooden rack wide is: 1829 (Part 1)-1961 Library Furniture and Fitting: Part 1 (Timber). These have been reaffirmed by the University Grants Commission's Library Committee. These are very much in use. These racks are meant for those libraries which are practising open access system. For libraries having closed access, almirahs with glass windows would be useful. These are very costly. In the alternative, wooden book racks with adjustable planks can also serve the purpose. Though these are more attractive than the steel racks, yet there remains always a danger that enemies of books may assault the books. The steel racks, on the other hand, are very much durable and also are free from being spoiled or eaten away by the white-ants, etc.

Stacking Systems: The real problem of accommodating more books is faced by either national libraries or other depository centres or libraries where the books of various sizes are continuously received in staggering numbers. The following methods have been brought into practice to solve this difficult problem.

Double Rows on Fixed Shelves: On normal fixed shelves, the books can be arranged in double rows as was experimented earlier. But due to inconvenience in selecting the books on the rear rows, it was replaced by two separate shelves to be used for two 'layers'. In this system in order to have access to the books in the rear row, the books on the front line could be easily swung on the side.

Hinged Stacks: In an experiment conducted on these lines at Bradford between 1878 and 1884 by the City Librarian, Charles G. Virgo, an equipment was introduced which foreshadowed very closely the hinged shelving for compact storage now in use in the United States. It consisted of a press, hinged at one side and mounted in front of fixed shelving, access to which was obtained by opening the hinged press in the manner of a door. The equipment was constructed of wood, and to give additional support to the hinged press a roller was attached to the outer edge, running on a curved metal track in the floor.

Bracket Stacks: Another method of shelving books is to use the bracket stack. "Tabular columns into which the shelf brackets engage are supported by a heavy shelf base and the shelves are easily adjusted at I in intervals.' Such stacks are found in the National Archives of India, New Delhi. In this method, lot of space and materials are saved and more books can be shelved in a given space.

Multi-tier Stacks: The multi-tier stacks method has been adopted by many large libraries of the world due to lack of space. "This system is constructed with a self-supporting mental framework extending from basement to roof, and designed to carry the weight of the book load, with the weight of the deck floors and line dead." Vertical extension of stacks is cheaper than the horizontal one if the multi-tier stack system is resorted to. This is because the floor on each stack is temporary one. It may be either a wooden framework of a lighter steel or concrete framework. The book and shelf load is on the basement every stack floor is connected with the others by joining the shelves in a vertical manner. In the Central Secretariat Library New Delhi' multi-tier stack system is followed and the floor of each stack except that of the ground floor consists of wooden frame. Each stack floor of the Indian National Scientific Documentation Centre Library New Delhi consists of concrete but it is incapable of bearing the heavy load of books and other equipment. "The close spacing of the supporting columns which are slotted to support the shelf brackets permits the use of thin slab concrete or metal plate floors."

Tower Stacks: One kind of tower stacks is the arranging of many shelves on one another, thus raising the shelf capacity. This kind of system is found in the Punjab and Haryana High Court Library, Chandigarh the stacks are arranged along the walls. These extend up to the roofs which are very high. But the stacks are made of lighter wood so that due to heavy load, the lower shelves do not give way. Another precaution is taken by providing appropriate wall support to the shelves by attaching the same to the walls in one way or the other. The whole of the weight is not on the lower shelves. But this kind of shelving is dangerous and expensive. This method does not put every volume within the reach of a normal reader. Staircases have to be used for having access to volumes placed on the upper stack.

The second kind of tower stacks is the provision of stacks on more than one floor, each floor being independent of the other. The floors of all the stack areas are made of concrete and the weight of books and other equipment is borne by each floor by itself. The height of the stack room is not more than 9 feet. This type of stacking is very popular now-a-days. It is very expensive. This system is found in many libraries of India. "In some of the older buildings, such as Widener at Harvard, and in new buildings, as at Princeton, underground stacks have played a prominent part in the storage of books." In such stacks the aisles which give access to the book shelves take up about 65 per cent of the space in the stack. In order to obviate these problems, the moving blacks and compact storage methods may be made use of.

Rolling Stacks: In order to meet the scarcity of space for stacking purposes, Rolling Stacks may be used. "These are metal stack units mounted on wide tread ball-bearing wheels. These cases are placed side by side forming a solid bank of books and by the use of this system about 50 per cent, more books can be stored in a given floor area than is possible by the normal fixed shelving system. Individual cases are easy to pull out provided a hard level floor exists.' Such stacks are available in many Indian libraries such as the National Library, Calcutta and the Planning Commission Library, New Delhi. A recent Swedish invention—already in use in Britain—enables rolling cases to be manipulated by electric power."

Compact Storage: Fremont Rider is a strong protagonist of compact storage. He bases his proposals on his experience as Librarian of Wesleyan University, Middle town, Connecticut. He advocates the use of compact storage methods for libraries facing space problems. Though microcopy methods can be used to meet the challenge of the ever-increasing number of accessions in bigger libraries, yet the cost of converting the conventional paper-books into microcards or microfilms, etc., is much more costly than the original texts. For actual shelves only 35 per cent space is available because as already pointed out, the aisles take away 65 per cent of the total volume of space. At least 50 per cent space which is now-a-days wasted in arranging books on.......................... selves, can be saved. The first step for achieving the stipulated 50 per cent saving is to arrange books by sizes so as to save 25 per cent space. Although explored since the days of Melvil Dewey, compact book shelving has been widely publicised and used since 1950. Robert H. Muller enumerates the following factors which should be taken into consideration by the librarians who plan to have compact storage:

1. Cost of shelving per linear foot;
2. Mechanical functioning of the equipment;
3. Relative accessibility and visibility of books;
4. Efficiency in shelving, collecting and shifting books;
5. Ease of shelf labelling;
6. Adaptability of the equipment to the floor area dimensions under consideration;
7. Adjustability of shelves and drawers;
8. Hazards and safety features;
9. Relative quietness and noisiness in operation;
10. Appearance;
11. Adaptability to non-book uses; and
12. Reconvertibility to non-compact storage;

> "This system consists of units of three stacks, the centre row of fixed double-sided stacks at each side. Each hinged stack is hung on ball-bearing pivots without rails or guides and is easily swung into the aisle to give access to material in the inner shelves."

> "The Vernier mobile book stack made by Messrs. Libraco, of Charlton, London, is a free-standing double-sided press mounted on casters with specially designed roller bearings which the makers claim, ensure that it does not 'wander' in use."

Another type of compact storage equipment manufactured by Messrs. Glover of Great Britain has been invented by a Swiss engineer. It is known as Compactus-System, the Foulkes Mobile Storage System or Compactus-Ingold System.

> "Compact storage is already employed in the United States and among the types of movable shelving designed for use in conjunction with fixed presses is that manufactured by Messrs. Snead and Co., of Orange, Va, one of the earliest installations of which is to be found in Midwest Inter-Library Centre. Chicago. The Snead System makes use of fixed and movable shelves, and takes the form of a triple bank of double-sided adjustable steel shelving, the centre presses being fixed and each having a double-sided press of the same width hinged to each face. There are, thus, six layers of shelves between stack aisles, and each outer compartment can be swung open like a door to afford access to books on its inner side and on the fixed centre shelving—a modern application of the principle introduced by Virgo at Bradford."

Many other kinds of compact storage equipments are found at many places out of which the following may be mentioned:

1. In the Hamilton Compo stack equipment, which is now being made in the United States, drawers take place of shelves, and a 'floating side' permits any drawer to be opened to its fullest extent without becoming dislodged.

2. Art Metal Company of James Town, N.Y. has made a shelving equipment which is known as Com-Pac-Case Storage System. This may be adopted for new installations, or applied to existing fixed shelving, where conditions permit. Unlike Snead equipment, the Com-Pac-Case movable presses are single-sided, the standard pattern is 7 ft. 3 inches high and has adjustable shelves 9 in. deep and 15 inches wide. Units are hinged to each side of the front of fixed presses 3 ft. wide; a space of 3¼ inches between the inner sides of the hinged units permits one-half to be opened without disturbing the other. The hinged units are secure in the closed position by a spring loaded bolt and many be fastened with a padlock.
3. "The Stor-Mor equipment made by the W.R. Ames Co. of San Francisco, employs double-headed drawers, designed to give 100 per cent increase in capacity with no decrease in the width of aisles. In the Charles Holbrook Library of the Pacific School of Religion at Berkeley Cal. An increase of 113 per cent was claimed to have been achieved through the introduction of Stor-Mor equipment. Like the Hamilton drawers these may be installed in existing library buildings; unlike them they have no shelf fitted across the front of the drawer and directly accessible, but books are shelved in two rows along the length of the drawer, fore-edge inward.

   The drawer assembly is such that it may be mounted on stack supports designed for fixed bracket type shelving and the two sizes of drawer advertised measure 16-3/8 inches wide and 68-5/8 or 76-5/8 inches long. Other sizes are available. Two drawers side by side have the same width as a standard 3 ft. shelf.

   The height of the front of the drawers is 7-5/8 inches To permit the removal of books there are no raised sides, while supports are fitted to hold books in place when the drawers are moved. The length of the drawers is such that when fixed shelving is replaced by Stor-Mor equipment, as with Hamilton, the space formerly occupied by alternative aisles is made available for books. The drawers run on ball-bearing rollers, will open with a pull of less than 3 lbs. and are held in place when closed by a locking catch. They are fitted with two 5 × 3 inches card holders at each end to enable the contents to be indicated. The makers state that all volumes are easily visible when the drawers are open. The equipment is in use in Stanford University Library; and is to be installed in the libraries of California and Michigan Universities.
4. The compact storage system advocated by Remington Rand employs four-way stack columns to make it possible to turn the direction of stack ranges by 90 degrees; it achieves compactness through aisle reduction from a width of about 36 inches to 20 inches and elimination of a centre aisle. If no centre aisle or cross aisles are provided both before and after the change, storage capacity can be increased by about 40 per cent. The claim made in advertisements that storage capacity can be increased by 60 per cent is true only if you assume a relatively comfortable provision of aisles before the change and no cross aisles after the change."

Evaluation of Compact Storage: The librarians who are faced with the space problem due to infinite increase in the number of accretions in the libraries feel tempted to adopt these latest stacking methods especially compact storage methods and mechanisms as advertised and demonstrated by various firms. But they should not take them at their face value. They should take them with a grain of salt because these systems do lessen the use of books which is not desirable. All the same, merits and demerits of various systems should be carefully studied before making a decision as to whether a particular stacking method is to be adopted or not. About compact storage many librarians have expressed their opinions.

> "The only place where savings would be affected would be in the amount (per book stored) of the stack building shell which would be required; and though this saving might be material, the extra cost of the stack installation in it would probably more than offset the saving. What we have here again, in other words, is a greater compactness and no overall economy."

Dr. Muller has brought into light the following kinds of savings which can be effected by the adoption of compact storage methods:

1. Lighting installation and maintenance;
2. The installation of floor covering and floor maintenance;
3. The cost of handling books to the delivery desk and returning them;
4. The installation and maintenance of heating and ventilating equipment; and
5. Janitorial maintenance.

He compares the cost of shelving (excluding building costs) per volume in various kinds of stacking equipments and systems as follows:

	Sh.
1. Fixed Shelving	0.16
2. Hamilton drawers	0.54
3. Ames 'Stor-Mor' drawers	0.57
4. Art Metal hinged units	
(a) Two units per face of fixed shelving	0.56
(b) Four units(double layer on each face)	0.65

> "The extensive use of compact storage equipment is, therefore, economically justifiable when building costs are very high, when land values are high and vertical extension impossible, or when for any reason extension or rebuilding is completely impossible."

The compact storage is not without disadvantages which should be taken into consideration when contemplating to introduce compact stacking. The following are the disadvantages of compact stacking:

1. Books are less directly accessible.
2. Movable parts may require maintenance.
3. Moving of drawers 6 hinged doors may cause noise.
4. Shelving, shifting and collecting of books may require more time and motion and may, therefore, involve greater labour costs.
5. Drawers and hinged doors may block aisles and become hazardous, causing accidents.
6. Time may have to be expended in teaching library users who are not mechanically inclined how to operate drawers or hinged doors with safety.
7. Compact storage units are perhaps not too practical in open stacks despite claims to the contrary.

Conclusion: For taking a decision as to whether compact shelving should be resorted to in a particular library in particular situations or not, the following questions must be considered:

1. Is the inconvenience that will result great enough to out-weight the saving in space that will be achieved?
2. What is the actual monetary saving that can be anticipated from adoption of any specific plan?

There are many drawbacks of special types of shelving materials other than those of ordinary standard fixed shelving. In the former non-accessibility of books, danger of damaging of books and stacking materials and the heavy costs of installations are some of the major drawbacks.

It can be concluded by observing that those libraries which stock books and other kindred materials. For constant use should prefer normal standard fixed stacking material. These are found especially in those libraries which have got open access system in vogue. The other methods of stacking can be and should be used with profit only by those libraries which are either national libraries or other copyright or depository libraries where the books are kept not for constant use but for storing and preserving purposes. Other methods given above can also be used for stacking those books in a library which are either lesser in demand or are otherwise not required. These methods are meant for bigger libraries which face problems of space. Smaller libraries should use only standard fixed shelves.

Shelving Methods

Introduction: Though there seems to be no difference between the meaning of 'storage' and 'shelving, 'yet the word 'storage' clearly indicates that the books are to be stored and proper care is be taken for their preservation. For this purpose, allotment of appropriate location marks would be useful instead of arranging books subject wise. In a growing library, if classified arrangement is not followed, the interpolation of books under various heads would become difficult and the very purpose of a service library will be marred altogether, and the use of books would be minimised.

Open access system which has been brought into practice in order to publicise books and induce the readers to do their selection easily and properly, will be put to a stop and thus it will be a retrograde step as the books will be kept in a medieval fashion. If the aim of a so-called library is to store books, the above-mentioned methods can be used besides the following methods:

1. Methods of shelving more books in the existing sections;
2. Methods of devoting a larger percentage of the available floor space to regular shelving; and
3. Methods of increasing the capacity of a given floor space by using special kinds of shelving.

The first method implies that less space should be left for future growth and books should be shelved by size, on their fore edges, in two or three deep and by increasing the height of shelving equipment.

The second method implies that shelves should have lesser width, space for aisles may be reduced, longer ranges of shelves may be adopted, and ranges of shelves may be lengthened and the width of the cross aisles should be reduced.

The third method implies the use of improved space-saving stacking and shelving methods. In case the books are collected for wider use, the arrangement of books on shelves should be decided keeping in constant view that books are meant for maximum use:

"The essence of efficient library service is to produce the book wanted, or to suggest a similar title, with the minimum of delay. All routines for the control of the book collection and all stock records stem from this. The fluidity of the private library of the earlier times, adequate enough for its owner was also often sole user and who could recall the contents of a given shelf easily produced a natural reaction in the nineteenth century, when a large public began to use libraries and, so as to minimise confusion, books were given fixed shelf numbers, made even more permanent by their inclusion in printed catalogue."

"The books should be arranged on the shelves so as to fulfil the Fourth Law of Library Science. The arrangement cannot be permanent in the changing library world. It will have to be judiciously varied and readjusted from time to time. Several factors will have to be examined from time to time for this purpose."

"Fixed location is an antiquarian method of shelving which should never be seen in a lending library and is justifiable only where collections are immutably complete and permanently placed. Such collections are usually important bequests which have to be preserved intact and found in cathedral libraries, large university or institutional libraries, or in the reference departments in municipal libraries. The books may be classified alphabetically, chronologically, or systematically by subject as circumstances may control or suggest."

Various Provisions

The books must be arranged on the shelves in some logical order if their proper use is to be ensured. One method which is commonly used by most of the libraries is the arrangement of books in a classified manner, i.e., in the order of a Classification scheme used in the library. Suppose, Dewey Decimal Classification is used in a library, the classified arrangement of books will be in the following order:

000	100	200	300	400
500	600	700	800	900

"So far as is practicable the stock should be arranged in unbroken sequence upon the shelves, but exceptions have sometimes to be allowed. For physical reasons it is frequently found necessary to have size grouping. Quartos and folios, including atlases, probably the whole of music, and all works of large size, cannot economically be placed with crown or demy octavos. To do so would be extremely wasteful of space, and this effect would not be pleasing."

Broken Order: In libraries, some books are in great demand while others may not be used by the reader's very frequently. The time of the readers is to be saved and efforts are to be made to ensure that all requisite books are brought to the notice of the readers. Reference books, children's books and other kindred materials are placed separately because these would be accessible easily if these are arranged in special sequences. All this implies a broken order. It implies that the arrangement of books is not strictly in accordance with the classified order. In a public library, books on fiction, biography and current topics are in constant demand.

These are taken out of the normal classified sequence, and are arranged in front rows so that the readers can select the books easily and without loss of time. This broken order may be as under:

800	920	320	
Reference Books	Juvenile Books.	100	200
300	400	500	600
700			

Parallel Arrangement: If the books are arranged in a classified manner and by size, a system of parallel order may be followed. It means that books of various sizes on a particular subject are arranged on the same shelves in such a manner that no space is wasted and books are made available without any extra labour. Books of smaller sizes on a particular subject may be arranged behind the books of normal size. The books of abnormal sizes may be arranged on the lower most shelf. Another method of ensuring parallel order may be to arrange books of smaller and bigger sizes on the 4th and 5th planks of shelves respectively on all subjects. This means that books of a particular size would be arranged in a separate sequence. But this arrangement would be classified.

"Having been obliged to disturb the schedule sequence and to arrange the books in so many collections, it is a great responsibility of the Maintenance Section to maintain correct sequence in the shelves and to see that every book is in its correct place. The mechanical apparatus invented by the library profession to cure this is what is known as the Shelf Register. It is made up of cards of standard size, viz., 125 × 75 mm. written on the principle—one title, one card—with the call number in the leading line."

Block Arrangement: "Block arrangement is the method of shelving books in regular shelf-to-shelf, case to case order according to classification. An interesting variation is accomplished by placing an occasional section of non-fiction in the congested fiction areas. This variation is designed quite practically to relieve the crowding that often exists when all the fiction is shelved close together in a busy public library."

Ribbon Arrangement: In this arrangement, the books of fiction are placed on the middle planks while non-fiction books are kept on the upper and lower planks. The purpose of this arrangement is to create interest amongst the readers to read non-fiction books and to dissuade them from reading fiction books. "Ribbon arrangement, which was on a definite decline when the American Library Association Survey was made, seems to be increasingly less popular except perhaps in the case of some school libraries and children's rooms in public libraries."

Shelving in Various Kinds of Libraries: In short, the arrangement of books should be decided keeping in view the needs of a particular library and its clientele. Classified order may be useful in general and academic libraries. In the case of national and other depository libraries, the arrangement of books may be accession wise or it be by sizes. The methods of compact storage may also be applied to secure maximum storage capacity.

Shelving Special Books and Non-book Materials

Bound Periodicals: A separate sequence may be prepared for keeping bound periodicals. If these are to be kept near the books on the related subjects, a parallel arrangement would be advisable. This Parallel arrangement implies two methods i.e., keeping periodicals on a particular subject just on the parallel shelves or by keeping periodicals on the uppermost or lower most planks of the shelves in which books on the related subjects are kept. Strict classified order though useful, is not economical. The former method is used in the Punjab University Library where each stack floor is divided into two wings i.e., in the one wing books on particular subjects are kept while in the second wing, bound periodicals on the related subjects are kept In Guwahati University Library, bound periodicals are shelved in the Periodicals and Reference Sections.

Rare Books and Manuscripts: Some books are rare because their duplicates are not easily available. Care must be taken for preserving them. The physique of such books is very weak. These should be handled with much attention and care. The following "Do's" and "Don'ts" for the treatment of rare books may be followed:

> "Do not mark on or in the book itself with ink; use pencil, use it lightly, and use it sparingly. Do not perforate. Do not stamp. Do no emboss. If call number is necessary, paste a label on the side of the book (not the spine) and write the call number on the label. Do not allow readers to use ink in taking notes. Put the book in a box or extra covers if it has to be housed in a dusty or dirty atmosphere or where there is much sunshine directly upon it. House in locked, dirt-proof bookcases, if possible. Guard more against physical harm to the book than against its theft, if a choice must be made. Shelving should be particularly smooth surfaced to prevent damage to the binding."

The manuscripts should be given a special care and treatment. All the manuscripts should be kept in a closed sequence and these should not be allowed to be handled by all persons.

Several Articles

Maps: For shelving maps, various kinds of storage cases are being used, such as oversize; legal size and correspondence size filing Cabinets and blueprint Cabinets. "When maps are frequently consulted, they probably should be laid flat in a blueprint Cabinet. Care should be taken that regardless of the case used, no more maps be put in a single folder or drawer than can be easily located, removed and refiled." In case of depository libraries, legal size Cabinets would be suitable but care should be taken that the paper used for such maps should be of superior quality, otherwise these would be spoiled by folding and refolding. The maps should be kept in envelops or folders which would also provide uniform surface for putting location numbers. A Cabinet of thirty 22-inch by 24-inch drawers may be used for filing maps horizontally and in alphabetical order. The maximum and minimum height of the Cabinets should be governed by the principle that the reading material were easily accessible. It should be about six feet high from the floor level.

Atlases: Atlases may be shelved in specially made ordinary cases or in drawers like cases. Larger atlases present problems of shelving because if these are shelved like books, the danger of damaging their bindings and pages looms large. If these are shelved in vertical fashion, the binding of the lowermost atlas is sure to be damaged. To avoid this, smaller volumes should be made to rest on larger and heavier atlases. Even the open-bar shelves are not suitable for shelving folio atlases because by friction the bindings are affected adversely.

Music: The music scores should be allowed to be used but without any damage because their physical construction is very fragile. In case the music scores are of book size, these should be bound and shelved like books. In case these are very thin, these may be bound in commercial pamphlet board bindings. The scores can also be tied by cardboard folders. Vertical file Cabinets may be used for shelving thinner music scores.

Pamphlets: The most practical solution for shelving pamphlets is the use of Manila folders which may be filed in the vertical file Cabinets. The pamphlets should be filed subject wise. The oft-used pamphlets should be got bound and be properly classified and catalogued. Comprehensive subject headings should be provided for the pamphlets. Periodical weeding of the out-of-date and unused pamphlets should be carried out in order to avoid unnecessary congestion in the files.

Films and Microfilms: Films and microfilms need 50 per cent relative humidity at 70°F like books. These must be kept free from dust. Films and microfilms being highly inflammable should be kept in metal storage Cabinets which may be filed in ordinary vertical files or file boxes. These need not be shelved along with books in a classified order because no special purpose will be served as these cannot be deciphered without projectors. Rather, these will be put to unnecessary dangers of mishandling.

Recordings: Recordings should be shelved vertically on specially constructed racks having pigeon holes at a distance of 4–5 inches, so that unnecessary lean may be avoided. But in those countries where the climate is warm and humid, it is better to shelve these in a horizontal manner otherwise the danger of warping increases.

9

LIBRARY STAFF

There are two broad classes of staff working in libraries-those involved in library and information work and those who provide back up services. These categories can be subdivided:

Qualified Librarian

Non-professional: The certificate Course after the school or a graduate is required.

Professional: The usual first step to professional degree from a university or college in library and information science. This degree should be followed by a post-graduate course from university or institute.

Fellow: Associates of five years' standing may be admitted to followship by submission of a thesis in librarianship (a significant and original contribution to the literature); by professional distinction; or by submission of published work in librarianship and information science which has made sustained and significant advancement in the field.

The Management: As a reflection of tile increase in demand for management skills, some library schools offer management emphasis. These are usually intended for experienced and qualified librarians, librarians with courses of advanced level, intended for experienced and qualified librarians.

Support Staff

Manual/ caretaking

Clerical/ secretarial

Technical and computer staff

Specialist

Library/information staff

Non-professional: Unqualified staff are usually educated to certificate or diploma in library science; national language as well as English should be known. They may have even higher qualifications which will enable them to take professional examinations. Non-professional staff are expected to undertake most of the routine work so that professionals can spend more time on intellectual work.

Some librarians have recognised the need for a career ladder for non-professional staff. Some libraries have three levels of library assistants: library assistants, senior library assistants, principal library assistants, These levels allow experienced and competent staff to progress to positions of responsibility, even though they don't wish to qualify.

Pre-professional: Broadly speaking all non-professional staff are pre-professional, but strictly the term relates to trainee librarians. The distinction is worth making, for trainees should be given some practice at professional duties and an attempt should be made to introduce them to a wider perspective of librarianship than they see in their immediate job. The use of trainees as a cheap source of high quality labour is unfair and on a par with the use of library school students on field work as convenient extra hands, available for clearing longstanding work and doing unpopular jobs.

Specialist: Professional librarians can specialise in many ways: by type of library, i.e., national, public, academic, special function, i.e., reference work, children's services, bibliographical services, etc.; or, perhaps, by subject interest, as in university libraries, where graduate qualified staff specialise in an area of the stock-selecting, cataloguing, classifying, and taking general responsibilities in that area. Some public libraries also employ subject specialist staff. In special libraries the knowledge of a particular subject area is very useful. Professional staff also carry out indexing, abstracting and translation work.

Managerial: Chief librarians are professional librarians with wider than average responsibilities, or professional managers comparable to industrial executives. Irrespective of the classification, it is evident that managerial expertise is now necessary for more senior posts in the profession.

Support Staff Manual/Caretaking: Libraries are expensive warehouses of knowledge. Equipment, stock, the buildings themselves are valuable. It makes good economic sense to employ people specifically to care for the library and its physical assets. Caretaking staff need to have qualities of reliabilities, responsibility and resourcefulness-many caretaking problems arise outside normal hours of work when senior staff cannot be consulted.

Clerical/Secretarial: The use of library assistants for clerical and secretarial work is inefficient: they are rarely trained clerical officers or typists and will not be effective at such tasks; they will be removed from library duties whilst undertaking other work. This is wasteful of their own skills; the work itself will be less accurate and will not have a professional finish. Many libraries employ secretarial and other clerical staff for these reasons; some libraries employ specialist receptionists.

Increased use of 'media resources' in libraries of all types, and the installation of computerised processes, have made technical knowledge essential. Although all staff concerned with handling new media should be trained in their use, large collections will require specialist technical staff. Computer processing in libraries has led to a need for trained operatives and, for libraries with in house systems, some technical expertise; such posts are often designated 'Technical Services Librarian'.

Specialist: Besides technical/ computer staff, libraries employ other classes of specialist. Some of these are:

- Large libraries often employ people with artistic talent to work on displays and exhibitions.
- Other specialist staff in libraries include advisory staff.

Library Information Staff

Non-professional

Pre-professional (trainee)

Professional

Specialist

Managerial

Other Personnel

Each department should be given supportive staff as detailed under the 'Norms'.

Filling Vacancies

Recruitment: Recruitment is the process of seeking and finding suitable people for jobs available in an organisation and includes the drawing up of a person specification for a job; the placing of advertisement and all those activities which aid the receipt of a number of applications from people qualified and experienced in the skills, knowledge and attitudes required. The prerequisites are job analysis and specification.

Person Specification: A person specification is the blueprint of an ideal employee; candidates for the job will be compared with it and close matches will be put on a 'short list'. There are seven headings under which a job and the ideal jobholder are judged, as given below:

1. Physical make-up;
2. Attainments;
3. Skills;
4. Work interests;
5. Work attitudes;
6. Personality;
7. Personal background.

Physical Make-up: Specifying physical requirements is harder than it first appears: vague statements like 'someone is needed who is fit'-do not actually describe standard levels of capability. For example, many people would consider, and describe, themselves as fit if they are capable of attending work and carrying out their duties: the job might, however, need someone who was strong enough to lift weights and carry them for distances-perhaps, a library assistant in a house bound readers' service with book boxes for users' individual choice, many of whom might live in flats with unreliable lifts. This heading also includes consideration of the impression the jobholder makes-i.e., personal manner, bearing and speech. Usually such features must be left to a personal interview when the general impression made by the candidate on the interviewing panel is taken as a measure of their impact on people in general.

Attainments: The job specification will usually define the knowledge and experience required to do the job adequately and so the question of qualifications and amounts of time spent in various types of work can be often answered direct from that specification. Jobs in libraries rarely leave this category blank, even the most junior of the library assistants in the smallest library must have a certain minimum standard of education.

Skills: There are various types of skill, for example, verbal influence is one, literacy another. It might be thought essential for anyone working in a library to be able to accurately file in alphabetical order. There are not many libraries who conduct tests of candidates' capability for alphabetisation all that is needed is a set of '5X3' cards with terms on them or authors' names which applicants could sort into either letter-by-letter or word-by-word order. Any skill required should be of specified standard, it is not an easy task as can be illustrated by looking at the difficulty of establishing a standard of verbal fluency.

Work interests: It is not an invasion on personal privacy to enquire about a candidate's interests both at work and away from it, as personal interests compatible with tasks performed at work are strong sources of job satisfaction. It is also sensible to appoint someone to a job as readers' adviser who expresses a personal interest in books and their contents.

Work Attitudes: Besides the importance of an individual's attitudes to work and the organisation, there is the question of aspects of job and the working situation which might cause dissatisfaction to the post-holder. The negative aspects of the job must be recognised and specified and attention must be paid to the characteristics of a person who would be least inconvenienced by them and happiest at work.

Personality: It is unrealistic to specify personality characteristics too closely, not only because terms are so imprecise and ambiguous, but also because we should only be concerned with those characteristics needed for adequate performance of the job. It is more useful to specify that 'flexibility' is sought, and to seek to establish this by investigating candidates' previous adaptability, that to rely on lists of traits like open-mindedness, honesty, etc. It is one of the paradoxes of the recruitment and selection process that personality, perhaps the most important of the variables, is the one least capable of identification prior to interview. Application forms do not give many clues to it, even references are unreliable.

Personal Background: Care must be taken with this category that unrealistic requirements are not set and that, in the subsequent selection process, candidates' privacy is not infringed. It is reasonable to specify that the candidate must live close to the work, or even occupy a service flat, if the job is a caretaking one which will need proximity. It is not reasonable to specify that the post-holder must be single and have no dependent, just because the panel feel that this will lead to better attendance at work. It is becoming rarer for application forms to require information on applicants' children and home circumstances. The wish expressed by some people that one's sex should not be asked for it is understandable, but the problem of gender and its possibility of impaired job chances is only postponed to the interview by such means.

One of the cheapest and most reliable ways of attracting candidates is by recommendation from present employees, at least this method is much used in industry and commerce. Libraries together with most other public service organisations, consider such methods incompatible with the aims of a fair recruitment policy and seek to fill posts by open competition.

Advertising: Professional posts are usually advertised in national papers, to ensure a wide audience.

Local papers are the best media for junior posts. It is unlikely that anyone would move to a new area for the post as a library assistant, and the expense of national coverage would be wasted.

Many libraries send application forms to prospective candidates. Reasons for doing this are:

(i) Personnel records can be standardised, it is easier to fill and compare applications on a standard form.

(ii) Incomplete applications can be avoided; the form can include all relevant headings.

(iii) Application forms are fairer to candidates-each receives an identical form and has, theoretically, an equal chance of success.

(iv) An application form is useful for cross checking in an interview.

Proof of Qualification

It is wise to ask candidates to bring documents proving qualifications, etc. to the interview. There is a risk of loss when original documents are sent by post, and obtaining copies is expensive. Documents which could be required include:

- Birth Certificate;
- Marriage Certificate;
- Degree or Qualification Certificates.

Selection: If recruitment is the process of casting the net and trawling for applicants, then selection is the stage of narrowing down the search; of discarding patently unsuitable people and investigating further those who seem to fit the person specification.

Short-listing: Short lists should be short. As a rule it is pointless to interview more than, perhaps, six candidates for anyone post. Interviewing time is expensive, especially when several senior staff comprise the panel, and there is a temptation to cut interview short when there are too many candidates to see. This is unfair to the applicants themselves and does not allow the panel time to make proper assessment.

It is important that a personal meeting should take place between an employer and a future employee. The mix of personalities will affect working performance and relations more than any other factor. The important qualifier to this is that the person doing the interviewing should be the one who will work with the post-holder otherwise the benefits of assessing the personality mix do not accrue. The interview as a method of selection has been heavily criticised; it is subjective, short and necessarily pressured occasion. Candidates who perform well at interview may not perform well in the job and, conversely, a bad interview is no true indicator of poor job performance. Interviewers are rarely well trained and adopt at the art of asking pertinent questions expertly, unless they have received specific training or are professional personnel department staff. Unfortunately, the interview is a popular and common feature of the selection process so that the best hope seems to be to limits its worst failings and maximise its benefits.

Panel Interview: A panel interview requires two or more people acting as interviewers at the same time. Panels are used for several reasons; bias can be lessened by a mix of opinions on a candidate; better information on the job is possible when several staff can answer questions; candidates are given an opportunity to meet a number of their future superiors. Disadvantages are: large numbers of interviewers can make candidates unduly nervous by creating an 'on-trial' atmosphere; as numbers on the panel increase the scenario becomes more difficult to stage, e.g., who will ask what?

Selection by Interview

A personal interview is conducted by one interviewer. Advantages are: a more relaxed style can be adopted, both by the candidate and the interviewer; the interview is easier to plan and the progression of topics likely to be more natural. Conversely, there is a possibility of bias as the interviewer must rely on his own personal opinion without the need to justify his reasons.

Serial interviews are sequential interviews with any number of interviewers. They can be arranged into a series of personal interviews, if informality is required, or they can be used to break up an unwieldy panel into digestible chunks. The main advantages depend on the particular structure of each interview i.e., candidates will feel relaxed only if each serial interview is informal- and the longer one taken up by this form of interview can be conducive to either increased relaxation, or anxiety. The problem of bias is avoided by this method.

Providing Training

Systematic Framework: Training is expensive, not only must the cost of the trainer's time be calculated, but the trainees' as well. Materials, premises used and the cost of any library equipment damaged also should be added to the total. In terms of the library's objectives, the only real justification for money spent in training is that it should contribute to the aims and purposes of the service and that the same objective could not have been achieved in any cheaper way. The most useful way of ensuring that training is cost-effective is to utilise a framework like the one outlined in figure.

The Diagnosis: This stage, although seeming far removed from training, is the vital first step. The manpower plan for the service is derived from long term objectives— a library planning to install a complete system of computerised charging in two years' time might be wise to specify some suitable training programmes for its staff well before the event and to plan for the recruitment of relevant staff if training were seen to be only partially a solution. Conversely, a library intending to subscribe to an on line system for bibliographic control and processing would be foolish to recruit and train librarians in cataloguing skills, under the old system.

The Requirements

With training the key to success is to put last things first. The simple equation for analysis requires first a statement of the knowledge, skills and attitudes needed in staff for adequate performance of the particular task. The setting of standards for these three components is a necessary and skilled part of professional training. Put very simply, the trainer must ask, 'What would I like the trainees to be able to do, or know, before?' This question addresses the crucial problem of training; the answer to it will often show that training is not the best solution to the library's problem. An example will clarify:

A library is having problems with long lunch time queues of borrowers at the books-returned desk. Furthermore, borrowers have been complaint that the counter staff are abrupt to the point of rudeness. One approach might be to train all counter staff in interpersonal skills with emphasis on courtesy and also to train them in processing of books and manipulation of files. This approach assumes that the staff are the problem and seeks to solve training.

Another could be to replace the Browne charging system manual filing of tickets by a faster, mechanised or even auto one. Job design approaches would also include looking methods employed by staff when dicharging books to see if better ones could be devised, without significant loss of accuracy studying the actions and reactions of staff and the movements by them to ensure that poor counter layout is not contributing problem. When terminal behaviour has been decided upon, the trainer set the standard of skills, knowledge and attitudes required as behaviour in each trainee. This does not mean-'What knowledge skills and attitudes does each trainee have?' but 'What is the minimum level of knowledge, skills and attitudes we wish trainee to have before they are considered suitable for training entry onto the programme?'

The training need, or gap, is simply the difference between the standards. The range of methods for training is almost as wide variety of phenomena that could be learning to take place-the essential difference being that training is purposive, i.e., that someone structured a learning experience for the benefit of someone.

Methods include lectures, demonstrations, programmed learning experiential earning (where the trainee experiences at first hand) role playing and other forms of simulation (case studies being intellectual equivalent), and, of course, reading staff manuals other texts. If the audio visual media are also included it becomes very long. Evidently trainers do not have a problem of limited range of methods for training. The method chosen will depend on the component of the knowledge, attitudes mix being developed as well as on the available funding. Lectures are cheap, for example lecturer and many listeners, but not noted for their value in training-you do not learn how to operate a computer keyboard by hearing about the layout. One of the vexed questions is whether or not to trail house. Libraries with very customised processes are obliged to train, their own staff internally. This does not often happen at professional level; it is assumed that the output of library schools meets at least the initial basic requirements of libraries.

The Assessment

Training is evaluated by measuring the total value of the training programme to the attainment of the library's objectives in terms of the cost/benefit equation. The validity of a training course is assessed in terms of its success or otherwise in attaining the objectives for it evaluation differs in that it must include an assessment of the costs of the training.

Libraries can test the value of their training programmes by observation of employee performance afterwards by testing formally the skills and knowledge learned; by conducting systematic performance appraisal and by various forms of follow-up investigation. There is no firm distinction between the terms training and education, but the difference can be explained as follows: Training should develop certain skills, knowledge and attitudes in the employee which will be useful in job performance. These skills can be practical, e.g., filing, or intellectual, e.g., handling users enquiries. Education should develop wider potential in the student by opening up new fields and perspectives without immediate relevance to any particular job. Teaching of practical skills is often incorporated in education; these can be necessary as a foundation for further learning but are only means to an end.

Induction Training: A new member of staff needs to be introduced to the library as an organisation and to understand what part his own job plays in achieving library objectives. Induction training begins before new employee comes to work and includes the information he is given about the library and the job he is applying for. Many librarians feel that the early weeks in a job are very important; too important for new staff to be left to sink or swim, collecting experience and information where they can. In many government departments, large industrial firms, and some academic institutions all new staff, including library staff, are given a short induction course. The usual length of such a course is between 3 to 10 days.

The nature of induction training makes delay unwise. A programme of induction is pointless if left until the employee has worked in the job for six months. The amount of training appropriate for induction depends on the size and complexity of the library system and the age and experience of the employee. There is tendency to rush induction programmes, especially in library where staff are scarce. Rushed 'courses usually result in information 'flooding', and participants retain little of what they hear, usually the less-important details. Lengthy courses, on the one hand, can create impatience in the employee who is anxious to get to grips with his 'new job'.

In-service/Job Training: The most obvious training need for any employee is instruction and practice in the tasks comprising his job. Job training is a way reducing expensive mistakes and accelerating learning on basic skills. The usual method is for colleagues, or immediate superiors to instruct the new entrant in the manner known as 'watch Nellie'. This casual approach can have drawbacks:

(i) Existing staff can pass on mistakes as well as experience;

(ii) Not all staff are competent instructors;

(iii) Traditional methods are not always best for present need rigidity of approach can result from such 'handed-down information.

On the plus side such training is the easiest, cheapest way of familiarising staff with new tasks. Existing staff are knowledged about the job in the context of that particular library.

Continuation/Development Training: As user's needs change so much library staff alter and the tasks they do and the ways they do them. Continuation trail aims to develop new skills in all staff-both newly arrived and more experienced-to prevent any divergence of purpose between library objectives and the tasks designed to achieve them.

Specialist Training: Professional staff may develop interests in specialist library work. Examples are: reference service, children's services, real advisory work; not everyone is clear about their special subjects at Library School. Specialist training is beneficial to both library and staff career development. Large systems, especially those with professional training officers, can run such course house.

Management Training: It is not easy to pinpoint the stage at which management skills become necessary; the librarian in charge of even the smallest library has a staff to deploy and a service to manage. The more senior posts, especially in large libraries, involve management of large staff, stocks, and budgets and increasingly require professional management expertise.

Increasing size and complexity of library systems-and changes in the technology and products they employ-make management training more and more necessary. The large management schools have been slow to respond to the needs of the public services, although now there are a variety of courses geared to a non-profit making sector. Another problem for senior librarians is that time away from work is hard to obtain-the very people who most need management training are the ones least able to be spared. Part time courses minimise the problem, at least as far as retention of a job is concerned; it does not alleviate workload, though, but adds to it and, for this reason, part time management courses are recognised as endurance tests in their own right.

Judging the Capability

An organisation which recruits and selects people with the appropriate skills, knowledge and experience and which conducts training systematically is likely to do performance appraisal. Performance appraisal is normally done annually and by the employee's immediate superior. The process is subjective, even though it is often given a veneer of objectivity by the use of rating scales; bias can be minimised by the superior discussing the employee's strengths and weaknesses with him and explaining the basis of the assessment by having more than one person make the appraisal; and by ensuring that all employees undergo the same process and with the same documentation. Performance appraisal is used for probation, for employee training and development, and for promotion purposes.

10

MANAGEMENT OF LIBRARY AND INFORMATION CENTRES

Historical Development

Difficulties arise in tracing the history of management. Some see it (by definition) as a late-modern (in the sense of late modernity) conceptualisation. On those terms it cannot have a pre-modern history, only harbingers (such as stewards). Others, however, detect management-like-thought back to Sumerian traders and to the builders of the pyramids of ancient Egypt. Slave-owners through the centuries faced the problems of exploiting/motivating a dependent but sometimes unenthusiastic or recalcitrant workforce, but many pre-industrial enterprises, given their small scale, did not feel compelled to face the issues of management systematically. However, innovations such as the spread of Hindu-Arabic numerals (5th to 15th centuries) and the codification of double-entry bookkeeping (1494) provided tools for management assessment, planning and control.

With the changing workplaces of industrial revolutions in the 18th and 19th centuries, military theory and practice contributed approaches to managing the newly-popular factories.

Given the scale of most commercial operations and the lack of mechanised record-keeping and recording before the industrial revolution, it made sense for most owners of enterprises in those times to carry out management functions by and for themselves. But with growing size and complexity of organisations, the split between owners (individuals, industrial dynasties or groups of shareholders) and day-to-day managers (independent specialists in planning and control) gradually became more common.

Early Writing

While management (according to some definitions) has existed for millennia, several writers have created a background of works that assisted in modern management theories. Some ancient military texts have been cited for lessons that civilian managers can gather. For example, Chinese general Sun Tzu in the 6th century BC, *The Art of War,* recommends being aware of and acting on strengths and weaknesses of both a manager's organisation and a foe's.

Various ancient and medieval civilizations have produced "mirrors for Princes" books, which aim to advise new monarchs on how to govern. Examples include the Indian Arthashastra by Chanakya (written around 300BC), and *The Prince* by Italian author Niccolo Machiavelli (c. 1515).

Written in 1776 by Adam Smith, a Scottish moral philosopher, *The Wealth of Nations* discussed efficient organisation of work through division of labour. Smith described how changes in processes could boost productivity in the manufacture of pins. While individuals could produce 200 pins per day, Smith analysed the steps involved in manufacture and, with 10 specialists, enabled production of 48,000 pins per day.

19th Century

Classical economists such as Adam Smith (1723–1790) and John Stuart Mill (1806–1873) provided a theoretical background to resource-allocation, production, and pricing issues. About the same time, innovators like Eli Whitney (1765–1825), James Watt (1736–1819), and Matthew Boulton (1728–1809) developed elements of technical production such as standardisation, quality-control procedures, cost-accounting, interchangeability of parts, and work-planning. Many of these aspects of management existed in the pre-1861 slave-based sector of the US economy. That environment saw 4 million people, as the contemporary usages had it, "managed" in profitable quasi-mass production.

Salaried managers as an identifiable group first became prominent in the late 19th century.

20th Century

By about 1900 one finds managers trying to place their theories on what they regarded as a thoroughly scientific basis. Examples include Henry R. Towne's *Science of management* in the 1890s, Frederick Winslow Taylor's *The Principles of Scientific Management* (1911), Frank and Lillian Gilbreth's *Applied motion study* (1917), and Henry L. Gantt's charts (1910s). J. Duncan wrote the first college management textbook in 1911. In 1912 Yoichi Ueno introduced Taylorism to Japan and became first management consultant of the "Japanese-management style". His son Ichiro Ueno pioneered Japanese quality assurance.

The first comprehensive theories of management appeared around 1920. The Harvard Business School offered the first Master of Business Administration degree (MBA) in 1921. People like Henri Fayol (1841–1925) and Alexander Church described the various branches of management and their interrelationships. In the early 20th century, people like Ordway Tead (1891–1973), Walter Scott and J. Mooney applied the principles of psychology to management, while other writers, such as Elton Mayo (1880–1949), Mary Parker Follett (1868–1933), Chester Barnard (1886–1961), Max Weber (1864–1920), Rensis Likert (1903–1981), and Chris Argyris (* 1923) approached the phenomenon of management from a sociological perspective. Peter Drucker (1909–2005) wrote one of the earliest books on applied management: *Concept of the Corporation* (published in 1946). It resulted from Alfred Sloan (chairman of General Motors until 1956) commissioning a study of the organisation. Drucker went on to write 39 books, many in the same vein.

H. Dodge, Ronald Fisher (1890–1962), and Thornton C. Fry introduced statistical techniques into management-studies. In the 1940s, Patrick Blackett worked in the development of the applied mathematics science of operations research, initially for military operations. Operations research, sometimes known as "management science" (but distinct from Taylor's scientific management), attempts to take a scientific approach to solving decision problems, and can be directly applied to multiple management problems, particularly in the areas of logistics and operations.

Some of the more recent developments include the Theory of Constraints, management by objectives, re-engineering, Six Sigma and various information-technology-driven theories such as agile software development, as well as group management theories such as Cog's Ladder.

As the general recognition of managers as a class solidified during the 20th century and gave perceived practitioners of the art/science of management a certain amount of prestige, so the way opened for popularised systems of management ideas to peddle their wares. In this context many management fads may have had more to do with pop psychology than with scientific theories of management.

Towards the end of the 20th century, business management came to consist of six separate branches, namely:

- Human resource management;
- Operations management or production management;
- Strategic management;
- Marketing management;
- Financial management;
- Information technology management responsible for management information systems.

21st Century

In the 21st century observers find it increasingly difficult to subdivide management into functional categories in this way. More and more processes simultaneously involve several categories. Instead, one tends to think in terms of the various processes, tasks, and objects subject to management.

Branches of management theory also exist relating to non-profits and to government: such as public administration, public management, and educational management. Further, management programmes related to civil-society organisations have also spawned programmes in non-profit management and social entrepreneurship.

Note that many of the assumptions made by management have come under attack from business-ethics viewpoints, critical management studies, and anti-corporate activism.

As one consequence, workplace democracy has become both more common, and more advocated, in some places distributing all management functions among workers, each of whom takes on a portion of the work. However, these models predate any current political issue, and may occur more naturally than does a command hierarchy. All management embraces to some degree a democratic principle—in that in the long term, the majority of workers must support management. Otherwise, they leave to find other work or go on strike. Despite the move towards workplace democracy, command-and-control organisation structures remain commonplace as *de facto* organisation structure. Indeed, the entrenched nature of command-and-control is evident in the way that recent layoffs have been conducted with management ranks affected far less than employees at the lower levels. In some cases, management has even rewarded itself with bonuses after laying off lower-level workers.

According to leadership academic Manfred F.R. Kets de Vries, a contemporary senior management team will almost inevitably have some personality disorders.

Topics

Basic Functions: Management operates through various functions, often classified as planning, organising, staffing, leading/directing, controlling/monitoring and motivation.

- *Planning:* Deciding what needs to happen in the future (today, next week, next month, next year, over the next five years, etc.) and generating plans for action.
- *Organising:* (Implementation) pattern of relationships among workers, making optimum use of the resources required to enable the successful carrying out of plans.
- *Staffing:* Job analysis, recruitment and hiring for appropriate jobs.
- *Leading/directing:* Determining what must be done in a situation and getting people to do it.
- *Controlling/monitoring:* Checking progress against plans.
- *Motivation:* Motivation is also a kind of basic function of management, because without motivation, employees cannot work effectively. If motivation does not take place in an organisation, then employees may not contribute to the other functions (which are usually set by top-level management).
- *Communicating:* Is giving, receiving, or exchange information.
- *Creating:* Ability to produce original Idea, thought through the use of imagination.

Basic Roles

- *Interpersonal:* Roles that involve coordination and interaction with employees.
- *Informational:* Roles that involve handling, sharing, and analysing information.
- *Decisional:* Roles that require decision-making.

Management Skills

- *Political:* Used to build a power base and establish connections.
- *Conceptual:* Used to analyse complex situations.
- *Interpersonal:* Used to communicate, motivate, mentor and delegate.
- *Diagnostic:* Ability to visualise most appropriate response to a situation.
- *Technical:* Expertise in one's particular functional area.

Formation of the Business Policy

- The mission of the business is the most obvious purpose—which may be, for example, to make soap.
- The vision of the business reflects its aspirations and specifies its intended direction or future destination.
- The objectives of the business refers to the ends or activity that is the goal of a certain task.
- The business's policy is a guide that stipulates rules, regulations and objectives, and may be used in the managers' decision-making. It must be flexible and easily interpreted and understood by all employees.
- The business's strategy refers to the coordinated plan of action it takes and resources it uses to realise its vision and long-term objectives. It is a guideline to managers, stipulating

how they ought to allocate and use the factors of production to the business's advantage. Initially, it could help the managers decide on what type of business they want to form.

Implementation of Policies and Strategies

- All policies and strategies must be discussed with all managerial personnel and staff.
- Managers must understand where and how they can implement their policies and strategies.
- A plan of action must be devised for each department.
- Policies and strategies must be reviewed regularly.
- Contingency plans must be devised in case the environment changes.
- Top-level managers should carry out regular progress assessments.
- The business requires team spirit and a good environment.
- The missions, objectives, strengths and weaknesses of each department must be analysed to determine their roles in achieving the business's mission.
- The forecasting method develops a reliable picture of the business's future environment.
- A planning unit must be created to ensure that all plans are consistent and that policies and strategies are aimed at achieving the same mission and objectives.

All policies must be discussed with all managerial personnel and staff that is required in the execution of any departmental policy.

- Organisational change is strategically achieved through the implementation of the eight-step plan of action established by John P. Kotter: Increase urgency, get the vision right, communicate the buy-in, empower action, create short-term wins, don't let up, and make change stick.

Policies and Strategies in the Planning Process

- They give mid and lower-level managers a good idea of the future plans for each department in an organisation.
- A framework is created whereby plans and decisions are made.
- Mid and lower-level management may add their own plans to the business's strategies.

Levels of Management

Most organisations have three management levels: first-level, middle-level, and top-level managers. These managers are classified in a hierarchy of authority, and perform different tasks. In many organisations, the number of managers in every level resembles a pyramid. Each level is explained below in specifications of their different responsibilities and likely job titles.

Top-level Managers

The top consists of the board of directors (including non-executive directors and executive directors), President, Vice-President, CEOs and other members of the C-level executives. They are responsible for controlling and overseeing the entire organisation. They set a tone at the top and develop strategic plans, company policies, and make decisions on the direction of the business. In addition, top-level managers play a significant role in the mobilisation of outside resources and are accountable to the shareholders and general public.

The board of directors is typically primarily composed of non-executives which owe a fiduciary duty to shareholders and are not closely involved in the day-to-day activities of the organisation, although this varies depending on the type (e.g., public versus private), size and culture of the organisation. These directors are theoretically liable for breaches of that duty and typically insured under directors and officers liability insurance. Fortune 500 directors are estimated to spend 4.4 hours per week on board duties, and median compensation was $212,512 in 2010. The board sets corporate strategy, makes major decisions such as major acquisitions, and hires, evaluates, and fires the top-level manager (Chief Executive Officer or CEO) and the CEO typically hires other positions. However, board involvement in the hiring of other positions such as the Chief Financial Officer (CFO) has increased. In 2013, a survey of over 160 CEOs and directors of public and private companies found that the top weaknesses of CEOs were "mentoring skills" and "board engagement", and 10 per cent of companies never evaluated the CEO. The board may also have certain employees (e.g., internal auditors) report to them or directly hire independent contractors; for example, the board (through the audit committee) typically selects the auditor.

Helpful skills of top management vary by the type of organisation but typically include a broad understanding competition, world economies, and politics. In addition, the CEO is responsible for executing and determining (within the board's framework) the broad policies of the organisation. Executive management accomplishes the day-to-day details, including: instructions for preparation of department budgets, procedures, schedules; appointment of middle level executives such as department managers; coordination of departments; media and governmental relations; and shareholder communication.

Middle-level Managers

Consist of general managers, branch managers and department managers. They are accountable to the top management for their department's function. They devote more time to organisational and directional functions. Their roles can be emphasised as executing organisational plans in conformance with the company's policies and the objectives of the top management, they define and discuss information and policies from top management to lower management, and most importantly they inspire and provide guidance to lower level managers towards better performance. Their functions include:

- Design and implement effective group and inter-group work and information systems.
- Define and monitor group-level performance indicators.
- Diagnose and resolve problems within and among work groups.
- Design and implement reward systems that support cooperative behaviour. They also make decision and share ideas with top managers.

First-level Managers

Consist of supervisors, section leaders, foremen, etc. They focus on controlling and directing. They usually have the responsibility of assigning employees tasks, guiding and supervising employees on day-to-day activities, ensuring quality and quantity production, making recommendations, suggestions, and up channelling employee problems, etc. First-level managers are role models for employees that provide:

- Basic supervision;
- Motivation;

- Career planning;
- Performance feedback.

Statistical Computing

The rapid and sustained increases in computing power starting from the second half of the 20th century have had a substantial impact on the practice of statistical science. Early statistical models were almost always from the class of linear models, but powerful computers, coupled with suitable numerical algorithms, caused an increased interest in non-linear models (such as neural networks) as well as the creation of new types, such as generalised linear models and multilevel models. Increased computing power has also led to the growing popularity of computationally intensive methods based on resampling, such as permutation tests and the bootstrap, while techniques such as Gibbs sampling have made use of Bayesian models more feasible. The computer revolution has implications for the future of statistics with new emphasis on "experimental" and "empirical" statistics. A large number of both general and special purpose statistical software are now available.

Misuse

There is a general perception that statistical knowledge is all-too-frequently intentionally misused by finding ways to interpret only the data that are favourable to the presenter. A mistrust and misunderstanding of statistics is associated with the quotation, "There are three kinds of lies: lies, damned lies, and statistics". Misuse of statistics can be both inadvertent and intentional, and the book *How to Lie With Statistics* outlines a range of considerations. In an attempt to shed light on the use and misuse of statistics, reviews of statistical techniques used in particular fields are conducted (e.g. Warne, Lazo, Ramos, and Ritter (2012)).

Ways to avoid misuse of statistics include using proper diagrams and avoiding bias. Misuse can occur when conclusions are overgeneralised and claimed to be representative of more than they really are, often by either deliberately or unconsciously overlooking sampling bias. Bar graphs are arguably the easiest diagrams to use and understand, and they can be made either by hand or with simple computer programmes. Unfortunately, most people do not look for bias or errors, so they are not noticed. Thus, people may often believe that something is true even if it is not well represented. To make data gathered from statistics believable and accurate, the sample taken must be representative of the whole. According to Huff, "The dependability of a sample can be destroyed by [bias]... allow yourself some degree of scepticism."

To assist in the understanding of statistics Huff proposed a series of questions to be asked in each case:

- Who says so? (Does he/she have an axe to grind?);
- How does he/she know? (Does he/she have the resources to know the facts?);
- What's missing? (Does he/she give us a complete picture?);
- Did someone change the subject? (Does he/she offer us the right answer to the wrong problem?);
- Does it make sense? (Is his/her conclusion logical and consistent with what we already know?).

Statistics Applied to Mathematics and Arts

Traditionally, statistics was concerned with drawing inferences using a semi-standardised methodology that was "required learning" in most sciences. This has changed with use of statistics in non-inferential contexts. What was once considered a dry subject, taken in many fields as a degree-requirement, is now viewed enthusiastically. Initially derided by some mathematical purists, it is now considered essential methodology in certain areas.

- In number theory, scatter plots of data generated by a distribution function may be transformed with familiar tools used in statistics to reveal underlying patterns, which may then lead to hypotheses.
- Methods of statistics including predictive methods in forecasting are combined with chaos theory and fractal geometry to create video works that are considered to have great beauty.
- The process art of Jackson Pollock relied on artistic experiments whereby underlying distributions in nature were artistically revealed. With the advent of computers, statistical methods were applied to formalise such distribution-driven natural processes to make and analyse moving video art.
- Methods of statistics may be used predicatively in performance art, as in a card trick based on a Markov process that only works some of the time, the occasion of which can be predicted using statistical methodology.
- Statistics can be used to predicatively create art, as in the statistical or stochastic music invented by Iannis Xenakis, where the music is performance-specific. Though this type of artistry does not always come out as expected, it does behave in ways that are predictable and tunable using statistics.

Etymology

The verb 'manage' comes from the Italian *maneggiare* (to handle, especially tools), which derives from the Latin word *manus* (hand). The French word *mesnagement* (later *menagement*) influenced the development in meaning of the English word *management* in the 17th and 18th centuries.

Definitions

Views on the definition and scope of management include:

- Management defined as the organisation and coordination of the activities of an enterprise in accordance with certain policies and in achievement of clearly defined objectives.
- Fredmund Malik defines as Management is the transformation of resources into utility.
- Management included as one of the factors of production - along with machines, materials and money.
- Peter Drucker (1909–2005) sees the basic task of a management as twofold: marketing and innovation. Nevertheless, innovation is also linked to marketing (product innovation is a central strategic marketing issue). Peter Drucker identifies marketing as a key essence for business success, but management and marketing are generally understood as two different branches of business administration knowledge.
- Directors and managers should have the authority and responsibility to make decisions to direct an enterprise when given the authority.
- As a discipline, management comprises the interlocking functions of formulating corporate policy and organising, planning, controlling, and directing a firm's resources to achieve a policy's objectives.

- The size of management can range from one person in a small firm to hundreds or thousands of managers in multinational companies.
- In large firms, the board of directors formulates the policy that the chief executive officer implements.

Library Management

Library management is a sub-discipline of institutional management that focuses on specific issues faced by libraries and library management professionals. Library management encompasses normal management tasks as well as intellectual freedom, anti-censorship, and fundraising tasks. Issues faced in library management frequently overlap those faced in management of non-profit organisations.

Basic Functions

Basic tasks in library management include:

- Planning the acquisition of materials;
- Negotiating borrowing materials from other libraries;
- Selection of library materials;
- Stacks maintenance;
- Fee collection in proper way;
- Membership management;
- Responding to challenges;
- Approving and designing events;
- Fundraising.

Common Library Constructs

Most physical libraries that store solid media, such as books, articles, film, and other artifacts, adhere to some derivative of the Dewey Decimal System as their method for tagging, storing, and retrieving artifacts based on unique identifiers. The use of such systems have caused librarians to develop and leverage common constructs that act as tools for, both, librarians and users of libraries, and which are now found in most libraries. These constructs include things like:

- *Master Catalogues:* A Master Catalogue acts as a catalogue of all domain or topic specific catalogues and often directs the user to a more specific area of a library, where the user can find a more specific Domain Catalogue. For example, upon entering a very large library, you may find a Master Catalogue that will direct you to specific wings of the library, where each wing focuses on a specific topic area, such as law, history, fiction, etc.
- *Domain Catalogues:* Domain Catalogues are usually a system of very large libraries, where the Master Catalogue cannot hold all information. As a result, the Master Catalogue leads the user to Domain Catalogues that contain homogeneous references to specific artifacts that fall within the category or domain assigned to that catalogue. For example, a very large library may have many Domain Catalogues; one for law, one for history, one for fiction, etc. In the case of smaller libraries where the use of Domain Catalogues are not needed, The Master Catalogue can contain all information.

- *Indexes:* An index represents a grouping of artifacts by some relevant grouping constraint. The most common index groupings are *"by title," "by subject,"* and *"by author."*
- *Unique Identifiers:* Unique identifiers, often referred to as IDs, represent a means of assigning and tagging an artifact with a readable string of characters that is unique to that single artifact. Such identifiers usually include the address or location of the artifact, within the library, and a unique character set that helps to distinguish artifacts that have common traits, such as common titles. Such unique identifiers are also broken into tokens. Such unique identifiers are usually placed somewhere on the surface of the artifact being stored, such as on the binder of a book, to facilitate location by the user.
- *Unique Identifier Tokens:* Unique identification strings are broken into predefined and fixed position segments or substrings. Each segment is called a token and represents a mapping to something meaningful. For example, one token may lead a user to a specific wing of a library, another might lead the user to a specific aisle within that wing, another to a specific bookcase within that ailse, etc., all ultimately leading to the artifact, itself. Such tokens are often separated by a character that is often referred to as a tokenizer (e.g. "." or ":").
- *Artifacts:* Artifacts represent those original things or authorised copies of things that are being categorised, stored within, and retrieved from libraries. Examples of artifacts include books, periodicals, research documentation, film, and computer disks.

Long-term Issues

Long-term issues include:

- Planning the construction of new libraries;
- Extensions to existing ones;
- Building maintenance;
- Updating the information books and new version.

Planning and Maintaining Library Facilities

An important aspect of library management is planning and maintaining library facilities. Planning the construction of new libraries or remodelling those that exist is integral as user needs are often changing. To supplement their operating budget, managers often secure funding through gifts and fundraising. The site for new construction must be located, the building must be designed, constructed, and then evaluated. Once established, it is important that the building management keep up on regular maintenance. This can also be completed by delegating tasks to maintenance personal or hiring an outside company through bids.

Associations

- Library Leadership and Management Association

The Library Leadership and Management Association (LLAMA), a division of the American Library Association, provides leaders with webinar, conferences, awards and grants, *Library Leadership and Management* (online quarterly magazine), and books. LLAMA membership includes a free subscription to great leadership *Library Leadership and Management* and discounts on conferences and publications.

Publications

The *Journal of Library Administration* began in 1980 and is currently published by Routledge, 8 times per year. It is a peer-reviewed academic journal that discusses issues pertaining to library management.

Coordinating Efforts

Management in business and organisations means to coordinate the efforts of people to accomplish goals and objectives using available resources efficiently and effectively. Management comprises planning, organising, staffing, leading or directing, and controlling an organisation or initiative to accomplish a goal. Resourcing encompasses the deployment and manipulation of human resources, financial resources, technological resources, and natural resources.

Since organisations can be viewed as systems, management can also be defined as human action, including design, to facilitate the production of useful outcomes from a system. This view opens the opportunity to 'manage' oneself, a prerequisite to attempting to manage others.

Theoretical Scope

Management involves the manipulation of the human capital of an enterprise to contribute to the success of the enterprise. This implies effective communication: an enterprise environment (as opposed to a physical or mechanical mechanism), implies human motivation and implies some sort of successful progress or system outcome. As such, management is not the manipulation of a mechanism (machine or automated programme), not the herding of animals, and can occur in both a legal as well as illegal enterprise or environment. Based on this, management must have humans, communication, and a positive enterprise endeavour. Plans, measurements, motivational psychological tools, goals, and economic measures (profit, etc.) may or may not be necessary components for there to be management. At first, one views management functionally, such as measuring quantity, adjusting plans, meeting goals. This applies even in situations where planning does not take place. From this perspective, Henri Fayol (1841–1925) considers management to consist of six functions:

1. Forecasting;
2. Planning;
3. Organising;
4. Commanding;
5. Coordinating;
6. Controlling.

Henri Fayol was one of the most influential contributors to modern concepts of management.

In another way of thinking, Mary Parker Follett (1868–1933), defined management as "the art of getting things done through people". She described management as philosophy.

Some people, however, find this definition useful but far too narrow. The phrase "management is what managers do" occurs widely, suggesting the difficulty of defining management, the shifting nature of definitions and the connection of managerial practices with the existence of a managerial cadre or class. One habit of thought regards management as equivalent to "business administration" and thus excludes management in places outside commerce, as for example in charities and in the public sector. More broadly, every organisation must manage its work, people, processes, technology, etc. to maximise effectiveness. Nonetheless, many people refer to university departments that teach management as "business schools". Some institutions (such as the Harvard Business School) use that name while others (such as the Yale School of Management) employ the more inclusive term "management".

English speakers may also use the term "management" or "the management" as a collective word describing the managers of an organisation, for example of a corporation. Historically this use of the term often contrasted with the term "Labour" - referring to those being managed.

Nature of Managerial Work

In for-profit work, management has as its primary function the satisfaction of a range of stakeholders. This typically involves making a profit (for the shareholders), creating valued products at a reasonable cost (for customers), and providing rewarding employment opportunities for employees. In non-profit management, add the importance of keeping the faith of donors. In most models of management and governance, shareholders vote for the board of directors, and the board then hires senior management. Some organisations have experimented with other methods (such as employee-voting models) of selecting or reviewing managers, but this is rare.

In the public sector of countries constituted as representative democracies, voters elect politicians to public office. Such politicians hire many managers and administrators, and in some countries like the United States political appointees lose their jobs on the election of a new President/ governor/mayor.

11

Classification Method

(Advance Knowledge Organisation)

The philosopher, John Dewey, claimed that knowledge is classification. Aristotle, Bacon and other philosophers had given concepts of systematic classification of knowledge, which have been utilised in library for many years and also influenced the library classification system. Dr. Ranganathan puts classification under law of library science. He says, 'A library is a growing organism as knowledge itself is growing; it is necessary that classification must be comprehensive, embracing all past and present knowledge and allowing places for any possible additions to knowledge'. Classification simplifies the process of thought. This is true of formal thinking or logic. When we design the course of study, pursue research or locate any information, we make use of classification, a kind of map of knowledge.

Classification is the process by which we group like things together. All the members of a group of like things share at least characteristics which members of other group do not possess. Characteristics are applied as the basis for finding out the likeliness between things. A characteristic is an attribute by which concept grouped or subjects divided. For example, we may keep lions, tigers and leopards close to each other by grouping them in a zoo; we observe that they are having a common characteristic of cat family which elephants, camel and hare do not possess.

The recognition of likenesses may be performed by machine by human beings. Human perception for like characteristics attributes may be intuitive or the result of conscious thought, for example we all are classifying things in our day to day life and we do in normal course. We never keep books and shoes together. We always separate each one according to their characteristics attribute, qualities and traits. There is always a purpose behind all classification. The same thing can be classified by different persons in different ways. We go to grocer shop we mark that grocer arranges his coins in numerical order, but a numismatist arranges them in a historical sequences. So the arrangement or classifications are made for the convenience. A grocer also arranges his commodities in such a way that he can locate which commodity is kept in which place. He classifies things in his own ways, so that he can directly go to the commodity that is asked for. So the object of classification is convenience. Convenience that matters the, particular way in which things are to be arranged and classified. Classification has everyday practical uses, for example supermarkets are organised so that all products of the similar nature are kept together whether it is meat or vegetables or dairy products or home appliances. Further they are subdivided into subgroups like mutton, chicken, potato, onion, garlic, butter, cooking oils, milk, cream, mixer, refrigerator, fan cooler and others. Without classification supermarkets would be unpleasant to use or carry on business. In the same way warehouses and factory stores arrange goods and parts together according to how they are used.

Classification is a mental process primarily. The idea or the concept of the thing is judged by experience of our mind, we develop a group or separate the dissimilar characteristic and create another group by our mental process. This mental process is an aid to our memory. This classification is an important work in library science. When library professionals classify books, they arrange in the most convenient order. This convenience is always directed towards storage and sorting of the documents. Classification gives the action of classifying and then result of classifying. The action of classifying indicates the physical action of sorting and the result of classifying indicates the mental process that dictates sorting.

Classification displays the relationships between things, and between classes of things. We see that members of the class PAINTINGS differ from the members of class DRAWINGS; but also that these two classes have a closer relationship with each other than either has with the class SCULPTURE, because they share the quality of being two dimensional. In the same way we appreciate that these three classes are related, because they are all kind of what is called Fine Art. The result of classification-is the display of network or Pattern of Relationships.

There are many possible ways of arranging books. Size, colour, binding, by press, by publisher, date of publication, by author, by title or by subjects are generally the factors. These factors are considered to determine the arrangement. But in practice this does not serve satisfactorily. Again we can say that the convenient way is to arrange by the thought content of the material. But this also can not be the basic principle, there are certain other factors to determine the arrangement of library material. These are children books; reference book; books of unusual size; date of printing; rare books; bound periodicals; fiction or non-fiction; local collections; magnetic discs and many other. When one has to locate a book in the huge collection of volumes, can realise the value of classified arrangement of books. Libraries employ classification system to make easier for readers as well as staff members to locate the volume on the shelves.

The normal procedure in the library is to identify the subject of a book and on the basis of decision taken with respect to the nature of library; a class number is being assigned from the classification system. This number indicates the subject of the volume according to the system used in the library. If the library also arranges its books under each subject alphabetically by author, an author number is assigned. The class number and author number together are known as the call number, which is used to obtain the volume from the shelves for the reader.

General Classification

This is a general classification of the whole of knowledge for use in libraries. It was devised by S.R. Ranganathan, who was one on world's foremost classification theorists, and was the first scheme to, be based entirely on faceted principles. Ranganathan introduct number of new ideas and terms, one of which was the term facet. In the Colon classification a 'facet formula' for combining concepts is provided for each basic subjects field and this is followed by lists of the concepts (called by Ranganathan 'foci') in each facet within that field. Here, for example, is the beginning of Class Education:

Classifying Subjects

It was possible to classify subjects by scanning the classification schedules. However, as the classification scheme develops into a more exhaustive and more complex system, such a scanning process becomes difficult, if not impossible. The scheme will therefore require an alphabetical index to make it more intelligible; so that the place in the schedules of a particular concept, and hence its notation, can be ascertained. In addition an introduction to the scheme would have to be written. This introduction will explain how the scheme may be used and will provide examples to illustrate this explanation. In a faceted scheme, among the more important things to be dealt with are the citation order and the method of notational combination. The introduction however should be as brief as possible subject to clarity and explicitness.

The compilation procedure for a complete scheme, one final, important point needs to be made. It can be noted that after examining the illustrative, alphabetic notations, the citation and schedule orders could be given a strong influence symbols. Therefore this allocation could, in many instances, more usefully be undertaken after decisions relating to those orders have been made. Taking this into account, the full procedure, therefore, would entail the following eight steps:

1. Analysis;
2. Grouping;
3. Order in array;
4. Citation order;
5. Schedule order;
6. Notation;
7. Index;
8. Introduction.

As we have seen, all of these would not be essential in every case, for example in a simple scheme for coding entities in a computerised information system.

Where analysis is concerned, appropriate concepts or terms are selected by an examination of the literature of the subject field or fields. It may be sufficient to use sources such as glossaries, dictionaries, encyclopaedias, indexing and abstracting journals and other classification schemes but it might become necessary to look at actual texts when such sources are inadequate or for current terms. The scheme for the estate agent, for example, used terms taken from actual advertisements.

This is a faceted classification of machine bolts for use in a computer based business system. It enables each type of bolt to be uniquely identified by a coding. Such bolts are available in different materials, in different thread sizes, in different head shapes and with different finishes.

Material

1 stainless steel 2 brass

3 steel

Thread size
- 1 0 BA
- 2 1 BA
- 3 2 BA
- and so on

Head shape
- 1 round
- 2 flat
- 3 hexagonal
- 4 square

Finish
- 1 unfinished
- 2 chromium plated
- 3 zinc plated
- 4 painted

The citation order is the same as the schedule order shown above so that sample classification numbers would be:

Chromium-plated brass square-head bolts of 2 BA thread	=	2342
Unfinished steel flat headed blots of 1 BA thread	=	3221

Classification for Office Organisations

The following are illustrative extracts from a possible enumerative classification for the organisation, by subject, of off in files.

16	TRAINING
16.1	MATERIALS
16.11	Visual aids Supplies
16.12	COURSES
16.2	Clerical
16.2.2	Management
16.2.3	Engineering

The index entries to the above schedule would be:

Clerical courses	16.2.1
Courses	16.2
Engineering courses	16.2.3
Management courses	16.2.2
Materials	16.1
Supplies	16.1.2
Training	16
Visual aids	16.1.1

A system might be suitable for the products, supplies, services and functions of an organisation. As an advantage the flexibility which the system offers, in that it is easy to subdivide and add topics, but, a disadvantage is the fact that an index is essential. Therefore a combination of systems for storing and retrieving information in the office and recommends 'direct filing', that is, alphabetical sequences by name, subject, and so on, where an index is not required.

A hierarchical enumerative scheme has the furthe problem that a subject can only be classified if it is enumerated, or listed. To take a simple example from the above scheme, the subject 'Visual aids for clerical courses', cannot be classified. A choice would have to made between 'Visual aids' (16.1.1) and 'Clerical courses' (16.2.1).

Bibliographic Classification

The 1940–53 edition of this general classification scheme for library materials by HE. Bliss is essentially enumerative but a certain amount of synthesis is provided for by 'systematic schedules', some of which may be applied throughout the scheme but others are applicable only in specific classes. Below are shown extracts from two schedules of the former variety:

Numerical Divisions of Any Class or Section

1. Reference books (including dictionaries, glossaries, encyclopaedias, indexes, handbooks)
2. Bibliography....
3. History....
4. Biography....

Geographical Division

a America

aa North America

ed Europe

ea Great Britain

'Education', in the Bibliographic classification, is J, and by use of the above schedules:

A history of education in Great Britain == J3ea

This number has been derived in a very similar way to the way in which classification is achieved in a faceted scheme. The subject is analysed into its constituent concepts and a notation assigned to each:

History = 3 Education = J Great Britain= ea

The instructions for citation order and method of combination given in the scheme must now be followed. Usually, classification would be first by subject then by 'place' and then by 'form', but when 'form' is 'history', as in this case, 'place' is cited last. As different symbols are used, a linking device is not required.

Bliss was a firm believer in brevity of notation. He thought that the economic limit should be three or four letters or digits. Perhaps because of this, he did not emphasise sufficiently what he refers to as 'composite notation', a general method of number building for complex subjects which he admitted might be necessary for specialist classification. He advocated the possible use of a hyphen to link numbers. Using this method, the classification number for the subject. 'The influence of politics upon the history of education in Great Britain', could therefore be:

J3ea-R where R is 'Politics'.

Dewey Decimal Classification: Like the Bibliographic classification, the Dewey scheme makes use of generally applicable special tables for standard subdivisions, areas, and so on. In addition, in more recent editions, there is a great deal of provision for synthesis, or number building, in many specific places throughout the scheme. The instructions at 636.8 'Cats', for instance, are:

636.8 Cats

636.800 3-7 800 9 Standard subdivisions Notations from Table

General principles

636.801-.808 Add to base number 636.80 the numbers following 636.0 in 636.01-636.08, e.g., breeding cats.

From Table = 'Encyclopaedias' and therefore, following the first instruction above:

An encyclopaedia of cats = 636.8003

Referring to 636.0, which is the general number for 'Animal husbandry':

636.801-.808

636	Animal husbandry
636.081	Selection and acquisition
636.0812	Judging
636.0811	Ownership makers
636.082	Breeding
636.084	Feeding

It can be ascertained that the classification number for:

Feeding cats = 636.8084

The above number is derived as follows:

Base number for cats	=	636.80
Add numbers following	=	636.0
Number for feeding	=	636.084
Add '34' to '636.80'	=	636.8084

The example given in the scheme, 'Breeding cats', is obtained in similar fashion.

Two Major Examples

There are two major examples of synthesis being grafted on to an enumerative scheme. The first dates back to the turn of the century when the Universal decimal classification was formulated. This scheme, which has been issued in a number of different languages and has progressed through a number of editions, was based upon the every decimal classification but a number of signs of combination and abbreviation were introduced to allow for number building. The second scheme is of much more recent origin and is the ongoing mission of the Bibliographic classification.

Universal Decimal Classification (UDC): General number building is allowed for by signs of combination, for example:

+ Addition

/ Extension (used for consecutive numbers)

= Relation

Here are some examples of UDC classification numbers. They are the same as their counterparts in the Dewey decimal classification except that the figure minimum is abolished, therefore

310 in Dewey becomes 31 in UDC:

31 Statistics

51 Mathematics

53 Physics

54 Chemistry

63 Agriculture

Applying the sings of combination to the above numbers in order to build up numbers for composite subjects would achieve results as illustrated in the following examples:

Mathematics and physics = 51 + 53

Physics and chemistry = 53/54

Statistics relating to agriculture = 63:31

or 31:63

There is no stipulated citation order in UDC, hence the possible alternative for the last number. This provides for great flexibility, if necessary, a double colon may be used to 'fix' the order of the constituent elements of a compound number, especially when UDC is used in a computer-based information system, for example:

Statistics relating to agriculture = 63::31

Unfortunately UDC retains a great deal of enumeration and this can result in conflict with the synthetic facilities. For example, a common auxiliary table for 'persons' (Table 1(k)—05) is applicable throughout the main schedules:

-05 Persons

-053 Persons according to age or age groups

.2 Children and infants

6 Young persons. Adolescents. Teenagers

.8 Adults. Grown ups

.9 Old persons. Persons in old age

-55 Persons according to sex and kinship

.1 Male persons. Men

.15 Boys

.2 Female persons. Women

.25 Girls

The subject Accident statistics' is classified at 313.12 and therefore, by applying the above table:

Accident statistics relating to women= 313.12-055.2

However, the table is not used consistently but is sometimes replaced by enumeration, for example:

343.91 Kinds of criminal

343.914 Women as criminals

362.8 Care of young persons

362.86 Care and welfare of girls and young women

However, that the number listed, or enumerated, in the schedule is shorter than the number that would have been obtained through the use of synthesis, for example:

343.91-055.2 Women as criminals

Bibliographic Classification Revised Edition: A new revision of the Bibliographic classification based upon facet analysis, began to appear in 1977 and is still in progress. It is the work of Jack Mills and his colleagues at the Polytechnic of North London. Within Class U Arts/ Useful arts, UVC in both the original scheme and the revision is 'Clothing industries'. Given below (some extracts from this class, on the left the original and on the right the revision, which illustrate the difference between the two.

UVC Clothing Industries

Original scheme	*Revision*
UVD Men's and 'boys' clothing UVDN Men's and boys' neckties, gloves, hats, caps	UVD Products By mode of manufacture, e.g., UVD C Knitwear
By material, e.g.,	
UVE Children's clothing	UVD E Textile
(No enumeration)	By occasion when worn, e.g.,
UVF Women's and girls' clothing	UVD KL Industrial
UVFL Women's and girls underwear, lingerie hosiery, gloves	'By sex, e.g., UVD Q Unisex. UVDS Female
By sex, e.g.,	
UVDV Child	
By part of body covered, e.g., (Trunk and arm)	

Colon Classification

The Colon Classification owes its name to the fact that the notational device first used by it to demarcate facets in Class Number was the symbol 1/:1/ (colon). Hereafter the word 'facet' will be used instead of 'dimension' or 'zone' in accordance with the terminology of the Colon Classification.

In the first three editions of the Colon classification, the implied assumption was that the number of facets in a universe of discourse is constant. Of course, among the fixed number of facets several arrangements are possible, some of which may be 'more or less helpful'. Of the 'more or less helpful' arrangements one is forcedly preferred for adoption. To mechanise the arrangement of facets in the preferred order, a rigorous face-formula is given for each universe of discourse called a Main or a Canonical class.

An important contribution of the Colon classification, the Library classification: Fundamentals and procedure (1944) and the Elements of library classification (1946) is the isolation of the concept of Universes with Loose Assemblage. They have introduced the term 'Phase' in describing an existent which is loosely assembled. In the first edition, the Colon classification (1933) prescribed the digit "0" (zero) as the symbol to connect the class numbers corresponding to the constituents of an existent with loose assemblage. Of course the resulting number is itself a class number. It may be called a Phased Class Number. Each constituent of a Phased Class Number is itself a Class Number. The second edition of the Colon classification (1939) recognised two species of phase-relation for which it prescribed zero and colon as the respective connecting symbols. The Fundamentals made an objective analysis of the problem. The Elements isolated one more species of phase-relation. The Agile has indications that the projected work in India includes a thorough analysis of phases, isolation of different species of phase-relations, and prescription of distinctive connecting symbols for them. It is hoped that this investigation will lay down a technique for handling new species of phases as and when they come to be known, though they may be unknown at present.

The Colon Classification is perhaps the first of the analytico-synthetic variety. It is a pure example of that variety. Its preliminary schedules include those of:

(1) Main Classes;

(2) Common Subdivisions;

(3) Geographical Divisions;

(4) Language Divisions; and

(5) Chronological Divisions.

Then follow one chapter for each 'of the Main Classes. In each chapter, if the Main Class is not broken down in the first instance into Canonical Divisions, there are usually one or two schedules corresponding to the one or two trains of characteristics which are relevant to its classification. In other words, the facets of the Main Class are mentioned and the foci in each of them are enumerated. If the Main Class is broken down into Canonical Divisions in the first instance, such of the Canonical Divisions as admit of them are provided with similar schedules based on the trains of characteristics relevant to their classification. Generally speaking the divisions in each of the above-mentioned schedules are enumerated in a 'more or less helpful' order. There are however regions where alphabetical arrangement is prescribed in the form 'Divide by Alphabetical Device'; and there are definite rules which prescribe the minimum arrangement is prescribed in the form 'Divide by Alphabetical Device'; and there are definite rules which prescribe the minimum arrangement is prescribed in the form number of the initial letters which should be used to secure individualisation. An example of this will be found in the Full Crop Schedule worked out for Agriculture in the Abgila of March 1950. It will be found in the Full Crop Schedule worked out for Agriculture in the Abgila of March 1950. It will be found that the international name of crops is prescribed to be used for Alphabetical Device. The Alphabetical Device is used only when there is strong evidence to show that there is no other arrangement which is at all helpful. The point is that when none of the possible arrangements has more of the element of helpfulness than the purely alphabetical one, the alphabetical arrangement scores because people are more familiar with it.

The first part of Colon classification is entitled 'Rules of classification'. It gives objective definition of Class Number and of most other concepts. In the preliminary chapters it describes various devices by which class numbers should be constructed. What are called Facet-and Phase-Formulae are defined. These formulae enable one to analyse a given specific subject in a systematic manner and rearrange the words in the name of the specific subject filling up ellipses if any, as a preliminary to the construction of the class number. The facet-formula of the main class or canonical division to which the specific subject belongs helps in this analysis and breakdown of the specific subject into its fundamental constituent elements. Connecting symbols are prescribed by the rules and also indicated in the facet-and phase-formulae for synthesising the fundamental constituent numbers, got by translating the fundamental constituent concept, into the derived composite class number as the translation of the name of the specific subject. It is this process of first analysing the specific subject and at the last stage synthesising the class number which makes the Colon Classification an analytico-synthetic classification.

The potential vocabulary of the Colon Classification is infinite. Its infinity is of a higher order than that of the Decimal Classification. The order of infinity of its potential vocabulary is that of the number of facets and phases its notation can accommodate. To take the example given in section 1521, we saw that it is impossible to get a Decimal Number for the specific subject 'Curriculum in secondary education'. But we can provide a Colon Number. It is T2 :44. Here

T = Education is Main Class

2 = Secondary education is a division in the Education schedule

44 = Curriculum is a number in the Problem schedule is the connecting symbol prescribed

The facet-formula prescribes the order in which the above symbols should be synthesised. Thus we get an individualising, coextensive number, i.e., a precise translation for the name of the specific subject. To use the old analogy of visitors and chairs, the Colon Classification can produce a greater abundance of chairs than the Decimal Classification. The occasions when two visitors will be obliged to sit on the same chair will be few and far between. Indeed the ideal is to eliminate such an occasion altogether.

There is one danger in an analytico-synthetic classification when viewed as language. Since an enumerative classification gives a ready-made translation (class number) made by the classificationist himself, it is ensured that no two different translations are made for the same original (specific) subject. But it is well known that when different translators translate with the aid of a dictionary, they may produce different translations. This is perhaps a desirable feature in literary translation. But it will be disastrous in classificatory translation. For, translating the name of a given specific subject into two different class numbers will mean inconsistency in arrangement.

That is why it has been stated that an essential quality of a classificatory language is that it must have no synonym and two different translations for the same original passage should not be allowed or possible. It is the facet-formula which protects Colon Classification from this potential danger. It is that formula which gives the necessary rigidity. But we have to beware that the facet formula does not introduce more rigidity than it is absolutely necessary for avoiding synonyms. If it introduces a greater amount of rigidity than it is necessary, to that extent it will restrict the potential vocabulary of the classificatory language.

To get a view of the map of the field of knowledge provided by the Colon Classification one must take into consideration fully worked-out class numbers, past, present and future. If that is done it will be found that a good map is provided. The conscious implementation of Hospitality in Chain and Hospitality in Array in the methodology of the Colon Classification, keeps co-ordinate classes and subordinate classes quite apart as and when new areas (specific subjects) are explored and have to be marked on the map. The facet-notation enables the Colon Classification to carry out these obligations of cartographers even more thoroughly than the Decimal Classification is able to do.

Viewing the problem from the angle of analogy with transformation, the facet and the phase-notation of the Colon Classification enables to avoid the fault of the Decimal Classification described in section 1523. It is not merely the end sub-cell in the multi-dimensional space of the field of knowledge, which is transformed into the end sub-interval in the linear space of class numbers, which is fully represented. But everyone of the sub-cells in a cluster constituting a compound cell is rightly transformed. In using the terminology of the Boolean Algebra the field of Colon Nu Numbers is a closed one in the sense that the product of any two sub-fields is contained within the total field. By throwing the search light of Boolean Algebra on the Colon Classification, it is expected that some of the subtler faults which are escaping unnoticed may be brought to light.

The notation or the Colon Classification is even more resourceful in its counter-tactics than that or the Decimal Classification. It has been able to withstand the grosser attacks of the field of knowledge. But in our days the field of knowledge has started, as it were, bacteria warfare. It has begun to play Hanuman's tactics as described' in section 1515. It is playing these tactics unendingly. Just as the vocal muscle of the witch in the Ramayana episode became too stiff at a certain stage for the jaws to be easily moved, we have been experiencing that the rigidity of the facet-formula is causing trouble in putting up the necessary counter-tactics. It is to take away this rigidity that the work on Optional Facets is being pursued.

The Colon Classification has virtually no patent medicine. Every mixture has to be compounded according to prescriptions written out by a competent doctor to meet the exact requirement of the disease diagnosed. This does not mean that mixtures in frequent demand should not be compounded and stored in advance to be handed over readily on demand.

Similarly the Colon Classification has virtually no ready-made toys. Every toy should be built up to suit the exact fancy of the child needing it. This does not mean that the toys in frequent demand should not be assembled in advance and kept in readiness, to be handed over readily on demand. The Colon Classification has closely followed the optical analogue in the design of its terminology, there is no need to elaborate further the statements made in that section. The structure of the Colon Number discloses more fully than any other classification number the structure of the specific subject.

A new feature of the Colon Classification which, however, needs to be mentioned here concerns the method it uses: (1) to secure theoretically infinite Hospitality in Array and in Chain severally. To secure Infinite Hospitality in Array the Colon Classification uses not only the Octave Notation but also other devices like Subject Device, Alphabetical Device, Geographical Device and Chronological Device. These are all described and illustrated in the Colon Classification. Of these, it is the Chronological Device which has usually facility to provide truly Infinite Hospitality in Array. It has stood the test admirably in accommodating Authors in Literature with neat individualising class numbers, no matter how many they are. It is also showing its capacity in individualising any number of special schools of thought in any region of knowledge. In the former, it consists in representing an author by the year of his birth. This makes classification of the authors belonging to any particular form of literature in any particular language chronological. This arranges the works by and on them in a manner which is not only helpful, in the ordinary sense, but also suggests the evolution of the literary art. Thus Hospitality in Chain is got by the decimal-fraction-notation which imitates the denudation process by which the links in the chain are successively derived.

When a link begins to throw forth its links of higher order, it often happens that all the links in the array of the next order are not thrown out at one time. If they are, it may be easy to determine a 'more or less helpful' arrangement among them and allot the extra digit or digits needed to represent them according to the octave notation or any of the devices mentioned above. When they are not thrown out at one time, it is difficult to surmise which place the first link which is thrown out should be given in the array—which octave and which place in the octave. It is here that the Colon Classification has contributed what has been described in the Prolegomena as Unscheduled Mnemonics. It is a subtle device and is therefore a powerful one. It gives a greater degree of autonomy to a classifier in sharpening Simple and Dependent Foci. It is difficult to explain it in general terms though it has been attempted in the Philosophy of library classification. Unscheduled Menmonics consists in using an ordinal digit to represent a primordial idea which is not often represented by any term in a natural language, when it is taken in isolation, but is represented by different terms when it is put in the context of the different subjects.

For example, the digit 3 represents Physiology in Biological Sciences, Social practices in Sociology, Functions of State in Political Science, Teaching Technique in Education, Distribution in Economics, Contract in Legal System and so on—all at bottom analogous at least in a thin or distant way. This mnemonic quality enable a classifier to form new foci in any facet without reference to the classificationist. What is more he need not wait to give numbers to these foci until all of them have appeared. Even when only one appears, he can number it with a high probability that it need not be changed and that very other classifier and the classificationist himself would be numbering it in the same way. The organisational set up on national and international basis for removing the effect of the small probability for inconsistency in fixing numbers by unscheduled mnemonics, has been described in Library classification and international documentation of the F.I.D. I have some vague information that there is a tradition of such unscheduled mnemonics current in the Tantric school. I wish something is done to collect, record and study this tradition of unscheduled mnemonics. Even among the common folk in western countries there is some trace of this which is brushed aside as sheer superstition. But scientific outlook requires that we should not brush aside anything on the sole ground that we cannot fit it into the rational matrix which intellect produces. We should be prepared to postulate and even grant trans-intellectual existents, though it is necessary to be on our guard not to become credulous subjects of fraud.

Universal Decimal Classification

In late 19th century there was an increasing concern for the problems of documentation. In earlier years cataloguers had concentrated on the problems of describing and recording books mostly in a bibliographic tradition, with a wealth of detail but with a corresponding delay in the dissemination of information. In the early 1890s Paul Otlet and Henri La Fontaine, in Belgium, translated the earlier cataloguers' efforts towards a universal catalogue into the world of documentation. They proposed a' universal index to recorded knowledge which must include non-book materials and ephemera as well as conventional material. In 1895 the First International Conference on Bibliography, for which Otlet and La Fontaine were largely responsible, approved their plans and established the Institute International de Bibliography (IIB). Otlet and La Fontaine had already agreed that such an index, and bibliographies based on it or contributing to it, must be organised systematically rather than alphabetically. They looked to the Dewey Decimal classification as the basis of a truly international scheme.

Otlet and La Fontaine negotiated with Dewey to use his scheme for the IIB's index. They wanted three things: to translate it into French, to expand its subject schedules and make it truly international in scope, and to allow arrangements to include non-book materials. Dewey was impressed and inclined to agree, but his assistants (in particular Dorcas Fellows) could not tolerate such changes to his original plan. Negotiations dragged on until in despair the Belgians went their own way. Without that reluctance of members of Dewey's staff we might now have only one decimal classification, and a realisation of Dewey's plan: a scheme of universal scope for documentation, a scheme for general use (as in DOC now), and an abridged scheme like the abridged DDC.

The adapted scheme was published for the first time in 1905 by the IIB as the Manual due repertoire universal bibliographique and became known in the English speaking world as the "Brussels classification". Even then it had more detail than the contemporary edition of the DOC, and it had most of the synthetic features peculiar to what is now the Universal Decimal Classification. It was quickly adopted by libraries in Europe, particularly special libraries with a scientific and technological orientation where non-book materials are common.

Computerised Classification

Allied to automatic indexing, although somewhat outside the scope of this present work, is automatic classification. At the Cambridge Language Research Unit, for instance, investigations panning a number of years from the early 1960s were involved with the machine analysis of documents for the discovery of 'keywords' for indexing purposes. Attempts were made to construct automatically a classification of key words based upon the way in which terms 'co-occur' in documents. Terms thus related are grouped together into 'clumps', terms 'outside'. Using clumps alone did not lead to very satisfactory results and later experiments utilised four different kinds of group, the original' clumps', together with 'strings', 'stars' and 'cliques'. A 'string', for example is a set of terms in which each term is found to be most strongly associated with the one next to it.

This is 'clearly and indisputably a newer form of classification' which may have far-reaching effects in the future. At present such work is still mainly at a theoretical level but there is a possibility that it could well improve the search capability in computerised databases to a marked degree.

Spark Jones considers that the immediate prospects for operational automatic classification are "not bright", because of the failure to fully establish appropriate methods and applications, and the high cost of experiments. Yet she believes that large files need more sophisticated tools, such as classification, and since automatic classification has not been conclusively shown to be unhelpful compared with human classification, its longer prospects should be interesting to all concerned with information systems. It is certainly possible that some form of classification, whether 'automatic' or not, 'built-in' to computerised databases could improve the search capability to a marked degree. It might, for instance, be feasible that a search on one term could be translated automatically into a search for other related coordinate or subordinate terms indicated by the classification. This could greatly improve the efficiency of the system. If, to take a simple example, an item dealing with the 'use of parachutes to stop ocean-going tankers' was searched for under 'parachutes' and 'slips', the automatic classification facility would reveal that 'tankers' was closely related to 'ships' and the relevant document would be retrieved.

Tool for Organising Documents

Classification is a tool for organising the document stores or library. A document is the physical carrier of a message. A document may be in various forms like book, films, slides, periodicals, newspapers, cards bearing the names and addresses of local organisations in a reference library files and machine readable media. The messages that documents bear may be simple facts, views, interpretations of events or works of art. For example Gita is message, just as Yojna is periodical, The Hindu is newspaper or name and address record is directory. When the number of documents become too much for a person seeking a particular information to scan through all those, it becomes necessary to organise them. When these tasks become too great to be performed informally, it is institutionalised. Specialists are appointed to carry out the task. These specialists are librarians and other information workers, whose function is to mediate between their clients and the documents containing the message.

Librarian's contribution to society is very precisely. He enables clients to find any required subject of documents from the total set as quickly and easily as possible. He selects and collects documents, organises his collection, cooperates with other librarians and information workers, and he helps as well as encourages his readers to use documents. The main task on which the user depends, is the organisation of collection which means the arrangement of documents in some helpful order and the provision of catalogues and indexes which act as both-keys and complements to that order. We call the techniques developed to bring about this organisation 'fixing'.

As indexing is concerned with the easy location of subsets or subclasses of documents. All the indexing techniques are application of classification. The characteristic which defines the different classes sought by a reader differ as the name of the author, the name of series of works (e.g. Library Science Series), the name of the translator, illustrator, composer, performer or film director; and the name of subject about which messages are required. In practice, we consider only classification by subject or in some cases forms of document.

Ideas and Concepts

Concepts are the ideas and it can be distinguished from the names of things. The same concept may have many names, for example in different languages-book, buch, livre; or in the same language, synonyms-firearms / guns, adolescents / teenagers, panthers / leopards. A name may stand for many different concepts in case of homonym. In concept indexing, the indicter recognises the concepts with which a document deals, rather than merely accepting the names he finds in the document. In practice, he provides the means for readers using the concept and not what is used the concept in the document and that he distinguishes the different meanings of homonyms, so that the client is not led to irrelevant documents by the indexing system. If we call the set of name or symbols which represent classes of documents the "index vocabulary", then we can say that in concept indexing the index vocabulary is controlled, because the indexer has controlled synonyms and homonyms. Failure to control the index vocabulary may lead to the failure to find material on a subject which is, in fact, available in a collection; or to the irritation of being presented with irrelevant documents.

Controlled vocabulary are usually structured that is they display the relationships between different concepts, either by means of references:

Systematic order between documents or records of documents in a catalogue is an order which displays the relationships between the subjects of documents it keeps together and works on the same subjects. This sequence illustrates the principle:

vertebrates

-fish

-birds

-mammals

-rodents

-rats

-mice

-insectivores

-hedgehogs.

Here we see the class RATS, kept with its closely related class MICE; these are preceded by the class which contains them, RODENTS, and followed by INSECTIVORES, which is related to the RODENTS; INSECTIVORES is in turn followed by the classes it contains, such as HEDGEHOGS. Systematic order is one method of displaying structure, so it brings the advantages of a structured vocabulary with the additional facility of easy browsing through the sequence.

Systematic order is the peculiar contribution of the classification scheme to indexing.

The common application of systematic order is the placing of books in order on the shelves of libraries, this is what most people think of as 'classification'. This use enables readers to browse for themselves among the stock, giving them greater autonomy, and making open access libraries possible. Systematic order is used in the classified catalogue, obviously; but a classification scheme can also provide the basis for the display of structure in an alphabetical subject catalogue-the references:

Vertebrates see also Mammals

Mammals see also Rodents

Rodents see also Rats

Mice see also Rats

could be easily derived from the systematic sequence above. In fact, a classification scheme is the basis of any kind of controlled and structured vocabulary. Alphabetical subject indexes to classified catalogues are derived from the classification scheme. By the technique of chain indexing, thesauri for post-coordinate indexes are often produced from classification schemes. So systematic order may be used for the records of documents on machine readable media, to save time in computer searches, and to make the broadening and narrowing of searches through the computer easier.

Hence classification is about the discovery and the display of relationships by means of systematic order.

Faceted Scheme

The Oxford dictionary defines facet as 'one side of a many-sided body'. Subjects can be divided into constituent sides or parts and the word facet may therefore be applied to a classification which can work on the principle of an analytico-synthetic method. Fundamental concepts are analysed and clubed together into facets. These concepts can be combined further to form more complex subjects. The following example should make this principle clearer.

A firm sells canned and bottled beers (mild, bitter, larger and stout) in various sizes from 330 ml to 31/2 litres. The firm wishes to devise a faceted classification scheme for coding items in its computerised sales system. In order to do this the relevant concepts, '330 ml', 'cans', 'bitter' and so on, are grouped into facets using the characteristics of 'capacity', 'container' and 'beer type', that is:

Capacity	*Container*	*Beer Type*
facet	facet	facet
330 ml	Cans	Mild
440 ml	Bottles	Bitter
550 ml		
1 litre		Stout
31/2litre		

Notational Symbol

Each concept within the classification scheme must be allocated a notational symbol which will enable the representation of that the concept by a 'shorthand' code or classification number. Numeric digits could perform this function. Here is such a notation added to the above scheme:

Capacity	*Container*	*Beer Type*
facet	facet	facet
1 330 ml	1 Cans	1 Mild
2 440 ml	2 Bottles	2 Bitter
3 550 ml		3 Larger
4 1 litre		4 Stout
531/2litre		

The process of classification is achieved by first ascertaining notation for each constituent concept and then combining the, notations to form a coding or classification number for the complete subject. For example, to classify 440 ml cans of lager' the subject first broken down into its constituent concepts:

440 ml cans lager

and the relevant notations ascertained from the classification scheme

2 1 3

These separate notations are combined to produce classification number:

213

Similarly:

1 litre bottles of mild = 421

31/2 litre cans of bitter = 512

In order to avoid confusion, when using a notation such as the shown here the notational length (that is, the number of digits must be constant and concepts from facets must be combined or cited in consistent order. In the above examples the order is that in who the facets have been written down, namely:

Capacity	*Container*	*Beer Type*
1 Cans 2 Bottles		
1 Mild		
2 Bitter 3 Lager 4 Stout		

If a coding in a computerised system were all that was required then the above scheme would be satisfactory but for other purposes for example a manual filing system, it would be inadequate.

Let us now review the steps that have been taken in order compile the faceted scheme.

Step 1 Analysis into relevant concepts, that is:

440 ml

bitter

cans lager

1 litre

bottles

etc.

Step 2 Grouping into facets characteristics, for example:

Capacity	*Container*	*Beer Type*
440ml	Cans	Bitter

Step 3 Adding a notation, for example:

2440 ml

4 1 litre

Step 4 Choosing a citation order, for example:

Capacity	*Container*	*Beer Type*

A further decision, which has not been specifically referred to, also had to be taken. This relates to the way in which the scheme is to be written down or printed, that is, the schedule order. In the above example the schedule order:

Capacity	*Container*	*Beer Type*

Schedule order would therefore become Step 5:

Step 5 Deciding upon the schedule order

For very brief schedules a tabular form of presentation can be used, but for lengthier schemes a continuous form is more appropriate, for example:

Capacity facet

1 330 ml

2 440 ml

3 550 ml

4 1 litre

5 31/2 litre

Container facet 1 Cans 2 Bottles

Type of beer facet

1 Mild

2 Bitter

3 Lager

4 Stout

Chapter T. Education

T(P): (E), (2P), (2P2)

Foci in (P)

1 Pre-secondary

13 Pre-school child

15 Elementary

2 Secondary

25 Intermediate

3 Adult

31 Literate

35 Foreigner

38 Illiterate

4 University

An examination of the concepts (or foci) in (P) and the first part of the 'facet formula' for the class, that is, T (P), will indicate that the subject 'University education' will have the class number T4, the square brackets in the formula are ignored.

Foci in (E) cum (2P)

1 Nomenclature

2 Curriculum

3 Teaching technique

Again an examination of the concepts in (E) and a further 100 at the formula will indicate that the classification number for 'Teaching methods' is T:3 and that for 'Teaching methods in universities' T4:3. The 'cum (2P)' tells us that the concepts in (E) should be linked whenever necessary to those in (2P) and the scheme states:

Foci in (2P)

1 2 3 to be got by (SD)

(SD) means subject device and this allows for the use of the classification number for any subject, from the whole of the Colon scheme, to be included here in parentheses. For example, 'Mathematics' is Class B and therefore the classification number for the subject 'The teaching of mathematics' would be T:3(B) and for 'The teaching of mathematics in universities' T4:3(B). The comma preceding (2P) is superfluous because of the parentheses.

Foci in (2P2)

1 Audiovisual

13 Audio

133 Gramophone

136 Radio

15 Visual

The concepts in the above facet would allow the classification of such subjects as 'The use of visual aids in the teaching of mathematics in universities', which would have the classification number T4:3(B),15.

Citation order in the Colon classification always conforms to the one formula, the PME5T formula, which stands for: Personality (relating to the most important facet which establishes the character of a subject)—Matter (relating to materials)—Energy (relating to processes, activities or operations)—Space (relating to geographical areas)—Time (relating to time periods). This does not mean that the maximum number of facets is five, which would be insufficient for many subjects and multiple 'personality' or other types of facet may be required. In the above Education class formula, for instance, (2P) stands for a 'second round' of the personality facet and (2P2) stands for a second, subsidiary level, of this second round of personality facet.

Hierarchial Classification

A 'hierarchy', as used in classification, is a series of classes or groups in successive subordination, for example:

Literature

English literature

Hindi literature

Punjabi literature

Poetry

Drama

Fiction

Thus each entity (for example English poetry) falls into a subgroup of a larger group (for example English literature), which in turn forms part of an even larger group (for example Literature). Such a classification is built up by a processes of division, according to certain characteristic of language, that is, English literature, Hindi literature, Punjabi literature. Each of these classes can then be further subdivided by the characteristic of form of literature, that is, English poetry, English drama, English fiction; Hindi poetry, Hindi drama, Hindi fiction; and so on. This is sometimes referred to as a 'top down' approach.

The tree structure shown above could be presented thus:

Literature

English literature

Poetry

Drama

Fiction

Hindi literature

Poetry

Drama

Fiction

Punjabi literature

Poetry

Drama

Fiction

As the process of division continues the hierarchical classification lists or 'enumerates' (hence 'enumerative' classification) complex subjects, for example 'English poetry', which comprises a language (English) and a literary form (poetry). This may be contrasted with the faceted approach, which would list 'English' and 'poetry' as separate concepts but not as a complete subject. In a properly designed hierarchical classification each subject should have only one place where it fits into the system.

Order of the Subjects

In a hierarchical scheme the order of subjects at a particular level of division is important. This order corresponds to the order of concepts within facets and should be as helpful to the user as possible. For example, in literature, at the language level it would be helpful to place the 'home' language, for example English, first, then related European languages followed by other languages.

The citation order in a hierarchical classification is derived from the order in which the characteristics of division are applied. In the literature example, the first characteristic of division is language and the second literary form. The citation order is therefore:

Language Form

but this citation order' is 'in-built' to classification numbers for complex subjects listed in the scheme.

Notation: Here is the above scheme with a simple notation consisting of numeric digits added:

1 Literature
11 English literature
111 Poetry
112 Drama
113 Fiction
12 Hindi literature
121 Poetry
122 Drama
123 Fiction
13 Punjabi literature
131 Poetry
132 Drama
133 Fiction

This notation may be described as:

Pure Expressive	Only one type of symbol is used (the numeric digit). It reflects the structure of the classification; 111 'English poetry' is a division of 11 'English literature', which in turn is a division of 1 'Literature'.
Hospitable	A decimal notation can be aided to indefinitely and therefore, in theory, is infinitely expansible.
Mnemonic	'Poetry' is always represented by the digit: 1. 'Drama' by the digit; 2. 'fiction' by the digit 3. This type of mnemonic aid is referred to as a 'systematic' mnemonic.

Index: The index to an enumerative hierarchical scheme lists complex subjects, for example 'Drama: English literature' Here is an to the above schedule:

Drama: English literature	112
Drama: Punjabi literature	132
Drama: Hindi literature	122
English litera' ıre	11
Fiction: English literature	113
Fiction: Punjabi literature	133
Fiction: Hindi literature	123
Punjabi literature	13
Hindi literature	12
Literature	1

Poetry: English literature	111
Poetry: Punjabi literature	131
Poetry: Hindi literature	121

The index brings together aspects of a subject which are separated in the scheme, for example poetry in various languages. It is therefore a relative index; it collocates distributed relatives.

An Enumerative Scheme

The process of classification, in an enumerative scheme achieved first by consulting the index and then by proceeding location pinpointed in the schedules. Although the index lists subjects rather than concepts one should never classify of index alone as this can lead to error. The relevant schedules examined in order to find the correct number. To take a example, if a book which deals with the work of famous such as Shakespeare, Dinkar and Nehru were to be classified, index entry for 'Literature' might be referred to and the class obtained. However after proceeding to in the schedules it apparent immediately that 'Literature' is divided by language the question whether all the authors dealt with are English authors must then be classified. Thus the structure classification scheme itself acts are as classifying.

If the classification of machine bolts were copied in a hierarchical scheme, dividing first by material, then by thread shape and head shape and finally by finish, it would begin to the following, appearance: brass bolts stainless steel machine bolts steel

Round

  Unfinished Chromium

  plated Zinc plated Painted

Flat

  Unfinished Chromium

  plated Zinc plated Painted

Hexagonal

  Unfinished Chromium

  plated Zinc plated Painted

Square

  Unfinished Chromium

  plated Zinc plated Painted

1 BA

Round

  Unfinished Chromium

  plated Zinc plated Painted

Flat

  Unfinished Chromium

  plated Zinc plated Painted

Hexagonal

Unfinished Chromium

plated Zinc plated Painted

Square

Unfinished Chromium

plated Zinc plated Painted

2BA

Round Unfinished Chromium

plated Zinc plated Painted

Flat

Unfinished Chromium

plated Zinc plated Painted and

so on. Several problems are apparent:

The extract from the scheme shown here has only progressed as far as the subject 'Painted flat 2 BA stainless steel bolts', yet already it is far longer than the faceted scheme.

As subjects, and not concepts, are being listed, constituent concept, such as 'unfinished' have to be repeated every time that they occur in a complex subject. However, it is still only possible to classify a subject if it is listed. For example, the subject 'Chromium plated stainless steel bolts' (that is, omitting the size) cannot be classified nor can the subject 'chromium plated bolts'.

Because of the problems (1) and (2), a hierarchical, enumerative scheme tends to become a compromise, and enumeration is not carried to its logical conclusion. Therefore the finished scheme it often very complex in nature and the basic principles of construction are difficult to identify.

Dewey Decimal Classification

This is a classification which covers the whole of knowledge was devised over a hundred years ago for shelf arrangement libraries. It has simple decimal, expansible notation. Here, is example, are some parts of the Literature class, which the reader '" see equate closely to the scheme shown above although the notations different:

800	Literature
810	American literature in English
811	Poetry
812	Drama
813	Fiction
829	Literature of English and Anglo-Saxon languages
821	English poetry
822	English drama
823	English fiction
830	Literature of Germanic (Teutonic) languages

831	German poetry
832	German drama
833	German fiction
840	Literature of Roman languages. French literature
841	French poetry
842	French drama
843	French fiction

With a decimal notation each subject is capable of division into nine subsidiary subjects, for example 821, 822, 823, 829, all of which are theoretically co-equal. As very few subject divide into nine parts naturally distortion is bound to occur, nevertheless this is an easily understood system and offers hospitality and expansibility The Dewey scheme utilises a three figure 'minimum' base, a illustrated above; further division continues after the decimal period for example:

822.3 English drama of the Elizabethan period where the '3' represents 'elizabe than period'. A fifth digit may then indicate a particular dramatist within this period, for example:

822.3 Shakespeare

If an item which deals with a work such as 'A criticism of Shakespeare's Macbeth' were classified by the above scheme, the classification is by subject, but if the actual text of Macbeth were to be defined, classification in this case would be by form, that is, literary form, it will be necessary in general classification to cater for this classes.

641.5	Cookery
641.52	For breakfast
641.53	For luncheon, brunch, elevenses, tea, supper, snacks
641.54	For dinner
641.55	Time and money-saving cookery
641.552	Money-saving cookery
641.555	Timesaving cookery
641.56	For special situations
641.561	For one or two persons
641.562	For persons of specific ages
641.5622	Infants and children
641.5627	Adults aged 65 and over
641.563	For health, appearancepersonal reasons
641.5631	For sick persons
641.56311	For persons with heart diseases
641.56314	For persons with diabetes
641.5632	Cookery with specified vitamin and mineral content

641.5634	High-calorie cookery
641.5635	Low-calorie cookery
641.5636	Vegetarian cookery
641.5637	Health-food cookery
641.5638	Protein, fat, carbohydrate cookery
641.504	For various specific times of year
641.506	For Christian church limitations and observances 641.507 For religious limitations and observances
641.508	For special occasions. Holidays, birthdays, etc.

The above extract illustrates the great detail of this scheme but it is also somewhat confusing and illustrates the problems of enumeration. A compromise has had to be reached and hierarchical process of division has not been continued at each step. For example, division by 'Meal' is not further subdivided by 'Special situations' and then by 'Health, etc.', but division by each of the characteristics is carried out separately. Thus it is impossible classify the subject 'Cooking dinner for one' or 'Cooking for aged 65 and over who suffer from heart disease'. A choice has to made in these instances between 'Cooking for dinner' or 'Cooking for one' and 'Cooking for adults aged 65 and over, or 'Cooking persons with heart disease'.

What is known as 'cross-classification' also occurs. This happens when different characteristics are applied at the one point division. For example, 'For special situations' is divided by characteristics of 'number of people' and' age' at the one step.

The index to the Dewey decimal classification is a very detailed often praised indeed and its relative nature, which was devised all lauded by Melvil Dewey' (the scheme's creator), has had considerable influence on many other indexes. Here is an illustrative example:

Sadism

Gen. med.	616.85835
geriatrics	618.97685835
paediatrics	618.9285835
psychology	157.7
statistics	312.385 835

other aspects were see Sexual deviations

This indicates that various aspects of the subject 'Sadism' can be found in five different places in the schedules, and the cross reference informs the user that additional aspects may be found consulting 'Sexual deviations'.

Dewey classification numbers can become quite lengthy and the digits after the decimal point are sometimes split into groups of the for greater convenience and ease of use.

Library of Congress Classification: This classification was constructed at the turn of the century for the US Library of Congress and it reflects knowledge as represented in the books which are included in this great library's stock. The following extracts are taken from Class T 'Technology'. Classes published in separate volumes and Class currently contains close 01 400 pages. This is only one of upwards of thirty volumes in the complete scheme, which gives some indication of the vast size that a classification which attempts to enumerate all subjects can reach.

Within Class T, Class This 'Building construction', and The 6000 onwards is concerned with 'Building fittings and their installation'. Here is a brief outline of this section of the scheme:

Building Fittings and their Classification

6010- GENERAL WORKS

6100- PLUMBING AND PIPEFITTING

7000- HEATING AND VENTILATION

7700- ILLUMINATION LIGHTING

8000- DECORATION AND DECORATIVE FURNISHINGS

9000- PROTECTION OF BUILDINGS

Each of these divisions is further subdivided, for example:

PROTECTION OF BUILDINGS

6488 6489 6490

9025 General works

9031 Against damage from natural causes 9100— Protection against fire

9700 Protection from burglary, sabotage, etc..

The above extracts illustrate the hierarchical nature of the scheme but fail to do the scheme justice in that Class TH from division 6000 onwards actually takes up 21 pages of complex schedules and the principles of construction become hidden in a wealth of enumerative detail. Here, for instance, are the divisions of one very small section, 'Plumbing of the bathroom':

Plumbing of bathrooms, Toilet rooms, Lavatories

6485 General works

6486 General special. Specifications, etc.

6487 Systems

Details Fixtures

6488 General works

6489 Catalogues of bathroom fixtures

6490 Basins Baths

6491 General works

6492 Shower baths, Sprays

6493 Tubs

6494 Foot baths

6495 Sintz baths

6496 Bidets

6497 Soil fixtures

6498 Water closets. Toilets

6499 Urinals

6500 Flush tanks and auxiliary valves, etc..

The subject 'Plumbing of a bidet', for example, would have the class number TH6496. Despite the detail displayed here, the true nature of the Library of Congress scheme is still not fully revealed. Here is a further extract from 'Heating of buildings':

Heating of buildings

7201 Periodicals, societies, etc.

7205 Congresses

7207 Collected works (non-serial)

7209 Dictionaries and encyclopaedias Directories

7212 General works

7216 Special localities

7215 History

7216 Country divisions, A-Z General works

7221 Early to 1860

7222 1869

Utility of Scheme

The process of classification in an enumerative scheme, achieved first by consulting the index and then by proceeding to the location pinpointed in the schedules. Although the index lists subjects rather than concepts, one should never classify from the index alone as this can lead to error. The relevant schedules must be examined in order to find the correct number. To take a simple example, if a book which deals with the work of famous authors such as Shakespeare, Dinkar and Nehru were to be classified, the index entry for 'Literature' might be referred to and the class number obtained. However after proceeding to 1 in the schedules it will be apparent immediately that 'Literature' is divided by language and the question whether all the authors dealt with are English language authors must then be classified.

It is possible to introduce an element of synthesis, or 'number building into a hierarchical enumerative scheme, in several different ways. This helps to reduce the length of the schedules but improves efficiency. One method is to provide auxiliary tables of terms which may be applicable throughout the schedules. These tables may include, for example: Common subdivisions, such as those of form of presentation, for example 'Encyclopaedia' or 'Serial'. Geographical tables for specifying 'place', for example 'United States' or 'United Kingdom'.

Permit tables for specifying 'time', for example 'Twentieth century'.

Another method is to include instructions within the schedules themselves for dividing one classification number in the same manner as answer. All plants, for instance, may suffer from 'injuries', 'disease' and 'pests'. Instead of enumerating each of these concepts under every individual plant, they can be listed once and instructions given for the division of each plant in, the same way.

Policies of Notation

Each concept within the classification scheme must be allocated a notational symbol which will enable the representation of that concept by a 'shorthand' code or classification number. Number digits could perform this function.

A common error is to think that choice of notation is the first in the compilation of a classification scheme. It should now be apparent that this is not so; the allocation of a notation is one of final steps.

Notation is, however, a very important feature. Poor note can reduce the value of even the best constructed scheme. Some of the policies which might be booked.

Uniqueness: There should be taken that one concept or subject cannot be mistaken for another. In a machine-based system, for example could be desirous if the coding for a component, say a ball-bearing were the same as that allocated to a completed product such gear box. A distinction must however be made between unique identification of a subject and identification of an actual item example, in a library the subject 'Use of artificial satellites telecommunication' might have the number XX 007 but there well be a great number of cooks dealing with this subject, all with the same class number. For unique identification of each book some must be added to this number, so that in effect it becomes a book number. This addition could consist of letters and digits could represent author, copy number, volume, and so on. A is situation exists in a computer-based system where a code used as the sole key for identification and location of a data record If several records have the same classification number then further coding must be added.

Simplicity: Notation should be easily comprehensible and must have ordinal value as it reflects and 'fixes' chosen orders, therefore:

1 A

2 or B

3 C

not

$

&

*

Confusion should be avoided, for example the use of both the upper case letter '0' and the digit '0', or the lower case letter 'I' and the digit '1'. It is advantageous if notation is easily memorised, written and spoken.

For classification and coding in industry, 'in order to assist the many functions of manufacture by providing a logical and meaningful system of identification for information, data and components" 'the best type of symbolisation is generally considered to be purely numerical and of uniform length'.

Brevity: Notation should be as brief as possible. Note that the longer the base, the shorter the classification numbers.. For example, using letters, with a base of 26, it is possible to allocate class numbers no longer than two letters to 676 subjects (that is 26 × 26). Using numerals, with a base of 10, only 100 subjects (that is, 10 × 10) can be allocated numbers no longer than two digits.

Hospitality: Notation should have the ability to accommodate new concepts or subjects as necessary. It should allow for the insertion of both subordinate and coordinate subjects. The former is catered for quite easily by the decimal use of numbers (or the use of letters on the same principle). If 1 represents 'Fiction' and 2 'Poetry' then further expansion is possible in this manner:

1 Fiction

11 Historical fiction

12 Romantic fiction

13 Science fiction

2 Poetry

21 Lyric poetry

The insertion of the coordinate subjects is more difficult but i could be provided for by leaving gaps, for example:

1 Construction

4 Testing

7 Maintenance

but the gaps may not be in appropriate places and therefore could interfere with the required order.

Flexibility: It may be useful to be able to alter citation order according to the needs of a particular set of users. Facet analysis lends itself admirably to variations in preferred citation order.

Expressiveness: This means that the notation reflects the structure of the scheme and such a notation may also be known as 'structural' or 'hierarchical', for example:

I Military ordinance;

II Artillery;

III Field artillery.

Although sometimes considered helpful (the user can understand the systematic order more easily and it can be effective tool in hierarchical computer searching), expressiveness is not essential if it results in longer classification numbers and limits hospitality.

Although the above features may be desirable, it is obviously going to be difficult to incorporate them all into a single scheme. It is particularly difficult in a faceted scheme for synthesis does not lend itself to brevity, simplicity, or expressiveness.

Retroactive Notation: One device which is sometimes used in faceted schemes in an attempt to shorten numbers is 'retroactive' notation. 'Retroactive' simply means 'backwards'. In notational terms a change of facets is indicated by a reversal of alphabetic or numeric direction from forwards to backwards. A classification number such as:

ABCD

shows no change of direction and therefore is derived from one facet only. However the classification number:

CDEBCDABC

shows a change of direction, and therefore a change of facet, between the E and the B, and the D and the A. It could have been written as:

CDE/BCD/ ABC

but the ' /' is superfluous because of the retroactive nature of the number.

In allocating such a notation, it will be seen that the first letters of the alphabet are used to introduce those facets which are to be cited last and not for the primary facets. The letter' A', having been used once, must not be used again in any earlier facet. Similarly 'B', having been used once, must not be used again. Thus the notational base, which is available, is progressively reduced. Care must therefore be taken that when the primary facets are reached, there are still sufficient notational symbols remaining. It is usual to ensure that an adequate amount of the notational base is reserved for the primary facets before allocating a notation to other facets.

Example: Hospitality-from the Library of Congress classification In the fifth edition of Class Q Science will be found:

QD CHEMISTRY

ORGANIC CHEMISTRY 241 Periodicals

243 Yearbooks

245 Collected works

248 History

'Encyclopaedias' are not enumerated or listed, and therefore An encyclopaedia of organic chemistry' cannot be classified. In the sixth edition of Class Q, however, appears:

246 Dictionaries and encyclopaedias

This class number has been neatly slotted into the appropriate place in the scheme by making use of the gap left, for hospitality purposes, in the notation between 245 and 248.

'An encyclopaedia of organic chemistry' can now be classified, the number being:

QD 246

The notation is 'mixed' comprising upper case letters and digits.

Example: Flexibility: From the London education classification. In this scheme the facets are arranged in an order of in CI concreteness, for example:

Lab Teaching methods

Mim Mathematics

Ras Primary schools

The recommended or preferred citation order is there for reverse of this, for example:

Ras Mim Lab = Teaching mathematics in primary schools

It is pointed out, however, by Foskett, the compiler individual libraries or information services may wish to vat; order: 'One of the greatest advantages of a faceted classification is that. . . the facets can be arranged in any sequence, to suit particular user'. If it were desired to bring together all items dealing with 'Teaching methods' and to sub-arrange first by subject and by environment, then the citation order could be altered to come to the schedule order and the classification number would become:

Lab Mim Ras = Teaching mathematics in primary schools

Note the 'pronounceable' notation. This led to some interesting mnemonic classification numbers, for example:

Bux = Documentation Pil = Sex education Ror = Choir schools

Unfortunately in the second edition four letter notation had I introduced and the pronounceable element was therefore reduced.

A change of facet as consistently indicated by a change from lower to an upper case letter. The upper case letter therefore as a facet indicator.

Example: Expression-from the Colon classification

X Economics

X7 Public finance

X72 Tax

X724 Income tax

X7244 on salary

Note the way in which the structure of the scheme is reflected in the notation.

Example: Retroactive notation-from the Dewey decimal classification

Perhaps without realising it. Dewey included a 'flavour' of retroactive notation in his 'History' class:

42 History of England

42.05 History of England in the Tudor period

42.1 History of London

42.105 History of London in the Tudor period

Note that whenever the notation returns to '0', that is goes backwards to '1', then the characteristics of division changes from 'Place' to 'Time'.

Impact of UDC

Probably the greatest impact of UDC on libraries has been through the abridged editions now published in some 16 languages. The first of these was not an official UDC abridgment but was a version used by S.C. Bradford in the Science Museum Library in London. Bradford was an early and enthusiastic supporter of UDC who attempted an index in English similar to the original index of the IIB. Bradford is the Science museum Library before the British Standards Institution became the official British publishers responsible for organising UDC revision and communication of changes as well as publication of English versions.

The first scheme with an analytico-synthetic element was the Universal Decimal Classification. Though the Universal Decimal Classification was not accessible at the time when the Colon Classification was designed and consequently it has not been possible to use it as a model in the designing of the Colon Classification, there is no denying that the latter appeared in the field only a generation later. In spite of it, it had been taken first for description because it has developed the features of an analytico-synthetic classification in a more pronounced and fundamental manner and the auxiliary books and writings centring round it have developed a terminology which makes communication easier. It was a good in disguise that the schedules of Universal Decimal Classification were not accessible for several years after the Colon Classification was designed and developed up to the third edition. If it had been, the pressure of its tradition would have inhibited free thought, even as the Decimal Classification had done. Indeed, it is being realised that many of the faults of the Colon Classification are due to the pressure of the tradition of the Decimal Classification.

In 1931 the IIB became the Institue Internationel de Documentation (II D) and in 1937 changed its name again to the Federation International de Documentation (FID) its present name. In the preparation of the 1927-1933 edition, Otlet and La Fontaine were joined by Frists Donker Duyivis of the Dutch Patent Office, who was to look after the natural science schedules. He became secretary of the II B in 1929 and stayed until his retirement in 1959. He was one of the principal influences on the development of UDC as we know it. The offices of the institute moved to the Hague, together with the master card file of the UDC. From these offices is conducted international coordination of the revision and development of the UDC. The ultimate coordinating body of the UDC is the Central Classification Committee (CCC). Originally this was made up of the editors of UDC and the secretary-general of FIC, but these members were joined in 1964 by representatives from the national committees responsible for publication of native-language editions and for the coordination of the work of special subject committees within each country. In addition there are international subject committees that report directly to the CCC.

Comment and criticism concerning existing schedules and proposals for revision or new classes travel up this committee structure, ultimately to the CCC. It is common for comments or draft schedules to be circulated at each level for future comment, so the process can be lengthy one, but it is also a process that involves the users of the scheme more directly than with any other major scheme. When draft schedules reach the CCC they are considered in the light of the scheme as whole, and after any modification to avoid clashes with any other schedules, they are issued as P-notes. At one time P stood for projects, and there were two kinds: projects provisions that had to be discussed and debated fully before official acceptance, and projects d' extensitions' that would become part of the UDC automatically if no objection was heard within 4 months. After a period of proliferation of different kinds of P-note, the system was simplified to the second of the original projects. After 4 months without objection the contents of P-notes are cumulated in Extensions and Corrections to the UDC published every 6 months and then cumulated triennially.

Revision takes place in three ways. The first is the obvious and natural extension of topics by more detailed subdivision. The second is by minor alternations of existing subdivision notation. The third and most important, since it is almost unique to UDC, is the "starvation policy" introduced by Donker Duyvis. This policy attempts to deal with a problem of particular significance to UDC that it is used mostly in scientific and technical libraries and is strongest in these dynamic and rapidly changing subject areas. It is difficult to apply a policy of changing the internal structure class as it stands-as LC has long done and as DDC now does "its II phoenix schedules'- since this policy assumes fairly static collections and the opportunity for fairly leisurely reclassification.

UDC is a synthetic scheme, using punctuation marks, auxiliary schedules to link and add to the basic notation derived from the DDC. The content of the schedules derived from UDC changed significantly over the years, but the basic outline is similar enough to DDC to assure anyone who knows the outline of DDC. They are dealing with a familiar scheme, at least for subject content. For most users, however, the characteristic feature of UDC is its v wide range of auxiliary signs and schedules, to allow for addition and extension of class numbers and for subdivisions of language form, place, time, etc. However, the main contribution in the auxiliaries is the use of non-decimal punctuation marks to signal use of DDC or DDC based decimal notation.

Auxiliaries: There are two kinds of auxiliaries: general, affecting the whole scheme; and special, affecting only specified parts of the scheme The general auxiliaries can in turn be divided into two groups: those that are simply signs that join other notational elements together a those that are signs that introduce explicit tables of subdivision.

To the first general group belong the signs of addition, extension and relation. The addition sign + is used to join together two subjects not adjacent in the schedules..

54+ 66 CHEMISTRY AND CHEMICAL TECHNOLOGY

It is an awkward combination to index and to file (54+66 shot file before 54 since it covers a larger subject area), and UDC does whole heartedly recommend its use. The extension sign / is used join consecutive notational elements, either two adjacent elements the beginning and end of a sequence.

537/538 ELECTRICITY AND MAGNETISM

22/28 THE CHRISTIAN RELIGION

When the extension sign is used with lengthy notation sharing common higher level, the notation for the higher level may omitted.

621.396/.397 THE EFFECT OF HOT-AIR CENTRAL HEATING ON INDOOR PLANTS

635.695:632.38 VIRUS DISEASES OF INDOOR PLANTS

635.695:582.675 INDOOR ANEMONES

The entity 635.695 INDOOR PLANTS, three laments have been added successively: notation from another class to indicate an effect on the entire notation from within the same class to indicate a problem of the entry, and notation from another class to indicate a kind or subclass of the entry. In other words, the colon is performing three separate functions. Notice also that the order listed here is an ideal arrangement for documents on shelves or in index files of general-to-special type. But the use of only the colon as a relational sign means that UDC numbers must be filed by the notation that fellows the colon, thus reversing that order-at least in this case; in fact the order will be arbitrary, depending on what notation follows the colon. There are further problems with the use of the colon. A collection on mathematics and its subdivisions written for engineering students might include:

51:62 MATHEMATICS FOR ENGINEERS

511 ARITHMETIC

511:62 ARITHMETIC FOR ENGINEERS

512 ALGEBRA

512:62 ALGEBRA FOR ENGINEERS

making it impossible to keep together all the textbooks for engineering students. For a long time, principally in the English editions of UDC, brackets were used to "intercalate" the related notation:

51 [62] MATHEMATICS FOR ENGINEERS

51[62]1 ARITHMETIC FOR ENGINEERS

51[62] 2 ALGEBRA FOR ENGINEERS

511 ARITHMETIC

512 ALGEBRA

The official use of brackets is now as a grouping device, for example:

54 + 66 (05)

might mean A JOURNAL (05) ON CHEMISTRY AND CHEMICAL TECHNOLOGY or CHEMISTRY AND JOURNALS ON CHEMICAL TECHNOLOGY

But UDC now offers

[54 + 66] (05)

to make it clear that the meaning is JOURNALS ON CHEMISTRY AND CHEMICAL TECHNOLOGY.

A more serious problem with the single colon as a relational all sign is that no order is specified or even recommended in DC for the elements that it joints. Thus using 633.491 POTATOES and 632.3 PARASITIC DISEASES, both 633.491P:632.3 and 632.3:633.491 may mean PARASITIC DISEASES OF POTATOES. UDC recognised the potential conclusion and took away most of the value of the sign by instruction to use both combinations in indexes or catalogue. This instruction effectively limited the relational sign to a link between only two components and prevented the exploration of assemblies of more than two components.

The use of the double colon can resolve the problem, by indicating that only the combination as expressed ::.may be used: 633.491 :: 632.3, but not 632.3:: 633.491.

Even with the later developments of : and :: the problems cited earlier remain the use of the relational sign in whatever form to indicate effects or influences (phases), problems (facets), and kinds can result in confused file order.

The remaining general auxiliaries are all tables of subdivision with distinctive punctuation marks to indicate their function.

Auxiliaries of Form and Language: The first two concern only the physical document: the common form auxiliary (0...) and the language auxiliary. Both are derived from the ADDC but with an interesting development that is echoed in some of the other auxiliaries. In DDC the list of common form subdivisions is a mixture of what Berwick. Sayers described, as' inner' and' outer form' on the one hand, the internal point of view or approach to the subject an, on the other hand, the physical arrangement or form of the material, for example, the philosophy of a subject and an ENCYCLOPAEDIA, respectively. UDC was able to recognise the distinction and to offer: 1 for the PHILOSOPHY of a subject, leaving the common subdivisions mostly for 'outer form'. It then enclosed DDCs 0... in parentheses to give it a clear indicator of its separateness from subject numbers. Such a concentration on 'outer form' freed notation used in DOC for 'inner form' for further expansion in UDC.

A similar development took place with the language auxiliary. DOC had no such facility; UDC included it because of its international and multilingual applications. Detail was taken from DOC's class 400 LANGUAGE and given the equals sign as an indicator of this separateness from the subject schedules. A further refinement took place when UDC ignored DOC's notational structure of three integers followed by a decimal point and decimal fraction notation. Instead, UDC regarded all notation as decimal and used a period after every three digits, breaking up a number in order to make it more mnemonic. This practice, together with the introduction of parentheses to introduction form and other subdivisions, free the 0 from its use in DOC only as an indictor and allowed it to be used as a specifying digit:

=42 THE ENGLISH LANGUAGE GROUP

=420 ENGLISH

Auxiliaries of Place, Time Race, and Persons time, and race found in varying degree in most major classification schemes. Like the group already discussed, the next group of general auxiliaries includes the common subdivisions of place, these too enjoy a development freed from the national constrictions of DOC.

The general auxiliary of place () took what was earlier the 'divide like' device of DOC (employing subdivisions of 940-999 to subdivide any other number) and is now the DOC Area Tables, and used those digits in parentheses. Because the parentheses indicated only place, the hitherto inaccessible 91 GEOGRAPHY and 92 BIOGRAPHY were now available as (1) and (2) for new meaning. UDC used them to indicate geographic or topographic detail not tied to politoco-geographic areas: rivers, mountains, seas, and even ideas like central, bordering, north, and south, rivers, mountains, and seas are listed and named in (2) as:

(237.15) SIERRE MADRE AND MEXICAN PLATEAU

Concepts like central, bordering, north, and south are listed at (1) as: (1-14) SOUTH

The (1) is simply a carrier digit to support the concept (-14) SOUTH; in fact, the concept may be added to any other geographical subdivisions in parentheses;

(468.1) ANDALUSIA

(468.1-14) SOUTH ANDALUSIA

For time subdivision UDC departed from all other traditions and used the date enclosed in quotation marks; "1976" means in 1970. The notation is decimal, so that "197" means the 1970s a "1970.01,.01" means January 1,1970.

Periods of time can also be indicated by the extension sing "196/197" means the 1960s and 1970s, and a negative sign-me, BC:

"-0055" 55 BC

The auxiliary for race is a combination of the auxiliaries of place and language, combining their signs. The language auxiliary sign= inside parentheses () indicates the race that speaks that language with form and place, the race auxiliary is able to expand beyond normal limits of the language specification by the freedom from p language numbers. For example, it is able to specify (=94: ESKIMOS, (96) NEGROES, and further, (1.493 = 40) WALLOONS by combining the race and the place specification using the carrier and a further subdivision.

The auxiliary-05 for person originated in class 3 social sciences but was clearly useful for general application:

62-055.2 WOMEN IN ENGINEERING

The only remaining general auxiliaries are the point of numbers .00 ..., and .000.' The first and original point view auxiliary .00 is used when many compounds joined by colons m; introduce confusion in a file, as in a collection of documents for business concern. It might be easier to organise the collection by the several aspects of the business and then subdivide b variety of subdivisions using colons. For example:

could be rearranged as:

635.965:582.675	INDOOR PLANTS :MARSH MARIGOLD
635.965:632.38	INDOOR PLANTS :VIRUS DISEASE
635.965:697.38	INDOOR PLANTS: EFFECTS OF CENTRAL HEATING
635.965.004:632.38	INDOOR PLANTS: MATERIAL MARSH MARIGOLD
635.965:002.3:582.675	INDOOR PLANTS:DETERIORATION /WEAR:EFFECT OF CENTRAL HEATING.

The introduction to the UDC has more examples of these of .00

A fairly recent addition to the point-of view auxiliary is one to account for an author's point of view. The notation is .000 and may be used as follows:

635.965.004:632.38	INDOOR PLANTS:USE/CARE:VIRUS DISEASE
162.6.000.335.5	DIALECTICS FROM THE MARXIST POINT OF VIEW

linking 162.6 DIALECTICSand 335.5 MARXISM

Special Auxiliaries: Special auxiliaries are subdivisions that deal only with limited ranges of subjects. They have the signs-, .0, and '. The-and .0 are equivalent and are so used throughout the scheme, occasionally being combined when more than one kind of special subdivision exists for combination, as in class VIII LITERATURE they may be applied anywhere in the area that they cover:

621-77	SAFETY DEVICES
621.039 5-77	SAFETY DEVICES IN NUCLEAR REACTORS
7.061	FORGERY IN ART
75.061	FORGERY IN PAINTINGS

There is no consistency in the use of and .0 in the scheme, as Dubuc points out (10), and proposals have been made to use only.

One other form of special auxiliary is the postrophe to indicate combinations of chemical elements:

546.33	SODIUM
546.13	CHLORINE
546.33'13	SODIUM CHLORIDE

Various Classes

The enumerated schedules themselves resemble the familiar decimal structure of the DDC, but the resemblance is more apparent than real. The same major classes are present and for the most part of the same divisions appear within these classes; but from that point onward (or downward) more and more differences can be seen, resulting from revisions within UDC. For example, RADIO ENGINEERING is represented by 621384 in the DOC but by 621.396 in DOC. This seems to be similar because both numbers begin with 621.3, but in fact the notation is distinctly different, as it is therefore for the whole of this large class. Differences in the schedules are not limited to notational differences of this kind. UDC has also restructured classes from the form used by DOC; for example, the use in 8 LITERATURE of the two special auxiliaries-AND .to accommodate the facets of form and of literary science and technique. The facet of period, if necessary, can of course, be represented by the Common auxiliary of time.

To describe in detail the enumerated content of the classes of UDC would be to repeat in large part a description of DOC, which has been laid out elsewhere in many textbooks and is in any case generally well known. Instead, the major differences are described here.

Generalities: UDC accepted most of this class as Dewey had laid it out in DOC. The major exception was in the early development of 00 as a class devoted to fundamentals of knowledge. DOC has now developed this class, but its form remains distinct from UDC, which divides the class as:

001 THE SCIENCES AND KNOWLEDGE IN GENERAL

002 DOCUMENTATION

003 SEMIOTICS, SYNTACTIC'S, SEMANTICS, WRITING, SCRIPTS, NOTATIONS, SIGNS AND SYMBOLS

005 ORGANISATION STUDY, METHODOLOGY, ANALYSIS AND SYSTEMATISATION GENERALLY.

007 ACTIVITY AND ORGANISING INFORMATION, COMMUNICATION, CONTROL THEORY (CYBERNETICS) INCLUDING 'HUMAN ENGINEERING'.

008 CIVILIZATION CULTURE PROGRESS

009 THE HUMANITIES THE" ARTS" IN GENERAL

Philosophy: With minor variations of terminology this class reflects the DOC from which it was originally taken, with the exception of the area of psychology. In DOC, 130 and 150 are devoted to the area of the mind; 130 concentrates on the ills of the mind and also on the occult and paranormal phenomena while 150 is concerned with the operations of the mind in its normal state. UDC anticipated DDC's re-organisation of these classes in using 13 for the occult and parapsychology, and 15 for the functions of the mind. Indeed, UDC introduced a new classification of the subject at 159.9, so as not to interfere with collections classified by the original 15. This new classification has since been reflected in DDC revisions.

Religion: There are few differences here between DDC and UDC The organisation of this class is biased towards Protestant Christianity because of the persuasion of melvil Dewey and his assistants to the extreme point of the absence of a single notation for Christianity itself, on the assumption that religion was Christianity and anything else was either variation or heresy. UDC fares better than DDC because the synthetic nature of UDC allows the construction of detailed notation for concepts and problems in non-Christian religions denied by the more enumerative structure of DDC.

Social Sciences: In many subdivisions of this major class there are minor differences between DDC and UDC occasioned, for example, by the ability of UDC to use the common auxiliary of place ( ) instead of DDC's "add" device, or by the allocation of specific notation for geographical extension, as in 310 STATISTICS. Otherwise the subdivisions of this class are the familiar ones, with the exception of LAW. Law is always a problem for classification schemes; the library of Congress has yet to publish a complete schedule. DOCs class 340 LAW for many editions was the most confused class in the scheme, though the revised version in DDEC 18 improved beyond measure. UDC adopted some of the early DOC class, changed some, and relied on synthesis to modify the rest sufficiently to solve most problems of subject description. Part of the problem lies in the use of legal literature by lawyers: in the dichotomy of the literature organised by problem (or kind of law) or by legal system.

UDC subdivided 340 LAW as:

340	LAW IN GENERAL
341	INTERNATIONAL LAW
342	PUBLIC LAW; CONSTITUTIONAL LAW
343	CRIMINAL LAW; PENAL OFFENCES; PENOLOGY, CRIMINOLOGY
344	SPECIAL LAW; CRIMINAL LAW.
347	PRIVATE LAW; CIVIL LAW
348	ECCLESIASTICAL AND CANONICAL LAW

This subdivision avoided the DDC inclusion of US and UK STATUTES AND CASES as major subdivisions of the class LAW, and of LAW OF OTHER COUNTRIES. These inclusions violated the fundamental laws of classification and caused severe confusion in the class and its practical application in law libraries.

As in so many cases, this approach by UDC, based on the analytico-synthetic philosophy, resulted in the later modification of DDC's class to a very similar overall organisation.

PHILOLOGY LANGUAGES

This is a non-class, since LANGUAGE has now been moved to class 8, to form LANGUAGE, LINGUISTICS, LITERATURE.

Mathematics and Natural Science: UDC kept close to the original DDC outline of this class, though it made minor changes that anticipated later DDC developments. Most developments were in extensions to the existing classes and in relatively minor shifts—for example, 541 QUALITATIVE ANALYSIS and 545 QUANTITATIVE ANALYSIS to 543.061 and 543.062, respectively, as part of 543 ANALYTICAL CHEMISTRY. In fact, UDC, in the area of science that was to be one of its major strengths, retained many of DDC's weaknesses; for example:

523.2 SOLAR SYSTEM 523.3 MOON

523.4 PLANETS 523.5 METEORS 523.6 COMETS

523.7 SUN

523.8 STARS

reflecting a distinctly geocentric view of the universe.

On the whole, however, UDC has successfully retained the century-old framework of this class from DOC because UDC's synthetic approach can restructure a notation to accommodate new topics.

The entry 608 includes an extremely useful area on patents and inventions, derived from DOC but expanded to reflect the scientific and technological orientation of UDC.

Medicine: This includes 618 as a special section on GYNECOLOGY, OBSTETRICS. Also, 619 is VETERINARY MEDICINE, a special class almost abandoned as a discipline by DOC and included with animal husbandry.

Engineering and Technology: In this group of subjects and disciplines UDC departed most radically from DOC. The adoption of UDC by European special libraries demanded the development of the scientific and technological areas, and in particular, the area of technology. Indeed, the UDC schedule for textile technology, developed for the French-language edition of 1928, was translated into English for inclusion in DOC 11 (1927) with the financial support of an American industrialist.

In particular, the dynamic area of telecommunications, especially RADIO AND TELEVISION ENGINEERING, called for expansion and revision. DOC had used 621.384; UDC, following Donker Duyvis's "starvation" policy, moved them to 621.396/ .397 and then later developed 621.38 for ELECTRONICS.

Agriculture: The early DOC had listed the operations and problems of agriculture in 631/632, and the products in 633/638. UDC's colon device has always allowed combination of entity and process, though DOC has recently allowed only limited combination.

65 MANAGEMENT, ORGANISATION OF INDUSTRY AND

COMMERCE, BUSINESS, COMMUNICATION AND TRANSPORT.

The structure of UDC includes a detailed subfacet on management theory that can be applied throughout the class. The rest of the class lists management areas. Unfortunately it still includes transport and communication services (at 654/656), which really belong elsewhere and are not part of management services.

Arts and Recreation: In general UDC accepted (and still accepts) DDC's basis for the organisation of this class, but the addition of a special auxiliary for the class allow more detail than does DDC.

For example, 7.025.4 RESTORATION allows

755.025.4 RESTORATION OF RELIGIOUS PAINTINGS.

8 LANGUAGE. LINGUISTICS, LITERATURE

Originally this class contained only LITERATURE; it now also contains LANGUAGE and LINGUISTICS. The entry 801 contains what used to be in 40/41; for example, 415 GRAMMAR has been moved to 801.5 GRAMMAR. The languages that used to be in 42/49 are now it:. 802/ 809, reflecting the auxiliary table of languages. Detail from 801 may be added to any specific language notation by replacing 801 with the dash that signifies a special auxiliary, so that 809.166 WELSH LANGUAGE may be extended to WELSH GRAMMAR by adding the 5 of 801.5 as a special auxiliary: 809.166-5 WELSH GRAMMAR.

UDC applied its special auxiliaries in 82/89 to improve the DDC model from which it was derived. DDC had subdivided the class hierarchically to produce chains like:

800	LITERATURE
820	ENGLISH LITERATURE
821	ENGLISH POETRY
821.3	English POETRY OF ELIZABETHAN PERIOD

UDC used two special and one common auxiliary to produce an even more sophisticated expression. Languages are left as an integer, and to them are added a special auxiliary to reflect form (e.g.,-1 POETRY) and, if necessary, another special auxiliary to reflect special processes like criticism or translation (e.g., 03 TRANSLATION).

Thus, with 820 ENGLISH LITERATURE we may find:

820"15"	ENGLISH LITERATURE OF THE SIXTEENTH CENTURY
820-1"15"	English POETRY OF THE SIXTEENTH CENTURY
820-1"15	English POETRY 03 TRANSLATIONS OF English POETRY OF THE SIXTEENTH CENTURY
820-1 " 820-1"15" .03=40	TRANSLATIONS INTO French (using the common auxiliary of language) OF English POETRY OF THE SIXTEENTH CENTURY.

9 GEOGRAPHY, BIOGRAPHY, HISTORY UDC retained the original outline of DDC's Class 900, with the exception of the introduction of the most useful class 908 — HOMELAND STUDIES. This includes comprehensive studies on the history, geography, economics, and culture of a country.

UDC has been used in several projects for the production of indexes or the control of information storage and retrieval systems using data-processing systems. The principal attractions are the synthetic nature of the scheme and its notation, which allows commands or search statements to be directed to selected components in document descriptions, and the hierarchical grouping, inherent in any classification scheme, which allows easy generic searching.

Other Classifications

Faceted: A faceted scheme lists concepts only-classification numbers for complex subjects are built up by means of synthesis.

Advantages: Because complex subjects are not listed, such schemes are easier to compile.

The schedules are shorter for the same reason but, despite their brevity, they permit the classification of both very simple and very complex subjects.

New subjects can very often be catered for by the combination of already existing concepts.

Disadvantages: The notation can become long and complex and why be unsuitable for the arrangement of documents on shelves as in a library. The problem of citation order can cause difficulty.

Enumerative: An enumerative scheme attempts to list all possible subjects, both simple and complex, within the defined subject field or fields.

Advantages: Such scheme have been generally accepted and widely used with considerable success throughout the world for a long period of time. A fairly short and uncomplicated notation can be used. 'Notationally', it is easier to display the structure of the scheme.

Disadvantages: It is impossible to list every conceivable subject.

There can be a lack of accommodation for even simple subject.

New subjects cannot be accommodated and regular revision may be required.

In relation to the use of general enumerative schemes in libraries, standardisation is facilitated because classification numbers may be included in centralised records. For example, Dewey decimal classification and Library of Congress classification numbers, are included in eye-readable and machine-readable records supplied by the Library of Congress and the British Library. With schemes such as the Dewey decimal classification there is also the possibility of 'integrity of numbers', that is, the stabilising of existing numbers, a policy initiated by Dewey.

However, general schemes may be unsuitable for certain purposes. For example, in libraries and information services which specialise in particular subject fields, they are not detailed enough specific areas. Special classification schemes, restricted by subject are therefore required. Although these may be enumerative faceted, the latter is now more common. Special schemes are useful for the manual filing of office papers and for the coding entities in computerised systems.

12

CIRCULATION PROCESS

The books are displayed on the shelves and a reference desk is provided so that readers may get guidance for selecting their reading material. A competent and sympathetic staff is provided so that reading interest of readers be aroused and efforts be made to sustain it for as long time as it is possible. The books may be used within the library premises but all persons who are animated with the desire of reading may not be able to find out so much spare time that they can sit in the library for reading purposes. All persons are busy throughout the day in their respective vocations for earning their livelihood. The students are busy in their classes in the daytime.

The question arises as to how the library resources can be utilised properly. Are the books to be preserved? Should these be allowed to be read out of the library premises so as to quench the thirst for knowledge of those persons, who cannot devote enough time for reading the books in the library premises? Moreover, would it be physically possible to provide enough space for accommodating thousands of readers who will have to come to library if they know that they cannot take home the books for reading purposes? Would it be economical? All these implications of not allowing the books to be issued out for home reading suggest the need for some device by which the urge for reading is fully satisfied without sacrificing any fundamental principle.

Since olden times, in order to solve these formidable questions the issuing of books for home reading has been resorted to. "Of all library activities, the circulation of books for home use represents by far the major public service provided by the American public library." In fact, all activities and processes are gone through so that lending out of books is facilitated. "The circulation function in libraries involves every use of library materials and the successful performance of the function is a measure of the effectiveness of all other duties to which librarians devote themselves. The best equipped library located in the most modern plant and staffed with the most capable librarians would be a mausoleum of recorded knowledge if the circulation function was omitted. The processes and services which result in-bringing users and library materials into productive relationship is the circulation function in libraries."

The old methods were rudimentary and primitive according to the needs of the time but with the increase in the number of readers and with a change in the concept of librarianship and libraries, it was felt that some satisfactory methods should be devised for facilitating the better use of books.

The Circulation work involves the following jobs:

1. Registration of Members;
2. Lending of Books;
3. Charging of Overdoes;
4. Reservation of Books;
5. Renewal of Books;
6. Maintenance of Records;
7. Maintenance of Statistics;
8. Lending of Books on Inter Library Loan Basis;
9. Miscellaneous Jobs.

Procedure of Admission

Registration of Members: As already pointed out, for putting the books to better use, the books may be allowed to be taken home for reading. The question arises as to whether there is any necessity of keeping some record of those persons who want to get books issued. Should we issue books to all persons without making note of them? Will it be economical or will it present any problem? The first objection to the liberal view that any book may be given to any reader without any record is that books are a public property and the librarian is accountable to the public authority for the disposal of books for which the public authorities have spent a lot of money. Even if we adopt the liberal view, it will be difficult to satisfy the demands of all readers if we do not keep any account of the books lent out. One book may be required by many readers and if the issued book is not got back, the other readers may not get the same book unless new copies of the same book are procured immediately for which unlimited funds are required but these are unfortunately not available in abundance.

Purposes of Registration

To know the Borrower: It is essential to know the whereabouts of a borrower because in case he does not return the issued book, he may be reminded to return the book. "This involves a contractual relationship between the library and its patron, a responsibility on the part of the library to safeguard the property entrusted to it and the protection of the rights of other individuals in the community who may wish to use the materials."

To have Dependable Statistics for Measuring the Usefulness or Effectiveness of a Library to the Population of the Area Served by it: "The principal data upon which the library depends in measuring its social significance to its patrons are the number of volumes circulated and the number of borrowers served during the year".

To Know the General Characteristics of the Borrowers: Whether they are young or old, male or female, officials, businessmen or peasants? Do they belong to rural or urban areas, lower, middle or upper classes?

To Know the Utility of the Library to the People of the Area, its Services and its Demands: These figures can also be used to compare the services rendered by one library in comparison with other libraries.

Registration Procedure: Keeping in view the purposes of registration, the registration procedures should be thought out. In other words, the permanent record which can be used easily should be kept. The generally accepted procedures include the filling up of a membership form; preferably in 5" x 3" card form which will contain the would-be member's name, permanent and present addresses, occupation and the name and address of the guarantor. A specimen of the membership form is given below:

Recto

To	Membership No.
The Librarian,	Category
....	Date of expiry
....	(For office use only)

Sir,

Kindly enrol me as a member of your library. I give below all my relevant particulars. I promise to abide by all library rules which may be made applicable from time to time. I would be liable to pay any dues, which I may owe due to my negligence or infringement of library rules. 1 certify that I am not already a member of this library in any capacity.

Name (Block letters)..

Present Local Address..

Class/Roll No...

Department/College/School......................................

Permanent Address...

Signature of the Guarantor.

Address.

Signature of the applicant.

Verso

(For office use only)

Receipt No. and Date (For Cash Deposit, if any)......................

....

Particulars checked and found in order.

(Initials of the Counter Assistant).

Librarian's Orders...

Date of enrolment..

Signature of the applicant with date..

Date of cancellation of the card and reason thereof.........................

....

Clearance certificate issued on...

Refund of cash deposit, if any..

Initials of the Assistant.

Librarian's Signature..

As already mentioned, these application forms should be in the form of 5" x 3" cards so that these may be arranged in a tray alphabetically. In this way, it is easier to find out any information regarding a member. If these application forms are kept in a file, it is difficult to consult the same because every time a new member is enrolled, the order in the file will be disturbed if it is to be maintained in an alphabetical order. If it is not kept in an alphabetical order, it becomes difficult to consult. Some libraries maintain this record in a register form just like an accession register.' It is difficult to consult it. But some libraries prefer to keep a duplicate record, i.e., on cards and registers. This can be resorted to in special circumstances provided staff is enough. Otherwise, it will be merely a duplicate record and may not serve any useful purpose.

In some libraries, a prospective member is asked to deposit a cash security. This may be resorted to where either a guarantor is not available or where the cost of the book exceeds a certain limit. Some libraries insist on depositing cash security in addition to the guarantee. This system, it has been amply experienced, puts a damper upon the enthusiasm of the prospective members to enrol themselves as members of the library and thus the library is not used to the extent it should be used. In foreign libraries, even the condition of guarantee is waived off in many cases. To increase the use of the libraries, it is desirable that the condition of cash deposit should not be insisted upon, rather it should be made an alternative in case of persons who cannot get a guarantor. In this case, a separate cash security register should be maintained.

Each member is allotted a membership number. It is quoted often in many cases. This number is allotted in a consecutive manner. It is easier to know the number of members at any time. A proper record should be kept of those members who have ceased to be the members of the library because it is desirable to know the number of active members at a time. For this purpose, it would be useful if fresh members are enrolled every year. In case of students in a school/college/university, it would be better if they are enrolled for the period they are normally expected to be in the institution. At the time of cancellation of membership, a proper record may be kept on the application form. In subscription libraries, prospective members have to pay a subscription fee at various intervals, may be monthly, quarterly, half-yearly and sometimes yearly. A subscription register should be maintained for this purpose. The subscription libraries are now becoming the things of the past. After a person is enrolled as a member, he is given a membership card or membership-cum-identity card along with as many membership tickets as he is entitled to according to his category and as are required under a specific charging system. The member is now eligible to draw books.

Lending of Books: There are different systems of lending books. In case of open access system which is now becoming more and more popular, a member is allowed access to the shelves. He makes selection of books either by consulting the catalogue, the Reference Assistant or by browsing amongst the books on the shelves which are generally arranged subjectwise.

Fees and Fine Structure

A member takes out the books from the shelves and takes them to the issue counter for getting them issued in his name. It is better if the member presents the books along with his membership card and tickets in such a manner that the Due Date Slip and Book Pocket along with Book Card are visible to the Issue Counter Assistant. The Assistant after verifying the *bona fides* of the member makes necessary records in accordance with the specific charging system followed in a particular library. The Counter Assistant takes out the Book Card out of the Book Pocket and keeps the Readers' Tickets and Book Cards in juxtaposition in a charging tray, especially prepared for the purpose, behind a date guide. The Book Cards which contain the Call Numbers and Accession Numbers of the book along with other requisite information about the book are arranged behind a date guide in a classified manner. In some libraries, particularly public libraries, these cards are arranged accessionwise. The Membership Card/Membership-cum-Identity Card is generally returned to the member along with the books. The due date/date of issue is put on the Due Date Slips either by a rubber stamp or by pen.

Issue of Gate Passes: In order to ensure that proper duplicate record is kept for each book issued out from a library, the author after assuming charge of the post of University Librarian, Himachal Pradesh University, Similar introduced the 'Gate Pass System'. Under this system, a card, thinner than an ordinary catalogue card, of the size of 2" x 1½" or 2½" x 2" is prepared for each book. The particulars of the book, *i e.,* Author, Title, Call No. and ACC. No. are either got printed or stamped (A special stamp is got prepared for the purpose) on both sides of the Gate Pass so that it can be used twice thereby economising stationery. At the time of issuing a book, the Issue Counter Assistant fills up the columns of the Gate Pass and inserts it in the book and the Janitor/Library Attendant at the check counter verifies the particulars of the Gate Pass with those of the issued book and allows the reader to take the book home and the Gate Pass is inserted in a locked box.

After the closing of the Issue counter, the Box containing Gate Passes is handed over to the Assistant Librarian (Readers Services). Simultaneously, the book cards of the issued books are also sent to him. The Assistant Librarian tallies the particulars of the issued books from the book cards and Gate Passes and after verification and rectification if some mistakes are detected, he returns the book cards to the Issue Counter Assistant and files the Gate Passes either in a classified order or by accession number in a locked Cabinet which remains with him. He makes an entry to this effect in a Register which is put up to the University Librarian for his information. This system ensures.

1. That for each book issued proper duplicate record is kept thereby eliminating the chances of tampering with the Issue Record. (In some libraries some irresponsible persons at the Issue Counter after issuing the books may destroy the book cards, thereby leaving no record with the library on the basis of which the library could claim back the unreturned books).
2. That the mistakes in recording the particulars of issued books are rectified at the earliest moment. (It has been found that due to rush at the counter book cards of books other than the issued books are filed).
3. That at least three persons (one of them being a senior staff member) are involved in the issuing of books thereby ensuring that no malpractices or irregularities are committed by the library staff.
4. That the readers are made to wait at the check counter for few seconds thereby giving enough time to the checking staff to find out if the reader is smuggling out a book unauthorisedly.
5. That the authorities are convinced that the library has been taking necessary steps to stop stealing or mutilation of records, thereby making the writing off of lost books easy. (when the books are returned, a reverse process is followed as explained in Sub-Section 'Cancellation of Gate Passes').

In open access libraries, one check counter is maintained where all the books issued are checked at this counter in order to check as to whether the books which are being taken out of the library premises have been issued properly or not. In closed access libraries, the members have to give a requisition slip. After some time, the reader comes to the counter and presents his membership card along with the membership tickets. The same process of issue is to be followed as is followed in case of open access libraries.

Discharging Procedure: The member after reading the books comes back to the library for returning the books. He presents the books at the Return Counter of the Library in such a manner that Due Date Slip pasted in the book is visible. The Counter Assistant after ascertaining the due date/date of issue from the Due Date Slip locates the corresponding card from the charging tray by looking up the cards behind the relevant date guide. The Call Number or the Accession Number is looked up and the corresponding cards are traced out from behind the particular date guide. These Book Cards along with the Readers' Tickets/Membership Cards are taken out of the charging tray and the book cards are slipped into the book pockets and the membership tickets are handed over to the member. Before the membership card/ticket is returned, the Counter Assistant makes sure that the book has been returned on the due date and no overdue charge is to be paid by the member. In case, the book has not been returned in time, the overdue fine is charged from the member before the membership ticket/card is returned to the member, otherwise it is presumed that the member has been absolved of the responsibility. In case there is lot of rush on the Return Counter, the Counter Assistant after locating the relevant card from the charging tray returns the membership ticket/card to the member after verifying that the book has been returned in time. The slipping of the book card is postponed for the time being and it is completed at some leisure hours. This system is called *Delayed Discharge.*

Cancellation of Gate Passes: In the evening the Incharge Circulation Section sends all the returned books along with their book cards to the Assistant Librarian (Readers Services, who verifies the particulars of each of the returned books and their book cards with those of the relevant Gate Passes after taking out one by one from the Gate Passes Cabinet and goes on cancelling the Gate Passes. If only one side of the Gate Passes is used these are sent to the circulation section for using them again. The books are sent to the stacks and the signature of the Stack Attendant to whom the books are handed over are taken in a Register meant for the purpose which is put up to the librarian daily for his information. In this way, it is ensured that the books have been duly sent back to the stacks thereby making the Incharge stacks responsible for the loss of the books.

Overdue Charges: An overdue charge is traditionally levied for those books which are returned after due date. Some people consider it as a primitive charge and denounce it while others consider it essential. They argue that in order to ensure that the books are returned in time and other members are not put to a disadvantage, some kind of punishment must be sanctioned and that monetary levy is the most appropriate and effective remedy. There are others who suggest that, no doubt, monetary levy is effective but the main purpose of levying this charge is to regularise the issue and return of book This can be achieved by disallowing the issue of books to the defaulter readers for a certain period.

This kind of arrangement can be successful as has been demonstrated by many foreign libraries. If monetary charge is levied for returning the books after due date, care should be taken that it does not take the shape of punishment. It should serve as a dissuading measure by which readers return the books at the proper time. The charge should be just a token amount, because it can neither become a source of revenue nor it should be considered as such.

In case such overdue charge is levied, the question of realisation presents many problems. Whether a regular receipt in token of its collection should be issued or a Conscience Box be used for this purpose. This depends upon the cost accounting done by taking into consideration the staff time spent and the amount to be paid as salary for the person who issues such receipts as compared to the amount realised as overdue fine. It has been experienced that in big libraries, some sort of Conscience Box is introduced. A Conscience Box is a contrivance by which the defaulter member puts the amount of overdue charge in coins as determined by the Counter Assistant in a box which is locked and has got a hole on the upper side cover and no receipt is issued.

The coins are counted in the evening and the amount is entered in the cash book of the library. The most important consideration which should be taken in this respect is that overdues should not be named as fine. Rather, it should indicate that due to not returning the books in time, the defaulter pays a little amount for his wrong.

Special Books

Due to general awakening and increased interest in reading amongst the general public and the increased emphasis on research and western impact on teaching methods, the demand for books has increased tremendously. Many books, especially text books and other related reading materials, remain in great demand. The libraries are incapable of meeting all the demands of the readers due to stringency of funds.

Due to this reason, an adequate number of copies of certain books cannot be purchased. If the requisite number of copies are purchased, it is feared that other standard and essential books may not be purchased because of limited funds.

Similarly, new and controversial books are in great demand. Moreover, the demand for textbooks and new and controversial books is very much temporary because when the examinations are over or when the controversy is over or subsides, the demand also slackens and if as many copies as are required by the readers at one time are acquired, it, though theoretically, fulfils the implications of the Second Law of Library Science, e.g., 'Every reader his/her book' but it will violate the Third Law of Library Science, e.g., 'Every book its readers' because after some time, most of the copies of such books will become idle and will curse the librarian for not putting them to best use.

The librarians have rightly thought out a proper method to control this situation. It will avoid unnecessary wastage of money and will fulfil the legitimate demands of the readers also. This method is known as 'Reservation of Books'. Dr. S. R. Ranganathan calls it 'Bespeaking work'.

This system will, in addition, check the unsocial habit of certain readers and members who somehow or other corner the books by keeping them issued in their names.

Reservation Procedures: When readers or members find some difficulty in getting particular books in a library, they are directed by the librarian to get such books reserved. The following procedure is followed for this purpose: The reader in need of a particular book gives in writing the particulars of the book on either a slip of paper along with his address or he fills up a printed card and hands over the same to the Counter Assistant. This reservation card is generally self addressed and self-stamped so that the intimation may be sent to the concerned reader whenever the book is returned. The specimen of such a card is given below:

Reservation Card

Recto

Call No.

Acc. No.

Author..

Title...

To

The Librarian,

Dear Sir,

Kindly reserve the above-mentioned book for me and inform me as soon as it is available for issue.

Yours faithfully,

(Signature of the member.)

Dated

Verso

Dear Sir,

Stamp

Please collect the book the particulars of which are given on reverse up to............ otherwise it will be issued to other members.

Address of

the member.......................

....

Librarian.

In order to ensure that the books are issued to all the readers in proper order of their reservation, the relevant information should be kept by the Issue Counter either in a separate card or in a counterfoil a sunder:

Recto

Name of the Library

Date and time of Deposit of Reservation Card.......................

Name of the Reader...

His Membership No..

For Staff Use only-Shelf Checked

Found/Not Found Initials of the Stack Attendant.

Dated......................

Issue Records Checked

1. Reserved for.. on.......................
2. Not Found..
3. Issued to..
4. Due on...

Verso

Recalled on..

Reminders sent vide office letter No................ dated..............

Referred to Librarian on...

Librarians's orders...

Further action..

Reservation Slip

Call No................... Author................... Ace. No.......................

Title...

Issued currently to..

Address:...

Due date of return..

Dale of reservation...

Date of receipt of the Book..

Date of sending intimation to the
reader for issuing the book..

Librarian/Deputy Lib./
Circulation Incharge.

Assistant.

On receipt of this bespeaking or reservation card, the Issue Counter Assistant puts this card in a tray meant for the purpose. At the appointed time on each day, the Assistant, by looking up the Call Number, Author and Title of the book locates the book card from the charged tray. It is a time-consuming job and so, for speedy work, the library must ensure that the arrangement of the cards in the charged tray is classified and that there are as few sequences of the cards in the charged tray as are possible because otherwise it will be a very difficult job.

After locating the particulars in the charged tray, the Assistant fills up the columns of the Reservation Slip and attaches the same with the book card of the reserved book. The Slip should exhibit in bold letters the words 'Reservation Slip' and this should be attached with the book card in such a manner that the words 'Reservation Slip or 'Reserved' should be projected. It should be visible easily. The relevant card is filed at the same place from where it was taken out. The Assistant at the Issue Counter sends the reservation card mentioned above to the member who got the book reserved and makes a note to this effect on the Reservation Slip which is lying in the book pocket of the reserved book. The said book is placed in the sequence 'Reserved Books' in a classified manner.

If the reader presents the 'Reservation Card' within the stipulated date or sends a letter requesting the extension of time due to certain tangible reasons, the Counter Assistant issues the book to the reader or replies in the affirmative or negative, as it is thought fit. If the reader does not turn up for getting issued the book or his request for extension of time is not accepted, the book, if reserved by other readers, the reservation card of which will also be found in the book pocket of the book at number 2, is informed accordingly and same procedure will be followed as is given above. If the book has not been reserved by other readers, the book is sent to the stacks for shelving purposes.

Renewal of Books: Some books are required by readers time after again, because they may require it constantly or that the books being lengthy, may require more time for studying them thoroughly. The books are to be put to maximum use constantly as is enjoined upon by the First and Third Laws of Library Science. Moreover, there is no harm if books are reissued to the same members when the particular books are not in demand. But care must be taken to ensure that the demand of such readers must be genuine. In other words, the books should not be renewed at the expense of other genuine readers.

The demand of other readers can be ascertained from the reservation cards received by the Counter Assistant. In certain special cases, if the expediency demands and if the demand of those readers whom the particular books have already been issued is found genuine, the departure may be made and the books may be reissued. "Agree to a long period loan only if

(a) The book is of a type for which there is not general demand;

(b) The reader needs it for a serious purpose;

(c) He agrees to return it to the library within twenty-four hours of receiving a request for it."

Renewal Procedures: The renewal of books can be effected in the following ways: 1. By presenting the books in person, 2. By post, 3. By telephone:

1. If the books are physically brought in the library and a request for renewal is made, these are reissued after locating the Book Card of the concerned book. New due dates are put on the Due Date Slip and the Book Card. The book is returned to the member and the Book Card along with the reader's ticket is placed in the charged tray behind a new due date guide.
2. If the request for renewal of a particular book is received by post, the relevant book card is located from the charged tray by ascertaining the call number from the letter of request which has been received by the Counter Assistant. The new due date is put on the Book Card of the relevant book and a reply is sent to the member concerned with a direction that new due date be put on the Date Slip of the concerned book. The Book Card of the renewed book is put either under the new due date guide with a dummy card which should bear the new due date against the old due date or the book card duly marked with the words 'Renewed until (Date)' is put behind the original due date guide.
3. If the request for renewal is received on telephone, the message is noted down and the reader is told to ring again. He is informed that he will be told about the renewal within a few minutes. This message is sent to the Counter Assistant who follows the usual procedure and sends back the requisite message to the librarian and requisite remarks are

put on the book card. If the telephone is on the issue counter, the reply can be given immediately by locating the book card from the charged tray. If some overdues are to be paid, the reader is told about the same and is directed to deposit the same within few days. It may be stipulated that the renewal would be valid only if the overdues are paid on the stipulated date. "In Dunedin, New Zealand, borrowers renewing by phone are given a renewal number of which a record is kept at the library and are asked to write this number on the date slip. This is a safeguard against a borrower's claiming that he renewed by phone a book now overdue."

4. If the member visits the library personally but does not bring the book to be renewed, the procedure that of renewals by post or telephone is followed, except that some kind of token signatures may be had from the member, if necessary.

Overnight Issues: In every library, there are certain books whose issue is to be restricted because these are required in the library at all hours. In other words, some books are such that these may be required in the library premises for consultation at any time, so these are not reference books in the strict sense of the word. For example, text books which are generally kept in a 'reserved section' are not reference books but these are not issued out on normal conditions. But because books are to be put to maximum use and every reader is to be given his requisite book, it is thought proper to devise a method by which the readers may be enabled to read the required books. This method is known as 'Overnight issue of books'. In this method, books are issued at the time of closing the library and the readers are asked to return the books within an hour of the opening of the library on the next day. Another condition for the issue of such book is that if it is not returned within the stipulated period a special overdue charge at enhanced rate may be charged. In some cases, the membership card/identity card of the member is kept in the library when such a book is issued for overnight and if he does not return the said book on the next day, he cannot get any other book issued on his membership/identity card.

Reserved Items

Postal Loans: Some readers who reside out of station, if enrolled as members, may be allowed to borrow books on special terms. These include the payment of postal charges to be incurred for sending and receiving the books. The books are issued for a longer period, say, for a month or so, to cover the time which is bound to be spent in transit. This is a very reasonable and practical solution to help the outstation members

Loans to Staff: Though in every library, staff members are provided certain special privileges. These include issue of more books, exemption from the payment of overdue charges and issue of new books before these are issued to other members. The staff members may be allowed such privileges but certain restrictions such as limit of number of books to be issued, the shorter period of issue and the obligation to return the new books immediately when demanded should be put. The same conditions may be put for other privileged members.

Loan of Pamphlets and Magazines: Though ephemeral materials are not generally issued out but on special conditions, these may be issued out for a very limited period. Since these pamphlets do not contain enough stiff paper cover, a proper binding is required otherwise there remains a danger of their early wear and tear. The pamphlets of permanent value are processed just like books.

Returning Books at Another Service Point: Though, strictly speaking, books must be returned at the counter where from these were got issued because in the absence of proper record at other service points neither it will be possible to find out the defaulters nor overdue charges can be calculated. This system will prove very costly. In this system, temporary receipt can be given to the reader who can get another book from the same library from which he originally borrowed the book. In England, some library systems allow such practices. The books returned at other branch libraries though borrowed from the central libraries, are returned on telephone to the latter and these are collected by the travelling vans of the central library whenever it visits the branch libraries during the week.

Inter-availability of Tickets: A person who is a member of one library system of a city and goes temporarily to another city may want to use the library of that city. On the production of the membership ticket of the library of which he is a member, the other library issues him books. Similarly those persons who are members of the latter library, are allowed to draw books from the former library. This system would be known to have inter-availability of tickets. It is based on reciprocity. This system is very useful because when people go on holidays for few days, they can make use of the library services without any-difficulty. It will, no doubt, to some extent entail an extra precaution, labour and expense on the part of libraries.

Transfer of Books to Branch Libraries: Those library systems which have got branch libraries and where all book purchases and their technical processing are centralised at the central library, must devise some methods by which the books can be sent to the branch libraries and a suitable record can be kept for that purpose. The same problem is faced in a University's central library tend its departmental libraries. The loans of books to the Branch and Departmental libraries are of two kinds, i.e., 1. Permanent Loan. 2. Temporary Loan.

All essential reference books and classics and standard works on various subjects should be transferred to the Branch and Departmental libraries permanently. These may only be replaced by new editions, whenever found necessary. Other books which include books on fiction, biography, and general and current topics should be transferred temporarily and these may be sent to various libraries in rotation. The rotation period may be about six months or so. The records of such transfers can be kept on the shelf list cards by marking these with the transfer numbers. Their book cards should be kept on the issue counter in a separate sequence so that it can be ascertained as to how many books and which books are with a particular library at any time. In the alternative, a Transfer Register may be kept in which all the particulars of the books transferred may be entered date wise under various Departments or Branch libraries. This system is not scientific because it will be difficult to trace out the particular books as the entries in the Transfer Register would be date wise and not in a classified order.

Inter-library Loan Methods: The Fifth Law of Library Science implies that a library is a growing organism which means that all its component parts grow constantly. Books, which constitute an important element of a library, are published every year in increasing numbers and if every library wants to purchase all these books, it requires huge amount of funds and space which are unluckily not available and it becomes difficult to control them. An alternative to this situation is the organisation of various kinds of libraries such as National, State and other kinds of libraries. Each kind of library is charged with a specific duty and the division of functions and responsibilities is effected. This implies that each library remains dependent upon each other for fulfilling the needs of its clientele. This can be achieved only if books of a library can be issued to the members of other libraries. For this purpose, the first pre-requisite is the provision of union catalogues of books covering various subjects and areas. By consulting these catalogues, the location of particular books can be determined.

As mentioned above, the readers of various libraries when in need of certain books which are not stocked by their libraries, request their librarians to help them to get these books because the readers cannot get books from the other libraries unless and until they enrol themselves as members. Every person cannot become a member of all the libraries due to certain restrictions. Moreover, rare books and manuscripts cannot be issued to ordinary members. Some such method is to be devised by which the reading material of any kind may be made available to the readers at any place. This method is known as Inter-Library Loan. By it various libraries mutually agree among themselves to issue books to each other on certain conditions.

Conditions of Inter-library Loan: The Inter-Library Loan system implies cooperation among various consenting libraries. "The purpose of Inter-Library Loans is to make available for research and for serious study library materials not in a given library, with due provisions made by the lending library for the rights of its primary clientele."' Further, it must be made clear that "Inter-library loan service is a courtesy and a privilege, not a right."' The borrowing of books on inter-library loan costs much as has been demonstrated by the Columbia University Libraries' findings that "It has cost them $ 2.70 per volume to borrow, and $ 1.27 to lend." The question arises as to whether the cost of such borrowing and lending must be charged from the readers or not. It may be charged from the readers, if not in full, at least about 50 per cent because on the one hand, "Libraries are generally hard pressed to find appropriations which would eliminate this fee. It has also been thought that the existence of the fee will discourage unnecessary borrowing."

Dr. S. R. Ranganathan in his book 'Library Administration' has given the details of those conditions which must be agreed to between the cooperating libraries. The IASLIC has recently drafted an Inter-Library Loan Code for libraries. An Inter-Library Loan Code was also adopted at the First National Seminar on University Libraries, Jaipur held few years ago. It is almost similar to that of Dr. Ranganathan who for this purpose divides the subject as under:

Prohibited Items

1. Books costing less than three rupees unless they are technical or specialist publications or they are more than five years old. (A limit of three rupees may be raised to five rupees due to the increase in the cost of book production.)
2. Text Books and other allied publications required for examination purposes.
3. Fiction, reference books and loose numbers of periodicals.
4. Those books the copy/copies of which are already available in the borrowing library.

Rights and Duties of Cooperating Libraries: Rights of the Lending Library:

1. The issue of the following types of books may be postponed:
   (a) Books of recent editions with local demand.
   (b) Books with unusual temporary demand.
2. Special conditions of loan may be specified.
3. Loans may be refused without any reason.

Duties of the Borrowing Libraries

1. The borrowing library must produce a certificate that it has got no copy of the publication requisitioned by it.

2. The borrowing library will have to pay the to and from charges and other incidental charges. (The libraries may agree to share these expenditures, i.e., one Library may pay the sending charges while the other may bear the charges of retaining the same.)
3. The borrowing library will have to be responsible for the safe custody and return of the borrowed book. If there is any damage, injury or loss, the borrowing library will have to make good the loss.
4. In case a book belonging to a set is lost or damaged, the borrowing library will have to replace the whole set, if required to do so.
5. The borrowing library has to abide by the other conditions imposed by the lending library, e.g., if asked to send a list of members who have used the lent book, the borrowing library must provide such a list.
6. The borrowed books are generally to be consulted within the library premises, especially if the books are rare ones.
7. The books must be returned within the stipulated period of loan. The books may be got renewed well within time, if these are required for some time more.

The Reference Services Division, acting on behalf of the American Library Association adopted on June 27, 1968, the National Inter-library Loan Code, 1968. The revised version of the Model Code adopted on January 28, 1969 makes for the following provisions which should be studied by the Indian Librarians for adopting those provisions of the code which they find useful and practicable:

Model Code (USA)

This code is a voluntary agreement adopted by........................ on .... to govern interlibrary lending among libraries [in the .... region, in the state of........................ in the metropolitan area of........................ or........................ group of........................ libraries]. Although correlated with the ALA National Interlibrary Loan Code, 1968 (adopted by the Reference Service Division, acting for the American Library Association on June 27, 1968) this local code is intended to promote a more liberalised interlibrary loan policy among the libraries adopting it. It is based on the premise that lending among libraries for the use of an individual [in the .... region, in the state of........................ etc.] is in the public interest and should be encouraged. However, liberal interlibrary lending should be no substitute for the development of adequate collections based on the needs of the service areas represented, in libraries and library systems.

This code may be further expanded or modified to meet the particular interests of participating libraries. The American Library Association has published a procedures manual suggested for use in implementing the national code; libraries requesting, materials on loan under the provisions of the local code are urged to follow the recommendations of the manual.

Definition: Interlibrary loans are transactions in which library materials are made available by one library to another; for the purposes of this code they also include the provision of copies as substitutes for loans of the original materials.

Purpose: Since it is increasingly evident that it is impossible for any one library to be self-sufficient, and in the belief that the furtherance of knowledge is in the general interest, interlibrary borrowing and lending is regarded by the libraries subscribing to this agreement as essential to library service.

Responsibility of Lending Libraries

1. Lending libraries have the responsibility of informing borrowing libraries of any failure to observe the provisions of this code, and if necessary may invoke the provisions stated in Sec. XII.
2. Lending libraries will practice as liberal and unrestrictive a policy as is possible in interlibrary loans, with due consideration to the interests of their primary clientele.

Responsibility of Borrowing Libraries

1. It is recognised that interlibrary lending does not relieve any library of the responsibility of developing its own collection. Each library will provide the resources to meet the ordinary study, educational, instructional, informational, and research needs of its users. Requests to borrow from other libraries will be limited to those items which the library might not be expected to own. No library should depend upon another to supply the normal needs of its clientele except under special agreement for such service.
2. Borrowing libraries will make every effort to exhaust their own resources before resorting to interlibrary loans.
3. Borrowing libraries will screen carefully all applications for loans, rejecting those which do not conform to this code.

Scope:

1. Any type of library material needed for the purposes of study, instruction, information or research may be requested on loan or in photocopy from another library. The lending library has the privilege of deciding in each case whether a particular item should or should not be provided, and whether the original or a copy should be sent. These decisions may be determined by the nature of the material or its physical condition, the degree of active demand for the material requested [or other reasons specifically indicated in this agreement].
2. Under the terms of this agreement it is permissible to request on interlibrary loan:
   a. Materials collected in specialised subject fields and in special non-restricted collections;
   b. Materials collected under special acquisition agreements;
   c. Materials bought under special grant or other programmes intended to promote economical use of the total resources of the area;
   d. Reference materials whenever lending might not hinder the service of the lending library.
3. Under the terms of this agreement, borrowing libraries will not ordinarily request:
   a. Books in current and/or recurring demand
   b. Bulky or fragile materials
   c. Rare materials
   d. A large number of titles for one person at any one time
   e. Duplicates of titles already owned
   f. Materials which can be copied cheaply
   g. Materials for class, reserve, or other group use.

4. Each participating library will prepare a statement of its interlibrary loan policies and procedures to further supplement the national and .... [regional, state, local] code and will make this statement, available to all participating libraries.

Expenses: The borrowing library should be prepared to assume any costs charged by the lending library as agreed upon in this code. If the charges are more than nominal, and not authorised beforehand by the borrowing library, the lending library will inform the requesting library and obtain authorisation to proceed with the transaction. Borrowing libraries should attempt to anticipate charges and authorise them on the initial request.

1. In the interests of efficiency the lending library may agree to absorb nominal costs for:
   a. Postage
   b. Photocopying
   c. Insurance.
2. Libraries may make special contractual or other arrangements, including financial reimbursement or other adjustments, in recognition of costs incurred by libraries whose resources are used extensively under this agreement.

Conditions of Loans:

1. The borrowing library will honour any limitations on use imposed by the lending library.
2. Unless specifically forbidden by the lending library, it is assumed that copying is permitted, provided that it is in accordance with copyright law and ALA policy and further, provided no damage to the original volume will result.
3. The borrowing library is responsible for returning loans promptly and in good condition.
4. The safety of borrowed materials is the responsibility of the borrowing library. The borrowing library will meet all costs of repair or replacement in accordance with the preferences of the lending library.

Placement of Requests:

1. Special arrangements for lending of materials by designated resource libraries may be made within the context of this agreement. Requests should be routed through such established channels as may be agreed upon by libraries participating in a local, state, or regional plan for library service.
2. Every effort will be made to locate materials through available local, state, and regional union catalogues, book catalogues, and union lists.
3. Requests may be made by mail, or transmitted by special or regularly scheduled messenger service, using the standard ALA form or the ALA photo duplication from (or a mutually acceptable from) or by teletype, using a format based on the standard from. When mutually agreeable, telephone requests are acceptable and shall be confirmed by the mailing of the standard form unless the lending library waives this record.
4. No library will lend directly to an individual on an interlibrary loan basis, except by mutual agreement between the borrowing and the lending libraries.

Form of Request:

1. Materials requested must be described as completely and accurately as possible following accepted bibliographic practice.

2. All items requested shall be verified in standard bibliographic tools and sources of verification cited. When the item requested cannot be verified, the statement "cannot verify" shall be indicated, and complete information as to source of reference furnished.
3. If verification is disregarded, or the bibliographic data is incorrect, and unless special agreement otherwise provides, the lending library may return the request unfilled without special effort to identify the reference.
4. The name and status (position or other identifying information) of the individual for whom the material is being requested shall appear on the request form.
5. All requests and shipments shall be conspicuously labelled "Interlibrary Loan."

Duration of Loan:

1. Unless otherwise specified by the lending library, the duration of the loan shall be calculated as the time the item is to be in the borrowing library, disregarding the time spent in transit. The period of loan shall be that ordinarily extended by the lending library.
2. Renewal requests shall be kept to a minimum. The renewal request shall be sent in time to reach the lending library before the due date. The lending library should respond to renewal requests promptly; if it does not, it will be assumed that renewal for the same period as the original loan is granted.
3. The loan period specified by the lending library should be appropriate to the type of material.
4. The borrowing library is responsible for returning interlibrary loans promptly and in good condition.
5. Material on loan is subject to recall at any time and the borrowing library shall comply promptly.

Notification and Acknowledgement

1. The lending library shall notify the borrowing library promptly whether or not the material is being sent; if the material cannot be supplied, the lending library shall state the reason.
2. Except in the case of very valuable shipments, no acknowledgement of receipt is necessary. If there is undue delay in receipt of shipments, the borrowing library shall notify the lending library so that a search may be initiated.

Violation of Code

1. Continued disregard of the provisions of this code shall be sufficient reason for suspension of borrowing privileges.

Interlibrary Loan Routines: A member of a library who wants to get a book from another library on interlibrary loan has to apply on an application form to its own library and has to deposit a sum of about ₹ 10/- to cover the postal and other charges for getting and sending back the book in question. The borrowing library, by consulting the requisite Union Catalogue and the individual catalogue of the other library, locates the availability of the book in question.

If not found in this way, a circular letter is sent to various important libraries of the country with whom the book may likely be in stock. On receipt of a reply, a requisition letter is sent to the library possessing the book in question for the loan of the book either per V.P.P. or per registered post. The Inter-Library Loan Committee of the Association of College and Research

Libraries has recently introduced a standard multiple-unit request form. "The advantages of this standardisation are apparent: a saving in typing and filing time, speed-up in the lending operation and general uniformity."

On behalf of the Interlibrary Loan Committee of the American Library Association, Sarah Katharine Thomson has published in 1970 an "Inter Library Procedure Manual" which interprets the 'National Interlibrary Loan Code, 1968 (Revised on January 28, 1969) and provides standardised methods of transacting interlibrary loan', and explains the details of the procedure to be followed for the purpose. These procedures should be studied by the Indian Librarians for standardising Interlibrary loan procedures in India.

On the receipt of the book, the borrower is informed accordingly. If the book is other than a manuscript, rare book or a periodical, it is issued to the borrower for home reading for a limited period, say, for ten days only, otherwise he is informed that he may consult the book within the premises of the library. After it has been duly read through by a reader, the book is sent back under registered or insured cover, depending upon the value and kind of the book.

The cost of all such processes is calculated and the balance is paid to the borrower if the expenditure was lesser than the deposit amount. In case the expenditure has exceeded the deposit amount, the borrower is asked to pay more so as to make good the deficiency. A proper account is kept for every such borrower. It would be better if accounts are maintained in a ledger. The following forms may be used for Interlibrary purposes:

To The Librarian

....

....

Sub.:—Procurement of books on Interlibrary Loan Basis.

Sir/Madam,

The following book/books are required by me for research. These are not available in this Library. Kindly oblige by procuring the same from some other Library on Inter-Library Loan basis:

1. ....
2. ....
3. ....
4. ....

Thanking you

Yours faithfully,

Dated.......................

Name and Address of the
Applicant

13

CATALOGUING PROCEDURE

(Advance Knowledge Organisation)

A catalogue is a list of and index to a collection of books and/or other materials. It enables the user to discover:

What material is present in the collection and where this material may be found.

The 'collection' may relate to one or a number of libraries or information service points. In the fitter case, the catalogue is termed a union catalogue.

The catalogue has much in common with the bibliography, which is also a list of books and/or other material. The same principles are applied to their compilation and they are used interchangeably. For example, the NECRT General catalogue of printed books or the National Book Trust catalogues also act as important bibliographies. The pure bibliography is not an index to a specific collection but simply a list of books and/or other materials within some restricted field, since it would clearly be impossible to list all materials from all countries and all periods on all subjects. This entry could also be used, without amendment, in a bibliography although there might not be any need to include the classification number and, on the other hand, further detail such as the price of the item might be required. Nevertheless the close relationship between the entry as used in a catalogue and the entry as used in a bibliography is obvious.

The art of cataloguing relates to both catalogues and bibliographies. It is the art of describing and listing material in such a way as to make it as easy as possible to discover the nature and extent of what is available and, if appropriate, where this material may be located or obtained.

Process of Cataloguing

Contemporary society has experienced an extraordinary explosion in knowledge; this has resulted in a corresponding increase in the publication of books and other materials which act as information carriers. In general terms, without the aid of technology it is now impractical, if not impossible, to ascertain what material exists and where it may be obtained.

Two Operations

The cataloguing process basically consists of two operations: first, the creation of the appropriate entry relating to a particular item and, second the subsequent manipulation of this and other entries to form the actual catalogue.

The computer cannot replace the first of these, that intellectual element which only a human being can, at present, supply. The creation of a catalogue entry involves the answering of questions such as: What is the title of the item? Which person or body is responsible for its content? Who published it? When by a machine, which could not, for instance, distinguish between an author, e.g., Charles Dickens, and a title, e.g., David Copperfield.

However, the computer is capable of performing the various clerical functions involved in the manipulation of entries. For example, the computer can quickly sort catalogue entries into any desired order, or search for entries which conform to a particular search profile. And the search facility that can be provided is a much more powerful one than would be possible in a manual index. Because the computer can rearrange entries into any desired order, it may be used as a means of producing a catalogue or bibliography in 'hard' copy, i.e., 'printed' on to paper or film. However, it is becoming far more common to use 'on-line' access, i.e., the catalogue entries are stored within the machine to use 'on-line' access, i.e., that catalogue entries are stored within the machine and searched for and displayed as necessitated by the requirements of a user.

Cutter's Definition

Cutter defined the functions of a library catalogue more than 100 years ago; he said that it should:

1. Enable a person to find as book of which either: the title is known the subject.
2. Show what the library has, by a given subject in a given kind of literature.
3. Assist in the choice of a book: as to its edition as to its character (literary or topical).

These objectives still hold good today, but the word 'book' should be replaced by 'item' or 'document' and the word 'author' should be replaced by 'responsible person or body'. This is because librarians are now concerned with far more than the printed word, e.g., audio and video recordings, micrograms, computer files, etc.

Flexible Search Facility

Further, it should be noted that today's computerised catalogues and bibliographies can offer a far more flexible search facility than Cutter could ever have envisaged. For example, the user may need to know only part of an author, or part of a title, in order to find a particular entry.

Cataloguing must not be considered a self-contained unit; the relationship with bibliographies has already been stressed for example. There are also obvious links between cataloguing and classification; the same mental process must take place when deciding on the subject of an item, whether this is described in alphabetical terms or by a classification number. In addition, the catalogue can form the basis of an integrated system with ordering, acquisition and circulation control modules. Indeed, when the computerisation of the cataloguing process is being planned, it should not be considered an isolation but as part of a larger entity.

Not everyone regards the catalogue as an essential tool. D.J. Urquhart showed, for instance, how effectively the National Lending Library for Science and Technology (now the British Library Document Supply Centre) in its early days could be administered without catalogue. It is seen by some people as a sacred cow and, in the 1960s, Grose and Line referred to it as a white elephant. Certainly there are many more keys to unlock the doors of knowledge in the form of bibliographies, indexes and databases, and library users can find out very quickly via a computer terminal what is available, in global terms, in any subject field. But what they so often want to know is whether a particular item is available in their particular library, whether it be public, academic or special. Most readers want subject arrangement in the library, so that they can browse and this means that a catalogue is desirable to show not only what is available but also where it is shelved. The descriptive part of the catalogue entry will help the user to decide whether an item not immediately available is likely to be relevant.

There are other reasons for maintaining a library catalogue. It can provide analytical entries for parts of an item and it can record all items in a library's stock, acting as a valuable supplement to published bibliographic tools. At present, bibliographical control of English and American books and periodical article is excellent but this is by no means true of, for instance, report literature, semi-published material and the many forms of non-book media.

Standardisation and the Road to AACR 2: The requirement of cooperative and centralised systems make the acceptance of standards of vital importance. Such standardisation might relate to the classification scheme used to arrange the stock of a library, to the alphabetical subject indexing methodology, or to the content and arrangement of the catalogue entry. It is the latter with which this chapter is primarily concerned.

The manner in which a catalogue entry is organised with regard to the amount of detail to be included will depend upon the requirements of the particular cataloguing agency.

Despite differences in the amount of detail required, it is clearly advantageous for various cataloguing agencies to agree to work to the one standard, i.e., a set of rules, to be used by all. The standard would prescribe how the content of the entry was to be organised and how the headings, or access points, under which an item was to be entered should be selected and presented. Whilst entries could be simple, because all elements advocated be compatible with those containing more detail because both had been produced using the same standard.

In USA: In the United States, standardisation of author-title cataloguing has been a way of life in libraries, especially since 1901 when the Library of Congress took over the printed catalogue card service begun by the Library Bureau in 1893.

In Britain: In Britain, progress towards standardisation was much slower perhaps due to the natural independence of British librarians, or perhaps because Britain's National Library did not attempt to take a central role in British librarianship until the 1970s, or possibly simply because no library was willing to accept the Anglo-American code of 1908 without considerable amendment. Even when the British national bibliography began to be published in 1950, using a much amended version of the 1908 code as the basis of its cataloguing, many libraries preferred to continue their own cataloguing practices.

When BNB started to issue printed catalogue cards in 1956 its cataloguing achieved greater acceptance, but there were still libraries which resisted, partly because they had reservation about the BNB's use of the Dewey decimal classification. What such libraries fail to appreciate is that standardisation does not mean accepting without question all of the data provided by a central cataloguing agency; rather it means using common practices as far as possible and allowing the agency to do work which cannot be done better locally. Even though Americans accepted AA 1908 and later the ALA revisions of 1941 and 1949, many of them were not happy with these rules.

Their dissatisfaction was voiced by Andrew Osborn on 1941 and, most notably, by Seymour Lubetzky in 1953. Lubetzky's Cataloguing rules and principles of that year came out strongly against the codification of catalogue rules via the elaborate and complex enumeration of innumerable 'cases' and pointed the way towards the possible formulation of a less complex set of rules based encyclopaedia, for example, would not be regarded as a particular 'case' or type of publication, but would be treated in a similar manner to all other works, i.e., according to the particular 'conditions' of authorship of responsibility pertaining to it.

Lubetzky's ideas were widely welcomed and helped pave the way for the International Conference on Cataloguing Principles held in Paris in 1961. A draft statement of principles based upon Lubetzky's Code of Cataloguing rules: author and title entry; an unfinished draft (ALA 1960) was submitted to this conference for discussion along with working papers on the various problems of rules prepared by delegates. A final version of the 'Statement of principles' was adopted and participants agreed to work in their separate countries revised rules which would be in agreement with these accepted principles.

The Anglo-American cataloguing rules of 1967 (AACR 1) was one of several codes reflecting the "Paris Principles'; though, unfortunately, it had to be published in two texts (British and North American) because there was not complete unanimity between the two countries' committees, particularly in the areas of description sand corporate headings.

AACR 1 was immediately accepted as a standard by the BNB and by several British libraries, but certainly not by all of them. In the United States its complete acceptance was hampered by the fact that the Library of Congress, one of the bodies responsible for the rules, adopted a superimposition or 'no conflict' policy-headings from A'ACR 1 were accepted only if they did not conflict with headings already in the catalogue.

Management of Cataloguing

The quality of good management lies in the application of the principles in such a way as to provide the most effective catalogue for a library and its users. Correct decisions must be made on such matters as the fullness of cataloguing required; whether to use a conventional classified or alphabetical subject catalogue required; whether to use a conventional classified or alphabetical subject catalogue or some other system; the method to be used for establishing subject headings or subject index entries; what filing system to use; policy with regard to analysis and annotation; the physical form of catalogue; and the extent to which CIP (Cataloguing-in-publication) information, centralised services and or the computer are used.

With regard to centralised services, writers such as Foster maintain that to process books efficiently, every library, large and small, must have a good portion of its cataloguing performed by an outside source. If a centralised service is utilised, some decisions may, of course, be taken out of the individual cataloguing agency's hands.

Cataloguing needs may vary, not only in different kinds of library but also within the same library system. In some special libraries the major demands may be for current subject information and more use may be made of a subject-based retrieval system than of an author catalogue constructed according to AACR 2. In others, such as the library of a professional organisation sending many items on postal loan, there may be a strong case for detailed cataloguing may vary according to the kind of material, some audiovisual materials may lack 'brows ability' and so be given more detailed cataloguing than books, and books which are on the open shelves may be catalogued less fully than those which are not. Whatever the kind of library, there are certain management techniques which can be applied to the cataloguing process. There is a bewildering number of techniques, 'more than 250 of them being described in Finch's excellent of guide', but it must be remembered that they are only a means to an end-aids to decision-making or problem-solving. Just as cataloguers should not become so immersed in their cataloguing rules or methods that they overlook the overriding purpose of the catalogue-to help users of the library to find what they want-so managers should avoid becoming so immersed in a particular technique that they forget its purpose-to improve or optimise performance, to measure value or to rectify faults.

Foster, in his Managing the cataloguing department, cites 'management by objectives' (MBO) as 'typical of the most innovative management concepts found in libraries today'. "MBO is so much a part of everyday normal management behaviour that the term is rarely used but it is still very relevant to cataloguing as 'an approach to assessing performance by reference to the achievement of results'. MBO involves formulating objectives (e.g. to ensure that library materials reach the public for whom they have been acquired with a minimum of delay); setting targets to allow these objectives to be met (e.g. cataloguing x number of items per day); and removing any obstacles to the achievement of these targets.

The cataloguing objectives can be defined as 'to ensure the maximum usefulness of the catalogue:

(a) Surveying the use of the COM catalogues;

(b) Reviewing the information required (i.e., considering the application of MARC and the latest edition of the Dewey Decimal Classification to new stock and old stock); and

(c) Considering new applications for the catalogue database (organising input and retrieving data to provide stock revision information, booklists on a subject and new accessions lists).

The specimen objective on cataloguing in the American Library Association's, 1980 planning manual for public libraries was concerned specifically with automation: 'to automate the acquisitions cataloguing, and circulation's functions within the five year period' with a view to lowering the elapsed time from receipt of materials to shelf to 20 days.

At New South Wales Institute of Technology the objectives of the cataloguing department were defined as 'to carry out the cataloguing and classification of all monographs, A/V and serials needed by the staff and students of the Institute, and the method of achieving these objectives reflected the underlying philosophy of the library: 'that the use of technological advances and resources sharing among libraries is the only effective and rational way of operating in these days of economic stringency.

Accepted Standards

In order to set targets it is necessary to have some generally accepted standards. In cataloguing, there are adequate standards of technique or practice but there are no generally accepted standards of timing or performance-inevitably, perhaps, in view of the different kinds of materials to be catalogued, the variation in difficulty of this material, and the differing amounts of information on catalogue entries.

A study at Cornell Lay Library, using the OCLC database, showed that the average cataloguing time was 8–9 minutes per record and, in a survey of members of OCLC network, 91 per cent of the libraries surveyed reported that the time required to catalogue items had been reduced by on-line cataloguing. A small study at Bath University Library showed that the cataloguing of 160 items took only 293 minutes, or an average of just under two minutes per item, but it must be borne in mind that this involved very brief catalogue entries. The average time taken to classify 148 items was just under five minutes per item, and classification normally forms part of the cataloguing process.

It should be possible for each library to determine its own standards. The Centre for Library and Information Management (CLAIM) at Loughboroughy University, United Kingdom has shown how this can be done using the ' diary' techniques, with each member of staff keeping an accurate record of the time spent on every activity. A study by CLAIM's predecessor, the Library Management Research Unit, of four libraries serving schools, colleges and institutes of a university, showed that one library spent an average of 8 minutes cataloguing each item, two spent an average of 10 minutes per item and one spent an average of 16 minutes per item. The four libraries were commensurate in size and staff involvement.

At La Trobe University, Melbourne, Australia, cataloguers kept detailed monthly statistics of the time spent on each operation. They did not object to the establishment of minimum output figures; rather, they requested such figures because they provided a target and a basis for assessing their performance. It should be borne in mind, however, that all human beings are different; they are not machines, and some people will inevitably perform tasks more quickly and efficiently than others.

Cataloguing Policy

Cataloguing policy, such as fullness of cataloguing, the rules to be used and the extent of analysis and annotation. The methods employed; for example, computerising the catalogue. The proper use of staff; for example, it may be cheaper to use clerical staff for routine cataloguing and checking. The extent to which cataloguing is coordinated with other operations.

The benefit part of the cost-benefit equation should not be ignored. Where (d) is concerned, for example, a major advantage of computerisation is that it allows on record to be used for many purposes, including ordering, cataloguing, circulation control, interlibrary loans, preparation of reading lists and production of management information. In a survey of OCLC members, 80 per cent of the libraries surveyed reported that their primary objectives had been met. For some libraries the primary objective was reduced costs, whilst for others it was faster cataloguing or improved interlibrary loans. Thus both cost and efficiency benefits had accrued form membership.

A study by the Bath University Programme of Catalogue Research undertaken in 1979 to establish the size and distribution of the market for automated cataloguing services, produced a considerable amount of data relating to the cost of cataloguing. Unfortunately, the report did not relate these figures to the kind of cataloguing or the value of the catalogue to the user, in other words the cost-benefit element was missing.

To change to AACR 2 (or to any other code of cataloguing rules) is major management decision. How many headings in the catalogue will need to be changed? How costly will the change be and, more important, how cost effective? Will it result in a better catalogue or allow more effective use of networks?

A study at La Trobe University Library, Melbourne, indicated that the time spend on cataloguing might rise by 2.3 per cent as a result of introducing AACR 2. Training would be an additional cost, though a one-off cost which need to be absorbed during a brief period of time. All in all, concluded George Sector, 'the adoption AACR 2 . . . is likely to cause financial disaster to libraries with up to date practices' .

Five possible methods of implementing a change to AACR 2 are:

1. Starting a new catalogue for all items acquired after a specified date
2. Starting a new catalogue for all items published after a specified date
3. Superimposition
4. Changing the old headings as required
5. Interfiling the new entries with the old ones and linking as necessary with see also references, e.g.:

   SMITH (W.H.) & SONS see also W.E. SMITH & SONS W.H. SMITH & SONS see also SMITH (W.H.) & SONS

Very large libraries are likely to opt for closure of the catalogue, but Rosenthal has pointed out that this step has implications for almost every library operation. He has also emphasised the importance of very careful planning of any change and that the public relations aspects should not be ignored. Any system must be properly explained to non-cataloguing staff and to the public. If a library opts to automate and to make use of MARC records in some way, e.g., by subscribing to the BLAISE Records Service or by joining a bibliographic utility such as OCLC, the decision to change to AACT 2 becomes implicit.

It is claimed that the 1988 revision of AACR 2 ' is a code supportive of the needs of library automation'. Libraries of all sizes use automated systems and 'there is a greater reliance on, and indeed, a greater expectation of the availability of derived cataloguing copy'. With such 'realities serving as a backdrop, and, with the urgings of ABACUS (Association of Bibliographic Agencies of Britain, Australia, Canada and the United States) to facilitate machine transfer of bibliographic information by further standardising, in particular, the choice and form of authors, titles, and series. JSCAACR has developed a revision more conducive to automated environments on the evolutionary scale of cataloguing codes, the 1988 revision of the Anglo American cataloguing rules carries us one step closer to the goal of universal bibliographic control'.

For those libraries maintaining non-MARC record-based systems there is more of an option to adopt AACR 2 or not. 'These non-MARC libraries must consider how not changing may effect exchange of information, or may impact on future plans for database or system conversion'.

The claims made for AACR 2 cited above are sweeping claims which some librarians might consider debatable but nevertheless the fact remains that the AACR 2 1988 revision exists; it does form the basis of the MARC record, and therefore the majority of libraries in English-speaking countries and even elsewhere must be prepared to take decisions about its use.

Pre-natal Cataloguing

For many years Ranganathan urged the inclusion of a catalogue entry in each book on publication-'pre-natal cataloguing', as he called it. During 1985-89 the Library of Congress's 'Cataloguing-in source' experiment attempted to establish the feasibility of this, in collaboration with publishers and with the assistance of a grant provided by the Council of Library Resources. At the in-Souse programme could not be justified from the viewpoint of financing technical considerations, or utility'. In 1971, 'cataloguing-in-source' was reborn in the United States as 'cataloguing-in-publication', initially for three-year experimental period, but it later became a permanent feature of Library of Congress record supply. For example, catalogue cards are printed from CIP records whenever full MARC cataloguing is not available. CIP entries differ from full

MARC cataloguing in that records are shorter and references to pagination and size are omitted. Brazil implemented a cataloguing-in-publication programme in the same year as the United States (1971). CIP schemes now operate in many countries and they have become an integral part of bibliographic services.

In the United Kingdom, British Library Bibliographic Services began to provide brief catalogue entries on the verso of the title page of some British books in 1976. CIP entries began to appear in the British national bibliography and on MARC tapes in 1977. In January 1985, the first of a new-style CIP entry, conforming generally to AACR 2 Level 2 for description and containing full subject data, appeared in the BNB. Prior to 1985, the CIP entry was not intended to be definitive but the new programme was designed to realise the full potential of CIP as a major input source for the creation of permanent UKMARC records of both high quality and high currency. Thus the CIP record formed the actual basis of the, definitive "national bibliographic" record'. It was a radical move away from the long-accepted principle of using the actual item as the primary source of cataloguing data. An essential requirement for an effective CIP programme is the fullest possible participation of publishers. By 1990 well over 1,0000 British publishers were participating in the scheme. 'It is a mutually advantageous service getting early information to libraries and offering increased marketing potential to participating publishers'.

In 1988 the British Library entered into an agreement with Book Data Ltd. which was intended to lead to improvements in both the quality of data and the coverage of the CIP programme. Book Data's declared objective is to serve publishers, booksellers and institutional buyers-including libraries, with particular emphasis on the acquisitions function-by creating a database of very full descriptive records about titles currently available or about to be published. By 1990 the list of participating publishers include some 900 imprints accounting for more than 25,000 titles a year.

The British Library has stated that from April 1991 it will cease to create CIP records from advance information supplied by publishers. In order to continue providing this service, however, the Library intends, as an interim arrangement, to continue to buy in CIP 1\ records from Book Data Ltd. These records will meet the minimum data requirement of AACR 2 Level 1 with some enhancement. They will include Book Data subject headings and will be classified according to Dewey Decimal Classification abridged edition. CIP records will continue to appear in BNB approximately six weeks before the expected date of publication.

As soon as the book has been published and received by the British Library Copyright Receipt Office a full authoritative record will be created which will then reappear in the main sequence of the BNB.

Whitaker is to supply CIP data to the British Library as from 1992.

Where Book Data is concerned, OCLC is also to mount a Book data file as part of its EPIC Reference Service.

Cataloguing at Low Cost

If necessary economies are not achieved by a more scientific approach to cataloguing, the library may resort to some form of 'limited cataloguing', an expedient useful also for reducing, cataloguing arrears and speeding up the cataloguing process and for reducing the bulk of the catalogue by eliminating unnecessary entries. The term 'limited cataloguing' is a generic one covering simplified cataloguing and selective cataloguing. The most usual form of simplified cataloguing is the reduction of the descriptive element of the catalogue, such as the omission of all or part of the publication area or physical description area. Other possibilities include the simplification of author headings and the elimination of certain added entries. These limitations apply to the whole of the library's stock, whereas selective cataloguing involves the use of a variant form of cataloguing" usually a simplified form, for certain items, and/ or the omission of a catalogue entry for some items.

Most libraries can practice some form of selective cataloguing with little inconvenience to their readers. There seems little point in cataloguing standards specifications, especially if a library takes all of them, since they are easily retrievable via published indexes; alternatively they can be given a subject entry but not an author entry. Similarly, libraries which receive all government publications may rely on the official indexes rather than cataloguing each item, though the quality of cataloguing and subject indexing in the official lists may not be satisfactory for the library. Where UK official publications are concerned, a catalogue is also available on CD-ROM (UKOP). This provides over 180,000 bibliographic records for official publications published since 1980. Such materials as town guides, trade catalogues and annual reports need not usually be catalogued as they may be regarded as 'self-indexing'. Some public libraries do not catalogue fiction, though many would consider this to be an undesirable economy.

The Library of Congress adopted a limited cataloguing policy between 1951 and 1963 when, in order to deal with arrears which had accumulated over the years, accessions were divided into four groups of documents considered primarily of interest as groups, and items given entry only. Care should be taken that the costs saved by adopting a limited cataloguing policy are not offset by greater inconvenience to library users because of reference and readers' advisory staff having to consult a large number of different sources for information. It is interesting that L.C. ended its limited cataloguing policy in August 1963 following comments from card subscribers and others. We are back to cost-benefit analysis.

In 1987, the British Library, as part of a plan for future development, identified certain categories of material to receive 'ARC 2 level I' treatment, i.e., 'minimal level' cataloguing. These categories included modern English fiction (15%). Children's literature (10%), science and technology (25%), material with 32 pages or less (9%) and religion (4%). With overlaps, these categories cover 50 per cent of BIB MACRO annual output and it was estimated that overall savings in record creation of 10 per cent would be made.

An Essential Task

Catalogue maintenance is an important part of a cataloguer's responsibility. It is essential that new and revised entries are filed regularly and correctly; superseded entries are withdrawn; worn cards or sheaf slips are replaced; filing errors and other inconsistencies are rectified; obsolete subject headings are replaced; and new subheadings are created when there are a large number of entries under one subject heading. Nowadays, simple instructions to the computer can often deal with these points.

An Important Aspect

An important aspect of catalogue maintenance is ensuring that library users are:

(a) Aware that a catalogue is available.

(b) Instructed in its use as required given guidance within the catalogue as necessary.

The catalogue is one of the most expensive commodities in the library, so we should surely do all we can to ensure that it is exploited to its full potential.

The first priority is to make the library user aware that a catalogue exists and where it may be found. This can be achieved by a general library plan, publicity leaflets, directional, e.g., hanging, guides, and the positioning of the catalogue in a prominent place. The space-eating card catalogue has, in some large libraries, have, however, rejected the idea of a separate, 'centre' for computer-based catalogues and indexes; the aim being to integrate machine-readable and eye-readable sources. The OPAC is itself a useful means of publicity.

External guides (instructions on how to use the catalogue) may take various forms; for example, a printed sheet or booklet either dealing with the catalogue alone or as part of a general library guide, a printed notice displayed near the catalogue or an introductory section in a book catalogue. The purpose of such guides is not to explain the niceties of cataloguing but to show the user how the catalogue can help him/her to find information. Professional jargon should be avoided and the judicious use of examples can be far more effective than verbose descriptions. The guidelines should be keep it simple made it clear, ensure that it is attractive and has impact.

It is important that the content of microtiches, card catalogue drawers, etc.., are clearly indicated and that labels are changed as reorganisation of the catalogue takes place.

Internal guides-such as cards, with protruding tabs in a card catalogue and headings at appropriate points in a book catalogue act as 'signposts' within the catalogue. A classified card catalogue is improved if 'feature headings' are used. In a card catalogue, different coloured cards could be used for different kinds of entries, e.g., author, subject, analytics.

In an online public-access catalogue there may be an initial screen containing general instructions on the use of the catalogue and further help screens dealing with specific features may be available as required at the touch of a key or upon typing "Help'. Some online catalogues have more than one mode to provide to both the uninitiated and the more experienced user. The interactive nature of the online catalogue can be utilised to provide clear guidance to the user and thus make it easier for required material to be located. Online tutorials are also a possibility.

Managing the Personnel

Communication is an essential feature of good staff management; staff must be kept informed of what is happening and why. Wherever possible some form of participative management is desirable, staff being involved in the decision-making process. One useful technique to employ is management by excepection, whereby matters are dealt with according to precise instructions or well defined objectives and only exceptional issues are referred to senior management.

The setting of objectives is an integral part of MBO techniques and there continues to be interest in MBO in British libraries, although the number of published references to its application has been on the decline. In the United States, however, academic libraries appear to have abandoned MBO in favour of Management Review and Analysis Programme (MRAP), an approach which relies very heavily on staff participation. MRAP was initially designed for use in large research libraries in the US in response to a perceived need to respond positively to the new economic, personal and external pressures of the 1970s. The focus is placed firmly on management functions: planning, budgeting, management information, policies, organisation, staff development, supervision and leadership, personnel and communication for example.

MRAP is not concerned with appraising or even developing a plan but with improving the procedures for planning. In more general terms, MRAP can be seen as a method of introducing participatory management into a library, for analysing the library's functions and for providing a new framework for decision-making. MRAP has been used in a considerable number of American libraries with, it must be said, very mixed results and does not seem to have caught on outside the United States.

Staff participation becomes absolutely essential when a library is implementing an automated system. In Norway, for example, the relevant trade union became interested in finding out what effect computerisation had on personnel. After interviewing staff who had recently experienced automation in their libraries, one of the major findings was that adequate training is a very important requisite and this training should include staff participation at all stages as the system develops.

Lovecy tells us that 'the most damaging element for staff morale is run our and speculation'. From the initial consideration of possible automation, it is important to involve members of staff in discussions. 'This makes sense from all points of view, since no librarian really wants to make a decision on whether or not to computerise without someone to discuss it with ... the more staff that can be drawn in to the discussion at this early stage the better.' Good staff management is helped by the use of a procedure manual, which should ensure consistency without endless repetition of verbal instructions.

Automated Cataloguing

The development of automated cataloguing methods, particularly the MARC (Machine-Readable Cataloguing) Project made the acceptance of an international standard more urgent, but already AACR 1 was being overtaken by events. Apart from the considerable influence of the computer, there were three factors which were of particular significance.

First, there were the rules being produced by a number of different countries throughout the world. Although these were also based upon the Paris Principles, there were some differences of opinion. European libraries, for instance, had never been happy with editors and compilers of collections being given the status of authors, preferring to enter collections under title, and so this rule was revised by the British and American in the interests of international cooperation. Corporate responsibility was another problematic area where unanimity was difficult to achieve.

Second, there were the rules developed specifically for non-book materials, an area which was undergoing rapid expansion and for which AACR 1 was not considered satisfactory. In Britain there was Non-book materials cataloguing rules, produced by the Library Association's Media Cataloguing Rules Committee, published by the National Council for Educational Technology in 1973, and known as LANCET (the initials of its two sponsoring organisations); in Canada there was Non-book materials: the organisation of integrated collections by Jean Riddle Welhs, Shirley Lewis, and Janet Macdonald, published by the Canadian Library Association in 1973; and in the United States there was Standards for cataloguing non-print materials— an interpretation and practical application by Alma Tillin and William J. Quinly, the fourth edition of which was published by the Association for Edicatopma; Communications and Technology (Washington) in 1976.

Third, there was the continuous work being undertaken by the International Federation of Library Associations (now the International Federation of Library Associations and Institutions), a Working Group on the co-ordination of Cataloguing Principles was set up by IFLA as early as 1954 and in 1957 the IFLA General Council adopted a proposal to hold a world-wide conference on basic cataloguing principles. The International Conference on Cataloguing Principles of'1961 was thus IFLA inspired, the necessary financial assistance being forthcoming from the Council on Library Resources in America. The ICCP achieved international agreement on the principles to be adopted for choice of headings but for the international exchange of bibliographic information, whether in written or machine-readable form, it is obviously also necessary to have a generally accepted standard which lists the elements to be included in the descriptive part of an entry the order in which the elements are to be cited the punctuation which is to be used to separate the elements.

An IFLA International Meeting of Cataloguing Experts in Copenhagen in 1969 set up a Working Party to study the possibilities for an International Standard Bibliographic Description for monographs. Such a standard ISBD (M), was subsequently drawn up and was officially adopted by the IFLA Committee on Cataloguing at its meeting in Liverpool in 1971. The publication of this standard necessitated the amendment of the relevant sections AACR 1, in order to achieve conformity. These amendments included the introduction of a new area to accommodate the recently introduced International Standard Book Number (ISBN) as a unique identifier. Later, the International Standard, Serial Number fISSN) also had to be catered for ISBD (M) was to be followed by similar standards for other } media such as ISBD (S) for serials and ISBD (NBM) for non-book materials. Almost inevitably, because a different committee was responsible for each standard, certain discrepancies became apparent and, to counteract this, a 'general' framework for description was produced, ISBD (G).

The above brief historical account clearly illustrates that there was a strong case for revision of AACR 1. There was a need to incorporate the ISBD (G) framework and to take account of other international developments. There was also the very important need for one unified Anglo-American text, which would incorporate all amendments issued since 1967. In addition, there was the need to consider other proposals for changes and the effects of library automation. The latter was particularly difficult because these effects are on-going and have yet to be completely assessed and understood.

The Council on Library Resources agreed to fund the revision, with certain conditions, the major one being that royalties from sale should be placed in a common fund for future activities associated with AACR. A Joint Steering Committee for AACR meeting in 1974 confirmed the participation of five bodies as 'authors' (ALA, LC, LA, BL, and the Canadian Committee on Cataloguing). It was agreed to set up national committees to consider issues and proposals for revision. The new rules, the results of collaboration between the national libraries and professional associations of three countries, were published in 1978. The main objectives were to a great extent achieved and not the least part of this remarkable achievement was the fact that any institution, organisation or individual with a point of view was given ample opportunity to express it during the process of revision.

Not Welcomed by All

The publication of AACR 2 was not welcomed by all librarians but, as Peter Lewis, later Director-General of the British Library Bibliographic Services Division, and former Chairman of the Joint Steering Committee for AACR, stated: 'for every powerful voice speaking against AACR 2, there is an equally powerful one calling for full implementation without delay'.

The major criticisms levelled against AACR 2 are that with the fast developing state of automation it is irrelevant, and its implementation increases library costs without increasing benefits. Despite objections, four national libraries (the British Library, the Library of Congress, the National Library of Australia and the National Library of Canada) adopted AACR 2 from January 1981. Initially, the Library of Congress decided to retain certain pre-AACR headings for economic reasons but it reconsidered its position and decided to abandon this 'compatible headings' policy from 1982. Thus all of the national libraries were then agreed that the adoption of the rules, as they stood, would bring long-term cost and user benefits.

Whether an, individual library decides to use AACR 2 will depend upon factors such as the use made of centralised services and the staff support available to amend existing catalogues. Cataloguing agencies which have adopted AACR 2 are using what is, in effect, an international standard. Work on the rules did not cease with the publication of AACR 2 in 1978, indeed, rather was the reverse the case in that a whole series of related activities was generated. These activities included .. the implementation of training programmes, and the production of adoption aids, interpretative manuals, illustrative examples and translations. AACR 2 has spread its influence into a number of Non-English-speaking countries, and translations have been made into languages such as Arabic, Finnish, French, Japan see, Norwegian, Portuguese, and Spanish.

In 1981 the first edition of Gorman's 'The concise AACR 2', a rewritten and simplified version of the rules, was published. This was intended to provide a readily comprehensible summary of AACR 2 practice for librarians and cataloguers in a number of different situations, such as librarianship students, persons working in small libraries, especially 'one-person' libraries, and cataloguers working in a non-English-language environment.

AACR 2 has also encouraged research. For example, cataloguing rules for choice of access points involve conditional decisions; i.e., if a certain condition applies then take a particular decision. A computerised expert system functions in a similar way using a knowledge base expressed as a set of rules. Because of this similarity, several researchers have investigated the feasibility of creating an expert system for cataloguing.

The international Joint Steering Committee for Recession of AACR continued to meet regularly, as did the various national committees, and in 1981 it was agreed to add an Australian representative to JSC. The revision process also continued and three sets of revisions were prepared and published in 1982, 1984 and 1986. Many of these revisions have formed part of a general' tidying-up' and correction process, whilst others have been of a more significant nature.

A major decision was taken by the Joint Steering Committee in 1985, when it was resolved to recommend that a consolidated was to incorporate all rule revisions passed, and topographical errors found, to that date. If possible, it was also intended to include revised rules for computer files, taking note of work that had already been done in this area such as that by Templeton and by Dodd, and for recently introduced media such as compact discs. This consolidation, including a new chapter for computer files and revised rules for recent media was published as Anglo-American cataloguing rules Second edition 1988 revision.

A survey of AACR 2 users taken in 1985 revealed that 98 per cent favoured a loose-leaf format, and the new revision is available in three versions: soft back, hardback and loose-leaf. A new version of the concise AACR 2 has also been published. The period in which AACR 2 has developed has been a time when applications of the computer in cataloguing have also been developing at a tremendous rate. Therefore there are bound to be questions posed by library automation which have not been answered by the rules, even though some new concepts have sprung from, or been precipitated by, advances in automation. Forman, the editor of AACR 2, considers that the fact that AACR 2 has not been able to take I; library automation fully into account is not really the fault of those responsible for AACR but rather is due to the fact that the effect of library automation on catalogues has yet to be completely assessed and understood.

For these reasons, Forman predicts that there will never be an AACR 3 but a new type of code which will deal with the creation of machine-readable records for use in national and international networks. However, in the meantime, revisions to AACR 2 will continue to be made; cataloguing cannot stand still, and the fact that the new revision is available in loose-leaf format reinforce this point.

Review Committee

An ISBD Review Committee was formed by IFLA in 1981 to implement a five-year review of the ISBDs for monographs, serials, cartographic materials and non-book materials, ISBD (M), ISBD (S), ISBD (CM) and ISBD (NBM), with the intention of publishing revisions in 1987. The Joint Steering Committee for AACR became concerned that ISBD(G), for which, as previously noted, the Joint Steering Committee was jointly responsible, might be effected by this review. Draft texts were circulated for comment in 1983-4; JSC AACR was one of the recipients of these drafts and was therefore given the opportunity to contribute to the review. Special attention has also been given to computer files; a Working Group net for the first time in 1986 and the final version of ISBD (CF) was published in 1990. The influence of AACR can be plainly seen in the latter publication with the ISBD adopting the AACR solution for differentiating between the type of file and physical carrier. A revised draft of the ISBD for rare, antiquarian books, ISBD (A), was circulated for study by appropriate persons in 1988.

The Main-entry Principle: Although rules for standardising a bibliographic description (as the ISBDs and AACR2) and for selecting and formulating access points (as ARCS 2) may be necessary, one other aspect of AACR 2 is completely redundant in the machine-readable context, namely the concept of main entry. AACR 2 considers 'the concept of main entry to be useful in assigning uniform title and in promoting the standardisation of bibliographic citation'. Some cataloguers defend AACR 2 on the ground that, although a number of on-line catalogues have appeared, the majority of present catalogues are still card catalogues. Other cataloguers would take issue with this defence. In Japan, for instance, cataloguers used codes based upon the main entry principle under the influence of AACR 2 and the Paris Principles until 1977, when a new code of Nippon cataloguing rules (NCR) was compiled. These rules abandon main entry not only because of progress in automation but also because of progress in automation but also because, in non-automated systems, it is seen to be less useful than the unit entry, which is now easy to produce and which ensures that each entry in the catalogue has an equal value.

The Japanese rules also differ from AACR 2 in another respect is that an attempt is made to define an item or unit more clearly. It is claimed that this leads to reader consistency where the cataloguing of multivolume sets and multipart items are concerned.

The Guidelines

AACR 2 reverses the pattern of all previous codes of cataloguing rules by placing the rules for description before the rules for choice of headings, because it is believed that this is the pattern followed in most libraries and bibliographic agencies. It also accepts the desirably of integrating bibliographic records of books and other kinds of materials.

Description: ACR 2 Part One-Description-is based upon the framework of ISBD(G). It begins with a general chapter containing rules which apply to all library materials. Each of the succeeding chapters in Part One, except for chapter 13, is concerned with more detailed rules for specific media, e.g.,: chapter 2 Printed monographs; chapter 5 Music; chapter 6 Sound recordings; chapter 9 Computer files; chapter 12 serials. More than one chapter, apart from the general chapter, may need to be consulted; a serial, for instance, may also be sound recording. When this sort of situation occurs, AACR 2 states that the description of an item should be based in the first instance on the chapter dealing with the class of materials to which the item belongs. For example, a printed monograph in microform should be described as a microform. The cataloguer brought up on earlier codes, which were concerned almost exclusively with printed material, must now, therefode, become familiar with some new terminology: publication, distribution, etc., area' instead of 'imprint', 'Physical description area' instead of 'collation'; and terms such as 'statement of responsibility', other 'title information' and 'statement of extent'. These new terms are largely a reflection of the integrated nature of the rules: 'statement of responsibility' includes the author of a book and the creator of a work of art; statement of responsibility includes the author of a book and the creator of a work of art; 'statement of extent' includes the pagination of a printed monograph or the playing time of a sound recording.

It is not necessary for all of the areas to be present in every case. An item may not, for instance, be influded in a series, or have a standard number. Similarly a note may not always be required. One area, the 'material specific details' are, in fact, used only for maps, music computer files and serials. The number given on the right is the relevant rule number for that particular area. These numbers are used logically and mnemonically so that rule 1.1 will deal with the recording of the title in general terms, rule 2.1 will deal more specifically with the recording of the title of a printed monograph, rule 6.1 with the recording of the title of a sound recording, and so on.

Each area may be further divided into constituent elements, for example the 'publication, distribution, etc.;. area could include such elements as the place of publication, distribution, publisher and date. These elements are separated by a prescribed punctuation.

Computerised Cataloguing

The quality of good management lies in the application of the principles in such a way as to provide the most effective catalogue for a library and its users. Correct decisions must be made on such matters as the fullness of cataloguing required; whether to use a conventional classified or alphabetical subject catalogue required; whether to use a conventional classified or alphabetical subject catalogue or some other system; the method to be used for establishing subject headings or subject index entries; what filing system to use; policy with regard to analysis and annotation; the physical form of catalogue; and the extent to which CIP (Cataloguing-in-publication) information, centralised services and the computer are used.

Increasing use of the computer; and of networks such as BLCMP and OCLC, is bound to have an effect on the management of cataloguing. The benefits of a computerised cataloguing system are indisputable but a decision to automate or not to automate the catalogue will depend upon a great many factors, including:

Size and type of library

Staffing levels

Financial support

Computer availability

Computerising the Catalogue: It might be difficult, for example, in a small one-person library with very restricted financial provision and no access to any sort of computer. It is appreciated that some small libraries, unfortunately, cannot afford even an adequate book, stock, let alone consider automation. On the other hand, a large academic library with considerable resources and, in all probability, access to a large mainframe computer might find it difficult to resist automation. It is not unknown, however, in the case of the small library, for things to change overnight and if, for instance, a chance were suddenly offered to purchase a microcomputer system, as might happen in a school or college library, then the possibility of automation would have to be reviewed.

This is not, of course, to imply that the larger library will always find it easy to automate. A number of sizable libraries, such as Liverpool City Libraries, continue to have to manage with manual catalogues. Before adopting an automated system it is necessary to carry out a process of systems analysis, which means that the existing method of operation must be examined in order to ascertain whether computerisation might lead to an improvement. Initially, objectives must be defined and a feasibility study undertaken.

The feasibility study will examine the various ways that the defined objectives might be achieved and it will look at the costs that might be incurred in relation to the benefit accrued (cost-benefit analysis). It will also investigate cost effectiveness in terms of manpower.

There are several options which a library planning to automate its catalogue might choose from:

> To develop a completely independent in-house system; to purchase a turnkey package; to join a bibliographic utility or cooperative network.

Whichever of the above is selected, it may be possible to make use of a centralised cataloguing service such as MARC in someway. Indeed, it may be obligatory to do so as in the case of the bibliographic utilities. Turnkey packages may not cater for the MARC format and for the importing of MARC records but many do and, in some instances, two approaches to the creation of the cataloguing database are offered-MARC and non-MARC. It should also be rioted that the bibliographic utilities usually offer some form of stand-alone turnkey system. This may also permit remote access to, and interaction with, the central database. There may well be, therefore, some overlap between options.

Go-in-One

The 'go-in-one', completely independent in-house system can vary from a single microcomputer configuration to a sophisticated setup with large mainframe-computer support. If in-house development is chosen, care should be taken to ensure that on-going back up and maintenance are available and that enhancement will be possible as and when necessary. It is not unknown for an in-house system to grind to a halt as it grows and develops, owing to the lack of such facilities. One library which preferred to use its own independent automated system was Derbyshire, UK, because it provided control over what to accept or reject, control over standards, and priority of access.

The prime example of an in-house development is probably that of the University of California's MELVYL catalogue system, which is recognised as one of the most sophisticated and advanced public online cataloguing systems in existence.

Follow-up studies have tended to confirm the above findings. For example, the University of Wyoming conducted a survey of online catalogue users in 1986. This was an adaptation of the Council on Library Resources study and the results were consistent with national findings, with very few exceptions.

Two Surveys

Liverpool Polytechnic has undertaken two surveys relating to PRECIS— a survey of reactions of indexers in all kinds of libraries, and a study of user reactions.

Of the 377 organisations respondings to the first survey, 255 (67%) had given no thought to its adoption, and of the remaining 122, only 25 were actually using the system for indexing. The reasons quoted most often for rejecting PRECIS were its complexity and labour-intensiveness and it is interesting to note that the British Library is now simplifying the methodology. Some indexes regarded the document-specificity of PRECIS and the open-endedness of its vocabulary as advantages, and others say them as disadvantages.

The small number of organisations using PRECIS in their own systems is not, of course, an indication of the total number of users. Anyone who makes use of the British National Bibliography or of UKMARC (1971–90) for subject access (including those he access British Library files online) can be considered a PRECIS user.

In the PRECIS user study, the main conclusion was that users generally reacted favourably, the document specificity was considered very useful. Users found the full subject statements more helpful than a string of terms, as in chain indexing, or broaded subject headings, as in the Library of Congress subject headings. Some non-librarian users found this aspect of PRECIS particularly Impressive. The ability of PRECIS to show relationships between terms was also appreciated.

Computerised Indexing

By removing the human intellectual element from indexing and allowing a machine, that is a computer, to select terms for index entries, a form of automatic indexing is obtained. Computerised 'keyword from title' indexes are automatic to a degree, but is there any way in which a computer can be programmed to identify appropriate terms from the text of an item? Initial attempts at automatic indexing were based upon determining, by statistical methods, the words which occur most frequently in a document. This method can be improved by comparing the number of times a particular word appears with the number of items it might be expected to appear. The advantage gained is immediately obvious; with the earlier technique a word occurring only a few times would be ignored but, using the latter method, the word might be proved to be very significant. Other experiments have concentrated upon the discovery that if words are 'paired' together in a document upon a number of occasions then this has an added significance.

In addition to the simple descriptors which are normally used in automatic indexing systems, it has also been shown that it may be possible to improve the quality of such systems by the addition of more complex descriptors, for example phrases, and other techniques evolve around the selection of sentences. Sentences can be weighed according to predetermined measure of significance. Sentences with the highest weights are likely to be those which best summarise the subject-content of an item. Examples of 'measures' are 'word frequency', as described above, and the position of a sentence-for example, the first sentence of a paragraph might be an important indication of the paragraph's subject-content.

An automatic indexing system can be linked with a machine-based thesaurus to provide controlled language indexing. Research into techniques such as those described above has continued over many years and operational systems have been devised. Some of these systems have been shown to possess a number of defects and inadequacies; others have been put to practical use and are claimed to be successful. For example,

Thonssen describes an automatic indexing system (PRIMUS-IDX) which interfaces with an automatic thesaurus management programme (INDEX) to enable large quantities of texts to be indexed quickly, consistently and cheaply. The recent application of expert system technology should also be noted. The overall objectives of research into automatic indexing can be said to be rather more than simply to represent the subject-content of a document by index terms; it is possible to produce an automatic extract ('autoextract') which compares reasonably well with an abstract prepared by a skilled abstractor. The SMART project, which was developed in the United States by Saltine, and which is sometimes referred to as Saltine's Magical Automatic Retrieval of Text, is concerned with the effectiveness of computer-based retrieval systems relying entirely or almost entirely on machine processing of text. Out of the early experiments evolved new techniques for the construction of computer-generated thesauri. The system could be used online and a comparison with MEDLARS proved that the SMART procedures worked well. A detailed discussion is outside the scope of this work but it is, perhaps, worth recording that Salton came to the sweeping conclusion that there is little jurisdiction for maintaining controlled many indexes.

The Embodiment

Part of the British Computer Society's approved definition states that an expert system is regarded as the embodiment within a computer of a knowledge-based component from an expert skill in such a form that the system can offer intelligent advice or take an intelligent decision about a processing decision. In other words, an expert system is a computer programme which can take the place of a human expert in some particular area of knowledge. As such, clearly there are possible applications within the cataloguing and indexing field.

For example, expert system techniques might be successfully applied to the task of selecting index terms. On such system is that operated by the Central Abstracting and Indexing Service of the American Petroleum Institute (API-CAUSE), which selects index terms from abstracts of articles appearing in the technical literature. A rule-based system has been created, using the API thesaurus as a base, which has been operational since 1985. The index terms selected by the computer are reviewed by a human index editor (as are the terms selected by CAIS's human indexers). After editing, the terms are used for printed indexes and for online computer searching.

Other examples include L-IDIA (L-Intelligent Document Information Analyser), which is the central part of an expert system designed to analyse automatically the content of documents in natural languages (relevant to well defined domains of knowledge) and an expert system described by Gauch and Smith for searching in full-text. Where the later is concerned, an intelligent search intermediary helps end-users to locate relevant passages.

An obvious possibility is automatic cataloguing based upon a set of rules as embodied in a code such as AACR 2, and there have been several pieces of research aimed at achieving this. One example of the research carried out by Hames at the University of Exeter, another is the work of Hjerppe at Linkoping University, and an investigation into automated title-page cataloguing has been carried out under the direction of Weibel at OCLC. However, 'for an expert system to generate the required conditions for a specifically designed goal, the logic in the knowledge base must be consistent. There have been problems in every attempt to convert AACR 2 into the highly structured rules necessary to run an expert system'. Meador and Whiting conclude that this may well lead to further changes in the rules because the impact of technology will demand greater consistency. Apart from this, Weibel cites other unsolved problems as the incorporation of the cataloguer's general knowledge into the system, the complexity of the rules, and a lack of reliable data capture techniques.

Language to Language: One of the problems that has exercised the minds of librarians over the years has been that of switching from one indexing language to another. Apart from direct one-to-one translation, there is the possibility of the use of having an intermediate neutral languages designed to switch indexing decisions recorded in one indexing language into equivalent decisions in other languages. The intermediary should have the same coverage and specificity as the languages with which it is to be used and should be hospitable to index languages with different structure; that is, faceted or enumerative classification, thesauri or alphabetical word lists. Horsnell investigated the feasibility of a switching language in the field of information science. She reported that switching is possible and that overall recall and precision values far normal indexes and indexing obtained by switching are similar.

Other developments in this area include work conducted under the auspices of UNISSIST to provide an international switching language which could be applied to all publications to indicate the subject fields covered. The original intention was that this would be an intermediate language between two established languages, for example:

German natural language-switching language-French natural language, but the eventual product was the Broad system of ordering. This is a general classification scheme, with a fairly low level of specificity (as the title suggests). Although the scheme, which was the work of an FID (International Federation for Documentation) /BSO Panel, is intended for information exchange and switching, it is not a true switching language in the context of the criteria explained above. It can be concluded that we should investigate and attempt to evaluate indexing systems rather than take their performance for granted, but we should not be too surprised if the results of these investigations are sometimes inconclusive. Cleverdon wrote, when reporting on the second Cornfield investigations: 'As with Cranfield I, the outcome of this test is to raise more questions than it answers. It would be absurd for any organisation to abandon conventional indexing and controlled index languages, whether thesauri or classification, on the basis of these test results.

Libraries Compared

A library may well find it helpful to compare its own activities and costs with those of their libraries in the same group, and published comparative statistics are useful from this point of view.

In the UK, for example, the Centre for Interfirm Comparison (CIFC), after its formation in 1959, carried out many comparisons of performance data in industry, showing that such comparisons can be a valuable management tool to help in the establishment of standards and in the evaluation of activities and procedures.

Flow of Work: A smooth workflow will help to streamline the cataloguing process, the various operations being performed in a reasonable chronological sequence and the layout of the cataloguing department being such that no member of staff has to exert himself more than necessary when carrying out his particular tasks. This 'is an example of ergonomics-the relationship between the worker, his environment, and the equipment he uses. Ergonomics is a technique which is sometimes overlooked in librarianship.

14

Library Material Selection and Acquisition

Library Acquisitions

Library acquisitions is the department of a library responsible for the selection and purchase of materials or resources. The department may select vendors, negotiate consortium pricing, arrange for standing orders, and select individual titles or resources.

Library Collection Development

According to the The International Federation of Library Associations and Institutions (IFLA), Acquisition and Collection Development focuses on methodological and topical themes pertaining to acquisition of print and other analogue library materials (by purchase, exchange, gift, legal deposit), and the licensing and purchase of electronic information resources.

Library collection development is the process of meeting the information needs of the people (a service population) in a timely and economical manner using information resources locally held, as well as from other organisations.

Collections are developed by Librarians and library staff by buying or otherwise acquiring materials over a period, based on assessment of the information needs of the library's users. In addition to ongoing materials acquisition, library collection development includes:

- The creation of policies to guide material selection;
- Replacement of worn or lost materials;
- Removal (weeding) of materials no longer needed in the collection;
- Planning for new collections or collection areas;
- Cooperative decision-making with other libraries or within library consortia.

Collection Evaluation Methods Some Library evaluation methods include: -Checklists Method -Circulation and Interlibrary Loan Statistics -Citation Analysis -Network Usage Analysis -Vendor-Supplied Statistics -Faculty Opinion. Checklists Method This method of collection evaluation is the practice of checking a library collection against a list of notable books or materials to see if the collection includes these titles. This is the oldest method of collection evaluation, and its first recorded use occurs in 1849 by Charles Jewett at the Smithsonian Institute.

Citation Analysis Citation Analysis is the method most used on the college and university level. This method looks at citations on bibliographies prepared by students' and faculty's written work to see if the resources used are included in the learning institute's partner library. The purpose is to see if the written work produced can be done using only the library located at the college or university. Citation analysis is a good research method to use in academic libraries on the university and college level when performing a collections evaluation. This method is performed by studying bibliographies from many sources such as student papers, faculty research publications, along with theses and dissertations. This information is then used to see what percentage of the items cited in the bibliographies have come from the academic library's collection. Citation analysis is used to see if the work produced at the university or college has been written using sources mainly from the academic library at that learning institution.

Faculty Opinion When faculty opinion about a library collection is asked the feelings, beliefs, values, and individual views about how well the library collection fits the curriculum of that learning institution are answered. Both librarians and teaching faculties opinions should be asked, and taken into account, as the evaluation of the library collection should be a cooperative effort that yields the best results possible. It is important to have the most current, and updated collection possible as a deficient collection could impact the learning institution negatively. The research method of faculty opinion to evaluate academic library collections will help aid the library with finding out what the strengths and weaknesses are so that these points can be corrected, and the gaps found can be filled. The faculty members who have the most responsibility for evaluating and building library collections are the Collection Development Librarians, and the institution's faculty especially professors.

Natural Science

As advances and specialisation have made new scientific research inaccessible to most audiences, the "literary" nature of science writing has become less pronounced over the last two centuries. Now, science appears mostly in journals. Scientific works of Aristotle, Copernicus, and Newton still exhibit great value, but since the science in them has largely become outdated, they no longer serve for scientific instruction. Yet, they remain too technical to sit well in most programmes of literary study. Outside of "history of science" programmes, students rarely read such works.

Philosophy

Philosophy has become an increasingly academic discipline. More of its practitioners lament this situation than occurs with the sciences; nonetheless most new philosophical work appears in academic journals. Major philosophers through history—Plato, Aristotle, Socrates, Augustine, Descartes, Kierkegaard, Nietzsche—have become as canonical as any writers. Some recent philosophy works are argued to merit the title "literature", such as some of the works by Simon Blackburn; but much of it does not, and some areas, such as logic, have become extremely technical to a degree similar to that of mathematics.

History

A significant portion of historical writing ranks as literature, particularly the genre known as creative non-fiction. So can a great deal of journalism, such as literary journalism. However these areas have become extremely large, and often have a primarily utilitarian purpose: to record data or convey immediate information. As a result the writing in these fields often lacks a literary quality, although it often and in its better moments has that quality. Major "literary" historians include Herodotus, Thucydides and Procopius, all of whom count as canonical literary figures.

Law

Law offers more ambiguity. Some writings of Plato and Aristotle, the law tables of Hammurabi of Babylon, or even the early parts of the Bible could be seen as legal literature. Roman civil law as codified in the Corpus Juris Civilis during the reign of Justinian I of the Byzantine Empire has a reputation as significant literature. The founding documents of many countries, including Constitutions and Law Codes, can count as literature; however, most legal writings rarely exhibit much literary merit, as they tend to be rather garrulous.

Literature

Literature (from Latin litterae (plural); letter) is the art of written work. The word literature literally means: "things made from letters". Literature is commonly classified as having two major forms—fiction and non-fiction—and two major techniques—poetry and prose.

Literature may consist of texts based on factual information (journalistic or non-fiction), a category that may also include polemical works, biography, and reflective essays, or it may consist of texts based on imagination (such as fiction, poetry, or drama). Literature written in poetry emphasises the aesthetic and rhythmic qualities of language—such as sound, symbolism, and metre—to evoke meanings in addition to, or in place of, ordinary meanings, while literature written in prose applies ordinary grammatical structure and the natural flow of speech. Literature can also be classified according to historical periods, genres, and political influences. While the concept of genre has broadened over the centuries, in general, a genre consists of artistic works that fall within a certain central theme; examples of genre include romance, mystery, crime, fantasy, erotica, and adventure, among others.

Important historical periods in English literature include Old English, Middle English, the Renaissance, the Elizabethan era of the 16th century (which includes the Shakespearean era), the 17th Century Restoration period, the 18th century Age of Enlightenment, the Romanticism of the early 19th century, the later 19th Century Victorian, and 20th Century Modernism and Post-modernism. Important intellectual movements that have influenced the study of literature include feminism, post-colonialism, psychoanalysis, post-structuralism, post-modernism, romanticism, and Marxism.

Poetry: A poem is a composition written in verse (although verse has also been used for epic and dramatic fiction). Poems make use of the aesthetic qualities of language to suggest differential meanings and to evoke emotive responses. Poems rely heavily on imagery and metaphor; they may have a rhythmic structure based on patterns of stresses (metric feet) or on patterns of different-length syllables (as in classical prosody); and they may or may not utilise rhyme. Due to the diversity of poetic forms and structures, poetry can be difficult to define and characterise. Typically though, poetry as a form of literature makes use of the *formal* properties of the words it uses – the properties of the written or spoken form of the words, independent of their meaning. For example, rhythm can be established by the number of syllables in the words or how these syllables are stressed; rhyme and alliteration depend on the sounds of the words.

Arguably, poetry pre-dates other forms of literature. Early examples include the Sumerian *Epic of Gilgamesh* (dated from around 2700 BC), parts of the Bible, the surviving works of Homer (the *Iliad* and the *Odyssey*), and the Indian epics *Ramayana* and *Mahabharata*. In cultures based primarily on oral traditions the formal characteristics of poetry often have a mnemonic function, and important texts: legal, genealogical or moral, for example, may appear first in verse form.

Some poetry uses specific forms. Examples include the haiku, the limerick, and the sonnet. A traditional haiku written in Japanese relate to nature, contain seventeen onji (syllables), distributed over three lines in groups of five, seven, and five, and should also have a kigo, a specific word indicating a season. A limerick has five lines, with a rhyme scheme of AABBA, and line lengths of 3,3,2,2,3 stressed syllables. It traditionally has a less reverent attitude towards nature. Poetry not adhering to a formal poetic structure is called "free verse".

Language and tradition dictate some poetic norms Persian poetry always rhymes whilst Greek poetry rarely does. Some languages contain more rhyming words than others. Italian, for example, has a rich rhyming structure permitting use of a limited set of rhymes throughout a lengthy poem. The richness results from word endings that follow regular forms. English, with its irregular word endings adopted from other languages, is less rich in rhyme. Perhaps the most paradigmatic style of English poetry, blank verse, as exemplified in works by Shakespeare and Milton, consists of unrhymed iambic pentameters. Some languages prefer longer lines; some shorter ones. Some of these conventions result from the ease of fitting a specific language's vocabulary and grammar into certain structures, rather than into others; For example, this may occur when a language typically has longer words than other languages, such us Greek and German. Other structural conventions come about as the result of historical accidents, where many speakers of a language associate good poetry with a verse form preferred by a particular skilled or popular poet.

Works for theatre traditionally took verse form. This has now become rare outside opera and musicals, although many would argue that the language of drama remains intrinsically poetic.

In recent years, digital poetry has arisen that utilises the artistic, publishing, and synthetic qualities of digital media.

Essays: An essay consists of a discussion of a topic from an author's personal point of view, exemplified by works by Michel de Montaigne or by Charles Lamb.

"Essay" in English derives from the French word for "to attempt," *essayer*. Thus, one can find open-ended, provocative, and inconclusive essays. The term "essays" first applied to the self-reflective musings of Michel de Montaigne, who has a reputation as the father of this literary form.

Genres related to the essay may include:

- The memoir, saying the story of an author's life from the author's personal point of view;
- The epistle: usually a formal, didactic, or elegant letter;
- Works by Lady Murasaki, the Arabic *Hayy ibn Yaqdhan* by Ibn Tufail, the Arabic *Theologus Autodidactus* by Ibn al-Nafis, and the Chinese *Romance of the Three Kingdoms* by Luo Guanzhong.

Early novels in Europe did not count as significant litera perhaps because "mere" prose writing seemed easy and unimportant. It has become clear, however, that prose writing can provide aesthetic pleasure without adhering to poetic forms. Additionally, the freedom authors gain in not having to concern themselves with verse structure translates often into a more complex plot or into one richer in precise detail than one typically finds even in narrative poetry. This freedom also allows an author to experiment with many different literary and presentation styles—including poetry—in the scope of a single novel.

Other Prose Literature: Philosophical, historical, journalistic, and scientific writings are traditionally ranked as literature. They offer some of the oldest prose writings in existence; novels and prose stories earned the names "fiction" to distinguish them from factual writing or non-fiction, which writers historically have crafted in prose.

Drama: A play or drama is another classical literary form that has continued to evolve over the years. It generally comprises chiefly dialogue between characters, and usually aims at dramatic / theatrical performance rather than at reading. During the 18th and 19th centuries, opera developed as a combination of poetry, drama, and music. Nearly all drama took verse form until comparatively recently. Shakespeare could be considered drama. Romeo and Juliet, for example, is a classic romantic drama generally accepted as literature.

Greek drama exemplifies the earliest form of drama of which we have substantial knowledge. Tragedy, as a dramatic genre, developed as a performance associated with religious and civic festivals, typically enacting or developing upon well-known historical or mythological themes. Tragedies generally presented very serious themes. With the advent of newer technologies, scripts written for non-stage media have been added to this form. War of the Worlds (radio) in 1938 saw the advent of literature written for radio broadcast, and many works of Drama have been adapted for film or television. Conversely, television, film, and radio literature have been adapted to printed or electronic media.

Oral Literature: The term oral literature refers not to written, but to oral tradition, folktales, and ballads. However the use of this oxymoron is controversial in the scientific community. Some prefer to avoid the Etyme.

Other Narrative Forms:

- Electronic literature is a literary genre consisting of works that originate in digital environments.
- Films, videos and broadcast soap operas have carved out a niche which often parallels the functionality of prose fiction.
- Graphic novels and comic books present stories told in a combination of sequential artwork, dialogue and text.

Genres of Literature: Literary genre is a mode of categorising literature. The term originates from French, designating a proposed type or class. However, such classes are subject to change, and have been used in different ways in different periods and traditions.

Literary Techniques: A literary technique or literary device can be used by authors in order to enhance the written framework of a piece of literature, and produce specific effects. Literary techniques encompass a wide range of approaches to crafting a work: whether a work is narrated in first-person or from another perspective, whether to use a traditional linear narrative or a non-linear narrative, or the choice of literary genre, are all examples of literary technique. They may indicate to a reader that there is a familiar structure and presentation to a work, such as a conventional murder-mystery novel; or, the author may choose to experiment with their technique to surprise the reader. In this way, use of a technique can lead to the development of a new genre, as was the case with one of the first modern novels, *Pamela* by Samuel Richardson. *Pamela* is written as a collection of letter-writing correspondence, called "epistolary technique"; by using this technique, *Pamela* strengthened the tradition of the epistolary novel, a genre which had been practised for some time already but without the same acclaim. Literary technique is distinguished from literary device, as military strategy is distinguished from military tactics. Devices are specific constructions within the narrative that make it effective. Examples include metaphor, simile, ellipsis, narrative motifs, and allegory. Even simple word play functions as a literary device. The narrative mode may be considered a literary device, such as the use of stream-of-consciousness narrative.

Literary criticism implies a critique and evaluation of a piece of literature and, in some cases, it is used to improve a work in progress or a classical piece, as with an ongoing theatre production. Literary editors can serve a similar purpose for the authors with whom they work. There are many types of literary criticism and each can be used to critique a piece in a different way or critique a different aspect of a piece.

International Standard Book Number

The International Standard Book Number (ISBN) is a unique numeric commercial book identifier based upon the 9-digit Standard Book Numbering (SBN) code created by Gordon Foster, Emeritus Professor of Statistics at Trinity College, Dublin, for the booksellers and stationers WHSmith and others in 1965. The 10-digit ISBN format was developed by the International Organisation for Standardisation (ISO) and was published in 1970 as international standard ISO 2108. (However, the 9-digit SBN code was used in the United Kingdom until 1974.) An SBN may be converted to an ISBN by prepending the digit "0". ISO has appointed the International ISBN Agency as the registration authority for ISBN worldwide and the ISBN Standard is developed under the control of ISO Technical Committee 46/Subcommittee 9 TC 46/SC 9. The ISO online facility only refers back to 1978.

Since 1 January 2007, ISBNs have contained 13 digits, a format that is compatible with "Bookland" EAN-13s. Occasionally, a book may appear without a printed ISBN if it is printed privately or the author does not follow the usual ISBN procedure; however, this can be rectified later. Another identifier, the International Standard Serial Number (ISSN), identifies periodical publications such as magazines.

An Overview

An ISBN is assigned to each edition and variation (except reprintings) of a book, for example an ebook, a paperback, and a hardcover would each have a different ISBN. The ISBN is 13 digits long if assigned on or after 1 January 2007, and 10 digits long if assigned before 2007. An International Standard Book Number consists of 4 parts (if it is a 10 digit ISBN) or 5 parts (for a 13 digit ISBN):

1. for a 13-digit ISBN, a prefix element - a *GS1 prefix*: so far 978 or 979 have been made available by GS1;
2. the *registration group element*, (language-sharing country group, individual country or territory);
3. the *registrant* element;
4. the *publication element;* and
5. a *checksum character* or check digit.

The 13 digit ISBN separates its parts (*prefix element, registration group, registrant, publication* and *check digit*) with either a hyphen or a space. Other than the prefix element and the check digit, no part of the ISBN has a fixed number of digits.

The 10 digit ISBN also separated its parts (*registration group, registrant, publication* and *check digit*) with either a hyphen or a space.

ISBN Issuance

International Standard Book Numbers issuance is country-specific, in that ISBNs are issued by the ISBN registration agency that is responsible for that country or territory. The ranges of ISBNs assigned to any particular country are based on the publishing profile of the country concerned - e.g., the number of books and the number, type and size of publishers that are active. Some ISBN registration agencies are based in National Libraries or within Ministries of Culture and thus may receive direct funding from government to support their services. In other cases the ISBN registration service is provided by organisations such as bibliographic data providers who are not government funded. In Canada the stated purpose of issuing International Standard Book Numbers for no cost was to encourage Canadian culture. In the United Kingdom, United States, and some other countries, where the service is provided by non-government funded organisations the issuing of International Standard Book Numbers is a chargeable service.

Australia: In Australia ISBNs are issued by the commercial library services agency Thorpe-Bowker, and prices range from $42 for a single ISBN (plus a $55 registration fee for new publishers) through to $2,890 for a block of 1,000 ISBNs.

Canada: In Canada Library and Archives Canada, a government agency, is the responsible entity, and there is no cost. Works in French are issued an ISBN by the Bibliotheque et Archives nationales du Quebec.

Pakistan: National Library of Pakistan is responsible for ISBN registrations for Pakistani Publishers, Authors, Universities, Institutions and Government Departments who are responsible for publishing books.

India: In India, Raja Rammohan National Agency for ISBN is responsible for registration of Indian Publishers, Authors, Universities, Institutions and Government Departments who are responsible for publishing books.

United Kingdom and Ireland: In the United Kingdom and Ireland the privately held company, Nielsen Book Services, part of Nielsen Holdings N.V., is the responsible entity, and there is a charge. ISBNs are sold in lots of ten or more.

United States: In the United States the privately held company RR Bowker is the responsible entity, and there is a charge, which varies depending upon the number of ISBNs purchased, with prices ranging from $125.00 for a single number.

Publishers and authors in other countries need to obtain ISBNs from their respective national ISBN registration Agency. A directory of ISBN Agencies is available on the International ISBN Agency website.

Registration Group Identifier

The registration group identifier is a 1 to 5 digit number. The single digit group identifiers are: 0 or 1 for English-speaking countries; 2 for French-speaking countries; 3 for German-speaking countries; 4 for Japan; 5 for Russian-speaking countries, 7 for People's Republic of China. An example 5 digit group identifier is 99936, for Bhutan. The allocated group IDs are: 0–5, 600–621, 7, 80–94, 950–989, 9927–9989, and 99901–99972. Books published in rare languages typically have longer group identifiers. The original standard book number (SBN) had no registration group identifier, but affixing a zero (0) as prefix to a 9-digit SBN creates a valid 10-digit ISBN.

Registrant Element

The national ISBN agency assigns the registrant element (cf. Category: ISBN agencies) and an accompanying series of ISBNs within that registrant element to the publisher; the publisher then allocates one of the ISBNs to each of his books. Generally, in most countries a book publisher is not required by law to assign an ISBN, however, most book stores only handle ISBN-bearing merchandise.

A listing of more than 900,000 assigned publisher codes is published, and can be ordered in book form (€1399, US$1959). The website of the ISBN agency does not offer any free method of looking up publisher codes. Partial lists have been compiled (from library catalogues) for the English-language groups: identifier 0 and identifier 1.

Publishers receive blocks of ISBNs, with larger blocks allotted to publishers expecting to need them; a small publisher may receive ISBNs of one or more digits for the registration group identifier, several digits for the registrant, and a single digit for the publication element. Once that block of ISBNs is used, the publisher may receive another block of ISBNs, with a different registrant element. Consequently, a publisher may have different allotted registrant elements. There also may be more than one registration group identifier used in a country. This might occur once all the registrant elements from a particular registration group have been allocated to publishers.

By using variable block lengths, registration agencies are able to customise the allocations of ISBNs that they make to publishers. For example, a large publisher may be given a block of ISBNs where the digits allocated for the registrant element are few and there are many digits allocated for the publication element; likewise countries publishing a large output of titles have few allocated digits for the registration group identifier, and many for the registrant and publication elements. Here are some sample ISBN-10 codes, illustrating block length variations.

ISBN	*Country or area*	*Publisher*
99921-58-10-7	Qatar	NCCAH, Doha
9971-5-0210-0	Singapore	World Scientific
960-425-059-0	Greece	Sigma Publications
80-902734-1-6	Czech Republic; Slovakia	Taita Publishers
85-359-0277-5	Brazil	Companhia das Letras
1-84356-028-3	English-speaking area	Simon Wallenberg Press
0-684-84328-5	English-speaking area	Scribner
0-8044-2957-X	English-speaking area	Frederick Ungar
0-85131-041-9	English-speaking area	J. A. Allen & Co.
0-943396-04-2	English-speaking area	Willmann–Bell
0-9752298-0-X	English-speaking area	KT Publishing

Pattern

English-language publisher codes follow a systematic pattern, which allows their length to be easily determined, as follows:

Item number length	*0- group identifier*			*1- group identifier*			
	From	*To*	*Publishers*	*From*	*To*	*Publishers*	*Total*
6 digits	0-00-xxxxxx-x	0-19-xxxxxx-x	20	1-00-xxxxxx-x	1-09-xxxxxx-x	10	30
5 digits	0-200-xxxxx-x	0-699-xxxxx-x	500	1-100-xxxxx-x	1-399-xxxxx-x	300	800
4 digits	0-7000-xxxx-x	0-8499-xxxx-x	1,500	1-4000-xxxx-x	1-5499-xxxx-x	1,500	3,000
3 digits	0-85000-xxx-x	0-89999-xxx-x	5,000	1-55000-xxx-x	1-86979-xxx-x	31,980	36,980
2 digits	0-900000-xx-x	0-949999-xx-x	50,000	1-869800-xx-x	1-998999-xx-x	129,200	179,200
1 digit	0-9500000-x-x	0-9999999-x-x	500,000	1-9990000-x-x	1-9999999-x-x	10,000	510,000
		Total	**557,020**		**Total**	**172,990**	**730,010**

Check Digits

A check digit is a form of redundancy check used for error detection, the decimal equivalent of a binary check bit. It consists of a single digit computed from the other digits in the message.

ISBN-10 Check Digits

The 2001 edition of the official manual of the International ISBN Agency says that the ISBN-10 check digit – which is the last digit of the ten-digit ISBN – must range from 0 to 10 (the symbol X is used for 10), and must be such that the sum of all the ten digits, each multiplied by its (integer) weight, descending from 10 to 1, is a multiple of 11.

For example, for an ISBN-10 of 0-306-40615-2:

$$s = (0\times10)+(3\times9)+(0\times8)+(6\times7)+(4\times6)+(0\times5)+(6\times4)+(1\times3)+(5\times2)+(2\times1)$$
$$= 0+27+0+42+24+0+24+3+10+2$$
$$= 132 = 12\times11$$

Formally, using modular arithmetic, we can say:

$$(10x_1 + 9x_2 + 8x_3 + 7x_4 + 6x_5 + 5x_6 + 4x_7 + 3x_8 + 2x_9 + x_{10}) \bmod 11 \equiv 0.$$

It is also true for ISBN-10's that the sum of all the ten digits, each multiplied by its weight in *ascending* order from 1 to 10, is a multiple of 11. For this example:

$$s = (0\times1)+(3\times2)+(0\times3)+(6\times4)+(4\times5)+(0\times6)+(6\times7)+(1\times8)+(5\times9)+(2\times10)$$
$$= 0+6+0+24+20+0+42+8+45+20$$
$$= 165 = 15\times11$$

Formally, we can say:

$$(x_1 + 2x_2 + 3x_3 + 4x_4 + 5x_5 + 6x_6 + 7x_7 + 8x_8 + 9x_9 + 10x_{10}) \bmod 11 \equiv 0.$$

The two most common errors in handling an ISBN (e.g., typing or writing it) are a single altered digit or the transposition of adjacent digits. It can be proved that all possible valid ISBN-10's have at least two digits different from each other. It can also be proved that there are no pairs of valid ISBN-10's with eight identical digits and two transposed digits. (These are true only because the ISBN is less than 11 digits long, and because 11 is a prime number.) The ISBN check digit method therefore ensures that it will always be possible to detect these two most common types of error, i.e., if either of these types of error has occurred, the result will never be a valid ISBN - the sum of the digits multiplied by their weights will never be a multiple of 11. However, if the error occurs in the publishing house and goes undetected, the book will be issued with an invalid ISBN.

In contrast, it is possible for other types of error, such as two altered non-transposed digits, or three altered digits, to result in a valid ISBN number (although it is still unlikely).

ISBN-10 Check Digit Calculation

Modular arithmetic is convenient for calculating the check digit using modulus 11. Each of the first nine digits of the ten-digit ISBN – excluding the check digit, itself – is multiplied by a number in a sequence from 10 to 2, and the remainder of the sum, with respect to 11, is computed. The resulting remainder, plus the check digit, must equal 11; therefore, the check digit is 11 minus the remainder of the sum of the products.

For example, the check digit for an ISBN-10 of 0-306-40615-? is calculated as follows:

$$s = (0\times10)+(3\times9)+(0\times8)+(6\times7)+(4\times6)+(0\times5)+(6\times4)+(1\times3)+(5\times2)$$
$$= 0+27+0+42+24+0+24+3+10$$
$$= 130 = 12\times11-2$$

Thus the check digit is 2, and the complete sequence is ISBN 0-306-40615-2. The value required to satisfy this condition might be 10; if so, an 'X' should be used.

Alternative calculation

```
//PHP
function is_isbn_10_valid($ISBN10){
   if(strlen($ISBN10) != 10)
      return false;

   $a = 0;
   for($i = 0; $i < 10; $i++){
      if ($ISBN10[$i] == "X" || $ISBN10[$i] == "x"){
         $a += 10*intval(10-$i);
      } else if (is_numeric($ISBN10[$i])) {
         $a += intval($ISBN10[$i]) * intval(10-$i);
      } else {
         return false;
      }
   }
   return ($a % 11 == 0);
}
#Python
def is_isbn10(isbn10):
   if len(isbn10) != 10:
      return False
   r = sum((10 - i) * (int(x) if x != 'X' else 10) for i, x in enumerate(isbn10))
   return r % 11 == 0

#Ruby
def is_valid?(isbn)
 (isbn.length == 10) && (isbn.split('').inject([10,0]){|a, c| i,s = a; [s+i*c.to_i,i-1]}.first%11==0)
end

#978-1-4349-1777-5 change code.
```

```
def is_valid?(isbn)
  (isbn.length == 10) && (isbn.split('').inject([10,0]){|a, c| i,s = a; [s+i*c.to_i,i-1]}.first%11==0)
end
```

ISBN-13 Check Digit Calculation

The 2005 edition of the International ISBN Agency's official manual describes how the 13-digit ISBN check digit is calculated. The ISBN-13 check digit, which is the last digit of the ISBN, must range from 0 to 9 and must be such that the sum of all the thirteen digits, each multiplied by its (integer) weight, alternating between 1 and 3, is a multiple of 10.

Formally, using modular arithmetic, we can say:

$$(x_1 + 3x_2 + x_3 + 3x_4 + x_5 + 3x_6 + x_7 + 3x_8 + x_9 + 3x_{10} + x_{11} + 3x_{12} + x_{13}) \bmod 10 \equiv 0.$$

The calculation of an ISBN-13 check digit begins with the first 12 digits of the thirteen-digit ISBN (thus excluding the check digit itself). Each digit, from left to right, is alternately multiplied by 1 or 3, then those products are summed modulo 10 to give a value ranging from 0 to 9. Subtracted from 10, that leaves a result from 1 to 10. A zero (0) replaces a ten (10), so, in all cases, a single check digit results.

For example, the ISBN-13 check digit of 978-0-306-40615-? is calculated as follows:

s = 9×1 + 7×3 + 8×1 + 0×3 + 3×1 + 0×3 + 6×1 + 4×3 + 0×1 + 6×3 + 1×1 + 5×3

= 9 + 21 + 8 + 0 + 3 + 0 + 6 + 12 + 0 + 18 + 1 + 15

= 93

93 / 10 = 9 remainder 3

10 – 3 = 7

Thus, the check digit is 7, and the complete sequence is ISBN 978-0-306-40615-7.

Formally, the ISBN-13 check digit calculation is:

$$x_{13} = (10 - (x_1 + 3x_2 + x_3 + 3x_4 + \cdots + x_{11} + 3x_{12}) \bmod 10) \bmod 10.$$

This check system – similar to the UPC check digit formula – does not catch all errors of adjacent digit transposition. Specifically, if the difference between two adjacent digits is 5, the check digit will not catch their transposition. For instance, the above example allows this situation with the 6 followed by a 1. The correct order contributes 3×6+1×1 = 19 to the sum; while, if the digits are transposed (1 followed by a 6), the contribution of those two digits will be 3×1+1×6 = 9. However, 19 and 9 are congruent modulo 10, and so produce the same, final result: both ISBNs will have a check digit of 7. The ISBN-10 formula uses the prime modulus 11 which avoids this blind spot, but requires more than the digits 0-9 to express the check digit.

Additionally, if the sum of the 2nd, 4th, 6th, 8th, 10th, and 12th digits is tripled then added to the remaining digits (1st, 3rd, 5th, 7th, 9th, 11th, and 13th), the total will always be divisible by 10 (i.e., end in 0).

```
// Java
public static boolean isISBN13Valid(String isbn) {
    int check = 0;
    for (int i = 0; i < 12; i += 2) {
```

```
        check += Integer.valueOf(isbn.substring(i, i + 1));
    }
    for (int i = 1; i < 12; i += 2) {
        check += Integer.valueOf(isbn.substring(i, i + 1)) * 3;
    }
    check += Integer.valueOf(isbn.substring(12));
    return check % 10 == 0;
}
//JavaScript
function isValidISBN13(ISBNumber) {
    var check, i;

    ISBNumber = ISBNumber.replace(/[-\s]/g,'');

    check = 0;
    for (i = 0; i < 13; i += 2) {
      check += parseInt(ISBNumber.charAt(i));
    }
    for (i = 1; i < 12; i += 2){
      check += 3 * parseInt(ISBNumber.charAt(i));
    }
    return check % 10 === 0;
}
//PHP
function is_isbn_13_valid($n){
    $check = 0;
    for ($i = 0; $i < 13; $i+=2) $check += substr($n, $i, 1);
    for ($i = 1; $i < 12; $i+=2) $check += 3 * substr($n, $i, 1);
    return $check % 10 == 0;
}
# Ruby
def isbn_checksum(isbn_string)
  digits = isbn_string.split(//).map(&:to_i)
  transformed_digits = digits.each_with_index.map do |digit, digit_index|
    digit_index.modulo(2).zero? ? digit : digit*3
  end
  sum = transformed_digits.reduce(:+)
```

```
end

def is_valid_isbn13?(isbn13)
  checksum = isbn_checksum(isbn13)
  checksum.modulo(10).zero?
end

def isbn13_checksum_digit(isbn12)
  checksum = isbn_checksum(isbn12)
  10 - checksum.modulo(10)
end
# Python
def is_valid_isbn13(isbn):
    check = (10 - (sum(int(digit) * (3 if idx % 2 else 1) for idx, digit in enumerate(isbn[:12]))
% 10)) % 10
    return check == int(isbn[-1])
// C/C++
bool is_valid_isbn13(char digits)
{
     int i, check=0;
     for (i=0; i<13; i+=2)
                                                                          check += digits[i];
     for (i=1; i<12; i+=2)
                                                                        check += 3*digits[i];
     return check%10==0;
}
— PL/SQL - for validation in Oracle database
FUNCTION validate_isbn_13(isbn VARCHAR2) RETURN INTEGER IS
    checksum INTEGER;
    weight INTEGER;
    modular INTEGER;
    valid INTEGER;
    reminder INTEGER;
BEGIN
    valid := -1;
    checksum := 0;
```

```
    FOR i IN 1 .. 12 LOOP
        IF MOD( i, 2) = 0 THEN
            weight := 3;
        ELSE
            weight := 1;
        END IF;
        checksum := checksum + weight * TO_NUMBER( SUBSTR( isbn, i, 1 ) );
    END LOOP;
    modular := MOD( checksum, 10 );

    IF modular = 0 THEN
        reminder := 0;
    ELSE
        reminder := 10 - modular;
    END IF;

    IF TO_CHAR( reminder) = SUBSTR(isbn, 13, 1) THEN
        valid := 0;
    END IF;

    RETURN valid;
END validate_isbn_13;
# Bourne-Again Shell
function is_valid_isbn13 () {
declare ISBN="${1//[^[:digit:]]}"
declare -i CheckDigit=0

  for i in $(seq 0 12); do
    CheckDigit+=$((${ISBN:$i:1}*(1 + 2*(i % 2))))
  done
  return $((CheckDigit % 10))
}
/* Maxima one-liner */
check_isbn13([x]):= is(mod(sum(x[2*i+1],i,0,6)+3*sum(x[2*i],i,1,6),10)=0)$
```

ISBN-10 to ISBN-13 Conversion

The conversion is quite simple as one only need to prepend prefix "978" and calculate new checksum with ISBN-13 algorithm.

```
function isbn10ToIsbn13(isbn10) {
    isbn13 = "978" + isbn10;
    return isbn13.substr(0, isbn13.length-1) + getIsbn13CheckSum(isbn13);
}
```

Errors in Usage

Publishers and libraries have varied policies about the use of the ISBN check digit. Publishers sometimes fail to check the correspondence of a book title and its ISBN before publishing it; that failure causes book identification problems for libraries, booksellers, and readers.

Most libraries and booksellers display the book record for an invalid ISBN issued by the publisher. The Library of Congress catalogue contains books published with invalid ISBNs, which it usually tags with the phrase "Cancelled ISBN". However, book-ordering systems such as Amazon.com will not search for a book if an invalid ISBN is entered to its search engine.

eISBN

There are no *e*-ISBN or eISBN numbers. Only the term ISBN should be used.

EAN Format used in Bar Codes, and Upgrading

Currently the bar codes on a book's back cover (or inside a mass-market paperback book's front cover) are EAN-13; they may have a separate bar code encoding five digits for the currency and the recommended retail price. For 10 digit ISBNs, the number "978", the Bookland "country code", is prefixed to the ISBN in the bar code data, and the check digit is recalculated according to the EAN13 formula (modulo 10, 1x and 3x weighting on alternate digits).

Partly because of an expected shortage in certain ISBN categories, the International Organisation for Standardisation (ISO) decided to migrate to a thirteen-digit ISBN (ISBN-13). The process began 1 January 2005 and was planned to conclude 1 January 2007. As of 2011, all the 13-digit ISBNs begin with 978. As the 978 ISBN supply is exhausted, the 979 prefix will be introduced. Part of the 979 prefix is reserved for use with the Musicland code for musical scores with an ISMN. 10 digit ISMN codes differed visually as they began with an "M" letter; the bar code represents the "M" as a zero (0), and for checksum purposes it counted as a 3. All ISMNs are now 13 digits commencing 979-0; 979-1 to 979-9 will be used by ISBN.

Publisher identification code numbers are unlikely to be the same in the 978 and 979 ISBNs, likewise, there is no guarantee that language area code numbers will be the same. Moreover, the ten-digit ISBN check digit generally is not the same as the thirteen-digit ISBN check digit. Because the EAN/UCC-13 is part of the Global Trade Item Number (GTIN) system (that includes the EAN/UCC-14, the UPC-12, and the EAN-8), it is expected that ISBN-generating software should accommodate fourteen-digit ISBNs.

Bar code format compatibility is maintained, because (aside from the group breaks) the ISBN-13 bar code format is identical to the EAN bar code format of existing ISBN-10s. So, migration to an EAN-based system allows booksellers the use of a single numbering system for both books and non-book products that is compatible with existing ISBN-based data, with only minimal changes to information technology systems. Hence, many booksellers (e.g., Barnes & Noble) migrated to EAN bar codes as early as March 2005. Although many American and Canadian booksellers were able to read EAN-13 bar codes before 2005, most general retailers could not read them. The upgrading of the UPC bar code system to full EAN-13, in 2005, eased migration to the ISBN-13 in North America.

International Standard Serial Number

An International Standard Serial Number (ISSN) is a unique eight-digit number used to identify a print or electronic periodical publication. Periodicals published in both print and electronic form may have two ISSNs, a print ISSN (p-ISSN) and an electronic ISSN (e-ISSN or eISSN). The ISSN system was first drafted as an ISO international standard in 1971 and published as ISO 3297 in 1975. The ISO subcommittee TC 46/SC 9 is responsible for the standard.

Code Format

The format of the ISSN is an eight digit number, divided by a hyphen into two four-digit numbers. The last digit, which may be 0–9 or an X, is a check digit. The ISSN of the journal *Hearing Research,* for example, is 0378-5955, the check digit is 5.

To calculate the check digit, the following algorithm may be used:

> Calculate the sum of the first seven digits of the ISSN multiplied by its position in the number, counting from the right—that is, 8, 7, 6, 5, 4, 3, and 2, respectively:

The modulus 11 of this sum is then calculated: divide the sum by 11 and determine the remainder.

If there is no remainder the check digit is 0, otherwise the remainder value is subtracted from 11 to give the check digit:

5 is the check digit.

An upper case X in the check digit position indicates a check digit of 10.

To confirm the check digit, calculate the sum of all eight digits of the ISSN multiplied by its position in the number, counting from the right (if the check digit is X, then add 10 to the sum). The modulus 11 of the sum must be 0. Also, there is an Online ISSN checker can check validity of ISSN base on above algorithm.

Code Assignment

ISSN codes are assigned by a network of ISSN National Centres, usually located at national libraries and coordinated by the ISSN International Centre based in Paris. The International Centre is an intergovernmental organisation created in 1974 through an agreement between UNESCO and the French government. The International Centre maintains a database of all ISSNs assigned worldwide, the *ISDS Register (International Serials Data System)* otherwise known as the *ISSN Register.* As of 2011, the ISSN Register contained records for 1,623,566 items.

Comparison with other Identifiers

ISSN and ISBN codes are similar in concept, where ISBNs are assigned to individual books. An ISBN might be assigned for particular issues of a periodical, in addition to the ISSN code for the periodical as a whole. An ISSN, unlike the ISBN code, is an anonymous identifier associated with a periodical title, containing no information as to the publisher or its location. For this reason a new ISSN is assigned to a periodical each time it undergoes a major title change.

Since the ISSN applies to an entire periodical a new identifier, the Serial Item and Contribution Identifier, was built on top of it to allow references to specific volumes, articles, or other identifiable components (like the table of contents).

Availability

The ISSN Register is not freely available for interrogation on the web but is available by subscription. There are several routes to the identification and verification of ISSN codes for the general public:

- The print version of a periodical typically will include the ISSN code as part of the publication information;
- Most periodical websites contain ISSN code information;
- Derivative lists of publications will often contain ISSN codes; these can be found through online searches with the ISSN code itself or periodical title;
- WorldCat permits searching their catalogue by ISSN by entering "issn:"+ISSN code in the query field. One can also go directly to an ISSN's record by appending. This does not query the ISSN Register itself but rather shows whether any Worldcat library holds an item with the given ISSN.

Use in URNs

An ISSN can be encoded as a Uniform Resource Name (URN) by prefixing it with "urn:ISSN:". For example *Rail* could be referred to as "urn:ISSN:1534-0481". URN namespaces are case-sensitive, and the ISSN namespace is all caps. If the checksum digit is "X" then it is always encoded in uppercase in a URN.

Young-adult Fiction

Young-adult fiction or young adult literature (often abbreviated as YA), also juvenile fiction, is fiction written, published, or marketed to adolescents and young adults, although recent studies show that 55 per cent of young-adult fiction is purchased by readers over 18 years of age. The Young Adult Library Services Association (YALSA) of the American Library Association (ALA) defines a young adult as someone between the ages of twelve and eighteen. Authors and readers of young adult (YA) novels often define the genre as literature as traditionally written for ages ranging from sixteen years up to the age of twenty-five, while Teen Fiction is written for the ages of ten and to fifteen. The terms young-adult novel, juvenile novel, young-adult book, etc. refer to the works in the YA category.

YA literature shares the following fundamental elements of the fiction genre: character, plot, setting, theme, and style. However, theme and style are often subordinated to the more tangible elements of plot, setting, and character, which appeal more readily to younger readers. The vast majority of YA stories portray an adolescent, rather than an adult or child, as the protagonist.

The subject matter and story lines of YA literature are typically consistent with the age and experience of the main character, but, beyond that, YA stories span the spectrum of fiction genres. Themes in YA stories often focus on the challenges of youth, sometimes referred to as problem novels or coming-of-age novels. Writing styles of YA stories range widely, from the richness of literary style to the clarity and speed of the unobtrusive and free verse.

Genre

Young Adult Literature has become a genre which covers various types of text including: novels, graphic novels, short stories, and poetry. Much of the literature published consists of young adult fiction which in itself contains several different types of text. The genre also contains other various types of non-fiction such as biographies, autobiographies, journal entries/diaries, and letters. Although many genres exist in young adult literature, the problem novel tends to be the most popular among young readers. Problem novel refers to young adult novels in the realistic-fiction category that "addresses personal and social issues across socioeconomic boundaries and within both traditional and non-traditional family structures" (Cole 98). Memoirs are also popular forms of Young Adult Literature. Another common genre within young adult fiction is Bildungsroman, a coming of age story that showcases the process of "growing up". The genre itself has been challenged due to its seemingly mature content by critics of Young Adult Literature, but "other converted critics have embraced Young Adult so dearly that they have scoured the canon for any classics they could adopt into the YA family" (Stephens 2007).

Themes

Young Adult Literature uses a wide array of themes in order to appeal to a wide variety of adolescent readers. Some of these themes include: identity, sexuality, science fiction, depression, suicide, drug abuse, alcohol abuse, familial struggles, bullying, and numerous others. Some issues discussed in Young Adult Literature include: friendship, love, race, money, divorce, relationships within families. "The culture that surrounds and absorbs young adults plays a huge role in their lives. Young Adult Literature explores themes important and crucial to adolescence such as relationships to authority figures, peer pressure and ensuing experimentations, issues of diversity as it relates to gender, sociocultural, and/or socioeconomic status. Primarily, the focus is centred around a young lead character and the reader experiences emotions, situations, and the like through this character and is able to see how these problems/situations are resolved. It also needs to play a significant role in how we approach this group and the books we offer them to read" (Lesesne 14). Reading about issues that adolescents can relate to allows them to identify with a particular character, and creates a sense of security when experiencing something that is going on within their lives. "Whether you call them archetypes or stereotypes, there are certain experiences and certain kinds of people that are common to adolescents. Reading about it may help a young person validate his or her own experience and make some kind of meaning out of it" (Blasingame, 12). In a paper written by April Dawn Wells, she discovers seventeen common traits of young adult novels. These include: "friendship, getting into trouble, interest in the opposite sex, money, divorce, single parents, remarriage, problems with parents, grandparents, younger siblings, concern over grades/school, popularity, puberty, race, death, neighbourhood, and job/working".

Characteristics

Young adult literature contains specific characteristics that are present throughout the genre. These characteristics encompass: "multi-themed story, tension versus shock effect, memorable characters, accurate facts and details, memorable voice, authentic dialogue, effective/clear writing style, sense of humour, widespread appeal, intriguing openings and memorable closings" (Cole 61-65). Other characteristics of Young Adult Literature include: "(1) Characters and issues young readers can identify with; those issues and characters are treated in a way that does not invalidate, minimise, or devalue them; (2) Is framed in language that young readers can understand; (3) Emphasises plot above everything else; and (4)Is written for an audience of young adults"

(Blasingame 11). Overall, Young Adult Literature needs to contain specific elements that will not only interest readers of this genre, but elements that relate directly to real situations adolescents in all generations may encounter, and contain believable, empathetic characters.

Usage in Education

Research suggests young adult literature can be advantageous to reluctant student readers by addressing their needs. Authors who write young adult literature have an adolescent's age and interests in mind. The language and plots of young adult literature are similar to what students are accustomed to finding in reality, television, movies, and popular culture (Bucher, Manning, 328-332).

The following are criteria that researchers have come up with to evaluate the effectiveness of young adult literature in the classroom (Bucher and Manning, 9-10):

- The subject matter should reflect age and development by addressing their interest levels, reading and thinking levels.
- The content should deal with contemporary issues and experiences with characters adolescents can relate.
- Subjects can relate to dealing with parents and adults, illness and death, peer pressure with regards to drugs, sex, and the complications of addiction and pregnancy.
- The content should consider existing global concerns such as cultural, social, and gender diversity; environmental and political issues as it relates to adolescents.

Young Adult Literature has been integrated into classrooms in order to increase student interest in reading. Research has been performed on what type of impact the introduction YA Literature has on students, particularly adolescent males and struggling readers: "Researchers have shown that introducing YA Literature to males improves their reading ability. YA Literature, because of its range of authors and story types, is an appropriate literature for every adolescent male who needs compelling material that speaks to him" (Gill). Research shows that not only adolescent males have been labelled as reluctant readers, struggling readers use reluctance as a coping mechanism. Young Adult Literature has been used to open up the door of reading literature to these readers as well: "When voluntary reading declines, the problems of struggling readers are only aggravated. By allowing adolescents to read good young adult literature, educators are able to encourage independent reading, which will, in turn, help adolescents develop the skills necessary to succeed." (Bucher and Manning)

Another reason that Young Adult Literature has been incorporated into classrooms is to be paired with classic texts that are traditionally read in classrooms, and required by many schools curricula. Using YA Lit alongside a canonical piece of text can increase a students comprehension of the common themes the various texts have, and make reading a classic text more enjoyable: "Young adult literature can spark interest in the classics and vice versa. Although it's clear that young adult literature is more accessible, that doesn't warrant denying the classics to struggling readers. The classics shouldn't be reserved for exceptional students, and Young Adult Literature shouldn't be reserved for at-risk readers." (Cole 513).

Situational Archetypes in Literature

The classic canon in high school literature classes can often be too overwhelming and far removed from the everyday life of an adolescent. Sarah K. Herz and Donald Gallo suggest using archetypes from traditional literature to "build bridges" to the classics through young adult literature. Young Adult Literature offers teachers an effective way to introduce the study of archetypes in literature by grouping a variety of titles around archetypal situations and characters. Herz and Gallo suggest before or amfter studying a traditional classic or contemporary novel it is a good time to introduce the concept of archetypes in literature. Based on the Jungian theory of archetypes, consider a literary archetype as a character type or theme which recurs frequently in literature (Herz and Gallo, 64-66). Recognisinmg archetypes in literature will help students build the foundation for making connection among various works of literature. Students can begin to grasp and identify the archetypal images and patterns that appear in new forms. Archetypes also help students become more conscious of an author's style and to think about and recognise the way in which a particular writer develops a character or story (Herz and Gallo, 66).

Using Classic Situational Archetypes in the Classroom

A partial list of classic situational literary archetypes as comprised by Herz and Gallo in two separate editions of their book, From Hinton to Hamlet: Building Bridges between Young Adult Literature and the Classics. The Young Adult Novels are paired with Classic Novels based on situational archetypes. (Herz and Gallo, 66-70).

Birth/Death/Rebirth

Presents the main character in a conflict. Through pain and suffering, the character's spirit survives the fight and through a development of self-awareness the main character is reborn. *Breathing Underwater* by Alex Flinn / *Hamlet* by William Shakespeare

The Fall: Expulsion from Eden

The main character is expelled because of undesirable actions on his or her part. *Speak* by Laurie Halse Anderson / *The Scarlet Letter* by Nathaniel Hawthorne

The Journey

The protagonist takes a journey, either physically or emotionally, that brings meaning in their life. *The Crazy Horse Electric Game* by Chris Crutcher / *The Odyssey* by Homer and *Of Mice and Men* by John Steinbeck.

The Test or Trial

The main character experiences growth and change; he or she experiences a transformation. *The True Confessions of Charlotte Doyle* by Avi, *Permanent Connections* by Sue Ellen Bridgers, *Dancing on Dark Waters* by Alden Carter, and *Driver's Ed* by Caroline Cooney / *The Red Badge of Courage* by Stephen Crane and *The Colour Purple* by Alice Walker.

Annihilation; Absurdity; Total Oblivion

In order to exist in an unbearable world, the main character accepts that life is "absurd, ridiculous, and ironic" *The Giver* by Lois Lowry / *Catch 22* by Joseph Heller and *Slaughterhouse Five* by Kurt Vonnegut Jr..

Parental Conflicts and Relationships

The protagonist deals with parental conflict by rejecting or bonding with parents. *Tiger Eyes* by Judy Blume, *Midnight Hour Encores* by Bruce Brooks, *Ironman* by Chris Crutcher, and *The Runner* by Cynthia Voigt / *Ordinary People* by Judith Guest, *Death of a Salesman* by Arthur Miller, *Romeo and Juliet* by William Shakespeare, *The Joy Luck Club* by Amy Tan, and *The Glass Menagerie* by Tennessee Williams.

The Wise Old Woman or Man

This figure protects or assists the main character in facing challenges. *Phoenix Rising* by Karen Hesse, *Memoirs of a Bookbat* by Kathryn Lasky, *Jacob I have Loved* by Katherine Paterson, and *Remembering The Good Times* by Richard Peck / *To Kill A Mocking Bird* by Harper Lee and *The Grapes of Wrath* by John Steinbeck.

The Hero

The main character leaves his or her community to go on an adventure, performing actions that bring honour to the community. *Staying Fat for Sarah Byrnes* by Chris Crutcher and *Make Lemonade* by Virginia Euwer Wolff / *A Tale of Two Cities* by Charles Dickens and *Cyrano de Bergerac* by Edmond Rostand.

The Sacrificial Redeemer

The protagonist is willing to die for a belief; the main character maintains a strong sense of morality. *Harry Potter* by J K Rowling, *The Hunger Games* by Suzanne Collins, *The Chocolate War* and *The Bumblebee Flies Anyway* by Robert Cormier / *Julius Caesar* by William Shakespeare and *Antigone* by Sophocles.

Hyphens

Recognition of the noun *young adult* and its punctuation as an adjectival modifier are inconsistent. Some dictionaries recognise *young adult* as a noun (Random House, 2nd 1987), while others do not (Webster's International, 3rd 2002). When recognised (as by Random House), *young adult* is treated as an open compound noun, with no hyphen.

When the noun *young adult* is placed before another noun (such as *fiction, novel, author*), however, the use of a hyphen varies widely. For example, an Internet search (of the Web or of news articles) using the key words *young adult fiction* shows widespread inconsistency in hyphenation. Although *the Chicago Manual of Style* falls short of declaring the omission of the hyphen as grammatically incorrect, it clearly addresses the issue in "Compounds and Hyphenation", sections 7.82-7.86: "When such compounds precede a noun, hyphenation usually makes for easier reading. With the exception of proper nouns (such as United States) and compounds formed by an adverb ending in *ly* plus an adjective, it is never incorrect to hyphenate adjectival compounds before a noun." (Chicago Manual of Style, 15th Edition 2003) The *Writer's Digest Grammar Desk Reference* is a little more forceful on the subject: "The most complicated business conducted by hyphens is uniting words into adjectival compounds that precede nouns. Many writers neglect to hyphenate such compounds, and the result is ramshackle sentences that often frustrate the reader." (Writer's Digest Grammar Desk Reference 2005, pp. 274–275) The *Wikipedia Manual of Style* also addresses the issue of hyphens for compound adjectives.

Although none of the sources cited above list *young adult* as an example, each clearly expresses a preference for hyphenating compound modifiers. With that in mind, *young adult* is a noun (without a hyphen) as defined by Random House. But when the noun *young adult* precedes another noun, it becomes a compound modifier and warrants a hyphen, as in young-adult fiction, young-adult author, young-adult novel, and so on. Because the sources do not declare the absence of a hyphen as grammatically incorrect, widespread inconsistencies in the punctuation of *young adult* are likely to continue, either out of ignorance or as conscious choice of style.

Trends

The category of YA fiction continues to expand into new genres: graphic novels, light novels, manga, fantasy, mystery fiction, romance novels, even subcategories such as cyberpunk, splatterpunk, techno-thrillers, and contemporary Christian fiction. New formats such as ebooks make it easier for teens to access these online.

The Young adult Problem Novel

Recently the term problem novel has been used to describe young adult literature that deal exclusively with an adolescent's first confrontation with a social or personal problem. The term was first used this way in the late 1960s with reference to contemporary works like *The Outsiders*, a coming-of-age novel by S. E. Hinton, first published in 1967. The adolescent problem novel is rather loosely defined. Rose Mary Honnold in *The Teen Reader's Advisor* defines them as dealing more with characters from lower-class families and their problems and as using "grittier", more realistic language, including dialects, profanity, and poor grammar, when it fits the character and setting. Sometimes, the term problem novel is used almost interchangeably with "young adult novel", but many young adult novels do not fit these criteria.

S. E. Hinton's *The Outsiders* (1967) and Paul Zindel's *The Pigman* (1968) are problem novels written specifically for teenagers. However, Sheila Egoff notes in *Thursday's Child: Trends and Patterns in Contemporary Children's Literature* that the Newbery Award winning novel *It's Like This, Cat* (1964) by Emily Cheney Neville may have established "the problem novel formula." *Go Ask Alice* (1971) is an early example of the sub-genre and is often considered an example of the negative aspects of the form (Although the author is "Anonymous", it is largely or wholly the work of its purported editor, Beatrice Sparks). A more recent example is Adam Rapp's *The Buffalo Tree* (1997).

Boundaries between Children's, YA, and Adult Fiction

The distinctions among children's literature, YA literature, and adult literature have historically been flexible and loosely defined. This line is often policed by adults who feel strongly about the border. At the lower end of the YA age spectrum, fiction targeted to readers age 9 to 12 is referred to as middle-grade fiction. Some novels originally marketed to adults have been identified as being of interest and value to adolescents, and *vice versa*, as in the case of books such as the Harry Potter series of novels.

New Adult Fiction

New-adult fiction (also known as post-adolescent literature) is a recent genre of fiction aimed towards post-adolescents and young-adults ages 18 to 30. The term is believed to have been first coined by St. Martin's Press in 2009. The genre tends to focus on issues prevalent in the young adult genre as well as focusing on issues experienced by individuals between the area of childhood and adulthood, such as leaving home for college and getting a job.

Children's Literature

Children's literature or juvenile literature includes stories, books, and poems that are enjoyed by children. Modern children's literature is classified in two different ways: genre or the intended age of the reader. One can trace children's literature back to stories and songs, part of a wider oral tradition, that adults shared with children before publishing existed. The development of early children's literature, before printing was invented, is difficult to trace. Even after printing became widespread, many classic "children's" tales were originally created for adults and later adapted for a younger audience. Since the 1400s, a large quantity of literature, often with a moral or religious message, has been aimed specifically at children. The late nineteenth and early twentieth centuries became known as the "Golden Age of Children's Literature" as this period included the publication of many books acknowledged today as classics.

An Overview

There is no single or widely used definition of children's literature. It can be broadly defined as anything that children read or more specifically defined as fiction, non-fiction, poetry, or drama intended for and used by children and young people. Nancy Anderson, of the College of Education at the University of South Florida, defines children's literature as "all books written for children, excluding works such as comic books, joke books, cartoon books, and non-fiction works that are not intended to be read from front to back, such as dictionaries, encyclopaedias, and other reference materials". The *International Companion Encyclopaedia of Children's Literature* notes that "the boundaries of genre... are not fixed but blurred". Sometimes, no agreement can be reached about whether a given work is best categorised as literature for adults or children. Meanwhile, others defy easy categorisation. J.K. Rowling's *Harry Potter* series was written and marketed for children, but it is also popular among adults. The series' extreme popularity led *The New York Times* to create a separate best-seller list for children's books. Despite the widespread association of children's literature with picture books, spoken narratives existed before printing, and the root of many children's tales go back to ancient storytellers Seth Lerer, in the opening of *Children's Literature: A Reader's History from Aesop to Harry Potter* says, "This book presents a history of what children have heard and read... The history I write of is a history of *reception*."

Background

Early children's literature consisted of spoken stories, songs, and poems, that would have ben used to educate, instruct, and entertain children. It was only in the 18th century, with the development of the concept of 'childhood', that a separate genre of children's literature began to emerge, with its own divisions, expectations, and canon.

French historian Philippe Aries argued in his 1962 book *Centuries of Childhood* that the modern concept of "childhood" only emerged in recent times, and that for the greater part of history, children were not viewed as greatly different from adults, and were not given significantly different treatment. As evidence for this position, he noted that, apart from instructional and didactic texts for children written by clerics like the Venerable Bede, and aelfric of Eynsham, there was a lack of any genuine literature aimed specifically at children before the 18th century. Other scholars have qualified this viewpoint by noting that there was a literature designed to convey the values, attitudes, and information necessary for children within their cultures, such as the *Play of Daniel* from the 1100s. Pre-modern children's literature, therefore, tended to be of a didactic and moralistic nature, with the purpose of conveying conduct-related, educational and religious lessons.

Antiquity and the Middle Ages

Every culture has its own mythology, unique fables, and other traditional stories that are told for instruction and entertainment. Early folk-type tales included the *Panchatantra* from India, which was composed about 200 AD and may be "the world's oldest collection of stories for children".

Oral stories would have been enjoyed by children, such as the tale of *The Asurik Tree,* which dates back at least 3,000 years in Persia.

In Imperial China, children attended public events with their parents, where they would listen to the complicated tales of professional storytellers. Children also watched the plays performed at festivals and fairs. Though not specifically intended for children, the elaborate costumes, acrobatics, and martial arts held even a young child's interest. The stories often explained the background behind the festival, covering folklore, history, and politics. Storytelling may have reached its peak during the Song Dynasty from 960-1279 AD. This traditional literature was used for instruction in Chinese schools until the 20th century.

Greek and Roman children would have enjoyed listening to stories such as the *Odyssey,* written by Homer and *Aesop's Fables* by the eponymous Aesop. Examples of medieval literature include *Gesta Romanorum,* the Roman fables of Avianus, the French *Livre pour l'enseignement de ses filles,* and the Welsh *Mabinogion.* In Ireland, many of the thousands of folk stories were recorded in the 11th and 12th centuries. Written in Old Irish on vellum, they began spreading through Europe, influencing other folk tales with stories of magic, witches, and fairies.

Early-modern Europe

During the 1600s, the concept of childhood began to emerge in Europe. Adults saw children as separate beings, innocent and in need of protection and training by the adults around them. The English philosopher John Locke developed his theory of the tabula rasa in his 1690 *An Essay Concerning Human Understanding.* In Locke's philosophy, *tabula rasa* was the theory that the (human) mind is at birth a "blank slate" without rules for processing data, and that data is added and rules for processing are formed solely by one's sensory experiences. A corollary of this doctrine was that the mind of the child was born blank, and that it was the duty of the parents to imbue the child with correct notions. Locke himself emphasised the importance of providing children with "easy pleasant books" to develop their minds rather than using force to compel them; "children may be cozened into a knowledge of the letters; be taught to read, without perceiving it to be anything but a sport, and play themselves into that which others are whipped for." He also suggested that picture books be created for children.

Another influence on this shift in attitudes came from Puritanism, which stressed the importance of individual salvation. Puritans were concerned with the spiritual welfare of their children, and there was a large growth in the publication of 'good godly books' aimed squarely at children. Some of the most popular works were by James Janeway, but the most enduring book from this movement, still widely read today, was *The Pilgrim's Progress* (1678) by John Bunyan.

Chapbooks, pocket-sized pamphlets that were often folded instead of being stitched, were published in Britain; illustrated by woodblock printing, these inexpensive booklets reprinted popular ballads, historical re-tellings, and folk tales. Though not specifically published for children at this time, young people enjoyed the booklets as well. Johanna Bradley in *From Chapbooks to Plum Cake* says that chapbooks kept imaginative stories from being lost to readers under the strict Puritan influence of the time.

Hornbooks also appeared in England during this time, teaching children basic information such as the alphabet and the Lord's Prayer. These were brought from England to the American colonies in the mid-17th century. The first such book was a catechism for children written in verse by the Puritan John Cotton. Known as *Spiritual Milk for Boston Babes,* it was published in 1646, appearing both in England and Boston. Another early book, *The New England Primer,* was in print by 1691 and used in schools for 100 years. The Primer begins, "In Adam's fall We sinned all..." and continues through the alphabet. It also contained religious maxims, acronyms, spelling help and other educational items, all decorated by woodcuts.

In 1634, the *Pentamerone* from Italy became the first major published collection of European folk tales. Charles Perrault began recording fairy tales in France, publishing his first collection in 1697. They were not well received among the French literary society, who saw them as only fit for old people and children. In 1658, Jan Amos Comenius in Bohemia published the informative illustrated *Orbis Pictus*, for children under six learning to read. It is considered as the first picture book produced specifically for children.

The first Danish children's book was *The Child's Mirror* by Niels Bredal in 1568, an adaptation of a Courtesy book by the Dutch priest Erasmus. *A Pretty and Splendid Maiden's Mirror*, an adaptation of a German book for young women, became the first Swedish children's book upon its 1591 publication. Sweden published fables and a children's magazine by 1766. In Italy, Giovanni Francesco Straparola released *The Facetious Nights of Straparola* in the 1550s. Called the first European storybook to contain fairytales, it eventually had 75 separate stories and written for an adult audience. Giulio Cesare Croce also borrowed from stories children enjoyed for his books.

Russia's earliest children's books, primers, appeared in the late 16th century. An early example is *ABC-Book*, an alphabet book published by Ivan Fyodorov in 1571. The first picture book published in Russia, Karion Istomin's *The Illustrated Primer*, appeared in 1694. Peter the Great's interest in modernising his country through Westernisation helped Western children's literature dominate the field through the 1700s. Catherine the Great wrote allegories for children, and during her reign, Nikolai Novikov started the first juvenile magazine in Russia.

Origin of the Modern Genre

The modern children's book emerged in mid-18th century England. A growing polite middle-class and the influence of Lockean theories of childhood innocence combined to create the beginnings of childhood as a concept. *A Little Pretty Pocket-Book*, written and published by John Newbery, is widely considered as the first modern children's book, published in 1744. It was a landmark as the first children's publication aimed at giving enjoyment to children, containing a mixture of rhymes, picture stories and games for pleasure. Newbery believed that play was a better enticement to children's good behaviour than physical discipline, and the child was to record their behaviour daily.

The book was child sized with a brightly coloured cover that appealed to children—something new in the publishing industry. Known as gift books, these early books became the precursor to the toy books popular in the 19th century. Newbery was also adept at marketing this new genre successfully. According to journal *The Lion and the Unicorn*, "Newbery's genius was in developing the fairly new product category, children's books, through his frequent advertisements ... and his clever ploy of introducing additional titles and products into the body of his children's books."

The improvement in the quality of books for children, as well as the diversity of topics he published, helped make Newbery the leading producer of children's books in his time. He published his own books as well as those by authors like Samuel Johnson and Oliver Goldsmith - the latter may have wrote *The History of Little Goody Two-Shoes*, Newbery's most popular book. Another philosopher influential on the development of children's literature, was Jean-Jacques Rousseau, who argued that children should be allowed to develop naturally and joyously. His idea of appealing to a children's natural interests took hold among writers for children. Popular examples included Thomas Day's *The History of Sandford and Merton*, four volumes that embody Rousseau theories. Furthermore, Maria and Richard Lovell Edgeworth's *Practical Education: The History of Harry and Lucy* (1780) urged children to teach themselves. Rousseau's ideas also had great influence in Germany, especially on German Philanthropism, a movement concerned with reforming both education and literature for children. Its' founder, Johann Bernhard Basedow, authored "Elementarwerk" as a popular textbook for children that included many illustrations by Daniel Chodowiecki. Another follower, Joachim Heinrich Campe's adaptation of *Robinson Crusoe* went into over 100 printings. He became Germany's "outstanding and most modern" writer for children. According to Hans-Heino Ewers in *The International Companion Encyclopaedia of Children's Literature*, "It can be argued that from this time, the history of European children's literature was largely written in Germany".

In the early 19th century, Danish author and poet Hans Christian Andersen travelled through Europe and gathered many well-known fairy tales. He was followed by the Brothers Grimm who preserved the traditional tales told in Germany. They were so popular in their home country that modern, realistic children's literature began to be looked down on there. This dislike of non-traditional stories continued there until the beginning of the next century. The Grimm's contribution to children's literature goes beyond their collection of stories, as great as that is. As professors, they had a scholarly interest in the stories, striving to preserve them and their variations accurately, recording their sources. A similar project was carried out by the Norwegian scholars, Peter Christen Asbjornsen and Jorgen Moe, who collected Norwegian fairy tales and published them as *Norwegian Folktales*, often referred to as *Asbjornsen and Moe*. By compiling these stories, they preserved Norway's literary heritage and helped create the Norwegian written language.

In Switzerland, Johann David Wyss published *The Swiss Family Robinson* in 1812, with the aim of teaching children about family values, good husbandry, the uses of the natural world and self-reliance. The book became popular across Europe after it was translated into French by Isabelle de Montolieu.

Golden Age

The shift to a modern genre of children's literature occurred in the mid-19th century, as the didacticism of a previous age began to make way for more humorous, child-oriented books, more attuned to the child's imagination. The availability of children's literature greatly increased as well, as paper and printing became widely available and affordable, the population grew and literacy rates improved.

Tom Brown's School Days by Thomas Hughes appeared in 1857, and is considered as the founding book in the school story tradition. However, it was Lewis Carroll's fantasy *Alice's Adventures in Wonderland*, published in 1865 in England, that signalled the change in writing style for children to an imaginative and empathetic one. Regarded as the first "English masterpiece written for children" and as a founding book in the development of fantasy literature, its publication opened the "First Golden Age" of children's literature in Britain and Europe that continued until the early–1900s. Another important book of that decade was *The Water-Babies, A Fairy Tale for a Land Baby* by Reverend Charles Kingsley in 1862, which became extremely popular in England, and has remained as a classic of British children's literature.

In 1883, Carlo Collodi wrote the first Italian fantasy novel, *The Adventures of Pinocchio*, which was translated many times. In Britain, *The Princess and the Goblin* and its sequel *The Princess and Curdie* by George MacDonald appeared in 1872 and '83, and the adventure stories *Treasure Island* and *Kidnapped*, both by Robert Louis Stevenson, were extremely popular in the 1880s. Rudyard

Kipling's *The Jungle Book* was first published in 1894, and J. M. Barrie told the story of Peter Pan in the novel *Peter and Wendy* in 1911. Johanna Spyri's two-part novel *Heidi* was published in Switzerland in 1880 and 1881. In the US, children's publishing entered a period of growth after the American Civil War in 1865. Boys' book writer Oliver Optic published over 100 books. 1868 brought the publication of the "epoch-making book" such as *Little Women*, the fictionalised autobiography of Louisa May Alcott. This *coming of age* story established the genre of realistic family books in the United States. Mark Twain released *Tom Sawyer* in 1876, and in 1880 another bestseller, *Uncle Remus: His Songs and His Sayings*, a collection of African American folk tales adapted and compiled by Joel Chandler Harris, appeared.

Later National Traditions

Britain: The Golden Age of Children's Literature ended with World War I in Great Britain and Europe, and the period before World War II was much slower in children's publishing. The main exceptions in England were the publications of *Winnie-the-Pooh* by A. A. Milne in 1926 and *The Hobbit* by J. R. R. Tolkien in 1937. T. H. White's sequence of Arthurian novels, *The Once and Future King*, began with *The Sword in the Stone*, published in 1938. In 1941, children's paperback books were first released in England under the Puffin Books imprint, and their lower prices helped make book buying possible for children during World War II.

In the 1950s, the book market in Europe began recovering from the effects of two world wars. In Britain, C. S. Lewis published the first instalment of *The Chronicles of Narnia* series in 1950, Dodie Smith's *The Hundred and One Dalmatians* was published in 1956, and Roald Dahl wrote *Charlie and the Chocolate Factory* in 1964. Children's fantasy literature remained strong in Great Britain throughout the 1900s. In Wales, the Welsh Joint Education Committee and the Welsh Books Council encouraged the publication of children's books in the Welsh language as well as books in English about Wales.

In 1997, J. K. Rowling published the first book in the *Harry Potter series* in England. Despite its huge success, the children's book market in Britain suffered at the end of the century due to a difficult economy and competition from television and video games. However, picture books continue to do well.

Continental Europe: The period from 1890 until World War I is considered the Golden Age of Children's Literature in Scandinavia. Erik Werenskiold, Theodor Kittelsen, and Dikken Zwilgmeyer were especially popular, writing folk and fairy tales as well as realistic fiction. The 1859 translation into English by George Webbe Dasent, helped increase the stories' influence. One of the most influential and internationally most successful Scandinavian children's books from this period is Selma Lagerlofs *The Wonderful Adventures of Nils*.

The interwar period saw a slow-down in output similar to Britain, although "one of the first mysteries written specifically for children", *Emil and the Detectives* by Erich Kastner, was published in Germany in 1930. The period during and following World War II became the Classical Age of the picture book in Switzerland, with works by Alois Carigiet, Felix Hoffmann, and Hans Fischer. 1963 was the first year of the Bologna Children's Book Fair in Italy, which was described as "the most important international event dedicated to the children's publishing". For four days it brings together writers, illustrators, publishers, and book buyers from around the world.

United States: One of American children's literature most famous books was L. Frank Baum's fantasy novel *The Wonderful Wizard of Oz, published in 1900.* "By combining the English fondness for word play with the American appetite for outdoor adventure", Connie Epstein in *International Companion Encyclopaedia Of Children's Literature* says Baum "developed an original style and form that stands alone". Baum wrote thirteen more Oz novels, and other writers continued the Oz series into the 1960s. Between the world wars, demand continued to grow in North America helped by the growth of libraries in both Canada and the United States. Children's reading rooms in libraries, staffed by specially trained librarians, helped create demand for classic juvenile books. Reviews of children's releases began appearing regularly in *Publishers Weekly* and in *The Bookman* magazine began to regularly publish reviews of children's releases, and the first Children's Book Week was launched in 1919. In that same year, Louise Seaman Bechtel became the first person to head a juvenile book publishing department in the country. She was followed by May Massee in 1922 and Alice Dalgliesh in 1934.

The American Library Association began awarding the Newbery Medal, the first children's book award in the world, in 1922. The Caldecott Medal for illustration followed in 1938. The first book by Laura Ingalls Wilder about her life on the American frontier, *Little House in the Big Woods* appeared in 1932. In 1937 Dr. Seuss published his first book, entitled, *And to Think That I Saw It on Mulberry Street*. The young adult book market developed during this period, thanks to sports books by popular writer John R. Tunis', the novel *Seventeenth Summer* by Maureen Daly, and the "Sue Barton" nurse book series by Helen Dore Boylston.

The already vigorous growth in children's books became a boom in the 1950s and children's publishing became big business. In 1952, American journalist E. B. White published *Charlotte's Web,* which was described as "one of the very few books for young children that face, squarely, the subject of death". Maurice Sendak illustrated more than two dozen books during the decade, which established him as an innovator in book illustration. The Sputnik crisis, that began in 1957, provided increased interest and government money for schools and libraries to buy science and math books and the non-fiction book market "seemed to materialise overnight".

USSR and Russia: In Russia, Russian folk tales were introduced to children by Aleksandr Afanasyev in his children's edition of his eight-volume *Russian Folk Tales* in 1871. By the 1860s, literary realism and non-fiction dominated children's literature. More schools were started, using books by writers like Konstantin Ushinsky and Leo Tolstoy, whose *Russian Reader* included an assortment of stories, fairy tales, and fables. Books written specifically for girls developed in the 1870s and 1880s. Publisher and journalist Evgenia Tur wrote about the daughters of well-to-do landowners, while Aleksandra Annenskaya's stories told of middle-class girls working to support themselves. Vera Zhelikhovsky, Elizaveta Kondrashova, and Nadezhda Lukhmanova also wrote for girls during this period. Children's non-fiction gained great importance in Russia at the beginning of the century. A ten-volume children's encyclopaedia was published between 1913 and 1914. Vasily Avenarius wrote fictionalised biographies of important people like Nikolai Gogol and Alexander Pushkin around the same time, and scientists wrote for books and magazines for children. Children's magazines flourished, and by the end of the century there were 61. Lidia Charskaya and Klavdiya Lukashevich continued the popularity of girls' fiction. Realism took a gloomy turn by frequently showing the maltreatment of children from lower classes. The most popular boys' material was Sherlock Holmes, and similar stories from detective magazines.

The state took control of children's literature during the October Revolution. Maksim Gorky edited the first children's, *Northern Lights,* under Soviet rule. People often label the 1920s as the Golden Age of Children's Literature in Russia. Samuil Marshak led that literary decade as the "founder of (Soviet) children's literature". As head of the children's section of the State Publishing House and editor of several children's magazines, Marshak exercised enormous influence by recruiting Boris Pasternak and Osip Mandelstam to write for children.

In 1932, professional writers in the Soviet Union formed the USSR Union of Writers, which served as the writer's organisation of the Communist Party. With a children's branch, the official oversight of the professional organisation brought children's writers under the control of the state and the police. Communist principles like collectivism and solidarity became important themes in children's literature. Authors wrote biographies about revolutionaries like Lenin and Pavlik Morozov. Alexander Belyayev, who wrote in the 1920s and 1930s, became Russia's first science fiction writer. According to Ben Hellman in the *International Companion Encyclopaedia of Children's Literature*, "war was to occupy a prominent place in juvenile reading, partly compensating for the lack of adventure stories", during the Soviet Period. More political changes in Russia after World War II brought further change in children's literature. Today, the field is in a state of flux because some older authors are being rediscovered and others are being abandoned.

India: Christian missionaries first established the Calcutta School-Book Society in the 19th century, creating a separate genre for children's literature in that country. Magazines and books for children in native languages soon appeared. In the latter half of the century, Raja Shivprasad wrote several well-known books in Hindustani. A number of respected Bengali writers began producing Bengali literature for children including Ishwar Chandra Vidyasagar, who translated some stories and wrote others himself. Nobel Prize winner Rabindranath Tagore wrote plays, stories, and poems for children, including one work illustrated by painter Nandalal Bose. They worked from the end of the 1800s into the beginning of the 20th-century. Tagore's work was later translated into English, with Bose's pictures. Behari Lal Puri was the earliest writer for children in Punjabi. His stories were didactic in nature.

The first full-length children's book was *Khar Khar Mahadev* by Narain Dixit, which was serialised in one of the popular children's magazines in 1957. Other writers include Premchand, and poet Sohan Lal Dwivedi. In 1919, Sukumar Ray wrote and illustrated nonsense rhymes in the Bengali language, and children's writer and artist Abanindranath Tagore finished *Barngtarbratn*. Benagli children's literature flourished in the later part of the twentieth century. Educator Gijubhai Badheka published over 200 children's books in the Gujarati language, and many of them are still popular. In 1957, political cartoonist K. Shankar Pillai founded the Children's Book Trust publishing company. The firm became known for high quality children's books, and many of them released in several languages. One of the most distinguished writers is Pandit Krushna Chandra Kar in Oriya literature, who wrote many good books for children like "Pari Raija", "Kuhuka Raija", "Panchatantra", and "Adi Jugara Galpa Mala". He wrote biography of many historical personalities like "Kapila Deva". In 1978, the firm organised a writer's competition to encourage quality children's writing. The following year, the Children's Book Trust began a writing workshop and organised the First International Children's Book Fair in New Delhi. Children's magazines, available in many languages, were widespread throughout India during this century.

China: The Chinese Revolution of 1911 and World War II brought political and social change that revolutionised children's literature in China. Western science, technology, and literature became fashionable. China's first modern publishing firm, Commercial Press, established several children's magazines, which included *Youth Magazine*, and *Educational Pictures for Children*. The first Chinese children's writer was Sun Yuxiu, an editor of Commercial Press, whose story *The Kingdom Without a Cat* was written in the language of the time instead of the classical style used previously. Yuxiu encouraged novelist Shen Dehong to write for children also. Dehong went on to rewrite 28 stories based on classical Chinese literature specifically for children. In 1932, Zhang Tianyi published *Big Lin and Little Lin*, the first full-length Chinese novel for children.

The Chinese Revolution of 1949 changed children's literature again. Many children's writers were denounced, but Tianyi and Ye Shengtao continued to write for children and created works that aligned with Maoist ideology. The 1976 death of Mao Zedong provoked more changes sweep China. Many writers from the early part of the century were brought back, and their work became available again. In 1990, *General Anthology of Modern Children's Literature of China,* a fifteen-volume anthology of children's literature since the 1920s, was released.

Classification

Children's literature can be divided into a number of categories, but it is most easily categorised according to genre or the intended age of the reader.

By Genre

A literary genre is a category of literary compositions. Genres may be determined by technique, tone, content, or length. According to Anderson, there are six categories of children's literature (with some significant subgenres):

- Picture books, including concept books that teach the alphabet or counting for example, pattern books, and wordless books;
- Traditional literature, including folktales, which convey the legends, customs, superstitions, and beliefs of people in previous civilizations. This genre can be further broken into subgenres: myths, fables, legends, and fairy tales;
- Fiction, including fantasy, realistic fiction, and historical fiction;
- Non-fiction;
- Biography and autobiography;
- Poetry and verse.

By Age Category

The criteria for these divisions are vague, and books near a borderline may be classified either way. Books for younger children tend to be written in simple language, use large print, and have many illustrations. Books for older children use increasingly complex language, normal print, and fewer (if any) illustrations. The categories with an age range are listed below:

- Picture books, appropriate for pre-readers or children ages 0–5.
- Early reader books, appropriate for children ages 5–7. These books are often designed to help a child build his or her reading skills.
- Chapter book, appropriate for children ages 7–12:
  - — Short chapter books, appropriate for children ages 7–9;
  - — Longer chapter books, appropriate for children ages 9–12.
- Young-adult fiction, appropriate for children ages 12–18.

Illustration

Pictures have always accompanied children's stories. A papyrus from Byzantine Egypt, shows illustrations accompanied by the story of Hercules' labours. Modern children's books are illustrated in a way that is rarely seen in adult literature, except in graphic novels. Generally, artwork plays a greater role in books intended for younger readers (especially pre-literate children). Children's picture books often serve as an accessible source of high quality art for young children. Even after children learn to read well enough to enjoy a story without illustrations, they continue to appreciate the occasional drawings found in chapter books.

According to Joyce Whalley in *The International Companion Encyclopaedia of Children's Literature*, "an illustrated book differs from a book with illustrations in that a good illustrated book is one where the pictures enhance or add depth to the text." Using this definition, the first illustrated children's book is considered to be *Orbis Pictus* which was published in 1658 by the Moravian author Comenius. Acting as a kind of encyclopaedia, *Orbis Pictus* had a picture on every page, followed by the name of the object in Latin and German. It was translated into English in 1659 and was used in homes and schools around Europe and Great Britain for years. Early children's books, such as *Orbis Pictus*, were illustrated by woodcut, and many times the same image was repeated in a number of books regardless of how appropriate the illustration was for the story. Newer processes, including copper and steel engraving were first used in the 1830s. One of the first uses of Chromolithography (a way of making multi-coloured prints) in a children's book was demonstrated in *Struwwelpeter*, published in Germany in 1845. English illustrator Walter Crane refined its use in children's books in the late 1800s.

Another method of creating illustrations for children's books was etching, used by George Cruikshank in the 1850s. By the 1860s, top artists were illustrating for children, including Crane, Randolph Caldecott, Kate Greenaway, and John Tenniel. Most pictures were still black-and-white, and many colour pictures were hand coloured, often by children. *The Essential Guide to Children's Books and Their Creators* credits Caldecott with "The concept of extending the meaning of text beyond literal visualisation". Twentieth-century artists such as Kay Nielson, Edmund Dulac, and Arthur Rackham produced illustrations that are still reprinted today. Developments in printing capabilities were reflected in children's books. After World War II, offset lithography became more refined, and painter-style illustrations, such as Brian Wildsmith's were common by the 1950s.

Scholarship

Professional organisations, dedicated publications, individual researchers and university courses conduct scholarship on children's literature. Scholarship in children's literature is primarily conducted in three different disciplinary fields: literary studies (literature and language departments), library and information science, and education. (Wolf, *et al.*, 2011).

Typically, children's literature scholars from literature departments in universities (English, German, Spanish, etc. departments) conduct literary analysis of books. This literary criticism may focus on an author, a thematic or topical concern, genre, period, or literary device. The results of this type of research are typically published as books or articles in scholarly journals, including *Children's Literature Association Quarterly, Children's Literature in Education, Children's Literature, The Lion and the Unicorn*, and *International Research in Children's Literature.*

The field of Library and Information Science has a long history of conducting research related to children's literature. Most educational researchers studying children's literature explore issues related to the use of children's literature in classroom settings. They may also study topics such as home use, children's out-of-school reading, or parents' use of children's books. Teachers typically use children's literature to augment classroom instruction.

Scholarly associations and centres include The Children's Literature Association, the International Research Society for Children's Literature, the Library Association Youth Libraries Group, the Society of Children's Book Writers and Illustrators the Irish Society for the Study of

Children's Literature, IBBY Canada and Centre for International Research in Childhood: Literature, Culture, Media (CIRCL), and the National Centre for Research in Children's Literature.

Illustrated Books

Modern English book-illustration—to which the present chapter is restricted -has no long or doubtful history, since to find its first beginnings, it is needless to go farther back than the last quarter of the eighteenth century. Not that "illustrated" books of a certain class were by any means unknown before that period. On the contrary, for many years previously, literature had boasted its "sculptures" of be-wigged and be-laurelled "worthies," its "prospects" and "land-skips," its phenomenal monsters and its "curious antiques." But, despite the couplet in the "Dunciad" respecting books where ". .. the pictures for the page atone, And Quarles is saved by beauties not his own;" - illustrations, in which the designer attempted the actual delineation of scenes or occurrences in the text, were certainly not common when Pope wrote, nor were they for some time afterwards either very numerous or very noteworthy.

There are Hogarth's engravings to "Hudibras" and "Don Quixote;" there are the designs of his crony Frank Hayman to Theobald's "Shakespeare," to Milton, to Pope, to Cervantes; there are Pine's "Horace" and Sturt's "Prayer- Book" (in both of which text and ornament were alike engraved); there are the historical and topographical drawings of Sandby, Wale, and others; and yet—notwithstanding all these—it is with Bewick's cuts to Gay's "Fables" in 1779, and Stothard's plates to Harrison's "Novelist's Magazine" in 1780, that book-illustration by imaginative compositions really begins to flourish in England. Those little masterpieces of the Newcastle artist brought about a revival of wood-engraving which continues to this day; but engraving upon metal, as a means of decorating books, practically came to an end with the "Annuals" of thirty years ago. It will therefore be well to speak first of illustrations upon copper and steel.

Stothard, Blake, and Flaxman are the names that come freshest to memory in this connection. For a period of fifty years Stothard stands pre-eminent in illustrated literature. Measuring time by poets, he may be said to have lent something of his fancy and amenity to most of the writers from Cowper to Rogers. As a draughtsman he is undoubtedly weak: his figures are often limp and invertebrate, and his type of beauty insipid. Still, regarded as groups, the majority of his designs are exquisite, and he possessed one all-pervading and un-English quality—the quality of grace. This is his dominant note. Nothing can be more seductive than the suave flow of his line, his feeling for costume, his gentle and chastened humour. Many of his women and children are models of purity and innocence.

But he works at ease only within the limits of his special powers; he is happier in the pastoral and domestic than the heroic and supernatural, and his style is better fitted to the formal salutations of "Clarissa" and "Sir Charles Grandison," than the rough horse-play of "Peregrine Pickle." Where Rowlandson would have revelled, Stothard would be awkward and constrained; where Blake would give us a new sensation, Stothard would be poor and mechanical. Nevertheless the gifts he possessed were thoroughly recognised in his own day, and brought him, if not riches, at least competence and honour. It is said that more than three thousand of his drawings have been engraved, and they are scattered through a hundred publications. Those to the "Pilgrim's Progress" and the poems of Rogers are commonly spoken of as his best, though he never excelled some of the old-fashioned plates (with their pretty borders in the style of Gravelot and the Frenchmen) to Richardson's novels, and such forgotten "classics" as "Joe Thompson", "Jessamy," "Betsy Thoughtless," and one or two others in Harrison's very miscellaneous collection.

Stothard was fortunate in his engravers. Besides James Heath, his best interpreter, Schiavonetti, Sharp, Finden, the Cookes, Bartolozzi, most of the fashionable translators into copper were busily employed upon his inventions. Among the rest was an artist of powers far greater than his own, although scarcely so happy in turning them to profitable account. The genius of William Blake was not a marketable commodity in the same way as Stothard's talent. The one caught the trick of the time with his facile elegance; the other scorned to make any concessions, either in conception or execution, to the mere popularity of prettiness.

"Give pensions to the learned pig, Or the hare playing on a tabor; Anglus can never see perfection But in the journeyman's labour," -he wrote in one of those rough-hewn and bitter epigrams of his. Yet the work that was then so lukewarmly received—if, indeed, it can be said to have been received at all—is at present far more sought after than Stothard's, and the prices now given for the "Songs of Innocence and Experience," the "Inventions to the Book of Job," and even "The Grave," would have brought affluence to the struggling artist, who (as Cromek taunted him) was frequently "reduced so low as to be obliged to live on half a guinea a week." Not that this was entirely the fault of his contemporaries. Blake was a visionary, and an untuneable man; and, like others who work for the select public of all ages, he could not always escape the consequence that the select public of his own, however willing, were scarcely numerous enough to support him.

His most individual works are the "Songs of Innocence," 1789, and the "Songs of Experience," 1794. These, afterwards united in one volume, were unique in their method of production; indeed, they do not perhaps strictly come within the category of what is generally understood to be copperplate engraving.

The drawings were outlined and the songs written upon the metal with some liquid that resisted the action of acid, and the remainder of the surface of the plate was eaten away with aquafortis, leaving the design in bold relief, like a rude stereotype. This was then printed off in the predominant tone— blue, brown, or yellow, as the case might be—and delicately tinted by the artist in a prismatic and ethereal fashion peculiarly his own. Stitched and bound in boards by Mrs. Blake, a certain number of these leaflets—twenty-seven in the case of the first issue—made up a tiny octavo of a wholly exceptional kind. Words indeed fail to exactly describe the flower-like beauty—the fascination of these "fairy missals," in which, it has been finely said, "the thrilling music of the verse, and the gentle bedazzlement of the lines and colours so intermingle, that the mind hangs in a pleasant uncertainty as to whether it is a picture that is singing, or a song which has newly budded and blossomed into colour and form."

The accompanying woodcut, after one of the illustrations to the "Songs of Innocence," gives some indication of the general composition, but it can convey no hint of the gorgeous purple, and crimson, and orange of the original.

Of the "Illustrations to the Book of Job," 1826, there are excellent reduced facsimiles by the recently-discovered photo-intaglio process, in the new edition of Gilchrist's "Life." The originals were engraved by Blake himself in his strong decisive fashion, and they are his best work. A kind of deisidaimonia—a sacred awe— falls upon one in turning over these wonderful productions of the artist's declining years and failing hand.

"Leaving the old, both worlds at once they view, That stand upon the threshold of the new," sings Waller; and it is almost possible to believe for a moment that their creator was (as he said) "under the direction of messengers from Heaven." But his designs for Blair's "Grave," 1808, popularised by the burin of Schiavonetti, attracted greater attention at the time of publication; and, being less rare, they are even now perhaps better known than the others. The facsimile here given is from the latter book. The worn old man, the trustful woman, and the guileless child are sleeping peacefully; but the King with his sceptre, and the warrior with his hand on his sword-hilt, lie open-eyed, waiting the summons of the trumpet. One cannot help fancying that the artist's long vigils among the Abbey tombs, during his apprenticeship to James Basire, must have been present to his mind when he selected this impressive monumental subject.

To one of Blake's few friends—to the "dear Sculptor of Eternity," as he wrote to Flaxman from Felpham—the world is indebted for some notable book illustrations. Whether the greatest writers—the Homers, the Shakespeares, the Dantes—can ever be "illustrated" without loss may fairly be questioned. At all events, the showy dexterities of the Dores and Gilberts prove nothing to the contrary. But now and then there comes to the graphic interpretation of a great author an artist either so reverential, or so strongly sympathetic at some given point, that, in default of any relation more narrowly intimate, we at once accept his conceptions as the best attainable. In this class are Flaxman's outlines to Homer and AEschylus. Flaxman was not a Hellenist as men are Hellenists to- day.

Nevertheless, his Roman studies had saturated him with the spirit of antique beauty, and by his grand knowledge of the nude, his calm, his restraint, he is such an illustrator of Homer as is not likely to arise again. For who—with all our added knowledge of classical antiquity—who, of our modern artists, could hope to rival such thoroughly Greek compositions as the ball-play of Nausicaa in the "Odyssey," or that lovely group from AEschylus of the tender- hearted, womanly Oceanides, cowering like flowers beaten by the storm under the terrible anger of Zeus? In our day Flaxman's drawings would have been reproduced by some of the modern facsimile processes, and the gain would have been great. As it is, something is lost by their transference to copper, even though the translators be Piroli and Blake. Blake, in fact, did more than he is usually credited with, for (beside the acknowledged and later "Hesiod," 1817) he really engraved the whole of the "Odyssey," Piroli's plates having been lost on the voyage to England. The name of the Roman artist, nevertheless, appears on the title-page (1793). But Blake was too original to be a successful copyist of other men's work, and to appreciate the full value of Flaxman's drawings, they should be studied in the collections at University College, the Royal Academy, and elsewhere.

Flaxman and Blake had few imitators. But a host of clever designers, such as Cipriani, Angelica Kauffmann, Westall, Uwins, Smirke, Burney, Corbould, Dodd, and others, vied with the popular Stothard in "embellishing" the endless "Poets," "novelists," and "essayists" of our forefathers. Some of these, and most of the recognised artists of the period, lent their aid to that boldly- planned but unhappily-executed "Shakespeare" of Boydell,—"black and ghastly gallery of murky Opies, glum Northcotes, straddling Fuselis," as Thackeray calls it.

They are certainly not enlivening- -those cumbrous "atlas" folios of 1803-5, and they helped to ruin the worthy alderman. Even courtly Sir Joshua is clearly ill at ease among the pushing Hamiltons and Mortimers; and, were it not for the whimsical discovery that Westall's "Ghost of Caesar" strangely resembles Mr. Gladstone, there would be no resting-place for the modern student of these dismal masterpieces. The truth is, Reynolds excepted, there were no contemporary painters strong enough for the task, and the honours of the enterprise belong almost exclusively to Smirke's "Seven Ages" and one or two plates from the lighter comedies. The great "Bible" of Macklin, a rival and even more incongruous publication, upon which some of the same designers were employed, has fallen into completer oblivion. A rather better fate attended another book of this class, which, although belonging to a later period, may be briefly referred to here. The "Milton" of John Martin has distinct individuality, and some of the needful qualities of imagination. Nevertheless, posterity has practically decided that scenic grandeur and sombre effects alone are not a sufficient pictorial equipment for the varied story of "Paradise Lost."

It is to Boydell of the Shakespeare gallery that we owe the "Liber Veritatis" of Claude, engraved by Richard Earlom; and indirectly, since rivalry of Claude prompted the attempt, the famous "Liber Studiorum" of Turner. Neither of these, however—which, like the "Rivers of France" and the "Picturesque Views in England and Wales" of the latter artist, are collections of engravings rather than illustrated books—belongs to the present purpose. But Turner's name may fitly serve to introduce those once familiar "Annuals" and "Keepsakes," that, beginning in 1823 with Ackermann's "Forget-me- Not," enjoyed a popularity of more than thirty years.

Their general characteristics have been pleasantly satirised in Thackeray's account of the elegant miscellany of Bacon the publisher, to which Mr. Arthur Pendennis contributed his pretty poem of "The Church Porch." His editress, it will be remembered, was the Lady Violet Lebas, and his colleagues the Honourable Percy Popjoy, Lord Dodo, and the gifted Bedwin Sands, whose "Eastern Ghazuls" lent so special a distinction to the volume in watered-silk binding. The talented authors, it is true, were in most cases under the disadvantage of having to write to the plates of the talented artists, a practice which even now is not extinct, though it is scarcely considered favourable to literary merit. And the real "Annuals" were no exception to the rule. As a matter of fact, their general literary merit was not obtrusive, although, of course, they sometimes contained work which afterwards became famous. They are now so completely forgotten and out of date, that one scarcely expects to find that Wordsworth, Coleridge, Macaulay, and Southey, were among the occasional contributors. Lamb's beautiful "Album verses" appeared in the "Bijou," Scott's "Bonnie Dundee" in the "Christmas Box," and Tennyson's "St. Agnes' Eve" in the "Keepsake."

But the plates were, after all, the leading attraction. These, prepared for the most part under the superintendence of the younger Heath, and executed on the steel which by this time had supplanted the old "coppers," were supplied by, or were "after," almost every contemporary artist of note. Stothard, now growing old and past his prime, Turner, Etty, Stanfield, Leslie, Roberts, Danby, Maclise, Lawrence, Cattermole, and numbers of others, found profitable labour in this fashionable field until 1856, when the last of the "Annuals" disappeared, driven from the market by the rapid development of wood engraving. About a million, it is roughly estimated, was squandered in producing them.

In connection with the "Annuals" must be mentioned two illustrated books which were in all probability suggested by them—the "Poems" and "Italy" of Rogers. The designs to these are chiefly by Turner and Stothard, although there are a few by Prout and others. Stothard's have been already referred to; Turner's are almost universally held to be the most successful of his many vignettes. It has been truly said—in a recent excellent life of this artist —that it would be difficult to find in the whole of his works two really greater than the "Alps at Daybreak," and the "Datur Hora Quieti," in the former of these volumes. Almost equally beautiful are the "Valombre Falls" and "Tornaro's misty brow." Of the "Italy" set Mr. Ruskin writes:- "They are entirely exquisite; poetical in the highest and purest sense, exemplary and delightful beyond all praise." To such words it is not possible to add much. But it is pretty clear that the poetical vitality of Rogers was secured by these well-timed illustrations, over which he is admitted by his nephew Mr. Sharpe to have spent about 7000 pounds, and far larger sums have been named by good authorities. The artist received from fifteen to twenty guineas for each of the drawings; the engravers (Goodall, Miller,

Wallis, Smith, and others), sixty guineas a plate. The "Poems" and the "Italy," in the original issues of 1830 and 1834, are still precious to collectors, and are likely to remain so. Turner also illustrated Scott, Milton, Campbell, and Byron; but this series of designs has not received equal commendation from his greatest eulogist, who declares them to be "much more laboured, and more or less artificial and unequal." Among the numerous imitations directly induced by the Rogers books was the "Lyrics of the Heart," by Alaric Attila Watts, a forgotten versifier and sometime editor of "Annuals," but it did not meet with similar success.

Many illustrated works, originating in the perfection and opportunities of engraving on metal, are necessarily unnoticed in this rapid summary. As far, however, as book-illustration is concerned, copper and steel plate engraving may be held to have gone out of fashion with the "Annuals." It is still, indeed, to be found lingering in that mine of modern art-books—the "Art Journal;" and, not so very long ago, it made a sumptuous and fugitive reappearance in Dore's "Idylls of the King," Birket Foster's "Hood," and one or two other imposing volumes. But it was badly injured by modern wood-engraving; it has since been crippled for life by photography; and it is more than probable that the present rapid rise of modern etching will give it the coup de grace.

By the end of the seventeenth century the art of engraving on wood had fallen into disuse. Writing circa 1770, Horace Walpole goes so far as to say that it "never was executed in any perfection in England;" and, speaking afterwards of Papillon's "Traite de la Gravure," 1766, he takes occasion to doubt if that author would ever "persuade the world to return to wooden cuts." Nevertheless, with Bewick, a few years later, wood-engraving took a fresh departure so conspicuous that it amounts to a revival. In what this consisted it is clearly impossible to show here with any sufficiency of detail; but between the method of the old wood-cutters who reproduced the drawings of Durer, and the method of the Newcastle artist, there are two marked and well-defined differences. One of these is a difference in the preparation of the wood and the tool employed.

The old wood-cutters carved their designs with knives and chisels on strips of wood sawn lengthwise—that is to say, upon the PLANK; Bewick used a graver, and worked upon slices of box or pear cut across the grain,—that is to say upon the END of the wood. The other difference, of which Bewick is said to have been the inventor, is less easy to describe. It consisted in the employment of what is technically known as "white line." In all antecedent wood-cutting the cutter had simply cleared away those portions of the block left bare by the design, so that the design remained in relief to be printed from like type. Using the smooth box block as a uniform surface from which, if covered with printing ink, a uniformly black impression might be obtained, Bewick, by cutting white lines across it at greater or lesser intervals, produced gradations of shade, from the absolute black of the block to the lightest tints. The general result of this method was to give a greater depth of colouring and variety to the engraving, but its advantages may perhaps be best understood by a glance at the background of the "Woodcock" on the following page.

Bewick's first work of any importance was the Gay's "Fables" of 1779. In 1784 he did another series of "Select Fables." Neither of these books, however, can be compared with the "General History of Quadrupeds," 1790, and the "British Land and Water Birds," 1797 and 1804. The illustrations to the "Quadrupeds" are in many instances excellent, and large additions were made to them in subsequent issues. But in this collection Bewick laboured to a great extent under the disadvantage of representing animals with which he was familiar only through the medium of stuffed specimens or incorrect drawings. In the "British Birds," on the contrary, his facilities for study from the life were greater, and his success was consequently more complete. Indeed, it may be safely affirmed that of all the engravers of the present century, none have excelled Bewick for beauty of black and white, for skilful rendering of plumage and foliage, and for fidelity of detail and accessory. The "Woodcock" (here given), the "Partridge," the "Owl," the "Yellow- Hammer," the "Yellow-Bunting," the "Willow-Wren," are popular examples of these qualities. But there are a hundred others nearly as good.

Among sundry conventional decorations after the old German fashion in the first edition of the "Quadrupeds," there are a fair number of those famous tail-pieces which, to a good many people, constitute Bewick's chief claim to immortality. That it is not easy to imitate them is plain from the failure of Branston's attempts, and from the inferior character of those by John Thompson in Yarrell's "Fishes." The genius of Bewick was, in fact, entirely individual and particular. He had the humour of a Hogarth in little, as well as some of his special characteristics,—notably his faculty of telling a story by suggestive detail. An instance may be taken at random from vol. I. of the "Birds." A man, whose wig and hat have fallen off, lies asleep with open mouth under some bushes. He is manifestly drunk, and the date "4 June," on a neighbouring stone, gives us the reason and occasion of his catastrophe. He has been too loyally celebrating the birthday of his majesty King George III. Another of Bewick's gifts is his wonderful skill in foreshadowing a tragedy. Take as an example, this truly appalling incident from the "Quadrupeds."

The tottering child, whose nurse is seen in the background, has strayed into the meadow, and is pulling at the tail of a vicious-looking colt, with back-turned eye and lifted heel. Down the garden-steps the mother hurries headlong; but she can hardly be in time. And of all this—sufficient, one would say, for a fairly-sized canvas—the artist has managed to give a vivid impression in a block of three inches by two! Then, again, like Hogarth once more, he rejoices in multiplications of dilemma. What, for instance, can be more comically pathetic than the head-piece to the "Contents" in vol. I. of the "Birds"? The old horse has been seized with an invincible fit of stubbornness. The day is both windy and rainy. The rider has broken his stick and lost his hat; but he is too much encumbered with his cackling and excited stock to dare to dismount. Nothing can help him but a Deus ex machina,—of whom there is no sign.

Besides his humour, Bewick has a delightfully rustic side, of which Hogarth gives but little indication. From the starved ewe in the snow nibbling forlornly at a worn-out broom, to the cow which has broken through the rail to reach the running water, there are numberless designs which reveal that faithful lover of the field and hillside, who, as he said, "would rather be herding sheep on Mickle bank top" than remain in London to be made premier of England. He loved the country and the country-life; and he drew them as one who loved them. It is this rural quality which helps to give such a lasting freshness to his quaint and picturesque fancies; and it is this which will continue to preserve their popularity, even if they should cease to be valued for their wealth of whimsical invention.

In referring to these masterpieces of Bewick's, it must not be forgotten that he had the aid of some clever assistants. His younger brother John was not without talent, as is clear from his work for Somervile's "Chace," 1796, and that highly edifying book, the "Blossoms of Morality." Many of the tail-pieces to the "Water Birds" were designed by Robert Johnson, who also did most of the illustrations to Bewick's "Fables" of 1818, which were engraved by Temple and Harvey, two other pupils. Another pupil was Charlton Nesbit, an excellent engraver, who was employed upon the "Birds," and did good work in Ackermann's "Religious Emblems" of 1808, and the second series of Northcote's "Fables." But by far the largest portion of the tail-pieces in the second volume of the "Birds" was engraved by Luke Clennell, a very skilful but unfortunate artist, who ultimately became insane. To him we owe the woodcuts, after Stothard's charming sketches, to the Rogers volume of 1810, an edition preceding those already mentioned as illustrated with steel- plates, and containing some of the artist's happiest pictures of children and amorini. Many of these little groups would make admirable designs for gems, if indeed they are not already derived from them, since one at least is an obvious copy of a well-known sardonyx—("The Marriage of Cupid and Psyche.") This volume, generally known by the name of the "Firebrand" edition, is highly prized by collectors; and, as intelligent renderings of pen and ink, there is little better than these engravings of Clennell's. Finally, among others of Bewick's pupils, must be mentioned William Harvey, who survived to 1866. It has been already stated that he engraved part of the illustrations to Bewick's "Fables," but his best known block is the large one of Haydon's "Death of Dentatus." Soon after this he relinquished wood-engraving in favour of design, and for a long period was one of the most fertile and popular of book-illustrators.

His style, however, is unpleasantly mannered; and it is sufficient to make mention of his masterpiece, the "Arabian Nights" of Lane, the illustrations to which, produced under the supervision of the translator, are said to be so accurate as to give the appropriate turbans for every hour of the day. They show considerable freedom of invention and a large fund of Orientalism.

Harvey came to London in 1817; Clennell had preceded him by some years; and Nesbit lived there for a considerable time. What distinguishes these pupils of Bewick especially is, that they were artists as well as engravers, capable of producing the designs they engraved. The "London School" of engravers, on the contrary, were mostly engravers, who depended upon others for their designs. The foremost of these was Robert Branston, a skilful renderer of human figures and indoor scenes. He worked in rivalry with Bewick and Nesbit; but he excelled neither, while he fell far behind the former. John Thompson, one of the very best of modern English engravers on wood, was Branston's pupil. His range was of the widest, and he succeeded as well in engraving fishes and birds for Yarrell and Walton's "Angler," as in illustrations to Moliere and "Hudibras." He was, besides, a clever draughtsman, though he worked chiefly from the designs of Thurston and others. One of the most successful of his illustrated books is the "Vicar of Wakefield," after Mulready, whose simplicity and homely feeling were well suited to Goldsmith's style. Another excellent engraver of this date is Samuel Williams. There is an edition of Thomson's "Seasons," with cuts both drawn and engraved by him, which is well worthy of attention, and (like Thompson and Branston) he was very skilful in reproducing the designs of Cruikshank. Some of his best work in this way is to be found in Clarke's "Three Courses and a Dessert," published by Vizetelly in 1830.

From this time forth, however, one hears less of the engraver and more of the artist. The establishment of the "Penny Magazine" in 1832, and the multifarious publications of Charles Knight, gave an extraordinary impetus to wood-engraving. Ten years later came "Punch," and the "Illustrated London News," which further increased its popularity. Artists of eminence began to draw on or for the block, as they had drawn, and were still drawing, for the "Annuals." In 1842-6 was issued the great "Abbotsford" edition of the "Waverley Novels," which, besides 120 plates, contained nearly 2000 wood- engravings; and with the "Book of British Ballads," 1843, edited by Mr. S. C. Hall, arose that long series of illustrated Christmas books, which gradually supplanted the "Annuals," and made familiar the names of Gilbert, Birket Foster, Harrison Weir, John Absolon, and a crowd of others. The poems of Longfellow, Montgomery, Burns, "Barry Cornwall," Poe, Miss Ingelow, were all successively "illustrated." Besides these, there were numerous selections, such as Willmott's "Poets of the Nineteenth Century," Wills's "Poets' Wit and Humour," and so forth. But the field here grows too wide to be dealt with in detail, and it is impossible to do more than mention a few of the books most prominent for merit or originality. Amongst these there is the

"Shakespeare" of Sir John Gilbert. Regarded as an interpretative edition of the great dramatist, this is little more than a brilliant tour de force; but it is nevertheless infinitely superior to the earlier efforts of Kenny Meadows in 1843, and also to the fancy designs of Harvey in Knight's "Pictorial Shakespeare." The "Illustrated Tennyson" of 1858 is also a remarkable production.

The Laureate, almost more than any other, requires a variety of illustrators; and here, for his idylls, he had Mulready and Millais, and for his romances Rossetti and Holman Hunt. His "Princess" was afterwards illustrated by Maclise, and his "Enoch Arden" by Arthur Hughes; but neither of these can be said to be wholly adequate. The "Lalla Rookh" of John Tenniel, 1860, albeit somewhat stiff and cold, after this artist's fashion, is a superb collection of carefully studied oriental designs. With these may be classed the illustrations to Aytoun's "Lays of the Scottish Cavaliers," by Sir Noel Paton, which have the same finished qualities of composition and the same academic hardness. Several good editions of the "Pilgrim's Progress" have appeared,—notably those of C. H. Bennett, J. D. Watson, and G. H. Thomas.

Other books are Millais's "Parables of our Lord," Leighton's "Romola," Walker's "Philip" and "Denis Duval," the "Don Quixote," "Dante," "La Fontaine" and other works of Dore, Dalziel's "Arabian Nights," Leighton's "Lyra Germanica" and "Moral Emblems," and the "Spiritual Conceits" of W. Harry Rogers. These are some only of the number, which does not include books like Mrs. Hugh Blackburn's "British Birds," Wolf's "Wild Animals," Wise's "New Forest," Linton's "Lake Country," Wood's "Natural History," and many more. Nor does it take in the various illustrated periodicals which have multiplied so freely since, in 1859, "Once a Week" first began to attract and train such younger draughtsmen as Sandys, Lawless, Pinwell, Houghton, Morten, and Paul Grey, some of whose best work in this way has been revived in the edition of Thornbury's "Ballads and Songs," recently published by Chatto and Windus. Ten years later came the "Graphic," offering still wider opportunities to wood-cut art, and bringing with it a fresh school of artists. Herkomer, Fildes, Small, Green, Barnard, Barnes, Crane, Caldecott, Hopkins, and others,—quos nunc perscribere longum est—have contributed good work to this popular rival of the older, but still vigorous, "Illustrated." And now again, another promising serial, the "Magazine of Art," affords a supplementary field to modern refinements and younger energies.

Not a few of the artists named in the preceding paragraph have also earned distinction in separate branches of the pictorial art, and specially in that of humorous design,—a department which has always been so richly recruited in this country that it deserves more than a passing mention. From the days of Hogarth onwards there has been an almost unbroken series of humorous draughtsmen, who, both on wood and metal, play a distinguished part in our illustrated literature. Rowlandson, one of the earliest, was a caricaturist of inexhaustible facility, and an artist who scarcely did justice to his own powers. He illustrated several books, but he is chiefly remembered in this way by his plates to Combe's "Three Tours of Dr. Syntax." Gillray, his contemporary, whose bias was political rather than social, is said to have illustrated "The Deserted Village" in his youth; but he is not famous as a book-illustrator.

Another of the early men was Bunbury, whom "quality"-loving Mr. Walpole calls "the second Hogarth, and first imitator who ever fully equalled his original (!);" but whose prints to "Tristram Shandy," are nevertheless completely forgotten, while, if he be remembered at all, it is by the plate of "The Long Minuet," and the vulgar "Directions to Bad Horsemen." With the first years of the century, however, appears the great master of modern humorists, whose long life ended only a few years since, "the veteran George Cruikshank"—as his admirers were wont to style him. He indeed may justly be compared to Hogarth, since, in tragic power and intensity he occasionally comes nearer to him than any artist of our time. It is manifestly impossible to mention here all the more important efforts of this indefatigable worker, from those far-away days when he caricatured "Boney" and championed Queen Caroline, to that final frontispiece for "The Rose and the Lily"—"designed and etched (according to the inscription) by George Cruikshank, age 83;" but the plates to the "Points of Humour," to Grimm's "Goblins," to "Oliver Twist," "Jack Sheppard," Maxwell's "Irish Rebellion," and the "Table Book," are sufficiently favourable and varied specimens of his skill with the needle, while the woodcuts to "Three Courses and a Dessert," one of which is here given, are equally good examples of his work on the block. The "Triumph of Cupid," which begins the "Table Book," is an excellent instance of his lavish wealth of fancy, and it contains beside, one—nay more than one—of the many portraits of the artist. He is shown en robe de chambre, smoking (this was before his regenerate days!) in front of a blazing fire, with a pet spaniel on his knee.

In the cloud which curls from his lips is a motley procession of sailors, sweeps, jockeys, Greenwich pensioners, Jew clothesmen, flunkies, and others more illustrious, chained to the chariot wheels of Cupid, who, preceded by cherubic acolytes and banner-bearers, winds round the top of the picture towards an altar of Hymen on the table. When, by the aid of a pocket-glass, one has mastered these swarming figures, as well as those in the foreground, it gradually dawns upon one that all the furniture is strangely vitalised. Masks laugh round the border of the tablecloth, the markings of the mantelpiece resolve themselves into rows of madly- racing figures, the tongs leers in a degage and cavalier way at the artist, the shovel and poker grin in sympathy; there are faces in the smoke, in the fire, in the fireplace,—the very fender itself is a ring of fantastic creatures who jubilantly hem in the ashes. And it is not only in the grotesque and fanciful that Cruikshank excels; he is master of the strange, the supernatural, and the terrible. In range of character (the comparison is probably a hackneyed one), both by his gifts and his limitations, he resembles Dickens; and had he illustrated more of that writer's works the resemblance would probably have been more evident. In "Oliver Twist," for example, where Dickens is strong, Cruikshank is strong; where Dickens is weak, he is weak too. His Fagin, his Bill Sikes, his Bumble, and their following, are on a level with Dickens's conceptions; his Monk and Rose Maylie are as poor as the originals. But as the defects of Dickens are overbalanced by his merits, so Cruikshank's strength is far in excess of his weakness. It is not to his melodramatic heroes or wasp-waisted heroines that we must look for his triumphs; it is to his delineations, from the moralist's point of view, of vulgarity and vice,—of the "rank life of towns," with all its squalid tragedy and comedy. Here he finds his strongest ground, and possibly, notwithstanding his powers as a comic artist and caricaturist, his loftiest claim to recollection.

Cruikshank was employed on two only of Dickens's books—"Oliver Twist" and the "Sketches by Boz." The great majority of them were illustrated by Hablot K. Browne, an artist who followed the ill-fated Seymour on the "Pickwick Papers." To "Phiz," as he is popularly called, we are indebted for our pictorial ideas of Sam Weller, Mrs. Gamp, Captain Cuttle, and most of the author's characters, down to the "Tale of Two Cities." "Phiz" also illustrated a great many of Lever's novels, for which his skill in hunting and other Lever-like scenes especially qualified him.

With the name of Richard Doyle we come to the first of a group of artists whose main work was, or is still, done for the time-honoured miscellany of Mr. Punch. So familiar an object is "Punch" upon our tables, that one is sometimes apt to forget how unfailing, and how good on the whole, is the work we take so complacently as a matter of course. And of this good work, in the earlier days, a large proportion was done by Mr. Doyle. He is still living, although he has long ceased to gladden those sprightly pages. But it was to "Punch" that he contributed his masterpiece, the "Manners and Customs of ye Englyshe," a series of outlines illustrating social life in 1849, and cleverly commented by a shadowy "Mr. Pips," a sort of fetch or double of the bustling and garrulous old Caroline diarist.

In these captivating pictures the life of thirty years ago is indeed, as the title-page has it, "drawn from ye quick." We see the Molesworths and Cantilupes of the day parading the Park; we watch Brougham fretting at a hearing in the Lords, or Peel holding forth to the Commons (where the Irish members are already obstructive); we squeeze in at the Haymarket to listen to Jenny Lind, or we run down the river to Greenwich Fair, and visit "Mr. Richardson, his show." Many years after, in the "Bird's Eye Views of Society," which appeared in the early numbers of the "Cornhill Magazine," Mr. Doyle returned to this attractive theme. But the later designs were more elaborate, and not equally fortunate. They bear the same relationship to Mr. Pips's pictorial chronicle, as the laboured "Temperance Fairy Tales" of Cruikshank's old age bear to the little-worked Grimm's "Goblins" of his youth. So hazardous is the attempt to repeat an old success!

Nevertheless, many of the initial letters to the "Bird's Eye Views" are in the artist's best and most frolicsome manner. "The Foreign Tour of Brown, Jones, and Robinson" is another of his happy thoughts for "Punch;" and some of his most popular designs are to be found in Thackeray's "Newcomes," where his satire and fancy seem thoroughly suited to his text. He has also illustrated Locker's well-known "London Lyrics," Ruskin's "King of the Golden River," and Hughes's "Scouring of the White Horse," from which last the initial at the beginning of this chapter has been borrowed. His latest important effort was the series of drawings called "In Fairy Land," to which Mr. William Allingham contributed the verses.

In speaking of the "Newcomes," one is reminded that its illustrious author was himself a "Punch" artist, and would probably have been a designer alone, had it not been decreed "that he should paint in colours which will never crack and never need restoration." Everyone knows the story of the rejected illustrator of "Pickwick," whom that and other rebuffs drove permanently to letters. To his death, however, he clung fondly to his pencil. In technique he never attained to certainty or strength, and his genius was too quick and creative—perhaps also too desultory—for finished work, while he was always indifferent to costume and accessory.

But many of his sketches for "Vanity Fair," for "Pendennis," for "The Virginians," for "The Rose and the Ring," the Christmas books, and the posthumously published "Orphan of Pimlico," have a vigour of impromptu, and a happy suggestiveness which is better than correct drawing. Often the realisation is almost photographic. Look, for example, at the portrait in "Pendennis" of the dilapidated Major as he crawls downstairs in the dawn after the ball at Gaunt House, and then listen to the inimitable context: "That admirable and devoted Major above all,—who had been for hours by Lady Clavering's side ministering to her and feeding her body with everything that was nice, and her ear with everything that was sweet and flattering—oh! what an object he was!

The rings round his eyes were of the colour of bistre; those orbs themselves were like the plovers' eggs whereof Lady Clavering and Blanche had each tasted; the wrinkles in his old face were furrowed in deep gashes; and a silver stubble, like an elderly morning dew, was glittering on his chin, and alongside the dyed whiskers, now limp and out of curl." A good deal of this—that fine touch in italics especially—could not possibly be rendered in black and white, and yet how much is indicated, and how thoroughly the whole is felt! One turns to the woodcut from the words, and back again to the words from the woodcut with ever-increasing gratification. Then again, Thackeray's little initial letters are charmingly arch and playful. They seem to throw a shy side-light upon the text, giving, as it were, an additional and confidential hint of the working of the author's mind. To those who, with the present writer, love every tiny scratch and quirk and flourish of the Master's hand, these small but priceless memorials are far beyond the frigid appraising of academics and schools of art.

After Doyle and Thackeray come a couple of well-known artists—John Leech and John Tenniel. The latter still lives (may he long live!) to delight and instruct us. Of the former, whose genial and manly "Pictures of Life and Character" are in every home where good- humoured raillery is prized and appreciated, it is scarcely necessary to speak. Who does not remember the splendid languid swells, the bright-eyed rosy girls ("with no nonsense about them!") in pork pie hats and crinolines, the superlative "Jeames's," the hairy "Mossoos," the music-grinding Italian desperadoes whom their kind creator hated so? And then the intrepidity of "Mr. Briggs," the Roman rule of "Paterfamilias," the vagaries of the "Rising Generation!" There are things in this gallery over which the severest misanthrope must chuckle—they are simply irresistible.

Let any one take, say that smallest sketch of the hapless mortal who has turned on the hot water in the bath and cannot turn it off again, and see if he is able to restrain his laughter. In this one gift of producing instant mirth Leech is almost alone. It would be easy to assail his manner and his skill, but for sheer fun, for the invention of downright humorous situation, he is unapproached, except by Cruikshank. He did a few illustrations to Dickens's Christmas books; but his best-known book-illustrations properly so called are to "Uncle Tom's Cabin," the "Comic Histories" of A'Beckett, the "Little Tour in Ireland," and certain sporting novels by the late Mr. Surtees. Tenniel now confines himself almost exclusively to the weekly cartoons with which his name is popularly associated. But years ago he used to invent the most daintily fanciful initial letters; and many of his admirers prefer the serio- grotesque designs of "Punch's Pocket-Book," "Alice in Wonderland," and "Through the Looking-Glass," to the always correctly-drawn but sometimes stiffly-conceived cartoons.

What, for example, could be more delightful than the picture, in "Alice in Wonderland," of the "Mad Tea Party?" Observe the hopelessly distraught expression of the March hare, and the eager incoherence of the hatter! A little further on the pair are trying to squeeze the dormouse into the teapot; and a few pages back the blue caterpillar is discovered smoking his hookah on the top of a mushroom. He was exactly three inches long, says the veracious chronicle, but what a dignity!—what an oriental flexibility of gesture! Speaking of animals, it must not be forgotten that Tenniel is a master in this line. His "British Lion," in particular, is a most imposing quadruped, and so often in request that it is not necessary to go back to the famous cartoons on the Indian mutiny to seek for examples of that magnificent presence. As a specimen of the artist's treatment of the lesser felidae, the reader's attention is invited to this charming little kitten from "Through the Looking-Glass."

Mr. Tenniel is a link between Leech and the younger school of "Punch" artists, of whom Mr. George du Maurier, Mr. Linley Sambourne, and Mr. Charles Keene are the most illustrious. The first is nearly as popular as Leech, and is certainly a greater favourite with cultivated audiences. He is not so much a humorist as a satirist of the Thackeray type,—unsparing in his denunciation of shams, affectations, and flimsy pretences of all kinds. A master of composition and accomplished draughtsman, he excels in the delineation of "society"—its bishops, its "professional beauties" and "aesthetes," its nouveaux riches, its distinguished foreigners,- -while now and then (but not too often) he lets us know that if he chose he could be equally happy in depicting the lowest classes.

There was a bar-room scene not long ago in "Punch" which gave the clearest evidence of this. Some of those for whom no good thing is good enough complain, it is said, that he lacks variety—that he is too constant to one type of feminine beauty. But any one who will be at the pains to study a group of conventional "society" faces from any of his "At Homes" or "Musical Parties" will speedily discover that they are really very subtly diversified and contrasted. For a case in point, take the decorously sympathetic group round the sensitive German musician, who is "veeping" over one of his own compositions. Or follow the titter running round that amused assembly to whom the tenor warbler is singing "Me-e-e-et me once again," with such passionate emphasis that the domestic cat mistakes it for a well-known area cry.

As for his ladies, it may perhaps be conceded that his type is a little persistent. Still it is a type so refined, so graceful, so attractive altogether, that in the jarring of less well-favoured realities it is an advantage to have it always before our eyes as a standard to which we can appeal. Mr. du Maurier is a fertile book-illustrator, whose hand is frequently seen in the "Cornhill," and elsewhere. Some of his best work of this kind is in Douglas Jerrold's "Story of a Feather," in Thackeray's "Ballads," and the large edition of the "Ingoldsby Legends," to which Leech, Tenniel, and Cruikshank also contributed.

One of his prettiest compositions is the group here reproduced from "Punch's Almanack" for 1877. The talent of his colleague, Mr. Linley Sambourne, may fairly be styled unique. It is difficult to compare it with anything in its way, except some of the happier efforts of the late Mr. Charles Bennett, to which, nevertheless, it is greatly superior in execution. To this clever artist's invention everything seems to present itself with a train of fantastic accessory so whimsically inexhaustible that it almost overpowers one with its prodigality. Each fresh examination of his designs discloses something overlooked or unexpected. Let the reader study for a moment the famous "Birds of a Feather" of 1875, or that ingenious skit of 1877 upon the rival Grosvenor Gallery and Academy, in which the late President of the latter is shown as the proudest of peacocks, the eyes of whose tail are portraits of Royal Academicians, and whose body-feathers are paint brushes and shillings of admission. Mr. Sambourne is excellent, too, at adaptations of popular pictures,—witness the more than happy parodies of Herrman's "A Bout d'Arguments," and "Une Bonne Histoire." His book-illustrations have been comparatively few, those to Burnand's laughable burlesque of "Sandford and Merton" being among the best.

Rumour asserts that he is at present engaged upon Kingsley's "Water Babies," a subject which might almost be supposed to have been created for his pencil. There are indications, it may be added, that Mr. Sambourne's talents are by no means limited to the domain in which for the present he chooses to exercise them, and it is not impossible that he may hereafter take high rank as a cartoonist. Mr. Charles Keene, a selection from whose sketches has recently been issued under the title of "Our People," is unrivalled in certain bourgeois, military, and provincial types. No one can draw a volunteer, a monthly nurse, a Scotchman, an "ancient mariner" of the watering-place species, with such absolutely humorous verisimilitude. Personages, too, in whose eyes—to use Mr. Swiveller's euphemism—"the sun has shone too strongly," find in Mr. Keene a merciless satirist of their "pleasant vices." Like Leech, he has also a remarkable power of indicating a landscape background with the fewest possible touches. His book- illustrations have been .mainly confined to magazines and novels. Those in "Once a Week" to a "Good Fight," the tale subsequently elaborated by Charles Reade into the "Cloister and the Hearth," present some good specimens of his earlier work. One of these, in which the dwarf of the story is seen climbing up a wall with a lantern at his back, will probably be remembered by many.

After the "Punch" school there are other lesser luminaries. Mr. W. S. Gilbert's drawings to his own inimitable "Bab Ballads" have a perverse drollery which is quite in keeping with that erratic text. Mr. F. Barnard, whose exceptional talents have not been sufficiently recognised, is a master of certain phases of strongly marked character, and, like Mr. Charles Green, has contributed some excellent sketches to the "Household Edition" of Dickens. Mr. Sullivan of "Fun," whose grotesque studies of the "British Tradesman" and "Workman" have recently been republished, has abounding vis comica, but he has hitherto done little in the way of illustrating books. For minute pictorial stocktaking and photographic retention of detail, Mr. Sullivan's artistic memory may almost be compared to the wonderful literary memory of Mr. Sala. Mr. John Proctor, who some years ago (in "Will o' the Wisp") seemed likely to rival Tenniel as a cartoonist, has not been very active in this way; while Mr. Matthew Morgan, the clever artist of the "Tomahawk," has transferred his services to the United States. Of Mr. Bowcher of "Judy," and various other professedly humorous designers, space permits no further mention.

There remains, however, one popular branch of book-illustration, which has attracted the talents of some of the most skilful and original of modern draughtsmen, *i.e.*, the embellishment of children's books. From the days when Mulready drew the old "Butterfly's Ball" and "Peacock at Home" of our youth, to those of the delightfully Blake-like fancies of E. V. B., whose "Child's Play" has recently been re-published for the delectation of a new generation of admirers, this has always been a popular and profitable employment; but of late years it has been raised to the level of a fine art. Mr. H. S. Marks, Mr. J. D. Watson, Mr. Walter Crane, have produced specimens of nursery literature which, for refinement of colouring and beauty of ornament, cannot easily be surpassed.

The equipments of the last named, especially, are of a very high order. He began as a landscapist on wood; he now chiefly devotes himself to the figure; and he seems to have the decorative art at his fingers' ends as a natural gift. Such work as "King Luckieboy's Party" was a revelation in the way of toy books, while the "Baby's Opera" and "Baby's Bouquet" are petits chefs d'oeuvre, of which the sagacious collector will do well to secure copies, not for his nursery, but his library. Nor can his "Mrs. Mundi at Home" be neglected by the curious in quaint and graceful invention. Another book—the "Under the Window" of Miss Kate Greenaway—comes within the same category. Since Stothard, no one has given us such a clear-eyed, soft-faced, happy-hearted childhood; or so poetically "apprehended" the coy reticences, the simplicities, and the small solemnities of little people.

Added to this, the old-world costume in which she usually elects to clothe her characters, lends an arch piquancy of contrast to their innocent rites and ceremonies. Her taste in tinting, too, is very sweet and spring-like; and there is a fresh, pure fragrance about all her pictures as of new-gathered nosegays; or, perhaps, looking to the fashions that she favours, it would be better to say "bow-pots." But the latest "good genius" of this branch of book-illustrating is Mr. Randolph Caldecott, a designer assuredly of the very first order. There is a spontaneity of fun, an unforced invention about everything he does, that is infinitely entertaining.

Other artists draw to amuse us; Mr. Caldecott seems to draw to amuse himself,—and this is his charm. One feels that he must have chuckled inwardly as he puffed the cheeks of his "Jovial Huntsmen;" or sketched that inimitably complacent dog in the "House that Jack Built;" or exhibited the exploits of the immortal "train- band captain" of "famous London town." This last is his masterpiece. Cowper himself must have rejoiced at it,—and Lady Austen. There are two sketches in this book—they occupy the concluding pages—which are especially fascinating. On one, John

Gilpin, in a forlorn and flaccid condition, is helped into the house by the sympathising (and very attractive) Betty; on the other he has donned his slippers, refreshed his inner man with a cordial, and over the heaving shoulder of his "spouse," who lies dissolved upon his martial bosom, he is taking the spectators into his confidence with a wink worthy of the late Mr. Buckstone. Nothing more genuine, more heartily laughable, than this set of designs has appeared in our day. And Mr. Caldecott has few limitations. Not only does he draw human nature admirably, but he draws animals and landscapes equally well, so one may praise him without reserve. Though not children's books, mention should here be made of his "Bracebridge Hall," and "Old Christmas," the illustrations to which are the nearest approach to that beau-ideal, perfect sympathy between the artist and the author, with which the writer is acquainted. The cut on page 173 is from the former of these works.

Many of the books above mentioned are printed in colours by various processes, and they are not always engraved on wood. But—to close the account of modern wood-engraving—some brief reference must be made to what is styled the "new American School," as exhibited for the most part in "Scribner's" and other Transatlantic magazines. Authorities, it is reported, shake their heads over these performances. "C'est magnifique, mais ce nest pas la gravure," they whisper. Into the matter in dispute, it is perhaps presumptuous for an "atechnic" to adventure himself. But to the outsider it would certainly seem as if the chief ground of complaint is that the new comers do not play the game according to the old rules, and that this (alleged) irregular mode of procedure tends to lessen the status of the engraver as an artist. False or true, this, it may fairly be advanced, has nothing whatever to do with the matter, as far, at least, as the public are concerned.

For them the question is, simply and solely—What is the result obtained? The new school, availing themselves largely of the assistance of photography, are able to dispense, in a great measure, with the old tedious method of drawing on the block, and to leave the artist to choose what medium he prefers for his design—be it oil, water-colour, or black and white—concerning themselves only to reproduce its characteristics on the wood. This is, of course, a deviation from the method of Bewick. But would Bewick have adhered to his method in these days? Even in his last hours he was seeking for new processes. What we want is to get nearest to the artist himself with the least amount of interpretation or intermediation on the part of the engraver. Is engraving on copper to be reproduced, we want a facsimile if possible, and not a rendering into something which is supposed to be the orthodox utterance of wood-engraving. Take, for example, the copy of Schiavonetti's engraving of Blake's Death's Door in "Scribner's Magazine" for June 1880, or the cut from the same source at page 131 of this book. These are faithful line for line transcriptions, as far as wood can give them, of the original copper-plates; and, this being the case, it is not to be wondered at that the public, who, for a few pence can have practical facsimiles of Blake, of Cruikshank, or of Whistler, are loud in their appreciation of the "new American School." Nor are its successes confined to reproduction in facsimile. Those who look at the exquisite illustrations, in the same periodical, to the "Tile Club at Play," to Roe's "Success with Small Fruits," and Harris's "Insects Injurious to Vegetation,"—to say nothing of the selected specimens in the recently issued "Portfolios"—will see that the latest comers can hold their own on all fields with any school that has gone before.

Besides copperplate and wood, there are many processes which have been and are still employed for book-illustrations, although the brief limits of this chapter make any account of them impossible. Lithography was at one time very popular, and, in books like Roberts's "Holy Land," exceedingly effective. The "Etching Club" issued a number of books circa 1841-52; and most of the work of "Phiz" and Cruikshank was done with the needle.

It is probable that, as we have already seen, the impetus given to modern etching by Messrs. Hamerton, Seymour Haden, and Whistler, will lead to a specific revival of etching as a means of book-illustration. Already beautiful etchings have for some time appeared in "L'Art," the "Portfolio," and the "Etcher;" and at least one book of poems has been entirely illustrated in this way,—the poems of Mr. W. Bell Scott. For reproducing old engravings, maps, drawings, and the like, it is not too much to say that we shall never get anything much closer than the facsimiles of M. Amand-Durand and the Typographic Etching and Autotype Companies. But further improvements will probably have to be made before these can compete commercially with wood-engraving as practised by the "new American School."

"Of making many books," 'twais said, "There is no end;" and who thereon The ever-running ink doth shed But probes the words of Solomon: Wherefore we now, for colophon, From London's city drear and dark, In the year Eighteen Eight-One, Reprint them at the press of Clark.

Books of the Collector

The easiest way to bring order into the chaos of desirable books, is, doubtless, to begin historically with manuscripts. Almost every age that has left any literary remains, has bequeathed to us relics which are cherished by collectors. We may leave the clay books of the Chaldeans out of the account. These tomes resemble nothing so much as sticks of chocolate, and, however useful they may be to the student, the clay MSS. of Assurbanipal are not coveted by the collector. He finds his earliest objects of desire in illuminated manuscripts.

The art of decorating manuscripts is as old as Egypt; but we need not linger over the beautiful papyri, which are silent books to all but a few Egyptologists. Greece, out of all her tomes, has left us but a few ill-written papyri. Roman and early Byzantine art are represented by a "Virgil," and fragments of an "Iliad"; the drawings in the latter have been reproduced in a splendid volume (Milan 1819), and shew Greek art passing into barbarism. The illumination of MSS. was a favourite art in the later Empire, and is said to have been practised by Boethius. The iconoclasts of the Eastern Empire destroyed the books which contained representations of saints and of the persons of the Trinity, and the monk Lazarus, a famous artist, was cruelly tortured for his skill in illuminating sacred works. The art was decaying in Western Europe when Charlemagne sought for painters of MSS. in England and Ireland, where the monks, in their monasteries, had developed a style with original qualities. The library of Corpus Christi at Cambridge, contains some of the earliest and most beautiful of extant English MSS. These parchments, stained purple or violet, and inscribed with characters of gold; are too often beyond the reach of the amateur for whom we write. The MSS. which he can hope to acquire are neither very early nor very sumptuous, and, as a rule, MSS. of secular books are apt to be out of his reach.

Yet a collection of MSS. has this great advantage over a collection of printed books, that every item in it is absolutely unique, no two MSS. being ever really the same. This circumstance alone would entitle a good collection of MSS. to very high consideration on the part of book-collectors. But, in addition to the great expense of such a collection, there is another and even more serious drawback. It is sometimes impossible, and is often extremely difficult, to tell whether a MS. is perfect or not.

This difficulty can only be got over by an amount of learning on the part of the collector to which, unfortunately, he is too often a stranger. On the other hand, the advantages of collecting MSS. are sometimes very great.

In addition to the pleasure—a pleasure at once literary and artistic—which the study of illuminated MSS. affords, there is the certainty that, as years go on, the value of such a collection increases in a proportion altogether marvellous.

I will take two examples to prove this point. Some years ago an eminent collector gave the price of 30 pounds for a small French book of Hours, painted in grisaille. It was in a country town that he met with this treasure, for a treasure he considered the book, in spite of its being of the very latest school of illumination. When his collection was dispersed a few years ago this one book fetched 260 pounds. In the celebrated Perkins sale, in 1873, a magnificent early MS., part of which was written in gold on a purple ground, and which was dated in the catalogue "ninth or tenth century," but was in reality of the end of the tenth or beginning of the eleventh, was sold for 565 pounds to a dealer. It found its way into Mr. Bragge's collection, at what price I do not know, and was resold, three years later, for 780 pounds.

Any person desirous of making a collection of illuminated MSS., should study seriously for some time at the British Museum, or some such place, until he is thoroughly acquainted (1) with the styles of writing in use in the Middle Ages, so that he can at a glance make a fairly accurate estimate of the age of the book submitted to him; and (2) with the proper means of collating the several kinds of service-books, which, in nine cases out of ten, were those chosen for illumination. A knowledge of the styles of writing can be acquired at second hand in a book lately published by Mr. Charles Trice Martin, F.S.A., being a new edition of "Astle's Progress of Writing." Still better, of course, is the actual inspection and comparison of books to which a date can be with some degree of certainty assigned.

It is very common for the age of a book to be misstated in the catalogues of sales, for the simple reason that the older the writing, the plainer, in all probability, it is. Let the student compare writing of the twelfth century with that of the sixteenth, and he will be able to judge at once of the truth of this assertion. I had once the good fortune to "pick up" a small Testament of the early part of the twelfth century, if not older, which was catalogued as belonging to the fifteenth, a date which would have made it of very moderate value.

With regard to the second point, the collation of MSS., I fear there is no royal road to knowing whether a book is perfect or imperfect. In some cases the catchwords remain at the foot of the pages. It is then of course easy to see if a page is lost, but where no such clue is given the student's only chance is to be fully acquainted with what a book OUGHT to contain. He can only do this when he has a knowledge of the different kinds of service-books which were in use, and of their most usual contents.

I am indebted to a paper, read by the late Sir William Tite at a meeting of the Society of Antiquaries, for the collation of "Books of Hours," but there are many kinds of MSS. besides these, and it is well to know something of them. The Horae, or Books of Hours, were the latest development of the service-books used at an earlier period. They cannot, in fact, be strictly called service-books, being intended only for private devotion.

But in the thirteenth century and before it, Psalters were in use for this purpose, and the collation of a Psalter is in truth more important than that of a Book of Hours. It will be well for a student, therefore, to begin with Psalters, as he can then get up the Hours in their elementary form. I subjoin a bibliographical account of both kinds of MSS. In the famous Exhibition at the Burlington Club in 1874, a number of volumes was arranged to show how persistent one type of the age could be. The form of the decorations, and the arrangement of the figures in borders, once invented, was fixed for generations. In a Psalter of the thirteenth century there was, under the month of January in the calendar, a picture of a grotesque little figure warming himself at a stove. The hearth below, the chimney-pot above, on which a stork was feeding her brood, with the intermediate chimney shaft used as a border, looked like a scientific preparation from the interior anatomy of a house of the period. In one of the latest of the MSS. exhibited on that occasion was the self-same design again. The little man was no longer a grotesque, and the picture had all the high finish and completeness in drawing that we might expect in the workmanship of a contemporary of Van Eyck. There was a full series of intermediate books, showing the gradual growth of the picture.

With regard to chronology, it may be roughly asserted that the earliest books which occur are Psalters of the thirteenth century. Next to them come Bibles, of which an enormous issue took place before the middle of the fourteenth century. These are followed by an endless series of books of Hours, which, as the sixteenth century is reached, appear in several vernacular languages. Those in English, being both very rare and of great importance in liturgical history, are of a value altogether out of proportion to the beauty of their illuminations. Side by side with this succession are the Evangelistina, which, like the example mentioned above, are of the highest merit, beauty, and value; followed by sermons and homilies, and the Breviary, which itself shows signs of growth as the years go on.

The real Missal, with which all illuminated books used to be confounded, is of rare occurrence, but I have given a collation of it also. Besides these devotional or religious books, I must mention chronicles and romances, and the semi-religious and moral allegories, such as the "Pelerinage de l'Ame," which is said to have given Bunyan the machinery of the "Pilgrim's Progress." Chaucer's and Gower's poetry exists in many MSS., as does the "Polychronicon" of Higden; but, as a rule, the medieval chronicles are of single origin, and were not copied. To collate MSS. of these kinds is quite impossible, unless by carefully reading them, and seeing that the pages run on without break.

I should advise the young collector who wishes to make sure of success not to be too catholic in his tastes at first, but to confine his attention to a single period and a single school. I should also advise him to make from time to time a careful catalogue of what he buys, and to preserve it even after he has weeded out certain items. He will then be able to make a clear comparative estimate of the importance and value of his collection, and by studying one species at a time, to become thoroughly conversant with what it can teach him. When he has, so to speak, burnt his fingers once or twice, he will find himself able to distinguish at sight what no amount of teaching by word of mouth or by writing could ever possibly impart to any advantage.

One thing I should like if possible to impress very strongly upon the reader. That is the fact that a MS. which is not absolutely perfect, if it is in a genuine state, is of much more value than one which has been made perfect by the skill of a modern restorer. The more skilful he is, that is to say the better he can forge the style of the original, the more worthless he renders the volume.

Printing seems to have superseded the art of the illuminator more promptly and completely in England than on the Continent. The dames galantes of Brantome's memoirs took pleasure in illuminated Books of Hours, suited to the nature of their devotions. As late as the time of Louis XIV., Bussy Rabutin had a volume of the same kind, illuminated with portraits of "saints," of his own canonisation. The most famous of these modern examples of costly MSS. was "La Guirlande de Julie," a collection of madrigals by various courtly hands, presented to the illustrious Julie, daughter of the Marquise de Rambouillet, most distinguished of the Precieuses, and wife of the Duc de Montausier, the supposed original of Moliere's Alceste.

The MS. was copied on vellum by Nicholas Jarry, the great calligraph of his time. The flowers on the margin were painted by Robert. Not long ago a French amateur was so lucky as to discover the MS. book of prayers of Julie's noble mother, the Marquise de Rambouillet. The Marquise wrote these prayers for her own devotions, and Jarry, the illuminator, declared that he found them most edifying, and delightful to study. The manuscript is written on vellum by the famous Jarry, contains a portrait of the fair Julie herself, and is bound in morocco by Le Gascon. The happy collector who possesses the volume now, heard vaguely that a manuscript of some interest was being exposed for sale at a trifling price in the shop of a country bookseller. The description of the book, casual as it was, made mention of the monogram on the cover. This was enough for the amateur. He rushed to a railway station, travelled some three hundred miles, reached the country town, hastened to the bookseller's shop, and found that the book had been withdrawn by its owner. Happily the possessor, unconscious of his bliss, was at home. The amateur sought him out, paid the small sum demanded, and returned to Paris in triumph. Thus, even in the region of manuscript-collecting, there are extraordinary prizes for the intelligent collector.

To Know, if a Manuscript is Perfect

If the manuscript is of English or French writing of the twelfth, thirteenth, fourteenth, or fifteenth centuries, it is probably either—(1) a Bible, (2) a Psalter, (3) a book of Hours, or (4), but rarely, a Missal. It is not worth while to give the collation of a gradual, or a hymnal, or a processional, or a breviary, or any of the fifty different kinds of service-books which are occasionally met with, but which are never twice the same.

To collate one of them, the reader must go carefully through the book, seeing that the catch-words, if there are any, answer to the head lines; and if there are "signatures," that is, if the foot of the leaves of a sheet of parchment has any mark for enabling the binder to "gather" them correctly, going through them, and seeing that each signed leaf has its corresponding "blank."

1. To collate a Bible, it will be necessary first to go through the catch-words, if any, and signatures, as above; then to notice the contents. The first page should contain the Epistle of St. Jerome to the reader. It will be observed that there is nothing of the nature of a title-page, but I have often seen title-pages supplied by some ignorant imitator in the last century, with the idea that the book was imperfect without one. The books of the Bible follow in order—but the order not only differs from ours, but differs in different copies.

The Apocryphal books are always included. The New Testament usually follows on the Old without any break; and the book concludes with an index of the Hebrew names and their signification in Latin, intended to help preachers to the figurative meaning of the biblical types and parables. The last line of the Bible itself usually contains a colophon, in which sometimes the name of the writer is given, sometimes the length of time it has taken him to write, and sometimes merely the "Explicit. Laus Deo," which has found its way into many modern books. This colophon, which comes as a rule immediately before the index, often contains curious notes, hexameters giving the names of all the books, biographical or local memoranda, and should always be looked for by the collector. One such line occurs to me. It is in a Bible written in Italy in the thirteenth century -

"Qui scripsit scribat. Vergilius spe domini vivat."

Vergilius was, no doubt, in this case the scribe. The Latin and the writing are often equally crabbed. In the Bodleian there is a Bible with this colophon -

"Finito libro referemus gratias Christo m.cc.lxv. indict. viij. Ego Lafracus de Pacis de Cmoa scriptor scripsi."

This was also written in Italy. English colophons are often very quaint—"Qui scripsit hunc librum fiat collocatus in Paradisum," is an example. The following gives us the name of one Master Gerard, who, in the fourteenth century, thus poetically described his ownership:-

"Si Ge ponatur—et rar simul associatur - Et dus reddatur—cui pertinet ita vocatur."

In a Bible written in England, in the British Museum, there is a long colophon, in which, after the name of the writer—"hunc librum scripsit Wills de Hales,"—there is a prayer for Ralph of Nebham, who had called Hales to the writing of the book, followed by a date- -"Fes. fuit liber anno M.cc.i. quarto ab incarnatione domini." In this Bible the books of the New Testament were in the following order:- the Evangelists, the Acts, the Epistles of S. Peter, S. James, and S. John, the Epistles of S. Paul, and the Apocalypse. In a Bible at Brussels I found the colophon after the index:- "Hic expliciunt interpretationes Hebrayorum nominum Do gris qui potens est p. sup. omia." Some of these Bibles are of marvellously small dimensions. The smallest I ever saw was at Ghent, but it was very imperfect. I have one in which there are thirteen lines of writing in an inch of the column. The order of the books of the New Testament in Bibles of the thirteenth century is usually according to one or other of the three following arrangements:-

(1) The Evangelists, Romans to Hebrews, Acts, Epistles of S. Peter, S. James, and S. John, Apocalypse.

(2) The Evangelists, Acts, Epistles of S. Peter, S. James, and S. John, Epistles of S. Paul, Apocalypse. This is the most common.

(3) The Evangelists, Acts, Epistles of S. Peter, S. James, and S. John, Apocalypse, and Epistles of S. Paul.

On the fly leaves of these old Bibles there are often very curious inscriptions. In one I have this:- "Haec biblia emi Haquinas prior monasterii Hatharbiensis de dono domini regis Norwegie." Who was this King of Norway who, in 1310, gave the Prior of Hatherby money to buy a Bible, which was probably written at Canterbury? And who was Haquinas? His name has a Norwegian sound, and reminds us of St. Thomas of that surname. In another manuscript I have seen

"Articula Fidei:- Nascitur, abluitur, patitur, descendit at ima Surgit et ascendit, veniens discernere cuncta."

In another this:-

"Sacramenta ecclesiae:- Abluo, fumo, cibo, piget, ordinat, uxor et ungit."

I will conclude these notes on MS. Bibles with the following colophon from a copy written in Italy in the fifteenth century:-

"Finito libro vivamus semper in Christo - Si semper in Christo carebimus ultimo leto. Explicit Deo gratias; Amen. Stephanus de Tantaldis scripsit in pergamo."

The "Psalter" of the thirteenth century is usually to be considered a forerunner of the "Book of Hours." It always contains, and usually commences with, a Calendar, in which are written against certain days the "obits" of benefactors and others, so that a well- filled Psalter often becomes a historical document of high value and importance. The first page of the psalms is ornamented with a huge B, which often fills the whole page, and contains a representation of David and Goliath ingeniously fitted to the shape of the letter. At the end are usually to be found the hymns of the

Three Children, and others from the Bible together with the Te Deum; and sometimes, in late examples, a litany. In some psalters the calendar is at the end. These Psalters, and the Bibles described above, are very frequently of English work; more frequently, that is, than the books of Hours and Missals. The study of the Scriptures was evidently more popular in England than in the other countries of Europe during the Middle Ages; and the early success of the Reformers here, must in part, no doubt, be attributed to the wide circulation of the Bible even before it had been translated from the Latin. I need hardly, perhaps, observe that even fragments of a Psalter, a Testament, or a Bible in English, are so precious as to be practically invaluable.

We are indebted to Sir W. Tite for the following collation of a Flemish "Book of Hours":-

1. The Calendar.
2. Gospels of the Nativity and the Resurrection.
3. Preliminary Prayers (inserted occasionally).
4. Horae—(Nocturns and Matins).
5. (Lauds).
6. (Prime).
7. (Tierce).
8. (Sexte).
9. (None).
10. (Vespers).
11. (Compline).
12. The seven penitential Psalms
13. The Litany.
14. Hours of the Cross.
15. Hours of the Holy Spirit.
16. Office of the Dead.
17. The Fifteen Joys of B. V. M.
18. The seven requests to our Lord.
19. Prayers and Suffrages to various Saints.
20. Several prayers, petitions, and devotions.

This is an unusually full example, but the calendar, the hours, the seven psalms, and the litany, are in almost all the MSS. The buyer must look carefully to see that no miniatures have been cut out; but it is only by counting the leaves in their gatherings that he can make sure. This is often impossible without breaking the binding.

The most valuable "Horae" are those written in England. Some are of the English use (Sarum or York, or whatever it may happen to be), but were written abroad, especially in Normandy, for the English market. These are also valuable, even when imperfect. Look for the page before the commencement of the Hours (No. 4 in the list above), and at the end will be found a line in red,—"Incipit Horae secundum usum Sarum," or otherwise, as the case may be. Missals do not often occur, and are not only very valuable but very difficult to collate, unless furnished with catch-words or signatures. But no Missal is complete without the Canon of the Mass, usually in the middle of the book, and if there are any illuminations throughout the volume, there will be a full page Crucifixion, facing the Canon. Missals of large size and completeness contain—(1) a Calendar; (2) "the proper of the Season;" (3) the ordinary and Canon of the Mass; (4) the Communal of Saints; (5) the proper of Saints and special occasions; (6) the lessons, epistles, and gospels; with (7) some hymns, "proses," and canticles. This is Sir W. Tite's list; but, as he remarks, MS. Missals seldom contain so much. The collector will look for the Canon, which is invariable.

Breviaries run to an immense length, and are seldom illuminated. It would be impossible to give them any kind of collation, and the same may be said of many other kinds of old service-books, and of the chronicles, poems, romances, and herbals, in which medieval literature abounded, and which the collector must judge as best he can.

The name of "missal" is commonly and falsely given to all old service-books by the booksellers, but the collector will easily distinguish one when he sees it, from the notes I have given. In a Sarum Missal, at Alnwick, there is a colophon quoted by my lamented friend Dr. Rock in his "Textile Fabrics." It is appropriate both to the labours of the old scribes and also to those of their modern readers:-

> "Librum Scribendo—Jon Whas Monachus laborabat - Et mane Surgendo—multum corpus macerabat."

It is one of the charms of manuscripts that they illustrate, in their minute way, all the art, and even the social condition, of the period in which they were produced. Apostles, saints, and prophets wear the contemporary costume, and Jonah, when thrown to the hungry whale, wears doublet and trunk hose. The ornaments illustrate the architectural taste of the day. The backgrounds change from diapered patterns to landscapes, as the modern way of looking at nature penetrates the monasteries and reaches the scriptorium where the illuminator sits and refreshes his eyes with the sight of the slender trees and blue distant hills. Printed books have not such resources.

They can only show varieties of type, quaint frontispieces, printers' devices, and fleurons at the heads of chapters. These attractions, and even the engravings of a later day, seem meagre enough compared with the allurements of manuscripts. Yet printed books must almost always make the greater part of a collection, and it may be well to give some rules as to the features that distinguish the productions of the early press. But no amount of "rules" is worth six months' practical experience in bibliography. That experience the amateur, if he is wise, will obtain in a public library, like the British Museum or the Bodleian. Nowhere else is he likely to see much of the earliest of printed books, which very seldom come into the market.

Those of the first German press are so rare that practically they never reach the hands of the ordinary collector. Among them are the famous Psalters printed by Fust and Schoffer, the earliest of which is dated 1457; and the bible known as the Mazarine Bible. Two copies of this last were in the Perkins sale. I well remember the excitement on that occasion. The first copy put up was the best, being printed upon vellum. The bidding commenced at 1000 pounds, and very speedily rose to 2200 pounds, at which point there was a long pause; it then rose in hundreds with very little delay to 3400 pounds, at which it was knocked down to a bookseller.

The second copy was on paper, and there were those present who said it was better than the other, which had a suspicion attaching to it of having been "restored" with a facsimile leaf. The first bid was again 1000 pounds, which the buyer of the previous copy made guineas, and the bidding speedily went up to 2660 pounds, at which price the first bidder paused. A third bidder had stepped in at 1960 pounds, and now, amid breathless excitement, bid 10 pounds more. This he had to do twice before the book was knocked down to him at 2690 pounds.

A scene like this has really very little to do with book-collecting. The beginner must labour hard to distinguish different kinds of printing; he must be able to recognise at a glance even fragments from the press of Caxton. His eye must be accustomed to all the tricks of the trade and others, so that he may tell a facsimile in a moment, or detect a forgery.

But now let us return to the distinctive marks of early printed books. The first is, says M. Rouveyre, -

1. The absence of a separate title-page. It was not till 1476-1480 that the titles of books were printed on separate pages. The next mark is -
2. The absence of capital letters at the beginnings of divisions. For example, in an Aldine Iliad, the fifth book begins thus-it was intended that the open space, occupied by the small epsilon ([epsilon symbol]), should be filled up with a coloured and gilded initial letter by the illuminator. Copies thus decorated are not very common, but the Aldine "Homer" of Francis I., rescued by M. Didot from a rubbish heap in an English cellar, had its due illuminations. In the earliest books the guide to the illuminator, the small printed letter, does not appear, and he often puts in the wrong initial.
3. Irregularity and rudeness of type is a "note" of the primitive printing press, which very early disappeared. Nothing in the history of printing is so remarkable as the beauty of almost its first efforts. Other notes are -
4. The absence of figures at the top of the pages, and of signatures at the foot. The thickness and solidity of the paper, the absence of the printer's name, of the date, and of the name of the town where the press stood, and the abundance of crabbed abbreviations, are all marks, more or less trustworthy, of the antiquity of books.

It must not be supposed that all books published, let us say before 1500, are rare, or deserve the notice of the collector. More than 18,000 works, it has been calculated, left the press before the end of the fifteenth century. All of these cannot possibly be of interest, and many of them that are "rare," are rare precisely because they are uninteresting. They have not been preserved because they were thought not worth preserving. This is a great cause of rarity; but we must not hastily conclude that because a book found no favour in its own age, therefore it has no claim on our attention. A London bookseller tells me that he bought the "remainder" of Keats's "Endymion" for fourpence a copy!

The first edition of "Endymion" is now rare and valued. In trying to mend the binding of an old "Odyssey" lately, I extracted from the vellum covers parts of two copies of a very scarce and curious French dictionary of slang, "Le Jargon, ou Langage de l'Argot Reforme." This treatise may have been valueless, almost, when it appeared, but now it is serviceable to the philologist, and to all who care to try to interpret the slang ballades of the poet Villon. An old pamphlet, an old satire, may hold the key to some historical problem, or throw light on the past of manners and customs. Still, of the earliest printed books, collectors prefer such rare and beautiful ones as the oldest printed Bibles: German, English,—as Taverner's and the Bishop's,—or Hebrew and Greek, or the first editions of the ancient classics, which may contain the readings of MSS. now lost or destroyed.

Talking of early Bibles, let us admire the luck and prudence of a certain Mr. Sandford. He always longed for the first Hebrew Bible, but would offer no fancy price, being convinced that the book would one day fall in his way. His foreboding was fulfilled, and he picked up his treasure for ten shillings in a shop in the Strand. The taste for incunabula, or very early printed books, slumbered in the latter half of the sixteenth, and all the seventeenth century.

It revived with the third jubilee of printing in 1740, and since then has refined itself, and only craves books very early, very important, or works from the press of Caxton, the St. Albans Schoolmaster, or other famous old artists. Enough has been said to show the beginner, always enthusiastic, that all old books are not precious. For further information, the "Biography and Typography of William Caxton," by Mr. Blades (Trubner, London, 1877), may be consulted with profit.

Following the categories into which M. Brunet classifies desirable books in his invaluable manual, we now come to books printed on vellum, and on peculiar papers. At the origin of printing, examples of many books, probably presentation copies, were printed on vellum. There is a vellum copy of the celebrated Florentine first edition of Homer; but it is truly sad to think that the twin volumes, Iliad and Odyssey, have been separated, and pine in distant libraries. Early printed books on vellum often have beautifully illuminated capitals. Dibdin mentions in "Bibliomania" (London, 1811), p. 90, that a M. Van Praet was compiling a catalogue of works printed on vellum, and had collected more than 2000 articles. When hard things are said about Henry VIII., let us remember that this monarch had a few copies of his book against Luther printed on vellum.

The Duke of Marlborough's library possessed twenty-five books on vellum, all printed before 1496. The chapter-house at Padua has a "Catullus" of 1472 on vellum; let Mr. Robinson Ellis think wistfully of that treasure. The notable Count M'Carthy of Toulouse had a wonderful library of books in membranis, including a book much coveted for its rarity, oddity, and the beauty of its illustrations, the "Hypnerotomachia" of Poliphilus (Venice, 1499). Vellum was the favourite "vanity" of Junot, Napoleon's general. For reasons connected with its manufacture, and best not enquired into, the Italian vellum enjoyed the greatest reputation for smooth and silky whiteness. Dibdin calls "our modern books on vellum little short of downright wretched." But the editor of this series could, I think, show examples that would have made Dibdin change his opinion.

Many comparatively expensive papers, large in format, are used in choice editions of books. Whatman papers, Dutch papers, Chinese papers, and even papier verge, have all their admirers. The amateur will soon learn to distinguish these materials. As to books printed on coloured paper—green, blue, yellow, rhubarb-coloured, and the like, they are an offence to the eyes and to the taste. Yet even these have their admirers and collectors, and the great Aldus himself occasionally used azure paper. Under the head of "large paper," perhaps "uncut copies" should be mentioned. Most owners of books have had the edges of the volumes gilded or marbled by the binders.

Thus part of the margin is lost, an offence to the eye of the bibliomaniac, while copies untouched by the binder's shears are rare, and therefore prized. The inconvenience of uncut copies is, that one cannot easily turn over the leaves. But, in the present state of the fashion, a really rare uncut Elzevir may be worth hundreds of pounds, while a cropped example scarcely fetches as many shillings. A set of Shakespeare's quartoes, uncut, would be worth more than a respectable landed estate in Connemara. For these reasons the amateur will do well to have new books of price bound "uncut." It is always easy to have the leaves pared away; but not even the fabled fountain at Argos, in which Hera yearly renewed her maidenhood, could restore margins once clipped away.

So much for books which are chiefly precious for the quantity and quality of the material on which they are printed. Even this rather foolish weakness of the amateur would not be useless if it made our publishers more careful to employ a sound clean hand-made paper, instead of drugged trash, for their more valuable new productions. Indeed, a taste for hand-made paper is coming in, and is part of the revolt against the passion for everything machine-made, which ruined art and handiwork in the years between 1840 and 1870.

The third of M. Brunet's categories of books of prose, includes livres de luxe, and illustrated literature. Every Christmas brings us livres de luxe in plenty, books which are no books, but have gilt and magenta covers, and great staring illustrations. These are regarded as drawing-room ornaments by people who never read. It is scarcely necessary to warn the collector against these gaudy baits of unregulated Christmas generosity. All ages have not produced quite such garish livres de luxe as ours. But, on the whole, a book brought out merely for the sake of display, is generally a book ill "got up," and not worth reading.

Moreover, it is generally a folio, or quarto, so large that he who tries to read it must support it on a kind of scaffolding. In the class of illustrated books two sorts are at present most in demand. The ancient woodcuts and engravings, often the work of artists like Holbein and Durer, can never lose their interest. Among old illustrated books, the most famous, and one of the rarest, is the "Hypnerotomachia Poliphili," "wherein all human matters are proved to be no more than a dream." This is an allegorical romance, published in 1499, for Francesco Colonna, by Aldus Manucius. Poliam Frater Franciscus Columna peramavit. "Brother Francesco Colonna dearly loved Polia," is the inscription and device of this romance. Poor Francesco, of the order of preachers, disguised in this strange work his passion for a lady of uncertain name. Here is a translation of the passage in which the lady describes the beginning of his affection. "I was standing, as is the manner of women young and fair, at the window, or rather on the balcony, of my palace.

My yellow hair, the charm of maidens, was floating round my shining shoulders. My locks were steeped in unguents that made them glitter like threads of gold, and they were slowly drying in the rays of the burning sun. A handmaid, happy in her task, was drawing a comb through my tresses, and surely these of Andromeda seemed not more lovely to Perseus, nor to Lucius the locks of Photis. On a sudden, Poliphilus beheld me, and could not withdraw from me his glances of fire, and even in that moment a ray of the sun of love was kindled in his heart." The fragment is itself a picture from the world of the Renaissance. We watch the blonde, learned lady, dreaming of Perseus, and Lucius, Greek lovers of old time, while the sun gilds her yellow hair, and the young monk, passing below, sees and loves, and "falls into the deep waters of desire."

The lover is no less learned than the lady, and there is a great deal of amorous archaeology in his account of his voyage to Cythera. As to the designs in wood, quaint in their vigorous effort to be classical, they have been attributed to Mantegna, to Bellini, and other artists. Jean Cousin is said to have executed the imitations, in the Paris editions of 1546, 1556, and 1561.

The "Hypnerotomachia" seems to deserve notice, because it is the very type of the books that are dear to collectors, as distinct from the books that, in any shape, are for ever valuable to the world. A cheap Tauchnitz copy of the Iliad and Odyssey, or a Globe Shakespeare, are, from the point of view of literature, worth a wilderness of "Hypnerotomachiae." But a clean copy of the "Hypnerotomachia," especially on VELLUM, is one of the jewels of bibliography. It has all the right qualities; it is very rare, it is very beautiful as a work of art, it is curious and even bizarre, it is the record of a strange time, and a strange passion; it is a relic, lastly, of its printer, the great and good Aldus Manutius. Next to the old woodcuts and engravings, executed in times when artists were versatile and did not disdain even to draw a bookplate (as Durer did for Pirckheimer), the designs of the French "little masters," are at present in most demand. The book illustrations of the seventeenth century are curious enough, and invaluable as authorities on manners and costume. But the attitudes of the figures are too often stiff and ungainly; while the composition is frequently left to chance. England could show nothing much better than Ogilby's translations of Homer, illustrated with big florid engravings in sham antique style.

The years between 1730 and 1820, saw the French "little masters" in their perfection. The dress of the middle of the eighteenth century, of the age of Watteau, was precisely suited to the gay and graceful pencils of Gravelot, Moreau, Eisen, Boucher, Cochin, Marillier, and Choffard. To understand their merits, and the limits of their art, it is enough to glance through a series of the designs for Voltaire, Corneille, or Moliere. The drawings of society are almost invariably dainty and pleasing, the serious scenes of tragedy leave the spectator quite unmoved. Thus it is but natural that these artists should have shone most in the illustration of airy trifles like Dorat's "Baisers," or tales like Manon Lescaut, or in designing tailpieces for translations of the Greek idyllic poets, such as Moschus and Bion. In some of his illustrations of books, especially, perhaps, in the designs for "La Physiologie de Gout" (Jouaust, Paris, 1879), M. Lalauze has shown himself the worthy rival of Eisen and Cochin. Perhaps it is unnecessary to add that the beauty and value of all such engravings depends almost entirely on their "state." The earlier proofs are much more brilliant than those drawn later, and etchings on fine papers are justly preferred.

For example, M. Lalauze's engravings on "Whatman paper," have a beauty which could scarcely be guessed by people who have only seen specimens on "papier verge." Every collector of the old French vignettes, should possess himself of the "Guide de l'amateur," by M. Henry Cohen (Rouquette, Paris, 1880). Among English illustrated books, various tastes prefer the imaginative works of William Blake, the etchings of Cruikshank, and the woodcuts of Bewick. The whole of the book of this sketch is devoted, by Mr. Austin Dobson, to the topic of English illustrated books. Here it may be said, in passing, that an early copy of William Blake's "Songs of Innocence," written, illustrated, printed, coloured, and boarded by the author's own hand, is one of the most charming objects that a bibliophile can hope to possess.

The verses of Blake, in a framework of birds, and flowers, and plumes, all softly and magically tinted, seem like some book out of King Oberon's library in fairyland, rather than the productions of a mortal press. The pictures in Blake's "prophetic books," and even his illustrations to "Job," show an imagination more heavily weighted by the technical difficulties of drawing.

The next class of rare books is composed of works from the famous presses of the Aldi and the Elzevirs. Other presses have, perhaps, done work as good, but Estienne, the Giunta, and Plantin, are comparatively neglected, while the taste for the performances of Baskerville and Foulis is not very eager. A safe judgement about Aldines and Elzevirs is the gift of years and of long experience. In this place it is only possible to say a few words on a wide subject. The founder of the Aldine press, Aldus Pius Manutius, was born about 1450, and died at Venice in 1514. He was a man of careful and profound learning, and was deeply interested in Greek studies, then encouraged by the arrival in Italy of many educated Greeks and Cretans. Only four Greek authors had as yet been printed in Italy, when (1495) Aldus established his press at Venice.

Theocritus, Homer, AEsop, and Isocrates, probably in very limited editions, were in the hands of students. The purpose of Aldus was to put Greek and Latin works, beautifully printed in a convenient shape, within the reach of all the world. His reform was the introduction of books at once cheap, studiously correct, and convenient in actual use. It was in 1498 that he first adopted the small octavo size, and in his "Virgil" of 1501, he introduced the type called Aldine or Italic. The letters were united as in writing, and the type is said to have been cut by Francesco da Bologna, better known as Francia, in imitation of the hand of Petrarch. For full information about Aldus and his descendants and successors, the work of M. Firmin Didot, ("Alde Manuce et l'Hellenisme a Venise: Paris 1875)," and the Aldine annals of Renouard, must be consulted. These two works are necessary to the collector, who will otherwise be deceived by the misleading assertions of the booksellers. As a rule, the volumes published in the lifetime of Aldus Manutius are the most esteemed, and of these the Aristotle, the first Homer, the Virgil, and the Ovid, are perhaps most in demand. The earlier Aldines are consulted almost as studiously as MSS. by modern editors of the classics.

Just as the house of Aldus waned and expired, that of the great Dutch printers, the Elzevirs, began obscurely enough at Leyden in 1583. The Elzevirs were not, like Aldus, ripe scholars and men of devotion to learning. Aldus laboured for the love of noble studies; the Elzevirs were acute, and too often "smart" men of business. The founder of the family was Louis (born at Louvain, 1540, died 1617). But it was in the second and third generations that Bonaventura and Abraham Elzevir began to publish at Leyden, their editions in small duodecimo. Like Aldus, these Elzevirs aimed at producing books at once handy, cheap, correct, and beautiful in execution.

Their adventure was a complete success. The Elzevirs did not, like Aldus, surround themselves with the most learned scholars of their time. Their famous literary adviser, Heinsius, was full of literary jealousies, and kept students of his own calibre at a distance. The classical editions of the Elzevirs, beautiful, but too small in type for modern eyes, are anything but exquisitely correct. Their editions of the contemporary. French authors, now classics themselves, are lovely examples of skill in practical enterprise. The Elzevirs treated the French authors much as American publishers treat Englishmen. They stole right and left, but no one complained much in these times of slack copyright; and, at all events, the piratic larcenous publications of the Dutch printers were pretty, and so far satisfactory. They themselves, in turn, were the victims of fraudulent and untradesmanlike imitations. It is for this, among other reasons, that the collector of Elzevirs must make M. Willems's book ("Les Elzevier," Brussels and Paris, 1880) his constant study. Differences so minute that they escape the unpractised eye, denote editions of most various value. In Elzevirs a line's breadth of margin is often worth a hundred pounds, and a misprint is quoted at no less a sum.

The fantastic caprice of bibliophiles has revelled in the bibliography of these Dutch editions. They are at present very scarce in England, where a change in fashion some years ago had made them common enough. No Elzevir is valuable unless it be clean and large in the margins. When these conditions are satisfied the question of rarity comes in, and Remy Belleau's Macaronic poem, or "Le Pastissier Francais," may rise to the price of four or five hundred pounds. A Rabelais, Moliere, or Corneille, of a "good" edition, is now more in request than the once adored "Imitatio Christi" (dateless), or the "Virgil"' of 1646, which is full of gross errors of the press, but is esteemed for red characters in the letter to Augustus, and another passage at page 92. The ordinary marks of the Elzevirs were the sphere, the old hermit, the Athena, the eagle, and the burning faggot. But all little old books marked with spheres are not Elzevirs, as many booksellers suppose.

Other printers also stole the designs for the tops of chapters, the Aegipan, the Siren, the head of Medusa, the crossed sceptres, and the rest. In some cases the Elzevirs published their books, especially when they were piracies, anonymously. When they published for the Jansenists, they allowed their clients to put fantastic pseudonyms on the title pages. But, except in four cases, they had only two pseudonyms used on the titles of books published by and for themselves. These disguises are "Jean Sambix" for Jean and Daniel Elzevir, at Leyden, and for the Elzevirs of

Amsterdam, "Jacques le Jeune." The last of the great representatives of the house, Daniel, died at Amsterdam, 1680. Abrahaın, an unworthy scion, struggled on at Leyden till 1712. The family still prospers, but no longer prints, in Holland. It is common to add duodecimos of Foppens, Wolfgang, and other printers, to the collections of the Elzevirs. The books of Wolfgang have the sign of the fox robbing a wild bee's nest, with the motto Quaerendo.

Curious and singular books are the next in our classification. The category is too large. The books that be "curious" (not in the booksellers' sense of "prurient" and "disgusting,") are innumerable. All suppressed and condemned books, from "Les Fleurs du Mal" to Vanini's "Amphitheatrum," or the English translation of Bruno's "Spaccia della Bestia Trionfante," are more or less rare, and more or less curious. Wild books, like William Postel's "Three Marvellous Triumphs of Women," are "curious." Freakish books, like macaronic poetry, written in a medley of languages, are curious. Books from private presses are singular.

The old English poets and satirists turned out many a book curious to the last degree, and priced at a fantastic value. Such are "Jordan's Jewels of Ingenuity," "Micro-cynicon, six Snarling Satyres" (1599), and the "Treatise made of a Galaunt," printed by Wynkyn de Worde, and found pasted into the fly-leaf, on the oak-board binding of an imperfect volume of Pynson's "Statutes." All our early English poems and miscellanies are curious; and, as relics of delightful singers, are most charming possessions. Such are the "Songes and Sonnettes of Surrey" (1557), the "Paradyce of daynty Deuices" (1576), the "Small Handful of Fragrant Flowers," and "The Handful of Dainty Delights, gathered out of the lovely Garden of Sacred Scripture, fit for any worshipful Gentlewoman to smell unto," (1584). "The Teares of Ireland" (1642), are said, though one would not expect it, to be "extremely rare," and, therefore, precious. But there is no end to the list of such desirable rarities. If we add to them all books coveted as early editions, and, therefore, as relics of great writers, Bunyan, Shakespeare, Milton, Sterne, Walton, and the rest, we might easily fill a book with remarks on this topic alone.

The collection of such editions is the most respectable, the most useful, and, alas, the most expensive of the amateur's pursuits. It is curious enough that the early editions of Swift, Scott, and Byron, are little sought for, if not wholly neglected; while early copies of Shelley, Tennyson, and Keats, have a great price set on their heads. The quartoes of Shakespeare, like first editions of Racine, are out of the reach of any but very opulent purchasers, or unusually lucky, fortunate book-hunters. Before leaving the topic of books which derive their value from the taste and fantasy of collectors, it must be remarked that, in this matter, the fashion of the world changes. Dr. Dibdin lamented, seventy years ago, the waning respect paid to certain editions of the classics. He would find that things have become worse now, and modern German editions, on execrable paper, have supplanted his old favourites.

Fifty years ago, M. Brunet expressed his contempt for the designs of Boucher; now they are at the top of the fashion. The study of old booksellers' catalogues is full of instruction as to the changes of caprice. The collection of Dr. Rawlinson was sold in 1756. "The Vision of Pierce Plowman" (1561), and the "Creede of Pierce Plowman" (1553), brought between them no more than three shillings and sixpence. Eleven shillings were paid for the "Boke of Chivalrie" by Caxton. The "Boke of St. Albans," by Wynkyn de Worde, cost 1 pounds: 1s., and this was the highest sum paid for any one of two hundred rare pieces of early English literature. In 1764, a copy of the "Hypnerotomachia" was sold for two shillings, "A Pettie Pallace of Pettie his Pleasures," (ah, what a thought for the amateur!) went for three shillings, while "Palmerin of England" (1602), attained no more than the paltry sum of fourteen shillings. When Osborne sold the Harley collection, the scarcest old English books fetched but three or four shillings. If the wandering Jew had been a collector in the last century he might have turned a pretty profit by selling his old English books in this age of ours. In old French, too, Ahasuerus would have done a good stroke of business, for the prices brought by old Villons, Romances of the Rose, "Les Marguerites de Marguerite," and so forth, at the M'Carthy sale, were truly pitiable. A hundred years hence the original editions of Thackeray, or of Miss Greenaway's Christmas books, or "Modern Painters," may be the ruling passion, and Aldines and Elzevirs, black letter and French vignettes may all be despised.

A book which is commonplace in our century is curious in the next, and disregarded in that which follows. Old books of a heretical character were treasures once, rare unholy possessions. Now we have seen so many heretics that the world is indifferent to the audacities of Bruno, and the veiled impieties of Vanini. The last of our categories of books much sought by the collector includes all volumes valued for their ancient bindings, for the mark and stamp of famous amateurs.

The French, who have supplied the world with so many eminent binders,—as Eve, Padeloup, Duseuil, Le Gascon, Derome, Simier, Bozerian, Thouvenin, Trautz-Bauzonnet, and Lortic—are the chief patrons of books in historical bindings. In England an historical binding, a book of Laud's, or James's, or Garrick's, or even of Queen Elizabeth's, does not seem to derive much added charm from its associations. But, in France, peculiar bindings are now the objects most in demand among collectors. The series of books thus rendered precious begins with those of Maioli and of Grolier (1479-1565), remarkable for their mottoes and the geometrical patterns on the covers. Then comes De Thou (who had three sets of arms), with his blazon, the bees stamped on the morocco.

The volumes of Marguerite of Angouleme are sprinkled with golden daisies. Diane de Poictiers had her crescents and her bow, and the initial of her royal lover was intertwined with her own. The three daughters of Louis XV. had each their favourite colour, and their books wear liveries of citron, red, and olive morocco. The Abbe Cotin, the original of Moliere's Trissotin, stamped his books with intertwined C's. Henri III. preferred religious emblems, and sepulchral mottoes—skulls, crossbones, tears, and the insignia of the Passion. Mort m'est vie is a favourite device of the effeminate and voluptuous Prince. Moliere himself was a collector, il n'es pas de bouquin qui s'echappe de ses mains,—"never an old book escapes him," says the author of "La Guerre Comique," the last of the pamphlets which flew from side to side in the great literary squabble about "L'Ecole des Femmes." M. Soulie has found a rough catalogue of Moliere's library, but the books, except a little Elzevir, have disappeared. Madame de Maintenon was fond of bindings. Mr. Toovey possesses a copy of a devotional work in red morocco, tooled and gilt, which she presented to a friendly abbess. The books at Saint-Cyr were stamped with a crowned cross, besprent with fleurs-de-lys. The books of the later collectors—Longepierre, the translator of Bion and Moschus; D'Hoym the diplomatist; McCarthy, and La Valliere, are all valued at a rate which seems fair game for satire.

Among the most interesting bibliophiles of the eighteenth century is Madame Du Barry. In 1771, this notorious beauty could scarcely read or write. She had rooms, however, in the Chateau de Versailles, thanks to the kindness of a monarch who admired those native qualities which education may polish, but which it can never confer. At Versailles, Madame Du Barry heard of the literary genius of Madame de Pompadour. The Pompadour was a person of taste. Her large library of some four thousand works of the lightest sort of light literature was bound by Biziaux. Mr. Toovey possesses the Brantome of this dame galante. Madame herself had published etchings by her own fair hands; and to hear of these things excited the emulation of Madame Du Barry. She might not be CLEVER, but she could have a library like another, if libraries were in fashion. One day Madame Du Barry astonished the Court by announcing that her collection of books would presently arrive at Versailles. Meantime she took counsel with a bookseller, who bought up examples of all the cheap "remainders," as they are called in the trade, that he could lay his hands upon. The whole assortment, about one thousand volumes in all, was hastily bound in rose morocco, elegantly gilt, and stamped with the arms of the noble house of Du Barry. The bill which Madame Du Barry owed her enterprising agent is still in existence. The thousand volumes cost about three francs each; the binding (extremely cheap) came to nearly as much. The amusing thing is that the bookseller, in the catalogue which he sent with the improvised library, marked the books which Madame Du Barry possessed BEFORE her large order was so punctually executed. There were two "Memoires de Du Barry," an old newspaper, two or three plays, and "L'Historie Amoureuse de Pierre le Long." Louis XV. observed with pride that, though Madame Pompadour had possessed a larger library, that of Madame Du Barry was the better selected. Thanks to her new collection, the lady learned to read with fluency, but she never overcame the difficulties of spelling.

A lady collector who loved books not very well perhaps, but certainly not wisely, was the unhappy Marie Antoinette. The controversy in France about the private character of the Queen has been as acrimonious as the Scotch discussion about Mary Stuart. Evidence, good and bad, letters as apocryphal as the letters of the famous "casket," have been produced on both sides. A few years ago, under the Empire, M. Louis Lacour found a manuscript catalogue of the books in the Queen's boudoir. They were all novels of the flimsiest sort,—"L'Amitie Dangereuse," "Les Suites d'un Moment d'Erreur," and even the stories of Louvet and of Retif de la Bretonne. These volumes all bore the letters "C. T." (Chateau de Trianon), and during the Revolution they were scattered among the various public libraries of Paris. The Queen's more important library was at the Tuileries, but at Versailles she had only three books, as the commissioners of the Convention found, when they made an inventory of the property of la fẹmme Capet. Among the three was the "Gerusalemme Liberata," printed, with eighty exquisite designs by Cochin, at the expense of "Monsieur," afterwards Louis XVIII. Books with the arms of Marie Antoinette are very rare in private collections; in sales they are as much sought after as those of Madame Du Barry.

With these illustrations of the kind of interest that belongs to books of old collectors, we may close this chapter. The reader has before him a list, with examples, of the kinds of books at present most in vogue among amateurs. He must judge for himself whether he will follow the fashion, by aid either of a long purse or of patient research, or whether he will find out new paths for himself. A scholar is rarely a rich man. He cannot compete with plutocrats who buy by deputy. But, if he pursues the works he really needs, he may make a valuable collection. He cannot go far wrong while he brings together the books that he finds most congenial to his own taste and most useful to his own studies. Here, then, in the words of the old "sentiment," I bid him farewell, and wish "success to his inclinations, provided they are virtuous." There is a set of collectors, alas! whose inclinations are not virtuous. The most famous of them, a Frenchman, observed that his own collection of bad books was unique. That of an English rival, he admitted, was respectable,—"mais milord se livre a des autres preoccupations!" He thought a collector's whole heart should be with his treasures. En bouquinant se trouve grand soulas. Soubent m'en vay musant, a petis pas, Au long des quais, pour flairer maint bieux livre. Des Elzevier la Sphere me rend yure, Et la Sirene aussi m'esmeut. Grand cas Fais-je d'Estienne, Aide, ou Dolet. Mais Ias! Le vieux Caxton ne se rencontre pas, Plus qu' agneau d'or parmi jetons de cuivre, En bouquinant! Pour tout plaisir que l'on goute icy-bas La Grace a Dieu. Mieux vaut, sans altercas, Chasser bouquin: Nul mal n'en peult s'ensuivre. Dr sus au livre: il est le grand appas. Clair est le ciel. Amis, qui veut me suivre En bouquinant?

15

Preservation and Conservation of Library Material

Preservation is a branch of library and information science concerned with maintaining or restoring access to artifacts, documents and records through the study, diagnosis, treatment and prevention of decay and damage. It should be distinguished from conservation, which refers to the treatment and repair of individual items to slow decay or restore them to a usable state. Conservation is occasionally used interchangeably with preservation, particularly outside the professional literature.

The Background

Antecedents

Preservation as a formal profession in libraries and archives dates from the twentieth century, but its philosophy and practice has roots in many earlier traditions. In many ancient societies, appeals to heavenly protectors were used to preserve books, scrolls and manuscripts from insects, fire and decay:

- To the ancient Egyptians, the scarab or dung beetle was a protector of written products. The scarab was also used as a holder or medium for personal name seals. A figurine of a scarab would be carved out of stone, and then on the smooth stomach of the scarab, the engraving of a seal was made. Later, this oval image was used for the representation of the cartouche, or name/title seals.
- In ancient Babylon, Nabu is the heavenly patron of books and protector of clay tablets. Nabu is the Babylonian god of wisdom and writing, and is the patron of the scribes, librarians and archivists. Nabu's symbols are the clay writing tablet with the cuneiform writing stylus. He usually wears a horned cap, and often stands with his hands clasped together, in the ancient gesture of priesthood. Nabu engraves the destiny of each person,

as the Gods have decided, on the tablets of sacred record. Thus, Nabu has the power to increase or diminish, at will, the length of human life. The image of Nabu is also one of the images on the brass doors designed by Lee Lawrie, entitled, "A History of the Written Word," on the John Adams Building of the Library of Congress. The figures on the doors also include: Thoth, an Egyptian god; Ts'ang Chieh or Cangjie, the Chinese patron of writing; Nabu, an Akkadian god; Brahma, the Indian god; Cadmus, the Greek sower of dragon's teeth; and Tahmurath or Tahmuras, a hero of the ancient Persians.

- In Hindu beliefs, Ganesh (Ganesvha or Ganapati) is the elephant-headed god of learning and new enterprises. As the god of wisdom, he knows all. Since he has the head of an elephant, he also has the reputed memory of the elephant, and thus does not forget anything. His statue is placed over the doors of and entrances of many buildings in India and Sri Lanka, including most libraries. Ganesh is the scribe who wrote the Mahabharata ("Great Epic of the Bharata Dynasty") from Vyasa's dictation. Ganesh is credited with inventing the Sanskrit alphabet, and he broke off his right tusk to make the first pen. As the inventor of the alphabet, as a scribe, and as a keeper of wisdom and knowledge, Ganesh is credited as a patron of libraries, librarians and book sellers and buyers.
- In Arabic and other eastern societies, sometimes a traditional method to protect books and scrolls was a metaphysical appeal to "Kabi: Kaj," the "King of the Cockroaches." By appealing to the King to protect a manuscript, cockroaches of less nobility (or lesser insects) would refrain from intruding on documents which could be eaten by the King only. Since many manuscripts were made with fish-glue, starch-paste, leather and other tasty substances, insect appetites were a constant and never ending problem to Arabic books and scrolls. A similar technique from Syria was to name the first and last page of a document or manuscript "The Page of the King of the Cockroaches", in the hope that the Cockroach King will control all other insects. Translated appeals include "O Kabi: kaj, save the paper!", "O Kabi: kaj, save this book from the worms!" and "O Kabi: kaj, do not eat this paper!" "In Maghribi manuscripts, the word appears in its evidently corrupt form, "Kaykataj" and is clearly used as a talisman... and mentions, after a certain Muhammad al-Samiri, that when one writes "Kaytataj" on the first and last folio of the book, one can be sure that worms will not attack it."
- There are three saints in the Christian church that are closely associated with libraries as patrons. Saint Lawrence is an early saint of the church, who seems to be more respected in European libraries than those in the Western Hemisphere. Saint Jerome is most often considered the patron saint of libraries in the US and Canada. Saint Catharine of Alexandria or Catherine of Alexandria is most often considered the patroness of libraries in the Orthodox tradition.
- In some Christian monasteries, prayers and curses were placed at the end of books to prevent theft, or to damn the thieves. Frequently called a "book curse", these were placed in the book to deter theft. "For him that stealth a book from this library, may it change into a serpent in his hand and rend him. May he be struck with palsy, and all his members blasted. May bookworms gnaw his entrails, in token of the worm which dieth not. And when at last he goeth to his final perdition, let the flames of Hell consume him forever and aye." Another example of a Christian curse is this medieval jingle placed at the end of a work: "Christ's curse upon the crook who takes away this book." Or in the Latin: "Sit maledictuus per Christum, Qui librum subraxerit istum."

- The ancient Chinese god Wei T'O is the patron god of libraries and books. Many examples of appeals to Wei T'O can be found in Chinese manuscripts dated five hundred or more years ago. Sometimes the last page of manuscripts would be dedicated to him, in a manner very similar to the Arabic prayer of protection to the King of the Cockroaches. "Wei T'o, an ancient Chinese god, protects books against destruction from fire, worms and insects, and robbers, big or small." Wei T'O is especially invoked for the protection of books and libraries against fire. Since the modern books are suffering from acid decomposition (slow fires), Wei T'O is especially relevant to modern librarianship. A modern product to deacidify paper is named in his honour.
- Sri Lankan symbols or images of the Sinhalese "Fire Demons" are hung in the corners of libraries and other buildings to appease the incendiary demons and to avert fire, lightning and cataclysm, according to Sinhalese mythology. The fire demons from Ceylon have no body, and show only a grinning face surrounded by flames. The expressions shown on the figures are of delirious glee or insane pleasure, as these demons eventually burn themselves up, leaving only charcoal and ashes and dust. These demons especially appreciate large amounts of paper such as books or magazines, as they are ready fuel for their infernal fires. Needless to say, these fire demons are hung up around banks and currency exchange offices as well, to avert catastrophe to other paper products. Since fire and acid decomposition (also known as "slow fires") are a special problem for libraries because of the concentration of paper products, the "Fire Demons" are also included when used to assuage these destroyers of libraries and books.
- The Aztec and Mayan Indians of Latin America also had deities concerned with libraries. The major god, Quetzalcoatl, is credited with the discoveries of the arts, the calendar, and of writing. A single feather or plume at the beginning or at the end of a document or stone carving would indicate a dedication to the "Feathered Serpent." This symbol degenerated over time to a single fringed line.

In library science, preservation is treated as an active and intentional process, as opposed to the passive sense of preservation that might be applied to palaeontological or archaeological finds. The survival of these items is a matter of chance, from an information science perspective, while the preservation of them after their discovery is a matter of intentional activity.

Human record-keeping arguably dates back to the cave painting boom of the upper palaeolithic, some 32,000-40,000 years ago. More direct antecedents are the writing systems that developed in the 4th millennium BC. Written record keeping and information sharing practices, along with oral tradition, sustain and transmit information from one group to another. This level of preservation has been supplemented over the last century with the professional practice of preservation and conservation in the cultural heritage community:

1. Oral tradition or oral culture, the transmission of information from one generation to the next without a writing system.
2. Antiquarian practices, including scribal practice, burial practice, the libraries at Pergamum, Alexandria and other ancient archives.
3. Medieval practices, including the scriptorium and relic collection.
4. Renaissance and the changing conception of artists and works of art.
5. Enlightenment and the Encyclopaedists.
6. Romantic movement's imperative to preserve.

Significant Events

- *1933:* William Barrow introduces the field of conservation to paper deacidification when he publishes a paper on the acid paper problem. In later studies, Barrow tested paper from American books made between 1900 and 1949 and learned that after forty years the books had lost on average 96 per cent of their original strength; after less than ten years, they had already lost 64 per cent. Barrow determined that this rapid deterioration was not the direct result of using wood-pulp fibres, since rag papers of this period were also aging rapidly, but rather due to the residual sulphuric acid produced in both rag and wood pulp papers. Manufacturing methods used after 1870 employed sulphuric acid for sizing and bleaching the paper. Earlier papermaking methods left the final product only mildly alkaline or even neutral. Such paper has maintained its strength for 300 to 800 years, despite sulphur dioxide and other air pollutants. Barrow's 1933 article on the fragile state of wood pulp paper predicted the life expectancy, or "LE," of this paper was approximately 40–50 years. At that point the paper would begin to show signs of natural decay, and he concluded that research for a new media on which to write and print was needed.
- *1966:* The Flood of the River Arno in Florence, Italy damaged or destroyed millions of rare books and led to the development of restoration laboratories and new methods in conservation. Instrumental in this process was conservationist Peter Waters, who led a group of volunteers, called "mud angels", in restoring thousands of books and papers. This event awakened many historians, librarians, and other professionals to the importance of having a preservation plan. Many consider this flood to be one of the worst disasters since the burning of the Alexandria Library in ancient Rome. It spurred a resurgence in the profession of preservation and conservation worldwide.
- *1987:* Terry Saunders releases the film Slow Fires: On the Preservation of the Human Record which examines paper embrittlement resulting from acid decay.
- *1989:* March 7 ["Commitment Day"] Major US print publishers convene at NYPL to endorse a community-wide commitment to utilising ISO 9706 certified permanent durable paper in order to combat the acid paper epidemic.

Significant People in the History of Preservation

- William Barrow (1904–1967) was an American chemist and paper conservator, and a pioneer of library and archives conservation. He introduced the field of conservation to paper deacidification through alkalisation.
- Paul N. Banks (1934–2000) was Conservator and Head of the Conservation Department at the Newberry Library from 1964 to 1981, and published regularly on bookbinding, book and paper conservation, and problems related to conservation. He designed and implemented a curriculum for Columbia University's School of Library Science that dealt directly with preservation training.
- Pamela Darling, author and historian, was Preservation Specialist for the Association of Research Libraries. Her works include materials to aid libraries in establishing their own comprehensive preservation programmes.
- Carolyn Harris worked as head of Columbia University Libraries' Preservation Division from 1981 until 1987, where she worked closely with Paul Banks. She published extensive research throughout her career, especially dealing with mass deacidification of wood-pulp paper.

- Peter Waters, former Conservation Officer at the Library of Congress in Washington, DC, worked in the areas of disaster recovery and preparedness, and the salvaging of water-damaged paper goods.
- Nicholson Baker is a contemporary American novelist and author of Double Fold, a criticism of libraries' destruction of paper-based media.
- Patricia Battin, as the first President of the Commission on Preservation and Access, worked to organise a national campaign both for the use of alkaline paper in publishing companies and for a national programme of preservation microfilming.
- John F. Dean, Preservation and Conservation Librarian at Cornell University, has made contributions towards improving preservation efforts in developing countries. Specifically, Dean has created online tutorials for library conservation and preservation in South East Asia and Iraq and the Middle East.

The Paul Banks and Carolyn Harris Preservation Award for outstanding preservation specialists in library and archival science, is given annually by the Association for Library Collections and Technical Services, a subdivision of the American Library Association. It is awarded in recognition of professional preservation specialists who have made significant contributions to the field. Banks/Harris award winners:

- Sally Buchanan 2001 - Buchanan received the award in recognition of years of service in the preservation field while an associate professor at the University of Pittsburgh School of Information Science.
- Ellen R. McCrady 2002-2008 - From 1975 to 2004, McCrady edited and published the "Abbey Newsletter", covering important information for preservation professionals. She also conducted research regarding papermaking and acid testing. From 1988-1997 she published the Alkaline Paper Advocate.
- John F. Dean 2003 - Since its inception in 1985, Dean has led the Department of Preservation and Conservation at Cornell University.
- Jan Merrill-Oldham 2004 - As the Malloy-Rabinowitz Preservation Librarian at Harvard University, Merrill-Oldham oversees the Weissman Preservation Centre and the Preservation and Imaging Department.
- Paul Conway 2005 - Conway is an associate professor in the University of Michigan School of Information and has worked with Yale and Duke University after beginning his career at the Gerald R. Ford Presidential Library. His research and educational work focuses primarily on digital preservation and electronic media.
- Gary Frost 2006 - Currently the University Conservator at the University of Iowa Libraries, Frost has been an educator and practitioner in the field of library preservation for almost 40 years. Frost is actively involved in library preservation and maintains an online blog at Futureofthebook.com.
- Walter Henry 2007 - Henry, a conservator at the Stanford University Libraries and Academic Information Resources, is the creator of Conservation OnLine and the Conservation DistList.
- Janet Gertz 2008 - Director for Preservation, Columbia University Libraries has been chair of ALCTS' Preservation and Reformatting Section (PARS). She has taught, spoken and published widely on topics ranging from traditional library preservation, disaster preparedness, commercial binding, and preservation microfilming to digital preservation,

audio preservation, preservation metadata and large-scale mass digitisation. She is an adjunct faculty member in the Palmer School of Library and Information Science, Long Island University, and has been a guest lecturer at Rutgers' Preservation Institute and at Queen's College.

- Barclay Ogden 2009.
- Michele Cloonan 2010.
- Roberta Pilette 2011.
- Julie Allen Page 2012.

Practices

Care and Handling

1. Exhibitions.
2. Circulating collections.
3. Special collections.

Environmental Controls

Environmental controls are necessary to facilitate the preservation of organic library materials and are especially important to monitor in rare and special collections. Key environmental factors to watch include temperature, relative humidity, pests, pollutants, and light exposure. In general, the lower the temperature is, the better it is for the collection. However, since books and other materials are often housed in areas with people, a compromise must be struck to accommodate human comfort. A reasonable temperature to accomplish both goals is 65-68°F however, if possible, film and photography collections should be kept in a segregated area at 55°F.

Books and other materials take up and give off moisture making them sensitive to relative humidity. Very high humidity encourages mould growth and insect infestations. Low humidity causes materials to lose their flexibility. Fluctuations in relative humidity are more damaging than a constant humidity in the middle or low range. Generally, the relative humidity should be between 30-50 per cent with as little variation as possible, however recommendations on specific levels to maintain vary depending on the type of material, i.e., paper-based, film, etc. A specialised dew point calculator for book preservation is available.

Pests, such as insects and vermin, eat and destroy paper and the adhesive that secures book bindings. Food and drink in libraries, archives, and museums can increase the attraction of pests. An Integrated Pest Management system is one way to control pests in libraries. Particulate and gaseous pollutants, such as soot, ozone, sulphur dioxide, oxides of nitrogen, can cause dust, soiling, and irreversible molecular damage to materials. Pollutants are exceedingly small and not easily detectable or removable. A special filtration system in the building's HVAC is a helpful defence.

Exposure to light also has a significant effect on library materials. It is not only the light visible to humans that can cause damage, but also ultraviolet light and infrared radiation. Measured in lux or the amount of lumens/m2, the generally accepted level of illumination with sensitive materials is limited to 50 lux per day. Materials receiving more lux than recommended can be placed in dark storage periodically to prolong the original appearance of the object.

Recent concerns about the impact of climate change on the management of cultural heritage objects as well as the historic environment has prompted research efforts to investigate alternative climate control methods and strategies that include the implementation of alternative climate control systems to replace or supplement traditional high-energy consuming HVAC systems as well as the introduction of passive preservation techniques. Rather than maintaining a flat line, consistent 24/7 condition for a collection's environment, fluctuation can occur within acceptable limits to create a preservation environment while also thinking of energy efficiency and taking advantage of the outside environment.

Bound materials are sensitive to rapid temperature or humidity cycling due to differential expansion of the binding and pages, which may cause the binding to crack and/or the pages to warp. Changes in temperature and humidity should be done slowly so as to minimise the difference in expansion rates. However, an accelerated aging study on the effects of fluctuating temperature and humidity on paper colour and strength showed no evidence that cycling of one temperature to another or one RH to another caused a different mechanism of decay.

Decision-making and Criteria

Making a proper decision is an important factor before starting preservation practices. Decision-making for preservation should be made considering significance and value of materials. Significance is considered to have two major components: importance and quality. "Importance" relates to the collection's role as a record, and "quality" covers comprehensiveness, depth, uniqueness, authenticity and reputation of the collection. Moreover, analysing the significance of materials can be used to uncover more about their meaning. Assessment of significance can also aid in documenting the provenance and context to argue the case for grant funding for the object and collection.

Forms of significance can be historically, culturally, socially, or spiritually significant. In the preservation context, libraries and archives make decisions in different ways. In libraries, decision-making likely targets existing holding materials, whereas in archives, decisions for preservation are often made when they acquire materials. Therefore, different criteria might be needed on different occasions. In general, for archive criteria, the points include: 1) the characteristics of a record (purpose, creator, etc.); 2) the quality of the information in the record; 3) the record in context (part of a series or not); 4) potential use and possible limitations; and 5) the cost against the benefits from its existence. For library criteria, the following are evidence of significance: 1) uniqueness, 2) irreplaceability, 3) high level of impact – over time or place, 4) high level of influence, 5) representation of a type, and 6) comparative value (rarity, completeness, integrity relative to others of its kind).

Selection

Since the 1970s, the Northeast Document Conservation Centre has stated that the study of understanding the needs of the library is inherently important to the survival of archives and libraries. In order for the preservation of a collection to survive for a long time it is important that a systematic preservation plan is in place. The first step in planning a preservation programme is to assess the institution's existing preservation needs. This process entails identifying the general and specific needs of the collection, establishing priorities, and gathering the resources to execute the plan.

Because budget and time limitations require priorities to be set, standards have been established by the profession to determine what should be preserved in a collection. Considerations include existing condition, rarity, and evidentiary and market values. With non-paper formats, the availability of equipment to access the information will be a factor (for example, playback equipment for audiovisual materials, or microform readers). An institution should determine how many, if any, other repositories hold the material, and consider coordinating efforts with those that do. Institutions should establish an environment conducive to preservation changes, involve staff, and create an understanding among administration and staff. The first steps an institution should implement, according to the NEDCC, are to establish a policy that defines and charts the course of action and create a framework fcr carrying out goals and priorities.

There are three methods for carrying out a preservation survey: general preservation assessment, collection condition surveys, and an item-by-item survey. General condition surveys can be part of a library inventory. Selection for treatment determines the survival of materials and should be done by a specialist, whether in relation to an established collection development policy or on an item by item basis. Once an object or collection has been chosen for preservation, the treatment must be determined that is most appropriate to the material and its repository. If the information is most important, reformatting or creation of a surrogate is a likely option. If the artifact itself is of value, it will receive conservation treatment, ideally of a reversible nature.

Research and Testing

With old media deteriorating or showing their vulnerabilities and new media becoming available, research remains active in the field of conservation and preservation. Everything from how to preserve paper media to creating and maintaining electronic resources is being explored by students and professionals in library and information science. The two main issues that most libraries tend to face are the rapid disintegration of acidic paper and water damage (due to flooding, plumbing problems, etc.). Therefore, these areas of preservation, as well as new digital technologies, receive much of the research attention.

The American Library Association has many scholarly journals that publish articles on preservation topics, such as College and Research Libraries, Information Technology and Libraries, and Library Resources and Technical Services. Scholarly periodicals in this field from other publishers include International Preservation News, Journal of the American Institute for Conservation, and Collection Management among many others.

Ethics

Conservators should refer to the AIC Code of Ethics and Guidelines for Practice, which states that the conservation professional must "strive to attain the highest possible standards in all aspects of conservation." Ethics will play an important role in many aspects of the conservator's activities. When choosing which objects are in need of treatment, the conservator should do what is best for the object in question and not yield to pressure or opinion from outside sources.

Preservation of Cultural Objects

One instance in which these decisions may get tricky is when the conservator is dealing with cultural objects. The AIC Code of Ethics and Guidelines for Practice has addressed such concerns, stating "All actions of the conservation professional must be governed by an informed respect for cultural property, its unique character and significance and the people or person who created it." This can be applied in both the care and long-term storage of objects in archives and institutions.

The AIC Code of Ethics and Guidelines for Practice also states: "While recognising the right of society to make appropriate and respectful use of cultural property, the conservation professional shall serve as an advocate for the preservation of cultural property." This statement speaks to the conservator's need to balance his or her duty to conserve objects and maintain a collection with society's right to have access and use of objects for their own cultural/religious purposes. While it is obvious that a member of a religion should be able to have access to an object or text that has spiritual value to them, it would be against the conservator's ethics to then allow that object to incur damage from such use. The conservator should make sure that the care of the object is kept in mind when access to an object is granted. The object should remain in the best condition possible not only so it is preserved for prosperity, but also so that it can be studied by researchers and by members of the cultural or religious group that created it.

It is important that preservation specialists to be respectful of cultural property and the societies that created it, it is also important for them to be aware of international and national laws pertaining to stolen items. The AIC Code of Ethics and Guidelines for Practice also states that:

> "The conservation professional should be cognisant of laws and regulations that may have a bearing on professional activity. Among these laws and regulations are those concerning the rights of artists and their estates, occupational health and safety, sacred and religious material, excavated objects, endangered species, human remains, and stolen property."

In recent years there has been a rise in nations seeking out artifacts that have been stolen and are now in museums. In many cases museums are working with the nations to find a compromise to balance the need for reliable supervision as well as access for both the public and researchers.

Conservators are not just bound by ethics to treat cultural and religious objects with respect, but also in some cases by law. For example, in the United States, conservators must comply with the Native American Graves Protection and Repatriation Act (NAGPRA). The First Archivists Circle, a group of Native American archivists, has also created Protocols for Native American Archival Materials. The non-binding guidelines are suggestions for libraries and archives with Native American archival materials.

With all these issues of respect and cultural sensitivity to consider, conservation and preservation issues are sure to arise. The care of cultural and sacred objects often affects the physical storage or the object. For example, sacred objects of the native peoples of the Western United States are supposed to be stored with sage to ensure their spiritual well being. The idea of storing an object with plant material is inherently problematic to an archival collection because of the possibility of insect infestation. When conservators have faced this problem, they have addressed it by using freeze-dried sage, thereby meeting both conservation and cultural needs.

Some individuals in the library science community have explored the possible moral responsibility to preserve all cultural phenomena, in regards to the concept of monumental preservation. Other advocates argue that such an undertaking is something that the indigenous or native communities that produce such cultural objects are better suited to perform. Currently, however, many indigenous communities are not financially able to support their own archives and museums. Still, indigenous archives are on the rise in the United States.

Preservation and the Library as a Sacred Institution

In her book "Sacred Stacks: The Higher Purpose of Libraries and Librarianship," Nancy Kalikow Maxwell discusses how libraries are capable of performing some of the same functions as religion. Many librarians feel that their work is done for some higher purpose. The same can be said for preservation librarians. One instance of the library's role as sacred is to provide a sense of immortality: with the ever changing world outside, the library will remain stable and dependable. Preservation is a great help in this regard. Through digitisation and reformatting, preservation librarians are able to retain material while at the same time adapting to new methods. In this way, libraries can adapt to the changes in user needs without changing the quality of the material itself. Through preservation efforts, patrons can rest assured that although materials are constantly deteriorating over time, the library itself will remain a stable, reliable environment for their information needs. Another sacred ability of the library is to provide information and a connection to the past. By working to slow down the processes of deterioration and decay of library materials, preservation practices help keep this link to the past alive.

Regional Centres

- The Conservation Centre for Art and Historic Artifacts in Philadelphia, PA. CCAHA is a non-profit conservation laboratory specialising in the treatment of art and historic artifacts on paper. The Centre also trains museum and library professionals in disaster planning, records and archives management.
- The Northeast Document Conservation Centre in Andover, MA. Since its inception in 1973, the Centre has instructed institutions and organisations, as well as librarians, conservators, preservationists and museum professionals in preservation care and procedures. From 1995 to 2007, NEDCC presented its School for Scanning conference eleven times in cities across the United States. The school takes a leading role for digital preservation.
- LYRASIS is a not-for-profit membership cooperative of libraries and other information organisations in the southeastern United States. Established in 1973, as the largest regional library network in the US, LYRASIS provides a variety of preservation education programmes and workshops.

Vendor Services

Many private entities provide preservation and conservation services and supplies.

Branches of Preservation

Standard functions of preservation programmes:

- Collections Care refers to the general maintenance and preventive care of a collection as a whole. This can include activities such as security, environmental monitoring, preservation surveys and more specialised activities such as mass deacidification.
- Conservation refers to the treatment and repair of individual items to slow decay or restore them to a usable state. Conservation is occasionally used interchangeably with preservation, particularly outside the professional literature.
- Digital preservation refers to the maintenance of digitally stored information. This should not be confused with digitisation, which is a process of creating digital information which must, in turn, be digitally preserved. Means of digital preservation include refreshing, migration, replication and emulation.
- Disaster Preparedness (RT: Disaster Plan / Business Continuation / Disaster Recovery / Disaster Mitigation Plan) refers to the practice of arranging for the necessary resources and planning the best course of action to prevent or minimise damage to a collection in the event of a disaster of any level of magnitude, whether natural or man-made.
- Reformatting refers to the practice of creating copies of an object in another type of data storage device. Reformatting processes include microfilming and digitisation.

Media Specific Issues and Treatments

- Books:
  - Sizing;
  - Leather Binding.
- Ephemera and Realia.
- Paper:
  - Acid-free paper;
  - Japanese tissue;
  - Mummy paper;
  - Paper splitting.
- Parchment:
  - Parchment repair;
  - Preservation of Illuminated Manuscripts.
- Moving image:
  - Film preservation;
  - Video recording.
- Sound recording:
  - Preservation of magnetic audiotape.
- Oral history preservation.
- Language Preservation.
- Visual material:
  - Still Photography;
  - Architectural reprography, a variety of technologies and media used to make multiple copies of original drawings or records created by architects, engineers, map makers and related professionals.
- Optical media preservation.
- Ink.

Education

One of the biggest challenges in the field of preservation today is educating a library's community, especially librarians and other staff, in the best ways to handle materials as well as the conditions in which particular materials will decay the least. This challenge is exacerbated by the fact that preservation is a peripheral element of most library science curricula; indeed, there are few places where one can receive a specialised education in preservation.

One of the primary degree granting institutions for library and archival preservation is the University of Texas at Austin's School of Information Science. The conservation and preservation programme is offered in partnership with the Kilgarlin Centre for Preservation of the Cultural Record and trains both conservators and preservation administrators. There are a number of other preservation administration programmes in the United States including the University of Michigan School of Information which specialises in digital preservation management. Recently the Institute for Museum and Library Services (IMLS) has funded a number of digital curation education programmes around the United States, including at the University of North Carolina at Chapel Hill. Digital curation includes the activity of digital preservation management. Other conservation programmes in the United States focus on Art Conservation and are considered to be more museum focused than library focused. These programmes are all part of the Association of North American Graduate Programmes in the Conservation of Cultural Property (ANAGPIC).

The Rutgers Preservation Management Institute provides post-graduate training in preservation administration for working librarians who have already completed a Master's degree. UT Austin also offers certificates of advanced study in conservation and preservation to librarians who already hold their MLS.

Another educational resource available to preservationists is the Northeast Document Conservation Centre or NEDCC. This institution was founded in 1973 as a reaction to the growing problem of paper deterioration occurring in repositories in the New England area. The Centre provides institutions and organisations, as well as librarians, conservators, preservationists, and museum professionals, with help in learning proper care and procedures to better preserve the integrity of their collections. The institution provides a variety of services such as imaging, surveys and consultations, and digitation. They also assist with disaster planning. The educational opportunities it provides include provision of workshops, conferences, and specialised trainings. Additional online courses are also available. For instance, some of the workshops offered by the NEDCC include: Basic Preservation, Collections Care, Emergency Preparedness, Integrated Pest Management (IPM), Identification and Care of Photographs, Basic and Intermediate Book Repair, Basic Paper Repair, Preservation of Scrapbooks, Preservation Technologies, Holdings Maintenance, Creating and Maintaining Digital Collections, Scanning Training, and Grant Writing. Additionally, the NEDCC is responsible for the creation of a Preservation Education Curriculum, which has been made available online to serve as an instructional aid for introductory preservation courses taught at Library and Information Science schools.

Additional preservation education is available to librarians through various professional organisations, such as:

- American Institute for Conservation of Historic and Artistic Works;
- American Library Association;
- Amigos Library Services Preservation Service;
- Association for Information and Image Management (AIIM);
- Association for Recorded Sound Collections (ARSC);
- Association of Moving Image Archivists (AMIA);
- Buffalo State College. Art Conservation Department, Buffalo, NY;
- Campbell Centre for Historic Preservation Studies, Mount Carroll, IL.;
- George Eastman House. School of Film and Video Preservation Rochester, NY;
- The Kilgarlin Centre for Preservation of the Cultural Record;
- Library Binding Institute;
- New York University. Conservation Centre, Institute of Fine Arts, New York, NY;
- North Bennet Street School. Boston, MA;
- Northeast Document Conservation Centre (NEDCC);

- The Conservation Centre for Art and Historic Artifacts in Philadelphia, PA;
- Queen's University. Master of Art Conservation Programme, Ont, Canada;
- Rare Book School (RBS) at the University of Virginia;
- Society of American Archivists;
- LYRASIS;
- University of Delaware. Winterthur Art Conservation Programme, Newark, DE;
- The National Archives.

Non-academic Facilities and Preservation

Public Libraries: Limited, tax-driven funding can often interfere with the ability for public libraries to engage in extensive preservation activities. Materials, particularly books, are often much easier to replace than to repair when damaged or worn. Public libraries usually try to tailor their services to meet the needs and desires of their local communities, which could cause an emphasis on acquiring new materials over preserving old ones. Librarians working in public facilities frequently have to make complicated decisions about how to best serve their patrons. Commonly, public library systems work with each other and sometimes with more academic libraries through interlibrary loan programmes. By sharing resources, they are able to expand upon what might be available to their own patrons and share the burdens of preservation across a greater array of systems.

Archival Repositories and Special Collections

Archival facilities focus specifically on rare and fragile materials. With staff trained in appropriate techniques, archives are often available to many public and private library facilities as an alternative to destroying older materials. Items that are unique, such as photographs, or items that are out of print, can be preserved in archival facilities more easily than in many library settings.

Museums

Because so many museum holdings are unique, including print materials, art, and other objects, preservationists are often most active in this setting.

Legal Issues

Reformatting, or in any other way copying an item's contents, raises obvious copyright issues. In many cases, a library is allowed to make a limited number of copies of an item for preservation purposes. In the United States, certain exceptions have been made for libraries and archives.

Criticism

There is a longstanding tension between preservation of and access to library materials, particularly in the area of special collections. Handling materials promotes their progression to an unusable state, especially if they are handled carelessly. On the other hand, materials must be used in order to gain any benefit from them. In a collection with valuable materials, this conflict is often resolved by a number of measures which can include heightened security, requiring the use of gloves for photographs, restricting the materials researchers may bring with them into a reading room, and restricting use of materials to patrons who are not able to satisfy their research needs with less valuable copies of an item. These restrictions are annoyances to researchers who feel that these measures are in place solely to keep materials out of the hands of the public.

There is also controversy surrounding preservation methods. A major controversy at the end of the twentieth century centred on the practice of discarding items that had been microfilmed. This was the subject of novelist Nicholson Baker's book Double Fold, which chronicled his efforts to save many old runs of American newspapers (formerly owned by the British Library) from being sold to dealers or pulped. A similar concern persists over the retention of original documents reformatted by any means, analogue or digital. Concerns include scholarly needs and legal requirements for authentic or original records as well as questions about the longevity, quality and completeness of reformatted materials. Retention of originals as a source or fail-safe copy is now a fairly common practice. Another controversy revolving around different preservation methods is that of digitisation of original material to maintain the intellectual content of the material while ignoring the physical nature of the book. Further, the Modern Language Association's Committee on the Future of the Print Record structured its "Statement on the Significance of Primary Records" on the inherent theoretical ideology that there is a need to preserve as many copies of a printed edition as is possible as texts and their textual settings are, quite simply, not separable, just as the artefactual characteristics of texts are as relevant and varied as the texts themselves (in the report mentioned herewith, G. Thomas Tanselle suggests that presently existing book stacks need not be abandoned with emerging technologies; rather they serve as vitally important original (primary) sources for future study).

Many digitised items, such as back issues of periodicals, are provided by publishers and databases on a subscription basis. If these companies were to cease providing access to their digital information, facilities that elected to discard paper copies of these periodicals could face significant difficulties in providing access to these items. Discussion as to the best ways to utilise digital technologies is therefore ongoing, and the practice continues to evolve. Of course, the issues surrounding digital objects and their care in libraries and archives continues to expand as more and more of contemporary culture is created, stored, and used digitally. These born-digital materials raise their own new kinds of preservation challenges and in some cases they may even require use new kinds of tools and techniques.

The Archive

An archives is an accumulation of historical records, or the physical place they are located. Archives contain primary source documents that have accumulated over the course of an individual or organisation's lifetime, and are kept to show the function of that person or organisation. Professional archivists and historians generally understand archives to be records that have been naturally and necessarily generated as a product of regular legal, commercial, administrative or social activities. They have been metaphorically defined as "the secretions of an organism", and are distinguished from documents that have been consciously written or created to communicate a particular message to posterity.

In general, archives consist of records that have been selected for permanent or long-term preservation on grounds of their enduring cultural, historical, or evidentiary value. Archival records are normally unpublished and almost always unique, unlike books or magazines for which many identical copies exist. This means that archives are quite distinct from libraries with regard to their functions and organisation, although archival collections can often be found within library buildings.

A person who works in archives is called an archivist. The study and practice of organising, preserving, and providing access to information and materials in archives is called archival science. The physical place of storage can be referred to as an archives, or repository.

When referring to historical records or the places they are kept, the plural form *archives* is chiefly used. The computing use of the term 'archive' should not be confused with the record-keeping meaning of the term.

Etymology

First attested in English in early 17th century, the word *archive* is derived from the French *archives* (plural), in turn from Latin *archium* or *archivum*, which is the romanised form of the Greek *arkheion*, "public records, town-hall, residence, or office of chief magistrates", itself from *arkhc*, amongst others "magistracy, office, government" (compare anarchy, monarchy), which comes from the verb *arkho*, "to begin, rule, govern".

The word originally developed from the Greek *arkheion*, which refers to the home or dwelling of the Archon, in which important official state documents were filed and interpreted under the authority of the Archon. The adjective formed from *archive* is *archival*.

Background

The use of keeping official documents is very old. Archaeologists have discovered archives of hundreds (and sometime thousands) of clay tablets going back to the third and second millennia BC in sites like Ebla, Mari, Amarna, Hattusas, Ugarit, Pylos. These discoveries have been fundamental to know ancient alphabets, languages, literatures and politics.

Archives were well developed by the ancient Chinese, the ancient Greeks, and ancient Romans (who called them *Tabularia*). However, they have been lost, since documents were written on organic materials like papyrus and paper. On the contrary, many archives founded since Middle Age by churches, kingdoms and cities survive and often have kept their official status uninterruptedly till now. They are the basic tool for historical research on these ages.

Modern archival thinking has many roots in the French Revolution. The French National Archives, who possess perhaps the largest archival collection in the world, with records going as far back as AD 625, were created in 1790 during the French Revolution from various government, religious, and private archives seized by the revolutionaries.

Users and Institutions

Historians, genealogists, lawyers, demographers, film-makers, and others conduct research at archives. The research process at each archive is unique, and depends upon the institution that houses the archive. While there are many kinds of archives, the most recent census of archivists in the United States identifies five major types: academic, business (for profit), government, non-profit, and other. There are also four main areas of enquiry involved with archives: material technologies, organising principles, geographic locations, and tangled embodiments of humans and non-humans. These areas help to further categorise what kind of archive is being created.

Academics

Archives in colleges, universities, and other educational facilities are typically housed within a library, and duties may be carried out by an archivist, professors may also run a smaller archive. Academic archives exist to preserve and celebrate the history of their school and academic community. An academic archive may contain items such as the administrative records of the institution, papers of former professors and Presidents, memorabilia related to school organisations and activities, and items the academic library wishes to remain in a closed-stack setting, such as rare books or thesis copies. Access to the collections in these archives is usually by prior appointment only; some have posted hours for making enquiries. Users of academic archives can be undergraduates, graduate students, faculty and staff, scholarly researchers, and the general public. Many academic archives work closely with alumni relations departments or other campus institutions to help raise funds for their library or school. Because of their library setting, a degree certified by the American Library Association is preferred for employment in an academic archive in the United States.

Business (for Profit)

Archives located in for-profit institutions are usually those owned by a private business. Examples of prominent business archives in the United States include Coca-Cola (which also owns the separate museum World of Coca-Cola), Procter and Gamble, Motorola Heritage Services and Archives, and Levi Strauss and Co. These corporate archives maintain historic documents and items related to the history and administration of their companies. Business archives serve the purpose of helping their corporations maintain control over their brand by retaining memories of the company's past. Especially in business archives, records management is separate from the historic aspect of archives. Workers in these types of archives may have any combination of training and degrees, from either a history or library background. These archives are typically not open to the public and only used by workers of the owner company, though some allow approved visitors by appointment. Business archives are concerned with maintaining the integrity of their company, and are therefore selective of how their materials may be used.

Government

Government archives include those maintained by local and state government as well as those maintained by the national (or federal) government. Anyone may use a government archive, and frequent users include reporters, genealogists, writers, historians, students, and people seeking information on the history of their home or region. Many government archives are open to the public and no appointment is required to visit. In the United States, National Archives and Records Administration (NARA) maintains central archival facilities in the District of Columbia and College Park, Maryland, with regional facilities distributed throughout the United States. Some city or local governments may have repositories, but their organisation and accessibility varies widely. State or province archives typically require at least a bachelor's degree in history for employment, although some ask for certification by test (government or association) as well.

In the UK the National Archives (formerly known as the Public Record Office) is the government archive for England and Wales. The English Heritage Archive is the public archive of English Heritage. The National Archives of Scotland, located in Edinburgh, serve that country while the Public Record Office of Northern Ireland in Belfast is the government archive for Northern Ireland.

A network of county record offices and other local authority-run archives exists throughout England, Wales and Scotland and holds many important collections, including local government, landed estates, church and business records. Many archives have contributed catalogues to the national "Access to Archives" programme and online searching across collections is possible. In France, the French Archives Administration (*Service interministeriel des Archives de France*) in the Ministry of Culture manages the National Archives (*Archives nationales*), which possess 406 km. (252 miles) of archives as of 2010 (the total length of occupied shelves put next to each other), with original records going as far back as AD 625, as well as the departmental archives (*archives departementales*), located in the *prefectures* of each of the 100 *departements* of France, which possess

2,297 km. (1,427 miles) of archives (as of 2010), and also the local city archives, about 600 in total, which possess 456 km. (283,4 miles) of archives (as of 2010). Put together, the total volume of archives under the supervision of the French Archives Administration is the largest in the world.

In India the National Archives (NAI) are located in New Delhi.

In Taiwan the National Archives Administration are located in Taipei.

Most intergovernmental organisations keep their own historical archives. However, a number of European organisations, including the European Commission, choose to deposit their archives with the European University Institute in Florence.

Church

A prominent Church Archives is the Vatican Secret Archive. Archdioceses, dioceses and parishes also have archives in the Roman Catholic and Anglican Churches. Very important are monastery archives, because of their antiquity, like the ones of Monte Cassino, Saint Gall and Fulda. The records in these archives include manuscripts, papal records, local Church records, photographs, oral histories, audiovisual materials, and architectural drawings. Most Protestant denominations have archives as well, including the Presbyterian USA Historical Society, The Southern Baptist Historical Library and Archives, the United Methodist Archives and History Centre of the United Methodist Church and the Christian Church (Disciples of Christ).

Films

Cinematheque: A cinematheque is a film archive with small cinemas that screens particularly classic and art-house films.

History

In 1935 Henri Langlois and Georges Franju founded a film club (Cercle du cinema) to show old films from which originated the Cinematheque Francaise in 1936.

The idea to archive old films was by no means self-evident at the time. Langlois was able to save many films the companies had intended to throw away. In 1933, the British Film Institute was founded in London. In 1938 Henri Storck, Andre Thirifays and Pierre Vermeylen founded the Cinematheque Royale de Belgique in Belgium. Also in 1938, the International Federation of Film Archives (FIAF) was founded in Paris.

Non-profit Things

Non-profit archives include those in historical societies, not-for-profit businesses such as hospitals, and the repositories within foundations. Non-profit archives are typically set up with private funds from donors to preserve the papers and history of specific persons or places. Often these institutions rely on grant funding from the government as well as the private funds. Depending on the funds available, non-profit archives may be as small as the historical society in a rural town to as big as a state historical society that rivals a government archives. Users of this type of archive may vary as much as the institutions that hold them. Employees of non-profit archives may be professional archivists, paraprofessionals, or volunteers, as the education required for a position at a non-profit archive varies with the demands of the collection's user base.

Web Archiving

Web archiving is the process of collecting portions of the World Wide Web and ensuring the collection is preserved in an archive, such as an archive site, for future researchers, historians, and the public. Due to the massive size of the Web, web archivists typically employ web crawlers for automated collection. Similarly, software code and documentation can be archived on the web, as with the example of CPAN.

Others

Some archives defy categorisation. There are tribal archives within the Native American nations in North America, and there are archives that exist within the papers of private individuals. Many museums keep archives in order to prove the provenance of their pieces. Any institution or persons wishing to keep their significant papers in an organised fashion that employs the most basic principles of archival science may have an archive. In the 2004 census of archivists taken in the United States, 2.7 per cent of archivists were employed in institutions that defied categorisation. This was a separate figure from the 1.3 per cent that identified themselves as self-employed.

Another type of archive is the Public Secrets project. This is an interactive testimonial, in which women incarcerated in the California State Prison System describe what happened to them. The archive's mission is to gather stories from women who want to express themselves, and want their stories heard. This collection includes transcripts and an audio recording of the women telling their stories. The archives of an individual may include letters, papers, photographs, computer files, scrapbooks, financial records or diaries created or collected by the individual – regardless of media or format. The archives of an organisation (such as a corporation or government) tend to contain other types of records, such as administrative files, business records, memos, official correspondence and meeting minutes.

Standardisation

The International Council on Archives (ICA) has developed a number of standards on archival description including the General International Standard Archival Description ISAD(G). ISAD(G) is meant to be used in conjunction with national standards or as a basis for nations to build their own standards. In the United States, ISAD(G) is implemented through Describing Archives: A Content Standard, popularly known as "DACS". In Canada, ISAD(G) is implemented through the Canadian Council of Archives: Rules for Archival Description, also known as "RAD".

ISO is currently working on standards.

Archivist

An archivist ("AR-kiv-ist" or "AR-kive-ist") is an information professional who assesses, collects, organises, preserves, maintains control over, and provides access to records and archives determined to have long-term value. The records maintained by an archivist can be any form of media (photographs, video or sound recordings, letters, documents, electronic records, etc.). As Richard Pearce-Moses wrote:

> "Archivists keep records that have enduring value as reliable memories of the past, and they help people find and understand the information they need in those records".

Determining what records have enduring value can be challenging. Archivists must also select records valuable enough to justify the costs of storage and preservation, plus the labour intensive expenses of arrangement, description, and reference service. The theory and scholarly work underpinning archives practices is called archival science. Although both are concerned with managing information, the profession of archivist is quite distinct from that of librarian. The two occupations have separate courses of training, adhere to separate and distinct professional principles, and are represented by separate professional organisations. In broad terms, the librarian tends to deal with published media (of which the metadata, such as author, title, and date of publication, are usually readily apparent and can be presented in standardised form), whereas the archivist deals with unpublished media (of which the metadata are usually less immediately apparent, more complex and varied, and more likely to depend on provenance). In addition, because archival records are frequently unique, the archivist may be as much concerned with the preservation and custody of the information carrier (i.e. the physical document) as with its informational content: in this regard, the skill-set and outlook of the archivist sometimes have more in common with those of the museum curator than with those of the librarian. The profession of archivist is also frequently distinguished from that of records manager, although in this case the distinction is less absolute: the archivist is predominantly concerned with records deemed worthy of permanent preservation, whereas the records manager is concerned with records of current administrative importance.

Duties and Work Environment

Archivists' duties include acquiring and appraising new collections, arranging and describing records, providing reference service, and preserving materials. In arranging records, archivists apply two important principles: provenance and original order. Provenance refers to the origin of records, essentially who created them. Many entities create records, including government, businesses, universities, and personal collections of individuals. Original order is applied by keeping records in their order as established and maintained by the creator(s). Both provenance and original order are closely related to the concept of *respect des fonds*, which states that records from one corporate body should not be mixed with records from another. There are two aspects to arrangement: intellectual and physical.

Both aspects follow the principle of original order. Archivists process the records physically by placing them in folders and boxes, usually acid free to ensure their long-term survival. They also process the records intellectually, by determining what the records consist of, how they are organised, and what, if any, finding aids need to be created. Finding aids can be box lists or descriptive inventories, or indexes. If the original arrangement is unclear or even unhelpful in terms of accessing the collection, it is not usually rearranged to something that makes more sense. This is because preserving the original order answers the most questions about the collection. It shows how the creator of the records functioned, why the records were created, and how he went about arranging them. If the archivist rearranged them, the records would lose the ability to answer these questions. It would also lose all significance, as the provenance and authenticity of the records may be lost. However, original order is not always the best way to maintain some collections and archivists must use their own experience and current best practices to determine the correct way to keep collections of mixed media or those lacking a clear original arrangement.

American archivists are also guided in their work by a code of ethics. Alongside their work behind the scenes arranging and caring for collections, archivists assist users in interpreting collections and answering enquiries. This reference work can be just part of an archivist's job in a smaller organisation, or consist of most of their occupation in a larger archive where specific roles (such as processing archivist and reference archivist) may be delineated. Archivists work for a variety of organisations, including government agencies, local authorities, museums, hospitals, historical societies, businesses, charities, corporations, colleges and universities, and any institution whose records may potentially be valuable to researchers, exhibitors, genealogists, or others. Alternatively, they could also work on the collections of a large family or even of an individual. Applicants for archives jobs usually outnumber positions available. Archivists are often educators as well; it is not unusual for an archivist employed at a university or college to lecture in a subject related to their collection. Archivists employed at cultural institutions or for local government frequently design educational or outreach programmes to further the ability of archive users to understand and access information in their collections. This might include such varied activities as exhibitions, promotional events or even media coverage. The advent of Encoded Archival Description, along with increasing demand for materials to be made available online, has required archivists to become more tech-savvy in the past decade. Many archivists are now acquiring basic XML skills in order to make their finding aids available to researchers online.

Skills

Because of the varied nature of the job and organisations and work environment, archivists need to have a wide range of skills:

- Those who work in reference and access-oriented positions need to be good with people, so that they are able to help them with their research.
- An ability to apply some basic knowledge of conservation is needed to help extend the useful life of cultural artifacts. Many different types of media (such as photographs, acidic papers, and unstable copy processes) can deteriorate if not stored and maintained properly.
- Although many archival collections consist solely of paper records, increasingly archivists must confront the new challenges posed by the preservation of electronic records, so they need to be forward-looking and technologically proficient.
- Because of the amount of sorting and listing, they need to be very logical and organised and be able to pay attention to detail.
- When cataloguing records, or when assisting users, archivists need to have some research skills.
- Archivists are occasionally called upon to comment or provide some context for the records in their collection and so should know as much about their collection as possible.

Educational Preparation

The educational preparation for archivists varies from country to country.

Colombia: In Colombia, the Universidad de La Salle offers the degree of Professional in Information Systems, Library and Archival Sciences. It is a vocational training programme, within existing legal standards aimed at providing knowledge, skills and abilities required for the design and management of information systems and documentation of various sorts. Its projection for the future is based on the application of new information technologies and communications for the management of information services economically viable. The programme was created in 1971.

Other institutions that offers a degree in Archival Science are:

- Universidad del Quindio – Professional degree: Professional in Information and Documentation, Library and Archival Sciences.
- Universidad de Antioquia, Escuela Interamericana de Bibliotecologia – Technological degree: Technologist in Archival Science.
- Universidad Catolica de Manizales – Technological degree: Technologist in Documentation and Archival Science.
- Servicio Nacional de Aprendizaje – SENA – in chain training with the Tecnologico de Antioquia Tecnologico de Antioquia – Technical degree: Professional Technical in Archives, Technological degree: Technologist in Documentation and Archival Science.

France: In France the oldest Archivist School is the *Ecole des chartes*, founded in 1821. This prestigious *grande ecole* offers a diploma in "Archivist-Palaeography" after a three-year curriculum. A part of its alumni pursue to a State archivist career after an 18 month formation at the *Institut national du patrimoine*. Most positions are reserved for European citizens. Some universities offer Master's degree in Archival Science : Angers, Caen, Dijon, Lille III, Lyon III, Mulhouse, Versailles Saint-Quentin.

Republic of Ireland: In Republic of Ireland, the University College Dublin School of History and Archives offers a Masters of Arts degree in Archives and Records Management, recognised by the Society of Archivists.

New Zealand: Victoria University of Wellington is the only tertiary institution in New Zealand provides post-graduate archival courses. Victoria Information Studies qualifications with ARCR endorsement have been recognised by Records and Information Management Professionals Australasia. Open Polytechnic of New Zealand provides undergraduate archival courses.

United Kingdom: In the United Kingdom, there are currently five full-or part-time post-graduate courses in archives administration or management which are recognised by the Archives and Records Association (United Kingdom and Ireland). Students are expected to have relevant paid or voluntary work experience before obtaining a place on the UK courses; many undertake a year's traineeship. Also, professional certification (after qualifying) can be pursued via the Registration Scheme offered by the Archives and Records Association.

United States: According to the most recent professional census of American Archivists published, most of those in the United States have earned a Masters degree. However, the exact type of degree can vary; the most common sorts of advanced degrees held by archivists are in archival science, public history, history, library science, or library and information science. It is also possible for archivists to earn a doctorate in library, or library and information, science. Archivists with a PhD often work at a teaching faculty or deans and directors of archival programmes. In 2002, the Society of American Archivists published Guidelines for a Graduate Programme in Archival Studies, as well as a code of ethics.

Also in the United States, the Academy of Certified Archivists offers supplemental archival training by means of a certification programme. When first established in 1989, some critics of ACA certification objected to its annual membership fees, the theoretical versus practical nature of its tests, and the need for members to re-certify every five years. However, in the decades since, it has been agreed that such requirements are comparable with certification programmes in other professions, and that certification strengthens professional standards and individual competencies. While some positions in archives require certification and many employers view certification as preferred, it is not required by all employers in the United States. Approximately 1,100 archivists were certified by ACA, as of 30 June 2011.

Professional Organisations and Continuing Education

Many archivists belong to a professional organisation, such as the Society of American Archivists, the Association of Canadian Archivists, the Archives and Records Association (UK/Ireland), the Colombian College of Archivists - CCA and the Australian Society of Archivists, as well as any number of local or regional associations. These organisations often provide ongoing educational opportunities to their members and other interested practitioners. In addition to formal degrees and or apprenticeships, many archivists take part in continuing education opportunities as available through professional associations and library school programmes. New discoveries in the fields of media preservation and emerging technologies require continuing education as part of an archivist's job in order to stay current in the profession.

History of Profession

In 1898 three Dutch archivists, Samuel Muller, Johan Feith, and Robert Fruin, published the first Western text on archival theory, entitled *Manual for the Arrangement and Description of Archives.* Produced for the Dutch Association of Archivists, it set out one hundred rules for archivists to base their work around. Notably, within these rules, the principle of preserving provenance and original order was first argued for as an essential trait of archival arrangement and description.

The next major text was the *Manual of Archive Administration* published in 1922 by Hilary Jenkinson, then employed at the British Public Record Office: a revised edition appeared in 1937. In this work Jenkinson states that archives are evidence and that the moral and physical defence of this evidential value is the central tenet of archival work. He further outlines his ideas of what an archive should be and how it should operate.

In 1956, T. R. Schellenberg, who is known as the "Father of American Archival Appraisal", published *Modern Archives.* Schellenberg's work was intended to be an academic textbook defining archival methodology and giving archivists specific technical instruction on workflow and arrangement. Moving away from Jenkinson's organic and passive approach to archival acquisition, where the administrator decided what was kept and what was destroyed, Schellenberg argued for a more active approach by archivists to appraisal. His primary (administrative) and secondary (research) value model for the management and appraisal of records and archives allowed government archivists greater control over the influx of material that they faced after the Second World War. As a result of the widespread adoption of Schellenberg's methods, especially in the United States of America, modern Records Management as a separate but related discipline was born.

In 1972, Ernst Posner published *Archives in the Ancient World.* Posner's work emphasised that archives were not new inventions, but had existed in many different societies throughout recorded history. In 1975, essays by Margaret Cross Norton were collected under the title of *Norton on Archives: The Writings of Margaret Cross Norton on Archival and Records Management.* Norton was one of the founders of the Society of American Archivists, and wrote essays based on her decades of experience working in the Illinois State Archives.

Archives 2.0

Archivists, like librarians, are taking advantage of Web 2.0 technologies such as blogs, wikis, as well as open access and open source philosophies.

Curator

A curator (from Latin: *curare* meaning "take care") is a manager or overseer. Traditionally, a curator or keeper of a cultural heritage institution (e.g., gallery, museum, library or archive) is a content specialist responsible for an institution's collections and involved with the interpretation of heritage material. The object of a traditional curator's concern necessarily involves tangible objects of some sort, whether it be artwork, collectibles, historic items or scientific collections. More recently, new kinds of curators are emerging: curators of digital data objects and biocurators.

Curator Responsibilities

In smaller organisations, a curator may have sole responsibility for the acquisition and care of objects. The curator will make decisions regarding what objects to take, oversee their potential and documentations, conduct research based on the collection and history that provides proper packaging of art for transportation, and shares that research with the public and community through exhibitions and publications. In very small volunteer-based museums, such as local historical societies, a curator may be the only paid staff member.

In larger institutions, the curator's primary function is as a subject specialist, with the expectation that he or she will conduct original research on objects and guide the organisation in its collecting. Such institutions can have multiple curators, each assigned to a specific collecting area (e.g., Curator of Ancient Art, Curator of Prints and Drawings, etc.) and often operating under the direction of a head curator. In such organisations, the physical care of the collection may be overseen by museum collections managers or museum conservators, and documentation and administrative matters (such as insurance and loans) are handled by a museum registrar.

In the United Kingdom, the term curator is also applied to government employees who monitor the quality of contract archaeological work under Planning Policy Guidance 16: Archaeology and Planning (PPG 16) and are considered to manage the cultural resource of a region. In the museum setting, a curator in the United Kingdom may also be called a "keeper".

In Scotland, the term "curator" is used to mean the guardian of a child.

In the United States, the term can also be used to refer to a member of the University of Missouri Board of Curators, the governing body of the University of Missouri System. The Board consists of nine members appointed by the state's governor.

More recently, advances in new technologies have led to a further widening of the role of curator. This has been focused in major art institutions internationally and has become an object of academic study and research.

In contemporary art, the title curator is given to a person who selects and often interprets works of art. In addition to selecting works, the curator often is responsible for writing labels, catalogue essays, and other supporting content for the exhibition. Such curators may be permanent staff members, be "guest curators" from an affiliated organisation or university, or be "freelance curators" working on a consultant basis. The late twentieth century saw an explosion of artists organising exhibitions. The artist-curator has a long tradition of influence. Notable among these was Sir Joshua Reynolds, founder of the Royal Academy, London.

In some American organisations, the term curator is also used to designate the head of any given division of a cultural organisation. This has led to the proliferation of titles such as "Curator of Education" and "Curator of Exhibitions". The term "literary curator" has been used to describe persons who work in the field of poetry, such as former 92nd Street Y poetry director Karl Kirchwey. This trend has increasingly been mirrored in the United Kingdom in such institutions as Ikon, Birmingham, UK and Baltic, Gateshead, UK.

In Australia and New Zealand, the term is also applied to a person who prepares a sports ground for use (especially a cricket ground) This job is equivalent to that of groundsman in some other cricketing nations.

In France, the term curator is translated as *conservateur*. There are two kinds of curators, Heritage curators (*conservateurs du patrimoine*) with five specialities (archaeology, archives, museums, historical monuments, natural science museums), and Librarian curators (*conservateurs des bibliotheques*). These curators are in public service, selected by competitive exam, the use of the title curator by private workers remains unofficial.

Education and Training

Curators generally hold a higher academic degree in their subject, typically a Doctor of Philosophy or a master's degree in subjects such as history, history of art, archaeology, anthropology, or classics. Curators are also expected to have contributed to their academic field, for example, by delivering public talks, publishing articles or presenting at specialist academic conferences. It is important that curators have knowledge of the current collecting market for their area of expertise, and are aware of current ethical practices and laws that may impact their organisation's collecting.

Recently, the increased complexity of many museums and cultural organisations has prompted the emergence of professional programmes in fields such as public history, museum studies, arts management, and curating/curatorial practice. In 1992, the Royal College of Art established an MA course co-funded by the Royal College of Art and the Arts Council of Great Britain, the first in Britain to specialise in curating with a particular focus on contemporary art.

The course is now funded by Arts Council England, and in 2001 the course title was amended to Curating Contemporary Art to more accurately reflect the content and primary focus of the programme. Other institutions that run programmes in curating include The Courtauld Institute of Art, London, UK Kingston University; Goldsmiths College, University of London; Birkbeck, University of London; Chelsea College of Art and Design; University of the Arts London; California College of the Arts; University of Southern California; Bard College; the Ecole du Louvre; University of Rennes 2—Upper Brittany; Ontario College of Art and Design and The University of Melbourne.

Technology and Society

In the same way that a museum curator may acquire objects of relevance or an art curator may select or interpret a work of art, the injection of technology and impact of social media into every aspect of our society has seen the emergence of technology curators; someone who is able to disentangle the science and logic of a particular technology and apply it to real world situations and society, whether for social change or commercial advantage.

The first UK Wired Conference had a test lab, where an independent curator selected technology that showcased radical technology advancements and their impact on society, such as the ability to design and "print" real world objects using 3D printers (such as a fully working violin) or the ability to model and represent accurate interactive medical and molecular models in Stereoscopic 3D. MLOVE, a Confestival started in 2010, celebrated the disruption of the perception of what a tech conference should be, using a radically more interactive format that drew on a variety of influences outside of the traditional world of technology, including religion, micro-banking for developing countries and interactive art installations/workshops such as the Future Cube and a giant interactive video projection.

Digital Preservation

Digital preservation can be understood as the series of managed activities necessary to ensure continued access to digital information for as long as necessary, involving the planning, resource allocation, and application of preservation methods and technologies to ensure that digital information of continuing value remains accessible and usable. It combines policies, strategies and actions to ensure access to reformatted and born digital content regardless of the challenges of media failure and technological change. The goal of digital preservation is the accurate rendering of authenticated content over time.

Challenges of Digital Preservation

Society's heritage has been presented on many different materials, including stone, vellum, bamboo, silk, and paper. Now a large quantity of information exists in digital forms, including e-mails, blogs, social networking websites, national elections websites, web photo albums, and sites which change their content over time. With digital media it is easier to create content and keep it up-to-date, but at the same time there are many challenges in the preservation of this content, both technical and economic. Unlike traditional analogue objects such as books or photographs where the user has unmediated access to the content, a digital object always needs a software environment to render it. These environments keep evolving and changing at a rapid pace, threatening the continuity of access to the content. Physical storage media, data formats, hardware, and software all become obsolete over time, posing significant threats to the survival of the content. This process can be referred to as digital obsolescence.

In the case of born-digital content (e.g., institutional archives, Websites, electronic audio and video content, born-digital photography and art, research data sets, observational data), the enormous and growing quantity of content presents significant scaling issues to digital preservation efforts. Rapidly changing technologies can hinder digital preservationists work and techniques due to outdated and antiquated machines or technology. This has become a common problem and one that is a constant worry for a digital archivist—how to prepare for the future.

Digital content can also present challenges to preservation because of its complex and dynamic nature, e.g., interactive Web pages, virtual reality and gaming environments, learning objects, social media sites. In many cases of emergent technological advances there are substantial difficulties in maintaining the authenticity, fixity, and integrity of objects over time deriving from the fundamental issue of experience with that particular digital storage medium and while particular technologies may prove to be more robust in terms of storage capacity, there are issues in securing a framework of measures to ensure that the object remains fixed while in stewardship.

For the preservation of software as digital content, a specific challenge is the typically non-availability of the source code as commercial software is normally distributed only in compiled binary form. Without the source code an adaption (Porting) on modern computing hardware or operating system is most often impossible, therefore the original hardware and software context needs to be emulated. Another potential challenge for software preservation can be the copyright who prohibits often the bypassing of copy protection mechanisms (Digital Millennium Copyright Act) incase software has become a orphaned work (Abandonware). An exemption from the United States Digital Millennium Copyright Act to permit to bypass copy protection was approved in 2003 for a period of 3 years to the Internet Archive who created an archive of "vintage software", as a way to preserve them. The exemption was renewed in 2006, and as of 27 October 2009, has been indefinitely extended pending further rule makings "for the purpose of preservation or archival reproduction of published digital works by a library or archive."

Another challenge surrounding preservation of digital content resides in the issue of scale. The amount of digital information being created along with the "proliferation of format types" makes creating trusted digital repositories with adequate and sustainable resources a challenge. The Web is only one example of what might be considered the "data deluge". For example, the Library of Congress currently amassed 170 billion tweets between 2006 and 2010 totalling 133.2 terabytes and each Tweet is composed of 23 fields of metadata. The economic challenges of digital preservation are also great. Preservation programmes require significant up front investment to create, along with ongoing costs for data ingest, data management, data storage, and staffing. One of the key strategic challenges to such programmes is the fact that, while they require significant current and ongoing funding, their benefits accrue largely to future generations.

Intellectual Foundations of Digital Preservation

"Preserving Digital Information (1996)"

The challenges of long-term preservation of digital information have been recognised by the archival community for years. In December 1994, the Research Libraries Group (RLG) and Commission on Preservation and Access (CPA) formed a Task Force on Archiving of Digital Information with the main purpose of investigating what needed to be done to ensure long-term preservation and continued access to the digital records. The final report published by the Task Force (Garrett, J. and Waters, D., ed. (1996). "Preserving digital information: Report of the task force on archiving of digital information.") became a fundamental document in the field of digital preservation that helped set out key concepts, requirements, and challenges.

The Task Force proposed development of a national system of digital archives that would take responsibility for long-term storage and access to digital information; introduced the concept of trusted digital repositories and defined their roles and responsibilities; identified five features of digital information integrity (content, fixity, reference, provenance, and context) that were subsequently incorporated into a definition of Preservation Description Information in the Open Archival Information System Reference Model; and defined migration as a crucial function of digital archives. The concepts and recommendations outlined in the report laid a foundation for subsequent research and digital preservation initiatives.

OAIS

To standardise digital preservation practice and provide a set of recommendations for preservation programme implementation, the Reference Model for an Open Archival Information System (OAIS) was developed. OAIS is concerned with all technical aspects of a digital object's life cycle: ingest, archival storage, data management, administration, access and preservation planning. The model also addresses metadata issues and recommends that five types of metadata be attached to a digital object: reference (identification) information, provenance (including preservation history), context, fixity (authenticity indicators), and representation (formatting, file structure, and what "imparts meaning to an object's bitstream").

Trusted Digital Repository Model

In March 2000, the Research Libraries Group (RLG) and Online Computer Library Centre (OCLC) began a collaboration to establish attributes of a digital repository for research organisations, building on and incorporating the emerging international standard of the Reference Model for an Open Archival Information System (OAIS). In 2002, they published "Trusted Digital Repositories: Attributes and Responsibilities." In that document a "Trusted Digital Repository" (TDR) is defined as "one whose mission is to provide reliable, long-term access to managed digital resources to its designated community, now and in the future." The TDR must include the following seven attributes: compliance with the reference model for an Open Archival Information System (OAIS), administrative responsibility, organisational viability, financial sustainability, technological and procedural suitability, system security, procedural accountability. The Trusted Digital Repository Model outlines relationships among these attributes. The report also recommended the collaborative development of digital repository certifications, models for cooperative networks, and sharing of research and information on digital preservation with regard to intellectual property rights.

In 2004 Henry M. Gladney proposed another approach to digital object preservation that called for the creation of "Trustworthy Digital Objects" (TDOs). TDOs are digital objects that can speak to their own authenticity since they incorporate a record maintaining their use and change history, which allows the future users to verify that the contents of the object are valid.

InterPARES

International Research on Permanent Authentic Records in Electronic Systems (InterPARES) is a collaborative research initiative led by the University of British Columbia that is focused on addressing issues of long-term preservation of authentic digital records. The research is being conducted by focus groups from various institutions in North America, Europe, Asia, and Australia, with an objective of developing theories and methodologies that provide the basis for strategies, standards, policies, and procedures necessary to ensure the trustworthiness, reliability, and accuracy of digital records over time.

The project began in 1999 with the first phase, InterPARES 1, which ran to 2001 and focused on establishing requirements for authenticity of inactive records generated and maintained in large databases and document management systems created by government agencies. InterPARES 2 (2002 – 2007) concentrated on issues of reliability, accuracy and authenticity of records throughout their whole life cycle, and examined records produced in dynamic environments in the course of artistic, scientific and online government activities. The third five-year phase (InterPARES 3) was initiated in 2007. Its goal is to utilise theoretical and methodological knowledge generated by InterPARES and other preservation research projects for developing guidelines, action plans, and training programmes on long-term preservation of authentic records for small and medium-sized archival organisations.

Strategies

In 2006, the Online Computer Library Centre developed a four-point strategy for the long-term preservation of digital objects that consisted of:

- Assessing the risks for loss of content posed by technology variables such as commonly used proprietary file formats and software applications.
- Evaluating the digital content objects to determine what type and degree of format conversion or other preservation actions should be applied.
- Determining the appropriate metadata needed for each object type and how it is associated with the objects.
- Providing access to the content.

There are several additional strategies that individuals and organisations may use to actively combat the loss of digital information.

Refreshing

Refreshing is the transfer of data between two types of the same storage medium so there are no bitrot changes or alteration of data. For example, transferring census data from an old preservation CD to a new one. This strategy may need to be combined with migration when the software or hardware required to read the data is no longer available or is unable to understand the format of the data. Refreshing will likely always be necessary due to the deterioration of physical media.

Migration

Migration is the transferring of data to newer system environments (Garrett *et al.*, 1996). This may include conversion of resources from one file format to another (e.g., conversion of Microsoft Word to PDF or OpenDocument) or from one operating system to another (e.g., Windows to GNU/ Linux) so the resource remains fully accessible and functional. Two significant problems face migration as a plausible method of digital preservation in the long terms. Due to the fact that digital objects are subject to a state of near continuous change, migration may cause problems in relation to authenticity and migration has proven to be time-consuming and expensive for "large collections of heterogeneous objects, which would need constant monitoring and intervention.

Replication

Creating duplicate copies of data on one or more systems is called *replication*. Data that exists as a single copy in only one location is highly vulnerable to software or hardware failure, intentional or accidental alteration, and environmental catastrophes like fire, flooding, etc. Digital data is more likely to survive if it is replicated in several locations. Replicated data may introduce difficulties in refreshing, migration, versioning, and access control since the data is located in multiple places.

Emulation

Emulation is the replicating of functionality of an obsolete system. According to van der Hoeven, "Emulation does not focus on the digital object, but on the hard- and software environment in which the object is rendered. It aims at (re)creating the environment in which the digital object was originally created.". Examples are having the ability to replicate or imitate another operating system. Examples include emulating an Atari 2600 on a Windows system or emulating WordPerfect 1.0 on a Macintosh. Emulators may be built for applications, operating systems, or hardware platforms. Emulation has been a popular strategy for retaining the functionality of old video game systems, such as with the MAME project. The feasibility of emulation as a catch-all solution has been debated in the academic community. (Granger, 2000)

Raymond A. Lorie has suggested a Universal Virtual Computer (UVC) could be used to run any software in the future on a yet unknown platform. The UVC strategy uses a combination of emulation and migration. The UVC strategy has not yet been widely adopted by the digital preservation community.

Jeff Rothenberg, a major proponent of Emulation for digital preservation in libraries, working in partnership with Koninklijke Bibliotheek and National Archief of the Netherlands, developed a software programme called Dioscuri, a modular emulator that succeeds in running MS-DOS, WordPerfect 5.1, DOS games, and more. Another example of emulation as a form of digital preservation can be seen in the example of Emory University and the Salman Rushdie's papers. Rushdie donated an outdated computer to the Emory University library, which was so old that the library was unable to extract papers from the hard drive. In order to procure the papers, the library emulated the old software system and was able to take the papers off his old computer.

Encapsulation

This method maintains that preserved objects should be self-describing, virtually "linking content with all of the information required for it to be deciphered and understood". The files associated with the digital object would have details of how to interpret that object by using "logical structures called "containers" or "wrappers" to provide a relationship between all information components that could be used in future development of emulators, viewers or converters through machine readable specifications. The method of encapsulation is usually applied to collections that will go unused for long periods of time.

Persistent Archives Concept

Developed by the San Diego Supercomputing Centre and funded by the National Archives and Records Administration, this method requires the development of comprehensive and extensive infrastructure that enables "the preservation of the organisation of collection as well as the objects that make up that collection, maintained in a platform independent form". A persistent archive includes both the data constituting the digital object and the context that the defines the provenance, authenticity, and structure of the digital entities. This allows for the replacement of hardware or software components with minimal effect on the preservation system. This method can be based on virtual data grids and resembles OAIS Information Model (specifically the Archival Information Package).

Metadata Attachment

Metadata is data on a digital file that includes information on creation, access rights, restrictions, preservation history, and rights management. Metadata attached to digital files may be affected by file format obsolescence. ASCII is considered to be the most durable format for metadata because it is widespread, backwards compatible when used with Unicode, and utilises human-readable characters, not numeric codes. It retains information, but not the structure information it is presented in. For higher functionality, SGML or XML should be used. Both markup languages are stored in ASCII format, but contain tags that denote structure and format.

Digital Sustainability

Digital sustainability encompasses a range of issues and concerns that contribute to the longevity of digital information. Unlike traditional, temporary strategies, and more permanent solutions, digital sustainability implies a more active and continuous process. Digital sustainability concentrates less on the solution and technology and more on building an infrastructure and approach that is flexible with an emphasis on interoperability, continued maintenance and continuous development. Digital sustainability incorporates activities in the present that will facilitate access and availability in the future.

Preservation Repository Assessment and Certification

A few of the major frameworks for digital preservation repository assessment and certification are described below. A more detailed list is maintained by the US Centre for Research Libraries.

Specific Tools and Methodologies

TRAC: In 2007, CRL/OCLC published Trustworthy Repositories Audit and Certification: Criteria and Checklist (TRAC), a document allowing digital repositories to assess their capability to reliably store, migrate, and provide access to digital content. TRAC is based upon existing standards and best practices for trustworthy digital repositories and incorporates a set of 84 audit and certification criteria arranged in three sections: Organisational Infrastructure; Digital Object Management; and Technologies, Technical Infrastructure, and Security. TRAC "provides tools for the audit, assessment, and potential certification of digital repositories, establishes the documentation requirements required for audit, delineates a process for certification, and establishes appropriate methodologies for determining the soundness and sustainability of digital repositories".

European Framework for Audit and Certification of Digital Repositories

The European Framework for Audit and Certification of Digital Repositories was defined in a memorandum of understanding signed in July 2010 between Consultative Committee for Space Data Systems (CCSDS), Data Seal of Approval (DSA) Board and German Institute for Standardisation (DIN) "Trustworthy Archives – Certification" Working Group.

The framework is intended to help organisations in obtaining appropriate certification as a trusted digital repository and establishes three increasingly demanding levels of assessment:

1. *Basic Certification:* Self-assessment using 16 criteria of the Data Seal of Approval (DSA).
2. *Extended Certification:* Basic Certification and additional externally reviewed self-audit against ISO 16363 or DIN 31644 requirements.
3. *Formal Certification:* Validation of the self-certification with a third-party official audit based on ISO 16363 or DIN 31644.

Nestor Catalogue of Criteria

A German initiative, *nestor* (the Network of Expertise in Long-Term Storage of Digital Resources) sponsored by the German Ministry of Education and Research, developed a catalogue of criteria for trusted digital repositories in 2004. In 2008 the second version of the document was published. The catalogue, aiming primarily at German cultural heritage and higher education institutions, establishes guidelines for planning, implementing, and self-evaluation of trustworthy long-term digital repositories. The *nestor* catalogue of criteria conforms to the OAIS reference model terminology and consists of three sections covering topics related to Organisational Framework, Object Management, and Infrastructure and Security.

Planets Project

In 2002 the *Preservation and Long-term Access through Networked Services* (PLANETS) project, part of the EU Framework Programmes for Research and Technological Development 6, addressed core digital preservation challenges. The primary goal for *Planets* was to build practical services and tools to help ensure long-term access to digital cultural and scientific assets. The outputs of the project are now sustained by the follow-on organisation, the Open Planets Foundation.

Platter

Planning Tool for Trusted Electronic Repositories (PLATTER) is a tool released by Digital Preservation Europe (DPE) to help digital repositories in identifying their self-defined goals and priorities in order to gain trust from the stakeholders. PLATTER is intended to be used as a complementary tool to DRAMBORA, NESTOR, and TRAC. It is based on ten core principles for trusted repositories and defines nine Strategic Objective Plans, covering such areas as acquisition, preservation and dissemination of content, finance, staffing, succession planning, technical infrastructure, data and metadata specifications, and disaster planning. The tool enables repositories to develop and maintain documentation required for an audit.

Audit and Certification of Trustworthy Digital Repositories

Audit and Certification of Trustworthy Digital Repositories (ISO 16363:2012), developed by the Consultative Committee for Space Data Systems (CCSDS), was approved as a full international standard in March 2012. Extending the OAIS Reference Model and based largely on the TRAC checklist, the standard is designed for all types of digital repositories. It provides a detailed specification of criteria against which the trustworthiness of a digital repository should be evaluated. The CCSDS Repository Audit and Certification Working Group has also developed and submitted for approval a second standard, Requirements for Bodies Providing Audit and Certification of Candidate Trustworthy Digital Repositories (ISO 16919), that defines the external auditing process and requirements for organisations responsible for assessment and certification of digital repositories.

Digital Preservation Best Practices

Although preservation strategies vary for different types of materials and between institutions, adhering to nationally and internationally recognised standards and practices is a crucial part of digital preservation activities. Best or recommended practices define strategies and procedures that may help organisations to implement existing standards or provide guidance in areas where no formal standards have been developed.

Best practices in digital preservation continue to evolve and may encompass processes that are performed on content prior to or at the point of ingest into a digital repository as well as processes performed on preserved files post-ingest over time. Best practices may also apply to the process of digitising analogue material and may include the creation of specialised metadata (such as technical, administrative and rights metadata) in addition to standard descriptive metadata. The preservation of born-digital content may include format transformations to facilitate long-term preservation or to provide better access.

Audio Preservation

Various best practices and guidelines for digital audio preservation have been developed, including:

- *Capturing Analogue Sound for Digital Preservation: Report of a Roundtable Discussion of Best Practices for Transferring Analogue Discs and Tapes* (2006), which defined procedures for reformatting sound from analogue to digital and provided recommendations for best practices for digital preservation.
- *Digital Audio Best Practices* (2006) prepared by the Collaborative Digitisation Programme Digital Audio Working Group, which covers best practices and provides guidance both on digitising existing analogue content and on creating new digital audio resources.
- *Sound Directions: Best Practices for Audio Preservation* (2007) published by the Sound Directions Project, which describes the audio preservation workflows and recommended best practices and has been used as the basis for other projects and initiatives.
- Documents developed by the International Association of Sound and Audiovisual Archives (IASA), the European Broadcasting Union (EBU), the Library of Congress, and the Digital Library Federation (DLF).

The Audio Engineering Society (AES) also issues a variety of standards and guidelines relating to the creation of archival audio content and technical metadata.

Moving Image Preservation

The term "moving images" includes analogue film and video and their born-digital forms: digital video, digital motion picture materials, and digital cinema. As analogue videotape and film become obsolete, digitisation has become a key preservation strategy, although many archives do continue to perform photochemical preservation of film stock.

"Digital preservation" has a double meaning for audiovisual collections: analogue originals are preserved through digital reformatting, with the resulting digital files preserved; and born-digital content is collected, most often in proprietary formats that pose problems for future digital preservation. There is currently no broadly accepted standard target digital preservation format for analogue moving images.

The following resources offer information on analogue to digital reformatting and preserving born-digital audiovisual content:

- The Library of Congress tracks the sustainability of digital formats, including moving images.
- *The Digital Dilemma 2: Perspectives from Independent Film-makers, Documentarians and Non-profit Audiovisual Archives (2012).* The section on non-profit archives reviews common practices on digital reformatting, metadata, and storage. There are four case studies.
- Federal Agencies Digitisation Guidelines Initiative (FADGI). Started in 2007, this is a collaborative effort by federal agencies to define common guidelines, methods, and practices for digitising historical content. As part of this, two working groups are studying issues specific to two major areas, Still Image and Audio Visual.
- PrestoCentre publishes general audiovisual information and advice at a European level. Its online library has research and white papers on digital preservation costs and formats.
- The Association of Moving Image Archivists (AMIA) sponsors conferences, symposia, and events on all aspects of moving image preservation, including digital. The *AMIA Tech Review* contains articles reflecting current thoughts and practices from the archivists' perspectives. *Video Preservation for the Millennia (2012)*, published in the *AMIA Tech Review*, details the various strategies and ideas behind the current state of video preservation.

E-mail Preservation

E-mail poses special challenges for preservation: *e*-mail client software varies widely; there is no common structure for *e*-mail messages; *e*-mail often communicates sensitive information; individual *e*-mail accounts may contain business and personal messages intermingled; and *e*-mail may include attached documents in a variety of file formats. E-mail messages can also carry viruses or have spam content. While *e*-mail transmission is standardised, there is no formal standard for the long-term preservation of *e*-mail messages.

Approaches to preserving *e*-mail may vary according to the purpose for which it is being preserved. For businesses and government entities, *e*-mail preservation may be driven by the need to meet retention and supervision requirements for regulatory compliance and to allow for legal discovery. (Additional information about *e*-mail archiving approaches for business and institutional purposes may be found under the separate article, *E*-mail archiving.) For research libraries and archives, the preservation of *e*-mail that is part of born-digital or hybrid archival collections has as its goal ensuring its long-term availability as part of the historical and cultural record. Several projects developing tools and methodologies for *e*-mail preservation have been conducted based on various preservation strategies: normalising *e*-mail into XML format, migrating *e*-mail to a new version of the software and emulating *e*-mail environments: Memories Using *E*-mail (MUSE), Collaborative Electronic Records Project (CERP), E-Mail Collection And Preservation (EMCAP), PeDALS *E*-mail Extractor Software (PeDALS), XML Electronic Normalising of Archives tool (XENA). Some best practices and guidelines for *e*-mail preservation can be found in the following resources:

- *Curating E-Mails: A Life-cycle Approach to the Management and Preservation of E-mail Messages* (2006) by Maureen Pennock.
- *Technology Watch Report 11-01: Preserving E-mail* (2011) by Christopher J Prom.
- *Best Practices: E-mail Archiving* by Jo Maitland.

Video Game Preservation

In 2007 the *Keeping Emulation Environments Portable* (KEEP) project, part of the EU Framework Programmes for Research and Technological Development 7, developed tools and methodologies to keep digital software objects available in their original context. Digital software objects as video games might get lost because of digital obsolescence and non-availability of required legacy hardware or operating system software; such software is referred to as abandonware. Because the source code is often not available any longer, emulation is the only preservation opportunity. KEEP provided an emulation framework to help the creation of such emulators. KEEP was developed by Vincent Joguin, first launched in February 2009 and was coordinated by Elisabeth Freyre of the French National Library.

Personal Archiving

There are many things consumers and artists can do themselves to help care for their collections at home.

- "Resource Centre: Caring For Your Treasures" by American Institute for Conservation of Historic and Artistic Works details simple strategies for artists and consumers to care for and preserve their work themselves.

The Library of Congress also hosts a list for the self-preserver which includes direction towards programmes and guidelines from other institutions that will help the user preserve social media, e-mail, and formatting general guidelines (such as caring for CDs). Some of the programmes listed include:

- *HTTrack Website Copier:* A site which allows the user to download a World Wide Website from the Internet to a local directory, building recursively all directories, getting HTML, images, and other files from the server to their computer.
- *Muse:* Muse (short for Memories Using E-mail) is a programme that helps users revive memories, using their long-term e-mail archives, run by Stanford University.

Education for Digital Preservation

Digital Preservation Outreach and Education: The Digital Preservation Outreach and Education (DPOE), as part of the Library of Congress, serves to foster preservation of digital content through a collaborative network of instructors and collection management professionals working in cultural heritage institutions. Composed of Library of Congress staff, the National Trainer Network, the DPOE Steering Committee, and a community of Digital Preservation Education Advocates, as of 2013 the DPOE has 24 working trainers across the six regions of the United States.

In 2010 the DPOE conducted an assessment, reaching out to archivists, librarians, and other information professionals around the country. A working group of DPOE instructors then developed a curriculum based on the assessment results and other similar digital preservation curricula designed by other training programmes, such as LYRASIS, Educopia Institute, MetaArchive Cooperative, University of North Carolina, DigCCurr (Digital Curation Curriculum) and Cornell

University-ICPSR Digital Preservation Management Workshops. The resulting core principles are also modelled on the principles outlined in "A Framework of Guidance for Building Good Digital Collections" by the National Information Standards Organisation (NISO).

Examples of Digital Preservation Initiatives

- The Library of Congress operates the National Digital Stewardship Alliance.
- The British Library is responsible for several programmes in the area of digital preservation and is a founding member of the Digital Preservation Coalition. Their digital preservation strategy is publicly available. The National Archives of the United Kingdom have also pioneered various initiatives in the field of digital preservation.

A number of open source products have been developed to assist with digital preservation, including DSpace, Fedora, EPrints and Research-Output Repository Platform. The commercial sector also offers digital preservation software tools, such as Ex Libris Ltd.'s *Rosetta*, Tessella Ltd.'s *Safety Deposit Box* and cloud based *Preservica*, CONTENTdm, Digital Commons, Equella, intraLibrary, Open Repository and Vital.

Large-scale Digital Preservation Initiatives

Many research libraries and archives have begun or are about to begin Large-Scale digital preservation initiatives (LSDIs). The main players in LSDIs are cultural institutions, commercial companies such as Google and Microsoft, and non-profit groups including the Open Content Alliance (OCA), the Million Book Project (MBP), and HathiTrust. The primary motivation of these groups is to expand access to scholarly resources.

LSDIs: Library Perspective

Approximately 30 cultural entities, including the 12-member Committee on Institutional Cooperation (CIC), have signed digitisation agreements with either Google or Microsoft. Several of these cultural entities are participating in the Open Content Alliance (OCA) and the Million Book Project (MBP). Some libraries are involved in only one initiative and others have diversified their digitisation strategies through participation in multiple initiatives. The three main reasons for library participation in LSDIs are: Access, Preservation and Research and Development. It is hoped that digital preservation will ensure that library materials remain accessible for future generations. Libraries have a perpetual responsibility for their materials and a commitment to archive their digital materials. Libraries plan to use digitised copies as backups for works in case they go out of print, deteriorate, or are lost and damaged.

The Binding

Library binding is the method of binding serials, and re-binding paperback or hardcover books, for use within libraries. Library binding increases the durability of books, as well as making the materials easier to use. The stiffening process is a low-cost, in-house alternative to library binding of paperbacks.

Purpose

Library binding is a way to increase the life of books and periodicals used in libraries. This is done by sewing the pages in place and by reinforcing the spine for each volume. The goal of library binding is long-term preservation. However, library bound books also benefit library patrons by ensuring that the volume in hand is complete, opened with ease, and easy to photocopy. In addition, many libraries re-bind damaged books in library bindings regardless of whether they were originally paperback or hardcover.

Methods and Materials

Most library binders use a method of bookbinding called *oversewing* to secure the volumes. Oversewing involves cutting or *milling* off the spines of the volumes, creating a block of loose pages. Then the loose sheets are combined into small units or *signatures*, which are secured with overlock stitching. The separate signatures then get sewn together, creating a single book block. Often a piece of linen is glued to the book block spine for further support. The spine of the volume sometimes is *rounded* and *backed* to keep the spine from caving in. But if the paper of the volume is too fragile, or the book block is too thick, the spine is left flat. The book block is placed in a sturdy cover or *case*, with special paper covering the inside covers (Boardway 1993).

The most common cloth used by library binders to cover the boards of the book is buckram coated with acrylic. Acrylic coatings are generally resistant to water, mould, insects, and ultraviolet light. The buckram used is a 100 per cent cotton, bulky fabric designed to withstand wear and tear (Jones 1993). Smaller books may be bound in *c-cloth*, a lighter weight cloth that may or may not have an acrylic coating. The information about the volume (such as title and call number) is hot-stamped onto the spine. Bound serials are typically all bound in the same colour of buckram, in order to indicate the relationship of the volumes.

Library Binders

Library binding is done at a commercial library binding company. Sending books to the library binder is a mass production process. The library will gather and set aside their volumes which they want library bound, and then box and ship off these books to a library binding company. The binding company handles each volume one at a time, and then places all the items from the shipment back into boxes and sends them back to the library.

- Commercial library binding factories were first established in America and England in the early twentieth century. Since then, there have emerged several prominent library binding companies (including Dague Bookbindery, Ocker and Trapp, or Wert Bookbinders). Although they are commercial enterprises, library binders act as partners to the library world. The operations they perform on books and serials help extend the life of these materials, making them more accessible to library users. The goal should always be to do as *little* damage to the volume as possible. A volume should not be sent to a commercial library binder if the papers in the volume are brittle, if the volume appears to have value as an artifact, if the item can be repaired or treated in-house, or if the item needs preparatory conservation treatment.
- Library binders and libraries must agree on the conditions of the services provided and the prices rendered, and then must sign a contract confirming these. The library binder should ensure against the loss of volumes and should correct any mistakes (such as the wrong colour buckram cloth, or the incorrect title stamped on the spine) (State of Connecticut Binding Contract 1993).
- The Library Binding Institute is the main source of information and standards on library binding. In conjunction with the National Information Standards Organisation, the Library Binding Institute has published standards of library binding that should be used by all binding companies. These include technical specifications (for the different methods of library binding) and material specifications (for the materials used in library binding).

Mass Deacidification

Mass deacidification is a term used in Library and Information Science for one possible measure against the degradation of paper in old books (the so-called "slow fires"). The goal of the process is to increase the pH of acidic paper on a large scale. Although acid-free paper has become more common, a large body of acidic paper still exists in books made after the 1850s because of its cheaper and simpler production methods. Acidic paper, especially when exposed to light, air pollution, or high relative humidity, yellows and becomes brittle over time. During mass deacidification an alkaline agent is deposited in the paper to neutralise existing acid and prevent further decay.

Current Services

There are several commercial deacidification techniques currently on the market:

- The BookKeeper process is a non-aqueous, liquid phase process that uses magnesium oxide. BookKeeper is available through Preservation Technologies, L.P. with plants in the US, Spain, Japan, Poland, The Netherlands, and South Africa.
- The CSC Book Saver uses carbonated magnesium propylate for deacidification. It is available through Conservacion de Sustratos Celulosicos S.L. (CSC) (Barcelona, Spain).
- The Papersave process was developed by Battelle Ingenieurtechnik GmbH and is, therefore, sometimes referred to as "the Battelle Process". The process uses magnesium titanium alkoxide. It is available in Europe through Nitrochemie Wimmis (Wimmis, Switzerland) under the name of Papersave Swiss and the Zentrum fur Bucherhaltung (Leipzig, Germany).
- The Wei T'o process uses methoxy magnesium methyl carbonate, or isopropoxy magnesium isopropyl carbonate, and new products are coming out in 2008. Wei T'o is less commonly used for mass deacidification treatment than for single item deacidification. Wei T'o products are available through Wei T'o Associates Inc. (Matteson, USA).

BookKeeper, CSC Booksaver, Papersave and Wei T'o are also available as a hand held sprays.

Goals

These are the results that the Library of Congress expected of an ideal mass deacidification treatment in 1994:

- Neutralise acidic paper and add an alkaline reserve.
- Produce a pH value between 6.8 and 10.4 which is evenly distributed throughout the book.
- Should not cause any damage to adhesives, inks or dyes.
- Should not cause any odour or any change in the colour of the paper.
- Should not cause loss of pliancy or mechanical strength.

Faculty members of the Slovak University of Technology added these further requirements:

- The chemicals used have to be safe.
- The process has to be able to be applied to any kind of paper.
- The process can not cause swelling or warping of the paper.

Effects

All of the processes imparted an adequately high pH in studies conducted by the European Commission on Preservation and Access, the Library of Congress, and a team of scientists from the Centre de Recherches sur la Conservation des Documents Graphiques in the early and mid-nineties. BookKeeper produced a pH of 9-10. CSC Book Saver gives a pH of 8.78-10.5. Wei T'o gives 7.5 to 10.4, and Papersave gives a pH of 7.5-9.

The same studies also found that the processes had negative cosmetic side effects. BookKeeper left "a palpable residue", clamp marks on the covers, and caused some of the coloured inks to rub off. CSC Book Saver left a "white powdery deposit" on books. Papersave caused "discolouration, white deposit, Newton rings, bleeding of inks and dyes, odour and different 'feel' of the paper." Wei T'o caused "odour, white residues, rings, cockling, (yellow) discolourations and adhesive bleeding."

However, these studies are now more than ten years old and several of the processes have changed their formulae since the mid-nineties. Conservators from the British Library acknowledge that the existing mass deacidification processes are still developing and further research needs to be conducted on their chemical and mechanical effects. The Library of Congress recommends libraries use mass deacidification to ensure that collections survive. Clearly, the conservators working for the Library of Congress believe that mass deacidification is vital to library collections, whatever the cosmetic effects may or may not be.

History of Research and Process Development

Mass deacidification - along with microfilm and lamination - was developed during the early- and mid-20th century as a response to the chemical process of hydrolysis by which the fibres that constitute paper, providing its structure and strength, have their bonds broken, resulting in paper that becomes increasingly brittle over time. Environmental pollutants can react with paper to form acids that promote oxidation, creating more acid as a by-product, which results in a positive feedback loop of autocatalytic destruction. Supported in part by grants from the Council on Library Resources, William J. Barrow conducted research into paper decay and found that no more than three per cent of the books published between 1900 and 1949 would survive more than fifty years. In response to this, a Standing Committee on the Preservation of Research Library Materials was formed by the Association of Research Libraries (ARL) in 1960.

Barrow also invented an aqueous process to neutralise acid in paper while depositing an alkaline buffer that would retard the rate of decay. In addition to Barrow's original method, both non-aqueous - employing organic solvents - and vaporous - the Library of Congress' DEZ (diethyl zinc) treatment - methods of achieving the same results have been researched in an attempt to reduce time, labour, and cost requirements.

One technique proposed was to place books in an evacuated chamber, then introduce diethylzinc (DEZ). In theory, the diethylzinc would react with acidic residues in the paper, leaving an alkaline residue that would protect the paper against further degradation. In practice, the heating required to remove trace water from the books before reaction (DEZ reacts violently with water) caused an accelerated degradation of the paper, and a range of other chemical reactions between DEZ and other components of the book (glues, bindings) caused further damage and the production of unpleasant smells. Regardless, in the 1980s, a pilot plant for mass deacidification using this process was constructed by NASA and was tested on books provided by the Library of Congress. However, it was discovered in 1986 that the DEZ had not been removed in one of the deacidification runs and was pooled in the bottom of the chamber, and probably remained within some of the plumbing. DEZ is violently flammable when it comes in contact with either oxygen or water vapour, so the vacuum chamber could not be opened to remove the books within. Eventually, explosives were used to rupture the suspect plumbing; suspicions of the presence of residual DEZ were confirmed by the subsequent fire that destroyed the plant. In his book Double Fold, Nicholson Baker discusses the failure of the NASA programme at great length.

The chemical company Akzo made later attempts at refining the process; though the risks of fire and explosions were reduced by better process design, damage and odours remained a problem. In the end, Akzo decided the process was not a viable commercial proposition, and shut down their research at the end of 1994.

Adoption and Costs

While deacidification has been adopted by major research libraries such as the Library of Congress and the New York Public Library, it is not clear that many archives, particularly those in the United States, have followed suit. Whereas some European national archives have tested deacidification techniques, the United States' National Archives and Records Administration (NARA), which pioneered an aqueous technique that improved upon Barrow's, has chosen to invest its preservation dollars elsewhere. In 2000, the Chief of the NARA Document Conservation Laboratory defended the lack of a mass deacidification programme by pointing to differences between library and archival collections, for example noting that many of the papers coming to NARA were of a higher quality than those in library collections; that the Archives does not receive records from Federal government agencies until they are at least 30 years old, by which time acidic paper will have already been irrevocably weakened; and that limited resources might best be applied elsewhere, such as climate control, as under the Archives' Twenty-Year Preservation Plan, the emphasis was on "maximum benefit for the greatest number of records."

Though now dated, several sources estimate the costs and suitability of deacidification treatment. Studies conducted by the Harry Ransom Humanities Research Centre and the General State Archive of the Netherlands found the DEZ method, properly used, might be particularly applicable to archival materials. It was estimated that deacidification costs, excluding transportation and handling, during the early 1990s was $5–10 per volume. During 1995-1997, the Library of Congress received $2 million in appropriations to deacidify 72,000 books using the Bookkeeper commercial method and evaluate alternative methods. The actual cost per book was $11.70. Finally, a recent cost comparison with reformatting options per volume yielded $125 for microfilming, $50 for scanning and minimal indexing, and, based on a New York Public Library project, $16.20 for deacidification.

Slow Fire

A slow fire is a term used in library and information science to describe paper embrittlement resulting from acid decay. The term is taken from the title of Terry Sanders' 1987 film *Slow Fires: On the preservation of the human record.*

Solutions to this problem include the use of acid-free paper stocks, reformatting brittle books by microfilming, photocopying or digitisation, and a variety of deacidification techniques.

16

INFORMATION SYSTEM AND MANAGEMENT

(Theory and Practice)

Information system (IS) is the study of complementary networks of hardware and software that people and organisations use to collect, filter, process, create, and distribute data. The study bridges business and computer science using the theoretical foundations of information and computation to study various business models and related algorithmic processes within a computer science discipline. Computer information system(s) (CIS) is a field studying computers and algorithmic processes, including their principles, their software and hardware designs, their applications, and their impact on society while IS emphasises functionality over design.

Any specific information system aims to support operations, management and decision-making. In a broad sense, the term is used to refer not only to the information and communication technology (ICT) that an organisation uses, but also to the way in which people interact with this technology in support of business processes. Some authors make a clear distinction between information systems, computer systems, and business processes. Information systems typically include an ICT component but are not purely concerned with ICT, focusing instead on the end use of information technology. Information systems are also different from business processes. Information systems help to control the performance of business processes.

Alter argues for advantages of viewing an information system as a special type of work system. A work system is a system in which humans and/or machines perform work (processes and activities) using resources to produce specific products and/or services for customers. An information system is a work system whose activities are devoted to processing (capturing, transmitting, storing, retrieving, manipulating and displaying) information. As such, information systems interrelate with data systems on the one hand and activity systems on the other. An information system is a form of communication system in which data represent and are processed as a form of social memory. An information system can also be considered a semi-formal language which supports human decision-making and action. Information systems are the primary focus of study for organisational informatics.

An Overview

Silver *et al.* (1995) provided two views on IS that includes software, hardware, data, people, and procedures. A second managerial view includes people, business processes and Information Systems. The Association for Computing Machinery defines "Information systems specialists [as] focusing on integrating information technology solutions and business processes to meet the information needs of businesses and other enterprises."

There are various types of information systems, for example: transaction processing systems, decision support systems, knowledge management systems, learning management systems, database management systems, and office information systems. Critical to most information systems are information technologies, which are typically designed to enable humans to perform tasks for which the human brain is not well suited, such as: handling large amounts of information, performing complex calculations, and controlling many simultaneous processes.

Information technologies are a very important and malleable resource available to executives. Many companies have created a position of Chief Information Officer (CIO) that sits on the executive board with the Chief Executive Officer (CEO), Chief Financial Officer (CFO), Chief Operating Officer (COO) and Chief Technical Officer (CTO). The CTO may also serve as CIO [Chief Information Officer], and vice versa. The Chief Information Security Officer (CISO) focuses on information security management.

The Background

The history of information systems coincides with the history of computer science that began long before the modern discipline of computer science emerged in the twentieth century. Regarding the circulation of information and ideas, numerous legacy information systems still exist today that are continuously updated to promote ethnographic approaches, to ensure data integrity, and to improve the social effectiveness and efficiency of the whole process. In general, information systems are focused upon processing information within organisations, especially within business enterprises, and sharing the benefits with modern society.

Disciplines of Information System

Several IS scholars have debated the nature and foundations of Information Systems which has its roots in other reference disciplines such as Computer Science, Engineering, Mathematics, Management Science, Cybernetics, and others. Information systems also can be defined as a collection of hardware, software, data, people and procedures that work together to produce quality information. Information may also be given from the person or application..

Types of Information Systems

The "classic" view of Information systems found in the textbooks in the 1980s was of a pyramid of systems that reflected the hierarchy of the organisation, usually transaction processing systems at the bottom of the pyramid, followed by management information systems, decision support systems, and ending with executive information systems at the top. Although the pyramid model remains useful, since it was first formulated a number of new technologies have been developed and new categories of information systems have emerged, some of which no longer fit easily into the original pyramid model.

Some examples of such systems are:

- Data warehouses;
- Enterprise resource planning;
- Enterprise systems;
- Expert systems;
- Search engines;
- Geographic information system;
- Global information system;
- Office automation.

A Computer(-Based) Information System is essentially an IS using computer technology to carry out some or all of its planned tasks. The basic components of computer based information system are:

- *Hardware*: These are the devices like the monitor, processor, printer and keyboard, all of which work together to accept, process, show data and information.
- *Software*: Are the programmes that allow the hardware to process the data.
- *Databases:* Are the gathering of associated files or tables containing related data.
- *Networks:* Are a connecting system that allows diverse computers to distribute resources.
- *Procedures:* Are the commands for combining the components above to process information and produce the preferred output.

The first four components (hardware, software, database and network) make up what is known as the information technology platform. Information technology workers could then use these components to create information systems that watch over safety measures, risk and the management of data. These actions are known as information technology services.

Certain information systems support parts of organisations, others support entire organisations, and still others, support groups of organisations. Recall that each department or functional area within an organisation has its own collection of application programmes, or information systems. These functional area information systems (FAIS) are supporting pillars for more general IS namely, business intelligence systems and dashboards.

As the name suggest, each FAIS support a particular function are within the organisation, e.g.: accounting IS, finance IS, production/operation management (POM) IS, marketing IS, and human resources IS. In finance and accounting, managers use IT systems to forecast revenues and business activity, to determine the best sources and uses of funds, and to perform audits to ensure that the organisation is fundamentally sound and that all financial reports and documents are accurate. Other types of organisational information systems are FAIS, Transaction processing systems, enterprise resource planning, office automation system, management information system, decision support system, expert system, executive dashboard, supply chain management system, and electronic commerce system.

Dashboards are a special form of IS that support all managers of the organisation. They provide rapid access to timely information and direct access to structured information in the form of reports. Expert systems attempt to duplicate the work of human experts by applying reasoning capabilities, knowledge, and expertise within a specific domain.

Information Systems Development

Information technology departments in larger organisations tend to strongly influence information technology development, use, and application in the organisations, which may be a business or corporation. A series of methodologies and processes can be used to develop and use an information system. Many developers have turned and used a more engineering approach such as the System Development Life Cycle (SDLC) which is a systematic procedure of developing an information system through stages that occur in sequence. An Information system can be developed in house (within the organisation) or outsourced. This can be accomplished by outsourcing certain components or the entire system. A specific case is the geographical distribution of the development team (Offshoring, Global Information System).

A computer based information system, following a definition of Langefors, is:

- A technologically implemented medium for recording, storing, and disseminating linguistic expressions;
- As well as for drawing conclusions from such expressions.

Which can be formulated as a generalised information systems design mathematical programme.

Geographic Information Systems, Land Information systems and Disaster Information Systems are also some of the emerging information systems but they can be broadly considered as Spatial Information Systems. System development is done in stages which include:

- Problem recognition and specification;
- Information gathering;
- Requirements specification for the new system;
- System design;
- System construction;
- System implementation;
- Review and maintenance.

Information Systems Research

Information systems research is generally interdisciplinary concerned with the study of the effects of information systems on the behaviour of individuals, groups, and organisations. Hevner *et al.* (2004) categorised research in IS into two scientific paradigms including *behavioural science* which is to develop and verify theories that explain or predict human or organisational behaviour and *design science* which extends the boundaries of human and organisational capabilities by creating new and innovative artifacts.

Salvatore March and Gerald Smith proposed a framework for researching different aspects of Information Technology including outputs of the research (research outputs) and activities to carry out this research (research activities). They identified research outputs as follows:

1. *Constructs* which are concepts that form the vocabulary of a domain. They constitute a conceptualisation used to describe problems within the domain and to specify their solutions.
2. A *model* which is a set of propositions or statements expressing relationships among constructs.

3. A *method* which is a set of steps (an algorithm or guideline) used to perform a task. Methods are based on a set of underlying constructs and a representation (model) of the solution space.
4. An *instantiation* is the realisation of an artifact in its environment.

Also research activities including:

1. *Build* an artifact to perform a specific task.
2. *Evaluate* the artifact to determine if any progress has been achieved.
3. Given an artifact whose performance has been evaluated, it is important to determine why and how the artifact worked or did not work within its environment. Therefore *theorise* and *justify* theories about IT artifacts.

Although Information Systems as a discipline has been evolving for over 30 years now, the core focus or identity of IS research is still subject to debate among scholars. There are two main views around this debate: a narrow view focusing on the IT artifact as the core subject matter of IS research, and a broad view that focuses on the interplay between social and technical aspects of IT that is embedded into a dynamic evolving context. A third view calls on IS scholars to pay balanced attention to both the IT artifact and its context.

Since the study of information systems is an applied field, industry practitioners expect information systems research to generate findings that are immediately applicable in practice. This is not always the case however, as information systems researchers often explore behavioural issues in much more depth than practitioners would expect them to do. This may render information systems research results difficult to understand, and has led to criticism. To study an information system itself, rather than its effects, information systems models are used, such as EATPUT.

The international body of Information Systems researchers, the Association for Information Systems (AIS), and its Senior Scholars Forum Subcommittee on Journals (23 April 2007), proposed a 'basket' of journals that the AIS deems as 'excellent', and nominated: Management Information Systems Quarterly (MISQ), Information Systems Research (ISR), Journal of the Association for Information Systems (JAIS), Journal of Management Information Systems (JMIS), European Journal of Information Systems (EJIS), and Information Systems Journal (ISJ).

A number of annual information systems conferences are run in various parts of the world, the majority of which are peer reviewed. The AIS directly runs the International Conference on Information Systems (ICIS) and the Americas Conference on Information Systems (AMCIS), while AIS affiliated conferences include the Pacific Asia Conference on Information Systems (PACIS), European Conference on Information Systems (ECIS), the Mediterranean Conference on Information Systems (MCIS), the International Conference on Information Resources Management (Conf-IRM) and the Wuhan International Conference on *E*-Business (WHICEB). AIS chapter conferences include Australasian Conference on Information Systems (ACIS), Information Systems Research Conference in Scandinavia (IRIS), Conference of the Italian Chapter of AIS (itAIS), Annual Mid-Western AIS Conference (MWAIS) and Annual Conference of the Southern AIS (SAIS).

Components

The 5 components that must come together in order to produce a Computer-Based Information system are:

1. *Hardware:* The term hardware refers to machinery. This category includes the computer itself, which is often referred to as the central processing unit (CPU), and all of its support

equipments. Among the support equipments are input and output devices, storage devices and communications devices.

2. *Software:* The term software refers to computer programmes and the manuals (if any) that support them. Computer programmes are machine-readable instructions that direct the circuitry within the hardware parts of the system to function in ways that produce useful information from data. Programmes are generally stored on some input/output medium, often a disk or tape.
3. *Data:* Data are facts that are used by programmes to produce useful information. Like programmes, data are generally stored in machine-readable form on disk or tape until the computer needs them.
4. *Procedures:* Procedures are the policies that govern the operation of a computer system. "Procedures are to people what software is to hardware" is a common analogy that is used to illustrate the role of procedures in a system.
5. *People:* Every system needs people if it is to be useful. Often the most overlooked element of the system are the people, probably the component that most influence the success or failure of information systems.

Information Systems Career Pathways

Information Systems have a number of different areas of work:

- IS strategy;
- IS management;
- IS development;
- IS iteration;
- IS organisation.

There is a wide variety of career paths in the information systems discipline. "Workers with specialised technical knowledge and strong communications skills will have the best prospects. Workers with management skills and an understanding of business practices and principles will have excellent opportunities, as companies are increasingly looking to technology to drive their revenue."

Impact on Economic Models

- Microeconomic theory model;
- Transaction cost theory;
- Agency theory.

Differentiating Information System from related Disciplines

Similar to computer science, other disciplines can be seen as both related and foundation disciplines of IS. The domain of study of IS involves the study of theories and practices related to the social and technological phenomena, which determine the development, use, and effects of information systems in organisation and society. But, while there may be considerable overlap of the disciplines at the boundaries, the disciplines are still differentiated by the focus, purpose, and orientation of their activities.

In a broad scope, the term *Information Systems* is a scientific field of study that addresses the range of strategic, managerial, and operational activities involved in the gathering, processing, storing, distributing, and use of information and its associated technologies in society and organisations. The term information systems is also used to describe an organisational function that applies IS knowledge in industry, government agencies, and not-for-profit organisations. *Information Systems* often refers to the interaction between algorithmic processes and technology. This interaction can occur within or across organisational boundaries. An information system is the technology an organisation uses and also the way in which the organisations interact with the technology and the way in which the technology works with the organisation's business processes. Information systems are distinct from information technology (IT) in that an information system has an information technology component that interacts with the processes' components.

One problem with that approach is that it prevents the IS field from being interested in non-organisational use of ICT, such as in social networking, computer gaming, mobile personal usage, etc. A different way of differentiating the IS field from its neighbours is to ask, "Which aspects of reality are most meaningful in the IS field and other fields?" This approach, based on philosophy, helps to define not just the focus, purpose and orientation, but also the dignity, destiny and responsibility of the field among other fields.

Systems and Management

Scope and Demarcation of Set-up

An organisation is a stable, formal social frame that takes resources from the environment and processes them to produce outputs. This definition concentrates on three aspects of an organisation. Capital and labour are primary factors of production provided by the environment. The organisation (the enterprise) changes these inputs into products and services in a production function. The products and services are consumed by environments in lien of supply inputs. An organisation is more stable than an informal group (like as a group of friends that meets every Friday for lunch) in terms of longevity and routineness. Organisations are formal legal structures with internal rules and procedures that must abide by laws. They are also social structures as they are a collection of social elements much as a machine has a structure — a certain arrangement of valves, cams, shafts, and other parts.

An organisation's behavioural definition is that it is a collection of rights, privileges, obligations, and responsibilities that are delicately balanced over a period of time by conflict and conflict resolution. In this behavioural view of the organisation, people who work in organisations develop customary means of working: they try to have access to attachments to existing relationships; and they make arrangements with subordinates and superiors about how work will be done, how much work will be done, and under what conditions. A bulk of these arrangements and feelings are not talked about in any formal rulebook. The technical and behavioural definitions of organisations are not contradictory. In fact, they complement each other. The technical definition reminds us about how thousands of enterprise in competitive markets combine capital, labour, and information technology, at the same time the behavioural model takes us inside the individual enterprise to see how that technology affects the organisation's inner workings.

Common Characteristics of Organisation

(a) *Formal Structure:* Modern business organisations such as IBM, Toyota, AT&T, Apple computer, 3M, GE, Alcatel, Tatas, Birlas, NTPC, ONGC more less are similar because they sharp the characteristics of Bureaucracy. Modern organisations are formal systems. They are in existence formally and legally through appropriate incorporation, registration, etc. with a board of directors who enjoy control over the organisation. The principal features common to all organisations are:

(i) division of labour,

(ii) hierarchy,

(iii) explicit rules and procedures

(iv) impartial judgement

(v) technical qualification for positions, etc.

(b) *Standard Operating Systems and Procedures (SOPs):* Inextricably linked to formal organisational structure is the set of standard operating systems and procedures.

Organisations that survive in a competitive business atmosphere over time become very efficient, producing a limited number of products and services by following standard routines. These standard routines get codified into reasonably precise rules, procedures, and practices known as Standard Operating Procedures (SOPs) that are developed to cope with nearly all expected situations. A few of these rules and procedures are written, formal procedures. Most are "rules of thumb" to be followed in choosen situations. The Business processes followed in enterprise are on the basis of SOPs.

These standard operating procedures significantly influence on the efficiency that modern organisations gain. For instance, in the assembly of a car, managers and workers adopt complex standard procedure to tackle thousands of motions in a precise fashion, allowing the finished product to roll off the assembly line. Any change in SOPs demands an enormous organisational effort. In fact, the organisation may require to halt the whole production process before the old SOPs can be retired.

The initial set of procedures that got codified were connected with financial transactions in the form of verification authority, approval authority, payment authority, and record-maintenance authority. The other set of systems and procedures that get formalised refer to the major business of organisation and its execution. For instance, for centuries the Registrar of a University has been the formally empowered authority to keep academic records such as degree certificates. As for construction and contracting companies as well as the manufacturing companies, the Chief Design Engineer formally holds the rights and responsibilities for designs. Accordingly, these designated authorities formally set up systems and procedures that guarantee clearly identifiable responsibilities so as to protect everyone at the juncture of any malpractice, mishap, etc.

Connected to these systems and procedures is a set of standards; like, standardised Account and Budget Heads, Codification of Expenses, Departments, Payment Terms, etc. Next come the standardised forms and even their usage. Sometimes, the very existence of different forms gives a convenient mechanism of separate yet standardised systems and procedures. The separation of tax forms for individuals and the corporate sector and their contents, formats, and instructions codifies in automatic way the respective systems and procedures. In enterprises that are far more organised, the standard operating procedures stretch out to office-layout, stationery, logo and its usage, policy for phone connections, policy for provision of company-transport, and even dress code, including uniform. Difficulty in changing standard operating procedures is one reason for inefficiency with a few organisations. Information systems are principal vehicles that implement these systems and procedures in a fast, flexible and cost-effective manner.

(c) *Transparency and Fairness as Organisation Culture:* To surmount the crises over a long period of time as acceptable business entities, where the best men and women would like to join, stay and grow as contributing to the corporate goals, organisations are supposed to have fairness in their operations. The fairness should be reflected in the hierarchy, sending a healthy signal that the top positions are open for any competent men and women accepting fair means to rise through the hierarchy. The standard operating norms should reflect practices that may be adopted by employees without fear or favour. The reward and punishment should be given in a transparent and fair manners.

Information systems are largely used to give evaluation-information like performance data, production data, defective data, etc., which are used to create incentive and bonus schemes for employees. A major chunk of these schemes would be ineffective in the absence of fair and transparent means of performance evaluation. Numerous information systems developed to help personnel departments in this country have failed to take off owing to the absence of such measures. Without fair, transparent and largely accepted performance measures, systems that compute such performance measures are likely to be resisted. This element must be taken into account in the design of information systems in areas like personnel, purchase, quality, etc.

(d) *Politics at Organisational Level:* People in organisations hold various positions with different specialities, views, concerns, and perspectives. Subsequently, they, naturally convergent as well as convergent viewpoints about how resources, rewards, and punishments should be distributed. To both managers and employees, these differences matter and they result in political struggle, competition, and often resultant conflict within every organisation. One of the great difficulties of bringing about organisational change is political resistance—especially the development of new information systems. Nearly all information systems that bring about major changes in goals, procedures, productivity, and personnel are politically charged and will elicit serious political opposition.

Systems in Organisational and Information System Structure: Successful development of information systems calls for a thorough awareness of the structure and dynamics of the organisations. As organisations oriented, the system analyst should be clear in his mind as to what information needs to be gathered, stored and analysed. As information has a context, only operational information that finally has some contribution to decision-making must be collected. This apart, the information collected and processed must be in conformity with the level of the organisation to which it is to be presented. In a seminal work on management control systems, Anthony classified and organised management into three levels—strategic, tactical and operational. It is classification is much deeper conceptually than a just classification of management into top management, middle management and operational, field or shop floor management. The levels of management necessarily do not reflect the level within the hierarchy of the organisation that can be the result of staffing policy, seniority of a person or a mere accident at any juncture. Anthony's classification is primarily grounded on the broad functional classification of management functions, regardless of the size and nature of business.

As there are many interests, specialities, and levels in an organisation, there are different types of systems. No single system is able to provide all the information needs of organisation.

The organisation is divided into strategic, management, knowledge, and operational levels and then is more divided into functional areas such as sales and marketing, manufacturing, finance, accounting, and human resources. Systems are established to serve these different organisational interests.

System of Information and Set-ups

The information systems are created for certain applications for use by an identified organisation. Thus, *understanding* the organisation—its primary goals and objectives, structure, dynamics, scale of operation, culture, tradition, social setting, level of competition, value system, and lastly, the environment under which the organisation is operating—plays a major part in the successful implementation of contemporary corporate information systems. Such an awareness is likely to supplement the technical soundness of the systems that are being designed. An Information system well designed from the technical accounts may fail if the dynamics of the organisation, where it is decided to be ultimately implemented, are not rightly understood. So, a vivid understanding of the organisational component of an information system is a major part of the education in the area of information system.

Both the information systems and organisations influence each other. Information systems must be linked with the organisation to give information that important groups within the organisation require. At the same time, the organisation must be aware of and be open to the impacts of information systems in order to benefit from recent technologies.

The interaction between information technology and organisations is much complex and is influenced by numerous mediating factors, including the organisations structure, standard operating procedure, politics, culture, surrounding atmosphere, and management decisions. Managers should bear in their minds that information system can enormously change life in the organisation. They are not able to design new systems or understand existing systems without understanding organisations. It is managers who have to decide what systems will be built, what they will do, how they will be implemented, and so forth. Often, however, the outcomes are the result of pure chance and of both good and bad luck.

Systems at Different Levels

There are main levels of information system such as:

(i) Strategic;

(ii) Management;

(iii) Knowledge; and

(iv) Operation level.

The volume of information decreases as we go up the pyramid. But, the value of information and quality of information increases as we go up:

(i) *Strategic-level systems* enable senior or top management address and solve strategic problems and issues. These also help in development of long-term trends, both in the firm and in the external environment. Their cardinal concern is matching changes in the external environment with prevailing organisational capability. For example what will the employment levels be in ten years ? What are the future industry-cost trends and where does our enterprise fit in? What products should we be making in ten years ?

(ii) *Management-level systems* help the monitoring, controlling, decision-making, and administrative functions of middle managers. The aim is to address questions like: Are things working well? Management-level systems in typed way provide periodic reports rather than instant information on operations. An instance is a relocation control system that reports on the total moving. Head hunting for head of HR, house-hunting, and home financing costs for employees in all company divisions, noting wherever actual costs that go beyond budgets.

A few management-level systems support non-routine decision-making. They tend to concentrate on less-structured decisions for which information needs are not always clear. Often these systems answer "what-if" questions: What would be the influence on production schedules if we were to double sales in the month of January ? What would happen to our return on investment in case a factory schedule were delayed for three months ? Answers to these very often require new data from outside the organisation, as well as data from inside that cannot be easily drawn from existing operational-level systems.

(iii) *Knowledge-level systems* help the organisation's knowledge and data workers. The objective of knowledge-level systems is to enable the business enterprise integrate fresh knowledge into the business and to help the organisation control the flow of paperwork. Knowledge-level systems, particularly in the form of workstations and office systems, are among the fastest-growing applications in business today.

(iv) *Operational-level systems* help operational managers by keeping track of the fundamental activities and transactions of the organisation, like quantity and quality of products or services, such as sales, receipts, cash deposits, payroll, credit decisions, and the flow of materials in a factory or service centre. The system's principal purpose at this level is to answer routine questions and to track the flow of transactions through the organisation. How many parts are in inventory? What happened to Dr. Suri's payment? To answer these sorts of questions, information must generally be easily available, reliable, current, and accurate. Instances of operational-level systems include a system to record bank's deposits from automatic teller machines or one that tracks the number of hours worked daily by employees on a factory floor.

Functioning of Specific-level Information System

Information systems prove to be the help for major business functions, like sales and marketing, manufacturing, finance, accounting, and human resources. An exemplary organisation every operational, management, knowledge, and strategic-level systems of every functional area. For instance, the sales-function generally has a sales system on the operational level to record daily sales figures and to process orders. A knowledge-level system designs promotional displays for the enterprise's products. As far as a management-level system is concerned, it tracks monthly sales figures by sales territory and reports on territories where sales increase or decrease below anticipated levels. A system to forecast sales trends over a ten-year period serves the strategic level.

Information System in various Hues

The organisation is equipped with executive support systems (ESS) at the strategic level, management information systems (MIS) and decision-support systems (DSS) at the management level, knowledge work systems (KWS) and office systems at the knowledge level, and transaction processing systems (TPS) at the operational level. Systems at each level are meant to serve each of the principal functional areas. Accordingly, the typical systems seen in organisations are design to help workers or managers at each level and in the functions of sales and marketing, manufacturing, finance, accounting, and human resources.

(i) *Executive Support Systems (ESS):* Information systems at the organisation's strategic level created to address unstructured decision-making through modern graphics and communications.

(ii) *Management Information Systems (MIS):* Information systems at the management level of an organisation that do the functions of planning, controlling, and decision-making by supplying routine summary and exception reports.

(iii) *Decision Support Systems (DSS):* Information systems at the organisation's management level that connect data and sophisticated analytical models or data analysis equipments to support semi-structured and unstructured decision-making.

(iv) *Knowledge Work Systems (KWS):* Information systems that help knowledge workers in the creation and integration of new knowledge in the organisation.

(v) *Office Systems.* Computer systems, like word processing, electronic mail systems, and scheduling systems, that are meant to enhance the productivity of data workers in the office.

(vi) *Transaction Processing Systems (TPS):* Computerised systems that perform and record the day-to-day routine transactions necessary to run the business; they serve the organisation's operational level.

Needs of Information and Managing Part

The entire management of an organisation would consist of many different functions. The functions would rely on the type of organisation. A numerous functions are, however, common to most organisations. For effective management of every function, specific strategic, tactical and operational information are required. In this section we discuss the important goals of some important functions and their information requirements. The information needs identified in the following subsections are not exhaustive but only indicative.

(I) *Production Management:* The aim of production management is to optimally deploy human resources, machines and materials to raise to the maximum the production of goods by the organisation. In order to accomplish this goal, the following types of information would be needed:

(i) Strategic

- Annually and monthly production quotas and alternate schedules
- Policies on machine replacement, enhancement, and modernisation
- Details on the introduction of new production technologies
- Recognising best product mix.

(ii) Tactical

- Identifying and regulating areas of high cost such as work-in-progress inventories
- Recognising crucial bottlenecks in production
- Identifying alternate production schedules on the basis of tools, machines, material, and personnel availability
- Performance aspects of machines (breakdown histories and cost of repair and failure) to decide on replacement.

(iii) Operational

- Monitoring up-to-date production information by monitoring assemblies, detecting likely shortages and giving early warning
- Scheduling better production in dynamic way
- Preventive maintenance schedules of machines
- Monitoring tools, machines, and availability of human resource.

Thus, manufacturing information system is required to be developed organisation:

(II) *Material Management:* The major objective of material management is to have readily available materials needed by the organisation and to keep optimal levels of stock of items. To accomplish this goal the following kinds of information would be needed:

(i) Strategic

- Developing vendors for critical items
- Deciding optimal levels of inventory
- Determining proportion of material to be ordered from various vendors
- Reducing varieties of inventory.

(ii) Tactical

- Developing vendor performance measures
- Deciding the impact on material cost, availability and procurement with design changes and fresh product introduction.
- Determining optimal reorder levels
- Regulating high-value inventory.

(iii) Operational

- Goods accepted and issued
- List of items rejected and issued
- List of items rejected
- Critical items accepted
- Backlog of supplies
- Scores in transit and in inspection
- Value of inventory in hand.

Hence material or inventory of storage information is needed to be developed.

(III) *Human Resource Management:* The important aim of human resource management is to make best use of the human resources available in the organisation. To accomplish this goal, the information necessary at different levels of management is as follows:

(i) Strategic Information

- Long-term human resource needs at different levels
- Policies on wages and incentives like stock options
- Policies on human resource development and training
- Policies on personnel welfare and facilities.

(ii) Tactical Information

- Appraisal of Performance
- Demographic make-up of personnel and its impact on retirement
- Production incentives and link to productivity
- Morale of personnel
- Absentee reduction
- Leave and overtime policies
- Personnel development policies.

(iii) Operational Information

- Routine assessment
- Skills inventory
- Loans/advances and recoveries
- Leave record.

In this way Human Resource system is needed to be developed in enterprise.

(IV) *Marketing Management:* The objective of this function is to maximise sales and ensure customer satisfaction. For attaining this goal, the various types of information needed are:

(i) Strategic

- Search for fresh markets and marketing strategies
- Analysis of competitor's strategy
- Technology and demographic forecasts and product changes.

(ii) Tactical

- Advertising techniques and analysis of their effect
- Customer preference surveys
- Correlation of prices and sales
- Sales force deployment and targets
- Exploring alternate marketing channels. Timing of specific sales campaigns

(iii) Operational

- Sales report by regions, customer class, sales persons
- Sales target versus accomplishment
- Market share and trends
- Seasonal variations
- Impact of model changes
- Performance of sales outlets
- Costs of sales campaigns and benefits

So, marketing information is needed and it will be discussed subsequently.

(V) *Finance Management:* The major objective of this function is to ascertain financial viability of the organisation, enforce financial discipline and plan and oversee the budget. The different levels of information needed to meet these goals are as follows:

(i) Strategic

- Methods of financing
- Pricing policies
- Tax planning

(ii) Tactical

- Variance between budget and expenses
- Large outstanding payments/receipts
- Credit and payment status
- Cost increases and pricing
- Impact of taxation on pricing.

(iii) Operational

- Time-bound financial reports
- Budget status to every functional manager
- Tax returns
- Share registration and transfers
- Account on profit and loss
- Payments and receipts
- Payroll, provident fund accounts
- Calculation of direct cost-overheads, standard cost.

Accordingly the Accounting and Financial information system is required.

(VI) *Research, Design and Development Management:* The aim of this function is to improve continuously existing products and develop fresh products and processes. For attaining this goal, following kinds of informations are needed:

(i) Strategic

- Which products are to be developed?
- What kind of improvements are required?
- What long-term research is most promising?
- What technical collaboration would be appropriate?
- What areas would need new human resource inputs?

(ii) Tactical

- Setting intermediate objectives for projects and assess progress.
- Checking availability of equipment and right selection.
- Determining proportion of resources to be given to various parts of a project.
- Deployment of personnel to projects, on the basis of talent and performance.
- Information on similar and connected research projects undertaken by other groups.

(iii) Operational

- Progress against goals.
- Budgeted expenses versus actual.
- Status of outstanding orders for equipment and components.

Grounds for Data Arrangement and Access: All organisations are all set to achieving goals or objectives. Accordingly, the managers are needed to get some particular activities executed.

The Managerial decisions are made based on the information at the disposal of staff executive. Data when set up to ensure that they are meaningful and of value to the recipient is referred as information. Data can be defined as facts and figures that are not currently being used in a decision-making process and normally take the shape of historical records that are recorded and filed without immediate intent to retrieve it for decision-making. As data is placed in a meaningful way, it becomes useful information. A manager action varied functions in an organisation POSDCORB. Decision-making is one of the major managerial jobs. For decision-making, a manager needs information. The quality of information decides the quality of decision. The principal objective of any CBIS is the acquisition and processing as it may be easily placed in a meaning context as a facilitation too for decision. CBIS relief upon the databases. Data is one of the key-elements of an information system. On being entered data, are organised and stored in successively more comprehensive groupings. Data must be organised in some logical manner on physical storage devices to make sure that they can be efficiently processed. Accordingly data is organised into logical data factors such as *characters, fields, records, files* and *databases.* Database structures such as hierarchical, network, relational and object-oriented models, are employed to organise the relationships among the data records stored in databases. The broad frame work has been described in earlier chapters. Putting together; these groupings are known as a data storage hierarchy. The broad grouping of any data storage hierarchy, is:

1. *The Characters:* Characters include all written language symbols like letters, numbers, and special symbols. The character is elaborately classified as numeric or alphanumeric. A character is the lowest level addressable element of a computer storage in which data value or content of a data element or an attribute of an entity is physically stored.
2. *Data Elements (Fields):* The meaningful collections of connected characters is referred as data elements. Data elements are also known as data terms or fields. The major examples of data elements are a small group of words, and a complete number. A field is one or more bytes of data stored on a storage medium. Every unit of information or a group of data items stored in a database record comprises discrete data elements or fields; each explaining a certain attribute or characteristics of an entity. Each field is assigned a unique identifier or tag which mentions the contents of the field. The fields may be fixed or variable. A fixed field includes predetermined or fixed number of characters. The length of such a field and its position in a record is permanent for all records. In variable length field, the number of characters which consist of a field may vary from record to record.

   The fixed length of field in fixed is 8 character for use in statistical analysis. For instance sex. Age as field name of 3 character.
3. *Records:* The records are collections of related data factors or field. For example, a student's name in a college computer file would seem in the "name" field. A logical grouping of related fields, such as student's name, age, sex, marks received, course opted, etc. comprise a record. The records may be of fixed length or variable length.

4. *Files:* File is a collection of connected information that may be score file, accounts file, inventory file, payroll file, etc. Data files employed in business have been classified into: (i) Master files (ii) Transaction files (iii) Reference files (iv) Table files (v) Report files (vi) Historical files (vii) Back up files

   (i) *Master Files:* Master file contains relatively permanent information which is used as a reference source and is generally updated from time to time. It comprises relatively permanent records for identification and summarising statistical information. An income tax return file, stock file, customer file, employee file, product file, etc., are master files. It may also consist of descriptive information like product description in a product file, statistical information in a stock file as product outstanding, number of orders, outstanding, etc.

   (ii) *Transaction Files:* The transaction files are made from source document or master file. Generally such files are used for recording events or transactions connecting to the master file. Transaction files are used to update master files. In case, the processing is of batch type, the transactions are gathered for a period and then at the end, transaction file is created from collected transactions. For instance, order received, account payable, customer file in a bank is a source document or master file. Transactions like 'withdrawal', 'deposit', 'new account', 'close account' are events stored in transaction file, and a new master-file is created by updating old master-file using transaction file.

   (iii) *Table Files:* These are tabular in nature e.g., exam, result catalogue or price lists.

   (iv) *Reference Files:* A file consisting of keys that have records in other files is known as reference file as for retrieving a record from a file, referenced file is searched first to locate the address of the record (or location).

   (v) *Report Files:* These files are concise, meaningful and are made from other data files. For example, sales-performance report of sales person in a company may contain yearly sale, zone sale, country sale, total figures.

   (vi) *Historical Files:* Files that comprised the information about the past are known as historical files. Generally these files contain statistical information for trend analysis or comparison, etc.

   (vii) *Back-up-files:* These are the copy of master files kept in computer library as a measure of security, that may be retrieved if disaster happens.

5. *Database:* Database is a collection of related files. The card catalogue employed by librarian is his database. For instance, student course file can be combined with files on student's personal histories to create a student database.

File organisation may be described as the organisation of the data of a file into records, blocks and access structure. So, the storing and accessing records/ file organisation.

Storing and Accessing Records/File Organisation: File organisation is the act by which the data in a some certain file are structured so that the different records may easily be entered, accessed and updated.

File Organisation Methods

The records on secondary storage media may be stored in various ways. The arrangement of record storage decides the manner in which the records can be accessed. File organisation consists of the way records and blocks are arranged on the storage medium and interlinked. On the other hand, access methods are set of operations that can be applied to a file. It is possible to apply different access methods to a file organised by you. A few access methods can be applied only to files that are organised in a specific way. Three kinds of access methods are there - *Sequential access method* are applied to and *direct access methods* indexed sequential file organisation. These methods are influenced by how the data is organised on a file. These are discussed below:

> The sequential/serial file organisation means a kind of storing or retrieving information that needs the programme to start reading at the beginning and continue until it finds the desired data.

In sequential organisation, records are placed one after another in a predetermined order whereas in serial organisation records are kept one after another in no special order but in chronological order in which records are added to the file.

Merits and Demerits of Sequential File Organisation: Advantages of sequential file organisation are:

(i) Records are arranged in a simple and contiguous manner. So, such files are easy to design and simple to access as only principal field is required.

(ii) The sequential file organisation is normally on magnetic tapes which is the cheapest medium.

(iii) The sequential organisations are easy to update the master files as number of transactions or file activity ratio is high and transactions are batched.

(iv) Less prone to errors, this kind of file organisation is very efficient and economical.

(v) Easy to maintain the back up.

Disadvantages of using sequential file organisation are:

(i) It is costly and time consuming if file activity ratio is low.

(ii) In order to update master-file, the transactions have to be batched and whole master-file has to be read even if only a few records are to be updated.

(iii) As the response from sequential file is low, thus on-line enquiry system cannot be generated using sequential files.

Direct (or Random) Access File Organisations: The direct access files keep the record in a manner that a desired record is found directly without searching sequentially. When records are stored in random order, records are also retrieved in any sequence regardless of their physical order on the storage medium. It is directly performed by the CPU to access the desired record employing randomising procedure without looking all other records in the file. This is referred as self (direct) addressing.

The random access file organisation needs direct access storage devices. Even if primary storage in CPU gives direct access, however, there are other devices-which give direct access feature such as, magnetic disk, floppy, drums, etc. This organisation is worth for on-line enquiry system where computer response is needed to be immediate.

Merits and Demerits of Random (Direct) Access File: Merits of direct file organisation are:

(i) Access to record is fast as it is not needed to search the whole file.

(ii) Records may be accessed both randomly and sequentially.

(iii) Records should not be sorted, it may be in any random order.

(iv) Transactions should not be batched as any single transaction is served as it is entered.

(v) This is useful in interactive, real-time on-line processing environment like Railway/Airline reservation, banks, etc.

Demerits of using direct file organisation are:

(i) It consists of extra computation to locate the address of the records.

(ii) It makes use of comparatively expensive media like magnetic disks.

(iii) Storage space is not efficiently used as location of the stored records is randomly arranged.

Indexed Sequential File Organisation: As for an indexed file organisation, the records are stored either in sequential or non-sequential way. The business data processing system employs a common file organisation in an ordered file with multi-level primary index on its ordering key field, like an organisation is known as indexed sequential file. These files have Indexed Sequential Access Method (ISAM). In indexed file organisation, an index is made. This index is similar to index in the Library or given at the end of the book. For finding a record, the cylinder index is searched to find cylinder address. Then, for that cylinder track index is looked for to find the track address of the wanted record. Every index entry matches a key value of the record and point to unique record. When index table usually consists the key value (unique) and address of that record (track number, cylinder number, surface numbers), the accessing is speedier in such file organisation as no sorting and additional block access is required.

Merits and Demerits of Indexed Sequential File: Merits of using indexed sequential access file organisation are:

(i) Could be employed in any kind of application.

(ii) This consists of the features of sequential and direct organisation. Direct access is accomplished by means of generating index.

(iii) If file activity ratio is high, then this file set up is efficient and economical.

Demerits of using indexed sequential file organisation are:

(i) It needs extra storage as record insertion causes overflow condition.

(ii) It augments the processing time as reading of indexes is required prior to accessing the record.

(iii) Needs expensive storage device like magnetic disk and software as well.

(iv) In comparison to random access, it needs more time because indexes are searched prior to record access.

(v) Requires more space.

Elements Influencing Selection of File Organisation: The factors influencing the selection of a file organisation vary from application to application. A few of the factors are:

(a) *File Activity Ratio:* It indicates the ratio of the number of records accessed in an execution divided by the total number of records in a master file. In case, in any application this ratio is less, then file should be on the disk so that it can be directly addressed.

This ratio is too small for real-time file, where only one master record is accessed and processed at a time. In such cases, direct access organisations are best suited. Whereas, if this is high, then indexed sequential processing is preferable.

If this ratio is 'one' than all the records are accessed at the time of an execution of the master file. In such cases, sequential file organisations are given preference. Examples of such file organisations are: payroll file, updating master file with transaction file at the end of the day in a bank.

(b) *File Interrogation:* It indicates to the retrieval of information from a file. For real-time processing retrieval of records is normally faster; accordingly, direct file organisation is opted. In batch-processing environment, where time of retrieval of records is not all that crucial, sequential file organisation can be more useful. Further, direct access method is preferred for large files over small files, as searching for records sequentially or with binary search in small files is easier than keeping complex indexes.

(c) *File Volatility:* It refers to the number of updations i.e., additions or deletions done to the file in a timeframe. Thus, high volatile file applications are those needing large number of additions/deletions. For high volatile applications, direct access file organisations are best suited, as in ISAM file organisations, addition of records would should be placed in the overflow area. At the same time, Sequential file organisations would be appropriate if there were no interrogation needs.

(d) *File Density:* It refers to the number of bits stored per inch. File density decides the actual utilisation of the storage space given to a file. The greater density mentions lower cost of storage and can be used for archival and back up storage purposes. As for the case of greatly densed files, sequential file organisation is preferred, as in such file organisation 100 per cent density can be accomplished.

Role of Communication Technology

Scope and Relevance

Distance Education has come to be recognised as a multimedia teaching-learning system. Since the learners in this system do not have to come to the classroom, except for short face-to-face contact they study most of the time at a distance, away from the teachers and the institution. It is for this reason that mere printed correspondence course material was not considered adequate to provide effective teaching-learning to the learners, although the printed course material will continue to be the mainstay of imparting instruction to the distant students in all Distance Education Institutions including the Open Universities. The tremendous developments in the field of communication technology in the world offers great possibilities for integrating appropriate communication media into the Distance Education System. These would help in reducing time and place restrictions on the learners and prove useful adjuncts of the printed word. Unfortunately this is one area which has not received proper attention of Distance Education Institutes, the Universities which are running these institutes and the bodies responsible for the overall supervision of the innovative system of education.

This paper highlights various devices of communication technology which are being used by Open Universities and Distance Education Institutes in most of the developed countries and in some developing countries as well. Most of these innovations have proved useful in imparting knowledge and skills to the distance education learners. In most cases these audiovisual programmes are put across to supplement or reinforce instruction imparted to the learners through the printed course material. However, instruction for some courses is provided exclusively by the audiovisual programmes as in some universities of the Air or Tele universities. Now there are indications of some electronic universities also coming up. These universities would be offering courses by computers. One distinct advantage of the Distance Education audio visual programmes is that apart from the students who enrol with the Distance education institutes, quite a number of other persons including students in the formal system, also benefit from these programmes. The use of communication technology, therefore, can help in wider spread of knowledge even among those who may not be interested in studying for a degree, diploma or certificate.

We must also reckon with the reality that the age-old system of class room teaching is losing its glamour and credibility. Moreover, education system in the modern age has to cope with the educational demands of adults because education now has to be a continuing lifelong process. Then there is the upsurge against elitism in the formal education system which cannot be ignored. We have got to democratise our educational system in order to extend and equalise opportunities for educational at all levels so that it is within the reach of all those who want it. The formal system cannot cope with these new demands. That is what explains the fast development and popularity of Distance teaching-learning system. The last two decades have brought this system to the fore front. Over 21 Open Universities have sprung up across the world to cope with the ever increasing and varied demands of varied clientele. The International Council for Distance Education and a number of National and Regional Associations are making positive contribution towards research on various aspects of distance education and collaboration among institutes of distance education. A number of journals and books on Distance education are helping in creating proper awareness about the potentialities, techniques and methodology of this innovative teaching-learning system by publishing research findings, developments, case studies, etc. Research and developments in communication technology related to distance education occupy an important place in these publications and this has generated a lot of interest among distance educators all over the world in the application of these new media to their teaching-learning processes.

Although the highly sophisticated communication technology may not be within the reach of distance education institutes in India and the other developing countries, a beginning can be made, and it must be made, if we really want our distance education system to be effective and responsive to the educational needs of our people. Of course we would have to make a judicious mix of the communication media available in our country keeping in mind their accessibility to our learners, not only in cities and towns but even in remote rural and backward areas, so that we may be able to take education to the very doorsteps of the people. The institutes of distance education by themselves may not be able to do much in this direction specially with regard to Radio and the Television, because unless the government lays down a clear-cut policy to provide Radio and TV support to Distance Education Institutes, no such programmes would be possible.

How Media is made use of ?: Now let us consider the various media which can be put to use for reinforcing our distance education programmes. In most of the developing countries, Radio on account of its wide acceptability and moderate cost, is used quite extensively for educational broadcasts and as a support service for teaching the distance learners. The only snag in this medium is that it provides just one-way communication. But the latest advance in radio technology has been utilised by some institutions in the advanced countries, such as New Zealand and Australia, to evolve Radio Tutorials and Radio-Conferences. Some of the advantages of Radio over other media are that Radio Programmes can relate a course of study to current events and it can be altered, brought up-to-date and improved. However, lot of imagination is required to make the Radio programmes really attractive and effective. Straight talks generally fail to sustain the listener's interest. Dramatisation, symposia, discussions, educational quiz and involvement of students can make these programmes more effective.

Television is also a very attractive and useful audiovisual medium which is widely used for imparting education in the developed as well as the developing countries. But it is not as easily accessible to the people in the developing countries as the radio. However, with the installation of satellites, introduction of microcomputer based system and reduction in costs, television is bound to come within the reach of fairly large segments of our population, even in rural areas. This medium is particularly useful for demonstration of laboratory experiments, etc. Some of the developed countries have evolved useful combinations of cable TV, electronic blackboard, fibre optics and telephone. These combinations, convert the simple television set into a powerful and educational tool called the Telidon—a Canadian Video System. The Video tape and Video disc are also very useful innovations which remove the constraint of viewing TV programmes at set times. The British Open University has developed an extremely versatile audiovisual teaching medium called the Cyclops which is based on the conventional TV set, standard audio cassettes and microcomputer technology. The Cyclops can be linked to telephone also and that increases its versatility as a teaching tool. It should not be difficult for us to develop and adopt, in due course of time, these innovations of Radio and television for imparting teaching to the Distant learners.

It is evident that the Radio and TV could constitute important inputs into the Distance Education programmes. Apart from being powerful also in the learning process, the radio and TV programmes would give a psychological satisfaction to the students of listening to the live voice of their teachers and seeing them. That would impart some sort of personal touch to their process of learning. Radio and TV programmes would facilitate comprehension, enliven learning, enrich the student's understanding of the subject matter and motivate them to do some independent thinking and reading. Thus, properly and well-prepared Radio and TV programmes could go a long way in supplementing and reinforcing the instruction imparted through the lessons. The UGC sponsored TV programmes of higher education and the school broadcasts have proved the utility of these media in the teaching process. Top priority should therefore, be given to the integration of TV and Radio into the Distance Education system.

Significant Steps

However, in order to make Radio & TV programmes really effective and useful it would be necessary to:

(i) Ensure sufficient autonomy in developing and broadcasting or telecasting educational programmes;

(ii) Provide special channels and frequencies for educational programmes;

(iii) Train teachers at different levels to produce good radio and television programmes;

(iv) Use care and imagination in selecting topics and talkers for these programmes;

(v) Allocate appropriate timings of these Radio broadcasts and TV programmes so as to attract the largest number of students to listen to and watch these programmes;

(vi) Organise an expert group which should monitor and evaluate the radio and television programmes to ensure regular improvements.

Audio Cassettes and Video tapes are also very useful teaching media. These have an advantage over the radio and TV in that they enable the learners to have control over the learning material; they can listen or view the programmes at any time convenient to them; they can stop the cassette or video tape at any stage, go back over any section of the cassette or tape as often as the need and use it again and again for revision or recall. Phonograph records and Flexidises too are good innovations and are cheaper and more easily accessible. Education film strips and films could also be very suitable and effective media for imparting education. The Computer is an excellent device that can be usefully employed for evaluating student's assignment. A fully developed Computer Assisted Education System (CADE) can be used for correction and comments on student's replies to multiple-choice questions will carefully selected distractors. In this system, an optical reader 'corrects' the student's replies, after which the computer selects relevant comments and explanations from among a great number of those programmes and stored for the purpose. The computer also checks and refers to the individual student's earlier performances and achievements when parallel or similar questions were attempted. A mistake in the student's answer or unsatisfactory answer elicits different comments from the computer, depending on the way in which the student has misunderstood or wrongly combined items.

Sometimes even correct replies are commented upon to underline something important or to strengthen the motivation of the students. Encouraging and counselling comments based on the overall performance of the students are also provided by the computer. All this is typed by the computer into a personal letter addressed to the individual student. However, this use of the computer is restricted to the objective assignments of the multiple choice type. Therefore, a number of subjects, themes within subjects and general types of learning e.g., free problem-oriented learning would require live tutors. Even the multiple-choice questions which can be marked by the computer are not always suited for all kinds of learning outcomes. The greatest advantage of computer-marked assignments is that it greatly reduces the average turn-round time of the assignments. The computer also eliminates the chances of erratic marking which has become the bane of our examination system. The computer ensures uniformity in evaluation. The computer can play a very important role even in the organisational setup of Distance Education Institutes which have large enrolments.

Telephone has tremendous potential for providing two way interaction between the learner and the teacher, as also among the learners themselves. This technology is particularly useful when students are scattered over vast areas and in countries where there is shortage of specialists. Some of the latest and significant innovations of telephone are Tele-tutoring and Teleconferencing. According to the World Bank study published in 1982, telephone has, in recent years, come to be used for direct teaching in the developed countries.

The study has listed six different methods in which telephones can be used for teaching:

1. *Tutor-learner:* When it is not possible to provide group teaching because of shortage of teachers or insufficient number of students, the learners are allocated to telephone tutors.
2. Learner-learner (self-help) to facilitate interaction among learners.
3. *Tutors-learners in a Group:* In case of shortage of tutors and long distance involved in reaching the learners, a tutor is linked to a class by means of loud speaker telephone in the study centre. The students can also communicate back to the tutor by means of a microphone linked to be study centre telephone. In this way a tutor can cover several groups of learners consecutively without having to travel.
4. *Tutors-learners in Several Groups:* By this method a teacher can lecture up to 200 classes or over 40,000 students simultaneously. This system has been successfully tried by Wisconsin University in the USA for its extension programmes.
5. *Conferencing (with Tutor):* This method can help in arranging telephone seminars without students or tutors having to leave their homes, if they have telephones. Seven different

numbers can be linked simultaneously with one another and every one can speak to and bear every one else. Alternatively, seven study centres could also be linked together.

6. *Self-help Conference Calls:* This method is exactly the same as method Five but no tutor is involved.

Equipments of various Nature

As pointed out earlier, while choosing the communication media, we must ensure that they are within the reach of our students. Individually, all the students may not have access to these media except the Radio. It would, therefore, be necessary to provide proper facilities for students at the study centres. Another way could be to organise mobile learning centres as tried by North Island College in Vancouver Island, Canada. The mobile centres should provide facilities for viewing and listening of videos, audio cassettes, flexi discs, etc., as also library and laboratory facilities. Such a mobile learning centre can travel to various places on a regular schedule and students informed in advance so that they may take full advantage of it. These mobile units serve the purpose of publicity vans also and enthuse a number of persons in the areas visited to enrol for various courses.

Thus we see that we now have a wide range of communication technology which can bring about a meaningful revolution and improvement in the teaching-learning processes. Although developing countries may not be in a position to make use of all these innovations, they should chalk out a phased programme for integration of these communication devices into their educational system to make it more effective. In the first phase, we should take immediate steps to introduce such communication technologies as are available to us, e.g., Radio, Television, Audio cassettes and Video tapes. In the second phase, we should aim at developing and adopting the various adaptations of Radio, Television and cassettes, such as Radio conference/tutorial facilities., Telidon, Video tape, Video disc, Cyclops, etc. For the third phase we should keep an eye on the future and try to develop the latest and sophisticated communication technologies in collaboration with the developed countries. The UNESCO, various Education Foundations and International Educational Organisations should launch special programmes to help the developing countries to integrate the latest communication technologies in their instructional programmes. The Government of India is now aware of the importance of Distance Education and new communication technology for imparting education at all levels. This is evident from the emphasis on these sectors in the new Education Policy document. The setting up of Indira Gandhi National Open University is the outcome of this awareness on the part of the government. Six State Governments—Andhra Pradesh, Kerala, West Bengal, Bihar, Madhya Pradesh and Uttar Pradesh have already decided to set up State Open Universities. I am sure other states would also be motivated to organise distance education on a sound footing and provide proper funding, support and recognition to this innovative system.

Distance Education has come to be recognised as an academically viable system for imparting higher education and is most relevant to the educational needs of our country. This system can ensure vertical as well as horizontal mobility to the motivated learners even after they take up employment. And it has the greatest potential for integrating new communication technologies in the teaching-learning processes. Distance education in a number of developed countries like the UK, USA, Canada, France, Sweden, Norway, West Germany, Japan, Australia, China, etc., has adopted the multimedia approach for imparting higher education, and integrated various communication media to make the teaching learning processes more effective and interesting.

Over the last decade and a half there have been very significant developments in this regard in a number of developing countries also, such as India, Pakistan, Sri Lanka, South Korea, Indonesia, Thailand, Malaysia, Spain, etc., and some of the African countries. This system has greatly helped in extending the equalising educational opportunities for all sections of society. It has taken education to the very doorsteps of people even in remote areas.

Distance education has the greatest social justification and deserves wholehearted support and generous financial backing for extending the widening the horizons of higher education, as well as continuing and adult education. If we support the Open Universities and Distance Education Institutes to develop and integrate new communication technologies in their teaching-learning techniques, the traditional universities and colleges too would be able to gain from their experience because ultimately they too will have to interweave relevant communication technologies in the traditional face-to-face teaching methodology. The sooner they do that the better would it be. I am sure, the establishment of Indira Gandhi National Open University would, in due course of time, provide guidance and help to the State's Open Universities and Distance Education Institutes in adopting multimedia teaching approach. But the State Governments must also provide financial support to such institutes in their States. We must march with the time and accept the relevant innovations of communication technology that can help in making the Distance teaching-learning processes more effective and meaningful.

17

Information, Knowledge and Communication

Knowledge Management

Knowledge management (KM) is the process of capturing, developing, sharing, and effectively using organisational knowledge. It refers to a multi-disciplined approach to achieving organisational objectives by making the best use of knowledge.

An established discipline since 1991, KM includes courses taught in the fields of business administration, information systems, management, and library and information sciences (Alavi & Leidner 1999). More recently, other fields have started contributing to KM research; these include information and media, computer science, public health, and public policy. Columbia University and Kent State University offer dedicated Master of Science degrees in Knowledge Management. Many large companies and non-profit organisations have resources dedicated to internal KM efforts, often as a part of their business strategy, information technology, or human resource management departments. Several consulting companies provide strategy and advice regarding KM to these organisations.

Knowledge management efforts typically focus on organisational objectives such as improved performance, competitive advantage, innovation, the sharing of lessons learned, integration and continuous improvement of the organisation. KM efforts overlap with organisational learning and may be distinguished from that by a greater focus on the management of knowledge as a strategic asset and a focus on encouraging the sharing of knowledge. It is seen as an enabler of organisational learning and a more concrete mechanism than the previous abstract research.

The Background

Knowledge management efforts have a long history, to include on-the-job discussions, formal apprenticeship, discussion forums, corporate libraries, professional training and mentoring programmes. With increased use of computers in the second half of the 20th century, specific adaptations of technologies such as knowledge bases, expert systems, knowledge repositories, group decision support systems, intranets, and computer-supported cooperative work have been introduced to further enhance such efforts.

In 1999, the term personal knowledge management was introduced; it refers to the management of knowledge at the individual level.

In the enterprise, early collections of case studies recognised the importance of knowledge management dimensions of strategy, process, and measurement. Key lessons learned include people and the cultural norms which influence their behaviours are the most critical resources for successful knowledge creation, dissemination, and application; cognitive, social, and organisational learning processes are essential to the success of a knowledge management strategy; and measurement, benchmarking, and incentives are essential to accelerate the learning process and to drive cultural change. In short, knowledge management programmes can yield impressive benefits to individuals and organisations if they are purposeful, concrete, and action-oriented.

More recently with the advent of the Web 2.0, the concept of knowledge management has evolved towards a vision more based on people participation and emergence. This line of evolution is termed Enterprise 2.0. However, there is an ongoing debate and discussions as to whether Enterprise 2.0 is a fad that does not bring anything new or useful or whether it is, indeed, the future of knowledge management.

Research

KM emerged as a scientific discipline in the earlier 1990s. It was initially supported solely by practitioners, when Skandia hired Leif Edvinsson of Sweden as the world's first Chief Knowledge Officer (CKO). Hubert Saint-Onge (formerly of CIBC, Canada), started investigating KM long before that. The objective of CKOs is to manage and maximise the intangible assets of their organisations. Gradually, CKOs became interested in practical and theoretical aspects of KM, and the new research field was formed. Discussion of the KM idea has been taken up by academics, such as Ikujiro Nonaka (Hitotsubashi University), Hirotaka Takeuchi (Hitotsubashi University), Thomas H. Davenport (Babson College) and Baruch Lev (New York University). In 2001, Thomas A. Stewart, former editor at Fortune magazine and subsequently the editor of Harvard Business Review, published a cover story highlighting the importance of intellectual capital in organisations. Since its establishment, the KM discipline has been gradually moving towards academic maturity. First, there is a trend towards higher cooperation among academics; particularly, there has been a drop in single-authored publications. Second, the role of practitioners has changed. Their contribution to academic research has been dramatically declining from 30 per cent of overall contributions up to 2002, to only 10 per cent by 2009 (Serenko *et al.* 2010).

A broad range of thoughts on the KM discipline exist; approaches vary by author and school. As the discipline matures, academic debates have increased regarding both the theory and practice of KM, to include the following perspectives:

- Techno-centric with a focus on technology, ideally those that enhance knowledge sharing and creation.
- Organisational with a focus on how an organisation can be designed to facilitate knowledge processes best.
- Ecological with a focus on the interaction of people, identity, knowledge, and environmental factors as a complex adaptive system akin to a natural ecosystem.

Regardless of the school of thought, core components of KM include people, processes, technology (or) culture, structure, technology, depending on the specific perspective (Spender & Scherer 2007). Different KM schools of thought include lenses through which KM can be viewed and explained, to include:

- Community of practice;
- Social network analysis;
- Intellectual capital (Bontis & Choo 2002);
- Information theory (McInerney 2002);
- Complexity science;
- Constructivism (Nanjappa & Grant 2003).

The practical relevance of academic research in KM has been questioned (Ferguson 2005) with action research suggested as having more relevance (Andriessen 2004) and the need to translate the findings presented in academic journals to a practice (Booker, Bontis and Serenko 2008).

Dimensions

Different frameworks for distinguishing between different 'types of' knowledge exist. One proposed framework for categorising the dimensions of knowledge distinguishes between tacit knowledge and explicit knowledge. Tacit knowledge represents internalised knowledge that an individual may not be consciously aware of, such as how he or she accomplishes particular tasks. At the opposite end of the spectrum, explicit knowledge represents knowledge that the individual holds consciously in mental focus, in a form that can easily be communicated to others. (Alavi & Leidner 2001). Similarly, Hayes and Walsham (2003) describe content and relational perspectives of knowledge and knowledge management as two fundamentally different epistemological perspectives. The content perspective suggest that knowledge is easily stored because it may be codified, while the relational perspective recognises the contextual and relational aspects of knowledge which can make knowledge difficult to share outside of the specific location where the knowledge is developed.

Early research suggested that a successful KM effort needs to convert internalised tacit knowledge into explicit knowledge to share it, and the same effort must permit individuals to internalise and make personally meaningful any codified knowledge retrieved from the KM effort. Subsequent research into KM suggested that a distinction between tacit knowledge and explicit knowledge represented an oversimplification and that the notion of explicit knowledge is self-contradictory. Specifically, for knowledge to be made explicit, it must be translated into information (i.e., symbols outside of our heads) (Serenko & Bontis 2004). Later on, Ikujiro Nonaka proposed a model (SECI for Socialisation, Externalisation, Combination, Internalisation) which considers a spiralling knowledge process interaction between explicit knowledge and tacit knowledge (Nonaka & Takeuchi 1995). In this model, knowledge follows a cycle in which implicit knowledge is 'extracted' to become explicit knowledge, and explicit knowledge is 're-internalised' into implicit knowledge. More recently, together with Georg von Krogh, Nonaka returned to his earlier work in an attempt to move the debate about knowledge conversion forwards (Nonaka & von Krogh 2009).

A second proposed framework for categorising the dimensions of knowledge distinguishes between embedded knowledge of a system outside of a human individual (e.g., an information system may have knowledge embedded into its design) and embodied knowledge representing a learned capability of a human body's nervous and endocrine systems (Sensky 2002).

A third proposed framework for categorising the dimensions of knowledge distinguishes between the exploratory creation of "new knowledge" (i.e., innovation) vs. the transfer or exploitation of "established knowledge" within a group, organisation, or community. Collaborative environments such as communities of practice or the use of social computing tools can be used for both knowledge creation and transfer.

Strategies

Knowledge may be accessed at three stages: before, during, or after KM-related activities. Organisations have tried knowledge capture incentives, including making content submission mandatory and incorporating rewards into performance measurement plans. Considerable controversy exists over whether incentives work or not in this field and no consensus has emerged.

One strategy to KM involves actively managing knowledge (push strategy). In such an instance, individuals strive to explicitly encode their knowledge into a shared knowledge repository, such as a database, as well as retrieving knowledge they need that other individuals have provided to the repository. This is commonly known as the Codification approach to KM.

Another strategy to KM involves individuals making knowledge requests of experts associated with a particular subject on an *ad hoc* basis (pull strategy). In such an instance, expert individual(s) can provide their insights to the particular person or people needing this (Snowden 2002). This is commonly known as the Personalisation approach to KM.

Hansen *et al.* propose a simple framework, distinguishing two opposing KM strategies: codification and personalisation. Codification focuses on collecting and storing codified knowledge in previously designed electronic databases to make it accessible to the organisation. Codification can therefore refer to both tacit and explicit knowledge. In contrast, the personalisation strategy aims at encouraging individuals to share their knowledge directly. Information technology plays a less important role, as it is only supposed to facilitate communication and knowledge sharing among members of an organisation.

Other knowledge management strategies and instruments for companies include:

- Rewards (as a means of motivating for knowledge sharing);
- Storytelling (as a means of transferring tacit knowledge);
- Cross-project learning;
- After action reviews;
- Knowledge mapping (a map of knowledge repositories within a company accessible by all);
- Communities of practice;
- Expert directories (to enable knowledge seeker to reach to the experts);
- Best practice transfer;
- Knowledge fairs;
- Competence management (systematic evaluation and planning of competences of individual organisation members);
- Proximity and architecture (the physical situation of employees can be either conducive or obstructive to knowledge sharing);
- Master-apprentice relationship;

- Collaborative technologies (groupware, etc.);
- Knowledge repositories (databases, bookmarking engines, etc.);
- Measuring and reporting intellectual capital (a way of making explicit knowledge for companies);
- Knowledge brokers (some organisational members take on responsibility for a specific "field" and act as first reference on whom to talk about a specific subject);
- Social software (wikis, social bookmarking, blogs, etc.);
- Inter-project knowledge transfer.

Motivations

There are a number of claims as to the motivations leading organisations to undertake a KM effort. Typical considerations driving a KM effort include:

- Making available increased knowledge content in the development and provision of products and services;
- Achieving shorter new product development cycles;
- Facilitating and managing innovation and organisational learning;
- Leveraging the expertise of people across the organisation;
- Increasing network connectivity between internal and external individuals;
- Managing business environments and allowing employees to obtain relevant insights and ideas appropriate to their work;
- Solving intractable or wicked problems;
- Managing intellectual capital and intellectual assets in the workforce (such as the expertise and know-how possessed by key individuals).

Debate exists whether KM is more than a passing fad, though increasing amount of research in this field may help to answer this question, as well as create consensus on what elements of KM help determine the success or failure of such efforts (Wilson 2002). Knowledge sharing remains a challenging issue for knowledge management, while there is no clear agreement barriers may include time issues for knowledge works, the level of trust, lack of effective support technologies and culture (Jennex 2008).

Technologies

Early KM technologies included online corporate yellow pages as expertise locators and document management systems. Combined with the early development of collaborative technologies (in particular Lotus Notes), KM technologies expanded in the mid-1990s. Subsequent KM efforts leveraged semantic technologies for search and retrieval and the development of *e*-learning tools for communities of practice (Capozzi 2007). Knowledge management systems can thus be categorised as falling into one or more of the following groups: Groupware, document management systems, expert systems, semantic networks, relational and object oriented databases, simulation tools, and artificial intelligence.

More recently, development of social computing tools (such as bookmarks, blogs, and wikis) have allowed more unstructured, self-governing or ecosystem approaches to the transfer, capture and creation of knowledge, including the development of new forms of communities, networks, or matrixed organisations. However such tools for the most part are still based on text and code, and thus represent explicit knowledge transfer. These tools face challenges in distilling meaningful reusable knowledge and ensuring that their content is transmissible through diverse channels (Andrus 2005).

Software tools in knowledge management are a collection of technologies and are not necessarily acquired as a single software solution. Furthermore, these knowledge management software tools have the advantage of using the organisation's existing information technology infrastructure. Organisations and business decision-makers spend a great deal of resources and make significant investments in the latest technology, systems and infrastructure to support knowledge management. It is imperative that these investments are validated properly, made wisely and that the most appropriate technologies and software tools are selected or combined to facilitate knowledge management.

Knowledge management has become a cornerstone in emerging business strategies such as Service Lifecycle Management (SLM) with companies increasingly turning to software vendors to enhance their efficiency in industries including, but not limited to, the aviation industry.

Knowledge

Knowledge is a familiarity, awareness or understanding of someone or something, such as facts, information, descriptions, or skills, which is acquired through experience or education by perceiving, discovering, or learning. Knowledge can refer to a theoretical or practical understanding of a subject. It can be implicit (as with practical skill or expertise) or explicit (as with the theoretical understanding of a subject); it can be more or less formal or systematic. In philosophy, the study of knowledge is called epistemology; the philosopher Plato famously defined knowledge as "justified true belief", though "well-justified true belief" is more complete as it accounts for the Gettier problems. However, several definitions of knowledge and theories to explain it exist.

Knowledge acquisition involves complex cognitive processes: perception, communication, and reasoning; while knowledge is also said to be related to the capacity of *acknowledgment* in human beings.

Theories of Knowledge

> The eventual demarcation of philosophy from science was made possible by the notion that philosophy's core was "theory of knowledge," a theory distinct from the sciences because it was their *foundation*... Without this idea of a "theory of knowledge," it is hard to imagine what "philosophy" could have been in the age of modern science.
> — *Richard Rorty, Philosophy and the Mirror of Nature*

The definition of knowledge is a matter of ongoing debate among philosophers in the field of epistemology. The classical definition, described but not ultimately endorsed by Plato, specifies that a statement must meet three criteria in order to be considered knowledge: it must be justified, true, and believed. Some claim that these conditions are not sufficient, as Gettier case examples allegedly demonstrate. There are a number of alternatives proposed, including Robert Nozick's arguments for a requirement that knowledge 'tracks the truth' and Simon Blackburn's additional requirement that we do not want to say that those who meet any of these conditions 'through a defect, flaw, or failure' have knowledge. Richard Kirkham suggests that our definition of knowledge requires that the evidence for the belief necessitates its truth.

In contrast to this approach, Wittgenstein observed, following Moore's paradox, that one can say "He believes it, but it isn't so," but not "He knows it, but it isn't so." He goes on to argue that these do not correspond to distinct mental states, but rather to distinct ways of talking about conviction. What is different here is not the mental state of the speaker, but the activity in which they are engaged. For example, on this account, to *know* that the kettle is boiling is not to be in a particular state of mind, but to perform a particular task with the statement that the kettle is boiling. Wittgenstein sought to bypass the difficulty of definition by looking to the way "knowledge" is used in natural languages. He saw knowledge as a case of a family resemblance. Following this idea, "knowledge" has been reconstructed as a cluster concept that points out relevant features but that is not adequately captured by any definition.

Communicating Knowledge

Symbolic representations can be used to indicate meaning and can be thought of as a dynamic process. Hence the transfer of the symbolic representation can be viewed as one ascription process whereby knowledge can be transferred. Other forms of communication include observation and imitation, verbal exchange, and audio and video recordings. Philosophers of language and semioticians construct and analyse theories of knowledge transfer or communication.

While many would agree that one of the most universal and significant tools for the transfer of knowledge is writing and reading (of many kinds), argument over the usefulness of the written word exists nonetheless, with some scholars sceptical of its impact on societies. In his collection of essays *Technopoly*, Neil Postman demonstrates the argument against the use of writing through an excerpt from Plato's work *Phaedrus* (Postman, Neil (1992) *Technopoly*, Vintage, New York, pp 73). In this excerpt the scholar Socrates recounts the story of Thamus, the Egyptian King and Theuth the inventor of the written word. In this story, Theuth presents his new invention "writing" to King Thamus, telling Thamus that his new invention "will improve both the wisdom and memory of the Egyptians" (Postman, Neil (1992) Technopoly, Vintage, New York, pp 74). King Thamus is sceptical of this new invention and rejects it as a tool of recollection rather than retained knowledge. He argues that the written word will infect the Egyptian people with fake knowledge as they will be able to attain facts and stories from an external source and will no longer be forced to mentally retain large quantities of knowledge themselves (Postman, Neil (1992) *Technopoly*, Vintage, New York, pp 74).

Classical early modern theories of knowledge, especially those advancing the influential empiricism of the philosopher John Locke, were based implicitly or explicitly on a model of the mind which likened ideas to words. This analogy between language and thought laid the foundation for a graphic conception of knowledge in which the mind was treated as a table (a container of content) that had to be stocked with facts reduced to letters, numbers or symbols. This created a situation in which the spatial alignment of words on the page carried great cognitive weight, so much so that educators paid very close attention to the visual structure of information on the page and in notebooks.

Media theorists like Andrew Robinson emphasise that the visual depiction of knowledge in the modern world was often seen as being 'truer' than oral knowledge. This plays into a longstanding analytic notion in the Wester intellectual tradition in which verbal communication is generally thought to lend itself to the spread of falsehoods as much as written communication. It is harder to preserve records of what was said or who originally said it – usually neither the source nor the content can be verified. Gossip and rumours are examples prevalent in both media. As to the value of writing, the extent of human knowledge is now so great, and the people interested in a piece of knowledge so separated in time and space, that writing is considered central to capturing and sharing it. Major libraries today can have millions of books of knowledge (in addition to works of fiction). It is only recently that audio and video technology for recording knowledge have become available and the use of these still requires replay equipment and electricity. Verbal teaching and handing down of knowledge is limited to those who would have contact with the transmitter or someone who could interpret written work. Writing is still the most available and most universal of all forms of recording and transmitting knowledge. It stands unchallenged as mankind's primary technology of knowledge transfer down through the ages and to all cultures and languages of the world.

Situated Knowledge

Situated knowledge is knowledge specific to a particular situation. It is a term coined by Donna Haraway as an extension of the feminist approaches of "successor science" suggested by Sandra Harding, one which "offers a more adequate, richer, better account of a world, in order to live in it well and in critical, reflexive relation to our own as well as others' practices of domination and the unequal parts of privilege and oppression that makes up all positions." This situation partially transforms science into a narrative, which Arturo Escobar explains as, "neither fictions nor supposed facts." This narrative of situation is historical textures woven of fact and fiction, and as Escobar explains further, "even the most neutral scientific domains are narratives in this sense," insisting that rather than a purpose dismissing science as a trivial matter of contingency, "it is to treat (this narrative) in the most serious way, without succumbing to its mystification as 'the truth' or to the ironic scepticism common to many critiques."

Haraway's argument stems from the limitations of the human perception, as well as the overemphasis of the sense of vision in science. According to Haraway, vision in science has been, "used to signify a leap out of the marked body and into a conquering gaze from nowhere." This is the "gaze that mythically inscribes all the marked bodies, that makes the unmarked category claim the power to see and not be seen, to represent while escaping representation." This causes a limitation of views in the position of science itself as a potential player in the creation of knowledge, resulting in a position of "modest witness". This is what Haraway terms a "god trick", or the aforementioned representation while escaping representation. In order to avoid this, "Haraway perpetuates a tradition of thought which emphasises the importance of the subject in terms of both ethical and political accountability".

Some methods of generating knowledge, such as trial and error, or learning from experience, tend to create highly situational knowledge. One of the main attributes of the scientific method is that the theories it generates are much less situational than knowledge gained by other methods. Situational knowledge is often embedded in language, culture, or traditions. This integration of situational knowledge is an allusion to the community, and its attempts at collecting subjective perspectives into an embodiment "of views from somewhere."

Knowledge generated through experience is called knowledge "a posteriori", meaning afterwards. The pure existence of a term like "a posteriori" means this also has a counterpart. In this case that is knowledge "a priori", meaning before. The knowledge prior to any experience means that there are certain "assumptions" that one takes for granted. For example if you are being told about a chair it is clear to you that the chair is in space, that it is 3D. This knowledge is not knowledge that one can "forget", even someone suffering from amnesia experiences the world in 3D. Even though Haraway's arguments are largely based on feminist studies, this idea of different worlds, as well as the sceptic stance of situated knowledge is present in the main arguments of post-structuralism. Fundamentally, both argue the contingency of knowledge on the presence of history; power, and geography, as well as the rejection of universal rules or laws or elementary structures; and the idea of power as an inherited trait of objectification.

Partial Knowledge

One discipline of epistemology focuses on partial knowledge. In most cases, it is not possible to understand an information domain exhaustively; our knowledge is always *incomplete* or partial. Most real problems have to be solved by taking advantage of a partial understanding of the problem context and problem data, unlike the typical math problems one might solve at school, where all data is given and one is given a complete understanding of formulas necessary to solve them.This idea is also present in the concept of bounded rationality which assumes that in real life situations people often have a limited amount of information and make decisions accordingly. Intuition is the ability to acquire partial knowledge without inference or the use of reason. An individual may "know" about a situation and be unable to explain the process that led to their knowledge.

Scientific Knowledge

The development of the scientific method has made a significant contribution to how knowledge of the physical world and its phenomena is acquired. To be termed scientific, a method of enquiry must be based on gathering observable and measurable evidence subject to specific principles of reasoning and experimentation. The scientific method consists of the collection of data through observation and experimentation, and the formulation and testing of hypotheses. Science, and the nature of scientific knowledge have also become the subject of Philosophy. As science itself has developed, knowledge has developed a broader usage which has been developing within biology/ psychology—discussed elsewhere as meta-epistemology, or genetic epistemology, and to some extent related to "theory of cognitive development".

Note that "epistemology" is the study of knowledge and how it is acquired. Science is "the process used everyday to logically complete thoughts through inference of facts determined by calculated experiments." Sir Francis Bacon was critical in the historical development of the scientific method; his works established and popularised an inductive methodology for scientific enquiry. His famous aphorism, "knowledge is power", is found in the Meditations Sacrae (1597).

Until recent times, at least in the Western tradition, it was simply taken for granted that knowledge was something possessed only by humans — and probably *adult* humans at that. Sometimes the notion might stretch to (ii) *Society-as-such*, as in (e.g.) "the knowledge possessed by the Coptic culture" (as opposed to its individual members), but that was not assured either. Nor was it usual to consider *unconscious* knowledge in any systematic way until this approach was popularised by Freud.

Other biological domains where "knowledge" might be said to reside, include: (iii) the *immune system*, and (iv) in the *DNA of the genetic code*. See the list of four "epistemological domains": Popper, (1975) and Traill (2008: Table S, page 31)—also references by both to Niels Jerne.

Such considerations seem to call for a separate definition of "knowledge" to cover the biological systems. For biologists, knowledge must be usefully *available* to the system, though that system need not be conscious. Thus the criteria seem to be:

- The system should apparently be dynamic and self-organising (unlike a mere book *on its own*).

- The knowledge must constitute some sort of representation of "the outside world", or ways of dealing with it (directly or indirectly).
- Some way must exist for the system to access this information quickly enough for it to be useful.

Scientific knowledge may not involve a claim to certainty, maintaining scepticism means that a scientist will never be absolutely certain when they are correct and when they are not. It is thus an irony of proper scientific method that one must doubt even when correct, in the hopes that this practice will lead to greater convergence on the truth in general.

Religious Aspects of Knowledge

In many expressions of Christianity, such as Catholicism and Anglicanism, knowledge is one of the seven gifts of the Holy Spirit. The Old Testament's tree of the knowledge of good and evil contained the knowledge that separated Man from God: "And the LORD God said, Behold, the man is become as one of us, to know good and evil..." (Genesis 3:22)

In Gnosticism divine knowledge or gnosis is hoped to be attained.

Vidya Daan, i.e. knowledge sharing is a major part of Daan, a tenet of all Dharmic Religions. Hindu Scriptures present two kinds of knowledge, *Paroksh Gyan* and *Prataksh Gyan*. *Paroksh Gyan* (also spelled *Paroksha-Jnana*) is secondhand knowledge: knowledge obtained from books, hearsay, etc. *Prataksh Gyan* (also spelled *Prataksha-Jnana*) is the knowledge borne of direct experience, i.e., knowledge that one discovers for oneself. Jnana yoga ("path of knowledge") is one of three main types of yoga expounded by Krishna in the Bhagavad Gita. (It is compared and contrasted with Bhakti Yoga and Karma yoga.)

In Islam, knowledge is given great significance. "The Knowing" is one of the 99 names reflecting distinct attributes of God. The Qur'an asserts that knowledge comes from God (2:239) and various *hadith* encourage the acquisition of knowledge. Muhammad is reported to have said "Seek knowledge from the cradle to the grave" and "Verily the men of knowledge are the inheritors of the prophets". Islamic scholars, theologians and jurists are often given the title *alim*, meaning "knowledgable".

In Jewish tradition, knowledge (Hebrew: *da'ath*) is considered one of the most valuable traits a person can acquire. Observant Jews recite three times a day in the Amidah "Favour us with knowledge, understanding and discretion that come from you. Exalted are you, Existent-One, the gracious giver of knowledge." The Tanakh states, "A wise man gains power, and a man of knowledge maintains power", and "knowledge is chosen above gold".

Measure of Religiosity

According to the sociologist Mervin Verbit, knowledge may be understood as one of the key components of religiosity. And religious knowledge itself may be broken down into four dimensions:

- Content;
- Frequency;
- Intensity;
- Centrality.

The content of one's religious knowledge may vary from person to person, as will the degree to which it may occupy the person's mind (frequency), the intensity of the knowledge, and the centrality of the information (in that religious tradition, or to that individual).

Information Technology

Information Technology (IT) is an ultramodern term in today's world. In fact, the technology used for the study, understanding, planning, design, construction, testing, distribution, support and operations of software, computers and computer related systems that exist for the purpose of Data, Information and Knowledge processing is Information Technology. It is the industry that has evolved to include the study, science, and solution-sets for all aspects of Data, Information and Knowledge management and/or processing. One may call it the Organisation in an enterprise or business that is held responsible and accountable for the technology, used for planning, design, construction, testing, distribution, support and operations of software, computers and computer related systems that exist for the purpose of Data, Information and Knowledge management and/or processing.

Definition

The Information Technology Association of America (ITAA) defines Information Technology as: The study, design, development, implementation, support or management of computer-based information systems, particularly software applications and computer hardware.

In practice, IT deals with the use of electronic computers and computer software to convert, store, protect, process, transmit, and securely retrieve information. This is the combination of telecommunication and computer science for the capture, storage and transmission of information to every nook and corner of the world. In other words, Information Technology is the technology (hardware and software) required for the processing of data and other information.

The Concept

Information Technology (IT), as defined by the Information Technology Association of America (ITAA), is "the study, design, development, implementation, support or management of computer-based information systems, particularly software applications and computer hardware." IT deals with the use of electronic computers and computer software to convert, store, protect, process, transmit, and securely retrieve information.

Today, the term information technology has ballooned to encompass many aspects of computing and technology, and the term has become very recognisable. The information technology umbrella can be quite large, covering many fields. IT professionals perform a variety of duties that range from installing applications to designing complex computer networks and information databases. A few of the duties that IT professionals perform may include data management, networking, engineering computer hardware, database and software design, as well as the management and administration of entire systems. When computer and communications technologies are combined, the result is information technology, or "infotech". Information Technology (IT) is a general term that describes any technology that helps to produce, manipulate, store, communicate, and/or disseminate information. Presumably, when speaking of Information Technology (IT) as a whole, it is noted that the use of computers and information are associated.

The term Information Technology (IT) was coined by Jim Domsic of Michigan in November 1981. Domsic created the term to modernise the outdated phrase "data processing". Domsic at the time worked as a computer manager for an automotive related industry. In recent years ABET and the ACM have collaborated to form accreditation and curriculum standards for degrees in Information Technology as a distinct field of study separate from both Computer Science and Information Systems. SIGITE is the ACM working group for defining these standards.

The Backdrop

In 1960s and 1970s, the term information technology (IT) was a little known phrase that was used only by those, who worked in places like banks and hospitals to describe the processes, that used to store information. With the paradigm shift to computing technology and 'paperless' workplaces, information technology has now come to be a household phrase. It depicts an industry that uses computers, networking, software programming and other equipment and processes to store, process, retrieve, transmit and protect information.

Now, the term information technology or IT is used to refer to an entire industry. In actuality, information technology is the use of computers and software to manage information. In some companies, this is referred to as Management Information Services (MIS) or simply as Information Services (IS). The information technology department of a large company would be responsible for storing information, protecting information, processing the information, transmitting the information as necessary, and later retrieving information as necessary.

It wasn't long ago that the Information Technology department might have consisted of a single computer operator, who might be storing data on magnetic tape, and then putting it in a box down, in the basement somewhere. The history of information technology is really fascinating. But, now the situation has changed.

In the early days of computer development, there was no such thing, as a college degree in IT. Software development and computer pro-gramming were best left to the computer scientists and mathematical engineers, due to their complicated nature. As time passed and technology advanced, such as with the advent of personal computer in 1980s and its everyday use at the home and the workplace, the world moved into the information age.

By early 21st century, nearly every child in the Western world, and many in other parts of the world, knew how to use a personal computer. Businesses information technology departments have gone from using storage tapes created by a single computer operator, to interconnected networks of employee workstations that store information in a server form, often somewhere away from the main business site. Communication has advanced, from physical postal mail, to telephone fax transmissions and to nearly instantaneous digital communication, through electronic mail.

Today, in order to perform the complex functions, information technology departments are required. A modern Information Technology Department would use computers, servers, database management systems and cryptography. Some of the most popular information technology skills include: Computer Networking; Information Security; IT Governance; Business Intelligence; Linux; Unix; Project Management, etc.

History of Information Technology

The term IT is ambiguous although mostly synonymous with computer technology. Haigh (2011) wrote:

> "In fact, the great majority of references to information technology have always been concerned with computers, although the exact meaning has shifted over time (Kline, 2006). The phrase received its first prominent usage in a Harvard Business Review article (Haigh, 2001b; Leavitt and Whisler, 1958) intended to promote a technocratic vision for the future of business management. Its initial definition was at the conjunction of computers, operations research methods, and simulation techniques. Having failed initially to gain much traction (unlike related terms of a similar vintage such as

> information systems, information processing, and information science) it was revived in policy and economic circles in the 1970s with a new meaning. Information technology now described the expected convergence of the computing, media, and telecommunications industries (and their technologies), understood within the broader context of a wave of enthusiasm for the computer revolution, post-industrial society, information society (Webster, 1995), and other fashionable expressions of the belief that new electronic technologies were bringing a profound rupture with the past. As it spread broadly during the 1980s, IT increasingly lost its association with communications (and, alas, any vestigial connection to the idea of anybody actually being informed of anything) to become a new and more pretentious way of saying "computer". The final step in this process is the recent surge in references to "information and communication technologies" or ICTs, a coinage that makes sense only if one assumes that a technology can inform without communicating".

• Some people use the term *information technology* about technologies used before the development of the computer. This is however to use the term as a retronym.

Boon to Business

Information Technology (IT) benefits the business world by allowing organisations to work more efficiently and to maximise productivity. Faster communication, electronic storage and protection of records are the advantages that IT can offer to any enterprise. Information Technology has to do with computer applications, on which nearly every work environment is dependent. Since, computerised systems are so widely used, it is advantageous to incorporate Information Technology, into any organisation. Information Technology creates electronic storage systems, to protect a company's valuable records. According to the Graziadio Business Report, published by Pepperdine University, securing maintenance of customer and patient files is vital to business integrity. Storage systems, such as virtual vaults, keep information safe by only allowing certain users, within a company to access, withdraw, add or change the documents. According to an article in Science Daily, IT security engineering systems protect one's electronic information, from being hacked, or wiped out during a technological disaster. Electronic security engineering means that valuable records would remain intact. Information Technology refers to the study and development of a support-management-based, computerised information system. The development is mainly observed in the form of dedicated software applications and a number of hardware programmes.

The advantages of IT include work place cost-effectiveness and essential globalisation. Information Technology or IT mainly deals with computer applications. The common work environment today is totally dependent on computers. This has led to the need to develop and consistently upgrade dedicated computer software like project management software, for a number of related requirements. These include storage and protection of content, processing and transmitting of dedicated information and the secured retrieval of information, when and as required.

IT promotes computing technology, covering everything from installing applications to developing databases. All work related applications are now completely automated, thanks to the IT sector. IT professionals are the people, involved in essential management of sensitive data, exclusive computer networking and systems-engineering. The advancement of the IT sector has resulted in automated administration of entire systems; production and manipulation of sensitive information; cultural development and communication; streamlining of business processes and timely upgrades, etc.

Branches of Information Technology

Computer Science

Computer Science or Computing Science (abbreviated CS or CompSci) is the scientific approach to computation, and specifically to the design of computing machines and processes. A computer scientist is a scientist who specialises in the theory of computation and the design of computers. Its subfields can be divided into practical techniques for its implementation and application in computer systems and purely theoretical areas. Some, such as computational complexity theory, which studies fundamental properties of computational problems, are highly abstract, while others, such as computer graphics, emphasise real-world applications. Still others focus on the challenges in implementing computations. For example, programming language theory studies approaches to description of computations, while the study of computer programming itself investigates various aspects of the use of programming languages and complex systems, and human-computer interaction focuses on the challenges in making computers and computations useful, usable, and universally accessible to humans.

The Background

The earliest foundations of what would become computer science predate the invention of the modern digital computer. Machines for calculating fixed numerical tasks such as the abacus have existed since antiquity. Wilhelm Schickard designed the first mechanical calculator in 1623, but did not complete its construction. Blaise Pascal designed and constructed the first working mechanical calculator, the Pascaline, in 1642. In 1694 Gottfried Wilhelm Leibnitz completed the Step Reckoner, the first calculator that could perform all four arithmetic operations. Charles Babbage designed a difference engine and then a general-purpose Analytical Engine in Victorian times, for which Ada Lovelace wrote a manual. Because of this work she is regarded today as the world's first programmer. Around 1900, punched card machines were introduced.

During the 1940s, as new and more powerful computing machines were developed, the term computer came to refer to the machines rather than their human predecessors. As it became clear that computers could be used for more than just mathematical calculations, the field of computer science broadened to study computation in general. Computer science began to be established as a distinct academic discipline in the 1950s and early 1960s. The world's first computer science degree programme, the Cambridge Diploma in Computer Science, began at the University of Cambridge Computer Laboratory in 1953. The first computer science degree programme in the United States was formed at Purdue University in 1962. Since practical computers became available, many applications of computing have become distinct areas of study in their own right.

Although, many initially believed it was impossible that computers themselves could actually be a scientific field of study, in the late fifties it gradually became accepted among the greater academic population. It is the now well-known IBM brand that formed part of the computer science revolution during this time. IBM (short for International Business Machines) released the IBM 704 and later the IBM 709 computers, which were widely used during the exploration period of such devices. "Still, working with the IBM [computer] was frustrating...if you had misplaced as much as one letter in one instruction, the programme would crash, and you would have to start the whole process over again". During the late 1950s, the computer science discipline was very much in its developmental stages, and such issues were commonplace. Time has seen significant improvements in the usability and effectiveness of computer science technology. Modern society has seen a significant shift from computers being used solely by experts or professionals to a more widespread user base. Initially, computers were quite costly, and for their most effective use, some degree of human aid was needed, in part by professional computer operators. However, as computers became widespread and far more affordable, less human assistance was needed, although residues of the original assistance still remained.

Major Achievements

Despite its short history as a formal academic discipline, computer science has made a number of fundamental contributions to science and society - in fact, along with electronics, it is a founding science of the current epoch of human history called the Information Age and a driver of the Information Revolution, seen as the third major leap in human technological progress after the Industrial Revolution (1750-1850 CE) and the Agricultural Revolution (8000-5000 BCE). These contributions include:

- The start of the "digital revolution," which includes the current Information Age and the Internet.
- A formal definition of computation and computability, and proof that there are computationally unsolvable and intractable problems.
- The concept of a programming language, a tool for the precise expression of methodological information at various levels of abstraction.
- In cryptography, breaking the Enigma code was an important factor contributing to the Allied victory in World War II.
- Scientific computing enabled practical evaluation of processes and situations of great complexity, as well as experimentation entirely by software. It also enabled advanced study of the mind, and mapping of the human genome became possible with the Human Genome Project. Distributed computing projects such as Folding@home explore protein folding.
- Algorithmic trading has increased the efficiency and liquidity of financial markets by using artificial intelligence, machine learning, and other statistical and numerical techniques on a large scale. High frequency algorithmic trading can also exacerbate volatility.
- Image synthesis, including video by computing individual video frames.
- Simulation of various processes, including computational fluid dynamics, physical, electrical, and electronic systems and circuits, as well as societies and social situations (notably war games) along with their habitats, among many others. Modern computers enable optimisation of such designs as complete aircraft. Notable in electrical and electronic circuit design are SPICE, as well as software for physical realisation of new (or modified) designs. The latter includes essential design software for integrated circuits.

Philosophy

A number of computer scientists have argued for the distinction of three separate paradigms in computer science. Peter Wegner argued that those paradigms are science, technology, and mathematics. Peter Denning's working group argued that they are theory, abstraction (modelling), and design. Amnon H. Eden described them as the "rationalist paradigm" (which treats computer science as branch of mathematics, which is prevalent in theoretical computer science, and mainly employs deductive reasoning), the "technocratic paradigm" (which might be found in engineering approaches, most prominently in software engineering), and the "scientific paradigm" (which approaches computer-related artifacts from the empirical perspective of natural sciences, identifiable in some branches of artificial intelligence).

Name of the Field

The term "computer science" was first coined by the numerical analyst George Forsythe in 1961. Despite its name, a significant amount of computer science does not involve the study of computers themselves. Because of this, several alternative names have been proposed. Certain departments of major universities prefer the term *computing science,* to emphasise precisely that difference. Danish scientist Peter Naur suggested the term *datalogy,* to reflect the fact that the scientific discipline revolves around data and data treatment, while not necessarily involving computers. The first scientific institution to use the term was the Department of Datalogy at the University of Copenhagen, founded in 1969, with Peter Naur being the first professor in datalogy.

The term is used mainly in the Scandinavian countries. Also, in the early days of computing, a number of terms for the practitioners of the field of computing were suggested in the *Communications of the ACM – turingineer, turologist, flow-charts-man, applied meta-mathematician,* and *applied epistemologist.* Three months later in the same journal, *comptologist* was suggested, followed next year by *hypologist.* The term *computics* has also been suggested. In Europe, terms derived from contracted translations of the expression "automatic information" (e.g. "informazione automatica" in Italian) or "information and mathematics" are often used e.g., *informatique* (French), *Informatik* (German), *informatica* (Italy), *informática* (Spain, Portugal) or *informatika* (Slavic languages) are also used and have also been adopted in the UK (as in *the School of Informatics of the University of Edinburgh*).

A folkloric quotation, often attributed to—but almost certainly not first formulated by—Edsger Dijkstra, states that "computer science is no more about computers than astronomy is about telescopes." The design and deployment of computers and computer systems is generally considered the province of disciplines other than computer science. For example, the study of computer hardware is usually considered part of computer engineering, while the study of commercial computer systems and their deployment is often called information technology or information systems. However, there has been much cross-fertilization of ideas between the various computer-related disciplines. Computer science research also often intersects other disciplines, such as philosophy, cognitive science, linguistics, mathematics, physics, statistics, and logic.

Computer science is considered by some to have a much closer relationship with mathematics than many scientific disciplines, with some observers saying that computing is a mathematical science. Early computer science was strongly influenced by the work of mathematicians such as Kurt Gödel and Alan Turing, and there continues to be a useful interchange of ideas between the two fields in areas such as mathematical logic, category theory, domain theory, and algebra.

The relationship between computer science and software engineering is a contentious issue, which is further muddied by disputes over what the term "software engineering" means, and how computer science is defined. David Parnas, taking a cue from the relationship between other engineering and science disciplines, has claimed that the principal focus of computer science is studying the properties of computation in general, while the principal focus of software engineering is the design of specific computations to achieve practical goals, making the two separate but complementary disciplines.

The academic, political, and funding aspects of computer science tend to depend on whether a department formed with a mathematical emphasis or with an engineering emphasis. Computer science departments with a mathematics emphasis and with a numerical orientation consider alignment with computational science. Both types of departments tend to make efforts to bridge the field educationally if not across all research.

Areas of Computer Science

As a discipline, computer science spans a range of topics from theoretical studies of algorithms and the limits of computation to the practical issues of implementing computing systems in hardware and software. CSAB, formerly called Computing Sciences Accreditation Board – which is made up of representatives of the Association for Computing Machinery (ACM), and the IEEE Computer Society (IEEE-CS) – identify four areas that it considers crucial to the discipline of computer science: theory of computation, algorithms and data structures, programming methodology and languages, and computer elements and architecture. In addition to these four areas, CSAB also identifies fields such as software engineering, artificial intelligence, computer networking and communication, database systems, parallel computation, distributed computation, computer-human interaction, computer graphics, operating systems, and numerical and symbolic computation as being important areas of computer science.

Theoretical Computer Science

The broader field of theoretical computer science encompasses both the classical theory of computation and a wide range of other topics that focus on the more abstract, logical, and mathematical aspects of computing.

Information and Coding Theory

Information theory is related to the quantification of information. This was developed by Claude E. Shannon to find fundamental limits on signal processing operations such as compressing data and on reliably storing and communicating data. Coding theory is the study of the properties of codes (systems for converting information from one form to another) and their fitness for a specific application. Codes are used for data compression, cryptography, error detection and correction, and more recently also for network coding. Codes are studied for the purpose of designing efficient and reliable data transmission methods.

Applied Computer Science

Artificial Intelligence: This branch of computer science aims to or is required to synthesise goal-orientated processes such as problem-solving, decision-making, environmental adaptation, learning and communication which are found in humans and animals. From its origins in cybernetics and in the Dartmouth Conference (1956), Artificial Intelligence (AI) research has been necessarily cross-disciplinary, drawing on areas of expertise such as applied mathematics, symbolic logic, semiotics, electrical engineering, philosophy of mind, neurophysiology, and social intelligence. AI is associated in the popular mind with robotic development, but the main field of practical application has been as an embedded component in areas of software development which require computational understanding and modelling such as finance and economics, data mining and the physical sciences.

The starting-point in the late 1940s was Alan Turing's question "Can computers think?", and the question remains effectively unanswered although the "Turing Test" is still used to assess computer output on the scale of human intelligence. But the automation of evaluative and predictive tasks has been increasingly successful as a substitute for human monitoring and intervention in domains of computer application involving complex real-world data.

Computer Architecture and Engineering

Computer architecture, or digital computer organisation, is the conceptual design and fundamental operational structure of a computer system. It focuses largely on the way by which the central processing unit performs internally and accesses addresses in memory. The field often involves disciplines of computer engineering and electrical engineering.

Computer Graphics and Visualisation

Computer graphics is the study of digital visual contents, and involves syntheses and manipulations of image data. The study is connected to many other fields in computer science, including computer vision, image processing, and computational geometry, and are heavily applied in the fields of special effects and video games.

Computer Security and Cryptography

Computer security is a branch of computer technology, whose objective includes protection of information from unauthorised access, disruption, or modification while maintaining the accessibility and usability of the system for its intended users. Cryptography is the practice and study of hiding (encryption) and therefore deciphering (decryption) information. Modern cryptography is largely related to computer science, for many encryption and decryption algorithms are based on their computational complexity.

Computational Science

Computational science (or scientific computing) is the field of study concerned with constructing mathematical models and quantitative analysis techniques and using computers to analyse and solve scientific problems. In practical use, it is typically the application of computer simulation and other forms of computation to problems in various scientific disciplines.

Health Informatics

Health Informatics in computer science is referred to as Computational health informatics and deals with computational techniques for solving problems in health care. It is a sub-branch of both computer science and health informatics.

Computer Engineering

Computer engineering is a discipline that integrates several fields of electrical engineering and computer science required to develop computer systems. Computer engineers usually have training in electronic engineering (or electrical engineering), software design, and hardware-software integration instead of only software engineering or electronic engineering. Computer engineers are involved in many hardware and software aspects of computing, from the design of individual microprocessors, personal computers, and supercomputers, to circuit design. This field of engineering not only focuses on how computer systems themselves work, but also how they integrate into the larger picture.

Usual tasks involving computer engineers include writing software and firmware for embedded microcontrollers, designing VLSI chips, designing analogue sensors, designing mixed signal circuit boards, and designing operating systems. Computer engineers are also suited for robotics research, which relies heavily on using digital systems to control and monitor electrical systems like motors, communications, and sensors. In many institutions, computer engineering students are allowed to choose areas of in-depth study in their junior and senior year, because the full breadth of knowledge used in the design and application of computers is beyond the scope of an undergraduate degree. Other institutions may require engineering students to complete one year of General Engineering before declaring computer engineering as their primary focus.

The Background

The first accredited computer engineering degree programme in the United States was established at Case Western Reserve University in 1971. As of October 2004, there were 170 ABET-accredited computer engineering programmes in the US. In Europe, accreditation of computer engineering schools is done by a variety of agencies part of the EQANIE network. Due to increasing job requirements for engineers, who can concurrently design hardware, software, firmware, and manage all forms of computer systems used in industry, some tertiary institutions around the world offer a bachelor's degree generally called computer engineering. Both computer engineering and electronic engineering programmes include analogue and digital circuit design in their curricula. As with most engineering disciplines, having a sound knowledge of mathematics and sciences is necessary for computer engineers. There are two major specialities in computer engineering: software and hardware.

Computer Software Engineering

Computer software engineers design, develop, and test software. Some software engineers design, construct and maintain computer programmes for companies. Some set up networks such as "intranets" for companies. Others make or install new software or upgrade computer systems. Computer software engineers can also work in application design. This involves designing or coding new programmes and applications to meet the needs of a business or individual.

Computer Hardware Engineering

Most computer hardware engineers research, develop, design, and test various computer equipment. This can range from circuit boards and microprocessors to routers. Some update existing computer equipment to be more efficient and work with newer software. Most computer hardware engineers work in research laboratories and high-tech manufacturing firms. Some also work for the federal government. According to BLS, 95 per cent of computer hardware engineers work in metropolitan areas. They generally work full time. Approximately 25 per cent of their work requires more than 40 hours a week. The median starting salary for employed qualified computer hardware engineers (2010) was $98,810 per year or $47.50 per hour. Computer hardware engineers held 70,000 jobs in 2010.

Speciality Areas

There are many speciality areas in the field of computer engineering.

Coding, Cryptography and Information Protection: According to the Sloan Career Cornerstone Centre, Computer engineers working in this area develop new methods for protecting various information, such as digital images and music, fragmentation, copyright infringement and other forms of tampering. Examples include work on wireless communications, multi-antenna systems, optical transmission, and digital watermarking.

Communications and Wireless Networks: Those focusing on com-munications and wireless networks work on advancements in communications systems and networks (especially wireless networks), modulation and error-control coding, and information theory. High-speed network design, interference suppression and modulation, design and analysis of fault-tolerant system, and storage and transmission schemes are all a part of this speciality.

Compilers and Operating Systems: This speciality focuses on compilers and operating systems design and development. Engineers in this field develop new operating system architecture, programme analysis techniques, and new techniques to assure quality. Examples of work in this field includes post-link-time code transformation algorithm development and new operating system development.

Computational Science and Engineering: Computational Science and Engineering is relatively new discipline. According to Sloan Career Cornerstone Centre, individuals working in this area, "computational methods are applied to formulate and solve complex mathematical problems in engineering and the physical and the social sciences. Examples include aircraft design, the plasma processing of nanometer features on semi-conductor wafers, VLSI circuit design, radar detection systems, ion transport through biological channels, and much more".

Computer Networks, Mobile Computing, and Distributed Systems: In this speciality, engineers build integrated environments for computing, communications, and information access. Examples include shared-channel wireless networks, adaptive resource management in various systems, and improving the quality of service in mobile and ATM environments. Some other examples include work on wireless network systems and fast Ethernet cluster wired systems.

Computer Systems: Architecture, Parallel Processing and Dependability: Engineers working in computer systems work on research projects that allow for reliable, secure, and high-performance computer systems. Projects such as designing processors for multi-threading and parallel processing are included in this field. Other examples of work in this field include development of new theories, algorithms, an other tools that add performance to computer systems.

Computer Vision and Robotics: In this speciality, computer engineers focus on developing visual sensing technology to sense an environment, representation of an environment, and manipulation of the environment. The gathered three-dimensional information is then implemented to perform a variety of tasks. These include, improved human modelling, image communication, and human-computer interfaces, as well as devices such as special-purpose cameras with versatile vision sensors.

Embedded Systems: Individuals working in this area design technology for enhancing the speed, reliability, and performance of systems. Embedded systems are found in many devices from a small FM radio to the space shuttle. According to the Sloan Cornerstone Career Centre, on going developments in embedded systems include "automated vehicles and equipment to conduct search and rescue, automated transportation systems, and human-robot coordination to repair equipment in space."

Integrated Circuits, VLSI Design, Testing and CAD: This speciality of computer engineering requires adequate knowledge of electronics and electrical systems. Engineers working in this area work on enhancing the speed, reliability, and energy efficiency of next-generation Very Large-Scale Integration (VLSI) circuits and microsystems. An example of this speciality is work done on reducing the power consumption of VLSI algorithms and architecture.

Signal, Image and Speech Processing: Computer engineers in this area develop improvements in human-computer interaction, including speech recognition and synthesis, medical and scientific imaging, or com-munications systems. Other work in this area includes computer vision development such as recognition of human facial features.

Education: Most entry-level computer engineering jobs require at least a bachelor's degree in computer engineering. Sometimes a degree in electrical engineering is accepted, due to the similarity of the two fields. According to BLS, "a computer engineering major is similar to electrical engineering but with some computer science courses added to the curriculum". Some large firms or specialised jobs require a master's degree. It is also important for Computer Engineers to keep up with rapid advances in technology. Therefore, many continue learning throughout their careers.

Software Engineering

Software engineering is the study of designing, implementing, and modifying software in order to ensure it is of high quality, affordable, maintainable, and fast to build. It is a systematic approach to software design, involving the application of engineering practices to software.

Software engineering deals with the organising and analysing software to get the best out of them. It doesn't just deal with the creation or manufacture of new software, but its internal maintenance and arrangement.

Education

Some universities teach computer science as a theoretical study of computation and algorithmic reasoning. These programmes often feature the theory of computation, analysis of algorithms, formal methods, concurrency theory, databases, computer graphics, and systems analysis, among others. They typically also teach computer programming, but treat it as a vessel for the support of other fields of computer science rather than a central focus of high-level study. Other colleges and universities, as well as secondary schools and vocational programmes that teach computer science, emphasise the practice of advanced programming rather than the theory of algorithms and computation in their computer science curricula. Such curricula tend to focus on those skills that are important to workers entering the software industry. The process aspects of computer programming are often referred to as software engineering.

While computer science professions increasingly drive the US economy, computer science education is absent in most American K-12 curricula. A report entitled "Running on Empty: The Failure to Teach K-12 Computer Science in the Digital Age" was released in October 2010 by Association for Computing Machinery (ACM) and Computer Science Teachers Association (CSTA), and revealed that only 14 states have adopted significant education standards for high school computer science. The report also found that only nine states count high school computer science courses as a core academic subject in their graduation requirements. In tandem with "Running on Empty", a new non-partisan advocacy coalition - Computing in the Core (CinC) - was founded to influence federal and state policy, such as the Computer Science Education Act, which calls for grants to states to develop plans for improving computer science education and supporting computer science teachers.

Within the United States a gender gap in computer science education has been observed as well. Research conducted by the WGBH Educational Foundation and the Association for Computing Machinery (ACM) revealed that more than twice as many high school boys considered computer science to be a "very good" or "good" college major than high school girls. In addition, the high school Advanced Placement (AP) exam for computer science has displayed a disparity in gender. Compared to other AP subjects it has the lowest number of female participants, with a composition of about 15 per cent women. This gender gap in computer science is further witnessed at the college level, where 31 per cent of undergraduate computer science degrees are earned by women and only 8 per cent of computer science faculty consists of women.

Algorithms and Data Structures

Programming Language Theory: Programming Language Theory (PLT) is a branch of computer science that deals with the design, implementation, analysis, characterisation, and classification of programming languages and their individual features. It falls within the discipline of computer science, both depending on and affecting mathematics, software engineering and linguistics. It is an active research area, with numerous dedicated academic journals.

Formal Methods

Formal Methods are a particular kind of mathematically based technique for the specification, development and verification of software and hardware systems. The use of formal methods for software and hardware design is motivated by the expectation that, as in other engineering disciplines, performing appropriate mathematical analysis can contribute to the reliability and robustness of a design. However, the high cost of using formal methods means that they are usually only used in the development of high-integrity and life-critical systems, where safety or security is of utmost importance. Formal methods are best described as the application of a fairly broad variety of theoretical computer science fundamentals, in particular logic calculi, formal languages, automata theory, and programme semantics, but also type systems and algebraic data types to problems in software and hardware specification and verification.

Concurrent, Parallel and Distributed Systems

Concurrency is a property of systems in which several computations are executing simultaneously, and potentially interacting with each other. A number of mathematical models have been developed for general concurrent computation including Petri nets, process calculi and the Parallel Random Access Machine model. A distributed system extends the idea of concurrency onto multiple computers connected through a network. Computers within the same distributed system have their own private memory, and information is often exchanged amongst themselves to achieve a common goal.

Databases and Information Retrieval

A database is intended to organise, store, and retrieve large amounts of data easily. Digital databases are managed using database management systems to store, create, maintain, and search data, through database models and query languages.

Job Outlook

Computer Software Engineering: According to BLS, "computer applications software engineers and computer systems software engineers are projected to be among the fastest growing occupations from 2008 to 2018". BLS reports an expected growth of 30 per cent for software developers from 2010 to 2020. In addition, growing concerns over cyber security add up to put computer software engineering high above the average rate of increase for all fields. However, some of the work will be outsourced in foreign countries. Due to this, job growth will not be as fast as during the last decade.

Computer Hardware Engineering

According to the BLS, "employment of computer hardware engineers is expected to increase 9 per cent from 2010 to 2020. Today, computer hardware is somehow equal to Electronic and Computer Engineering (ECE) and has divided to many subcategories, the most significant of them is Embedded system design. This field has developed all around us, from tiny controllers to huge computers.

Information Technology Operations

Information Technology operations, or IT operations, are the superset of all processes and services that are both provisioned by an IT staff to their internal or external clients and used by themselves, to run themselves as a business.

The definition of IT operations differs throughout the IT industry, where vendors and individual organisations often create their own custom definitions of such processes and services for the purpose of marketing their own products. Usually, they include management, envisioning, planning, design, implementation, construction, deployment, distribution, verification, installation, instantiation, execution and maintenance. They endeavour to define common processes and procedures, policies, roles, responsibilities, terminology, best practices and standards for running an enterprise. Best practice subsets of IT operations are ITIL, RUP, SDLC, MSF and MOF, which, while productive and focused, cover limited areas of what an enterprise needs.

Role of Information Technology in Libraries

Next-generation Library Catalogues

An online public access catalogue (often abbreviated as OPAC or simply "library catalogue") is an online database of materials held by a library or group of libraries. Users typically search a library catalogue to locate books, periodicals, audio/visual materials or other items under control of a library.

As access to the internet became more accessible to more people library users have grown more and more accustomed to these sites and search engines. They have become increasingly dissatisfied with the search mechanisms of older library catalogue systems. This has, in turn, led to vocal criticisms of these systems within the library community itself, and in recent years to the development of newer (often termed 'next-generation') catalogues. However, the large cost associated with these new systems has significantly hindered the widespread use of new systems. The newest generation of library catalogue systems are distinguished from earlier OPACs by their use of more sophisticated search technologies, in particular faceted search, and features aimed at greater user interaction and participation with the system, including tagging, reviewing, and RSS feeds.

However, the usefulness of these catalogues is limited by inconsistent metadata standards that vary from publisher to publisher. There is also the concern that only newly digitised material can be found while older material, published on different platforms that are no longer supported is effectively lost. Libraries are then faced with the expensive and time consuming task of reapplying new metadata tags to ensure these older records can become discoverable. At present there is no single standard for metadata records. Next generation library catalogue systems.

Proprietary

- Aquabrowser;
- Axiell Arena;
- Bibliocommons;
- Carmen (LANius);
- CS Library;
- DIMDATA ILS;

- Ebsco Discovery Service;
- Encore;
- Libramatic;
- LS2 PAC and LS2 Kids from The Library Corporation (TLC);
- POLARIS PAC, Mobile PAC, Polaris Library Systems;
- Primo (ExLibris);
- Prism 3 (Capita);
- Retrievo (KEEP SOLUTIONS);
- Serials Solutions Summon;
- VTLS Inc.;
- WorldCat Local (OCLC).

Open Source

- Avanti MicroLCS;
- Blacklight OPAC;
- Evergreen;
- Invenio;
- jOPAC;
- Koha;
- Omeka;
- OpenBiblio;
- OpenSiteSearch;
- PhpMyBibli;
- Rapi package;
- Scriblio;
- Social Online Public Access Catalogue (SOPAC);
- Steve.museum;
- VuFind.

SFX

SFX was the first OpenURL link resolver or link server. It remains the most widely used OpenURL resolver, being used by over 1,500 libraries.

Librarians Herbert van de Sompel, Patrick Hochstenbach and their colleagues at Ghent University in Belgium developed the OpenURL framework from 1998 to 2000. At that time they called it by the working title *Special Effects* (*SFX*). As part of the OpenURL development, they implemented the linking server software called *SFX server*. In early–2000, Ex Libris, Ltd. acquired the SFX server software from Ghent University. Ex Libris re-engineered the software and marketed it to libraries as an autonomous component of the OpenURL framework.

Ex Libris continues to develop the software and add enhancements recommended by its customers. SFX is the most widely known OpenURL link server within the library and scholarly publishing community, and occasionally the product name has been used as a generic term for OpenURL link servers.

VDX

VDX (standing for *Virtual Document eXchange*) is a software product for interlibrary loan (ILL) and document request management. VDX was developed by UK company Fretwell-Downing Informatics, a company which in 2005 was taken over by OCLC PICA, itself wholly acquired by OCLC Online Computer Library Centre in 2007.

VDX allows library staff to create and manage document borrowing and lending requests between participating libraries. VDX manages all the stages of the ILL process. It is also an efficient way to collect copyright fees for copyright holders such as authors and publishers.

How VDX Works?: ILL requests are sent to VDX through a process called automediation. VDX validates the request for the necessary information — author, title, date of publication — and searches for the item. It then creates a routing list (or "rota") of libraries that own the item. The request is sent to the first library on the rota, which indicates whether it can supply the item. If the library cannot lend or process the request, it will be automatically directed to the next library on the routing list, and so on, until a library is found that can supply the document. The document is then sent to the requesting library. Throughout the document exchange process, the requesting library can check the status of the request at any time.

ISO Standards

VDX is based on ISO 10161, which is the international standard for ILL. ISO 10161 defines communication protocols and guarantees that ILL information can be communicated between different ILL programmes (such as VDX and similar products). Another standard, ISO 10160, determines the terminology that is used for ILL transactions across various document exchange systems.

Koha

Koha is an open source Integrated Library System (ILS), used world-wide by public, school and special libraries. The name comes from a Maori term for a gift or donation.

Features

Koha is web-based ILS, with a SQL database (MySQL preferred) back end with cataloguing data stored in MARC and accessible via Z39.50 or SRU. The user interface is very configurable and adaptable and has been translated into many languages. Koha has most of the features that would be expected in an ILS, including:

- Simple, clear interface for librarians and members (patrons);
- Various Web 2.0 facilities like tagging, comment, Social sharing and RSS feeds;
- Union catalogue facility;
- Customisable search;
- Circulation and borrower management;
- Full acquisitions system including budgets and pricing information (including supplier and currency conversion);
- Simple acquisitions system for the smaller library;

- Ability to cope with any number of branches, patrons, patron categories, item categories, items, currencies and other data;
- Serials system for magazines or newspapers;
- Reporting;
- Reading lists for members.

Background

Koha was created in 1999 by Katipo Communications for the Horowhenua Library Trust in New Zealand, and the first installation went live in January 2000.

From 2000, companies started providing commercial support for Koha, building to more than 20 today.

In 2001, Paul Poulain (of Marseille, France) began adding many new features to Koha, most significantly support for multiple languages. By 2010, Koha has been translated from its original English into French, Chinese, Arabic and several other languages. Support for the cataloguing and search standards MARC and Z39.50 was added in 2002 and later sponsored by the Athens County Public Libraries. In France Paul Poulain co-founded BibLibre in 2007.

In 2005, an Ohio-based company, Metavore, Inc., trading as LibLime, was established to support Koha and added many new features, including support for Zebra sponsored by the Crawford County Federated Library System. Zebra support increased the speed of searches as well as improving scalability to support tens of millions of bibliographic records. In 2007 a group of libraries in Vermont began testing the use of Koha for Vermont libraries. At first a separate implementation was created for each library. Then the Vermont Organisation of Koha Automated Libraries (VOKAL) was organised to create one database to be used by libraries. This database was rolled out in 2011. Thirty-seven libraries have chosen to adopt Koha and moved to the shared production environment hosted and supported by ByWater Solutions. Previously Vermont used software from Follett.

In 2011 the Spanish Ministry of Culture maintains KOBLI, a tailored version of Koha based on an earlier report.

International Conferences

- KohaCon 2006, May 2–3, Paris, France;
- KohaCon 2009, April 15–17, Plano, Texas;
- KohaCon 2010, Oct. 25 - Nov. 2, Wellington, New Zealand;
- KohaCon 2011, Oct. 31 - Nov. 6, Thane, India;
- KohaCon 2012, June 5–11, Edinburgh, Scotland, UK;
- KohaCon 2013 October 16 - 22 Reno, Nevada.

Dispute with LibLime/PTFS

In 2009 a dispute arose between LibLime and other members of the Koha community. The dispute centred on LibLime's apparent reluctance to be inclusive with the content of the http://koha.org/ sites and the non-contribution of software patches back to the community. A number of participants declared that they believed that LibLime had forked the software and the community. A separate web presence, source code repository and community was established at http://koha-community.org/. The fork continued after March 2010, when LibLime was purchased by PTFS.

In November, 2011, LibLime announced they had been granted a provisional trademark on the use of the name *Koha* in New Zealand by Intellectual Property Office of New Zealand. The provisional trademark grant was successfully appealed by the Koha community lead by Catalyst, with a decision handed down in December 2013 and with Liblime to pay costs.

Current Status

The latest stable release of Koha is 3.14.1

Koha is currently a very active project. According to ohloh, it has a *very large, active development team* and a *mature, well-established codebase*. The analysis of the size of the code base may be deceptive because Koha stores user interface translations alongside actual source code and ohloh cannot always distinguish them.

Alexandria

Alexandria is cross-platform library automation software used by thousands of libraries around the world, both public libraries and school libraries. These include the Houston Independent School District, Philadelphia Public Schools, and the Berkeley Unified School District.

Background

COMPanion Corporation was founded in 1987 by company President Bill Schjelderup.

Version History:

- v6 released 2009.

Selected Features

- Library management;
- MARC cataloguing;
- Lexile integration;
- Supports reading programmes such as Accelerated Reader;
- Due date and policy flexibility;
- Thousands of flexible reports;
- Integration with book vendors such as Bound To Stay Bound;
- Web-based patron interface;
- Access to third-party databases such as netTrekker.

Information Communication and Society

"Freedom, Prosperity and the Development of society and individuals are fundamental human values. They will only be attained through the ability of well-informed citizens to exercise their democratic rights and to play an active role in society. Constructive participation and the development of democracy depend on satisfactory education as well as on free and unlimited access to knowledge, thought, culture and information.

The public library, the local gateway to knowledge, provides a basic condition for lifelong learning, independent decision-making and cultural development of the individual and social groups."

So says UNESCO in the introduction to its Public Library Manifesto. The manifesto goes on to say:

> "The librarian is an active intermediary between users and resources. Professional and continuing education of the librarian is indispensable to ensure adequate services."

Professional librarians are dedicated to providing access to information and resources and work to a strong ethical code. The Chartered Institute of Library and Information Professionals (CILIP) Code of Professional Practice contains the following clause which emphasises the role librarians must fulfil:

> "One of the distinguishing features of professions is that their knowledge and skills are at the service of society at large, and do not simply serve the interests of the immediate customer. Members should therefore:

1. Consider the public good, both in general and as it refers to particular vulnerable groups, as well as the immediate claims arising from their employment and their professional duties.
2. Promote equitable access for all members of society to public domain information of all kinds and in all formats.
3. Strive to achieve an appropriate balance within the law between demands from information users, the need to respect confidentiality, the terms of their employment, the public good and the responsibilities outlined in this Code.
4. Encourage and promote wider knowledge and acceptance of, and wider compliance with, this Code, both among colleagues in the information professions and more widely among those whom we serve."

This website will publish the facts about Public Library Services in the UK, and about the work librarians do. Its aim is to provide a balanced view of the service and the profession, and to discuss some ideas for the way forward. We don't want to lose our libraries, and we aim to ensure future generations continue to enjoy access to the fundamental values identified by UNESCO and provided by free unbiased public libraries and librarians.

Libraries, Information and Society

This module aims to:

- Provide students with an understanding of the various library models and sectors.
- Introduce students to the range of management challenges and services offered across the various library and information sectors.
- Provide an understanding of the role of libraries and information services within society.

On completion of this module, students will:

- Understand the role of the different library sectors in providing services to their user communities;
- Understand the nature and differences in services provided by various libraries;
- Understand the management and marketing issues concerning the various library sectors;
- Be aware of how to identify and investigate the social value provided to society by libraries and associated information services.

Indicative topics:

- Library sectors and models;
- Libraries in the Commercial sector;
- Marketing information services;
- Measuring service value and impact;
- Impact and Social value of information and library services within society;
- The professional librarian;
- The information society.

Social Orientation

Digital Divide

A digital divide is an economic inequality between groups, broadly construed, in terms of access to, use of, or knowledge of information and communication technologies (ICT). The divide within countries (such as the digital divide in the United States) can refer to inequalities between individuals, households, businesses, and geographic areas at different socioeconomic and other demographic levels, while the divide between countries is referred to as the global digital divide, which designates nations as the units of analysis and examines the gap between developing and developed countries on an international scale.

Approaches

Conceptualisation of the digital divide is often as follows:

1. Subjects of connectivity, or who connects: individuals, organisations, enterprises, schools, hospitals, countries, etc.
2. Characteristics of connectivity, or which attributes: demographic and socio-economic variables, such as income, education, age, geographic location, etc.
3. Means of connectivity, or connectivity to what: fixed or mobile, Internet or telephony, digital TV, etc.
4. Intensity of connectivity, or how sophisticated the usage: mere access, retrieval, interactivity, innovative contributions.
5. Purpose of connectivity, or why individuals and their cohorts are (not) connecting: reasons individuals are and are not online and uses of the Internet and information and communications technologies (ICTs).
6. Dynamics of evolution, or whether the gap of concern would increase or decrease in the future, when the gap of concern would be maximised.

In research, while each explanation is examined, the others should be controlled for in order to eliminate interaction effects or mediating variables, but these explanations are meant to stand as general trends, not direct causes. Each of the above listed items can be looked at from different angles, which leads to a myriad of ways to look at (or define) the digital divide. For example, measurements for the intensity of usage, such as incidence and frequency, vary by study. Some report usage as access to Internet and ICTs while others report usage as having previously connected to the Internet. Some studies focus on specific technologies, others on a combination (such as Infostate, proposed by Orbicom-UNESCO, the Digital Opportunity Index, or ITU's ICT Development Index). Based on different answers to the questions of who, with which kinds of characteristics, connects how and why, to what there are hundreds of alternatives ways to define the digital divide. "The new consensus recognises that the key question is not how to connect people to a specific network through a specific device, but how to extend the expected gains from new ICTs". In short, the desired impact and "the end justifies the definition" of the digital divide.

Explanatory Variables

Obtaining access to ICTs and using them actively has been linked to a plethora of demographic and socio-economic characteristics: among them income, education, race, gender, and geographic location (urban-rural), age, skills, awareness, political and cultural and psychological attitudes. Multiple regression analysis across countries has shown that income levels and educational attainment are identified as providing the most powerful explanatory variables for ICT access and usage. Evidence was found that Caucasians are much more likely than non-caucasians to own a computer as well as have access to the Internet in their homes. As for geographic location, people living in urban centres have more access and show more usage of computer services than those in rural areas. Gender was previously thought to provide an explanation for the digital divide, many thinking ICT were male gendered, but controlled statistical analysis has shown that income, education and employment act as confounding variables and that women with the same level of income, education and employment actually embrace ICT more than men.

Means of Connectivity

Infrastructure

The infrastructure by which individuals, households, businesses, and communities connect to the Internet address the physical mediums that people use to connect to the Internet such as desktop computers, laptops, basic mobile phones or smart phones, iPods or other MP3 players, Xboxes or PlayStations, electronic books readers, and tablets such as iPads.

Location

Internet connectivity can be utilised at a variety of locations such as homes, offices, schools, libraries, public spaces, Internet cafe and others. There are also varying levels of connectivity in rural, suburban, and urban areas.

Applications

Common Sense Media, a non-profit group based in San Francisco, surveyed almost 1,400 parents and reported in 2011 that 47 per cent of families with incomes more than $75,000 had downloaded apps for their children, while only 14 per cent of families earning less than $30,000 had done so.

Overcoming Digital Divide

An individual must be able to connect in order to achieve enhancement of social and cultural capital as well as achieve mass economic gains in productivity. Therefore, access is a necessary (but not sufficient) condition for overcoming the digital divide. Access to ICT meets significant challenges that stem from income restrictions. The borderline between ICT as a necessity good and ICT as a luxury good is roughly around the "magical number" of US$10 per person per month, or US$120 per year, which means that people consider ICT expenditure of US$120 per year as a basic necessity. Since more than 40 per cent of the world population lives on less than US$ 2 per day, and around 20 per cent live on less than US$ 1 per day (or less than US$ 365 per year), these income segments would have to spend one third of their income on ICT (120/365 = 33%). The global average of ICT spending is at a mere 3 per cent of income. Potential solutions include driving down the costs of ICT, which includes low cost technologies and shared access through Telecentres.

Furthermore, even though individuals might be capable of accessing the Internet, many are thwarted by barriers to entry such as a lack of means to infrastructure or the inability to comprehend the information that the Internet provides. Lack of adequate infrastructure and lack of knowledge are two major obstacles that impede mass connectivity. These barriers limit individuals' capabilities in what they can do and what they can achieve in accessing technology. Some individuals have the ability to connect, but they do not have the knowledge to use what information ICTs and Internet technologies provide them. This leads to a focus on capabilities and skills, as well as awareness to move from mere access to effective usage of ICT.

The United Nations is aiming to raise awareness of the divide by way of the World Information Society Day which has taken place yearly since May 17, 2001. It also sets up the Information and Communications Technology (ICT) Task Force in November 2001. Social media websites serve as both manifestations of and means by which to combat the digital divide. The former describes phenomena such as the divided users demographics that make up sites such as Facebook and Myspace or Word Press and Tumblr. Facebook and Word Press are considered "white" in their more complicated and up-to-date user interfaces while Tumblr and Myspace are considered "black" due to their less sophisticated appearance and functions. While this dichotomy does exist, black communities are using the internet, especially websites like Tumblr and Twitter, to narrow the gap of the digital divide. Each of these sites host thriving communities that engage with otherwise marginalised populations. An example of this is the large online community devoted to Afrofuturism, a discourse that critiques dominant structures of power by merging themes of science fiction and blackness. Social media brings together minds that may not otherwise meet, allowing for the free exchange of ideas and empowerment of marginalised discourses.

Effective Use

Community Informatics (CI) provides a somewhat different approach to addressing the digital divide by focusing on issues of "use" rather than simply "access". CI is concerned with ensuring the opportunity not only for ICT access at the community level but also, according to Michael Gurstein, that the means for the "effective use" of ICTs for community betterment and empowerment are available. Gurstein has also extended the discussion of the digital divide to include issues around access to and the use of "open data" and coined the term "data divide" to refer to this issue area.

Implications

Social Capital

Once an individual is connected, Internet connectivity and ICTs can enhance his or her future social and cultural capital. Social capital is acquired through repeated interactions with other individuals or groups of individuals. Connecting to the Internet creates another set of means by which to achieve repeated interactions. ICTs and Internet connectivity enable repeated interactions through access to social networks, chat rooms, and gaming sites. Once an individual has access to connectivity, obtains infrastructure by which to connect, and can understand and use the information that ICTs and connectivity provide, that individual is capable of becoming a "digital citizen".

Criticism

Second-level Digital Divide

The second-level digital divide, also referred to as the production gap, describes the gap that separates the consumers of content on the internet from the producers of content. As the technological digital divide is decreasing between those with access to the internet and those without, the meaning of the term digital divide is evolving. Previously, digital divide research has focused on accessibility to the internet and internet consumption. However, with more and more of the population with access to the internet, researchers are examining how people use the internet to create content and what impact socioeconomics are having on user behaviour. New applications have made it possible for anyone with a computer and an internet connection to be a creator of content, yet the majority of user generated content available widely on the internet, like public blogs, is created by a small portion of the internet using population. Web 2.0 technologies like Facebook, YouTube, Twitter, and Blogs enable users to participate online and create content without having to understand how the technology actually works, leading to an ever increasing digital divide between those who have the skills and understanding to interact more fully with the technology and those who are passive consumers of it. Many are only nominal content creators through the use of Web 2.0, posting photos and status updates on Facebook, but not truly interacting with the technology.

Some of the reasons for this production gap include material factors like the type of internet connection one has and the frequency of access to the internet. The more frequently a person has access to the internet and the faster the connection, the more opportunities they have to gain the technology skills and the more time they have to be creative. Other reasons include cultural factors often associated with class and socioeconomic status. Users of lower socioeconomic status are less likely to participate in content creation due to disadvantages in education and lack of the necessary free time for the work involved in blog or website creation and maintenance. Additionally, there is evidence to support the existence of the second-level digital divide at the K-12 level based on how educators' use technology for instruction. Schools' economic factors have been found to explain variation in how teachers use technology to promote higher-order thinking skills.

Knowledge Divide

Since gender, age, racial, income, and educational gaps in the digital divide have lessened compared to past levels, some researchers suggest that the digital divide is shifting from a gap in access and connectivity to ICTs to a knowledge divide. A knowledge divide concerning technology presents the possibility that the gap has moved beyond access and having the resources to connect to ICTs to interpreting and understanding information presented once connected.

Digitising

Digitising or digitisation is the representation of an object, image, sound, document or a signal (usually an analogue signal) by a discrete set of its points or samples. The result is called *digital representation* or, more specifically, a *digital image*, for the object, and *digital form*, for the signal. Strictly speaking, digitising means simply capturing an analogue signal in digital form. For a document the term means to trace the document image or capture the "corners" where the lines end or change direction. McQuail identifies the process of digitisation having immense significance to the computing ideals as it "allows information of all kinds in all formats to be carried with the same efficiency and also intermingled".

Process

The term digitisation is often used when diverse forms of information, such as text, sound, image or voice, are converted into a single binary code. Digital information exists as one of two digits, either 0 or 1. These are known as bits (a contraction of *binary digits*) and the sequences of 0s and 1s that constitute information are called bytes.

Analogue signals are continuously variable, both in the number of possible values of the signal *at* a given time, as well as in the number of points in the signal *in* a given period of time. However, digital signals are discrete in both of those respects – generally a finite sequence of integers – therefore a digitisation can, in practical terms, only ever be an approximation of the signal it represents.

Digitisation occurs in two parts:

Discretisation: The reading of an analogue signal *A*, and, at regular time intervals (frequency), sampling the value of the signal at the point. Each such reading is called a *sample* and may be considered to have infinite precision at this stage.

Quantisation

Samples are rounded to a fixed set of numbers (such as integers), a process known as quantisation. In general, these can occur at the same time, though they are conceptually distinct.

A series of digital integers can be transformed into an analogue output that approximates the original analogue signal. Such a transformation is called a DA conversion. The sampling rate and the number of bits used to represent the integers combine to determine how close such an approximation to the analogue signal a digitisation will be.

Examples

The term is often used to describe the scanning of analogue sources (such as printed photos or taped videos) into computers for editing, but it also can refer to audio (where sampling rate is often measured in kilohertz) and texture map transformations. In this last case, as in normal photos, sampling rate refers to the resolution of the image, often measured in pixels per inch.

Digitising is the primary way of storing images in a form suitable for transmission and computer processing, whether scanned from two-dimensional analogue originals or captured using an image sensor-equipped device such as a digital camera, tomographical instrument such as a CAT scanner, or acquiring precise dimensions from a real-world object, such as a car, using a 3D scanning device.

Digitising is central to making a digital representations of geographical features, using raster or vector images, in a geographic information system, i.e., the creation of electronic maps, either from various geographical and satellite imaging (raster) or by digitising traditional paper maps or graphs (vector).

"Digitisation" is also used to describe the process of populating databases with files or data. While this usage is technically inaccurate, it originates with the previously proper use of the term to describe that part of the process involving digitisation of analogue sources, such as printed pictures and brochures, before uploading to target databases.

Digitising may also used in the field of apparel, where an image may be recreated with the help of embroidery digitising software tools and saved as embroidery machine code. This machine code is fed into an embroidery machine and applied to the fabric. The most supported format is DST file.

Analogue Signals to Digital

Analogue signals are continuous electrical signals; digital signals are non-continuous. Analogue signal can be converted to digital signal by ADC.

Nearly all recorded music has been digitised. About 12 per cent of the 500,000+ movies listed on the Internet Movie Database are digitised on DVD.

Handling of analogue signal becomes easy when it is digitised because the signal is digitised before modulation and transmission. The conversion process of analogue to digital consists of two processes: sampling and quantising. Digitisation of personal multimedia such as home movies, slides, and photographs is a popular method of preserving and sharing older repositories. Slides and photographs may be scanned using an image scanner, but videos are more difficult.

Analogue Texts to Digital

About 5 per cent of texts have been digitised as of 2006.

Older print books are being scanned and optical character recognition technologies applied by academic and public libraries, foundations, and private companies like Google.

Unpublished text documents on paper which have some enduring historical or research value are being digitised by libraries and archives, though frequently at a much slower rate than for books. In many cases, archives have replaced microfilming with digitisation as a means of preserving and providing access to unique documents.

Implications of Digitisation

This shift to digitisation in the contemporary media world has created implications for traditional mass media products, however these "limitations are still very unclear" (McQuail, 2000:28). The more technology advances, the more converged the realm of mass media will become with less need for traditional communication technologies. For example, the Internet has transformed many communication norms, creating more efficiency for not only individuals, but also for businesses. However, McQuail suggests traditional media have also benefited greatly from new media, allowing more effective and efficient resources available (2000: 28).

Collaborative Digitisation Projects

There are many collaborative digitisation projects throughout the United States. Two of the earliest projects were the Collaborative Digitisation Project in Colorado and NC ECHO - North Carolina Exploring Cultural Heritage Online, based at the State Library of North Carolina.

These projects establish and publish best practices for digitisation and work with regional partners to digitise cultural heritage materials. Additional criteria for best practice have more recently been established in the UK, Australia and the European Union. Wisconsin Heritage Online is a collaborative digitisation project modelled after the Colorado Collaborative Digitisation Project. Wisconsin uses a wiki to build and distribute collaborative documentation. Georgia's collaborative digitisation programme, the Digital Library of Georgia, presents a seamless virtual library on the state's history and life, including more than a hundred digital collections from 60 institutions and

100 agencies of government. The Digital Library of Georgia is a GALILEO initiative based at the University of Georgia Libraries.

In South-Asia Nanakshahi trust is digitising manuscripts of Gurmukhiscript.

Library Preservation

Digital preservation in its most basic form is a series of activities maintaining access to digital materials over time. Digitisation in this sense is a means of creating digital surrogates of analogue materials such as books, newspapers, microfilm and videotapes. Digitisation can provide a means of preserving the content of the materials by creating an accessible facsimile of the object in order to put less strain on already fragile originals. For sounds, digitisation of legacy analogue recordings is essential insurance against technological obsolescence.

The prevalent Brittle Books issue facing libraries across the world is being addressed with a digital solution for long term book preservation. For centuries, books were printed on wood-pulp paper, which turns acidic as it decays. Deterioration may advance to a point where a book is completely unusable. In theory, if these widely circulated titles are not treated with deacidification processes, the materials upon those acid pages will be lost forever. As digital technology evolves, it is increasingly preferred as a method of preserving these materials, mainly because it can provide easier access points and significantly reduce the need for physical storage space.

Cambridge University Library is working on the Cambridge Digital Library, which will initially contain digitised versions of many of its most important works relating to science and religion. These include examples such as Isaac Newton's personally annotated first edition of his Philosophiae Naturalis Principia Mathematica as well as college notebooks and other papers, and some Islamic manuscripts such as a Quran from Tipoo Sahib's library.

Google, Inc. has taken steps towards attempting to digitise every title with "Google Book Search". While some academic libraries have been contracted by the service, issues of copyright law violations threaten to derail the project. However, it does provide - at the very least - an online consortium for libraries to exchange information and for researchers to search for titles as well as review the materials.

Lean Philosophy

The broad use of internet and the increasing popularity of Lean philosophy has also increased the use and meaning of "digitising" to describe improvements in the efficiency of organisational processes. This will often involve some kind of Lean process in order to simplify process activities, with the aim of implementing new "lean and mean" processes by digitising data and activities.

Fiction

Works of science-fiction often include the term digitise as the act of transforming people into digital signals and sending them into a computer. When that happens, the people disappear from the real world and appear in a computer world (as featured in the cult film *Tron*, the animated series *Code: Lyoko*, or the late 1980s live-action series *Captain Power and the Soldiers of the Future*). In the video game *Beyond Good and Evil*, the protagonist's holographic friend digitises the player's inventory items.

Information Access

Information access is an area of research at the intersection of Informatics, Information Science, Information Security, Language Technology, Computer Science, and Library Science.

The objective of the various research efforts in information access is to simplify and more effective for human users to access and further process large and unwieldy amounts of data and information.

Several technologies applicable to the general area are Information Retrieval, Text Mining, Machine Translation, and Text Categorisation.

During discussions on free access to information as well as on information policy, information access is understood as concerning the insurance of free and closed access to information. Information access covers many issues including copyright, open source, privacy, and security.

Provision was made in copyright and patent law for information in the public domain. However the extent of the public domain has been under attack in recent years, as database vendors expand the copyright and contract laws to eliminate concepts such as fair use. UCITA, the Uniform Computer Information Transactions Act has been defeated in most jurisdictions, but restrictions on the public domain still exist in more recent laws such as the Digital Millennium Copyright Act (DMCA).

Librarians have always advocated free and open access to government information. Groups such as the American Library Association, the American Association of Law Libraries, Ralph Nader's Taxpayers Assets Project have advocated for free access to legal information. The vendor neutral citation movement in the legal field is working to ensure that courts will accept citations from cases on the web which do not have the traditional (copyrighted) page numbers from the West Publishing company. There is a worldwide Free Access to Law Movement which advocates free access to legal information. The Wired Magazine Article Who Owns The Law is a good introduction to the access to legal information issue.

Acts following the September 11 attacks, such as the Patriot Act, in the interest of security has led to restrictions on access to certain types of information as well as an increased government attempts at surveillance of individual's private information, such as their library records.

Links to Free Software

Free software takes the approaches of openly accessible information and applies them to software code. Based on the tenets of open information practices, free and open source software takes a freedom based approach to software development and maintenance. The free software movement has impacted areas such as software and free access to scholarly journals. Lawrence Lessig, himself a board member of Free Software Foundation advocates free software and argues that computer code can regulate conduct in much the same way that legal codes do.

18

SOCIAL SCIENCE INFORMATION SYSTEM

The society in which we live has been so profoundly affected by information systems that historians refer to the present time as the information age. This is due to our ability to collect, process, store, disseminate and manipulate large amount of information using information system. As an information society, it is very imperative we consider both the social and ethical implications of the use of information system in our society.

Information systems as described by Whitten is an arrangement of people, data, process and interface that interacts to support and improve day-to-day operations in a business as well as support the problem-solving and decision-making needs of the management and users. Also, Laudon and Laudon technically defined information systems as a set of interrelated components that collects (or retrieve), process, store and distribute information to support decision-making, coordination, and control in an organisation. Information systems contain information about significant people, places and things within the organisation or in the environment surrounding it. By information we mean data that have been shaped into a form that is meaningful and useful to human beings. Data in contrast is a collection of raw facts representing events occurring in the organisations or within our physical environment. According to Pollack people have become much more technologically savvy largely due to the dramatically increased scope of information available via Internet, the ease of access to information, and the broadened scope of computer literacy; the security of information and privacy of individuals have become areas of significant concern. Considering the fact that computers and information systems have become a fundamental part of our lives, the opportunities to misuse and abuse computer, the information it generates and systems now abound.

The increase in the applications of information systems in our society and its escalating growth has altered the face of almost every aspects of the society. The most obvious effects of information systems have been the rise of the internet and its consequences in terms of how of information systems have changed the face of almost every aspect of our societies, most remarkably in terms of economics and culture or behavioural approach. Information systems can be viewed as a factor of production that can be freely substituted for capital and labour. As the cost of information systems continues to reduce, it is substituted for labour and capital, which historically has been a rising cost. Also, it helps organisations to lower the cost of their transactions thereby making it worthwhile for organisations to contrast with external suppliers instead of using internal sources. However, behavioural researchers have theorised that information systems could change the hierarchy of decision-making in organisation by lowering the costs of information acquisition and broadening the distribution of information. As an information society, we must consider both the ethical and social implications of the use of information systems in our society.

The digital world we are presently leaving is posing some important and new ethical questions such as who owns information, particularly information about us. Who is responsible for making the information accurate? Should we set guidelines on how business organisations and business professionals should use information, computer systems and information? And if that is so, what should these guidelines be? What penalties should be accessed for unethical norms and abuses? This topic is becoming increasingly so important so as to successfully manage the use of information systems in our society.

Social Impact of Information Systems

The increase in the application of information systems in our society has changed the face of almost every aspect of our society and cultures. The most obvious effect of information system has been the rise of the internet and its consequences in terms of how we communicate, socialise, learn and do business to mention but few. However, before considering the implications of the internet, which is basically linked to that of the computer, we shall foremost explore some important features of information systems and what they mean to us.

Firstly, we must not forget that the computer was primarily designed as a means of solving arithmetic and logic problems, and data storage. The development of the computer from these modest roots are the complex machines of today which allow us to work out more complex problems in a way that would have otherwise been impossible and store more information. This affects our society in two ways: On an individual basis it means that any person in possession of some kind of a computer has the capacity to store every document they will ever need in a single compact machine. This connotes that computer allows people to set up businesses and work from home on a scale never seen before, not to mention taking the human progress a step beyond that of the printing press by removing the need for hand writing for the first time in our history. On a larger scale, it allows scientific progress to accelerate as mathematical problems incomprehensible to humans can be worked out by simple programmed machines. The effect of computer storage capacity is to totally change how large scale businesses function, by assisting inventory management, by facilitating and expediting the storage of data important to organisations, for instance: customer preferences or phone numbers.

Another effect of information systems is the rise in computer games. This has caused serious worries over how they affect those who use them, and especially their effects on youth. The debate still rages over whether the large number of violent computer games available influences those who play to imitate such behaviour, with a host of scientific research being done on the issue. Yet almost worrying are the statistics which seem to be highly addictive to the quality of such games - most notably internet based ones. In contrast many have begun to see the potential computers held as a means of education, since, unlike other traditional forms of teaching tools, computer game based learning has a propensity to entertain the student. Businesses and organisations are already using computers as educational devices and technology development tools, especially in the field of virtual reality games and more would still follow. Whatever one's feelings on the growth of these video games, in both recreational and educational formats they are becoming ever more of a reality, for instance the United States military uses one of such game as a recruitment device.

Another interesting and undeniable effect is the use of internet in the societies worldwide; in fact, it could be said to connect and eliminate differences between geographically and culturally separated societies. The effects of the computer are still developing; nevertheless it is already obvious that they are sufficiently wide reaching to far surpass an answer of this length. Ultimately the internet is a means of communication. One of the results is to make learning democratic. At the click of a mouse anyone with a computer, regardless of their wealth, status, or education, can access a practically limitless supply of knowledge. A benefit of this is that with the correct internet know-how, one can find out almost anything in a matter of seconds; it revolutionises the way people go about research.

However, the same capacity for multiplying information which makes the internet great and threatens the whole organisations as music, films and other forms of entertainment and information are released free of charge onto the web. Inevitably sales of CD's and DVD's have fallen as the use of the internet has grown, and indeed the speed of the web's growth has made it nearly impossible for media companies to find ways of stemming the problem. Equally, in the same way that the internet gives every single person with a computer a voice with which they can share their thoughts and ideas with the world, so too has the number of offensive sites grown with the development of the internet, from pornographic sites to the more worrying cases of websites designed for the sharing of paedophilic materials, as well as racism and even terrorism supporting sites. The technology field has been overtaken with other types of behaviour that can affect anyone who uses technology such as computer crime

Computer crime is another prevalent social impact of information system in our society. The term computer crime as described by Valacich is the act of using a computer to commit an illegal act, such as targeting a computer while committing an offence, using a computer to commit an offence, or using computers in the course of a criminal activity. Computer virus and hacker attacks are intended to destroy data and software and disrupt computer services. In the year 2002 alone, more than 7,000 computer viruses were reported. Phishing attacks frequently target a specific group of people and are intended to secure personal information, usually financially related, from innocent and unsuspecting responders.

Other types of the crime that are ubiquitous include carding, cloning, data diddling, phishing, shoulder-surfing, salami slicing and social engineering Correspondingly, the increasing recognition of social networking sites is a double-edged sword. On the one hand it has allowed people to connect and communicate with one another with ease and scale never seen before. At the most basic level this began with e-mail, which alone can be seen as nearly equal to the invention of the telephone in terms of communication. Some social sites like the www.facebook.com have more members than the average national population. The fact that the internet allows such.

Forms of communication to be free makes it democratic. The potential of such sites to be used for the good of the people can be seen recently in the part played by Face book in Middle Eastern uprisings of Egypt, Tunisia, Algeria and Libya, when it was used by rebelling citizens as a way of coordinating strikes and marches. Yet equally there are many cases of children being groomed by sex offenders through *these websites.*

Ethics in an Information Society

Codes of Ethical Conduct in Society

According to Woodbury, instead of investing in "the perfect crime detection tool, a better approach might be to virtue ethics", and goes on to suggest that perhaps an "honour code" would be a better solution. The essence of creating codes of ethical conduct in our society is to give the public a sense of trust in a group of professionals. These professionals make good use of these codes to define the limits of their activities and to help guide them in their businesses and organisations. The codes of ethics are promises by professions to control themselves in the general interest of the society.

Most organisations have developed guidelines for the ethical use of information system and computers and most computer-related professional institutes have also published guidelines for their members. Higher institutions of learning and public schools have developed guidelines for their students, faculty members and employees about the ethical use of computers. In addition, they encourage all their system users to act responsibly, ethically and legally whenever they are using computers and to obey accepted rules of online etiquette. Some of the impacted ethics and public policy guidelines prohibit the followings:

- To interfere with other people's computer files;
- Spying other peoples files;
- To harm other people with the use of computers;
- Stealing with the use of computers;
- Using computer to bear false witness;
- Copying and using proprietary software without license;
- Using other peoples computer resources without legal authority.

Future Scope

The introduction of information systems in our society can be usefully divided into three phases, two of which have already occurred: the introduction stage and the circulation stage. We have only recently entered the third and most important phase which is the control phase; in which many of the most serious social, political, legal and ethical questions involving information systems will present themselves on a large scale. Some of the discussions in this paper will give one an insight that the future developments in information systems will make ethics and social impacts more vibrant and more important than ever.

Conclusion

The study was carried out with a view of assessing the emerging technological trends that information systems are posing on the society. New challenges that have not been dealt with before in the society are beginning to materialise. There is no doubt, the society is becoming more aware of the increasing complexity of information security and the ethical concerns that revolves around the massive amount of possible infringes. Since it's our world and future, we should be concerned and involved in its resolution. In view of this, various organisations in the country especially the oil and gas industries are taking preventive actions through the enactment of codes of ethics and codes of conduct. Government agencies have also supported the society with legislation for the protection of data integrity and privacy of individuals.

Despite the benefits associated with the applications of information systems in our society, there are some underlying issues that arose from the main discussions. Based on these, the following recommendations are suggested:

- The society must ensure each person is accountable for everything he or she does, no matter how inexplicable his or her action may appear.
- Since there are growing complexities of ethical and social issues that revolve around multiple breaches, it becomes imperative for the educators and computer professional bodies to develop curriculum on ethical and professional codes of conduct in the information society
- There is need to lay emphases on information systems security controls
- The government should develop a comprehensive laws and legislations to create a sense or awareness of compliance requirements that affects information systems professionals.
- Our law enforcement agents should be more sophisticated in their computer crime investigation. This can be enhanced with the use of computer forensics, which is a formal investigative technique used in evaluating digital information for judicial *review*.

Ethical and Social Impact of Information Systems

As a matter of fact, changes in technology often affect the society. This can change individuals, jobs, education, government and social interactions. As component of a society, each group has rights and responsibilities to one another, such as right to privacy and obligations regarding ethics. The effect of technology on individuals can be beneficial or detrimental. But in most cases an alteration in technology may help a group of individuals and be harmful to another set of people. Typical challenges include loss of privacy, depersonalisation and change in incentives. The benefits include lower prices, better products and services. Many of these issues does not only affect our society as a whole, but also raise lots of questions for organisations and our working place at large.

Ethical Concerns of Information Systems

Laudon and Laudon described ethics as the principle of right and wrong that individuals, acting as free moral agents, use to make choices to guide their behaviours. Information systems raise new ethical questions for both individuals and society because they create opportunities for intense social change, and this threaten existing distributions of power, funds, rights and obligations. Just like other technologies such as steam engines, electricity, the telephone and radios, information system can be used to achieve social progress, but can also be used to commit crimes and threaten treasured social values. The development of information systems will produce benefits for many and cost for others. Another ethical issue that is giving a new urgency is the rise in the internet and electronic commerce. The internet and digital technology have made it much easier than ever for organisations to assemble, integrate and distribute information, thereby unleashing concerns about the appropriate use of customers' information, personal privacy and intellectual property. Other ethical issues include establishing accountability for the consequences of information systems, setting standards to safeguard system quality that protects the safety of individuals and society, and preserving values and institutions considered to be the quality of life in an information society. According to Haag as we prepare future professionals for employment in technological fields, it is important we develop a sense of awareness of the potential types of ethical issues that are common to information systems organisations. Included in a long list of issues that are covered by policies in most organisations are policies for ethical computer use, information privacy, acceptable use, *e*-mail, Internet use, and an anti-spam policy. Pearlson pointed out that managers must be involved in monitoring outward activities of the business because customers and their privacy are affected when there are outward breaches. Other ethical issues related to information systems are:

(i) *Health Risks:* A lot of health related concerns such as Carpal Tunnel Syndrome (CTS), Repetitive Stress Injury (RSI), Techno-stress and Computer Vision Syndrome (CVS) are related to prolonged use of information systems. One should be aware of this health issues because it costs business huge amount of money annually in medical treatment claims and affects productivity. Although, ergonomics, which can be described as the science that studies safe work environments, or the study of the relationship between human and machines has helped to determine that it is cheaper to purchase equipment that will reduce the health risk associated with information systems such as different keyboards, monitors that reduce eyes strain and desks that allows proper body positioning.

(ii) *Employment:* Re-engineering work is typically hailed in the information systems community as a major benefit of new information technology. It is much less frequently noted that redesigning business processes could potentially cause millions of middle-level managers and clerical workers to lose their jobs. One economist has raised the possibility that we will create a society run by a small "high tech elite of corporate professionals... in a nation of the permanently unemployed".

(iii) *Information Privacy:* The invasion of privacy is a very big challenge associated with information systems, because it can accommodate vast amounts of data, we must therefore decide what information is proper to store or not, and who should have access to the information. Every time you use a credit card, make a phone call, withdraw money, reserve a flight, or register at school, all these transactions of yours are recorded by the systems. These records can be used to learn a great deal about you, where you have been, when you were there, and how much money was spent. Should this information be available to everyone? Information systems are also used to store information about individuals' credit rating, which may determine their abilities to borrow money.

Ethical Analysis

This section presents various step processes of how one should analyse ethical concerns when confronted with such a situation:

(i) *Identify and Clearly Describe the Facts:* This involves finding out who did what to whom, and where; when and how. In most cases, you will be astonished of the mistakes in the initially reported facts, and you will find that simply getting the facts straight helps in defining the solution. Also, this assists other opposing parties involved in an ethical quandary to agree with the facts.

(ii) *State the Inconsistency and Identify the Higher-Order Values Involved:* The parties involved in disputes over ethical, social and political concerns always claim to pursue higher values such as privacy, freedom and protection of property. It is very important to clearly define the conflict in ethical concerns and identify the ones with higher values.

(iii) *Identify the Stakeholders:* You must find out the identity of the stakeholders as every ethical, social and political issues have stakeholders; players in the game who have an interest in the outcome and that have invested in the situation and what they want.

(iv) *Identify the Reasonable Options to Select:* It may be discovered that none of the options may ever satisfy all the interest involved while some of the options performs a better job than others. So, sometimes concluding at a good or ethical solution may not always be a balancing of consequences to stakeholders.

(v) *Identify the Potential Consequences of Selected Options:* Some options may be ethically right but disastrous from other points of view. Other options may work in one instance and not work in another similar instance. But always ask yourself the consequences of any option chosen.

Quality of Life: Equity, Access and Boundaries

Balancing Power: Centre versus Periphery

Lower level employees many be empowered to make minor decisions but the key policy decisions may be as centralised as in the past.

Rapidity of Change: Reduced Response Time to Competition

Information systems have helped to create much more efficient national and international market. The now-more-efficient global marketplace has reduced the normal social buffers that permitted businesses many years to adjust to competition. We stand the risk of developing a "just-in-time society" with "just-in-time jobs" and "just-in-time" workplaces, families, and vacations.

Maintaining Boundaries: Family, Work, and Leisure

The danger to ubiquitous computing, telecommuting, nomad computing, and the "do anything anywhere" computing environment is that it is actually coming true. The traditional boundaries that separate work from family and just plain leisure have been weakened. The work umbrella now extends far beyond the eight-hour day.

Quality of System

This has to do with data quality and system errors. As we rely more on information systems, data quality issues are gaining more importance. These issues affect you as a consumer and as a user.

Quality of Life

An interesting quality of life issue that affects more and more people personally is the ability to work from home. Before the advent of information systems most people used to have a regular day job 8.00 a.m. to 5.00 p.m., five days a week in a typical office setting in our society. But with the introduction of information systems people can work seven days a week, all hours of the day, at home and on their ways especially the management staff in a company. Also, the quality of life issues would be incomplete without mentioning online love affairs. People also lose their jobs and ways of life because of information systems. All these are valid concerns of information systems.

Information Right and Obligations

What information rights do individuals and organisations possess with respect to themselves? What can they protect? What obligation do individuals and organisation have concerning this information?

Property Rights and Obligations

How will traditionai intellectual property rights be protected in a digital society in which tracing and accounting for ownership is difficult and ignoring such property rights is so easy?

Accounting Liability and Control

Determining who should take responsibility for decisions and actions. Many of the laws and court decisions and actions establishing precedents in the area of accountability, liability and control were firmly in place long before information systems were invented.

Basic Concepts: Responsibility, Accountability, and Liability

Ethical choices are decisions made by individuals who are responsible for the consequences of their actions. Responsibility is a key element and means that you accept the potential costs, duties, and obligations for the decisions you make. Accountability is a feature of systems and social institutions and means mechanisms are in place to determine who took responsible action, and who is responsible. Liability is a feature of political systems in which a body of laws is in place that permits individuals to recover the damages done to them by other actors, systems, or organisations. Due process is a related feature of law-governed societies and is a process in which laws are known and understood, and there is an ability to appeal to higher authorities to ensure that the laws are applied correctly.

Information Rights

Privacy is the claim of individuals to be left alone, free from surveillance or interference from other individuals or organisations, including the state. Most American and European privacy law is based on a regime called Fair Information Practices (FIP) first set forth in a report written in 1973 by a federal government advisory committee (U.S. Department of Health, Education, and Welfare, 1973).

Property Rights: Intellectual Property

Intellectual property is considered to be intangible property created by individuals or corporations. Information technology has made it difficult to protect intellectual property because computerised information can be so easily copied or distributed on networks. Intellectual property is subject to a variety of protections under three different legal traditions: trade secrets, copyright, and patent law.

Trade Secrets

Any intellectual work product – a formula, device, pattern, or compilation of data-used for a business purpose can be classified as a trade secret, provided it is not based on information in the public domain.

Copyright

Copyright is a statutory grant that protects creators of intellectual property from having their work copied by others for any purpose during the life of the author plus an additional 70 years after the author's death.

Patents

A patent grants the owner an exclusive monopoly on the ideas behind an invention for 20 years. The congressional intent behind patent law was to ensure that inventors of new machines, devices, or methods receive the full financial and other rewards of their labour and yet make widespread use of the invention possible by providing detailed diagrams for those wishing to use the idea under license from the patent's owner.

Internet Challenges to Privacy

Internet technology has posed new challenges for the protection of individual privacy. Information sent over this vast network of networks may pass through many different computer systems before it reaches its final destination. Each of these systems is capable of monitoring, capturing, and storing communications that pass through it.

Cookies are small text files deposited on a computer hard drive when a user visits to the websites. Cookies identify the visitor's web browser software and track visits to the website. Web beacons, also called web bugs, are tiny objects invisibly embedded in *e*-mail messages and Web pages that are designed to monitor the behaviour of the user visiting a website or sending *e*-mail. Spyware can secretly install itself on an Internet user's computer by piggybacking on larger applications. Once installed, the spyware calls out to Websites to send banner ads and other unsolicited material to the user, and it can also report the user's movements on the Internet to other computers.

System Quality: Data Quality and System Errors

Three principle sources of poor system performance are (1) software bugs and errors (2) hardware or facility failures caused by natural or other causes and (3) poor input data quality. The software industry has not yet arrived at testing standards for producing software of acceptable but not perfect performance.

Computer Crime and Abuse

New technologies, including computers, create new opportunities for committing crimes by creating new valuable items to steal, new way to steal them, and new ways to harm others. Computer crime is the commission illegal acts through the use of a computer or against a computer system. Simply accessing a computer system without authorisation or with intent to do harm, even by accident, is now a federal crime.

Computer abuse is the commission of acts involving a computer that may not illegal but that are considered unethical. The popularity of the Internet and *e*-mail has turned one form of computer abuse – spamming – into a serious problem for both individuals and businesses. Spam is junk *e*-mail sent by an organisation or individual to a mass audience of Internet users who have expressed no interest in the product or service being marketed.

Employment: Trickle-Down Technology and Re-engineering Job Loss

Re-engineering work is typically hailed in the information systems community as a major benefit of new information technology. It is much less frequently noted that redesigning business processes could potentially cause millions of mid-level managers and clerical workers to lose their jobs. One economist has raised the possibility that we will create a society run by a small "high tech elite of corporate professionals...in a nation of permanently unemployed" (Rifkin, 1993). Careful planning and sensitivity to employee needs can help companies redesign work to minimise job losses.

Equity and Access: Increasing Racial and Social Class Cleavages

Several studies have found that certain ethnic and income groups in the United States are less likely to have computers or online Internet access even though computer ownership and Internet access have soared in the past five years. A similar digital divide exists in US schools, with schools in high-poverty areas less likely to have computers, high-quality educational technology programmes, or internet access availability for their students. Public interest groups want to narrow this digital divide by making digital information services – including the Internet – available to virtually everyone, just as basic telephone service is now.

Health Risks: RSI, CVS, and Technostress

The most common occupational disease today is repetitive stress injury (RSI). RSI occurs when muscle groups are forced through repetitive actions often with high-impact loads (such as tennis) or tens of thousands of repetitions under low-impact loads (such as working at a computer keyboard).

The single largest source of RSI is computer keyboards. The most common kind of computer-related RSI is carpal tunnel syndrome (CTS), in which pressure on the median nerve through the wrist's bony structure, called a carpal tunnel, produces pain. Millions of workers have been diagnosed with carpal tunnel syndrome. Computer vision syndrome (CVS) refers to any eyestrain condition related to display screen use in desktop computers, laptops, *e*-readers, smart-phones, and hand-held video games. Its symptoms, which are usually temporary, include headaches, blurred vision, and dry and irritated eyes.

The newest computer-related malady is technostress, which is stress induced by computer use. Its symptoms include aggravation, hostility towards humans, impatience, and fatigue. Technostress is thought to be related to high levels of job turnover in the computer industry, high levels of early retirement from computer-intense occupations, and elevated levels of drug and alcohol abuse.

Dependence and Vulnerability

Today our businesses, governments, schools, and private associations, such as churches are incredibly dependent on information systems and are, therefore, highly vulnerable if these systems fail. The absence of standards and the criticality of some system applications will probably call forth demands for national standards and perhaps regulatory oversight.

Summary

Technology can be a double-edged sword. It can be the source of many benefits but it can also create new opportunities for invading your privacy, and enabling the reckless use of that information in a variety of decisions about you. The computer has become a part of our lives – personally as well as socially, culturally, and politically. It is unlikely that the issues and our choices will become easier as information technology continues to transform our world. The growth of the Internet and the information economy suggests that all the ethical and social issues we have described will be heightened further as we move into the first digital century.

19

Bussiness Information System

Types of Business Information Systems

No single system can provide all the information an organisation needs. Even small firms have a collection of different systems: *e*-mail systems, sales tracking systems, etc. Different systems can be described through:

- *A Functional Perspective:* Identifying systems by their major business function;
- *A Constituency Perspective:* Identifying systems in terms of the major organisational groups that they serve.

There are four main types of information systems that serve different functional systems:

1. Sales and marketing information systems help the firm with marketing business processes (identifying customers for the firm's products or services, developing products and services to meet their needs, promoting products and services) and sales processes (selling the products and services, taking orders, contacting customers, and providing customer support).
2. Manufacturing and production information systems deal with the planning, development, and production of products and services, and controlling the flow of production.
3. Finance and accounting information systems keep track of the firm's financial assets and fund flows.
4. Human resources information systems maintain employee records, track employee skills, job performance and training, and support planning for employee compensation and career development.

There are four main categories of systems from a constituency perspective:

1. Transaction processing systems (TPS) are basic business systems that serve the operational level of the organisation by recording the daily routine transactions required to conduct business, such as payroll and sales receipts.

2. Management information systems (MIS) serve middle managers' interests by providing current and historical performance information to aid in planning, controlling, and decision-making at the management level. MIS typically compress TPS data to present regular reports on the company's basic operations.
3. Decision support systems (DSS), or business intelligence systems, help managers with non-routine decisions that are unique, rapidly changing, and not easily specified in advance. DSS are more analytical than MIS, using a variety of models to analyse internal and external data or condense large amounts of data for analysis.
4. Executive support systems (ESS) provide a generalised computing and communications environment that help senior managers address strategic issues and identify long-term trends in the firm and its environment. ESS address non-routine decisions requiring judgement, evaluation, and insight because there is no agreed-on procedure for arriving at a solution. ESS present graphs and data from many internal and external sources through an interface that is easy for senior managers to use. Often the information is delivered to senior executives through a portal, which uses a Web interface tc present integrated personalised business content.

Ideally, these constituency-based systems are interrelated. TPS are typically a major source of data for other systems, whereas ESS are primarily a recipient of data from lower-level systems and external sources.

The various types of systems in the organisation have interdependencies. TPS are major producers of information that is required by many other systems in the firm, which, in turn, produce information for other systems. These different types of systems are loosely coupled in most business firms, but increasingly firms are using new technologies to integrate information that resides in many different systems.

Information Systems Function in Business

In all but the smallest of firms, the information systems department is the formal organisational unit responsible for information technology services. The information systems department is responsible for maintaining the hardware, software, data storage, and networks that comprise the firm's IT infrastructure. The information systems department suggests new business strategies and new information-based products and services, and coordinates both the development of the technology and the planned changes in the organisation.

The information systems department consists of specialists, such as:

- *Programmers:* Technical specialists who write the software instructions for computers;
- *Systems Analysts:* The principal liaisons between the information systems groups and the rest of the organisation;
- *Information Systems Managers:* Leaders of teams of programmers and analysts, project managers, physical facility managers, telecommunications managers, or database specialists.

In many companies, the information systems department is headed by a chief information officer (CIO), a senior manager who oversees the use of information technology in the firm. End users are representatives of departments outside of the information systems group for whom applications are developed.

Small companies may not have a formal information systems group. Larger companies will have a separate information systems department, which may be organised along several different lines, depending on the nature and interests of the firm, such as:

- *Decentralised Arrangement:* Each functional area of the business has its own information systems department and management that typically reports to a senior manager or chief information officer.
- *Separate Department:* In this arrangement, the information systems function operates as a separate department similar to the other functional departments with a large staff, a group of middle managers, and a senior management group.

Divisional Groups

Very large "Fortune 1,000"-size firms with multiple divisions and product lines might allow each division (such as the Consumer Products Division or the Chemicals and Additives Division) to have its own information systems group. All of these divisional information systems groups report to a high-level central information systems group and CIO.

Business Processes and Information Systems

Business processes refer to the manner in which work is organised, coordinated, and focused to produce a valuable product or service. Business processes also refer to the unique ways in which organisations coordinate work, information, and knowledge, and the ways in which management chooses to coordinate work. Every business can be seen as a collection of business processes. To a large extent, the performance of a business firm depends on how well its business processes are designed and coordinated. Many business processes are tied to a specific functional area, such as sales and marketing, while others cross many different functional areas and require coordination across departments.

Information systems enhance business processes in primarily two ways:

1. *Increasing the Efficiency of Existing Processes:* Enabling entirely new processes that are capable of transforming the business.

Developing Information Systems

"The actions that are taken to create an information system that solves an organisational problem are called system development". These include system analysis, system design, computer programming/implementation, testing, conversion, production and finally maintenance. These actions usually take place in that specified order but some may need to repeat or be accomplished concurrently.

Conversion is the process of changing or converting the old system into the new. This can be done in three basic ways, though newer methods (prototyping, Extreme Programming, JAD, etc.) are replacing these traditional conversion methods in many cases:

- Direct cut – The new system replaces the old at an appointed time.
- Pilot study – Introducing the new system to a small portion of the operation to see how it fares. If good then the new system expands to the rest of the company.
- Phased approach – New system is introduced in stages.

Corporate Governance

Information and technology (IT) governance is a subset discipline of corporate governance, focused on information and technology (IT) and its performance and risk management. The interest in IT governance is due to the on-going need within organisations to focus value creation efforts on an organisation's strategic objectives and to better manage the performance of those responsible for creating this value in the best interest of all stakeholders. It has evolved from The Principles of Scientific Management, Total Quality Management and ISO 9001 Quality Management Systems.

Historically, board-level executives deferred key IT decisions to the company's IT management and business leaders. Short-term goals of those responsible for managing IT can be in conflict with the best interests of other stakeholders unless proper oversight is established. IT governance systematically involves everyone: board members, executive management, staff, customers, communities, investors and regulators. An IT Governance framework is used to identify, establish and link the mechanisms to oversee the use of information and related technology to create value and manage the risks associated with using information and technology.

Various definitions of IT governance exist. Whilst in the business world the focus has been on managing performance and creating value, in the academic world the focus has been on "specifying the decision rights and an accountability framework to encourage desirable behaviour in the use of IT." The IT Governance Institute's definition is: "*...leadership, organisational structures and processes to ensure that the organisation's IT sustains and extends the organisation's strategies and objectives.*"

AS8015, the Australian Standard for Corporate Governance of Information and Communication Technology (ICT), defines Corporate Governance of ICT as "*The system by which the current and future use of ICT is directed and controlled. It involves evaluating and directing the plans for the use of ICT to support the organisation and monitoring this use to achieve plans. It includes the strategy and policies for using ICT within an organisation.*"

Background

The discipline of information technology governance first emerged in 1993 as a derivative of corporate governance and deals primarily with the connection between an organisation's strategic objectives, business goals and IT management within an organisation. It highlights the importance of value creation and accountability for the use of information and related technology and establishes the responsibility of the governing body, rather than the chief information officer or business management.

The primary goals for information and technology (IT) governance are to (1) assure that the use of information and technology generate business value, (2) oversee management's performance and (3) mitigate the risks associated with using information and technology. This can be done through board-level direction, implementing an organisational structure with well-defined accountability for decisions that impact on the successful achievement of strategic objectives and institutionalise good practices through organising activities in processes with clearly defined process outcomes that can be linked to the organisation's strategic objectives.

Following corporate governance failures in the 1980s, a number of countries established codes of corporate governance in the early 1990s:

- Committee of Sponsoring Organisations of the Treadway Commission (USA);
- Cadbury Report (UK);
- King Report (South Africa).

As a result of these corporate governance efforts to better govern the leverage of corporate resources, specific attention was given to the role of information and the underpinning technology to support good corporate governance. It was soon recognised that information technology was not only an enabler of corporate governance, but as a resource, it was also a value creator that was in need of better governance.

In Australia, the AS8015 Corporate Governance of ICT was published in January 2005. It was fast-track adopted as ISO/IEC 38500 in May 2008. IT governance process enforces a direct link of IT resources & process to enterprise goals in line of strategy. There is a strong correlation between maturity curve of IT governance and overall effectiveness of IT.

Problems with IT Governance

IT governance is often confused with IT management, compliance and IT controls. The problem is increased by terms such as "governance, risk and compliance (GRC)" that establish a link between governance and compliance. The primary focus of IT governance is the stewardship of IT resources on behalf of various stakeholders whose ranking is established by the organisation's governing body. A simple way to explain IT governance is: *what* is to be achieved from the leveraging of IT resources. While IT management is about "planning, organising, directing and controlling the use of IT resources" (that is, the *how*), IT governance is about creating value for the stakeholders based on the direction given by those who govern. ISO 38500 has helped clarify IT governance by describing a model to be used by company directors.

While directors are responsible for this stewardship it is not unusual that will delegate this responsibility to management (business and IT) who are expected to develop the necessary capability to deliver the performance expected. Whilst managing risk and ensuring compliance are essential components of good governance, the primary focus is on delivering value and managing performance (i.e. "Governance, Value delivery and Performance management" (GVP)).

Frameworks

There are quite a few supporting references that may be useful guides to the implementation of information and technology (IT) governance. Some of them are:

- AS8015-2005 Australian Standard for Corporate Governance of Information and Communication Technology. AS8015 was adopted as ISO/IEC 38500 in May 2008
- ISO/IEC 38500:2008 Corporate governance of information technology, (very closely based on AS8015-2005) provides a framework for effective governance of IT to assist those at the highest level of organisations to understand and fulfil their legal, regulatory, and ethical obligations in respect of their organisations' use of IT. ISO/IEC 38500 is applicable to organisations from all sizes, including public and private companies, government entities, and not-for-profit organisations. This standard provides guiding principles for directors of organisations on the effective, efficient, and acceptable use of Information Technology (IT) within their organisations.
- COBIT (Control Objectives for Information and related Technology) is regarded as the world's leading IT governance and control framework. COBIT provides a reference model of 37 IT processes typically found in an organisation. Each process is defined together with process inputs and outputs, key process activities, process objectives, performance measures and an elementary maturity model. Originally created by ISACA, COBIT is now the responsibility of the ITGI (IT Governance Institute).

Others include:

- CMM - The Capability Maturity Model: focus on software engineering

Non-IT specific frameworks of use include:

- The Balanced Scorecard (BSC) - method to assess an organisation's performance in many different areas.

Various Information Systems

Enterprise systems create a standard data structure and are invaluable in eliminating the problem of information fragmentation caused by multiple information systems within an organisation. An EIS differentiates itself from legacy systems in that it self-transactional, self-helping and adaptable to general and specialist conditions. Unlike an enterprise information system, legacy systems are limited to department wide communications.

A typical enterprise information system would be housed in one or more data centres, would run enterprise software, and could include applications that typically cross organisational borders such as content management systems.

Enterprise Information System

An enterprise information system (EIS) is any kind of information system which improves the functions of an enterprise business processes by integration. This means typically offering high quality of service, dealing with large volumes of data and capable of supporting some large and possibly complex organisation or enterprise. An EIS must be able to be used by all parts and all levels of an enterprise.

The word enterprise can have various connotations. Frequently the term is used only to refer to very large organisations such as multinational companies or public sector organisations. However, the term may be used to mean virtually anything, by virtue of it having become the latest corporate-speak buzzword.

Purpose

Enterprise information systems provide a technology platform that enables organisations to integrate and coordinate their business processes on a robust foundation. An EIS is currently used in conjunction with customer relationship management and supply chain management to automate business processes. An enterprise information system provides a single system that is central to the organisation and that ensures information can be shared across all functional levels and management hierarchies.

An EIS can be used to increase business productivity and reduce service cycles, product development cycles and marketing life cycles. It may be used to amalgamate existing applications. Other outcomes include higher operational efficiency and cost savings.

Financial value is not usually a direct outcome from the implementation of an enterprise information system.

Executive Information System

An executive information system (EIS) is a type of management information system that facilitates and supports senior executive information and decision-making needs. It provides easy access to internal and external information relevant to organisational goals. It is commonly considered a specialised form of decision support system (DSS). EIS emphasises graphical displays and easy-to-use user interfaces. They offer strong reporting and drill-down capabilities. In general, EIS are enterprise-wide DSS that help top-level executives analyse, compare, and highlight trends in important variables so that they can monitor performance and identify opportunities and problems. EIS and data warehousing technologies are converging in the marketplace.

In recent years, the term EIS has lost popularity in favour of business intelligence (with the sub areas of reporting, analytics, and digital dashboards).

The Background

Traditionally, executive information systems were mainframe computer-based programmes. The purpose was to package a company's data and to provide sales performance or market research statistics for decision-makers, such as financial officers, marketing directors, and chief executive officers, who were not necessarily well acquainted with computers. The objective was to develop computer applications that highlighted information to satisfy senior executives' needs. Typically, an EIS provides only data that supported executive level decisions, not all company data.

Today, the application of EIS is not only in typical corporate hierarchies, but also at personal computers on a local area network. EIS now cross computer hardware platforms and integrate information stored on mainframes, personal computer systems, and minicomputers. As some client service companies adopt the latest enterprise information systems, employees can use their personal computers to get access to the company's data and identify information relevant to their decision-making. This arrangement lets all users customise their access to company data, and provides relevant information to upper and lower corporate levels.

Components

EIS components can typically be classified as:

- Hardware;
- Software;
- User interface;
- Telecommunications.

Hardware

When talking about computer hardware for an EIS environment, we should focus on the hardware that meet the executive's needs. The executive must be put first and the executive's needs must be defined before the hardware can be selected. The basic hardware needed for a typical EIS includes four components:

1. Input data-entry devices. These devices allow the executive to enter, verify, and update data immediately
2. The central processing unit (CPU), which is the important because it controls the other computer system components
3. Data storage files. The executive can use this part to save useful business information, and this part also help the executive to search historical business information easily
4. Output devices, which provide a visual or permanent record for the executive to save or read. This device refers to the visual output device such as monitor or printer

In addition, with the advent of local area networks (LAN), several EIS products for networked workstations became available. These systems require less support and less expensive computer hardware. They also increase EIS information access to more company users.

Software

Choosing the appropriate software is vital to an effective EIS. Therefore, the software components and how they integrate the data into one system are important. A typical EIS includes four software components:

1. Text-handling software—documents are typically text-based
2. Database—heterogeneous databases on a range of vendor-specific and open computer platforms help executives access both internal and external data
3. Graphic base—graphics can turn volumes of text and statistics into visual information for executives. Typical graphic types are: time series charts, scatter diagrams, maps, motion graphics, sequence charts, and comparison-oriented graphs (i.e., bar charts)
4. Model base—EIS models contain routine and special statistical, financial, and other quantitative analysis

User Interface

An EIS must be efficient to retrieve relevant data for decision-makers, so the user interface is very important. Several types of interfaces can be available to the EIS structure, such as scheduled reports, questions/answers, menu driven, command language, natural language, and input/output.

Telecommunication

As decentralising is becoming the current trend in companies, telecommunications will play a pivotal role in networked information systems. Transmitting data from one place to another has become crucial for establishing a reliable network. In addition, telecommunications within an EIS can accelerate the need for access to distributed data.

Applications

EIS helps executives find data according to user-defined criteria and promote information-based insight and understanding. Unlike a traditional management information system presentation, EIS can distinguish between vital and seldom-used data, and track different key critical activities for executives, both which are helpful in evaluating if the company is meeting its corporate objectives. After realising its advantages, people have applied EIS in many areas, especially, in manufacturing, marketing, and finance areas.

Manufacturing

Manufacturing is the transformation of raw materials into finished goods for sale, or intermediate processes involving the production or finishing of semi-manufactures. It is a large branch of industry and of secondary production. Manufacturing operational control focuses on day-to-day operations, and the central idea of this process is effectiveness and efficiency.

Marketing

In an organisation, marketing executives' duty is managing available marketing resources to create a more effective future. For this, they need make judgements about risk and uncertainty of a project and its impact on the company in short term and long term. To assist marketing executives in making effective marketing decisions, an EIS can be applied. EIS provides sales forecasting, which can allow the market executive to compare sales forecast with past sales. EIS also offers an approach to product price, which is found in venture analysis. The market executive can evaluate pricing as related to competition along with the relationship of product quality with price charged.

In summary, EIS software package enables marketing executives to manipulate the data by looking for trends, performing audits of the sales data, and calculating totals, averages, changes, variances, or ratios.

Financial Aspects

Financial analysis is one of the most important steps to companies today. Executives needs to use financial ratios and cash flow analysis to estimate the trends and make capital investment decisions. An EIS integrates planning or budgeting with control of performance reporting, and it can be extremely helpful to finance executives. EIS focuses on financial performance accountability, and recognises the importance of cost standards and flexible budgeting in developing the quality of information provided for all executive levels.

Advantages and Disadvantages

Advantages of EIS:

- Easy for upper-level executives to use, extensive computer experience is not required in operations;
- Provides timely delivery of company summary information;
- Information that is provided is better understood;
- EIS provides timely delivery of information. Management can make decisions promptly;
- Improves tracking information;
- Offers efficiency to decision-makers.

Disadvantages of EIS

- System dependent;
- Limited functionality, by design;
- Information overload for some managers;
- Benefits hard to quantify;
- High implementation costs;
- System may become slow, large, and hard to manage;
- Need good internal processes for data management;
- May lead to less reliable and less secure data.

Future Trends

The future of executive info systems is not bound by mainframe computer systems. This trend free executives from learning different computer operating systems, and substantially decreases implementation costs. Because this trend includes using existing software applications, executives don't need to learn a new or special language for the EIS package.

Management Information System

A management information system (MIS) provides information that organisations require to manage themselves efficiently and effectively. Management information systems are typically computer systems used for managing. The five primary components: 1.) Hardware 2.) Software 3.) *Data (information for decision-making)*, 4.) Procedures (design, development and documentation), and 5.) People (individuals, groups, or organisations). Management information systems are distinct from other information systems because they are used to analyse and facilitate strategic and operational activities.

Academically, the term is commonly used to refer to the study of how individuals, groups, and organisations evaluate, design, implement, manage, and utilise systems to generate information to improve efficiency and effectiveness of decision-making, including systems termed decision support systems, expert systems, and executive information systems. Most business schools (or colleges of business administration within universities) have an MIS department, alongside departments of accounting, finance, management, marketing, and sometimes others, and grant degrees (at undergrad, masters, and PhD levels) in MIS.

Historical Backdrop

[laudom] and Jane Laudon identify five *eras* of Management Information System evolution corresponding to the five phases in the development of computing technology: 1) mainframe and minicomputer computing, 2) personal computers, 3) client/server networks, 4) enterprise computing, and 5) cloud computing.

The *first era* (mainframe and minicomputer) was ruled by IBM and their mainframe computers; these computers would often take up whole rooms and require teams to run them - IBM supplied the hardware and the software. As technology advanced, these computers were able to handle greater capacities and therefore reduce their cost. Smaller, more affordable minicomputers allowed larger businesses to run their own computing centres in-house.

The *second era* (personal computer) began in 1965 as microprocessors started to compete with mainframes and minicomputers and accelerated the process of decentralising computing power from large data centres to smaller offices. In the late 1970s minicomputer technology gave way to personal computers and relatively low cost computers were becoming mass market commodities, allowing businesses to provide their employees access to computing power that ten years before would have cost tens of thousands of dollars. This proliferation of computers created a ready market for interconnecting networks and the popularisation of the Internet.

As technological complexity increased and costs decreased, the need to share information within an enterprise also grew—giving rise to the *third era* (client/server), in which computers on a common network access shared information on a server. This lets thousands and even millions of people access data simultaneously. The *fourth era* (enterprise) enabled by high speed networks, tied all aspects of the business enterprise together offering rich information access encompassing the complete management structure. Every computer is utilised.

The *fifth era* (cloud computing) is the latest and employs networking technology to deliver applications as well as data storage independent of the configuration, location or nature of the hardware. This, along with high speed cellphone and wifi networks, led to new levels of mobility in which managers access the MIS remotely with laptop and tablet computers, plus smartphones.

Types and Terminology

The terms *Management Information System* (MIS), *information system, Enterprise Resource Planning* (ERP), and *information technology management* are often confused. Information systems and MIS are broader categories that include ERP. Information technology management concerns the operation and organisation of information technology resources independent of their purpose.

Most management information systems specialise in particular commercial and industrial sectors, aspects of the enterprise, or management substructure.

- *Management information systems,* produce fixed, regularly scheduled reports based on data extracted and summarised from the firm's underlying transaction processing systems to middle and operational level managers to identify and inform structured and semi-structured decision problems.
- *Decision Support Systems (DSS)* are computer programme applications used by middle and higher management to compile information from a wide range of sources to support problem solving and decision-making. DSS is majorly used for semi-structured and unstructured decision problems.
- *Executive Information Systems (EIS)* is a reporting tool that provides quick access to summarised reports coming from all company levels and departments such as accounting, human resources and operations.
- *Marketing Information Systems* are Management Information Systems designed specifically for managing the marketing aspects of the business.
- *Office Automation Systems (OAS)* support communication and productivity in the enterprise by automating work flow and eliminating bottlenecks. OAS may be implemented at any and all levels of management.
- *School Information Management Systems* (SIMS) cover school administration, and often including teaching and learning materials.
- *Enterprise Resource Planning* facilitates the flow of information between all business functions inside the boundaries of the organisation and manage the connections to outside stakeholders.

Advantages

The following are some of the benefits that can be attained for different types of MISs.

- Companies are able to highlight their strengths and weaknesses due to the presence of revenue reports, employees' performance record, etc. The identification of these aspects can help the company improve their business processes and operations.
- Giving an overall picture of the company and acting as a communication and planning tool.
- The availability of customer data and feedback can help the company to align their business processes according to the needs of the customers. The effective management of customer data can help the company to perform direct marketing and promotion activities.
- MISs can help a company gain a competitive advantage. Competitive advantage is a firm's ability to do something better, faster, cheaper, or uniquely, when compared with rival firms in the market.

Enterprise Applications

- *Enterprise systems*—also known as *enterprise resource planning (ERP)* systems—provide integrated software modules and a unified database that personnel use to plan, manage, and control core business processes across multiple locations. Modules of ERP systems may include finance, accounting, marketing, human resources, production, inventory management, and distribution.
- *Supply chain management (SCM)* systems enable more efficient management of the supply chain by integrating the links in a supply chain. This may include suppliers, manufacturers, wholesalers, retailers, and final customers.
- *Customer relationship management (CRM)* systems help businesses manage relationships with potential and current customers and business partners across marketing, sales, and service.
- *Knowledge management system (KMS)* helps organisations facilitate the collection, recording, organisation, retrieval, and dissemination of knowledge. This may include documents, accounting records, unrecorded procedures, practices, and skills. Knowledge management (KM) as a system covers the process of knowledge creation and acquisition from internal processes and the external world. The collected knowledge is incorporated in organisational policies and procedures, and then disseminated to the stakeholders.

20

HEALTH SCIENCE INFORMATION SYSTEM

Health Information System

Health informatics (also called health information systems, health care informatics, health care informatics, medical informatics, nursing informatics, clinical informatics, or biomedical informatics) is a discipline at the intersection of information science, computer science, social science, behavioural science and health care. It deals with the resources, devices, and methods required to optimise the acquisition, storage, retrieval, and use of information in health and biomedicine. Health informatics tools include computers, clinical guidelines, formal medical terminologies, and information and communication systems. It is applied to the areas of nursing, clinical care, dentistry, pharmacy, public health, occupational therapy, physical therapy and (bio)medical research, and alternative medicine too.

- The international standards on the subject are covered by ICS 35.240.80 in which ISO 27799:2008 is one of the core components.
- Molecular bioinformatics and clinical informatics have converged into the field of translational bioinformatics.

Health Care Informatics

Clinical Informatics

Clinical Informatics is concerned with the use of information in health care by clinicians.

Clinical informaticians transform health care by analysing, designing, implementing, and evaluating information and communication systems that enhance individual and population health outcomes, improve [patient] care, and strengthen the clinician-patient relationship. Clinical informaticians use their knowledge of patient care combined with their understanding of informatics concepts, methods, and health informatics tools to:

- Assess information and knowledge needs of health care professionals and patients,
- Characterise, evaluate, and refine clinical processes,
- Develop, implement, and refine clinical decision support systems, and
- Lead or participate in the procurement, customisation, development, implementation, management, evaluation, and continuous improvement of clinical information systems.

Clinicians collaborate with other health care and information technology professionals to develop health informatics tools which promote patient care that is safe, efficient, effective, timely, patient-centred, and equitable.

In October 2011 American Board of Medical Specialities (ABMS), the organisation overseeing the certification of physician specialists in the United States, announced the creation of physician certification in Clinical Informatics. The first examination for board certification in the subspeciality of Clinical Informatics was offered in October 2013 by American Board of Preventive Medicine with 432 passing to become the 2014 inaugural class of Diplomates (ABPM) in Clinical Informatics. Fellowship programmes exist for physicians who wish to become board-certified in Clinical Informatics. Physicians must have graduated from a medical school in the United States or Canada, or a school located elsewhere that is approved by the ABPM. In addition, the must complete a primary residency programme such as Internal Medicine (or any of the 24 subspecialities recognised by the ABMS) and be eligible to become licensed to practice medicine in the state where their fellowship programme is located. The fellowship programme is 24 months in length, with fellows dividing their time between Informatics rotations, didactics, research, and clinical work in their primary speciality.

Human Bioinformatics

Translational Bioinformatics

With the completion of the human genome and the recent advent of high throughput sequencing and genome-wide association studies of single nucleotide polymorphisms, the fields of molecular bioinformatics, biostatistics, statistical genetics and clinical informatics are converging into the emerging field of translational bioinformatics.

The relationship between bioinformatics and health informatics, while conceptually related under the umbrella of biomedical informatics, has not always been very clear. The TBI community is specifically motivated with the development of approaches to identify linkages between fundamental biological and clinical information. Along with complementary areas of emphasis, such as those focused on developing systems and approaches within clinical research contexts, insights from TBI may enable a new paradigm for the study and treatment of disease.

Community Health Informatics

Computational Health Informatics

Computational health informatics is a branch of Computer Science that deals specifically with computational techniques that are relevant in health care. Computational health infcrmatics is also a branch of Health Informatics, but is orthogonal to much of the work going on in health informatics because computer scientist's interest is mainly in understanding fundamental properties of computation. Health informatics, on the other hand, is primarily concerned with understanding fundamental properties of medicine that allow for the intervention of computers. The health domain provides an extremely wide variety of problems that can be tackled using computational techniques, and computer scientists are attempting to make a difference in medicine by studying the underlying principles of computer science that will allow for meaningful (to medicine) algorithms and systems to be developed. Thus, computer scientists working in computational health informatics and health scientists working in medical health informatics combine to develop the next generation of health care technologies.

Using computers to analyse health data has been around since the 1950s, but it wasn't until the 1990s that the first sturdy models appeared. The development of the internet has helped develop computational health informatics over the past decade. Computer models are used to examine various topics such as how exercise affects obesity, health care costs, and many more.

Examples of projects in computational health informatics include the COACH project.

Clinical Research Informatics

Clinical Research Informatics (or, CRI) takes the core foundations, principles, and technologies related to Health Informatics, and applies these to clinical research contexts. As such, CRI is a sub-discipline of sorts of Health Informatics, and interest and activities in CRI have increased greatly in recent years given the overwhelming problems associated with the explosive growth of clinical research data and information. There are a number of activities within clinical research that CRI supports, including:

- More efficient and effective data collection and acquisition;
- Optimal protocol design and efficient management;
- Patient recruitment and management;
- Adverse event reporting;
- Regulatory compliance;
- Data storage, transfer, processing and analysis.

Health Informatics Laws

Health informatics law deals with evolving and sometimes complex legal principles as they apply to information technology in health-related fields. It addresses the privacy, ethical and operational issues that invariably arise when electronic tools, information and media are used in health care delivery. Health Informatics Law also applies to all matters that involve information technology, health care and the interaction of information. It deals with the circumstances under which data and records are shared with other fields or areas that support and enhance patient care.

As many health care systems are making an effort to have patient records more readily available to them via the internet, it is important that providers be sure that there are a few security standards in place in order to make sure that the patients information is safe. They have to be able to assure confidentiality and the security of the people, process, and technology. Since there is also the possibility of payments being made through this system, it is vital that this aspect of their private information will also be protected through cryptography.

Health Information Management

'Health information management (HIM) is the practice of acquiring, analysing and protecting digital and traditional medical information vital to providing quality patient care. HIM professionals are highly trained in the latest information management technology applications and understand the workflow in any health care provider organisation from large hospital systems to the private physician practice. They are vital to the daily operations management of health information and electronic health records.

With the widespread computerisation of health records, traditional (paper-based) records are being replaced with Electronic Health Records (EHRs). The tools of health informatics and health information technology are being increasingly utilised to introduce efficiency in information management practices in the health care sector. Both hospital information systems and health human resources information systems (HRHIS) are common implementations of HIM.

Health information management professionals plan information systems, develop health policy, and identify current and future information needs. In addition, they may apply the science of informatics to the collection, storage, analysis, use, and transmission of information to meet legal, professional, ethical and administrative records-keeping requirements of health care delivery. They work with clinical, epidemiological, demographic, financial, reference, and coded health care data. Health information administrators have been described to "play a critical role in the delivery of health care in the United States through their focus on the collection, maintenance and use of quality data to support the information-intensive and information-reliant health care system".

The World Health Organisation (WHO) stated that the proper collection, management and use of information within health care systems "will determine the system's effectiveness in detecting health problems, defining priorities, identifying innovative solutions and allocating resources to improve health outcomes."

History and Developments

HIM Standards began with Establishment of AHIMA: Health information management's standards history is dated back to the introduction of the American Health Information Management Association, founded in 1928 "when the American College of Surgeons established the Association of Record Librarians of North America (ARLNA) to 'elevate the standards of clinical records in hospitals and other medical institutions.'"

In 1938, AHIMA was known as American Association of Medical Record Librarians (AAMRL) and its members were known as medical record experts or librarians who studied medical record science. The goal was to raise the standards of records keeping in hospitals and other health care facilities. The individuals involved in this profession were promoters for the successful management of clinical records to guarantee accuracy and precision. Over time, the organisation's name changed to reflect the evolving field of health information management practices, eventually becoming the American Health Information Management Association. The association's current name is meant to cover the wide variety of areas which health professionals work in today.

AHIMA members affect the quality of patient information and patient care at every touch point in the health care delivery cycle. They often serve in bridge roles, connecting clinical, operational, and administrative functions.

Modern Developments

Electronic Health Records: The electronic health record has been continually expressed as an evolvement of health record-keeping. Because it is electronic, this means of record keeping has been both supported and debated in the health professional community and within the public realm. In the United States, 89 per cent of those who responded to a recent Wall Street Journal poll described themselves as "Very/Somewhat Confident" in their health care provider who used electronic health records compared to 71 per cent of respondents who responded positively about their providers who didn't or don't use electronic health records. As of 2008, more than fifty-percent of Chief Information Officers polled listed that they wanted ambulatory electronic health records in order to have the health information record available to move across each stage of health care.

Health information managers are charged with the protection of patient privacy and are responsible for training their employees in the proper handling and usage of the confidential information entrusted to them. With the rise of technology's importance in health care, health information managers must remain competent with the use of information databases that generate crucial reports for administrators and physicians.

Educational Programmes

The requisites and accreditation processes for health information management education and professional activity vary across jurisdictions.

In the United States, the CAHIIM requires continued accreditation for accredited programmes in health information management. The current standard is that accreditation may be maintained with periodic site visits, submission of an annual report, informing CAHIIM of adverse changes within the programme and paying CAHIIM administrative fees. HIM students may opt to participate in a full-time bridge programme called the Joint Bachelor of Science/Masters Programme. With this programme, students can achieve both the Bachelor of Science in Health Information Management and the Master of Health Services Administration Programme (BSHIM/MHSA). The full-time bridge programme allows students to achieve both degrees in five years. Students pursuing the BSHIM/MHSA will be prepared to assume management and executive positions in health-related organisations such as: hospitals, managed care organisations, health information system developers and vendors, and pharmaceutical companies, and bring their knowledge in HIM to these positions.

In Canada, graduates of Canadian Health Information Management Association (CHIMA) programmes are eligible to write a national certification examination to pursue a profession in HIM.

21

Information Sources, Systems and Services

Throughout the course of your studies you will need to use a variety of different information sources such as:

- Reference material;
- Books and ebooks;
- Academic journals;
- Magazines;
- Newspapers;
- Statistics;
- Internet sites; and
- Specialist information.

The type of information source you use will differ based on the questions you are trying to answer and the assignment requirements set out by your Course Co-ordinators.

Primary, Secondary and Tertiary Sources

As you conduct research, you will consult different sources of information. A professor may request primary, secondary, or tertiary sources. What does that mean? This guide explains these terms and gives examples for each category.

The types of information that can be considered primary sources may vary depending on the subject discipline, and also on how you are using the material.

For example:

- A magazine article reporting on recent studies linking the reduction of energy consumption to the compact fluorescent light bulb would be a secondary source.

- A research article or study proving this would be a primary source.
- However, if you were studying how compact fluorescent light bulbs are presented in the popular media, the magazine article could be considered a primary source.

Primary Sources

Definition: Primary sources are original materials. They are from the time period involved and have not been filtered through interpretation or evaluation. Primary sources are original materials on which other research is based. They are usually the first formal appearance of results in physical, print or electronic format. They present original thinking, report a discovery, or share new information.

Note: The definition of a primary source may vary depending upon the discipline or context.

Examples include:

- Artifacts (e.g. coins, plant specimens, fossils, furniture, tools, clothing, all from the time under study);
- Audio recordings (e.g. radio programmes);
- Diaries;
- Internet communications on *e*-mail, listservs;
- Interviews (e.g., oral histories, telephone, *e*-mail);
- Journal articles published in peer-reviewed publications;
- Letters;
- Newspaper articles written at the time;
- Original Documents (i.e. birth certificate, will, marriage license, trial transcript);
- Patents;
- Photographs;
- Proceedings of Meetings, conferences and symposia;
- Records of organisations, government agencies (e.g. annual report, treaty, Constitution, government document);
- Speeches;
- Survey Research (e.g., market surveys, public opinion polls);
- Video recordings (e.g. television programmes);
- Works of art, architecture, literature, and music (e.g., paintings, sculptures, musical scores, buildings, novels, poems);
- Website.

Secondary Sources

Definition: Secondary sources are less easily defined than primary sources. Generally, they are accounts written after the fact with the benefit of hindsight. They are interpretations and evaluations of primary sources. Secondary sources are not evidence, but rather commentary on and discussion of evidence. However, what some define as a secondary source, others define as a tertiary source. Context is everything.

Note: The definition of a secondary source may vary depending upon the discipline or context. Examples include:

- Bibliographies (also considered tertiary);
- Biographical works;
- Commentaries, criticisms;
- Dictionaries, Encyclopaedias (also considered tertiary);
- Histories;
- Journal articles (depending on the disciple can be primary);
- Magazine and newspaper articles (this distinction varies by discipline);
- Monographs, other than fiction and autobiography;
- Textbooks (also considered tertiary);
- Website (also considered primary).

Tertiary Sources

Definition: Tertiary sources consist of information which is a distillation and collection of primary and secondary sources.

- Almanacs;
- Bibliographies (also considered secondary);
- Chronologies;
- Dictionaries and Encyclopaedias (also considered secondary);
- Directories;
- Fact books;
- Guidebooks;
- Indexes, abstracts, bibliographies used to locate primary and secondary sources;
- Manuals;
- Textbooks (also be secondary).

Reference Sources

Reference sources such as dictionaries, encyclopaedias, almanacs, atlases, etc. are research tools that can help you with your paper or project. Reference sources provide answers to specific questions, such as brief facts, statistics, and technical instructions; provide background information; or direct you to additional information sources. In most libraries, reference sources do not circulate and are located in a separate reference collection. This practice makes reference sources readily available and easily accessible.

Reference sources are designed to be consulted rather than read through. Their design is generally dependent on the type of information and treatment provided. Reference materials can be arranged alphabetically, topically, or chronologically. Many will contain cross listed information and more than one index. If it is not obvious how a reference source is organised, take a moment to look through the explanatory or how-to-use information, which is usually presented at the beginning of the book, or in HELP screens for online products. There are thousands of reference sources available that cover practically every subject.

Although the term reference "book" is frequently used, reference sources can be books, serials, on-line databases or the Internet. A large part of using reference sources well is choosing the right one. Despite the wide variety available, reference sources can be categorised into a handful of groups. Think about the kind of information you need and how you will use it. If you are unsure which reference tool is best suited to your information need, a reference librarian will be able to assist you.

Quick guide for selecting the right type of reference source (Collins, 151):

For information about...	Choose...
Words	Dictionaries
General information/Overview of topic	Encyclopaedias
Names and addresses of people, organisations, institutions, companies	Directories
Profiles of people	Biographical Dictionaries
Places/Maps	Gazetteers or Atlases
Facts and Statistics	Almanacs
Formula, Tables, How-To-Do-It	Handbooks and Manuals
A person's work	Reviews or Criticisms
Dates, outlines, historical timelines	Historical tables, Chronologies, Historical yearbooks
Periodical Articles	Indexes or Abstracts
Books and other sources	Bibliographies or Guides to Literature...

Clippings from Newspapers

Information of current interest in newspapers and periodicals may be made known to the users either by keeping their complete files or indexing the individual item of information or by cutting out appropriate items and filing these in some suitable sequence. News-clippings or press-cuttings are pasted on thicker sheet for easy handling and arranged in a systematic order. Clippings constitute a source of information supplementing the general reference materials. Generally it records information of transitionary interest and a frequent weeding is essential. News summaries are covered by some current news-indexes like *Indian Press Index.*

Indexes to individual newspapers as well as general indexes are also available. With the availability of these services the necessity of maintaining clippings and press-cuttings in individual libraries are reduced to a minimum. However, these constitute an important source of information in newspaper libraries and other information agencies, etc., particularly till they are incorporated in the indexes.

Use: The newspaper clippings are pasted on a mount which may consist of a sheet of paper or a cardboard. The subject heading or class number, source and date are recorded on the mount so as to facilitate its arrangement. Some libraries may not prefer to mount the clippings and may put the cuttings straight-way in manila folders or envelopes. The clippings are quite often placed along with pamphlets in vertical files arranged subject-wise and sub-arranged chronologically. In academic institutions, industries and other organisations press-clippings will be found of great interest and use for knowing all the latest information.

Some libraries do not maintain regular clipping service but they display the newspaper cuttings on notice boards.

Government Gazette: A government gazette is an important reference tool. It contains very useful information, like important notifications issued by the government and their organisations, orders, ordinances, acts, advertisements and other miscellaneous information. Gazettes are frequently consulted by a large number of readers. They are the newspapers of the Central and State governments. As such any piece of information appearing in a gazette is considered to be most authentic and reliable, but the way in which the information appears in a gazette poses insurmountable difficulties for the users, many of whom are often uninstructed in the layout of its various parts, sections and their arrangement, pagination and frequency, etc. To use it effectively, it is necessary to know the outlay or the presentation of the information in the gazette.

Use: Every gazette is issued in two main editions—ordinary and extraordinary. Ordinary issues of the gazette are published weekly or at regular intervals, whereas extraordinary gazettes are brought out on any day of the week and contain timely and very urgent information. A gazette is primarily divided into some parts which are further subdivided into sections and subsections depending upon the nature of the information.

Usually gazettes appear in loose leaf form. In libraries the information contained is scanned and sorted out on the basis of the contents and arranged according to the specific parts or sections. A separate file is maintained for each part or division or section and on completion of the volume, this file is got bound. Libraries may prepare index entries for every important information giving reference to the part, section, year and date of publication and page number arranging these entries either alphabetically or in a classified order. Extraordinary gazettes are also arranged similarly but in a separate sequence.

Gazettes, as said above, are brought out by the Central as well as State Governments. *The Gazette of India,* for instance, is basically divided into four parts. Each part is further categorised into sections. The table of contents provides full description of the subject headings covered in each part. Any information not covered in these parts is provided in supplements. The following are the contents of a *Government of India Gazette.*

The Gazette of India

Part I. *Section I.* Notification relating to Non-Statutory Rules, Regulations, Orders and Resolutions issued by the Ministries of the Government of India (Other than the Ministry of Defence) and by the Supreme Court.

Section 2. Notification regarding appointments promotions, leave, etc. of Government Officers issued by the Ministries of the Government of India (Other than the Ministry of Defence) and by the Supreme Court.

Section 3. Notification relating to Non-Statutory Rules, Regulations, Orders and Resolutions issued by the Ministry of Defence.

Section 4. Notifications regarding appointments, promotions, leave, etc. of Officers issued by the Ministry of Defence.

Part II. *Section 1.* Acts, Ordinances and Regulations.

Section 2. Bills and Reports of Select Committees on Bills.

Section 3. Sub-sec. (i) General Statutory Rules (including orders, by laws, etc. of general character) issued by the Ministries of the Government of India (Other than the Ministry of Defence) and by the Central Authorities (other than the Administration of Union Territories).

Section 4. Subsection (ii) Statutory Orders and Notifications issued by the Ministries of the Government of India (other than the Ministry of Defence) and by the Central Authorities (other than the Administrations of Union Territories).

Section 5. Statutory Rules and Orders by issued the Ministry of Defence.

Part III. *Section 1.* Notifications issued by the Auditor General, Union Public Service Commission, Railway Administration, High Courts and the attached and subordinate Offices of the Government of India.

Section 2. Notifications and Notices issued by the Patents Office, Calcutta.

Section 3. Notifications issued by or under the authority of Chief Commissioners.

Section 4. Miscellaneous Notifications including Notifications, orders, advertisements and notices issued by Statutory Bodies.

Part VI. Advertisements and Notices by Private Individual and Private Bodies.

State Gazettes: Besides, the *Gazette of India* almost all the constituent States also publish gazettes, e.g., *Rajasthan Gazette* published by the Government Central Press, Jaipur, is an official organ of the Rajasthan Government. It is divided into seven main parts which are further subdivided into sections and subsections. A user intending to consult a gazette should first ascertain the type of information he desires to look for and then he should go through the table of contents, where he should find useful indication. A reader interested in knowing patents, standards, specifications and trade marks should go through the *Gazette of India* Part III Section 2 wherein complete information on the desired subject is reported weekly. Similarly one interested in knowing the latest rules and regulations of Municipalities, District Boards and Village Panchayats of Rajasthan should consult the *Rajasthan Gazette* Part 6 wherein he will find complete information on the subject.

Other Government Publications: A government document is a publication printed at government expenses or published under the authority of a governmental body. These documents reflect the policies and the activities of a government and form an important source material in libraries. The contents of government publications are as varied as the departments and various agencies which issue them. They include annual reports, parliamentary proceedings, statistical analysis, manuals of instructions, speeches, rules and regulations, proceedings, bibliographies directories, results of research, travel information, etc. They may be printed or mimeographed and may appear in either loose form or bound as book or pamphlets, issues of periodicals, or poster, leaflet, motion pictures, etc.

Government documents may be issued at any level of administration, Federal, State or local government and by the their organisations. US Government claims to be the largest single publisher in the world. In USSR all publications are official, The governments of UK, Germany, France, Japan and India also publish a large number of documents of different varieties. They relate to matters like legislature, education, agriculture, statistics, social welfare, defence, community development, etc. These publications are specially useful for studies and research in history, social sciences, personnel management, physical and biological sciences, and applications of science in industry. The government documents are considered most authoritative. Many government publications provide bibliographies which may be found useful for further study and research. The parliamentary proceedings, documents on foreign affairs, white papers, departmental reports, economic and industrial surveys, statistical publications, plan reports, various commission and committee reports form very important and useful source material in all types of libraries.

Types: According to the nature of the contents of the publications and the issuing body, government documents may be categorised as follows:

(i) Executive publications;

(ii) Legislative publications;

(iii) Judicial publications; and

(iv) Other publications.

Executive Publications: These comprise of various executive orders, notifications, manuals and other information issued by the executive heads or under their authority by various agencies like ministries and departments under them. Any person doing research in the field of economics, industry, education, science and technology will inevitably need executive publications.

Legislative Publications: These are primarily a record of parliamentary or legislative activities such as the proceedings of Parliaments, findings of a committee appointed by Parliament for a specific purpose, and reports of various standing Committees like 'Public Accounts Committee', etc. Various bills and resolutions published by legislative bodies also form a very useful and authentic source material for the students of history, political science, public administration, economics, law, labour, etc.

Judicial Publications: The judgements and interpretations of Supreme Courts, High Courts and other courts and similar agencies fall in the category of judicial publications. These would be found of utmost value by the students of law and practising lawyers and advocates.

Use: Quite often, the library users feel puzzled by the great number and variety of government documents. They do not know how to select or locate and use them. Hence, an understanding of the nature and purpose of government documents and of the way in which these are arranged in libraries is essential. Different libraries adopt different methods for organising government documents. Some libraries shelve these along with the reading material without making any distinction whereas some libraries place these prominently in a separate section which may be known as *Government Document Section*. Arrangement of publications depends upon the volume of such documents and their use by the different categories of users. If the government documents are treated like other library materials they will be assigned a call number and arranged accordingly on the shelves along with books on the same subject. In this case the users will have to locate them with the help of library catalogue which may or may not bear a symbol indicating Government Document marked on the catalogue card. Libraries which have a sizable collection of government documents, generally keep them in a separate section where they may be arranged in a classified order. Government documents which are issued successively in a numerical order are arranged in their numerical sequence on the library shelves like 1st report, 2nd report, 3rd report and so on. A good number of guides explaining the scope and contents of different varieties of government documents have been brought out and may be found useful in the selection and use of these documents.

The Patents: Patents contain information about the discoveries and inventions which have not yet appeared either, in print or in any other form. These provide information about the technical processes and methods of testing. Patents are today, the most popular forms of technological information. Patents protect inventors against misuse by other inventors. Their inventions are patented so that these may not be copied by other.

The United International Bureau For the Production of International Property (BIRPI) is considered to be the earliest and most important international institution for the protection of industrial and intellectual property. The BIRPI is situated at Geneva and has an extensive library. Its two most important publications, *viz: Bibliography of the Official Publications of National Industrial Property Affairs* and *Model Patent Law of Developing Countries* provide very useful information on patent literature. Another important international patent agency is International Patent Institute (IPI), the Hague. It serves the Governments and individuals of the countries who have signed the agreement and also the countries who are members of BIRPI. IPI offers services through the respective national patent offices on nominal charges. The services of IPI include examination of patent applications; selection of patents and other documents; preparation of a list and selection of specified subjects and compilation of bibliography on selected subjects. Besides these, almost all countries have established patent offices.

Use: Patents are very useful sources of information for the persons engaged in industrial research e.g., scientists, technologists, production engineers, etc. The researchers at university level may also require the patent literature. Patents are invariably known to the users by their code numbers assigned by the issuing Patent Office. For this reason many libraries prefer to put the patents separately arranged country-wise, and sub-arranged by code number, and not in a classified order. These are indexed indicating the patent office name, assignee, subject and number. To consult the subject index to the patents would be helpful to the users in knowing the various patents under each of the subjects like buildings, bridges, machine, etc. Most of the patents are very thin and therefore filed loosely either in ordinary file folders or loose binders or placed in pamphlet boxes or vertical files. The further amendments and reissues are filed along with the earlier patents so as to provide up-to-date information to the users. Some patent offices have brought out useful publications explaining the handling of patent literature which also provide details of the various patents granted by them.

Books, Dictionaries and Directories

Library is a collection of antique manuscript, printed and non-print materials maintained for use. The collection may comprise of clay tablets, papyrus rolls, engravings, archival material, manuscripts, early printed books, modern printed matter like books, periodicals, reports, etc. and non-print matter like music sheets, sound tapes, audiovisual aids and micro documents. A library may or may not possess all the varied forms of collection. The collection in a library would vary in format, subject matter, academic level of the thought content and the quality depending upon the nature and requirements of the community it serves, e.g., the nature of collection in a children's library would be entirely different from that of a library for adults. Similarly, the collection in a special library would vary from that of a public or academic library. Thus, it is the users and their requirements which shape the collection of a library. Of course, comprehensive, balanced and up-to-date collection enhances the importance of a library.

In India, libraries are in a developing stage. Majority of these possess printed matter alone and a few may possess non-print material as well. Among the printed material, the book is the most familiar form, it plays an important role in the dissemination of knowledge and helps in establishing cultural links between the people of different lands and different times. Although, users frequently make use of books, many users hardly know about its various parts, and its systematic use. Scanning the books or just reading the whole of it from first page to the last and not get the desired information would not mean the proper use of a book. As a result of this, majority of the users fail to derive maximum information from the books. Knowledge of various parts of the book and use of these effectively would greatly benefit the users in locating information in a short time.

Parts of a Book: A book may usually be divided into three major parts:

(i) The preliminaries (prelims);

(ii) The text; and

(iii) The supplementaries.

The sequence of information in each of the above parts depends upon the nature of the book. The 'prelims' include half-title page, title page, dedication, table of contents, list of illustrations, foreword and preface, etc.

Text matter makes up the bulk of the book. The supplementaries comprise of the appendix(es), glossary, bibliography, index(es), etc. Pagination of preliminaries is generally provided in Roman numerals and that of the text and supplementaries in Indian numbers. The front (or the first or the right-hand side of each page) is called the *recto;* and the reverse of it (or the left hand side) is called the *verso.* The recto bears an odd page number and the verso bears an even page number. A short description of some parts of a book is provided below for the information of the users.

Title Page: Title page gives the first impression about the book to the users. The information it includes is about the title, author(s), imprint and other useful information on the back. Title may be short or lengthy, sometimes it may include subtitle and alternative title. Author is the person or a corporate body responsible for the thought content expressed in the book. Accordingly, it is known as personal author or corporate author. For compilations, edited works and translated works collaborators may be taken as authors in the absence of author information. The bottom of the title page includes imprint information i.e., the name of the publisher, the name of the place(s) where its principal office(s) is (are) located and the year of publication. The title page information may be found helpful in judging the utility of the book, standing of the author and publisher and recency of ideas included in the book. The scope of the book can also be scanned from its title page.

Copyright: The copyright information appears on the back of the title page. The copyright year may follow the symbolic. This indicates the legal relationship between the publisher and the author. Some books may bear a note following the copyright symbol stating that—'All rights are reserved'. It means the prohibition of any unauthorised taking of any information from the book. The user should obtain prior permission either from the author or the publisher before quoting or taking any piece of information. Imprint or copyright dates may or may not be the same. The users should not get confused between the edition and reprint. The edition means that book has been brought up-to-date with certain changes and modifications whereas reprint simply means printing the book again without any changes made in the previous edition. It is much more important in case of books on scientific, economic or socio-economic areas which need frequent updating. Readers engaged in research in comparative studies on socio-economic, or scientific subjects emphasise the need for up-to-date and latest books. Edition and reprint information may be found mentioned on the title page or on its back.

Table of Contents: The table of contents contains the subject headings suitably divided into parts, chapters or sections along with their location in the book. The arrangement of the text matter in the table of contents depends much upon the flair of the author and as such no uniformity is found in the order of contents page in books. However, care is taken to bring a filiatary or logical sequence. Books of corporate nature or collections of papers or chapters by different authors have information provided in the table of contents along with the names of the contributors. Books on technical subjects, survey reports or those covering a wide range of miscellaneous topics are found divided into parts, chapters, sections and subsections.

Preface and Forward: Preface is usually written by the author stating the need and reasons for undertaking the work. The author also states the scope of his work and if it is a book of practical nature, he may suggest the ways as to how to consult the book and make best use of it. In preface, the author acknowledges assistance, guidance and help received by him from individuals and institutions in successfully completing the work. For a new edition of a book, a new preface may be written. In case of an edited or revised work, the preface may be provided by the editor or the reviser, in addition to the preface by the original author.

Forward is a statement often written by some one other than the author that is either by a subject specialist or a person of pre-eminence. The purpose of the forward is to recommend the book and highlight its feature.

Books: Books may be broadly categorised into two classes: *regular* books and *reference* books. Generally speaking *regular* books are those that are read from cover to cover, whereas the *reference* books are used for consultation of specific information. Regular books include manuals, handbooks, textbooks, histories, etc. Every user is familiar with these books. The most useful aid to research is contained in reference books which comprise of dictionaries, encyclopaedias, directories, yearbooks, etc.

It is essential that the use of these books is taught at the secondary school stage and gradually encouraged to make the students self-reliant when they have to get and use a lot of information.

Dictionaries: The dictionary is the most common and familiar type of reference source. Basically it is a book containing words of a language or subject arranged in an alphabetical arrangement giving their meaning, spelling, pronunciation and derivation. The words 'lexicon', 'thesaurus', 'wordbook', 'vocabulary' and 'glossary' are also used as synonyms for 'dictionary, although technically speaking they have limited meaning. Dictionaries mainly deal with the word meanings but some dictionaries provide more details, e.g., origin and history of the words, their synonyms and antonyms, definitions, quotations and illustrations and some dictionaries do also provide maps, plates, charts, etc.

Types: Dictionaries may be divided according to the number of words contained and their contents, approach and usefulness. The dictionaries may also be categorised as language dictionaries, and subject dictionaries.

Languages Dictionaries: They are so called because they deal with the words of a language, *viz.*, Hindi, English, German, French, Spanish, Bengali, Marathi, etc. Dictionaries may be unilingual, bilingual or multilingual. It is called unilingual if the meaning is provided in the same language as the word itself, e.g., Funk and Wagnall's *New Standard Dictionary of the English Language; Shorter Oxford English Dictionary; Webster's New International Dictionary of the English Language.* A dictionary is bilingual or multilingual if the meaning of the word is provided in another language or languages e.g., *Comprehensive English-Hindi Dictionary; A practical English-Chinese pronouncing Dictionary; Oxford English-Arabic Dictionary of Current usage; Bhartiya Byabhar Kosh or Dictionary of Sixteen Indian Languages including English, etc.*

Dictionaries may be comprehensive or abridged depending upon the number of words included therein. The maximum limit of words for an abridged dictionary is 1,50,000. If it contains more than 1,50,000 words it is regarded as a comprehensive dictionary, e.g., *Oxford English Dictionary* (13 *volumes); Webster's Third New International Dictionary of the English Language* (2 volumes); *Hindi Shabdasagar* (11 volumes); *Shabdakalpadruma* (5 volumes), etc. There are some encyclopaedic dictionaries. They differ from general dictionaries in more ways than one; (i) besides words, these have entries for the names of the persons and places; (ii) these include general information and (iii) these do not only define the words but give background information about them. Thus an encyclopaedic dictionary serves both as an encyclopaedia as well as a dictionary, e.g., *Reader's Digest Great Encyclopaedic Dictionary* (3 volumes); *Century Dictionary and Encyclopaedia...* (12 volumes), etc.

Subject Dictionaries: On account of the rapid developments in the various fields of knowledge—specially in science and technological subjects, new words are coming up which require correct and precise definition. This has resulted in demand for subject dictionaries. Though, generally, language dictionaries are fairly comprehensive, it may be difficult to cover specialised words of various disciplines. It is much more difficult when new terms are being coined continuously. Subject dictionaries may, therefore, be considered as complementary to general language dictionaries. Subject dictionaries are found very useful in overcoming the language barriers and translating the research results. There has been a tremendous proliferation of subject dictionaries during the past few years. The subject dictionaries are also termed as 'glossaries.' Normally they provide explanatory definitions of specialised terms which may be difficult to understand without such aids. The difference is explicit as "the general dictionary aims to report the meanings that a word has in use. The basis for the definition is whatever meaning the people who use the word intend to convey. A specialised dictionary, by contrast, considers the meaning of terms in relation to a large body of knowledge. It not only reports what speakers and writers mean by a given word, but also attempts to assess the suitability of such usage" (I). Some frequently used subject dictionaries are: *Chamber's Technical Dictionary; Henderson's Dictionary of Biological Terms; Dictionary of Politics; Mozley and Whiley's Law Dictionary,* etc.

Special Purpose Dictionaries: Dictionaries which do not fall exclusively under either of the two categories discussed above and serve a specific purpose are known as special-purpose dictionaries. Though, the pronunciation, spelling, dialect, abbreviation, etc. are generally dealt with in general dictionaries, these aspects are not tackled in detail. There exist special dictionaries for this purpose, e.g., pronouncing dictionary: spelling dictionary; etymological dictionary; dictionary of synonyms and antonyms; dictionary of phrases; dictionary of usage; dictionary of difficult words, new words, obsolete words; dialect dictionary, dictionary of slang; dictionary of abbreviations, etc. Some such special-purpose dictionaries are; *Daniel Jone's English pronouncing dictionary; Cassell's spelling dictionary; Skeat's Etymological dictionary of the English language; Webster's dictionary of synonyms; Roget's Thesaurus of English words and phrases; John Walker's rhyming dictionary of the English language; Oxford dictionary of English Proverbs; Brewer's dictionary of phrase and fables; Fowler's dictionary of modern English usage; Robert Hill's dictionary of difficult words; Berg's dictionary of new words; Joseph Wright's English dialect dictionary; Eric Partidge's dictionary of slang and unconventional English; Stevenson's book of quotations; Classical and modern dictionary of anagrams,* etc.

Use: Although, the nature and scope of dictionaries may vary enormously, the majority have common features such as approach, arrangement and information. Dictionaries are consulted for either finding out a word meaning or checking the pronunciation and the spelling of a word. For this purpose any abridged dictionary like *Oxford Shorter Dictionary or Chamber's Twentieth Dictionary* may be consulted. If further details like the origin, variant spellings, etymology and usage, etc. are required, a comprehensive dictionary like the *Oxford English Dictionary* (13 volumes) or *Universal Dictionary of English Language or* Webster's *Third New International Dictionary of the English Language,* etc. should be consulted. Usually, an average dictionary comprises of: (i) introduction or preface; (ii) key to abbreviations used in the dictionary; (iii) key to pronunciation and other important features. Many dictionaries provide a 'A guide to the dictionary' for easy and effective use. Users intending to use any dictionary should first go through these preliminaries to ascertain the purpose and scope of the dictionary. Usually, the words are arranged in alphabetical order either letter by letter or word by word. To facilitate quick handling and to find a word, each page within an alphabetical sequence will have running headings. Some dictionaries provide a thumb index indicating where different letters of the alphabets begin. Explanatory notes on two important dictionaries are provided below:

> *The Oxford English Dictionary;* being corrected reissue with an introduction, supplement and bibliography of *A New English Dictionary* on historical principles; founded mainly on the materials collected by Philological Society. Oxford, Clarendon Press, 1933, (reprint 1970) 13 V.

The Oxford English Dictionary popularly known as OED is the most authoritative and comprehensive multi-volumed dictionary of English language. The aim of this dictionary is to present in alphabetical series the words that have formed the English vocabulary from the time of the earliest records down to the present day, with all the relevant facts concerning their form, sense, history, pronunciation and etymology. It embraces not only the standard language of literature and conversation, whether current at the moment or obsolete or archaic, but also the main technical vocabulary and a large measure of dialectal usage and slang (preface). The OED provides in details the vocabulary, classification of vocabulary and pronunciation in a separate heading entitled 'General explanations.' Generally, the words and phrases are classed as:

(i) Main words;

(ii) Subordinate words; and

(iii) Combination.

The main words and subordinate words are arranged in a single alphabetical sequence. Further, the main words comprise of the identification, morphology, significance, the illustrative quotations, etc. Although the OED is primarily concerned with the words and their meanings but virtually it is regarded as a treasury of information. On account of its wide popularity and usage, Oxford dictionaries based upon the OED have come out in various editions and different forms such as The *Shorter Oxford English Dictionary* (2v); *Concise Oxford dictionary of Current English; Pocket Oxford dictionary; Little Oxford dictionary of current English,* etc.

> *The Random House Dictionary of the English Language.* Ed. by Jess Stein New York, Random House, 1966. 2059 p.

The Random House Dictionary of the English Language (RHD) is perhaps the most comprehensive single volume dictionary of 20th century. It provides the information regarding meaning, spelling, pronunciation, usage, etymology, etc. As a general language dictionary, the RHD satisfies the needs of general as well as specialist readers. Besides words, it covers, to a large, extent biographical terms, abbreviations, titles of major literary works and similar useful information. In the preliminary pages, there appear some important chapters on 'Historical sketch of the English language'; usage, dialects and functional varieties of pronunciation of English. These are very useful, especially for the students of philology. The RHD also provides a detailed chapter on 'A guide to the dictionary' which may prove useful to the users in understanding the entry word, pronunciation, parts of speech, inflected forms, definitions, cross references, etymologies, run-on-entries are supported by diagrams, charts, maps and illustrations.

The last 400 pages of the RHD are full of miscellaneous information of general interest, e.g., signs and symbols, directory of colleges and universities, concise dictionary of French-English,

Spanish-English, Italian-English, German-English; major reference works, a select bibliography, historical and political information—major dates in world history; Constitution of United States; Charter of the United Nations; list of independent States; geographical information; atlas of the world and the gazetteer. These are hardly found in other dictionaries. For easy location of words 'Thumb Index' has been provided.

Encyclopaedias: An encyclopaedia is a compendium of knowledge. Its primary purpose is to present information on all branches of knowledge. It may be referred to as a mine of information from Alchemy to Zoology. All questions of general information such as the population of India; height of Mt. Everest; the invention of aeroplane; the situation of Island of St. Helena, as well as the specialised questions of advanced subjects like the glass and its industrial use; textile industry; isotopes; problems in surgery, etc. can be answered with the help of an encyclopaedia.

Encyclopaedias differ from dictionaries in the sense that dictionaries generally deal with the words whereas encyclopaedias deal with things. This difference is illustrated in the following example. The term 'LIBRARY' is defined in *Webster's Third New International Dictionary of the English Language as:*

"1. (a) a room, a section or series of a building, or a building itself given over to books, manuscripts, musical scores or other literary and sometimes artistic materials as paintings or musical recordings usually kept in some convenient order for use but not for sale."

(b) (1) a collection of books, manuscripts or other literary materials kept (as in library) for study or reading or a collection of paintings, musical scores, musical recordings, photographs, maps or films kept for convenient use, study or enjoyment.

(2) an institution for the custody of administration of such a collection (Library of Congress)...

Whereas for the same term in *Encyclopaedia Britannica*, provides more detailed description as:

> "A library is a collection of written, printed or other graphic material (including films, slides, phonographs, records and tapes) organised for use. In this article the general term 'books' is used to denote collectively the varied forms taken by the contents of libraries, unless a particular form, e.g.; manuscripts, films, requires to be specified. Libraries may be roughly classified in two ways: by owner-ship or purpose, e.g.; national, county or municipal, university, research, school, industrial, club, private, etc., or by contents, e.g.; general, special (including medical, legal, theological, scientific, engineering, music, etc.,)...

The article is divided into following divisions:

1. History;
2. Modern libraries; and
3. Library organisation.

Each of these divisions are further subdivided into section and subsections and the complete article is spread over in 31 pages duly supported by illustrations and diagrams. Comprehensive bibliographies arranged by sections enhance the value of the articles. Encyclopaedias contain articles on various concepts, persons, places, and events. The length of articles may vary from a few lines to several pages. These are written by experts. Some dictionaries provide descriptions of words and concepts at length and are thus encyclopaedic in nature. In many encyclopaedias the names and initials of the authors appear at the end of the article and that adds to their authenticity. In some encyclopaedias a bibliography is provided at the end of each article which may be handy for further reading. Encyclopaedias are mostly multi-volumed, because it is difficult to compress the information on all the subjects in a single volume. The most well-known multi-volumed encyclopaedias are: *Encyclopaedia Britannica; Encyclopaedia Americana; Chamber's Encyclopaedia; World Book Encyclopaedia; Collier's Encyclopaedia, Viswa Kosh,* etc.

Encyclopaedias are available in single volume as well. Though they are not comprehensive like the multi-volumed ones, they serve as useful sources of information in a compact and handy manner. Some of the important single volume encyclopaedias are: *Columbia Encyclopaedia, Pears Encyclopaedia; Funk and Wagnell's Standard Encyclopaedia of Modern Knowledge; Worldmark Encyclopaedia of Nations, Sansar Gyan,* etc.

General Encyclopaedias: Encyclopaedias cover a wide field of knowledge, these may be general or devoted to specialised subjects. The scope of general encyclopaedias is further dictated mainly by two considerations:

(i) Age level; and

(ii) Emphasis.

From the age point of view encyclopaedias are known as adult encyclopaedias and children's Encyclopaedias.

The children's encyclopaedias supplement the curriculum and informational needs of the children of secondary level. These provide reading which would be found of interest not only by the children but by non-expert adults as well. The purpose of children's encyclopaedias is to help the children to build up a solid foundation of knowledge. These are aided by bright illustrations which arouse interest among the children, e.g., *Golden Book Encyclopaedia; Compton's Picture Encyclopaedia; Oxford Junior Encyclopaedia; Shishu Bharti; Sachitra Viswa Kosh,* etc. These are appreciated by the children because the illustrations greatly help the children in understanding many of the complicated things, difficult to understand otherwise.

Adult encyclopaedias are meant for the scholars and educated adults. They may be used by subject experts as well as by lay men. They serve as basic reference source in all types of libraries. The most important and well-known adult general Encyclopaedias are the *Encyclopaedia Britannica; Encyclopaedia Americana; Hindi Viswa-Bharti,* etc. Most adult encyclopaedias lay much emphasis on a subject point of view that determines the scope of the encyclopaedia. The emphasis is primarily a matter of editorial decision if compromise is made between scholarship and popularity, or between the coverage of one subject and other. Encyclopaedia Britannica is considered strong in arts, literature and biological sciences whereas the Encyclopaedia Americana is considered strong in science, technology and literature. On the lines of general Encyclopaedias some notable attempts have been made in India as well, e.g., *Hindi Viswa Kosh* published by Nagari Pracharni Sabha, Varanasi.

Subject Encyclopaedias: The general Encyclopaedias are meant to serve the requirements of the users in quest of specific facts and background material on any specific subject or on all subject areas. The articles provided therein are shorter, general and informative, and do not mean to serve the requirements of the specialists. As a result of ever expanding knowledge and specialisation in the fields of science, technology and social science new subjects are coming up in ever increasing number, which cannot be comprehensively covered in general Encyclopaedias. Hence the subject Encyclopaedias have emerged during the 20th century to deal with such subjects more exhaustively. There are many subject Encyclopaedias, single volumed and multi-volumed. Some popular

Encyclopaedias are: *Encyclopaedia of the Social Sciences; Encyclopaedia of Religion and Ethics; Encyclopaedia of the Life-Sciences, McGraw-Hill Encyclopaedia of Science and Technology; Encyclopaedia of Educational Research*, etc.

Use: Using an Encyclopaedia is an art which can be acquired through careful, patient and persistent use. Many users may find it difficult to use an Encyclopaedia whereas it is as easy as the consultation of any dictionary. The main problem in using an Encyclopaedia is a knowledge of its arrangement. Before actually proceeding to use an Encyclopaedia, one should decide which Encyclopaedia would provide the desired information. If the desired information is of general nature, it should be first looked up a general Encyclopaedia like the *Encyclopaedia Britannica or the Encyclopaedia Americana* or the *Hindi Viswa Kosh*, etc. If the desired information is of specialised nature like the frequency of radio waves; mechanical use of isotopes; edifice of some religious or social tradition, some subject Encyclopaedias like, *Encyclopaedia of Physics; International Encyclopaedia of Social Sciences or Encyclopaedia of Religion and Ethics*, should be consulted to advantage.

Most of the Encyclopaedias follow alphabetical arrangement. The arrangement of entry headings may be letter-by-letter or word-by-word. Some Encyclopaedias provide information under broad subject headings. It is also possible that the desired information may not have been provided as an independent article but it may have been included as part of another article. It is also possible that the information on a subject may have been provided in several different places in relation to other subjects. Unless systematically approached, it will be time-consuming and a make an easy task difficult in search of an information spread over in several volumes of an Encyclopaedia. The best way to search information would be to proceed with the help of an index which is usually provided at the end of each volume or a cumulative index provided in the last volume of a set. Different patterns of references are adopted in different Encyclopaedias which are generally explained in the introduction or preface appearing in volume 1 or in the index volume itself. It will be helpful for the users first to look at this information and then to proceed to find out the desired information in the Encyclopaedia. The knowledge, how to use an index of an Encyclopaedia is essential for all potential users. A few minutes spent in understanding this will save much of their time and trouble in locating the information.

The significant features of some important Encyclopaedias and how to use them are explained below:

> *Encyclopaedia Britannica: a new survey of universal knowledge.* Chicago, Encyclopaedia Britannica, Inc. Ed 14, 24 volumes.

Encyclopaedia Britannica is one of the oldest and most popular English language Encyclopaedia used throughout the world. It has appeared in many editions. Each edition has its peculiarity for the readers. The eleventh edition, known as the War Edition is still of much importance for retrospective value to the researchers and persons interested in history. The last edition was in 24 volumes and published in 1969. A comprehensive index has been provided in the last volume. In 1969 edition main entry headings are provided in bold face capital letters and the portion of articles covered within the main articles are provided in light face in capital and small letters, e.g.,

ANDHRA PRADESH, State, Indian —	1	—	903b
Area & Population	12	—	37
Circars	5	—	780b
Madras	14	—	556a
Physiography	12	—	3Id

References are made to the volume number and page numbers. The volume and page numbers have been indicated in Indo-Arabic numerals. Volume numbers appear in bold face and the page numbers appear in light face. For the purpose of exact reference, each page is considered divided into four parts by means of the letters a, b, c, d, signifying respectively the upper and lower halves of the first and second columns; for example, if one needs to look for the 'Physiography of Andhra Pradesh' he should look up volume 12, page 31 in the lower of the right column.

Entries in the Encyclopaedia are arranged alphabetically letter by letter and a comprehensive bibliography is provided at the end of each article. The running headings at the top of the *recto* and *verso* (Right and the left pages) indicate the subjects covered in the pages. A separate index for atlases has been provided in the index volume. All entries whether consisting of one or more words have been treated as a complete heading for the purpose of alphabetisation. The use of index would highly facilitate the search for information spread over in any volume of Encyclopaedia.

Encyclopaedia Americana. New York, Americana Corp. 30 volumes, 1971.

Like Encyclopaedia Britannica, Encyclopaedia Americana is also a comprehensive general adult Encyclopaedia in English language. The index volume provides in the preliminaries a detailed guide to the use of the Encyclopaedia. The aim of the index is to facilitate the users in finding out specific information easily and quickly. The index provides entries under various headings which have been provided with independent articles followed by volume and page numbers. There are three types of references:

(1) Main articles are provided in boldface capital letters, e.g.,

BASKET 3–319

CROMWELL, OLIVER 8–237; 13–312, 313

HINDUISM 14–207

INDUSTRIAL REVOLUTION 15–122; 10–30;
20–359; 29–197

(2) Entries for topics not provided with main articles but covered in another article appear in boldface capital and lower case letters, e.g.,

Head Valve 27–868

Maratha Wars (India): Baji Rao II 3–66

(3) See references have been provided for the alternative spellings, inverted headings, pseudonyms and abbreviations. Reference is made to the heading under which the information would be available e.g.,

Commonwealth Prime Minister's Meetings: If a topic is discussed in more than one place, it is indicated in the index by sub-entries that follow the main entry. The key words are arranged alphabetically.

MARATHAS (Asian people) 18–262; 14–946, 950]:

Asia	2--501
Gujarat	13–595
Gwalior	13–636
Holkar	14–294
Maharashtra	18–135, 136
Peshwa	29–652c

International Encyclopaedia of Social Science, Ed. by David L. Sills. New York, MacMillan and Free Press, 17 vols, 1968.

The proliferation of knowledge has given rise to several new subjects and concepts especially in the field of social science disciplines. The major aim of this Encyclopaedia is to reflect and encourage the rapid developments of the social sciences throughout the world. Its subject matter covers concepts, principles, theories, methods and characteristics relating to social science. Articles treat significant concepts and research areas in social sciences as well as methodological problems and techniques and the lives and contributions of important social scientists. Information is arranged in alphabetical order according to subjects or concepts; cross references are also provided.

Major topics are discussed by a series of articles bringing together the various aspects of the topics and facilitates the users to study the subject in the right perspective. Encompassing all disciplines in Social Sciences it lays stress on the explanations of concepts and theories rather than their chronological analysis.

For example 'History' is included in the form of articles dealing with varying connections of the nature of history and its subject matter spread over under the divisions, like:

(1) Philosophy of history;

(2) History of the social sciences;

(3) Ethno-history;

(4) Cultural history;

(5) Social history;

(6) International history;

(7) Economic history;

(8) Business history—each of these divisions are written by subject specialists duly supported by adequate bibliographical references, but the Encyclopaedia does not cover specific historical period or events.

Biographical sketches of about 600 social scientists whose research and writings have had impact upon the society, have been included. Bibliographies provided at the end of each article enable the users to further study the desired discipline. Exhaustive index provided in the last volume facilitates the users in locating the desired information and also enhances the utility of Encyclopaedia as a whole.

McGraw-Hill Encyclopaedia of Science and Technology. New York. McGraw-Hill. 15 Volumes, 1971.

This is a commendable effort to satisfy the needs and requirements of library users in the field of science and technology. It first started in 1960. The subject matter of the Encyclopaedia covers all important fields in natural, behavioural and applied sciences. Each article has been defined and written in such an easy and understandable manner that even a non-specialist may follow the scientific concepts. Illustrations are provided along with the text making the articles more useful. The Encyclopaedia caters not only to the new entrants but also the specialists. Articles are written by subject specialists. In volume 1, there appears a 'Guide for Readers' which indicates the basic plan of the Encyclopaedia and the way titles are arranged. Usually each article first defines the article, its scope and coverage.

Cross references provided in the Encyclopaedia take the readers from the general articles to the other related articles. Most of the titles of articles are arranged alphabetically word-by-word. Index appears in the last volume. The index volume is divided in four parts, viz.

(a) Contributors;

(b) Scientific notation;

(c) Analytic index; and

(d) Topical index.

Analytical index satisfies the users' approach to a subject through a particular aspect whereas the topical index groups all articles under a few headings and thus it serves as a broader guide. Scientific notation explains the usages of symbols, abbreviations and nomenclature, etc. To make the Encyclopaedia more up-to-date, comprehensive and recent, it brings out a 'Year Book' incorporating all important interpretations, inventions and innovations, etc. of the year under coverage.

Directories: Directory is a list of persons or organisations arranged usually in a systematic order either alphabetically or classified, giving addresses, affiliations, etc. of individuals; and addresses, officers, functions and similar data for organisations." The purpose of the directory is to direct the user to the address of a person or an organisation. There are few directories which appear combined with yearbooks like 'the *Times of India Directory and Year Book including Who's Who*. In these, directory type of information may or may not be comprehensive. Directories provide information about the learned societies, educational and research institutions, national and international organisations, social welfare institutions, clubs, political associations, professional and trade organisations, etc. Some directories appear annually and the others at irregular intervals.

Kinds: Directories may be categorised as general and special depending upon their general or specialised coverage. Directories may also be categorised as local, national, international and at the same time be institutional, governmental, professional and trade directories depending upon their scope. A brief description of some of the important categories is given below:

Local and National Directories: These enlist the important persons and organisations of a town or a locality either in alphabetical order or classified order according to trades or occupations. The most common directory of this type is the local telephone directory and the other examples may be the directories of local schools, gardens, clubs, departmental stores, theatres and social organisations, etc. National: Times of India, Directory and Year Book including Who's Who and International directories (UN directories) similarly have wider geographical scope.

They list the academic institutions, museums, libraries, hospitals, professional and learned organisations, etc. These are available at national and international levels, e.g., *World of Learning* is an international directory which provides information about the academic and research institutions, museums and libraries and similar organisations all over the world. *India at a glance* is a national directory of learned institutions and other organisations of academic and professional institutions in India. *Institutions of Higher Education and Technical Education in India* is another example of a directory of educational institutions at national level.

Government Directories: Many governments and their agencies issue at regular intervals a register of officials, mentioning their official details and residential addresses, etc. within the country and abroad. Such directories may also be issued for the parliamentarians and legislators giving the names of their constituencies, biographical notes and addresses list of offices, etc., e.g., *Directory of Post-Offices and Foreign Service List*, etc.

Professional and Trade Directories: These are the lists of the members and organisations engaged in a particular field, profession or interested in specific trade or business. These may be found useful in knowing other persons and firms in the same trade their qualifications research contribution and the positions held, their addresses, etc. in case of persons, and composition, financial and trade information regarding firms, etc. Some suitable directories are:

International Directory of Anthropologists; Thacker's Indian Directory.

Use: Any one interested in knowing what courses and research facilities are available in the field of their specialisation; what scholarships and travel grants are available; who is the professor of economics at a university; what library facilities are available in certain universities; what is the address of a person or an institution. Government officers, parliamentarians, businessmen and traders may feel interested in knowing who is the latest incumbent to an office; which are the exporting establishments; which are the firms dealing in specific equipment, etc. Answers to such questions can be had in different kinds of directories. Arrangement of information would vary from one directory to another. *World of learning* arranges information alphabetically by country. Under each country information is further provided in a sequence—Academic, learned societies, research institutions, libraries and archives, museums and art galleries, universities, etc.

The *Commonwealth University Year Book* also arranges information alphabetically by country. Further under each country various universities are arranged alphabetically. Under each university lists of teaching departments and affiliated colleges are provided. *Study Abroad* provides information classified according to the subjects in which the scholarships are available as well as under various countries where these are available. Some directories follow the classified arrangement under the headings education, industry, transport and communication, etc. *Times of India Directory and Year Book including Who's Who* is a case of an unorganised directory providing information under major headings like, the country, natural resources, agro-based industries, education and social welfare, demography, etc. which are further subdivided under important subjects in an alphabetical sequence. The scope, coverage and arrangement of information are found explained in the preface. It is advisable first to go through the preface and list of contents of the directory for effective use. Almost all directories are provided with a comprehensive index at the end, use of which can be made for locating the information quickly.

Year Books and Almanacs

Year Books: A yearbook is a publication issued annually to give current information on a multitude of subjects. It may adopt narrative or statistical pattern for providing the information. It contains the record of progress and embodies the current developments in different fields of human activity. It covers all important events which are likely to be of interest to the people in general. It is a chronicle of events of the year (given on title page) or the one preceding.

Types: Yearbooks differ in scope and arrangement from other types of reference books already discussed. These can be divided into the following main categories:

(i) Encyclopaedia annuals;

(ii) General yearbooks—International, National, local, and

(iii) Subject year books.

Encyclopaedia Annuals: An Encyclopaedia can not keep pace with latest developments, unless supplemented with annuals. Hence to make it up-to-date all standard Encyclopaedias publish a yearbook, e.g., *Britannica Book of the Year; Americana Annual; Collier's Encyclopaedia Yearbook and*

World Book Encyclopaedia Yearbook, etc. These yearbooks keep the main Encyclopaedia up-to-date and present a summary of the major events of the year. The contents of the yearbook seldom corresponds to the articles of the Encyclopaedia and each yearbook has a separate index of its own.

General Yearbooks: General yearbooks cover a wide range of information such as governments, international and national organisations, Constitution, recent political developments, legal system, areas, population, education, trade and commerce, defence and transport, etc. General yearbooks may cover either the information about the whole world like the *Statesman's Yearbook;* about a continent like *Europe Yearbook* or a country like *India: a reference annual.* Such yearbooks form a very useful source of ready reference enquires. Sometimes they contain useful information on weights and measures, latest discoveries and well-established facts. Some yearbooks also contain directory type information like the addresses and biographies of some important institutions and persons.

Subject Yearbooks: Subject yearbooks cover the progress of activities in specified subject fields during the year covered, such as the *Yearbook of Medicine; the Municipal Yearbook; Yearbook of Agricultural Cooperation; the Bowker's Annual of Library and Book Trade,* etc. The United Nations and its specialised agencies also bring out annual publications depicting the progress and important events in different fields, e.g., *Yearbook of Human Rights; United Nations' Yearbook or Yearbook of the United Nations; Yearbook of the International Law Commission,* etc.

Almanacs: An almanac is the record of astronomical data and information of current events and developments generally presented in a statistical manner. It is grouped with yearbooks as it is also an annual publication with similar objectives. In the beginning the almanacs used to be arranged by months, weeks, and days providing information about the rising and setting of sun and moon, times of low and high tide, a calendar of holidays and miscellaneous information. Subsequently, some almanacs started providing other useful information on international, national, and regional affairs. Some well-known general almanacs are: *World Almanac and Book of the Facts; Reader's Digest Almanac; Information Please Almanac and Whitaker's Almanac,* etc.

Use: Yearbooks and Almanacs are very useful sources for finding out answers to a great variety of questions like the awards of government recognition given during a particular year; winners of Sahitya Akademi award; newly admitted members to the United Nations; population of Israel; research advances in plastic surgery; percentage of literacy in a country; currency of a nation; day of the week on a particular date, etc. Most of the yearbooks and almanacs provide information under topical headings—subjects and countries—which are enumerated in the list of contents. A look into preface would explain the scope, coverage and arrangement of information in the yearbook or the almanac. Use of the index is generally provided at the end and facilitates the use of this reference source. For finding out factual and statistical information one should look into a general yearbook or an almanac. For finding out new trends in a subject, one should look into a subject yearbook. Some yearbooks and almanacs provide maps and illustrative matter which add to their usefulness.

Panchang: Panchang is an astronomical almanac; it is an annual publication. Besides stellar position, it also depicts the important dates of the religious, social, cultural, historical and national importance. Panchang is often used to decide an auspicious moment (called Muhurut) for various religious and social occasions, such as marriages, travel, inauguration of new building, etc.

Panchang was originally used to determine the auspicious time for performing certain religious practices. Later on its scope was extended to social and other functions as well. Among the existing panchangs, Hindu Panchang is considered to be the oldest. Arya Bhatt is said to be the maker of first systematic Hindu Panchang. Hindu Panchang is comprised of five salient features, viz., 'vaar', 'tithi', 'nakshtra', 'karan' and 'yog'. It is worked out mathematically. On the recommendations of the 'Panchang Revision Committee', Government of India has devised a new 'Rastriya Panchang', which is very exact and accurate. In addition to the dates of Vikram era the 'Rastriya Panchang' also provides the dates according to Christian and Islamic era. There are as many as 30 different kinds of panchangs available in India today.

Some of the most important panchang are:

(i) Bharatiya Rastriya Panchang;

(ii) Islamic Panchang;

(iii) Persian Panchang; and

(iv) Christian (also known as Gregorian Panchang) Panchang.

The Christian Panchang has been modified and brought out as a 'World Calendar' (Vishwa Panchang) which is most popular. This panchang makes it easy for anyone to ascertain the day of the week on a certain date in any year in a number of decades. The combination of days and dates is easy and one can learn it quickly.

Biographical Source Material: Biographies provide information about the lives of important personalities and great men of the past and present. Shores has defined biographical sources as "Essentially a directory of notable persons usually arranged alphabetically by surnames with biographical identifications that range from brief outline to extended narrative" (2). Biographical sources have mainly developed during later half of 19th century. These emerged as tools for providing a variety of information about the people, parliamentarians or politicians, nobility or royalty and those having gained prominence for one reason or the other—inventors, sportsmen, actors, writers, artists, etc. whether living or dead. Generally biographical sources provide information about the dates of birth (and death), family, academic and professional achievements, vocation, honours and decorations, important publications and addresses.

Encyclopaedias may also provide biographical information for a few notable persons who are very prominent in their respective fields but biographical sources mainly specialise in providing such information. Biographical sources are alphabetically arranged like the words in a dictionary so they are also referred to as biographical dictionaries. The most notable biographical sources are: *McGraw-Hill Encyclopaedia of World Biography; Dictionary of National Biography; Dictionary of Indian National Biography*, etc. Biographical sources can be divided into these categories: Universal or International; National; and Professional or Occupational which may be universal or national. Each of these may be retrospective for persons no more living or current, of people who are alive, or both include all persons (dead or alive). These are known as 'Who's Who' or 'Who was Who'. Among notable current biographical sources are: *International Who's who; Who's Who; Chamber's Dictionary of Scientists;* etc. Among the retrospective biographical sources are such works as *Who was Who, Dictionary of National Biography*. Sometimes biographical sources form part of a bigger work e.g., *The Times of India Directory and Yearbook including Who's Who.* The Who's Who part of this directory provides very useful biographical source for Indian people. Recently some Indian publishers have made good attempts in bringing out biographical sources in general and also in specialised fields.

Use: It may sometimes be necessary to ascertain the nationality, occupation and dates of a person in order to make a choice for a suitable biographical source, i.e., Universal: The *International Who's Who;* National: *Dictionary of National Biography,* Retrospective *Who was Who;* Current—*Who's Who in India* or biographical dictionaries limited to persons belonging to one profession. Generally biographical sources follow alphabetical arrangement under the surname of the person. The introduction is an important part of the source book which should invariably be consulted before referring to the actual text. Necessary tips regarding special features, abbreviations and symbols, etc. are provided in the introduction.

Geographical Source Material: Geography is a description of the world and its inhabitants or it is the science of earth and its life or human ecology. Enquiries about geographical information are common in all types of libraries. Questions may pertain to the situation of a country, height of various places above the sea level, etc. Answers to such queries can be found in geographical sources. The social and economic progress is very much interdependent on the mutual understanding among nations and breaking the geographical barriers. As such, a knowledge of the physical features, environment, physical resources, mineral resources, means of transport, population, climate and other geographical phenomena, are necessary for an understanding of the civilization in that area. Geographical sources aim at making such knowledge available. The important kinds of geographical sources are the gazetteer, maps, atlases, guidebooks, etc.

Gazetteer: Gazetteer is a mine of geographical information about the location of a city, town or district. In addition to the location, gazetteers also provide information about the people, their historical, cultural, economic, industrial, demographic background and about the natural wealth of the region. Gazetteers are available at the international, national, state and district level. *Columbia Lippincott Gazetteer of the World* provides information about the countries of the world, their divisions and subdivisions.

Imperial Gazetteer of India (1907–31) in 26 volumes still serves as an authoritative source of information for various parts of the country. It had first appeared in 1881. The second edition was published in 1885–87 and later a new and comprehensive edition in 26 volumes was published (1907–31). The break-up of the information in the Imperial Gazetteer is in four groups: (i) V 1 to 4 deal with the Indian Empire-Description; Historical; Economic; and Administrative; (ii) V 5 to 24 deal with big and small administrative units arranged alphabetically; (iii) V 25 is Index; and (iv) V 26 contains an atlas and general index to provincial maps.

The information in the volumes appears alphabetically under names of places and administrative units. The entries under districts cover the information in respect of physical aspect; history; population; agriculture, trade and commerce; finance and administration, etc. More coverage has been provided for presidency towns like Calcutta, Bombay and Madras. Although the Imperial Gazetteer has become very old, it still serves as a useful source for detailed and authentic description of India.

A gazetteer provides geographical, historical, industrial and educational information in a nutshell and forms a very useful source for knowing important places and the people. It is necessary that it should contain latest and up-to-date information. For this reason the Imperial Gazetteer though comprehensive enough still fails to satisfy the queries of readers on modern Indian life and society. It serves a historical purpose, because of the tremendous changes in the physical economical, political, social and cultural spheres particularly since 1947. In view of these considerations the representatives of the State Governments and the various ministries of Government of India at a conference observed that the existing gazetteers were conceived and devised to meet a particular and limited need under the British regime but they are nevertheless a storehouse of authentic information in a convenient form and of great value for the general public and particularly for those concerned with administration. It was therefore agreed that the Imperial Gazetteer should be thoroughly revised and updated. As such it was ultimately decided that the Central Government should take up the work of revising the Indian Empire portion of the Imperial Gazetteer in the new light and the State Governments should either revise and bring up-to-date the concerned volumes of Imperial Gazetteer or compile entirely new gazetteers at district level. With this decision, Government of India has brought out two of the four volumes in a radically changed new edition the four volumes are:

Vol. 1. Country and people;

Vol. 2. History and culture;

Vol. 3. Economic structure and activities;

Vol. 4. Administration and public welfare.

Use: In making use of a gazetteer, users should first note the copy-right date as an indication of the recency and up-to-dateness of the work otherwise it is of no use to consult outdated sources. Further, they should go through the preface of the gazetteer which explains the layout of the information; distribution of chapters, the abbreviations used, and any additional information. A look at the list of the contents would also be found useful. Appendices, usually provided at the end, contain very important and useful information. Use of the index helps the users in locating the information specifically and pinpointedly, particularly in case of sites not treated under an entry name.

Maps and Atlases: A map is a representation of the earth's surface or a part of it. It gives knowledge about the physical features of land and sea. It may cover area as wide as the whole world or be limited to a small area only. A physical map represents the physical features of the area such as the rivers, valley, mountains, etc. A route map indicates various routes of transport like the roads, rails, bridges, sea routes and air routes, etc. A political map represents the political boundaries of the various regions. Maps which are prepared for indicating special features, like the meteorological, ethnological or historical, are known as thematic maps. Maps also show ocean currents, air currents, national wealth, flora and fauna, hospitals and post-offices, etc. The diverse information needed by geographers and other map users have led to the development of a number of styles of map making.

The art of drawing a map is known as cartography. Special training, high degree of accuracy and precision is required to prepare the maps. Some specialised agencies, government bodies and geographical societies have brought out accurate and up-to-date maps and atlases. General Encyclopaedias provide maps either in a separate volume, e.g., *Encyclopaedia Britannica* or along with the text, e.g., *Encyclopaedia Americana.* Annuals of the important Encyclopaedias give latest maps. Besides these directories, handbooks, yearbooks, almanacs and other reference sources also provide maps but these may be used in absence of an atlas, for an atlas is more useful when maps have to be consulted. An atlas is a collection of maps representing different regions of the world along with a table of contents and followed by an adequate index to indicate the location of every place or feature shown in the maps. An atlas may or may not contain a text. It may not be confined to maps alone. It may also contain photographs charts, tables, etc. Some-times an atlas may represent subjects in tabular form. Atlases vary in quality and content. Usually it is recognised that atlases are meant for the study of history, geography and other subjects of social sciences. Today maps and atlases have become very essential and necessary tools for general references such as verifying names of places and their location while reading news about places in newspapers or on the radio and television, etc. For authentic information users should rely only on maps and atlases brought out by the governments or their approved agencies.

Magazines and Periodicals

Periodicals are the backbone of modern library collections. They are the means of communication of new ideas and research results and a variety of other useful information which may interest the users. Growth of periodicals has been phenomenal with the growth of knowledge. Periodicals started appearing in the 16th century. They had started as pamphlets and by the turn of 17th century had acquired the characteristics of modern periodicals when some pioneer and learned societies, research bodies and professional organisations were established. It gave impetus to periodical publications which became numerous during the 19th century.

During the 20th century, these are available in almost all fields of specialisation and cover about 75 per cent of the total publication. Estimates vary regarding the total world production of periodicals but accordings to one reliable guess there are something like 35 thousand titles in science and technology alone and these are increasing at the rate of 5 to 10 per cent every year. Not only librarians, information specialists, computer engineers, system analysts and documentalists but management people also feel concerned about the unprecedented rate of growth of knowledge. In one of such studies Dr. George Andrela observes "...some 10 to 12 million authors are regularly or occasionally producing new information in the exact and human science, technology and engineering, medicine and education. Their papers are published at an increasingly rapid rate in some 50,000 to 100,000 journals and form the subject of more than 150,000 abstracts every year, which in turn are issued by more than 1800 services specialising in bibliographical description" He feels that further growth of new information in the coming years will pose serious problems of management beyond control of automation.

Periodical Publications: Serials and periodicals are the terms which are loosely used for any publication coming in successive issues at certain intervals. As a matter of fact a 'Serial' is a comprehensive term which includes periodicals, newspapers, memoirs and transactions of learned societies, annual publications like reports and yearbooks. Thus a serial may be defined as a publication in continuous series bearing consecutive numbers and supposed to continue indefinitely. A periodical is also a publication which is issued in successive parts at regular intervals and supposed to continue indefinitely. It bears a distinctive title. Each issue contains contributions (articles) by several contributors. When all issues for a definite period are put together they constitute a single volume. The other words which are synonymously used for the periodical are the *journal* and the *magazine*. The word journal had originally meant a daily newspaper, but now it is generally used to cannot any publication containing news and current information in a particular field of knowledge like, *Journal of Astronomy; Journal of Radiology; Indian Economic Journal; and Indian Journal of Chemical Education*, etc. The word magazine is generally used for literary periodical publications consisting of stories, articles, essays, poems and other information and general interest such as *Carvan; Imprint* and *Modern Review*, etc.

Types: The periodical publication may be broadly categorised as general periodicals and subject periodicals.

General Periodicals: A general periodical is not confined to a single area of interest but covers many interests and areas. These are non-technical and are popularly referred to as magazines. The main purpose of the type of publication is to inform the users of the latest developments in a number of fields like politics, economics, science and technology, etc. which affect human life as a whole. These publications also contain literary pieces like short stories, short novels, comics and other similar materials which provide information, inspiration and recreation to the users. These generally form the leisure reading for the users. These are issued in different formats and appear at varied periodicity like—monthly, fortnightly, weekly, etc. Some of these are very popular among all classes of people irrespective of their age, sex and other considerations, e.g., *Illustrated Weekly of India; Dharmyug; Saptahik Hindustan; Readers Digest;* whereas some of these are specially meant for a specific group of people by age and sex, e.g., *Modern Review* and *Bhawans Journal* would be of interest to the adult users. *Eves Weekly, Femina, Woman and Home,* etc. would be of interest to women. The teenagers and children would enjoy *Junior Statesman* (Popularly known as *JS), Nandan, Parag* and *Chandamama,* etc.

Subject Periodicals: A subject periodical is generally confined to a specific field or at the most to some related fields. It is often termed as a professional journal. It includes articles on topics usually written by subject experts. Subject periodicals offer contemporary information and results of specialised studies and research on a topic which may take years to appear in the form of books. Thus they supplement the information already contained in books and provide the latest ideas which are necessary for furtherance of knowledge. Now, subject periodicals exist in almost all subject areas, e.g., *The Education Quarterly, Current History, Indian Journal of Applied Psychology, The Astronomical Journal, Science and Culture, Herald of Library Science, etc.*

Use: The general periodicals are mainly used for entertainment and keeping up-to-date with the developments of general interest, whereas the subject periodicals are the information carriers for the subject specialists, advanced students and researchers. They supplement the information already available in books. They are invaluable sources of current thought and view points and are inevitable for research. Both types of periodicals—General and Subject—are received in libraries. All the current issues are displayed appropriately, either arranged alphabetically or subjectwise. The back issues are placed either separately or along with the current issues. The back issues are placed in specially designed shelves below the slanting cover on which the current issues are displayed. Each issue has a list of contents which may appear either on the title page itself or few pages behind it or the backover. This helps the users in knowing the titles of the articles which have appeared in a particular issue. Their usefulness may be determined by actually examining the articles. All important journals and periodicals provide an annual index on the completion of a volume. This is useful for the users.

Generally the back files of general magazines and periodicals are not retained because they are not in frequent demand whereas the back files of the subject periodicals are frequently demanded by the users. Hence, all libraries maintain complete flies of back volumes of all subject periodicals. To look for relevant articles on a current subject like devaluation, impact of oil crisis on modern technology, etc. one should look into the contents or the index of the various volumes of the concerned periodicals. It is a complicated and time consuming task. So, to facilitate the information searching in periodicals some tools have been designed, known as 'Indexes' and 'Abstracts'. These greatly simplify the task of information searching in periodical literature. The use of indexes and abstracts will be explained in the succeeding pages.

Sources of Periodical Publications: Looking to the immense utility of periodical publications in the study and research, lists or directories of periodicals have been compiled. These lists or directories provide complete details for each title in respect of the publisher, frequency, editor, annual subscription and year of establishment, etc.

Various other Materials

Indexes: An index is a list of names, terms, subjects, places and other significant items identifying the exact page or place where it has been included in the work. It is a means of easy identification and location of information in a work. It is generally provided at the end of a book or a monograph and other publications. In a periodical publication comprising several issues, an index will be a useful aid in the identification and location of desired information. Several articles may have appeared simultaneously on the same topic in different periodicals. Index to an individual volume of a periodical publication will provide clue to the articles which have appeared in that individual volume alone, but a general periodical index provides information about all such articles which may have appeared on a subject in different periodicals during a span of time. The general periodical index is thus a great relief for the students and researchers who are collecting date and source material for their research.

The first major index in English language was compiled by Alexander Cruden in 1737 'A Concordance to Bible.' The art of indexing has improved ever since. Index to 'Encyclopaedia Britannica' and 'Poole's Index to periodicals' are the landmarks in the 19th century indexing effort. By the turn of 20th century index was established as an essential and effective tool in literature search. Some good firms like H.W. Wilson (New York) and Library Association (London), etc. are well established agencies publishing a great variety of very useful indexes. *'The Readers' Guide to Periodical Literature'* brought out by H. W. Wilson in 1901 was unprecedented and unique in itself. It was followed by a large number of indexes in almost every field of knowledge. Looking to the large number of indexes published during the 20th century it may be appropriately called as an age of indexing. The 1960's saw the establishment of societies of indexes in UK and USA to improve the indexing techniques.

Kinds: Mainly two kinds of indexes are found in libraries, viz.:

(i) General indexes; and

(ii) Subject indexes.

General Indexes: These cover periodicals on a wide range of subjects like Social Sciences and Humanities, etc. Such indexes are available for retrospective materials, also. Mostly indexes are available for current literature. Some of the important general indexes are:

Index India, Ed by N. N. Gidwani, Jaipur, University of Rajasthan, 1965-----(Q)

Index India is an epoch making reference publication from Rajasthan University Library, Jaipur. It is a quarterly documentation list of articles on India in English language combining newspaper index, periodical index, composite publications index and book reviews index, etc. all in one sequence. It provides a separate author and subject index.

The contents provide a list of the subjects covered. It is mainly devoted to the subjects in social sciences and humanities, like economics, politics and government, history, geography, psychology, education, religion, philology, and arts, etc. It also includes subjects like science and technology, engineering, agriculture and medicine. A helpful guide on 'How to use the Index' has been provided. A study of the same would be found useful by the users of this index. Next to it are provided abbreviations, the list of periodicals, and the list of composite books covered by the index.

It is a classified index wherein the main subjects are arranged in the order mentioned in the contents, e.g., generally, planning, economics, politics and government, elections, public administration, foreign relations, history, geography, sociology and anthropology, etc. Entries on each of these subjects are further arranged in a classified order wherein the main headings are given in capital letters in 10 point type and subdivisions are printed in capital letters in 8 point. The subsections are printed in capital and lower case letters, e.g.,

BANKS

RURAL

BANKS

Rural Banks & Savings

The names of countries and constituent states have been given in alphabetical order under each of the headings, e.g.,

BANKS
STATES
MAHARASHTRA
MYSORE
PUNJAB
TAMIL NADU
WEST BENGAL

Entries for personal names have been made under the surnames where-ever available, otherwise they are entered under their forenames. Arrangement within a heading is alphabetical letter by letter. Each page comprises of three columns and each entry is assigned a serial number which is provided at the bottom of each column. For making an efficient use of this useful source one has to understand the arrangement of the subjects and the entries in it. Any one looking for the latest publications on a subject like Industrial Economics, Government policy on as pacific subjects, Social tension and Public Health and Hygiene should first choose the appropriate subject in the list of contents where the information on the desired subjects would be available. After looking at the main subject he should further look into the subheadings and sub-divisions, appropriate or nearest to the subject of his choice. The various entries under each of the subdivisions and subsections are provided in alphabetical order by author or title when author information is not available, but the quickest approach will be through the index.

Guide to Indian Periodical Literature, Ed by V. K. Jain. Gurgaon (Haryana), Indian Documentation Service. 1964——(Q).

The 'Guide' is an index to articles and other reading material, covering nearly 300 Indian journals in Social Sciences and Humanities. Subject and author entries have been combined and arranged in a dictionary order. All main headings have been divided into subheadings and second subheadings, all arranged alphabetically. Main headings appear in bold face with first word or key word in 'capital'. The sub-heads also appear in bold face, but the second sub-heads in light face italics. Certain articles carry two entries—one under author and other under subject. It also provides additional subject entries in case of articles dealing with more than one subject. Adequate cross references have also been provided, which enhance its use.

Reader's Guide to Periodical Literature. New York, H. W. Wilson. 1901——.

It indexes 125 periodicals of general nature. It is the most popular general index in many libraries all over the world. Periodical articles are referred to by author and subject. An abridged Readers Guide to Periodical literature indexes 40 magazines of popular interest.

Social Sciences and Humanities Index. New York, H.W. Wilson. 1965——.

The Social Sciences and Humanities Index is perhaps the most widely used means of access to scholarly literature in the subjects covered by it. It indexes more than 200 journals in sociology, anthropology, political science, economics, history, geography, literature, religion and other fields of humanities. Originally it had started in the year 1907 under the title *International Index to Periodicals* and continued till it changed to the above title in 1965. It is only next to the *Reader's*

Guide in importance and popularity in libraries. *Social Sciences and Humanities Index* is an ideal example of the periodical literature in a very wide range of topics but at the same time users may not find it suitable tool for comprehensive searching of the literature of any particular field.

British Humanities Index. London, Library Association. 1915——.

Till 1962 it was published under the title *Subject Index to Periodicals.* Primarily, it covers a wide range of periodicals in medical sciences, business, technology, social sciences and humanities. Since 1962 it has omitted medical sciences, business and education which have been taken up by other indexes. It is confined to British journals in the field of political science, economics, history and literature.

Subject Indexes: These are confined to narrow fields of studies like, education, medicine, applied science—engineering and technology, etc. Though the purpose is to index materials in a particular field, the material in related fields is also given due coverage. These are not confined solely to periodical publications. Many subject indexes include books, monographs, pamphlets, bulletins, reports, and government documents, as well. Generally, they tend to be wide in scope. Subject indexes are available in almost all fields of specialisation. Some of the important subject indexes are:

Biology and Agricultural Index. New York, H.W. Wilson. 1916——.

Until 1964 it was published under the title *Agricultural Index.* It analyses 146 journals published in the United States, Canada and the Commonwealth countries. A few government publications bearing on the subject are included. There is an index with every issue which is cumulated annually.

Applied Science and Technology Index. New York, H.W. Wilson. 1958——.

This is one of the two indexes that came out on the splitting of *Industrial Art Index* in 1958. It analyses 225 periodicals in the field of aeronautics, automation, chemistry, construction, machinery and physics, etc. It is published every month except August and cumulated annually.

On account of the shortcomings of indexing periodicals, viz., the time lag, cost and coverage, many libraries have started bringing out local indexes to serve the immediate requirements of the user. These indexes are confined to the periodicals received in a library or a group of libraries and to the interest of their users. These have proved useful in making the information readily available to the concerned users and in saving huge amounts of money which would be required in subscribing to the indexing periodicals. Such attempts have been made locally by some libraries and the outcome is known as either a *'documentation list'* or an *'index'*. These are either mimeographed or printed and may also be circulated to the other libraries.

A few such important indexes are: *Select articles on current affairs; Public Administration: abstracting and indexing of articles; Current administration literature;* Similar documentation lists and indexes are being brought out by Lok Sabha Secretariat, Planning Commission and libraries of various ministries and other organisations. Some organised attempts have been made to index all important Indian periodicals in a specialised subject fields, e.g., *Indian Legal Periodicals; Index to Statistical Literature; Index to Indian Economic Journal; Index to Indian Medical Periodicals,* etc.

Use: An Index is an aid to use the countless pieces of information in periodicals. The arrangement of the entries in indexing periodicals is either classified or alphabetical. Different indexing periodicals have different arrangements. To enable easy use of an indexing periodical, it is necessary to understand the system of indexing, the kinds of articles covered, the subjects and the periodicals covered, the arrangement of information in each entry, the abbreviations used, etc. All such information is generally explained in each issue of indexing periodicals or at least with first issue of each volume under the heading 'How to Use'.

Generally, an indexing periodical provides a list of subject headings, its divisions and sub-divisions under which the entries have been arranged. The main subject headings are arranged alphabetically and their divisions may be further arranged alphabetically under each of the subject headings. The entries under each of the division may be arranged alphabetically under author or title, e.g.,

INDUSTRIAL accidents India.

INDUSTRIAL administration.

INDUSTRIAL arbitration.

INDUSTRIAL communication.

INDUSTRIAL Development Bank of India.

INDUSTRIAL Finance Corporation of India.

INDUSTRIAL hygiene.

INDUSTRIAL law and legislation India.

INDUSTRIAL relations.

APO symposium on productivity and industrial relations (Tokyo, 22–26 Oct., 1973) Productivity 14(4) Ja-Mr '74, 500–01.

Employer-employee relationship. Pawan Choudhary Indian Worker 22(36) 3 Je '74.

Industrial peace and productivity. R.P. Billimoria Productivity 14(4) Jan.-March '74 502–12.

Industrial relations management in a changing environment. M.R. Meher Capital 172 (4307) 4 Apr. 74 464.

Productivity and industrial relations. V. G. Gopal Productivity 14(4) Jan.-March. 74 513–15 India.

Customary rights in industrial relations. S. R. Mohandas Management 13(4) Apr. 74 15–17.

Industrial peace necessary to increase production. Amarnath Vidyalankar Haryana Lab. J 5(1) Jan. '74 12.

Industrial relations: Implications of the recent changes in I.D. Act. S.K. Choudhary Capital 109 (4243)14 Dec. '72 995–96.

No prerogatives of management pet workers self-management. Janata 29(13) 5 May. '74 13/14.

Problems of industrial relations in companies with all India base S. K. Choudhary Capital 170 (4260) 19 Apr. '73 621–22.

Some implications of industrial relations policies for government and public sector. R. C. Goyal Haryana Lab' J 5(1) Jan. '74 13–14.

Towards better industrial relations. M.R. Meher Eastern Econ 62(8) 22 Feb. '74 305–06.

(Abstracted from Guide to Indian Periodical Literature V 11 (2) Ap-Je '74 p. 114–5).

A list of journals indexed along with abbreviations used in the indexing periodical, is generally provided at the beginning of each issue. An alphabetical author and subject index may at times be provided separately.

Abstracts: An abstract means a concise summary of an article or a pamphlet. An index helps in locating the reading material, an abstract is a step forward. It provides the summary of the reading material in addition to its location. The abstract or summary briefly describes the salient features in a short paragraph indicating the primary point of view and the essential features. Sometimes it may be evaluative. An abstracting journal is a bibliography of current literature providing the summaries under each entry with adequate bibliographical description. Generally it includes periodical articles only, but they may include other varieties of reading material as well. An abstract serves two purposes:

(i) It saves the time of the users by providing the summary of the contents of the periodical articles which may help him in quickly deciding whether they would like to see the articles; and

(ii) It serves as a rapid method of surveying the retrospective literature without actually looking at the primary materials.

Need: The abstracting periodicals have emerged out of the need for providing quick information and saving the time of the scholars and researchers. With the growing volume of periodical literature it is difficult for a scholar to leisurely consult every reference provided in an index and then search and read the articles only to realise that are they of no use to him. An abstract would have saved him the both erasion of locating unnecessary articles. A user needs explicit information about the useful reading in the least possible time and that is possible only through abstracts. The abstracting periodicals provide concise summaries of thousands of articles published during a particular period, month, quarter or a year on a particular subject. Survey reports, learned articles and research results are the products of the mental work performed by the engineers, scientists and scholars engaged in different studies and research projects. The outcome of research is published in more than fifty languages. An average user may know 2–3 languages and thus it will be difficult for him to make use of the literature in the languages other than what he knows. An abstract helps the users to know the contents and help him to decide if he needs translations of some of these. Abstracts provide an opportunity to make a worthy selection of articles.

The earliest attempt to publish abstracting periodicals were made in Germany, where 'Chemisches Zentrablatt' was published in 1830. By the turn of 20th century several abstracting periodicals were available in different fields, viz., *The Chemical Abstracts; The Psychological Abstract; The Electrical and Electronical Abstract; The Physics Abstract;* etc. Like the bibliographies and indexes the abstracting journal may be selective or comprehensive. An abstract may be prepared by an individual institution for retrospective use by its researchers and scholars, or it may be brought out by commercial organisations. Abstracts are produced and published on cards also.

Major Abstracting Services: Among the major abstracting services, the *'Chemical Abstracts'* has grown to the highest peak. National Federation of Science Abstracting and Indexing Services, Washington, is another very important abstracting agency. Another source for abstracting services in science, technology, medicine, agriculture, social sciences and humanities is International Federation of Documentation, the Hague (Netherlands). *Physics Abstracts (UK); Electrical and Electronical Abstracts* (UK) and Referativnyi Zhurnal (USSR) are among the world's foremost abstracting services covering a wide range of subjects. These services aim at providing complete coverage of the subjects, including articles in foreign languages. In addition to these many abstracting services exist which are bringing out abstracting periodicals in different subject fields. In United States alone there are more than 450 abstracting and indexing services. The USSR and UK also have well organised abstracting services. The developing countries are not blind to their usefulness.

Problems: There are a number of problems which the users and libraries may have to face regarding abstracts. Library's main problem is to bring to the users only those abstracts which are of greatest potential concern to them. It is estimated that 200,000 abstracts of chemical papers are brought out per year.

How to select among these and disseminate only those which are of prime importance to the researchers, is a big problem. Another big problem is the delay in appearance of the original document and its abstract. Scanning of articles, reports, etc. requires time before they can be abstracted, the publication of the abstract generally takes 6 to 8 months and by that time the researcher may not feel interested in the information any more. Thus, the currency is a major problem in abstracting journals and they fall far behind the current indexes. To overcome the problems many countries and organisations have started bringing out indexes of titles, formulas and the like and abstracts of the local periodicals.

Use of Abstracts: Like indexing periodicals, abstracting periodicals also vary in arrangement. These may follow either alphabetical arrangement under broad subject headings with appropriate author index or a classified arrangement under class numbers with appropriate author and alphabetical subject index. Some abstracting periodicals cumulate annually; some cover periodical articles only and others cover books, reports, dissertations, monographs and similar publications, also. In addition to the author and subject index some abstracting periodicals like *Chemical Abstracts* and *Index Medicos* include an index to formulas, patents and ring systems, also.

The majority of the abstracting periodicals aim at complete coverage in narrow subject fields like *Solid State Abstracts;* and *Geomorphological Abstracts.* They have almost all the characteristics of an indexing periodical, including the bibliographical details. In addition, they provide short summaries or the abstracts for each entry. Generally, each abstracting periodical provides necessary information regarding its use either in the first issue of each volume, or in each issue. It makes a mention of the scope, i.e., the subjects and periodicals covered, the arrangement and information about the abstracts, etc.

> *Indian Science Abstract,* Ed. by M.S. Dutta. New Delhi, Indian National Scientific Documentation Centre, 1965.

Indian Science Abstract is a monthly abstracting periodical reporting the work in the field of pure and applied sciences by Indian authors published either in India or abroad. It provides a list of contents giving the UDC class numbers for each subject and its subdivisions along with the entry number, e.g.:

UDC Number		Subject	(4) Entry Number
(1) 54	(2)	Chemistry	5683-801
	(3)	Physical Chemistry	5683-702
		Chemical Compound	5704-27
		Analytical Chemistry	5728-49
		Inorganic Chemistry	5750-51
		Organic Chemistry	5752-93
		Natural Substances	5794-98
		Crystallography	5799
		Mineralogy	5800-01

In the above illustration:

(1) Is the Class number according to the Universal Decimal Classification Scheme;

(2) Is the Main Subject heading;

(3) Is list of divisions or subheadings; and

(4) Is a list of numbers of entries for each subject and its divisions in the classified part.

Indian Science Abstract has classified arrangement wherein all the main entries and their abstracts are arranged in the order of these class numbers. The Class Numbers of the major divisions appear in capital letters in antic face. These are followed by their names in natural language. Technically these are known as feature headings. Entries in this part are assigned serial numbers; they are arranged alphabetically by author's name under each of the subheadings.

Pamphlets: A publication dealing with the specific aspect of a subject and consisting of fifty or less pages is generally known as a pamphlet. It is also known as minor publication and differs from books and periodicals in physical shape and content. Books have stiff covers, pamphlets have paper covers; books are bound, pamphlets are generally stapled. Usually a pamphlet is a separate entity without regular periodicity of publication, although it may be published in a series.

A pamphlet generally contains current information on a subject or a group of subjects which may not have yet been covered in the book form. Thus the purpose of a pamphlet is to supplement knowledge and to keep the users supplied with up-to-date information. Pamphlets include patents, small booklets, leaflets, research reports, reprints of articles, occasional papers and speeches, etc.

Pamphlets are sponsored by international, national and local agencies on topics of current interest in the field of politics, economics, social service, religion, scientific progress, industrial development, etc. Most governments issue a large number of pamphlets relating to their policies. Sometimes pamphlets contain controversial issues of current interest—religious, political, economic, social, etc.

Pamphlets are ephemeral material. The utility of these is over as soon as the information contained in them is included in the books or it losses the interest of the users. A large number of pamphlets is distributed free of cost as a part of publicity programme by various governments and organisations. There is danger of a library being flooded with pamphlets unless a process of proper checking and weeding is used to control the heavy bulk of each material. Many established organisations have brought out useful pamphlet publications.

Arrangement and Use: Arrangement of pamphlets differs from library to library. In some libraries pamphlets are placed with books and given full classification and cataloguing treatment. However, some libraries prefer to put these on a separate shelf, or in vertical files, and others bind together pamphlets on a subject and put them on the shelves. The practice of putting pamphlets into vertical files is more common and convenient to use.

The vertical files are the folders hung up in steel filing Cabinets. Each folder bears a tab in which the subject heading of the contents of the folders may be provided and these files may be arranged either alphabetically or in any other appropriate order. Some libraries put them in boxes which are placed with books on the same subject or these boxes are arranged separately in a classified order.

Pamphlets being ephemeral material, librarians choose select cataloguing or no cataloguing at all. Hence, the users should find from the library staff whether pamphlets have been catalogued or not, and where they have been placed. In case, pamphlets have been catalogued, to trace the pamphlet will not be difficult, but in most of libraries these are not catalogued. In such cases they may be arranged alphabetically under subject headings. In vertical files pamphlets may be arranged chronologically in each folder so that the latest pamphlet is placed first and the oldest, the last. As soon as the last pamphlet losses its utility it may be withdrawn from the folder. Users may find the handling of vertical files very easy and interesting.

Reference Services

The function of libraries is three-fold. Libraries acquire information, organise that information in a way it can be retrieved, and disseminate the information the library has acquired. Reference services fulfils this last function. Reference services may vary from library to library, but most libraries have an information or Reference Desk where assistance from a librarian is available. Almost all libraries also provide reference services via the telephone and in many libraries you can *e*-mail your reference question, or Ask a Librarian, to a reference librarian who will *e*-mail you back with the answers.

There are three main types of reference assistance:

- Assistance or instruction in the use of the library, including location of materials, use of the catalogue, use of computers to access information, and the use of basic reference sources.
- Assistance in identifying library materials needed to answer a question.
- Providing brief, factual answers to questions, such as addresses, statistics, phone numbers, etc. that can be quickly located.

Reference Tools

Two major categories of reference materials are general and subject. General sources include all subjects and present overviews of topics. Reference materials focused on specific subjects can provide more in-depth coverage.

There are reference sources that provide information on specific subjects as well as general sources that provide information on many subjects. In general, reference sources are either general or subject specific. If you need an overview of a subject, perhaps a general information source will suit your needs. If you need specialised information, a subject specific tool may be better suited.

The following reference sources and others are available in the main Reference Collection on Level 4, and/or via the Internet.

Dictionaries

Dictionaries provide information about words.

- General dictionaries are the most familiar to us. You may even own one. This group includes *Webster's International Dictionary*, the *Random House Dictionary of the English Language*, and the *Merriam-Webster Collegiate Dictionary*. These sources generally provide definitions, pronunciations, syllabication, and usage.
- Historical dictionaries provide the history of a word from its introduction into the language to the present. *The Oxford English Dictionary* is an excellent example of this type of dictionary.
- Etymological dictionaries are dictionaries which emphasise the analysis of components of words and their cognates in other languages. These dictionaries emphasise the linguistic

and grammatical history of the word usage. The *Oxford Dictionary of English Etymology* is an example of an etymological dictionary.

- Period or scholarly specialised dictionaries focus on a particular place or time period. For example, try the *Dictionary of Alaskan English* if you would like to know when the word "cheechako" was first used.
- Foreign language dictionaries are fairly self-explanatory. We've all looked up words in a French or Spanish or other Western European language. Don't forget other wonderful dictionaries, such as the *Yup'ik Eskimo Dictionary* or the *Inupiat Eskimo dictionary.*
- Subject dictionaries focus on word definitions in a subject area, such as finance, law, botany, electronics, physics, etc.
- Other dictionaries include dictionaries of slang, abbreviations, synonyms, antonyms, abbreviations, acronyms, reversals, rhyming, idioms, phrases, and guides to correct usage. *Dictionary of Acronyms and Abbreviations, The Macmillan Dictionary of Historical Slang, Roget's II: The New Thesaurus, The American Language, Strunk's Elements of Style.*

Dictionaries, like other reference sources, may belong to more than one category. For example, an English-Russian engineering dictionary is both a foreign language and a subject dictionary. Dictionaries may be abridged or unabridged. Abridged dictionaries are smaller and contained the most commonly used words. Unabridged dictionaries try to include all words in current usage. Like other reference sources, dictionaries may become outdated as language evolves. Care should be taken to carefully identify the publication date and focus of the dictionary selected. General dictionaries begin with LC call numbers starting with AG. Specialised dictionaries will have subject specific call numbers.

Encyclopaedias

Encyclopaedias provide general background information; they are a good place to start researching a topic that you know little about. Large subject areas or disciplines are covered in broad articles that explain basic concepts. These overview articles often contain references to more specific aspects of the larger topic and may include a bibliography that leads you to more in-depth sources. Encyclopaedias may be general or subject specific:

- General encyclopaedias usually arrange articles alphabetically by topic. Look for an accompanying index which may list cross-references to other articles. Included in this category are *Encyclopaedia Britannica* (29 volumes), *The Cambridge Encyclopaedia, Encyclopaedia Americana,* and the *Columbia Encyclopaedia.* General encyclopaedia LC call numbers begin with AE.
- Subject encyclopaedias are available for almost every academic discipline. They provide more in-depth and technical information than general encyclopaedias. Subject encyclopaedias generally assume some prior knowledge of the subject. There is no general rule for how these tools are arranged. Look for an index. A few examples of subject encyclopaedias include the *McGraw-Hill Encyclopaedia of Science and Technology, International Encyclopaedia of the Social Sciences, Encyclopaedia of World Art, Encyclopaedia of Philosophy,* and the *Encyclopaedia of Archaeology.* Subject encyclopaedias will have subject specific call numbers.

Directories

Directories provide names, addresses, affiliations, etc. of people, organisations, or institutions. They can be used to verify addresses, name spellings, and provide contact information. As in other reference sources, directories may be general or focused on a particular subject:

- *General Directories:* Zip Code and Post Office Directory, Encyclopaedia of Associations;
- *Subject Directories:* Fairbanks Phone Directory, Museums of the World, A Directory of Eskimo Artists in Sculpture and Prints, Directory of Multinationals, Federal Government Agencies Directory (Hierarchical), Thomas Register of American Manufacturers, Scholarly Societies Project.

Biographical Dictionaries

Biographical dictionaries contain short articles about people's lives. Biography resources have call numbers that begin with CT.

- General biographical dictionaries include *Current Biography, Dictionary of American Biography, Who's Who, Encyclopaedia of World Biography,* etc.
- Subject biographical dictionaries may focus on a subject area or group. These sources include *Dictionary of Scientific Biography, Contemporary Authors, Biographical Dictionary of Psychology, New Grove Dictionary of Music and Musicians, Women of Science,* etc.

Gazetteers and Atlases

Geographic information is located in gazetteers, atlases and maps. Geography resources have call numbers that begin with G.:

- Atlasescontain collections of maps. They provide information on geographical/political changes. There are world, national, and thematic atlases and these may be current or historical:
  - — World atlases include *National Geographic Atlas of the World;*
  - — National atlases: *National Atlas of the United States, Atlas of the American Revolution;*
  - — Thematic atlases focus on a specific subject area, such as astronomy or agriculture. Examples include, *The Oxford Economic Atlas of the World* and the *Environmental Atlas of Alaska.*
- Gazetteersare sometimes referred to as geographical dictionaries and provide descriptions of places, but no maps:
  - — General gazetteers include *Webster's New Geographical Dictionary, The Columbia Lippincott Gazetteer of the World, Gazetteer of Undersea Features, The World Gazetteer,* etc.;
  - — Regional gazetteers, such as *Dictionary of Alaska Place Names,* by D. Orth, focus on a specific geographical region and are good places to look if you want to know the location of a town, its population, or where its name came from.

Sometimes atlases and gazetteers are combined, as in the *Alaska Atlas and Gazetteer,* by DeLorme Mapping, which publishes similar products for the other states.

Almanacs

Almanacs contain statistics and facts about countries, events, personalities, or subjects. Almanac resources have call numbers that begin with AY:

- General almanacs include the *Statistical Abstract of the United States, The New York Public Library Desk Reference, World Almanac* (an American focus), *Information Please Almanac* (print ed. called *Time Almanac*), *Whitaker's Almanak* (United Kingdom focus).
- Subject almanacs include *The Weather Almanac, The Almanac of Renewable Energy, Political Reference Almanac, Alaska Almanac,* and more.

Handbooks/Manuals

Handbooks and manuals are subject area tools. Handbooks provide facts, terms, concepts, movements, etc. of a topic. Manuals provide detailed instructions on a particular subject, such as how-to-do something or how something works:

- *Handbooks:* Handbook of North American Indians, Guide to Alaska Trees, Words and Ideas: A Handbook for College Writing, Handbook of Mathematical Formulas, MLA Handbook For Writers of Research Papers.
- *Manuals:* Manual of Photography, Manual for Environmental Impact Evaluation, Alaska Craftsman Home Building Manual, United States Government Manual.

Review and Criticism Sources

These tools provide reviews or critiques of a person's work:

- *General:* Book Review Digest (OCLC FirstSearch, hereafter called FirstSearch), MLA (FirstSearch), New York Times Book Review, Contemporary Literary Criticism.
- *Subject:* Children's Literature Review, Popular Music Record Reviews.

Historical Tables, Chronologies, Historical Yearbooks

Historical tables and chronologies present historical facts in different formats. Historical tables provide facts chronologically in columns with each column representing another geographical area or other major area, such as history, economics, religions, etc. Chronologies use narrative form to present facts. Historical tables and chronologies may span long or very short time periods. Historical yearbooks provide facts and statistics for a single year and may be published annually:

- *Historical Tables:* The Timetables of History, Historical Tables, 58 BC-AD 1985.
- *Chronologies:* Chronology of World History, The New York Public Library Book of Chronologies, Chronology of the Expanding World, 1492-1762, A Chronology of the People's Republic of China from October 1, 1949, Annals of European Civilization, 1501-1900.
- *Historical Yearbooks:* The Statesman's Year-Book.

Indexes and Abstracts

Indexes and abstracts lead to additional sources of periodical articles. Indexes only provide author, title, and subject information. Abstracts tend to be more descriptive. Some online index databases also include the full-text of the article:

- *General:* Reader's Guide to Periodic Index (FirstSearch), Book Review Index, Periodicals Abstracts (FirstSearch).
- *Subject:* Art Abstracts (FirstSearch), New York Times Index (ABI Inform), Biography Index (FirstSearch), Chemical Abstracts.

Bibliographies

Bibliographies lead to other information sources. They are lists of books and other materials that provide author, title, and publication information. Annotated bibliographies also include a brief description or summary of the item. Bibliographies are available on almost every topic and may focus on specific persons, groups, subjects, or time periods. Many bibliographies are selective and do not attempt to include all publications. Bibliographies are sometimes referred to as "Guides to the Literature..."

Examples: American Fiction, 1774-1850, Bibliography of Education, Utilisation of Wood Residues: An Annotated Bibliography, A Bibliography of Sir Walter Scott, MLA Bibliography (FirstSearch), Current Bibliographies in Medicine (NLM), Equity Issues in Science and Math (State of AK, Dept. of ED), Alutiiq Ethnographic Bibliography (ANKN).

Ready References

The Ready Reference Collection contains reference sources that are used most frequently. The Ready Reference shelves are located adjacent to the Reference Desk. The collection includes reference tools such as *The Encyclopaedia of Associations, The Encyclopaedia of Associations, The Dictionary of Alaska Place Names,* Style guides (MLA, APA, Chicago), a thesaurus, *The Physician's Desk Reference,* Alaska phone directories, *Black's Law Dictionary, World Almanac, The Merck Manual of Medical Information,* Zip Code Directories, etc.

Web Resources for Reference Tools: The number of Internet reference tools increases every year. If you are looking for reliable online versions of your favourite print research tools, some good places to start are university sponsored reference sites, such as, Internet subject directories or virtual libraries.

Virtual Libraries, websites created by librarians that index quality web links, can also help you find quality Internet reference tools. Many of these sites have specific "general reference" sections. Try some of the virtual libraries listed here:

- *Reference Desk:* Librarian's Index to the Internet. Includes links to other information sources including almanacs, calendars, dictionaries, encyclopaedias, holidays, names, phone books, and statistics.
- *General Reference:* WWW Virtual Library. One of the first virtual library sites, started by Tim Berners-Lee, the creator of html and the web itself.
- *Reference and Periodicals:* Awesome Library. This virtual library provides separate indexes for teachers, kids, teens, parents, librarians and "community."
- *Reference Resources:* Internet Public library. Maintained by the University of Michigan. Reference works are broken into over twenty sub categories from almanacs to trivia.
- *Electronic Resources:* For The Reference Desk - A selective list of reference sites from the Library of Congress.
- See this linked Academic Info Digital Library site for a list of subject specific virtual libraries.

Other good online reference tools can be found on the WWW. The selected sites below represent the variety of online resources:

- Bartleby.com This site features full text of several reference standards, including *Columbia Encyclopaedia, American Heritage Dictionary,* Strunk and White's *Elements of Style, Bartlett's Familiar Quotations, Gray's Anatomy, Roget's Thesaurus,* the *World Factbook,* and more.
- *The Riley Guide:* Career information, including preparing a resume, job listings, and links to professional organisations.
- *NIH Health Information:* Created by the National Institutes of Health. Health Information provides links to reliable web sources on a wide range of health issues.
- *Encyclopaedia Smithsonian:* Features answers to frequently asked questions about the Smithsonian and links to Smithsonian resources on subjects from Art to Zoology.

- *E-Conflict World Encyclopaedia:* Country information from around the world. A resource for business, tourists, students and teachers.
- *Currency Conversion:* A conversion tool sponsored by Yahoo.
- *Essentials of Music:* A W.W. Norton. site. Includes overviews of historical periods of classical music, biographies of composers, and a dictionary of music terms.
- *Mammals Species of the World (MSW):* Sponsored by the Smithsonian national Museum of Natural History, this site contains the names of the 4,629 currently recognised species of mammals, in a taxonomic hierarchy that includes Order, Family, Subfamily, and Genus.
- *Nobel Foundation:* The official site for the Nobel Prize Foundation. Includes information on all recipients, arranged by prize category.
- *Online Literary Criticism Collection:* The Internet Public Library Online Literary Criticism Collection contains 4689 critical and biographical websites about authors and their works that can be browsed by author, by title, or by nationality and literary period.
- *ZIP Code Look-Up and Address Information:* A. US Postal Service site.

Abstracts

An abstract is a brief summary of a research article, thesis, review, conference proceeding or any in-depth analysis of a particular subject or discipline, and is often used to help the reader quickly ascertain the paper's purpose. When used, an abstract always appears at the beginning of a manuscript or typescript, acting as the point-of-entry for any given academic paper or patent application. Abstracting and indexing services for various academic disciplines are aimed at compiling a body of literature for that particular subject.

The terms precis or synopsis are used in some publications to refer to the same thing that other publications might call an "abstract". In management reports, an executive summary usually contains more information (and often more sensitive information) than the abstract does.

Purpose and Limitations

Academic literature uses the abstract to succinctly communicate complex research. An abstract may act as a stand-alone entity instead of a full paper. As such, an abstract is used by many organisations as the basis for selecting research that is proposed for presentation in the form of a poster, platform/oral presentation or workshop presentation at an academic conference. Most literature database search engines index only abstracts rather than providing the entire text of the paper. Full texts of scientific papers must often be purchased because of copyright and/or publisher fees and therefore the abstract is a significant selling point for the reprint or electronic form of the full text.

Abstracts are protected under copyright law just as any other form of written speech is protected. However, publishers of scientific articles invariably make abstracts publicly available, even when the article itself is protected by a toll barrier. For example, articles in the biomedical literature are available publicly from MEDLINE which is accessible through PubMed. It is a common misconception that the abstracts in MEDLINE provide sufficient information for medical practitioners, students, scholars and patients. The abstract can convey the main results and conclusions of a scientific article but the full text article must be consulted for details of the methodology, the full experimental results, and a critical discussion of the interpretations and conclusions. Consulting the abstract alone is inadequate for scholarship and may lead to inappropriate medical decisions.

An abstract allows one to sift through copious amounts of papers for ones in which the researcher can have more confidence that they will be relevant to his or her research. Once papers are chosen based on the abstract, they must be read carefully to be evaluated for relevance. It is commonly surmised that one must not base reference citations on the abstract alone, but the entire merits of a paper.

Structure

An academic abstract typically outlines four elements relevant to the completed work:

- The research focus (i.e. statement of the problem(s)/research issue(s) addressed);
- The research methods used (experimental research, case studies, questionnaires, etc.);
- The results/findings of the research; and
- The main conclusions and recommendations.

It may also contain brief references, although some publications' standard style omits references from the abstract, reserving them for the article body (which, by definition, treats the same topics but in more depth). Abstract length varies by discipline and publisher requirements. Typical length ranges from 100 to 500 words, but very rarely more than a page and occasionally just a few words. An abstract may or may not have the section title of "abstract" explicitly listed as an antecedent to content. Abstracts are typically sectioned logically as an overview of what appears in the paper, with any of the following subheadings: Background, Introduction, Objectives, Methods, Results, Conclusions. Abstracts in which these subheadings are explicitly given are often called structured abstracts by publishers. In articles that follow the IMRAD pattern (especially original research, but sometimes other article types), structured abstract style is the norm. (The "A" of abstract may be added to "IMRAD" yielding "AIMRAD".) Abstracts that comprise one paragraph (no explicit subheadings) are often called unstructured abstracts by publishers. They are often appropriate for review articles that don't follow the IMRAD pattern within their bodies.

Example

Example taken from the *Journal of Biology, Volume 3, Issue 2.*:

The hydrodynamics of dolphin drafting

by Daniel Weihs, Faculty of Aerospace Engineering, Technion, Israel Institute of Technology, Haifa 32000, Israel.

Abstract:

Background Drafting in cetaceans is defined as the transfer of forces between individuals without actual physical contact between them. This behaviour has long been surmised to explain how young dolphin calves keep up with their rapidly moving mothers. It has recently been observed that a significant number of calves become permanently separated from their mothers during chases by tuna vessels. A study of the hydrodynamics of drafting, initiated inmechanisms causing the separation of mothers and calves during fishing-related activities, is reported here.

Results Quantitative results are shown for the forces and moments around a pair of unequally sized dolphin-like slender bodies. These include two major effects. First, the so-called Bernoulli suction, which stems from the fact that the local pressure drops in areas of high speed, results in an attractive force between mother and calf. Second is the displacement effect, in which the motion of the mother causes the water in front to move forwards and radially outwards, and water behind the body to move forwards to replace the animal's mass. Thus, the calf can gain a 'free ride' in the forward-moving areas. Utilising these effects, the neonate can gain up to 90 per cent of the thrust needed to move alongside the mother at speeds of up to 2.4 m/s. A comparison with observations of eastern spinner dolphins (*Stenella longirostris*) is presented, showing savings of up to 60 per cent in the thrust that calves require if they are to keep up with their mothers.

Conclusions A theoretical analysis, backed by observations of free-swimming dolphin schools, indicates that hydrodynamic interactions with mothers play an important role in enabling dolphin calves to keep up with rapidly moving adult school members.

Abstract Types

Informative: The informative abstract, also known as the complete abstract, is a compendious summary of a paper's substance including its background, purpose, methodology, results, and conclusion. Usually between 100 and 200 words, the informative abstract summarises the paper's structure, its major topics and key points. A format for scientific short reports that is similar to an informative abstract has been proposed in recent years. Informative abstracts may be viewed as standalone documents.

Descriptive Abstracts: The descriptive abstract, also known as the limited abstract or the indicative abstract, provides a description of what the paper covers without delving into its substance. A descriptive abstract is akin to a table of contents in paragraph form.

Graphical Abstracts: During the late 2000s, due to the influence of computer storage and retrieval systems such as the Internet, some scientific publications, such as *Journal of Colloid and Interface Science*, started including graphical abstracts alongside the text abstracts. The graphic is intended to summarise or be an exemplar for the main thrust of the article. It is not intended to be as exhaustive a summary as the text abstract, rather it is supposed to indicate the type, scope, and technical coverage of the article at a glance.

Abstract Quality Assessment

Various methods can be used to evaluate abstract quality, e.g., rating by readers, checklists (not necessary in structured abstracts), and readability measures (such as Flesch Reading Ease).

Electronic Documents

An electronic document is any electronic media content (other than computer programmes or system files) that are intended to be used in either an electronic form or as printed output. Originally, any computer data were considered as something internal — the final data output was always on paper. However, the development of computer networks has made it so that in most cases it is much more convenient to distribute electronic documents than printed ones. And the improvements in electronic display technologies mean that in most cases it is possible to view documents on screen instead of printing them (thus saving paper and the space required to store the printed copies).

However, using electronic documents for final presentation instead of paper has created the problem of multiple incompatible file formats. Even plain text computer files are not free from this problem — e.g., under MS-DOS, most programmes could not work correctly with UNIX-style text files, and for non-English speakers, the different code pages always have been a source of trouble.

Even more problems are connected with complex file formats of various word processors, spreadsheets and graphics software. To alleviate the problem, many software companies distribute free file viewers for their proprietary file formats (one example is Adobe's Acrobat Reader). The other solution is the development of standardised non-proprietary file formats (such as HTML and OpenDocument), and electronic documents for specialised uses have specialised formats–the specialised electronic articles in physics use TeX or PostScript.

E-books

An electronic book (variously: *e*-book, eBook, *e*-Book, ebook, digital book, or even *e*-edition) is a book-length publication in digital form, consisting of text, images, or both, readable on computers or other electronic devices. Although sometimes defined as "an electronic version of a printed book", many *e*-books exist without any printed equivalent. Commercially produced and sold *e*-books are usually intended to be read on dedicated *e*-book readers, however, almost any sophisticated electronic device that features a controllable viewing screen, including computers, many mobile phones, and all smartphones can also be used to read *e*-books.

The Background

The inventor of the first *e*-book is not widely agreed upon. Some notable candidates include the following:

> The first *e*-book may be the Index Thomisticus, a heavily annotated electronic index to the works of Thomas Aquinas, prepared by Roberto Busa beginning in the late 1940s. However, this is sometimes omitted, perhaps because the digitised text was (at least initially) a means to developing an index and concordance, rather than as a published edition in its own right.

Some years earlier the idea of the *e*-reader came to Bob Brown after watching his first "talkie" (movies with sound). In 1930, he wrote an entire book on this invention and titled it "The Readies" playing off the idea of the "talkie". In his book, Brown says that movies have out manoeuvred the book by creating the "talkies" and as a result reading should find a new medium: A machine that will allow us to keep up with the vast volume of print available today and be optically pleasing (this was a big point for Brown).

Though Brown may have come up with the idea intellectually in the 1930s, early commercial *e*-readers did not follow his model. Nevertheless, Brown in many ways predicted what *e*-readers would become and what they would mean to the medium of reading. In an article Jennifer Schuessler writes, "The machine, Brown argued, would allow readers to adjust the type size, avoid paper cuts and save trees, all while hastening the day when words could be 'recorded directly on the palpitating ether.'" However, Brown would likely have found our *e*-readers today to be much too bookish and not unique enough in their own right. He felt that the *e*-reader should bring a completely new life to the medium of reading. Schuessler relates it to a DJ spinning bits of old songs to create a beat or an entirely new song as opposed to just a remix of a familiar song.

In 1949 a teacher from Galicia, Spain - Angela Ruiz - patents the first electronic book. Her intention was to decrease the number of books that her pupils carried to the school.

Alternatively, some historians consider electronic books to have started in the early 1960s, with the NLS project headed by Doug Engelbart at Stanford Research Institute (SRI), and the Hypertext Editing System and FRESS projects headed by Andries van Dam at Brown University. Augment ran on specialised hardware, while FRESS ran on IBM mainframes. FRESS documents were structure-oriented rather than line-oriented, and were formatted dynamically for different users, display hardware, window sizes, and so on, as well as having automated tables of contents, indexes, and so on. All these systems also provided extensive hyperlinking, graphics, and other capabilities. Van Dam is generally thought to have coined the term "electronic book", and it was established enough to use in an article title by 1985.

FRESS was used for reading extensive primary texts online, as well as for annotation and online discussions in several courses, including English Poetry and Biochemistry. Brown faculty made extensive use of FRESS; for example the philosopher Roderick Chisholm used it to produce several of his books. Thus in the Preface to *Person and Object* (1979) he writes "The book would not have been completed without the epoch-making File Retrieval and Editing System ..."

Brown University's leadership in electronic book systems continued for many years, including navy-funded projects for electronic repair-manuals; a large-scale distributed hypermedia system known as InterMedia; a spin-off company Electronic Book Technologies that built DynaText, the first SGML-based book-reader system; and the Scholarly Technology Group's extensive work on the still-prevalent Open eBook standard.

Despite the extensive earlier history, several publications report Michael S. Hart as the inventor of the *e*-book. In 1971 the operators of the Xerox Sigma V mainframe at the University of Illinois gave Hart extensive computer-time. Seeking a worthy use of this resource, he created his first electronic document by typing the United States Declaration of Independence into a computer. *Project Gutenberg* was launched afterwards to create electronic copies of more texts - especially books.

One early *e*-book implementation was the desktop prototype for a proposed notebook computer, the *Dynabook*, in the 1970s at PARC: a general-purpose portable personal computer capable of displaying books for reading.

In 1992, Sony launched the Data Discman, an electronic book reader that could read *e*-books that were stored on CDs. One of the electronic publications that could be played on the Data Discman was called *The Library of the Future.*

Early *e*-books were generally written for speciality areas and a limited audience, meant to be read only by small and devoted interest groups. The scope of the subject matter of these *e*-books included technical manuals for hardware, manufacturing techniques and other subjects. In the 1990s, the general availability of the Internet made transferring electronic files much easier, including *e*-books.

E-book Formats

As *e*-book formats emerged and proliferated, some garnered support from major software companies such as Adobe with its PDF format, and others supported by independent and open-source programmers. Different readers followed different formats, most of them specialising in only one format, and thereby fragmenting the *e*-book market even more. Due to exclusiveness and limited readerships of *e*-books, the fractured market of independent publishers and speciality authors lacked consensus regarding a standard for packaging and selling *e*-books.

However, in the late 1990s a consortium formed to develop the Open eBook format as a way for authors and publishers to provide a single source-document which many book-reading software and hardware platforms could handle. Open eBook as defined required subsets of XHTML and CSS; a set of multimedia formats (others could be used, but there must also be a fallback in one of the required formats); and an XML schema for a "manifest", to list the components of a given *e*-book, identify a table of contents, cover art, and so on. Google Books has converted many public-domain works to this open format. In 2010 *e*-books continued to gain in their own underground markets. Many *e*-book publishers began distributing books that were in the public domain. At the same time, authors with books that were not accepted by publishers offered their works online so they could be seen by others. Unofficial (and occasionally unauthorised) catalogues of books became available on the web, and sites devoted to *e*-books began disseminating information about *e*-books to the public.

Libraries

US Libraries began providing free *e*-books to the public in 1998 through their websites and associated services, although the *e*-books were primarily scholarly, technical or professional in nature, and could not be downloaded. In 2003, libraries began offering free downloadable popular fiction and non-fiction *e*-books to the public, launching an *e*-book lending model that worked much more successfully for public libraries. The number of library *e*-book distributors and lending models continued to increase over the next few years. From 2005 to 2008 libraries experienced 60 per cent growth in *e*-book collections. In 2010, a Public Library Funding and Technology Access Study found that 66 per cent of public libraries in the US were offering *e*-books, and a large movement in the library industry began seriously examining the issues related to lending *e*-books, acknowledging a tipping point of broad *e*-book usage. However, some publishers and authors have not endorsed the concept of electronic publishing, citing issues with demand, piracy and proprietary devices. Demand-driven acquisition (DDA) has been around for a few years in public libraries, which allows vendors to streamline the acquisition process by offering to match a library's selection profile to the vendor's *e*-book titles. The library's catalogue is then populated with records for all the *e*-books that match the profile. The decision to purchase the title is left to the patrons, although the library can set purchasing conditions such as a maximum price and purchasing caps so that the dedicated funds are spent according to the library's budget. The 2012 meeting of the Association of American University Presses included a panel on patron-drive acquisition (PDA) of books produced by university presses based on a preliminary report by Joseph Esposito, a digital publishing consultant who has studied the implications of PDA with a grant from the Andrew W. Mellon Foundation.

Dedicated Hardware Readers and Mobile Reader Software

There have been several generations of dedicated hardware *e*-book readers. The Rocket eBook and several others were introduced around 1998, but did not gain widespread acceptance. The establishment of the E Ink Corporation in 1997 led to the development of electronic paper, a technology which allows a display screen to reflect light like ordinary paper without the need for a backlight; electronic paper was incorporated first into the Sony Librie (released in 2004) and Sony Reader (2006), followed by the Amazon Kindle, a device which, upon its release in 2007, sold out within five hours.

As of 2009, new marketing models for *e*-books were being developed and a new generation of reading hardware was produced. *E*-books (as opposed to *e*-book readers) have yet to achieve global distribution. In the United States, as of September 2009, the Amazon Kindle model and Sony's PRS-500 were the dominant *e*-reading devices. By March 2010, some reported that the Barnes and Noble Nook may be selling more units than the Kindle in the US.

On January 27, 2010 Apple Inc. launched a multi-function device called the iPad and announced agreements with five of the six largest publishers that would allow Apple to distribute *e*-books. The iPad includes a built-in app for *e*-books called iBooks and the iBookstore. The iPad, the first commercially-profitable tablet computer, was followed in 2011 by the release of the first Android-based tablets as well as LCD versions of the Nook and Kindle; unlike previous dedicated *e*-readers, tablet computers are multi-function, utilise LCD displays (and usually touchscreens), and (like iOS and Android) be more agnostic to *e*-book vendor applications, allowing for installation of other *e*-book vendors. The growth in general-purpose tablet computer use allowed for further growth in popularity of *e*-books in the 2010s.

In July 2010, online bookseller Amazon.com reported sales of *e*-books for its proprietary Kindle outnumbered sales of hardcover books for the first time ever during the second quarter of 2010, saying it sold 140 *e*-books for every 100 hardcover books, including hardcovers for which there was no digital edition. By January 2011, *e*-book sales at Amazon had surpassed its paperback sales. In the overall US market, paperback book sales are still much larger than either hardcover or *e*-book; the American Publishing Association estimated *e*-books represented 8.5 per cent of sales as of mid-2010, up from 3 per cent a year before. At the end of the first quarter of 2012, *e*-book sales in the United States surpassed hardcover book sales for the first time.

In Canada, *The Sentimentalists* won the prestigious national Giller Prize. Owing to the small scale of the novel's independent publisher, the book was initially not widely available in printed form, but the *e*-book edition became the top-selling title for Kobo devices in 2010.

Use of an *e*-book reader is disallowed on commercial airliners during takeoff and landing. A comparison of available *e*-book readers can be found at comparison of *e*-book readers.

Comparison to Printed Books

Advantages:

Spatial Benefits: Over 2 million free *e*-books were available between July 4 and August 4 in 2009. Mobile availability of *e*-books may be provided for users with a mobile data connection, so that these *e*-books need not be stored on the device. An *e*-book can be offered indefinitely, without ever going "out of print". In the space that a comparably sized print book takes up, an *e*-reader can potentially contain thousands of *e*-books, limited only by its memory capacity. If space is at a premium, such as in a backpack or at home, it can be an advantage that an *e*-book collection takes up little room and weight.

Mechanical and Multimedia Benefits

E-book websites can include the ability to translate books into many different languages, making the works available to speakers of languages not covered by printed translations. Depending on the device, an *e*-book may be readable in low light or even total darkness. Many newer readers have the ability to display motion, enlarge or change fonts, use Text-to-speech software to read the text aloud for visually impaired, partially sighted, elderly or dyslectic people or just for convenience, search for key terms, find definitions, or allow highlighting bookmarking and annotation. Additionally, *e*-books allow for readers to look up words or find more information about the topic immediately. Material can be organised however the author prefers and is not limited to a linear path through the book as hyper-text can allow a number of paths through the material.

Printed books use 3 times more raw materials and 78 times more water to produce than *e*-books. However, the manufacture and distribution of *e*-book hardware (both the readers and the servers from which books are downloaded) consume materials and energy; the disposal of *e*-book hardware creates electronic waste; and the storage, distribution, and reading of *e*-books consume energy. Depending upon the software support and used formats, non-textual multimedia can also be embedded into *e*-book pages as widgets, including images (and image galleries), videos, audio files and interactive (still or animated) models; this is similar to HTML elements which allow for presentation of multimedia content through embedding of the content inside web pages. This results in *e*-books offering richer reading experiences than is possible through traditional, physical books.

E-books, while often presented as "flipping" between "pages" (in a skeumorphic nod to traditional book design), are not necessarily limited to such presentation, and entries can be presented through downward scrolling; further, more novel widgets interactive widgets for revealing additional textual information can be added to an *e*-book.

Distributive and Access Benefits

While an *e*-book reader costs much more than one book, the electronic texts are at times cheaper. Moreover, a great share of *e*-books are available online for free, minus the minimal costs of the electronics required. For example, all fiction from before the year 1900 is in the public domain. Also, libraries lend more current *e*-book titles for limited times, free samples are available of many publications, and there are other lending models being piloted as well. *E*-books can be printed for less than the price of traditional new books using new on-demand book printers.

An *e*-book can be purchased/borrowed, downloaded, and used immediately, whereas when one buys or borrows a book, one must go to a bookshop, a home library, or public library during limited hours, or wait for a delivery.

Depending on possible digital rights management, *e*-books can be backed up to recover them in the case of loss or damage and it may be possible to recover a new copy without cost from the distributor. Compared to printed publishing, it is cheaper and easier for authors to self-publish *e*-books. Also, the dispersal of a free *e*-book copy can stimulate the sales of the printed version.

Digital Rights Management

Anti-circumvention techniques may be used to restrict what the user may do with an *e*-book. For instance, it may not be possible to transfer ownership of an *e*-book to another person, though such a transaction is common with physical books. Some devices can phone home to track readers and reading habits, restrict printing, or arbitrarily modify reading material. This includes restricting the copying and distribution of works in the public domain through the use of "click-wrap" licensing, effectively limiting the rights of the public to distribute, sell or use texts in the public domain freely.

Most *e*-book publishers do not warn their customers about the possible implications of the digital rights management tied to their products. Generally they claim that digital rights management is meant to prevent copying of the *e*-book. However in many cases it is also possible that digital rights management will result in the complete denial of access by the purchaser to the *e*-book. With some formats of DRM, the *e*-book is tied to a specific computer or device. In these cases the DRM will usually let the purchaser move the book a limited number of times after which they cannot use it on any additional devices. If the purchaser upgrades or replaces their devices eventually they may lose access to their purchase. Some forms of digital rights management depend on the existence of online services to authenticate the purchasers. When the company that provides the service goes out of business or decides to stop providing the service, the purchaser will no longer be able to access the *e*-book.

As with digital rights management in other media, *e*-books are more like rental or leasing than purchase. The restricted book comes with a number of restrictions, and eventually access to the purchase can be removed by a number of different parties involved. These include the publisher of the book, the provider of the DRM scheme, and the publisher of the reader software. The *e*-books sold by most major publishers and electronic retailers, including notably Amazon.com and Apple Inc., are DRM-protected and tied to the publisher's *e*-reader software or hardware. The first major publisher to omit DRM was Tor Books, one of the largest publishers of science fiction and fantasy, in 2012. Smaller *e*-book publishers such as O'Reilly Media, Carina Press and Baen Books had already forgone DRM previously. In recent years, some websites including library.nu, BookFinder and Library Genesis have emerged which allow downloading ebooks by violating copyright.

Production

Some *e*-books are produced simultaneously with the production of a printed format, as described in electronic publishing, though in many instances they may not be put on sale until later. Often, *e*-books are produced from pre-existing hard-copy books, generally by document scanning, sometimes with the use of robotic book scanners, having the technology to quickly scan books without damaging the original print edition. Scanning a book produces a set of image files, which may additionally be converted into text format by an OCR programme. Occasionally, as in some *e*-text projects, a book may be produced by re-entering the text from a keyboard. As a newer development, sometimes only the electronic version of a book is produced by the publisher. It is even possible to release an *e*-book chapter by chapter as each chapter is written. This is useful in fields such as information technology where topics can change quickly in the months that it takes to write a typical book. It is also possible to convert an electronic book to a printed book by print on demand. However these are exceptions as tradition dictates that a book be launched in the print format and later if the author wishes an electronic version is produced.

As of 2010, there is no industry-wide *e*-book bestseller list, but various *e*-book vendors compile bestseller lists, such as those by Amazon Kindle Bestsellers and Fictionwise.

e-Readers

e-book reader, also called an *e*-book device or *e*-reader, is a mobile electronic device that is designed primarily for the purpose of reading *e*-books and digital periodicals. An *e*-book reader is similar in form to a limited purpose tablet computer.

e-Reader Applications: Additionally, some of the major book retailers and multiple third-party developers offer free (and in some third-party cases, premium paid) *e*-Reader applications for the Mac and PC desktops as well as for Android, Blackberry, iPad, iPhone and Palm OS devices to allow the reading of eBooks and other documents independently of dedicated *e*-book devices (such as the Amazon Kindle, Barnes and Noble Nook, Kobo eReader, and Sony Reader).

Timeline

Until 1979

~1949

- Roberto Busa begins planning the *Index Thomisticus*

~1963

- Doug Engelbart starts the NLS (and later Augment) projects

~1965

- Andries van Dam starts the HES (and later FRESS) projects, with assistance from Ted Nelson, and other faculty at Brown University develop and use electronic textbooks for poetry and biology.

1971

- Michael S. Hart types the US Declaration of Independence into a computer and launches Project Gutenberg to create electronic copies of more books.

1978

- The *Hitchhiker's Guide to the Galaxy* radio series launches (first novel published in 1979), featuring an electronic reference book containing all knowledge in the Galaxy (plus much more). Unlike real electronic books, this vast amount of data could be fit into something the size of a large paperback book, with updates received over the "Sub-Etha" (possibly a play on ethernet, which in turn is a play on the concept of the aether.)

1980–1999

1985–1992

- Robert Stein starts Voyager Company Expanded Books and books on CD-ROM.

1990

- Eastgate Systems publishes the first hypertext fiction, "Afternoon, a story", by Michael Joyce, available on floppy disk.
- Electronic Book Technologies releases DynaText, the first SGML-based system for delivering large-scale books such as aircraft technical manuals. It was later tested on a US aircraft carrier as replacement for paper manuals, allowing the ship to rest 6" higher in the water.

1992

- Sony launches the Data Discman electronic book reader.
- Charles Stack's Book Stacks Unlimited begins selling new physical books online.

1992–1993

- F. Crugnola and I. Rigamonti design and create the first *e*-book reader, called Incipit, as a thesis project at the Politecnico di Milano.

1993

- Digital Book, Inc. offers digital books on floppy disk in Digital Book Format (DBF).
- Hugo Award for Best Novel nominee texts published on CD-ROM by Brad Templeton.
- Bibliobytes, a project of free digital books online in Internet, launches.

1994

- C&M Online is founded in Raleigh, North Carolina and publishes *e*-books through its imprint, Boson Books. Authors include Fred Chappell, Kelly Cherry, Leon Katz, Richard Popkin, and Robert Rodman.

1995

- Amazon starts to sell physical books on the Internet.
- Online poet Alexis Kirke discusses the need for wireless internet electronic paper readers in his article "The Emuse".

1996

- Project Gutenberg reaches 1,000 titles. The target is 1,000,000.

1997

- E Ink Corporation is co-founded in 1997 by Joseph Jacobson, whose technology is later used to develop products like the Sony Reader, Barnes and Noble Nook, and Amazon Kindle.

1998

- Kim Blagg obtained the first ISBN issued to an ebook and began marketing multimedia-enhanced ebooks on CDs through retailers including amazon.com, bn.com and borders.com. Shortly thereafter, through her company Books OnScreen, she introduced the ebooks at the Book Expo America in Chicago, IL to an impressed, but unconvinced bookseller audience.
- The first ebook readers - Rocket ebook and SoftBook - were introduced.
- The Cybook / Cybook Gen1 was sold and manufactured at first by Cytale (1998–2003) then by Bookeen.
- Websites began selling ebooks in English, such as eReader.com and eReads.com.

1999

- Baen Books opens up the Baen Free Library.
- Webscriptions (since renamed Baen Ebooks) starts selling Baen titles as unencrypted eBooks.

2000's

2000

- Microsoft Reader with ClearType technology.
- Stephen King offers his book *Riding the Bullet* as a digital file; it can only be read on a computer.
- Digital Book Index begins operation. DBI and the Online Books Page both organise electronic books from disparate sites into single, searchable indexes, creating large virtual libraries of ebooks.

2001

- Todoebook.com, the first website selling ebooks in Spanish.

2002

- Random House and HarperCollins start to sell digital versions of their titles in English.

2004

- Sony Librie, first ebook using *e*-ink.
- Google announces plans to digitise the holdings of several major libraries, as part of what would later be called the Google Books Library Project.

2005

- Amazon buys Mobipocket.
- Google is sued for copyright infringement by the Authors Guild for scanning books still in copyright.

2006

- Sony Reader with *e*-ink.

- LibreDigital launched BookBrowse as an online reader for publisher content.
- BooksOnBoard, one of the largest independent ebookstores, opens and sells ebooks and audiobooks in six different formats.

2007

- Amazon launches Kindle in US.
- Bookeen launches Cybook Gen3 in Europe.

2008

- Adobe and Sony agree to share their technologies (Adobe Reader and DRM).
- Sony sells the Sony Reader PRS-505 in UK and France.
- BooksOnBoard is first to sell ebooks for iPhones.

2009

- Bookeen releases the Cybook Opus in the US and in Europe.
- Sony releases the Reader Pocket Edition and Reader Touch Edition.
- Amazon releases the Kindle 2.
- Amazon releases the Kindle DX in the US.
- Barnes and Noble releases the NOOK in the US.

2010

- Amazon releases the Kindle DX International Edition worldwide.
- Bookeen reveals the Cybook Orizon at CES.
- *TurboSquid Magazine* announces first magazine publication using Apple's iTunes LP format, however, this project was cancelled before it reached the market.
- Apple releases the iPad with an *e*-book app called iBooks. Between its release in April 2010, to October, Apple had sold 7 million iPads.
- Kobo Inc. releases its Kobo eReader to be sold at Indigo/Chapters in Canada and Borders in the United States.
- Amazon reports that its ebook sales outnumbered sales of hardcover books for the first time ever during the second quarter of 2010.
- Amazon releases the third generation Kindle, available in 3G+Wi-Fi and Wi-Fi versions.
- BeBook releases the BeBook Neo, first *e*-reader in Europe with Wi-FI.
- Kobo Inc. releases an updated Kobo eReader, which now includes Wi-Fi.
- Barnes and Noble releases the new NOOK Colour.
- Sony releases its second generation Daily Edition PRS-950.
- Google launches Google eBooks.
- PocketBook expands its line with an Android ereader.

2011

- Amazon.com announces in May that its *e*-book sales in the US now exceed all of its printed book sales.
- Barnes and Noble releases the NOOK Simple Touch ereader and NOOK Tablet.

- Bookeen launches its own *e*-books store, BookeenStore.com, and starts to sell digital versions of titles in French.
- Nature Publishing publishes *Principles of Biology*, a customisable, modular textbook, with no corresponding paper edition.
- The *e*-reader market grows in Spain, and companies like Telefonica, Fnac, and Casa del Libro (the most important Spanish bookshop) launches their *e*-readers with the Spanish brand bq readers.
- Amazon launches the Kindle Fire and Kindle Touch.

2012

- PocketBook starts selling PocketBook Touch, an *e*-ink Pearl eReader, winning awards from German magazines *Tablet PC* and *Computer Bild*.
- Kbuuk released the cloud based eBook self-publishing SaaS platform.
- Apple releases iBooks Author, software for creating iPad *e*-books to be directly published in its iBooks bookstore or to be shared as PDF files.
- Apple opens a textbook section in its iBooks bookstore.
- The publishing companies Random House, Holtzbrinck, and arvato get an *e*-book library called Skoobe on the market.
- US Department of Justice prepares anti-trust lawsuit against Apple, Simon and Schuster, Hachette Book Group, Penguin Group, Macmillan, and HarperCollins, alleging collusion to increase the price of books sold on Amazon.
- Amazon.com releases the Kindle Paperwhite, its first *e*-reader with a built-in light.
- Library.nu - previously called ebooksclub.org and gigapedia.com, a popular linking website for downloading ebooks - was accused of copyright infringement and shut down by court order on February 15, 2012.
- Ebooks sold in the US market collects over 3 billion in revenue.

2013

- Barnes and Noble releases the 7 and 8.9 inch NOOK HD. On April 27, 2013, the company posts losses of $475 million on its NOOK business for the prior fiscal year and in June 2013 announces its intention to discontinue manufacturing NOOK tablets (although Barnes and Noble stated it plans to continue making and designing black-and-white *e*-readers like the Nook Simple Touch, which "are more geared to serious readers, who are its customers, than to tablets".
- The Association of American Publishers announces that ebooks now account for about 20 per cent of book sales. Barnes and Noble estimates it has a 27 per cent share of the US *e*-books market.
- Apple executive Keith Moerer testifies in the ongoing *e*-book price fixing trial that the iBookstore held approximately 20 per cent of the ebook market share in the United States within the months after launch - a figure that *Publishers Weekly* reports is roughly double many of the previous estimates made by third parties. Moerer further testified that iBookstore acquired about an additional 20 per cent by adding Random House in 2011.

- Five major US *e*-book publishers, as part of their settlement of a price-fixing suit, will have to refund about $3 for every electronic copy of a New York Times bestseller that they sold from April 2010 to May 2012.
- Oyster launched as the first unlimited-access *e*-book subscription service.

Electronic Journals

Electronic journals, also known as *ejournals, e-journals,* and *electronic serials,* are scholarly journals or intellectual magazines that can be accessed via electronic transmission. In practice, this means that they are usually published on the Web. They are a specialised form of electronic document: they have the purpose of providing material for academic research and study, and they are formatted approximately like journal articles in traditional printed journals. Being in electronic form, articles sometimes contain metadata that can be entered into specialised databases, such as DOAJ or OACI, as well as the databases and search-engines for the academic discipline concerned.

Some electronic journals are online-only journals; some are online versions of printed journals, and some consist of the online equivalent of a printed journal, but with additional online-only (sometimes video and interactive media) material. Most commercial journals are subscription-based, or allow pay-per-view access. Many universities subscribe in bulk to packages of electronic journals, so as to provide access to them to their students and faculty. It is generally also possible for individuals to purchase an annual subscription to a journal, via the original publisher.

An increasing number of *e*-journals are now available as open access journals, requiring no subscription and offering free full-text articles and reviews to all. Individual articles from electronic journals will also be found online for free in an *ad hoc* manner: in working paper archives; on personal homepages; and in the collections held in institutional repositories and subject repositories. Some commercial journals do find ways to offer free materials. They may offer their initial issue or issues free, and then charge thereafter. Some give away their book reviews section for free. Others offer the first few pages of each article for free. Most electronic journals are published in HTML and/or PDF formats, but some are available in only one of the two formats. A small minority publish in DOC, and a few are starting to add MP3 audio. Some early electronic journals were first published in ASCII text, and some informally published ones continue in that format.

Electronic Publishing

Electronic publishing (also referred to as ePublishing or digital publishing) includes the digital publication of *e*-books, EPUBs, digital magazines (also sometimes known as electronic articles), and the development of digital libraries and catalogues.

An Overview

Electronic publishing has become common in scientific publishing where it has been argued that peer-reviewed scientific journals are in the process of being replaced by electronic publishing. It is also becoming common to distribute books, magazines, and newspapers to consumers through tablet reading devices, a market that is growing by millions each year, generated by online vendors such as Apple's iTunes bookstore, Amazon's bookstore for Kindle, and books in the Google Play Bookstore. Market research suggests that half of all magazine and newspaper circulation will be via digital delivery by the end of 2015 and that half of all reading in the United States will be done without paper by 2015. Although distribution via the Internet (also known as online publishing or web publishing when in the form of a website) is nowadays strongly associated with electronic publishing, there are many non-network electronic publications such as Encyclopaedias on CD and DVD, as well as technical and reference publications relied on by mobile users and others without reliable and high speed access to a network. Electronic publishing is also being used in the field of test-preparation in developed as well as in developing economies for student education (thus partly replacing conventional books) - for it enables content and analytics combined - for the benefit of students. The use of electronic publishing for textbooks may become more prevalent with iBooks from Apple Inc. and Apple's negotiation with the three largest textbook suppliers in the US.

Electronic publishing is increasingly popular in works of fiction as well as with scientific articles. Electronic publishers are able to provide quick gratification for late-night readers, books that customers might not be able to find in standard book retailers (erotica is especially popular in eBook format), and books by new authors that would be unlikely to be profitable for traditional publishers.

While the term "electronic publishing" is primarily used today to refer to the current offerings of online and web-based publishers, the term has a history of being used to describe the development of new forms of production, distribution, and user interaction in regard to computer-based production of text and other interactive media.

Electronic Publishing Process

The electronic publishing process follows a traditional publishing process but differs from traditional publishing in two ways: 1) it does not include using an offset printing press to print the final product and 2) it avoids the distribution of a physical product. Because the content is electronic, it may be distributed over the Internet and through electronic bookstores. The consumer may read the published content on a website, in an application on a tablet device, or in a PDF on a computer. In some cases the reader may print the content using a consumer-grade ink-jet or laser printer or via a print on demand system.

Distributing content electronically as apps has become popular due to the rapid consumer adoption of smartphones and tablets. At first, native apps for each mobile platform were required to reach all audiences, but in an effort towards universal device compatibility, attention has turned to using HTML5 to create web apps that can run on any browser.

The benefit of electronic publishing comes from using three attributes of digital technology: XML tags to define content, style sheets to define the look of content, and metadata to describe the content for search engines. With the use of tags, style sheets, and metadata, this enables reflowable content that adapts to various reading devices or delivery methods.

Because electronic publishing often requires text mark-up to develop online delivery methods, the traditional roles of typesetters and book designers have changed. Designers must know more about mark-up languages, the variety of reading devices available, and the ways in which consumers read. However, new design software is becoming available for designers to publish content in this standard without needing to know programming, such as Adobe Systems' Digital Publishing Suite and Apple's iBooks Author. The most common file format is .epub, used in many *e*-book formats, which is a free and open standard available in many publishing programmes. Another common format is .folio, which is used by the Adobe Digital Publishing Suite to create content for Apple's iPad tablets and apps.

Academic Publishing

After an article is submitted to a journal for consideration, there can be a delay ranging from several months to more than two years before it is published in a journal, rendering journals a less than ideal format for disseminating current research. In some fields such as astronomy and some parts of physics, the role of the journal in disseminating the latest research has largely been replaced by pre-print repositories such as arXiv.org. However, scholarly journals still play an important role in quality control and establishing scientific credit. In many instances, the electronic materials uploaded to pre-print repositories are still intended for eventual publication in a peer-reviewed journal.

There is statistical evidence that electronic publishing provides wider dissemination. A number of journals have, while retaining their peer review process, established electronic versions or even moved entirely to electronic publication.

Electronic Publishing and Copyright

Copyright laws are currently tailored to printed books. Electronic publishing brings up new questions in relation to copyright. ePublishing may be more collaborative, often involving more than one author, and more accessible, since it is published online. This opens up more doors for plagiarism or theft.

Some publishers are trying to change this. For example, HarperCollins limited the number of uses that one of its ebooks can be lent in a public library. Others, such as Penguin, are attempting to incorporate the elements of the eBook into their publications instead.

Examples: Electronic versions of traditional media:

- CD-ROM;
- E-book;
- Electronic journal;
- Online magazine;
- Online newspaper;
- PDF.

New media:

- Blog;
- Collaborative software;
- Digital publication app;
- File sharing;
- Mobile apps;
- Podcast.

Business models:

- Digital distribution platform;
- Online advertising;
- Online distribution;
- Open access (publishing);
- Pay-Per-View;

- Print on demand;
- Subscriptions;
- Self-publishing;
- Non-Subsidy Publishing.

Database

Most databases are organised collections of information. A telephone directory is an example of a database in print form. It is organised alphabetically by last name, and it contains fields for name, address, telephone number, etc. When you want someone's phone number you access the database (phone book) by the person's last name. Similarly, libraries have databases, although these are usually in electronic or computerised form. Library databases are organised by fields such as title, author, subject, etc. When you want to find something in a library database you access the database by one or more of these fields to retrieve the information you need.

Examples of the databases at the FIU library include:

- The online library catalogue for FIU - WebLUIS Catalogue;
- Indexes and abstracts - such as Readers' Guide to Periodical Literature, ERIC, and Medline;
- Full text databases - such as Encyclopaedia Britannica, Lexis-Nexis, and Literature Resource Centre.

In order to use databases effectively, it is helpful to be familiar with the following:

- The structure of a database;
- Types of databases;
- Database coverage;
- Types of searches.

Structure of Databases

Structure of Databases

- Understanding the structure of a database will help you locate and retrieve information more efficiently.
- The information about each item in a database is called a record. For example, the WebLUIS Catalogue has a record for each item (each book, journal, newspaper, video, map, etc.) located in the library.
- A record is composed of individual elements of information called fields. All the records in a given database are composed of a common set of fields. These fields can be used as access points when searching a database. For example, in WebLUIS the records share common fields such as author, title, call number, and subject.

Types of Databases

There are several types of databases. The kind of information contained in a database determines its type. The most common types of databases include:

- Bibliographic databases - provide citations (a listing of information about the item), and sometimes include abstracts (summaries) or descriptions of the items.

- Full-text databases - contain the full text of a work.
- Numeric databases - provide mostly numeric data (numbers) such as statistics or financial data.
- Image databases - could include art prints, photos, animations, and other types of images.
- Audio/Video databases - could include audio clips of sound effects and music samples or video excerpts from speeches, television shows, or other broadcast media.
- Mixed databases - combine two or more of the other database types.

Full-Text and Numeric Databases: Full-text databases contain the full text of a work right on the screen. Full-text databases are usually bibliographic databases that contain the complete article.

For example, Britannica Online contains entire encyclopaedia articles, and Lexis-Nexis provides the full-text of articles from newspapers, magazines, and other publications.

Numeric databases provide mostly numeric data such as statistics, financial data, census information, economic indicators, etc.